Frommer's®
Maui 2013

by Jeanette Foster

WILEY

John Wiley & Sons, Inc.

Published by:
John Wiley & Sons, Inc.
111 River St.
Hoboken, NJ 07030-5774

ISBN 978-1-118-28759-0 (paper); ISBN 978-1-118-33367-9 (ebk); ISBN 978-1-118-33145-3 (ebk);
ISBN 978-1-118-33477-5 (ebk)

Editor: Christine Ryan
Production Editor: Eric T. Schroeder
Cartographer: Liz Puhl
Photo Editor: Cherie Cincilla, Richard Fox
Design and Layout by Vertigo Design
Graphics and Prepress by Wiley Indianapolis Composition Services
Front cover photo: ©David Olsen / Photo Resource Hawaii / Alamy Images.
Back cover photo: ©Ryan Siphers

For information on our other products and services or to obtain technical support, please contact
our Customer Care Department within the U.S. at 877/762-2974, outside the U.S. at 317/572-3993
or fax 317/572-4002.

Wiley also publishes its books in a variety of electronic formats. Some content that appears in print
may not be available in electronic formats.

Manufactured in China

5 4 3 2 1

CONTENTS

4 EXPLORING MAUI 97

5 FUN ON & OFF THE BEACH 152

6 WHERE TO EAT 190

7 SHOPS & GALLERIES 230

8 ENTERTAINMENT & NIGHTLIFE 245

9 WHERE TO STAY 255

10 MOLOKAI, THE MOST HAWAIIAN ISLE 302

LIST OF MAPS

ABOUT THE AUTHOR

A resident of the Big Island, **Jeanette Foster** has skied the slopes of Mauna Kea—during a Fourth of July ski meet, no less—and gone scuba diving with manta rays off the Kona Coast. A prolific writer widely published in travel, sports, and adventure magazines, she's also the editor of *Zagat's Survey to Hawaii's Top Restaurants,* and the Hawaii chapter author of *1,000 Places to See in the USA and Canada Before You Die.* In addition to writing this guide, Jeanette is the author of *Frommer's Hawaii; Frommer's Kauai; Frommer's Hawaii Day by Day; Frommer's Honolulu, Waikiki & Oahu; Frommer's Maui Day by Day;* and *Frommer's Honolulu & Oahu Day by Day.*

ACKNOWLEDGMENTS

Special thanks to Priscilla Life, the world's best researcher.

HOW TO CONTACT US

In researching this book, we discovered many wonderful places—hotels, restaurants, shops, and more. We're sure you'll find others. Please tell us about them, so we can share the information with your fellow travelers in upcoming editions. If you were disappointed with a recommendation, we'd love to know that, too. Please write to:

Frommer's Maui 2013
John Wiley & Sons, Inc. • 111 River St. • Hoboken, NJ 07030-5774

ADVISORY & DISCLAIMER

Travel information can change quickly and unexpectedly, and we strongly advise you to confirm important details locally before traveling, including information on visas, health and safety, traffic and transport, accommodation, shopping and eating out. We also encourage you to stay alert while traveling and to remain aware of your surroundings. Avoid civil disturbances, and keep a close eye on cameras, purses, wallets and other valuables.

While we have endeavored to ensure that the information contained within this guide is accurate and up-to-date at the time of publication, we make no representations or warranties with respect to the accuracy or completeness of the contents of this work and specifically disclaim all warranties, including without limitation warranties of fitness for a particular purpose. We accept no responsibility or liability for any inaccuracy or errors or omissions, or for any inconvenience, loss, damage, costs or expenses of any nature whatsoever incurred or suffered by anyone as a result of any advice or information contained in this guide.

The inclusion of a company, organization or Website in this guide as a service provider and/or potential source of further information does not mean that we endorse them or the information they provide. Be aware that information provided through some Websites may be unreliable and can change without notice. Neither the publisher or author shall be liable for any damages arising herefrom.

FROMMER'S STAR RATINGS, ICONS & ABBREVIATIONS

Every hotel, restaurant, and attraction listing in this guide has been ranked for quality, value, service, amenities, and special features using **a star-rating system.** In country, state, and regional guides, we also rate towns and regions to help you narrow down your choices and budget your time accordingly. Hotels and restaurants are rated on a scale of zero (recommended) to three stars (exceptional). Attractions, shopping, nightlife, towns, and regions are rated according to the following scale: zero stars (recommended), one star (highly recommended), two stars (very highly recommended), and three stars (must-see).

In addition to the star-rating system, we also use **seven feature icons** that point you to the great deals, in-the-know advice, and unique experiences that separate travelers from tourists. Throughout the book, look for:

🎁   Special finds—those places only insiders know about

💬   Fun facts—details that make travelers more informed and their trips more fun

☺   Best bets for kids and advice for the whole family

📷   Special moments—those experiences that memories are made of

✋   Places or experiences not worth your time or money

✐   Insider tips—great ways to save time and money

🏷   Great values—where to get the best deals

The following **abbreviations** are used for credit cards:

AE	American Express	**DISC**	Discover	**V**	Visa
DC	Diners Club	**MC**	MasterCard		

TRAVEL RESOURCES AT FROMMERS.COM

Frommer's travel resources don't end with this guide. Frommer's website, **www. frommers.com**, has travel information on more than 4,000 destinations. We update features regularly, giving you access to the most current trip-planning information and the best airfare, lodging, and car-rental bargains. You can also listen to podcasts, connect with other Frommers.com members through our active-reader forums, share your travel photos, read blogs from guidebook editors and fellow travelers, and much more.

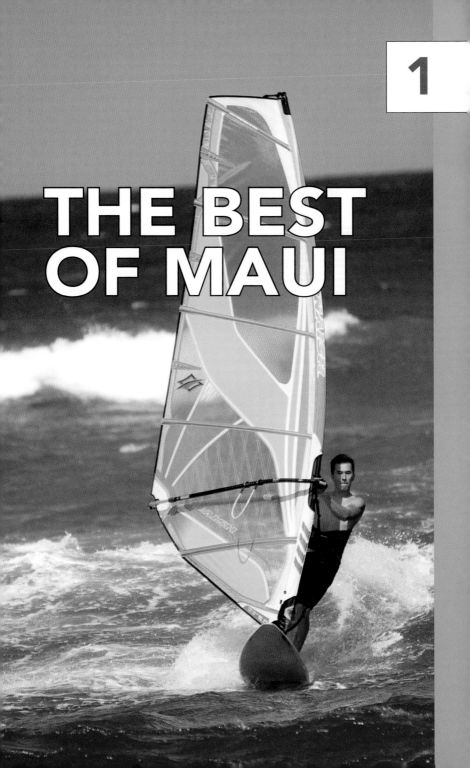

THE BEST OF MAUI

Only 75 miles from urban Honolulu on Oahu, Maui is a totally different island—a collection of mostly small towns, plus natural wonders like Haleakala National Park, that introduce visitors to a slower way of life. It's famous for its extensive beaches, tumbling waterfalls, romantic sunsets, and variety of adventures—from golf to snorkeling to scuba diving. The island's as lush as an equatorial rainforest in Hana, as hot and dry as Mexico in Lahaina, and as cool and misty as Oregon in Kula.

Beaches   If you're a hedonist looking for a day of lying on the soft sand and feeling the trade winds caress your body, head to **D.T. Fleming Beach Park.** Jacques Cousteau types can don a mask, fins, and snorkel to float weightlessly through rainbows of tropical fish at **Wailea Beach** or the islet of **Molokini,** one of Hawaii's most popular dive spots. When the big waves are up, surfers and surfer wannabes make way to **Hookipa Beach Park.**

Things to Do   For an awe-inspiring experience, drive to the highest point on Maui, the 10,000-foot volcano **Haleakala,** just before dawn, and watch the sunrise. Or take an entire day to drive along the **Hana Highway,** a barely-two-lane road with the tropical jungle on one side and the churning ocean on the other. Get close to marine life at the **Maui Ocean Center,** a 5-acre facility housing sharks, reefs, and touch pools.

Eating & Drinking   A trip to Maui is not complete without experiencing Hawaii's culinary specialty, the **luau.** At the oceanfront **Old Lahaina Luau,** you're treated to a traditional feast of **kalua pig** cooked in an *imu* (an underground pit lined with hot rocks). If you want a more formal dining experience, Maui's star chefs at restaurants like **Sansei Seafood Restaurant & Sushi Bar** create menus with local ingredients and fresh fish like ahi and Kona lobster. Upcountry, look for low-key ethnic spots that serve *manapua,* a bready, doughy sphere filled with sweetened pork or sweet beans.

D.T. Fleming Beach Park.

PREVIOUS PAGE: **Windsurfing at Hookipa Beach.**

Nature   On the outskirts of **Hana,** visit the shiny black-sand **Waianapanapa Beach,** or venture to the **Seven Sacred Pools** of **Oheo Gulch.** The pools are fern-shrouded, dazzlingly beautiful, and swimmable (mostly). If you're going to **Molokai,** don't miss the **Molokai Mule Rides.** Well-trained mules take you from the top of the nearly perpendicular ridge down a rocky switchback trail to **Kalaupapa,** a national park that was historically home to those who suffered from leprosy.

THE most unforgettable
MAUI EXPERIENCES

○ **Taking the Plunge:** Don mask, fins, and snorkel to explore the magical underwater world, where kaleidoscopic clouds of tropical fish flutter by exotic corals; a sea turtle might even come over to check you out. Molokini is everyone's favorite snorkeling destination (see "Snorkel Cruises to Molokini," p. 168), but the shores of Maui are lined with magical spots as well (see "Beaches," p. 153). Can't swim? No problem: Hop on a submarine with **Atlantis Adventures** (© **800/548-6262;** p. 169) for a plunge beneath the waves without getting wet.

○ **Hunting for Whales on Land:** No need to shell out megabucks to go out to sea in search of humpback whales—you can watch these majestic mammals breach and spy-hop from shore. I recommend scenic McGregor Point, at mile marker 9 along Honoapiilani Highway, just outside Maalaea in south Maui. The humpbacks arrive as early as November, but the majority travel through

Visitors to Maui can whale-watch from shore or join a boat tour to get up close to these majestic creatures.

Maui's waters from mid-December to mid-April. See "Whale-Watching," p. 170.

o **Watching the Windsurfers:** World-championship contests are held at Hookipa, on the north shore, one of the greatest windsurfing spots on the planet. Sit on a grassy bluff or stretch out on the sandy beach, and watch the world's top-ranked windsurfers twirling and dancing on the wind and waves like colorful butterflies. See "Windsurfing," p. 172, and "Driving the Road to Hana," p. 131.

o **Experiencing Maui's History:** Wander the historic streets of the old whaling town of Lahaina, where the 1800s are alive and well thanks to the efforts of the Lahaina Restoration Society. Drive the scenic Kahekili Highway, where the preserved village of Kahakuloa looks much as it did a century ago. Stand in awe at Piilanihale, Hawaii's largest *heiau* (temple), located just outside Hana. See "Lahaina & West Maui," p. 104.

o **Greeting the Rising Sun from Haleakala's Summit:** Bundle up in warm clothing, fill a thermos full of hot java, and drive up to the summit to watch the sky turn from inky black to muted charcoal as a small sliver of orange forms on the horizon. Standing at 10,000 feet, breathing in the rarefied air, and watching the first rays of light streak across the sky is a mystical experience of the first magnitude. See "House of the Sun: Haleakala National Park," p. 175.

o **Exploring a Different Hawaii—Upcountry Maui:** On the slopes of Haleakala, cowboys, farmers, ranchers, and other country people make their homes in serene, neighborly communities such as Makawao, Kula, and Ulupalakua—worlds away from the bustling beach resorts. Acres of onions, lettuce, tomatoes, carrots, cabbage, and flowers cover the hillsides. Maui's only winery

Sunrise at Haleakala.

Cruising along the Hana Highway.

is located here, offering the perfect place for a picnic. See "More in Upcountry Maui," p. 129.

o **Driving Through a Tropical Rainforest:** The Hana Highway is not just a drive but an adventure: Stop along the way to plunge into icy mountain ponds filled by cascading waterfalls; gaze upon vistas of waves pummeling soaring ocean cliffs; inhale the sweet aroma of blooming ginger; and take a walk back in time, catching a glimpse of what Hawaii looked like before concrete condos and fast-food joints washed ashore. See "Driving the Road to Hana," p. 131.

o **Taking a Day Trip to Lanai:** From Lahaina, join **Trilogy** (*©* **888/MAUI-800** [628-4800]) for a snorkel cruise to Lanai, or take the **Expeditions Maui-Lanai Passenger Ferry** over and rent a four-wheel-drive jeep on your own. It's a two-for-one island experience: Board in Lahaina Harbor and admire Maui from offshore; then get off at Lanai and go snorkeling in the clear waters, tour the tiny former plantation island, and catch the last ferry home. See "Day Cruises to Lanai," p. 162, and chapter 11.

THE best BEACHES

o **D.T. Fleming Beach Park:** This quiet, out-of-the-way beach, located north of the Ritz-Carlton hotel, starts at the 16th hole of the Kapalua Golf Course (Makaluapuna Point) and rolls around to the sea cliffs on the other side of the cove. Ironwood trees provide shade on the land side. Offshore, a shallow sandbar extends out to the edge of the surf. The waters are generally good for swimming and snorkeling, but sometimes, near the sea cliffs, the waves are big enough to suit body boarders and surfers. See p. 153.

o **Kapalua Beach:** On an island of many great beaches, this one takes the prize. A golden crescent with swaying palms protected from strong winds and currents by two outstretched lava-rock promontories, Kapalua has calm waters that are perfect for snorkeling, swimming, and kayaking. Even though it borders the Kapalua Resort, the beach is long enough for everyone to enjoy. Facilities include showers, restrooms, and lifeguards. See p. 154.

o **Kaanapali Beach:** Four-mile-long Kaanapali stands out as one of Maui's best beaches, with grainy gold sand as far as the eye can see. Most of the beach parallels the sea channel, and a paved beach walk links hotels and condos, open-air restaurants, and the Whalers Village shopping center. Summertime swimming is excellent. The best snorkeling is around Black Rock, in front of the Sheraton; the water is clear, calm, and populated with brilliant tropical fish. See p. 154.

o **Wailea Beach:** This is the best gold-sand, crescent-shaped beach on Maui's sun-baked southwestern coast. One of five beaches within Wailea Resort, Wailea Beach is big, wide, and protected on both sides by black-lava points. It serves as the front yard for the Four Seasons Resort, Maui's most elegant hotel, and the Grand Wailea Resort, its most outrageous. From the beach, the view out to sea is magnificent, framed by neighboring Kahoolawe and Lanai and the tiny crescent of Molokini. The clear waters tumble to shore in waves just the right size for gentle riding, with or without a board. All the beaches on the west and south coasts are great for spotting whales, but Wailea, with its fairly flat sandy beach that gently slopes down to the ocean, provides exceptionally good whale-watching from shore in season (Dec–Apr). See p. 157.

o **Maluaka Beach (Makena Beach):** On the southern end of Maui's resort coast, development falls off dramatically, leaving a wild, dry countryside punctuated by green kiawe trees. This wide, palm-fringed crescent of golden sand is set between two black-lava points and bounded by big sand dunes topped by a grassy knoll. Makena can be perfect for swimming when it's flat and placid, but it can also offer excellent bodysurfing when the waves come rolling in. Molokini and Kahoolawe can be seen off in the distance. See p. 157.

o **Waianapanapa State Park:** In east Maui, a few miles before Hana, the 120 acres of this state park offer 12 cabins, a caretaker's residence, a picnic area, a shoreline hiking trail, and, best of all, a black-sand beach (it's actually small black pebbles). Swimming is generally unsafe, though, due to strong waves and rip currents. But it's a great spot for picnicking, hiking along the shore, and simply sitting and relaxing. See p. 181.

o **Hamoa Beach:** This half-moon-shaped, gray-sand beach (a mix of coral and lava) in a truly tropical setting is a favorite among sunbathers, snorkelers, and bodysurfers in Hana. The 100-foot-wide beach is about 900 feet long and sits below 30-foot, black-lava sea cliffs. An unprotected beach open to the ocean, Hamoa is often swept by powerful rip currents. The surf breaks offshore and rolls in, making this a popular surfing and bodysurfing area. The calm left side is best for snorkeling in the summer. See p. 146.

Maui

PACIFIC OCEAN

Pailolo Channel

Auau Channel

LANAI

Alenuihaha Channel

Alalakeiki Channel

KAHOOLAWE

KANAIO COAST

Nanualele Pt.
Hamoa Beach
Muolea Pt.
Waianapanapa State Park
Hana Airport
Hana
Kipahulu
Kaupo
Kailio Pt.
Apole Pt.

Hana Hwy. 360

Hanawi Natural Area Reserve
Hana Forest Reserve
Hanakauhi
Kipahulu Valley
Kipahulu Forest Reserve
Kuiki
Haleakala
Haleakala Crater HALEAKALA NATIONAL PARK
Kalikimui Forest Reserve
Piilani Hwy.

Keanae Pt.
Keanae
Koolau Forest Reserve
Keanae Valley
Makawao Forest Reserve
Puu Ulaula
Kanaio Natural Area Reserve

Honokala Pt.
Huelo
Opana Pt.
Pauwela
Haiku
Makawao
Haliimaile
Hookipa Beach
H.P. Baldwin Beach Park
Paia
Pukalani
Kula
Kula Forest Reserve
Waiohuli
Ulupalakua
Ahihi-Kinau Natural Area Reserve

Hana Hwy.
Haleakala Hwy. 37
377
378
37
36
Kula Hwy.

Kahului Airport
Kahului
Puunene
Wailuku
311
380
Kealia Pond
Kihei
Maalaea Bay
31
Kamaole III Beach
Ulua Beach
Wailea
Wailea Beach
Makena
Maluaka Beach
Makena State Park
Oneloa Beach
Molokini I.
La Perouse Bay

WEST MAUI MOUNTAINS
West Maui Natural Area Reserve
West Maui Forest Reserve
Iao Valley
Puu Kukui
Honoapiilani Hwy.
Waihee
Waiehu
Waikapu
Maalaea
Papawai Pt.
Olowalu

Nakalele Pt.
Hakuee Pt.
Kahakuloa
Lipoa Pt.
Kapalua
Kapalua Beach
Napili
Honokowai
Kaanapali
Kaanapali Beach
Wahikuli County Wayside
Puunoa Pt.
Lahaina
Launiupoko County Wayside

Kapalua-West Maui Airport

340
30

5 mi
5 km

Kapalua Beach is perfect for snorkeling, swimming, and kayaking.

- **Hulopoe Beach (Lanai):** This golden, palm-fringed beach off the south coast of Lanai gently slopes down to the azure waters of a Marine Life Conservation District, where clouds of tropical fish flourish and spinner dolphins come to play. A tide pool in the lava rocks defines one side of the bay, while the other is lorded over by the Four Seasons Lanai at Manele Bay, which sits prominently on the hill above. Offshore, you'll find good swimming, snorkeling, and diving; onshore, there's a full complement of beach facilities, from restrooms to camping areas. See p. 350.

THE most unforgettable
MAUI ADVENTURES

Branch out while you're in Maui. Do something you wouldn't normally do—after all, you're on vacation. Some of the following adventures are a bit pricey, but these splurges are worth every penny.

o **Scuba Diving:** You're in love with snorkeling and the chance to view the underwater world, but it's just not enough—you want to get closer and see even more. Take an introductory scuba dive: After a brief lesson on how to use the diving equipment, you'll plunge into the deep to swim with the tropical fish and go eyeball to eyeball with other marine critters. See "Scuba Diving," p. 165.

o **Skimming over the Ocean in a Kayak:** Glide silently over the water, hearing only the sound of your paddle dipping beneath the surface. This is the way the early Hawaiians traveled along the coastline. You'll be eye level and up close and personal with the ocean and the coastline, exploring areas you can't get to any other way. Venture out on your own or go with an experienced guide—either way, you won't be sorry. See "Ocean Kayaking," p. 164.

o **Seeing the Stars from Inside a Volcanic Crater:** Driving up to see the sunrise is a trip you'll never forget, but to *really* experience Haleakala, plan to hike in and spend the night. To get a feel for why the ancient Hawaiians considered this one of the most sacred places on the island, you simply have to wander into the heart of the dormant volcano, where you'll find some 27 miles of hiking trails, two camping sites, and three cabins. See "Hiking & Camping," p. 355, and "Haleakala National Park," p. 122.

o **Hiking to a Waterfall:** There are waterfalls and then there are *waterfalls:* The magnificent 400-foot Waimoku Falls, in Oheo Gulch outside of Hana, are worth the long drive and the uphill hike you have to take to get there. The falls are surrounded by lush green ferns and wild orchids, and you can even stop to take a dip in the pool at the top of Makahiku Falls on the way. See "Hiking & Camping," p. 355.

o **Flying over the Remote West Maui Mountains:** Your helicopter streaks low over razor-thin cliffs, then flutters past sparkling waterfalls and down into the canyons and valleys of the inaccessible West Maui Mountains. There's so much beauty to absorb that it all goes by in a rush. You'll never want to stop flying over this spectacular, surreal landscape—and it's the only way to see the dazzling beauty of the prehistoric area of Maui. See "Flying High: Helicopter Rides," p. 100.

o **Taking a Drive on the Wild Side:** Mother Nature's wild side, that is—on the Kahekili Highway on Maui's northeast coast. This back-to-nature experience will take you past ancient Hawaiian *heiau* (temples); along steep ravines; and by rolling pastures, tumbling waterfalls, exploding blowholes, crashing surf, and jagged lava coastlines. You'll wander through the tiny Hawaiian village of Kahakuloa and around the "head" of Maui to the Marine Life Conservation Area of Honolua-Mokuleia and on to the resort of Kapalua. You'll remember this adventure for years. See "Lahaina & West Maui," in chapter 4.

Get a different perspective of Maui's coastline from a kayak.

o **Riding a Mule to Kalaupapa:** Even if you have only 1 day to spend on Molokai, spend it on a mule. The **Kalaupapa Rare Adventure** ★ (formerly known as the Molokai Mule Ride) from "topside" Molokai to the Kalaupapa National Historical Park (Father Damien's world-famous leper colony) is a once-in-a-lifetime adventure. The cliffs are taller than 300-story skyscrapers,

Taking a mule ride down the cliffs to Kalaupapa, on Molokai.

and the narrow 3-mile trail includes 26 dizzying switchbacks; but Buzzy Sproat has never lost one of his trustworthy mules (or any riders) on the difficult trail. The mules make the trek daily, rain or shine. See "The Legacy of Father Damien: Kalaupapa National Historical Park," p. 312.

THE best OF UNDERWATER MAUI

An entirely different Maui greets anyone with a face mask, snorkel, and fins. Under the sea, you'll find schools of brilliant tropical fish, green sea turtles, quick-moving game fish, slack-jawed moray eels, and prehistoric-looking coral. It's a kaleidoscope of color and wonder.

○ **Black Rock:** This spot, located on Kaanapali Beach just off the Sheraton Maui Resort, is excellent for beginning snorkelers during the day and for scuba divers at night. Schools of fish congregate at the base of the rock and are so used to snorkelers that they go about their business as if no one was around. If you take the time to look closely at the crannies of the rock, you'll find lion fish in fairly shallow water. At night (when a few outfitters run night dives here), lobsters, Spanish dancers, and eels come out. See "Kaanapali Beach," p. 154.

○ **Olowalu:** When the wind is blowing and the waves are crashing everywhere else, Olowalu, the small area 5 miles south of Lahaina, can be a scene of total calm—perfect for snorkeling and diving. You'll find a good snorkeling area around mile marker 14. You might have to swim about 50 to 75 feet; when you get to the large field of finger coral in 10 to 15 feet of water, you're there. You'll see a turtle-cleaning station, where turtles line up to have small cleaner wrasses pick off small parasites. This is also a good spot to see crown-of-thorns starfish, puffer fish, and lots of juvenile fish. See "Snorkeling," p. 167, and "Lahaina & West Maui," p. 104.

There are plenty of great snorkeling spots along Maui's coast.

○ **Hawaiian Reef:** Scuba divers love this area off the Kihei-Wailea coast because it has a good cross section of topography and marine life typical of Hawaiian waters. Diving to depths of 85 feet, you'll see everything from lava formations and coral reef to sand and rubble, plus a diverse range of both shallow- and deep-water creatures. See "An Expert Shares His Secrets: Maui's Best Dives," p. 166.

○ **Third Tank:** Scuba divers looking for a photo opportunity will find it at this artificial reef, located off Makena Beach at 80 feet. This World War II tank acts like a fish magnet: Because it's the only large solid object in the area, any fish or invertebrate looking for a safe home comes here. Surrounding the tank is a cloak of schooling snappers and goatfish just waiting for a photographer with a wide-angle lens. It's small, but Third Tank is loaded with more marine life per square inch than any site off Maui. See "An Expert Shares His Secrets: Maui's Best Dives," p. 166.

○ **Molokini:** Shaped like a crescent moon, this islet's shallow concave side serves as a sheltering backstop against sea currents for tiny tropical fish; on its opposite side is a deep-water cliff inhabited by spiny lobsters, moray eels, and white-tipped sharks. Neophyte snorkelers report to the concave side; experienced scuba divers, the cliff side. Either way, the clear water and abundant marine life make this islet off the Makena coast one of Hawaii's most popular dive spots. See "Water-sports," p. 160.

○ **Ahihi-Kinau Natural Preserve:** Fishing is strictly *kapu* (forbidden) in Ahihi Bay (at the end of the road in south Maui), and the fish seem to know it—they're everywhere in this series of rocky coves and black-lava tide pools. The black, barren, lunarlike land stands in stark contrast to the green-blue water, which is home to a sparkling mosaic of tropical fish. Scuba divers might want to check out **La Pérouse Pinnacle** in the middle of La Pérouse Bay; clouds of damselfish and triggerfish will greet you on the surface. See "Snorkeling," p. 167, and "An Expert Shares His Secrets: Maui's Best Dives," p. 166.

Molokini.

THE best FAMILY EXPERIENCES

○ **Best for Thrill Seekers:** Jules Vern comes to life as you and your kids climb aboard a real submarine with **Atlantis Adventures,** which will take you beneath the waves, into the shallow coastal waters off Lahaina to see plenty of fish (maybe even a shark!). Kids will love it, and you'll stay dry the entire time. See p. 169.

○ **Best Activity for Small Kids:** Riding **the Sugar Cane Train** will appeal not only to small kids, but to train buffs of all ages as well. A steam engine pulls open passenger cars of the Lahaina/Kaanapali & Pacific Railroad on a 30-minute, 12-mile round-trip through sugar cane fields between Lahaina and Kaanapali. The conductor sings and calls out the landmarks, and along the way you can see Molokai, Lanai, and the hidden parts of Kaanapali. See p. 87.

○ **Best Place to Run & Play: The Kamaole Beach Parks I, II, and III,** in Kihei, are heaven-sent for parents with very active *keiki* (children). Grass lawn fronts the ocean, so your little ones can run off all that energy built up and the white-sand beaches gently slope to the water. Keep an eye on the little ones (especially those not used to ocean conditions) when they venture into the water, but on land, they have plenty of room to roam. See p. 156.

○ **Best for Keeping the Kids Quiet:** Take the entire family underground, to the thousand-year-old caves found underground in Hana at the **Hana Lava Tube.** The safe, inexpensive tours offers a glimpse into this unique geological feature. The kids will be astounded. See p. 189.

○ **Best for Wearing the Kids Out:** After a day walking around the lunarlike surface of the 10,000-foot volcano, located at **Haleakala National Park,** the kids will be worn out from a day of exploring and hiking. See p. 175.

○ **Best Nighttime Activity:** Not all the great sites on Maui, are "on" Maui. The stars over the island shine big and bright because the tropical sky is almost entirely free of pollutants and the interference of big-city lights. Amateur astronomers can probe the Milky Way, see Saturn's rings and Jupiter's moons, and scan the Sea of Tranquillity at the Hyatt Regency Maui Resort's **Tour of the Stars** (p. 267), a 60-minute star search on a recreational computer-driven telescope. Great activity for kids of any age.

Taking a ride on the sugar cane train.

- **Best Way to Introduce Your Kids to the Ocean:** Hawaii's largest aquarium, the **Maui Ocean Center,** has a range of sea critters—from tiger sharks to tiny starfish—that are sure to fascinate kids of all ages. Take the family to this 5-acre facility in Maalaea, where, without getting wet, you can be introduced to the ocean as you wind your way among the tanks and exhibits, starting at the beach exhibits and going down to the ocean depths via the three dozen tanks, countless exhibits, and 100-foot-long main oceanarium. See p. 78.

- **Best "Way Cool" Look at Hawaii's Ecosystem:** Kids will think this is too much fun to be educational. Don a face mask and get the dizzying perspective of what a dragonfly sees as it flies over a mountain stream, or watch the tiny *oopu* fish climb up a stream at the **Hawaii Nature Center** in beautiful Iao Valley, where you'll find some 30 hands-on, interactive exhibits and displays of Hawaii's natural history. See p. 103.

THE best GOLF COURSES

- **Kaanapali Golf Resort:** All golfers, from high handicappers to near pros, will love the two challenging courses here. The North Course is a true Robert Trent Jones, Sr., design: an abundance of wide bunkers; several long, stretched-out tees; and the largest, most contoured greens on Maui. The South Course is an Arthur Jack Snyder design; although shorter than the North Course, it requires more accuracy on the narrow, hilly fairways. Just like its sibling course, it has a water hazard on its final hole, so don't tally up your score card until you sink your final putt. See p. 184.

- **Kapalua Resort:** Kapalua Resort has probably the best nationally known golf resort in Hawaii, due to the PGA Hyundai Tournament of Champions played here each January. The Bay Course and the Village Course are vintage Arnold Palmer designs; the Plantation Course is a strong entry from Ben Crenshaw and Bill Coore. All sit on Maui's wind-swept northwestern shore, at the rolling foothills of Puu Kukui, the summit of the West Maui Mountains. See p. 184.

- **Makena Golf Courses:** Here you'll find 36 holes by "Mr. Hawaii Golf"—Robert Trent Jones, Jr.—at his best. Add to that spectacular views: Molokini islet looms in the background, humpback whales gambol offshore in winter, and the tropical sunsets are spectacular. The South Course has magnificent views (bring your camera) and is kinder to golfers who haven't played for a while. The North Course is more difficult but also more stunning. The 13th hole, located partway up the mountain, has a view that makes most golfers stop and stare. The next hole is even more memorable: a 200-foot drop between tee and green. See p. 184.

o **Wailea Golf Club:** On the sunbaked south shore of Maui stands the Wailea Golf Club, *the* hot spot for golf in the islands. You'll find great golf at these three resort courses: The Blue Course is an Arthur Jack Snyder design, while the Emerald and Gold courses are both by Robert Trent Jones, Jr. All boast outstanding views of the Pacific and the mid–Hawaiian Islands. See p. 185.

o **The Lanai Courses:** For quality and seclusion, nothing in Hawaii can touch Lanai's two golf-resort offerings. The **Experience at Koele,** designed by Ted Robinson and Greg Norman, and the **Challenge at Manele,** a wonderful Jack Nicklaus course, with ocean views from every hole, rate among Hawaii's best courses. Both are tremendous fun to play, with the Experience featuring the par-4 8th hole, which drops some 150 yards from tee to fairway, and the Challenge boasting the par-3 12th, which plays from one cliff side to another over a Pacific inlet—one of the most stunning holes in Hawaii. See p. 356 and 357.

Kapalua Plantation Golf Course.

THE best RESORT SPAS

- **Spa Moana at the Hyatt Regency Maui Resort & Spa:** The island's first oceanfront spa, this 20,000-square-foot facility offers an open-air exercise lanai, wet-treatment rooms, massage rooms, a relaxation lounge, sauna and steam rooms, a Roman pool illuminated by overhead skylights, and a duet treatment suite for couples. See p. 267.

- **Spa at the Ritz-Carlton Kapalua:** Book a massage on the beach. The spa itself is welcoming and wonderful, but there is nothing like smelling the salt in the air and feeling the gentle caress of the wind in your hair while experiencing a true Hawaiian massage. See p. 277.

- **Spa Kea Lani at the Fairmont Kea Lani Maui:** This intimate, Art Deco boutique spa (just a little over 5,000 sq. ft., with nine treatment rooms) is the place for personal and private attention. The fitness center downstairs is open 24 hours (a rarity in Hawaiian resorts) with a personal trainer on duty some 14 hours a day. See p. 287.

- **Spa at the Four Seasons Resort Maui at Wailea:** Imagine the sound of the waves rolling on Wailea Beach as you are soothingly massaged in the privacy of your cabana, tucked in among the beachside foliage. This is the place to come to be absolutely spoiled. Yes, there's an excellent workout area and tons of great classes, but the specialty here is hedonistic indulgence. See p. 288.

- **Spa Grande at the Grand Wailea:** This is Hawaii's biggest spa, at 50,000 square feet and with 40 treatment rooms. The spa incorporates the best of the Old World (romantic ceiling murals, larger-than-life Roman-style sculptures, mammoth Greek columns, huge European tubs), the finest Eastern traditions (a full Japanese-style traditional bath and various exotic treatments from India), and the lure of the islands (tropical foliage, ancient Hawaiian treatments, and island products). It has everything from a top fitness center to a menu of classes and is constantly on the cutting edge of the latest trends. See p. 289.

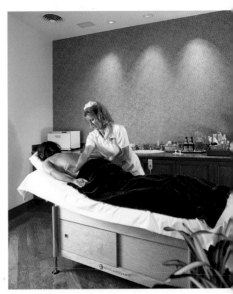

- **Spa at the Four Seasons Resort Lanai at Manele Bay:** The spa facility here features a variety of massages, facials, wraps, and scrubs (don't miss the signature Ali'i banana-coconut scrub). In addition, the Four Seasons has added a 1,500-square-foot fitness center (with one of the best ocean views in the resort) that features the latest cardiovascular and strength-training equipment, free weights, and a wood-floor studio for classes (spinning, yoga, Pilates, and meditation). See p. 364.

Go for ultimate relaxation at the Spa Kea Lani at the Fairmont Kea Lani Maui.

Hawaii's spas have raised the art of relaxation and healing to a new level. The traditional Greco-Roman-style spas, with lots of marble and big tubs in closed rooms, have evolved into airy, open facilities that embrace the tropics. Spagoers in Hawaii are looking for a sense of place, steeped in the culture. They want to hear the sound of the ocean, smell the salt air, and feel the caress of the warm breeze. They want to experience Hawaiian products and traditional treatments they can get only in the islands.

The spas of Hawaii, once nearly exclusively patronized by women, are now attracting more male clients. There are also special massages for children and pregnant women, and some spas have created programs to nurture and relax brides on their big day.

Today's spas offer a wide diversity of treatments. Massage options include Hawaiian lomilomi, Swedish, aromatherapy (with sweet-smelling oils), craniosacral (massaging the head), shiatsu (no oil, just deep thumb pressure on acupuncture points), Thai (another oil-less massage involving stretching), and hot stone. There are even side-by-side massages for couples. The truly decadent might try a duo massage—not one, but two massage therapists working on you at once.

Body treatments, for the entire body or just the face, involve a variety of herbal wraps, masks, or scrubs using a range of ingredients from seaweed to salt to mud, with or without accompanying aromatherapy, lights, and music.

After you have been rubbed and scrubbed, most spas offer an array of water treatments—a sort of hydromassage in a tub with jets and an assortment of colored crystals, oils, and scents.

Those are just the traditional treatments. Most spas also offer a range of

alternative healthcare treatments, such as acupuncture and chiropractic, and more exotic treatments, such as ayurvedic and *Siddha* from India or *Reiki* from Japan. Some offer specialized, cutting-edge treatments, such as the Grand Wailea Resort's full-spectrum color-light therapy pod (based on NASA's work with astronauts).

Once your body has been pampered, spas also offer a range of fitness facilities (weights, racquetball, tennis, golf, and so on) and classes (such as yoga, aerobics, spinning, tai chi, and kickboxing). Several offer adventure fitness packages (from bicycling to snorkeling). For the less active, most spas also have salons dedicated to hair and nail care.

If all this sounds a bit overwhelming, not to worry: All the spas in Hawaii have individual consultants who will help you design an appropriate treatment program to fit your individual needs.

Of course, all this pampering doesn't come cheap. Massages are generally $180 to $275 for 50 minutes and $240 to $300 for 80 minutes, body treatments are in the $150-to-$250 range, and alternative healthcare treatments can be as high as $200 to $300. But you may think it's worth the expense to banish your tension and stress.

THE most unforgettable
FOOD & DRINK EXPERIENCES

- **Colleen's at the Cannery:** This chic, fabulous find in rural Haiku is way, way, way off the beaten path. It's worth the drive to enjoy Colleen's fabulous culinary creations, such as wild-mushroom ravioli with sautéed portobello mushrooms, tomatoes, herbs, and a roasted-pepper *coulis*. See p. 225.

- **Gannon's:** Dine on award-winning chef Bev Gannon's fabulous cuisine at this restaurant perched high on a hill. You'll enjoy spectacular views of the ocean and Molokini in the distance. See p. 219.

- **Haliimaile General Store:** This foodie haven is another of Bev Gannon's creations. You'll dine at tables set on old wood floors under high ceilings. The food, a blend of eclectic American with ethnic touches, bridges Hawaii and Gannon's Texas roots to put an innovative spin on Hawaii Regional Cuisine. See p. 220.

- **Ko:** This successful restaurant is pure genius—taking the various ethnic cuisines from Maui's old plantation days (Hawaiian, Filipino, Portuguese, Korean, Puerto Rican, and European) and cooking them up in a gourmet fashion. See p. 217.

- **Mala Ocean Tavern:** This tiny "tavern" is the brainchild of Mark and Judy Ellman, owners of Maui Tacos and Penne Pasta Café. The atmosphere could not be more enticing, with just a handful of tables out on the oceanfront lanai and several more tables in the warmly decorated interior. They use healthy, organically grown food and fresh fish to make intriguing dishes. See p. 202.

- **Old Lahaina Luau:** Maui's best luau serves top-quality food that's as much Pacific Rim as authentically Hawaiian, served from an open-air thatched structure. It's one-third entertainment, one-third good food, and one-third ambience and should not be missed. See p. 247.

- **Pineapple Grill:** If you had only a single night to eat on the island, I'd send you here. In fact, if you eat here at the beginning of your Maui trip, you might

Sit back at Maui's Old Lahaina Luau and enjoy the show.

Sansei Seafood Restaurant & Sushi Bar

end up coming back! Chef Ryan Luckey is a genius at turning fresh local ingredients into culinary masterpieces, such as the Maui-style seafood paella with Portuguese sausage and Kula herbs. See p. 212.

- **Roy's Kahana Bar & Grill:** Hawaii's now-iconic cuisine, Hawaii Regional, was created by 12 chefs, one of whom was Roy Yamaguchi. His restaurant bustles with young, hip servers impeccably trained to deliver blackened ahi or perfectly seared lemon grass *shutome* (broadbill swordfish) hot to your table, in rooms that sizzle with cross-cultural tastings. See p. 209.

- **Sansei Seafood Restaurant & Sushi Bar:** Come here for the best Japanese & Japanese Fusion cuisine on the island. Sansei serves sushi and then some: hand rolls warm and cold, *udon* and ramen, and the signature Asian rock-shrimp cake with the oh-so-complex lime-chili butter and cilantro pesto. This place is flavor central—simplicity is not its strong suit, so be prepared for some busy tasting. See p. 213.

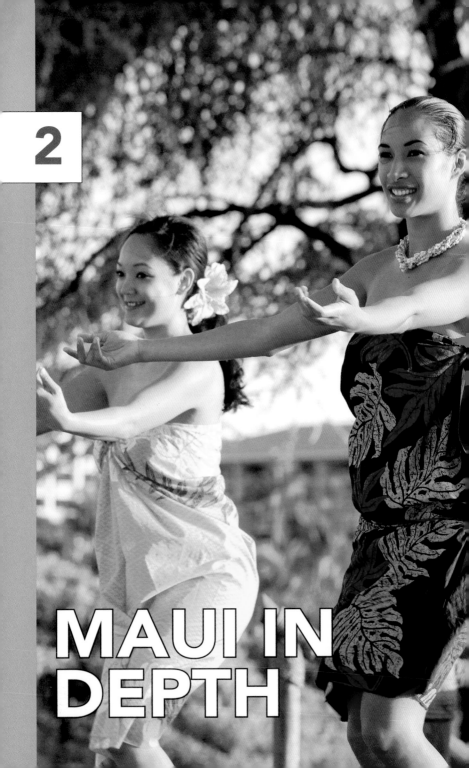

2

MAUI IN DEPTH

S ince the Polynesians ventured across the Pacific to the Hawaiian Islands more than 1,000 years ago, these floating jewels have continued to call visitors from around the globe.

Located in one of the most remote and isolated places on the planet, Maui, as part of the Hawaiian Islands chain, floats in the warm waters of the Pacific, blessed by a tropical sun and cooled by gentle year-round trade winds—creating what might be the most ideal climate imaginable. Centuries of the indigenous Hawaiian culture have given the people of the islands the "spirit of aloha," a warm, welcoming attitude that invites visitors to come and share this exotic paradise. Mother Nature has carved out verdant valleys, hung brilliant rainbows in the sky, and trimmed the islands with sandy beaches in a spectrum of colors, from white to black and even red.

Visitors are drawn to Maui not only for its incredible beauty, but also for its opportunities for adventure: bicycling down a 10,000-foot dormant volcano, swimming in a sea of rainbow-colored fish, hiking into a rainforest, or watching whales leap out of the ocean as you tee off on one of the country's top golf courses. Others come to rest and relax in a land where the pace of life moves at a slower rate and the sun's rays soothe and allow both body and mind to regenerate and recharge.

Venturing to Maui is not your run-of-the-mill vacation, but rather an experience in the senses that will remain with you, locked into your memory, way, way, way after your tan fades. Years later, a sweet smell, the warmth of the sun on your body, or the sound of the wind through the trees will take you back to the time you spent in the islands.

Incidentally, Maui is the only island in the Hawaiian chain named after a god—well, actually a demigod (half man, half god). Hawaiian legends are filled with the escapades of Maui, who had a reputation as a trickster. In one story, Maui is credited with causing the birth of the Hawaiian Islands when he threw his "magic" fishhook down to the ocean floor and pulled the islands up from the bottom of the sea. Another legend tells how Maui lassoed the sun to make it travel more slowly across the sky so that his mother could more easily dry her clothes. Maui's status as the only island to carry the name of a deity seems fitting, considering its reputation as the perfect tropical paradise, or as Hawaiians say, *"Maui no ka oi"* ("Maui is the best").

MAUI TODAY

A CULTURAL RENAISSANCE A conch shell sounds, a young man in a bright feather cape chants, torchlight flickers at sunset on the beach, and hula dancers begin telling their graceful centuries-old stories. It's a cultural scene out of the past come to life once again—for Hawaii is enjoying a renaissance of hula, chant, and other aspects of its ancient culture.

PREVIOUS PAGE: **Traditional hula dancing.**

The biggest, longest, and most elaborate celebrations of Hawaiian culture are the Aloha Festivals, which encompass more than 500 cultural events from August to October. "Our goal is to teach and share our culture," says Gloriann Akau, a former manager of the Aloha Festivals. "In 1946, after the war, Hawaiians needed an identity. We were lost and needed to regroup. When we started to celebrate our culture, we began to feel proud. We have a wonderful culture that had been buried for a number of years. This brought it out again. Self-esteem is more important than making a lot of money."

In 1985, native Hawaiian educator, author, and *kupuna* (respected elder) George Kanahele started integrating Hawaiian values into hotels like Maui's Kaanapali Beach Hotel. "You have the responsibility to preserve and enhance the Hawaiian culture, not because it's going to make money for you, but because it's the right thing to do," Kanahele told the Hawaii Hotel Association. "Ultimately, the only thing unique about Hawaii is its Hawaiian-ness. Hawaiian-ness is our competitive edge."

From general managers to maids, resort employees went through hours of Hawaiian cultural training. They held focus groups to discuss the meaning of aloha—the Hawaiian concept of unconditional love—and applied it to their work and their lives. Now many hotels have joined the movement and instituted Hawaiian programs. No longer content with teaching hula as

Piilanihale Heiau

a joke, resorts now employ a real *kumu hula* (hula teacher) to instruct visitors and have a *kupuna* take guests on treks to visit *heiau* (temples) and ancient sites.

THE QUESTION OF SOVEREIGNTY The Hawaiian cultural renaissance has also made its way into politics. Many *kanaka maoli* (native people) are demanding restoration of rights taken away more than a century ago when the U.S. overthrew the Hawaiian monarchy. Their demands were not lost on President Bill Clinton, who was picketed at a Democratic political fundraiser at Waikiki Beach in July 1993. Four months later, Clinton signed a document stating that the U.S. Congress "apologizes to Native Hawaiians on behalf of the people of the United States for the overthrow of the Kingdom of Hawaii on January 17, 1893, with the participation of agents and citizens of the United States, and deprivation of the rights of Native Hawaiians to self-determination."

But even neonationalists aren't convinced that complete self-determination is possible. Each of the 30 identifiable sovereignty organizations (and more than 100 splinter groups) has a different stated goal, ranging from total independence to nation-within-a-nation status, similar to that of Native Americans. In 1993, the state legislature created a Hawaiian Sovereignty Advisory Commission to "determine the will of the native Hawaiian people." The commission plans to pose the sovereignty question in a

referendum open to all persons over age 18 with Hawaiian blood, no matter where they live. More than 2 decades later, the question still remains unanswered.

LOOKING BACK AT MAUI

Paddling outrigger canoes, the first ancestors of today's Hawaiians followed the stars and birds across the sea to Hawaii, which they called "the land of raging fire." Those first settlers were part of the great Polynesian migration that settled the vast triangle of islands stretching between New Zealand, Easter Island, and Hawaii. No one is sure exactly when they came to Hawaii from Tahiti and the Marquesas Islands, some 2,500 miles to the south, but a bone fishhook found at the southernmost tip of the Big Island has been carbon-dated to A.D. 700. Chants claim that the Mookini Heiau, also on the Big Island, was built in A.D. 480. Some recent archaeological digs at Maluuluolele Park in Lahaina even predate that.

All we have today are some archaeological finds, some scientific data, and ancient chants to tell the story of Hawaii's past. The chants, especially the *Kumulipo*, which is the chant of creation and the litany of genealogy of the *alii* (high-ranking chiefs) who ruled the islands, talk about comings and goings between Hawaii and the islands of the south, presumed to be Tahiti. In fact, the channel between Maui, Kahoolawe, and Lanai is called *Kealaikahiki*, or "the pathway to Tahiti."

Around 1300, the transoceanic voyages stopped for some reason, and Hawaii began to develop its own culture in earnest. The settlers built temples, fishponds, and aqueducts to irrigate taro plantations. Sailors became farmers and fishermen. Each island was a separate kingdom. The *alii* created a caste system and established taboos. Violators were strangled. High priests asked the gods Lono and Ku for divine guidance. Ritual human sacrifices were common.

Maui's history, like that of the rest of Hawaii, is one of wars and conquests, with one king taking over another king's land. The rugged terrain of Maui and the water separating Maui, Molokai, Lanai, and Kahoolawe made for natural boundaries of kingdoms. In the early years, there were three kingdoms on Maui: Hana, Waikulu, and Lahaina. The chants are not just strict listings of family histories. Some describe how a ruler's pride and arrogance can destroy a community. For example, according to the chants, Hana's King Hua killed a priest in the 12th century, and as a result the gods sent a severe drought to Hana as a punishment.

Three centuries later, another ruler came out of Hana who would change the course of Maui's history: Piilani, the first ruler to unite all of Maui. His rule was a time not only of

A statue of King Kamehameha.

peace but also of community construction projects. Piilani built fishponds and irrigation fields and began creating a paved road some 4 to 6 feet wide around the entire island. Piilani's sons and grandson continued these projects and completed the *Alalou,* the royal road that circled the united island. They also completed Hawaii's largest *heiau* to the god of war, Piilanihale, which still stands today.

Maui was a part of a pivotal change in Hawaii's history: After conquering Maui in 1795, Kamehameha united all of the islands into one kingdom. It started in 1759, when yet another battle over land was going on. This time Kalaniopuu, a chief from the Big Island, had captured Hana from the powerful Maui chief Kahikili. Kahikili was busy overtaking Molokai when the Big Island chief stole Hana from him. The Molokai chief escaped and fled with his wife to Hana, where the Big Island chief welcomed him. A few years later, the Molokai chief and his wife had a baby girl in Hana, named Kaahumanu, who later married Kamehameha.

THE "FATAL CATASTROPHE" No ancient Hawaiian ever imagined a *haole* (a white person; literally, one with "no breath") would ever appear on one of these "floating islands." But then one day in 1778, just such a person sailed into Waimea Bay on Kauai, where he was welcomed as the god Lono.

The man was 50-year-old Capt. James Cook, already famous in Britain for "discovering" much of the South Pacific. Now on his third great voyage of exploration, Cook had set sail from Tahiti northward across uncharted waters to find the mythical Northwest Passage that was said to link the Pacific and Atlantic oceans. On his way, Cook stumbled upon the Hawaiian Islands quite by chance. He named them the Sandwich Islands, for the Earl of Sandwich, first lord of the admiralty, who had bankrolled the expedition.

Overnight, Stone Age Hawaii entered the age of iron. Nails were traded for fresh water, pigs, and the affections of Hawaiian women. The sailors brought syphilis, measles, and other diseases to which the Hawaiians

Captain James Cook.

A statue in Lahaina commemorates the area's rich whaling history.

had no natural immunity, thereby unwittingly wreaking havoc on the native population.

After his unsuccessful attempt to find the Northwest Passage, Cook returned to Kealakekua Bay on the Big Island, where a fight broke out over an alleged theft, and the great navigator was killed by a blow to the head. After this "fatal catastrophe," the British survivors sailed home. But Hawaii was now on the sea charts, and traders on the fur route between Canada and China anchored in Hawaii to get fresh water. More trade—and more disastrous liaisons—ensued.

Two more sea captains left indelible marks on the islands. The first was American John Kendrick, who in 1791 filled his ship with sandalwood and sailed to China. By 1825, Hawaii's sandalwood forests were gone, enabling invasive plants to take charge. The second captain was Englishman George Vancouver, who in 1793 left cows and sheep, which spread out to the high-tide lines. King Kamehameha I sent for cowboys from Mexico and Spain to round up the wild livestock, thus beginning the islands' *paniolo* (cowboy) tradition.

The tightly woven Hawaiian society began to unravel after the death in 1819 of King Kamehameha I, who had used guns seized from a British ship to unite the islands under his rule. One of his successors, Queen Kaahumanu, abolished old taboos, such as that of women eating with men, and opened the door for religion of another form when she converted to Christianity.

STAYING TO DO WELL   In 1819, the first whaling ship dropped anchor in Lahaina. Sailors on the *Bellina* were looking for fresh water and supplies, but they found beautiful women, mind-numbing grog, and a tropical paradise. A few years later, in 1823, the whalers met rivals for this hedonistic playground: the missionaries. The God-fearing missionaries arrived from New England bent on converting the pagans. They chose Lahaina because it was the capital of Hawaii.

Intent on instilling their brand of rock-ribbed Christianity in the islands, the missionaries clothed the natives, banned them from dancing the hula, and nearly dismantled their ancient culture. They tried to keep the whalers and sailors out of the bawdy houses, where a flood of whiskey quenched fleet-size thirsts and where the virtue of native women was never safe.

The missionaries taught reading and writing, created the 12-letter Hawaiian alphabet, started a printing press in Lahaina, and began writing the islands' history, which until then had existed only as an oral account in memorized chants. They also started the first school in Lahaina, which still exists today: the Lahainaluna High School.

Children of the missionaries became the islands' business leaders and politicians. They married Hawaiians and stayed on in the islands, causing one wag to remark that the missionaries "came to do good and stayed to do well."

In Lahaina's heyday, some 500 whaling ships a year dropped anchor in the Lahaina Roadstead. In 1845, King Kamehameha III moved the capital of Hawaii from Lahaina to Honolulu, where more commerce could be accommodated in the natural harbor there. Some whaling ships started skipping Lahaina for the larger port of Honolulu. Fifteen years later, the depletion of whales and the emergence of petroleum as a more suitable oil signaled the beginning of the end of the whaling industry.

IS EVERYONE hawaiian IN HAWAII?

The plantations brought so many different people to Hawaii that the state is now a rainbow of ethnic groups: Living here are Caucasians, African Americans, American Indians, Eskimos, Japanese, Chinese, Filipinos, Koreans, Tahitians, Vietnamese, Hawaiians, Samoans, Tongans, and other Asian and Pacific Islanders. Add a few Canadians, Dutch, English, French, Germans, Irish, Italians, Portuguese, Scottish, Puerto Ricans, and Spaniards. Everyone's a minority here.

In combination, it's a remarkable potpourri. Many people retain an element of the traditions of their homeland. Some Japanese Americans in Hawaii, generations removed from the homeland, are more traditional than the Japanese of Tokyo. And the same is true of many Chinese, Koreans, Filipinos, and others, making Hawaii a kind of living museum of various Asian and Pacific cultures.

KING SUGAR EMERGES   When the capital of Hawaii moved to Honolulu, Maui might have taken a back seat in Hawaii's history had it not been for the beginning of a new industry: sugar. In 1849, George Wilfong, a cantankerous sea captain, built a mill in Hana and planted some 60 acres of sugar cane, creating Hawaii's first sugar plantation. At that time, the gold rush was on in California, and sugar prices were wildly inflated. Wilfong's harsh personality and the demands he placed on plantation workers did not sit well with the Hawaiians. In 1852, he imported Chinese immigrants to work in his fields. By the end of the 1850s, the gold rush had begun to diminish, and the inflated sugar prices dropped. When Wilfong's mill burned down, he finally called it quits.

A photo of sugar cane workers from the Alexander & Baldwin Sugar Museum in Puunene.

Sugar production continued in Hana, however. In 1864, two Danish brothers, August and Oscar Unna, started the Hana Plantation. Four years later they imported Japanese immigrants to work the fields.

Some 40 miles away, in Haiku, two sons of missionaries, Samuel Alexander and Henry Baldwin, planted 12 acres of this new crop. The next year, Alexander and Baldwin added some 5,000 acres in Maui's central plains and started Hawaii's largest sugar company. They quickly discovered that without the copious amounts of rainfall found in Hana, they would need to get water to their crop, or it would fail. In 1876, they constructed an elaborate ditch system that brought water from rainy Haiku some 17 miles away to the dry plains of Wailuku, a move that cemented the future of sugar in Hawaii.

Around the same time, another sugar pioneer, Claus Spreckels, bought up property in the arid desert of Puunene from Hawaiians who sold him the "cursed" lands at a very cheap price. The Hawaiians were sure they had gotten the better part of the deal because they believed that the lands were haunted.

Spreckels was betting that these "cursed" lands could be very productive if he could get water rights up in the rainy hills and bring that water to Puunene, just as Alexander and Baldwin had done. But first he needed that water. Thus began a series of late-night poker games with the then-king Kalakaua. Spreckels's gamble paid off: He beat the king at poker (some say he cheated), then built the elaborate 30-mile Haiku Ditch system, which transported 50 million gallons of water a day from rainy Haiku to dry Puunene.

The big boost to sugar, not only on Maui but also across the entire state, came in 1876, when King Kalakaua negotiated the Sugar Reciprocity Treaty with the United States, giving the Hawaiian sugar industry a "sweet" deal on prices and tariffs.

In 1891, King Kalakaua visited chilly San Francisco, caught a cold, and died in the royal suite of the Sheraton Palace. His sister, Queen Liliuokalani, assumed the throne.

A SAD FAREWELL On January 17, 1893, a group of American sugar planters and missionary descendants, with the support of U.S. Marines, imprisoned Queen Liliuokalani in her own palace, where she later penned the sorrowful lyric "Aloha Oe," Hawaii's song of farewell. The monarchy was dead.

A new republic was established, controlled by Sanford Dole, a powerful sugar cane planter. In 1898, through annexation, Hawaii

Statue of Queen Liliuokalani.

DO YOU HAVE TO SPEAK HAWAIIAN IN HAWAII?

Almost everyone here speaks English. But many folks in Hawaii now speak Hawaiian as well. All visitors will hear the words *aloha* and *mahalo* (thank you). If you've just arrived, you're a *malihini*. Someone who's been here a long time is a *kamaaina*. When you finish a job or your meal, you are *pau* (finished). On Friday it's *pau hana*, work finished. You eat *pupu* (Hawaii's version of hors d'oeuvres) when you go *pau hana*.

The Hawaiian alphabet, created by the New England missionaries, has only 12 letters: the five regular vowels (*a, e, i, o,* and *u*) and seven consonants (*h, k, l, m, n, p,* and *w*). The vowels are pronounced in the Roman fashion: that is, *ah, ay, ee, oh,* and *oo* (as in "too")— not *ay, ee, eye, oh,* and *you,* as in English. For example, *huhu* is pronounced *who-who*. Most vowels are sounded separately, though some are pronounced together, as in Kalakaua: Kah-lah-*cow*-ah.

Following are some basic Hawaiian words that you'll often hear in Hawaii and see throughout this book. For a more complete list of Hawaiian words, go to **http://hawaiian dictionary.hisurf.com**.

alii   Hawaiian royalty

aloha   greeting or farewell

halau   school

hale   house or building

heiau   Hawaiian temple or place of worship

kahuna   priest or expert

kamaaina   old-timer

kapa   tapa, bark cloth

kapu   taboo, forbidden

keiki   child

kupuna   respected elder

lanai   porch or veranda

lomilomi   massage

mahalo   thank you

makai   a direction, toward the sea

mana   spirit power

mauka   a direction, toward the mountains

muumuu   loose-fitting gown or dress

ono   delicious

pali   cliff

paniolo   Hawaiian cowboy(s)

wiki   quick

became an American territory ruled by Dole. His fellow sugar cane planters, known as the Big Five, controlled banking, shipping, hardware, and every other facet of economic life on the islands.

Planters imported more contract laborers from Puerto Rico (in 1900), Korea (in 1903), and the Philippines (1907–31). Most of the new immigrants stayed on to establish families and become a part of the islands. Meanwhile, the native Hawaiians became a landless minority in their homeland.

For nearly a century on Hawaii, sugar was king, generously subsidized by the U.S. federal government. The sugar planters dominated the territory's economy, shaped its social fabric, and kept the islands in a colonial plantation era with bosses and field hands.

WORLD WAR II & ITS AFTERMATH   On December 7, 1941, Japanese Zeros came out of the rising sun to bomb American warships based at Pearl Harbor, on the island of Oahu. This was the "day of infamy" that plunged the United States into World War II.

The attack brought immediate changes to the islands. Martial law was declared, stripping the Big Five cartel of its absolute power in a single day. Japanese Americans and German Americans were interned. Hawaii was "blacked out" at night, Waikiki Beach was strung with barbed wire, and Aloha Tower was painted in camouflage.

During the postwar years, the men of Hawaii returned after seeing another, bigger world outside of plantation life and rebelled. Throwing off the mantle of plantation life, the workers struck for higher wages and improved working conditions. Within a few short years after the war, the

The attack at Pearl Harbor is the "day of infamy" that plunged the United States into World War II.

Pearl Harbor today.

white, Republican leaders who had ruled since the overthrow of the monarchy were voted out of office, and labor leaders in the Democratic Party were suddenly in power.

TOURISM & STATEHOOD In 1959, Hawaii became the 50th state of the union. But that year also saw the arrival of the first jet airliners, which brought 250,000 tourists to the fledgling state.

Tourism had already started on Maui shortly after World War II, when Paul I. Fagan, an entrepreneur from San Francisco who had bought the Hana Sugar Co., became the town's angel.

Fagan wanted to retire to Hana, so he focused his business acumen on this tiny town with big problems. Years ahead of his time, he thought tourism might have a future in Hana, so he built a small six-room inn, called Kauiki Inn, which later became the Hotel Hana Maui (recently renamed Travaasa Hana Hotel). When he opened it in 1946, he said it was for first-class, wealthy travelers (just like his friends). Not only did his friends come, but he also pulled off a public relations coup that is still talked about today. Fagan owned a baseball team, the San Francisco Seals. He figured they needed a spring-training area, so why not use Hana? He brought out the entire team to train in Hana, and, more important, he brought out the sportswriters. The sportswriters penned glowing reports about the town, and one writer gave the town a name that stuck: "Heavenly Hana."

However, it would be another 3 decades before Maui became a popular visitor destination in Hawaii. Waikiki was king in the tourism industry, seeing some 16,000 visitors a year by the end of the 1960s, and some 4 million a year by the end of the 1970s. In 1960, Amfac, owner of Pioneer Sugar Co., looked at the area outside of Lahaina that was being used to dump sugar cane refuse and saw another use for the beachfront land. The company decided to build a manicured, planned luxury resort in the Kaanapali area. They built it, and people came.

A decade later, Alexander & Baldwin, now the state's largest sugar company, looked at the arid land they owned south of Kihei and also saw possibilities: The resort destination of Wailea was born.

By the mid-1970s, some one million visitors a year were coming to Maui. Ten years later, the number was up to two million.

At the beginning of the 21st century, the visitor industry replaced agriculture as Maui's number-one industry. Maui is the second-largest visitor destination in Hawaii. For 17 years in a row, the readers of *Condé Nast Traveler* and *Travel + Leisure* magazines have voted Maui the "Best Island in the World."

Hawaii was at record-breaking visitor counts (6.9 million) in 2000. After the September 11, 2001, terrorist attacks, tourism dropped abruptly in Hawaii, sending the state's economy into a tailspin. But people eventually started traveling again, and in 2003, visitor arrivals were up to 6.3 million. By 2005, Hawaii's economy was recovering, the number of visitors to the state shot up to 6.75 million, business was booming in construction, and real estate sales were higher than ever.

> ### Pidgin: 'Eh Fo' Real, Brah
>
> If you venture beyond the tourist areas, you might hear another local tongue: pidgin English, a conglomeration of slang and words from the Hawaiian language. "Broke da mouth" (tastes really good) is the favorite pidgin phrase and one you might hear; "'Eh fo' real, brah" means "It's true, brother." You could be invited to hear an elder "talk story" (relating myths and memories). But because pidgin is really the province of the locals, your visit to Hawaii is likely to pass without your hearing much pidgin at all.

Just 3 years later, the economic pendulum swung the opposite way. Real estate in Hawaii, as on the mainland, dropped in value and sales plummeted. A record number of visitors, some nine million, had come to Hawaii in 2007, but the economic downturn in 2008 caused the closure of Aloha Airlines (which had served Hawaii for 61 years) and ATA Airlines, as well as Molokai Ranch, that island's largest employer and landowner.

After more than a decade in the new century, Maui is still climbing out of the recession, and the tourism industry has not yet recovered to its former healthy state.

MAUI IN POPULAR CULTURE

In addition to the books discussed below, you may want to peruse *Frommer's Maui Day by Day.* Those planning an extended trip to Hawaii should check out *Frommer's Honolulu, Waikiki & Oahu; Frommer's Honolulu & Oahu Day by Day; Frommer's Kauai; Frommer's Hawaii;* and *Frommer's Hawaii with Kids* (all published by John Wiley & Sons).

Books

FICTION

Perhaps the best-known book about the islands is James A. Michener's *Hawaii* (Fawcett Crest, 1974). This epic novel manages to put the island's history into chronological order, but remember, it is still fiction, and very sanitized fiction, too. For a more contemporary look at life in Hawaii today, one of the best novels is *Shark Dialogues,* by Kiana Davenport (Plume, 1995). The novel tells the story of Pono, a larger-than-life matriarch, and her four daughters of mixed races. Davenport skillfully weaves legends and myths of Hawaii into the "real life" reality that Pono and her family face in the complex Hawaii of today. Lois-Ann Yamanaka uses a very "local" voice and stark depictions of life in the islands in her fabulous novels *Wild Meat and the Bully Burgers* (Farrar, Straus, and Giroux, 1996), *Blu's Hanging* (Avon, 1997), and *Heads by Harry* (Avon, 1999).

A recent book, *The Descendants* by Kaui Hart Hemmings (Random House Trade Paperbacks, 2008) is a wonderful novel about the head of a Hawaiian land-owning clan who has drifted through his charmed life but suddenly has to wake up when a boating accident leaves his wife in a coma. The protagonist has to come to terms with his family (both his daughters and his wife, who had taken a lover) and decide what to do with the family's large land holdings. The novel was the basis for the movie of the same name that was released in 2011 and starred George Clooney.

NONFICTION

Mark Twain's writing on Hawaii in the 1860s offers a wonderful introduction to Hawaii's history. One of his best books is *Mark Twain in Hawaii: Roughing It in the Sandwich Islands* (Mutual Publishing, 1990). A great depiction of the Hawaii of 1889 is *Travels in Hawaii,* by Robert Louis Stevenson (University of Hawaii Press, 1973).

For a contemporary perspective on Hawaii's unique culture, read *Voices of Wisdom: Hawaiian Elders Speak,* by M. J. Harden (Aka Press, 1999). Some 24 different *kahuna* (experts) in their fields were interviewed about their talent, skill, or artistic practice. These living treasures talk about how Hawaiians of yesteryear viewed nature, spirituality and healing, preservation and history, dance and music, arts and crafts, canoes, and the next generation.

Native Planters in Old Hawaii: Their Life, Lore, and Environment (Bishop Museum Press, 2004) was originally published in 1972 but is still one of the most important ethnographic works on traditional Hawaiian culture, portraying the lives of the common folk and their relationship with the land before the arrival of Westerners. This revised edition, with a great index that allows you to find anything, is an excellent resource for anyone interested in Hawaii.

Honolulu Stories: Two Centuries of Writing (Mutual Publishing, 2008),

MARK TWAIN IN HAWAII
Roughing It
In The Sandwich Islands
Hawaii in the 1860's
Foreword By A. Grove Day

Mark Twain's writing on Hawaii offers a wonderful introduction to Hawaiian history.

edited by Gavan Daws and Bennett Hymer, is a fascinating 1,000-plus-page book filled with the writings of various authors over the past 200 years. More than 350 selections—ranging from short stories; excerpts from novels; and scenes from plays, musicals, and operas to poems, songs, Hawaiian chants, cartoons, slams, and even stand-up comedy routines—are contained in this must-read for anyone interested in Hawaii. The authors range from Hawaiian kings and queens to Hawaiian chefs and commoners, including some well-known writers (translated from seven different languages)—all telling their own stories about Honolulu.

FLORA & FAUNA Because Hawaii is so lush with nature and blessed with plants, animals, and reef fish seen nowhere else on the planet, a few reference books can help you identify what you're looking at and make your trip more interesting. In the botanical world, Angela Kay Kepler's *Hawaiian Heritage Plants* (University of Hawaii Press, 1998) is the standard for plant reference. In a series of essays, Kepler weaves culture, history, geography, botany, and even spirituality into her vivid descriptions of plants. You'll never look at plants the same way again. There are great color photos and drawings to help you sort through the myriad species. Another great resource is *Tropicals,* by Gordon Courtright (Timber Press, 1988), which is filled with color photos identifying everything from hibiscus and heliconia to trees and palms.

The other necessary reference to have in Hawaii is one that identifies the colorful reef fish you will see while snorkeling. The best of the bunch is John E. Randall's *Shore Fishes of Hawaii* (University of Hawaii Press, 1998). Two other books on reef-fish identification, with easy-to-use spiral bindings, are *Hawaiian Reef Fish: The Identification Book* (Blue Kirio Publishing, 1993), by Casey Mahaney, and *Hawaiian Reef Fish* (Island Heritage, 1998), by Astrid Witte and Casey Mahaney.

To learn everything you need to identify Hawaii's unique birds, try H. Douglas Pratt's *A Pocket Guide to Hawaii's Birds* (Mutual Publishing, 1996).

For fans of the Hawaiian lei, *Na Lei Makamae: The Treasured Lei* (University of Hawaii Press, 2003), by Marie McDonald and Paul Weissich, is a comprehensive work on this incredible art form. McDonald is one of Hawaii's top lei makers, and Weissich is the director emeritus of Honolulu Botanical Gardens; together they cover some 88 flowers and plants used for leis.

For a complete rundown on where to see the best botanical gardens on Maui (and other Hawaiian islands), get Kevin Whitton's *A Pocket Guide to Hawaii's Botanical Gardens* (Mutual Publishing, 2009).

HISTORY There are many great books on Hawaii's history, but one of the best to start with is David E. Eyre's *By Wind, By Wave: An Introduction to Hawaii's Natural History* (Bess Press, 2000), which vividly describes the formation of the Hawaiian Islands. In addition to chronicling the natural history of Hawaii, Eyre discusses the complex interrelationships among the plants, animals, ocean, and people. He points out that Hawaii has become the "extinction capital of the world," but rather than dwelling on that fact, he urges readers to do something about it and carefully spells out how.

For an even more complete tome, get the University of Hawaii Press's *Hawaiian Natural History, Ecology, and Evolution* (2002), by Alan C. Ziegler. Readers can trace the natural history of the Hawaiian archipelago through the book's 28 chapters, or focus on specific topics such as island formation by plate tectonics, plant and animal evolution, flightless birds and their fossil sites, Polynesian migrational history and ecology, the effects of humans and exotic animals on the environment, current conservation efforts, and the contributions of the many naturalists who visited the islands over the centuries and the stories behind their discoveries.

For a history of "precontact" Hawaii (before Westerners arrived), David Malo's *Hawaiian Antiquities* (Bishop Museum Press, 1976) is the preeminent source. Malo was born around 1793 and wrote about the Hawaiian lifestyle at that time, as well as the beliefs and religion of his people. It's an excellent reference book, but not a fast read. For more readable books on old Hawaii, try *Stories of Old Hawaii* (Bess Press, 1997), by Roy Kakulu Alameida; *Hawaiian Folk Tales* (Mutual Publishing, 1998), by Thomas G. Thrum; and *The Legends and Myths of Hawaii* (Charles E. Tuttle Company, 1992), by David Kalakaua.

The best story of the 1893 overthrow of the Hawaiian monarchy is told by Queen Liliuokalani, in her book *Hawaii's Story by Hawaii's Queen, Liliuokalani* (Mutual Publishing, 1990). When it was written, it was an international plea for justice for her people, but it is a poignant read even today. It's also a must-read for people interested in current events and the recent rally for sovereignty in the 50th state. Two contemporary books on the question of Hawaii's sovereignty are Tom Coffman's *Nation Within: The Story of America's Annexation of the Nation of Hawaii* (Epicenter, 1998) and Thurston Twigg-Smith's *Hawaiian Sovereignty: Do the Facts Matter?* (Goodale, 2000), which explores the opposite view. Twigg-Smith, former publisher of the former statewide newspaper the *Honolulu Advertiser,* is the grandson of Lorrin A. Thurston, one of the architects of the 1893 overthrow of the monarchy. His so-called politically incorrect views present a different look on this hotly debated topic.

For more recent history, Lawrence H. Fuchs's *Hawaii Pono* (Bess Press, 1991) is a carefully researched tome on the contributions of each of Hawaii's main immigrant communities (Chinese, Japanese, and Filipino) between 1893 and 1959.

An insightful look at history and its effect on the Hawaiian culture is *Waikiki, A History of Forgetting & Remembering* (University of Hawaii Press, 2006), by Andrea Feeser. A beautiful art book (designed by Gaye Chan), this is not your typical coffee-table book, but a different look at the cultural and environmental history of Waikiki. Using historical texts, photos, government documents, and interviews, this book lays out the story of how Waikiki went from a self-sufficient agricultural area to a tourism mecca, detailing the price that was paid along the way.

Another great cultural book is Davianna Pomaikai McGregor's *Na Kua'aina: Living Hawaiian Culture* (University of Hawaii Press, 2007). I love this book for so many reasons—first, it focuses not on the Hawaiian royalty, but on the common people of Hawaii and how they lived. McGregor, a professor of ethnic studies at the University of Hawaii, examines how people lived in rural lands and how they kept the Hawaiian traditions alive. She describes the cultural significance of each area (the island of Molokai; Hana, Maui; and Puna), the landscape, the Hawaiian gods who lived there, the chants and myths about the area, and how the westernization of the area has changed the land and the Hawaiian people.

Film

My favorite films made in Hawaii but about other places are listed here:

o **Bird of Paradise:** Delmer Daves's 1951 remake of the 1932 film stars Debra Paget as an island princess who falls in love with a visiting Frenchman (Louis Jourdan) against the wishes of the princess's people. It was filmed on the island of Kauai with a new (at the time) technology called Technicolor.

o **The Devil at Four O'Clock:** Mervyn LeRoy directed this 1961 movie about faith and redemption (filmed on Maui), which tells the story of an alcoholic priest (Spencer Tracy) who enlists the aid of three condemned convicts (one played by Frank Sinatra) to help in the rescue of native children threatened by an erupting volcano.

o **Donovan's Reef:** John Ford directed this 1963 John Wayne romantic comedy about two ex-navy men who remain on a South Seas island (played by Kauai) after World War II. "Guns" Donovan (Wayne) runs the local bar, while Doc Dedham (Jack Warden) has married a local princess. A former shipmate (Lee Marvin) arrives, followed by a high-society Bostonian (Elizabeth Allen).

o **The Enemy Below:** This classic story (released in 1957) of a U.S. destroyer chasing a German submarine during World War II stars Robert Mitchum and Curt Jurgens in the lead roles as the American and German captains. While all of the ocean scenes take place in the North Atlantic, they were actually filmed in Hawaii.

o **Islands in the Stream:** Filmed on Kauai, this 1977 movie is based on Ernest Hemingway's last published novel. Set on the island of Bimini in the Caribbean, it is about artist Thomas Hudson's renewed relationship with his three young sons and former wife.

o **Joe Versus the Volcano:** This least-well-known of the Tom Hanks/Meg Ryan movies is a romantic comedy filmed in 1990. John Shanley's film tells the tale of a hypochondriac who, when told that he is dying, accepts an offer to throw himself into the volcano of a remote tropical island. En route, however, he learns that there are many reasons to keep on living.

o **Jurassic Park:** Filmed on the islands of Kauai and Oahu, Steven Spielberg's 1993 megahit, which was billed as "an adventure 65 million years in the making," is the story of dinosaurs on the loose at the site of the world's only dinosaur farm and theme park, where creatures from the past are produced using harvested DNA.

o **The Karate Kid, Part II:** In one of those instances where the sequel is actually better than the original, this 1986 movie takes our hero Daniel LaRusso (Ralph Macchio) and his mentor, Mr. Miyagi (Pat Morita), to Miyagi's homeland, Okinawa, to visit his dying father and confront his old rival. An entire Okinawan village was re-created on Oahu's Windward Coast.

o **King Kong:** John Guillermin's 1976 version of the classic story of the great ape and the girl (Jessica Lange) was filmed on parts of Kauai rarely seen by visitors or residents.

o **The Lost World: Jurassic Park:** In Steven Spielberg's 1997 follow-up to *Jurassic Park,* dinosaurs have been bred and then escaped following the abandonment of the project in the first installment. The sequel features much more Hawaiian scenery than the original.

- **Mister Roberts:** John Ford's 1955 comedy-drama, set aboard an insignificant ship stationed in the Pacific during World War II, was nominated for three Academy Awards, including Best Picture. Jack Lemmon won the Oscar for Best Supporting Actor for his role as Ensign Pulver. The film also stars Henry Fonda in the title role and James Cagney as Captain Morton.

- **None But the Brave:** Frank Sinatra directed and starred in this 1965 story of American and Japanese soldiers who, when stranded on a tiny Pacific island during World War II (filmed on Kauai), must make a temporary truce and cooperate to survive. This is the only film directed by Sinatra.

- **Outbreak:** Wolfgang Petersen directed this 1995 tale of a lethal virus that is transported to the United States by an African monkey host. Federal agencies rush to find an antidote before the planet's population is wiped out. The scenes of the African village were filmed near the Wailua River on Kauai.

- **Planet of the Apes:** Tim Burton's 2001 remake of the 1968 science fiction classic, which starred Charlton Heston, is more faithful to the original Pierre Boulle novel, but also much more dark and sinister. Exterior battle scenes were filmed on lava fields on the Big Island of Hawaii.

- **Raiders of the Lost Ark:** Filmed on Kauai, Steven Spielberg's 1981 film follows archaeologist Indiana Jones on a search for the Ark of the Covenant, which is also sought by the Nazis under orders from Hitler.

- **Six Days Seven Nights:** Ivan Reitman's 1998 adventure-comedy is about a New York magazine editor and a gruff pilot who are forced to put aside their dislike for each other in order to survive after crash landing on a deserted South Seas island (filmed on Kauai). It stars Harrison Ford and Anne Heche.

- **South Pacific:** The 1958 motion picture adaptation of the Rodgers and Hammerstein musical was filmed on Kauai. The film has an all-star cast, with Rossano Brazzi and Mitzi Gaynor in the lead roles. It was nominated for three Academy Awards but won only for Best Sound.

- **Uncommon Valor:** Ted Kotcheff's 1983 story tells of a retired Marine colonel (Gene Hackman) who reunites his son's former unit to organize a secret raid on a Vietnamese prison camp, where he hopes to rescue his son and other American POWs. The climactic scenes set in Laos were filmed on the island of Kauai.

- **The Wackiest Ship in the Army:** Richard Murphy directed this 1960 comedy set during World War II and filmed on Kauai and Oahu. The crew and captain (played by Jack Lemmon) are sent on a secret mission in waters patrolled by the Japanese. The film is based on the true story of a mission ordered by General Douglas MacArthur.

- **Waterworld:** Kevin Costner directed and stars in this 1995 film about a future in which the polar ice caps have melted, leaving most of the world's surface deep beneath the oceans. The survivors live poorly on the water's surface, dreaming of finding "dry land." Some of the water scenes were filmed off Kauai. The final and most beautiful scenes in the movie were filmed in the Waipio Valley on the Big Island.

My favorite films made in Hawaii and about Hawaii are these:

- **Blue Hawaii:** Chad Gates (Elvis Presley), upon discharge from the army, returns to Hawaii to enjoy life with his buddies and girlfriend, against the wishes of his parents, who want him to work for the family business. Presley, Joan Blackman, and Angela Lansbury make this 1961 film a classic, with great music and beautiful Hawaiian scenery from the early 1960s.

o **The Descendants:** Directed by Alexander Payne and starring George Clooney, this 2011 movie is about Matt King, a wealthy landowner in Hawaii. King is forced to reexamine his life in the islands after his wife is in a coma due to a boating accident, leaving him with his estranged daughters, the recent discovery of his wife's infidelity, and decisions regarding the family's land holdings and his family's connection to the past. Beautifully filmed on Oahu, the Big Island, and Kauai.

o **50 First Dates:** This 2004 romantic comedy stars Drew Barrymore and Adam Sandler in a story about a young woman (Barrymore) who has lost her short-term memory in a car accident and who now relives each day as if it were October 13. She follows the same routine every day, until she meets Henry Roth (Sandler), who falls in love with her and seeks a way to forge a long-term relationship.

o **From Here to Eternity:** Fred Zinnemann's 1953 multiple-Oscar winner, set in pre–World War II Hawaii, tells the story of several army soldiers stationed on Oahu on the eve of Pearl Harbor. The film won Best Picture, Best Supporting Actor (Frank Sinatra), Best Supporting Actress (Donna Reed), and five other awards.

o **Hawaii:** George Roy Hill's 1966 adaptation of the James Michener novel features amazing island scenery and stars Julie Andrews, Max von Sydow, and Richard Harris. It is a great introduction to the early history of Hawaii.

o **Honeymoon in Vegas:** Andrew Bergman's 1992 comedy starring James Caan, Nicolas Cage, Sarah Jessica Parker, and Pat Morita is primarily set in Las Vegas, but has a wonderful segment shot on Kauai at the fictional home of millionaire Tommy Korman (Caan).

o **In Harm's Way:** Otto Preminger's 1965 classic drama of the war in the Pacific focuses on several navy officers (and the women in their lives) who are suddenly catapulted into the war following the Japanese attack on Pearl Harbor. It stars John Wayne, Kirk Douglas, Patricia Neal, Tom Tryon, and Paula Prentiss.

o **Molokai: The Story of Father Damien:** This 1999 film follows the life of Belgian priest Damien de Veuster from 1872, the year before his arrival in Kalaupapa, through his years ministering to

St. Joseph's Church, built by Father Damien in 1876.

the patients with Hansen's disease at Kalaupapa, until his death at the Molokai settlement in 1889.

o **Pearl Harbor:** Michael Bay's 2001 film depicts the time before, during, and after the December 7, 1941, Japanese attack (with the best re-creation of the Pearl Harbor attack ever filmed) and tells the story of two best friends and the woman they both love.

o **Picture Bride:** Japanese director Kayo Hatta presents this 1995 film about a Japanese woman who travels to Hawaii to marry a man whom she has never met but has seen only through photos and letters. She soon discovers that he is twice her age and that much turmoil awaits her in her new home. Beautifully filmed on the North Shore of Oahu and the Hamakua Coast of the Big Island, with a special appearance by Toshiro Mifune.

o **Tora! Tora! Tora!:** This 1970 film tells the story of the Japanese attack on Pearl Harbor as seen from both the American and the Japanese perspectives.

Music

Hawaiian music ranges from traditional ancient chants and hula to slack-key guitar, to contemporary rock and a new genre, Jawaiian, a cross of reggae, Jamaican, and Hawaiian. To listen to Hawaiian music, check out Hawaiian 105 (www.hawaiian105.com). Below are my picks.

An LP of traditional Hawaiian songs.

o **Best of the Gabby Band,** by Gabby Pahinui (traditional Hawaiian)

o **Gently Weeps,** by Jake Shimabukuro (contemporary Hawaiian)

o **Hapa,** by Hapa (contemporary Hawaiian)

o **Hawaiian Blossom,** by Raiatea Helm (traditional Hawaiian)

o **Hawaiian Tradition,** by Amy Hanaiali'i Gilliom (traditional Hawaiian)

o **Honolulu City Lights,** by Keola & Kapono Beamer (contemporary Hawaiian)

o **Legends of Hawaiian Slack Key Guitar,** by various artists (a collection of slack-key guitar music and a 2007 Grammy winner)

o **Masters of Hawaiian Slack Key Guitar, Vol. 1,** by various artists (a collection of slack-key guitar music and a 2006 Grammy winner)

o **Na Leo Hawaii Kaniko,** by the Master Chanters of Hawaii (chanting)

o **Na Pua O Hawaii,** by Makaha Sons (contemporary Hawaiian)

o **Wonderful World,** by Israel Kamakawiwo'ole (contemporary Hawaiian)

EATING & DRINKING ON MAUI
Tried & True: Hawaii Regional Cuisine

Peter Merriman, a founding member of Hawaii Regional Cuisine (HRC) and a recipient of the James Beard Award for Best Chef: Northwest/Hawaii (along with George Mavrothalassitis of Chef Mavro Restaurant), describes the current trend in Hawaii as a refinement, a tweaking upward, of everything from fine dining to down-home local cooking. This means sesame- or nori-crusted fresh catch on plate-lunch menus, and *huli-huli* chicken at five-diamond eateries, paired with Beaujolais and leeks and gourmet long rice.

At the same time, says Merriman, HRC, the style of cooking that put Hawaii on the international culinary map, has become watered down, a buzz-word: "A lot of restaurants are paying lip service."

As it is with things au courant, it is easy to make a claim but another thing to live up to it. As Merriman points out, HRC was never solely about technique; it is equally about ingredients and the chef's creativity and integrity. "We continue to get local inspiration," says Merriman. "We've never restricted ourselves." If there is a fabulous French or Thai dish, chefs like Merriman will prepare it with local ingredients and add a creative edge that makes it distinctively Hawaiian.

HRC was established in the mid-1980s in a culinary revolution that catapulted Hawaii into the global epicurean arena. The international training, creative vigor, fresh ingredients, and cross-cultural menus of the 12 original HRC chefs have made the islands a dining destination applauded nationwide. (In a tip of the toque to island tradition, *ahi*—a word ubiquitous in Hawaii—has replaced *tuna* on many chic New York menus.)

Here's a sampling of what you can expect to find on a Hawaii Regional Cuisine menu: seared Hawaiian fish with *lilikoi* shrimp butter; taro crab cakes; Pahoa corncakes; Molokai sweet-potato or breadfruit vichyssoise; Ka'u orange sauce and Kahua Ranch lamb; fern shoots from Waipio Valley; Maui onion soup; Hawaiian bouillabaisse with fresh snapper, Kona crab, and fresh aquacultured shrimp; blackened ahi summer rolls; herb-crusted onaga; and gourmet Waimanalo greens, picked that day. You may also encounter locally made cheeses, squash and taro risottos, Polynesian *imu*-baked foods, and guava-smoked meats. If there's pasta or risotto or rack of lamb on the menu, it could be nori (red algae) linguine with opihi (limpet) sauce, or risotto with local seafood served in taro cups, or rack of lamb in cabernet and hoisin sauce (fermented soybean, garlic, and spices). Watch for ponzu sauce too; it's lemony and zesty, much more flavorful than the soy sauce it resembles.

Plate Lunches & More: Local Food

At the other end of the spectrum is the vast and endearing world of "local food." By that, I mean plate lunches and poke, shave ice and saimin, bento lunches and *manapua*—cultural hybrids all.

Reflecting a polyglot population of many styles and ethnicities, Hawaii's idiosyncratic dining scene is eminently inclusive. Consider surfer chic: Barefoot in the sand, in a swimsuit, you chow down on a **plate lunch** ordered from a lunch wagon, consisting of fried mahimahi, "two scoops rice," macaroni salad, and a few leaves of green, typically julienned cabbage. (Generally, teriyaki beef and shoyu chicken are options.) Heavy gravy is often the condiment of choice, accompanied by a soft drink in a paper cup or straight out of the can. Like **saimin**—the local version of noodles in broth topped with scrambled eggs, green onions, and sometimes pork—the plate lunch is Hawaii's version of high camp.

But it was only a matter of time before the humble plate lunch became a culinary icon in Hawaii. These days, even the most chichi restaurant has a version of this modest island symbol (not at plate-lunch prices, of course), while vendors selling the real thing—carb-driven meals served from wagons—have queues that never end.

Because this is Hawaii, at least a few licks of poi—cooked, pounded taro (the traditional Hawaiian staple crop)—are a must. Other **native foods** include those from before and after Western contact, such as laulau (pork, chicken, or fish steamed in ti leaves), kalua pork (pork cooked in a Polynesian underground oven known here as an *imu*), lomi salmon (salted salmon with tomatoes and green onions), squid luau (cooked in coconut milk and taro tops), poke (cubed raw fish seasoned with onions and seaweed and the occasional sprinkling of roasted *kukui* nuts), haupia (creamy coconut pudding), and *kulolo* (steamed pudding of coconut, brown sugar, and taro).

Bento, another popular quick meal available throughout Hawaii, is a compact, boxed assortment of picnic fare usually consisting of neatly arranged sections of rice, pickled vegetables, and fried chicken, beef, or pork. Increasingly, however, the bento is becoming more health-conscious, as in macrobiotic or vegetarian brown-rice bentos. A derivative of the modest lunch box for Japanese immigrants who once labored in the sugar and pineapple fields, bentos are dispensed everywhere, from department stores to corner delis and supermarkets.

Also from the plantations comes *manapua,* a bready, doughy sphere filled with tasty fillings of sweetened pork or sweet beans. In the old days, the Chinese "*manapua* man" would make his rounds with bamboo containers balanced on a rod over his shoulders. Today you'll find white or whole-wheat *manapua* containing chicken, vegetables, curry, and other savory fillings.

The daintier Chinese delicacy **dim sum** is made of translucent wrappers filled with fresh seafood, pork hash, and vegetables, served for breakfast and lunch in Chinatown restaurants. The Hong Kong–style dumplings are ordered fresh and hot from bamboo steamers rolled on carts from table to table. Much like hailing a taxi in Manhattan, you have to be quick and loud for dim sum.

For dessert or a snack, particularly on Oahu's North Shore, the prevailing choice is **shave ice,** Hawaii's version of a snow cone. Particularly on hot, humid days, long lines of shave-ice lovers gather for heaps of finely shaved ice topped with sweet tropical syrups.

Traditional Hawaiian foods include taro, poi, and kalua pork.

(The sweet-sour *li hing mui* flavor is a current favorite.) The fast-melting mounds, which require prompt, efficient consumption, are quite the local summer ritual for sweet tooths. Aficionados order shave ice with ice cream and sweetened adzuki beans plopped in the middle.

Ahi, Ono & Opakapaka: A Hawaiian Seafood Primer

The seafood in Hawaii has been described as the best in the world. And why not? Without a doubt, the islands' surrounding waters, including the waters of the remote northwestern Hawaiian Islands, and a growing aquaculture industry contribute to the high quality of the seafood here.

The reputable restaurants in Hawaii buy fresh fish daily at predawn auctions or from local fishermen. Some chefs even catch their ingredients themselves. "Still wiggling" and "just off the hook" are the ultimate terms for freshness in Hawaii.

Although some menus include the Western description for the fresh fish used, most often the local nomenclature is listed, turning dinner into a confusing, quasi-foreign experience for the uninitiated. To help familiarize you with the menu language of Hawaii, here's a basic glossary of Hawaii's fish:

ahi   yellowfin or big-eye tuna, important for its use in sashimi and poke at sushi bars and in Hawaii Regional Cuisine

aku   skipjack tuna, heavily used by local families in home cooking and poke

ehu   red snapper, delicate and sumptuous, yet lesser known than opakapaka

hapuupuu   grouper, a sea bass whose use is expanding

hebi   spearfish, mildly flavored, and frequently featured as the "catch of the day" in upscale restaurants

kajiki   Pacific blue marlin, also called *au,* with a firm flesh and high fat content that make it a plausible substitute for tuna

kumu   goatfish, a luxury item on Chinese and upscale menus, served *en papillote* or steamed whole, Oriental-style, with scallions, ginger, and garlic

mahimahi   dolphin fish (the game fish, not the mammal) or dorado, a classic sweet, white-fleshed fish requiring vigilance among purists because it's often disguised as fresh when it's actually "fresh-frozen"—a big difference

monchong   bigscale or sickle pomfret, an exotic, tasty fish, scarce but gaining a higher profile on Hawaiian Island menus

nairagi   striped marlin, also called *au,* good as sashimi and in poke, and often substituted for ahi in raw-fish products

onaga   ruby snapper, a luxury fish, versatile, moist, and flaky

ono   wahoo, firmer and drier than the snappers, often served grilled and in sandwiches

opah   moonfish, rich and fatty, and versatile—cooked, raw, smoked, and broiled

opakapaka   pink snapper, light, flaky, and luxurious, suited for sashimi, poaching, sautéing, and baking; the best-known upscale fish

papio   jack trevally, light, firm, and flavorful, and favored in Hawaiian cookery

shutome   broadbill swordfish, of beeflike texture and rich flavor

tombo   albacore tuna, with a high fat content, suitable for grilling

uhu   parrotfish, most often encountered steamed, Chinese-style

uku   gray snapper of clear, pale-pink flesh, delicately flavored and moist

ulua   large jack trevally, firm fleshed and versatile

WHEN TO GO

Most visitors don't come to Maui when the weather's best on the island; rather, they come when it's at its worst everywhere else. Thus, the **high season**—when prices are up and resorts are often booked to capacity—is generally from mid-December to March or mid-April. The last 2 weeks of December, in particular, are the prime time for travel to Hawaii. If you're planning a holiday trip, make your reservations as early as possible, expect crowds, and prepare to pay top dollar for accommodations, car rentals, and airfare.

The **off season,** when the best rates are available and the islands are less crowded, is spring (mid-Apr to mid-June) and fall (Sept to mid-Dec)—a paradox because these are the best seasons to be in Hawaii, in terms of reliably great weather. If you're looking to save money, or if you just want to avoid the crowds, this is the time to visit. Hotel rates and airfares tend to be significantly lower, and good packages are often available.

Note: If you plan to come to Maui between the last week in April and early May, be sure you book your accommodations, interisland air reservations, and car rentals in advance. In Japan, the last week of April is called **Golden Week** because three Japanese holidays take place one after the other.

Due to the large number of families traveling in **summer** (June–Aug), you won't get the fantastic bargains of spring and fall. However, you'll still do much better on packages, airfare, and accommodations than you will in the winter months.

Climate

Because Hawaii lies at the edge of the tropical zone, it technically has only two seasons, both of them warm. There's a dry season that corresponds to **summer** (Apr–Oct) and a rainy season in **winter** (Nov–Mar). It rains every day somewhere in the islands any time of the year, but the rainy season sometimes brings enough gray weather to spoil your tanning opportunities. Fortunately, it seldom rains in one spot for more than 3 days straight.

The **year-round temperature** doesn't vary much. At the beach, the average daytime high in summer is 85°F (29°C), while the average daytime high in winter is 78°F (26°C); nighttime lows are usually about 10° cooler. But how warm it is on any given day really depends on *where* you are on the island.

Each island has a leeward side (the side sheltered from the wind) and a windward side (the side that gets the wind's full force). The **leeward** sides (the west and south) are usually hot and dry, while the **windward** sides (east and north) are generally cooler and moist. When you want arid, sunbaked, desertlike weather, go leeward. When you want lush, wet, junglelike weather, go windward.

Maui is also full of **microclimates,** thanks to its interior valleys, coastal plains, and mountain peaks. It can be hot, dry, and sunny on the island's leeward side in Lahaina and Kihei, but it's downright chilly at 3,000 feet and above in the upcountry region of Kula—there is snow on top of 10,000-foot Haleakala. On the windward side, an abundance of rain is what makes Kahului, Haiku, and Hana so verdant. If the weather doesn't suit you where you are, just head to the other side of the island—or into the hills.

On rare occasions, the weather can be disastrous, as when Hurricane Iniki crushed Kauai in September 1992 with 225-mph winds. Tsunamis have swept Hilo and the south shore of Oahu. But those are extreme exceptions. Mostly, one day follows another here in glorious, sunny procession, each quite like the other.

Average Monthly High/Low Temperatures, Water Temperature & Precipitation in Lahaina

	JAN	FEB	MAR	APR	MAY	JUNE	JULY	AUG	SEPT	OCT	NOV	DEC
HIGH (°F)	81	80	82	84	85	86	87	88	88	87	85	83
HIGH (°C)	27	27	28	29	29	30	31	31	31	31	29	29
LOW (°F)	66	63	64	65	64	68	69	70	69	69	67	65
LOW (°C)	19	17	18	18	18	20	21	21	21	21	19	18
WATER TEMP. (°F)	75	74	74	75	76	77	78	79	80	79	77	76
WATER TEMP. (°C)	24	23	23	24	24	25	26	26	27	26	25	24
AVG. PRECIP. (IN INCHES)	3.3	2	2	1	0.5	0.1	.02	0.3	0.3	1	2	3

Average Monthly High/Low Temperatures, Water Temperature & Precipitation in Kihei

	JAN	FEB	MAR	APR	MAY	JUNE	JULY	AUG	SEPT	OCT	NOV	DEC
HIGH (°F)	80	81	81	82	86	86	87	87	88	87	84	82
HIGH (°C)	27	27	27	28	30	30	31	31	31	31	29	28
LOW (°F)	63	63	65	66	69	69	66	71	70	69	68	65
LOW (°C)	17	17	18	19	20	21	19	22	21	21	20	18
WATER TEMP. (°F)	75	74	74	75	76	77	78	79	80	79	77	76
WATER TEMP. (°C)	24	23	23	24	24	25	26	26	27	26	25	24
AVG. PRECIP. (IN INCHES)	4	3	2	2	0.6	0.1	0.1	0.3	0.3	1	2	3

Holidays

When Hawaii observes holidays (especially those over a long weekend), travel between the islands increases, interisland airline seats are fully booked, rental cars are at a premium, and hotels and restaurants are busier.

Federal, state, and county government offices are closed on all federal holidays.

SYMBOL OF A CULTURE: the outrigger canoe

Hawaiians have been masters of the outrigger canoe since the first Polynesians landed on the islands' shores about 1,500 years ago. Today, outrigger canoeing is the official state sport, and dozens of canoeing clubs throughout the islands cater to a growing interest—and pride—in this oldest of Hawaiian traditions.

Far more than a simple mode of transportation, the canoe in ancient Hawaii was inextricably woven into the culture: as an expression of royal power, the basis of its early naval fleet, a favorite sport, an essential tool for fishing and survival, and an art form. Outrigger canoes have one or more lateral support floats (outriggers), or can be double-hulled, like today's catamarans. Historically, the one-piece hulls were carved from the hardwood koa tree; the floats and other parts were lashed together with coconut-fiber cord. Sails were mats woven from pandanus leaves. Because the canoe's performance in Hawaii's rough ocean waters could determine life or death, a priest often oversaw the building of the vessel, and offerings of fish, pigs, and flowers were made upon completion of a canoe. Canoe racing was a physically rigorous sport, and races were held primarily for serious gambling purposes. It's estimated that when the Europeans arrived in the 18th century there were as many as 12,000 canoes in Hawaii, though canoe racing, like surfing, was banned once missionaries arrived, around 1820.

Centuries before European explorers were plying the world's oceans, the Hawaiians' ancestors, the Polynesians, were using sophisticated long-distance navigation techniques and large, double-hulled outrigger canoes to travel thousands of miles in the vast Pacific. From their earliest origins in Southeast Asia, these early navigators traveled to the western edge of Polynesia (Micronesia) between 3,000 and 1,500 B.C. From there, they steadily moved west and north to colonize eastern Polynesian islands like Samoa and Tonga. Sometime between 300 and 700 A.D., the Polynesians arrived in New Zealand, the Easter Islands (Rapa Nui), and Hawaii. The Polynesians and Hawaiians practiced star map navigation, which uses the rising points of the stars, and observation of the sun, moon, ocean swells, and flight patterns of birds, as a natural compass to steer the course.

—by Megan McFarland

State and county offices are also closed on local holidays, including Prince Kuhio Day (Mar 26), honoring the birthday of Hawaii's first delegate to the U.S. Congress; King Kamehameha Day (June 11), a statewide holiday commemorating Kamehameha the Great, who united the islands and ruled from 1795 to 1819; and Admissions Day (third Fri in Aug), which honors the admittance of Hawaii as the 50th state on August 21, 1959.

Other special days celebrated in Hawaii by many people but that involve no closing of federal, state, and county offices are the Chinese New Year (which can fall in Jan or Feb), Girls' Day (Mar 3), Buddha's Birthday (Apr 8), Father Damien's Day (Apr 15), Boys' Day (May 5), Samoan Flag Day (in Aug), Aloha Festivals (Sept–Oct), and Pearl Harbor Day (Dec 7).

Maui, Molokai & Lanai Calendar of Events

Please note that as with any schedule of upcoming events, the following information is subject to change; always confirm the details before you plan your trip around an event.

For an exhaustive list of events beyond those listed here, check http://events.frommers.com, where you'll find a searchable, up-to-the-minute roster of what's happening in cities all over the world.

JANUARY

Hyundai Tournament of Champions, Kapalua Resort, Maui. Top PGA golfers compete for $5.6 million. Call ✆ **808/669-2440** or go to www.kapalua-maui.com. First weekend in January.

Ka Molokai Makahiki, Kaunakakai Town Baseball Park, Mitchell Pauole Center, Kaunakakai, Molokai. Makahiki, a traditional time of peace in ancient Hawaii, is re-created with performances by Hawaiian music groups and hula *halau* (schools), ancient Hawaiian games, a sporting competition, and Hawaiian crafts and food. It's a wonderful chance to experience the Hawaii of yesteryear. Call ✆ **800/800-6367** or 808/553-3876 or go to www.molokaievents.com. Late January.

Chinese New Year, Maui. Lahaina town rolls out the red carpet for this important event with a traditional lion dance at the historic Wo Hing Temple on Front Street that's accompanied by fireworks, food booths, and a host of activities. Call ✆ **888/310-1117** or 808/667-9175 or go to www.visitlahaina.com. Also on Maui, at the Maui Mall in Kahului; call ✆ **808/878-1888.** Chinese New Year can fall in January or February; 2013 ushers in the year of the Snake on February 10; in 2014, the year of the Horse comes in on January 14.

FEBRUARY

Kaanapali Champions Skins Game, Kaanapali Golf Courses, Maui. Longtime golfing greats participate in this four-man tournament for $770,000 in prize money. Call ✆ **808/661-3691** or go to www.kaanapali-golf.com. Late January or early February.

Whale Day Celebration, Kalama Park, Kihei. A daylong celebration in the park, with a parade of whales, entertainment, a crafts fair, games, and food. Call ✆ **808/249-8811,** ext. 1, or go to www.mauiwhalefestival.org. Early or mid-February.

Ocean Arts Festival, Lahaina. The entire town of Lahaina celebrates the annual migration of Pacific humpback whales with this festival in Banyan Tree Park. Artists display their best ocean-themed art for sale, while Hawaiian musicians and hula troupes entertain. Enjoy marine-related activities, games, and a Creature Feature touch-pool exhibit for children. Call ✆ **888/310-1117** or 808/667-9194 or go to www.visitlahaina.com. Mid-March.

📎 Daylight Saving Time

Since 1966, most of the United States has observed daylight saving time from the first Sunday in April to the last Sunday in October. In 2007, these dates changed, and now daylight saving time lasts from 2am on the second Sunday in March to 2am on the first Sunday in November. ***Note: Hawaii does* not** **observe daylight saving time.** So when daylight saving time is in effect in most of the U.S., Hawaii is 3 hours behind the West Coast and 6 hours behind the East Coast. When the U.S. reverts to standard time in November, Hawaii is 2 hours behind the West Coast and 5 hours behind the East Coast.

MARCH

Prince Kuhio Day Celebrations. Various festivals are held throughout Hawaii to celebrate the birth of Jonah Kuhio Kalanianaole, who was born on March 26, 1871, and elected to Congress in 1902. Molokai also hosts a 1-day celebration; call ℂ **808/567-6027** or go to www.visitmolokai.com to learn more.

APRIL

East Maui Taro Festival, Hana, Maui. Taro, a Hawaiian staple food, is celebrated through music, hula, arts, crafts, and, of course, food. Call ℂ **808/264-1553** or go to www.tarofestival.org. Varying dates in April.

Buddha Day, Lahaina Jodo Mission, Lahaina, Maui. Each year on the first Saturday in April, this historic mission holds a flower festival pageant honoring the birth of Buddha. The first Saturday in April.

Celebration of the Arts, Ritz-Carlton Kapalua, Kapalua Resort, Maui. Contemporary and traditional artists give free hands-on lessons during this 2-day festival, which begins the Friday before Easter. Call ℂ **808/665-7084** or go to www.celebrationofthearts.org. Late March or early April.

Polo Spring Season Begins. For a complete list of all the polo matches in the cool, upcountry area of Maui, call ℂ **808/877-7744** or go to www.mauipoloclub.com.

David Malo Day, Lahainaluna High School, Lahaina. This daylong event, with hula and other Hawaiian cultural celebrations, commemorates Hawaii's famous scholar and ends with a luau. Call ℂ **808/662-4000** or go to www.visitmaui.com. Mid- or late April.

Banyan Tree Birthday Party, Lahaina. Come celebrate the birthday of Lahaina's famous Banyan Tree with a weekend of activities. Call ℂ **888/310-1117** or 808/667-9175 or go to www.visitlahaina.com. Generally the end of April.

MAY

Outrigger Canoe Season, all islands. From May to September, canoe paddlers across the state participate in outrigger canoe races nearly every weekend. Call ℂ **808/383-7798** or go to www.y2kanu.com for this year's schedule of events.

Lei Day Celebrations, various locations on all islands. May Day is Lei Day in Hawaii, celebrated with lei-making contests, pageantry, arts and crafts, and music. For a list of Maui events go to www.visitmaui.com/maui/calendar, which includes the Lei Day Brothers Cazimero concert at the **Maui Arts & Cultural Center** (ℂ **808/242-2787;** www.mauiarts.org).

Maui Onion Festival, Whalers Village, Kaanapali, Maui. Everything you ever wanted to know about the sweetest onions in the world. There is food, entertainment, tastings, and the Maui Onion cook-off. Call ℂ **808/661-4567** or go to www.whalersvillage.com/onionfestival.htm. Early May.

Molokai Ka Hula Piko Festival, Mitchell Pau'ole Center, Kaunakakai, Molokai. This 3-day-long celebration of the hula takes place in mid-May on the island where it was born. It features performances by hula schools, musicians, and singers from across Hawaii, as well as local food and Hawaiian crafts, including quilting, woodworking, feather work, and deer-horn scrimshaw. Call ℂ **800/800-6367** or 808/553-3876 or go to www.molokaievents.com.

JUNE

Hawaiian Slack-Key Guitar Festival, Maui Arts & Cultural Center, Kahului, Maui. This festival features great music performed by the best musicians in Hawaii. It's 5 hours long and free. Call ℂ **808/226-2697** or go to www.slackkeyfestival.com. Late June. Check the website for festivals on the other islands and their dates.

King Kamehameha Celebration, all islands. This state holiday (officially June 11, but celebrated on different dates on

Traditional hula is a feature of many Hawaiian festivals.

each island) features a massive floral parade, *hoolaulea* (party), and much more. Call ☎ **808/667-9194** for Maui events, ☎ **808/553-3876** for Molokai events, or go to http://hawaii.gov/dags/kamehameha. Most events in 2013 will be held early to mid-June.

Kapalua Wine & Food Festival, Ritz-Carlton and various locations, Maui. One of Hawaii's best food-and-wine festivals features Hawaii's top chefs as well as international chefs and sommeliers showing off their culinary talents and wines from around the world. The event's 31st year will be 2013. Not to be missed. Call ☎ **808/665-5493** or go to www.kapaluamaui.com. Early June.

Maui Film Festival, Wailea Resort, Maui. Five days and nights of screenings of premieres and special films, along with traditional Hawaiian storytelling, chants, hula, and contemporary music. It begins the Wednesday before Father's Day. Call ☎ **808/579-9244** or go to www.mauifilmfestival.com. Mid-June.

JULY

Fourth of July. Lahaina holds an old-fashioned Independence Day

celebration with fireworks lighting the night sky over Lahaina's roadstead. Call ☎ **888/310-1117** or 808/667-9194 or go to www.visitlahaina.com.

Makawao Parade & Rodeo, Makawao, Maui. The annual parade and rodeo event has been taking place in this upcountry cowboy town for generations. Go to www.visitmaui.com or call 808/572-9565. July 4.

Lanai Pineapple Festival, Lanai City, Lanai. This festival celebrates Lanai's history of pineapple plantations and ranching, including a pineapple-eating contest, a pineapple-cooking contest, entertainment, arts and crafts, food, and fireworks. Call ☎ **808/565-7600** or go to www.gohawaii.com/lanai. Last Saturday in July.

Polo Season, Olinda Polo Field, Makawao. Polo matches featuring Hawaii's top players, often joined by famous international players, are held every Sunday at 1pm throughout the summer. Call ☎ **808/877-7744** or go to www.mauipoloclub.com.

Bon Dance & Lantern Ceremony, Lahaina, Maui. This colorful Buddhist ceremony honors the souls of the dead. Call ☎ **808/661-4304.** Usually the first Saturday in July.

Molokai to Oahu Paddleboard Race, starts on Molokai and finishes on Oahu. Some 70 participants from an international field journey to Molokai to compete in this 32-mile race, considered to be the world championship of long-distance paddle-board racing. The race begins at Kepuhi Beach on Molokai at 7am and finishes at Maunaloa Bay on Oahu around 12:30pm. Call ☎ **808/638-8208** or go to www.visitmolokai.com. Mid- to late July.

AUGUST

Hawaii State Windsurfing Championship, Kanaha Beach Park, Kahului, Maui. Top windsurfers compete. Call ☎ **808/877-2111** or go to www.surfmaui.com. Late July or early August.

Tahiti Fete, War Memorial Gym, Wailuku, Maui. This is an annual festival with Tahitian dance competition, arts and crafts, and food. Call ☎ **808/270-7389** or go to www.ipolynesia.com.

Admissions Day, all islands. This is a state holiday honoring the day (August 21, 1959) that Hawaii became the 50th state. All state-related facilities are closed. Third Friday in August.

SEPTEMBER

Aloha Festivals, various locations on all islands. Parades and other events celebrate Hawaiian culture and friendliness throughout the state. Call or go to www. festivalsofaloha.com or call
☎ **808/268-9285.**

A Taste of Lahaina, Lahaina Civic Center, Maui. Some 30,000 people show up to sample 40 signature entrees from Maui's premier chefs during this weekend festival, which includes cooking demonstrations, wine tastings, and live entertainment. The event begins Friday night with Maui Chefs Present, a dinner/

ONGOING events ON MAUI

Every Friday night from 7 to 10pm, as part of **Friday Night Is Art Night** in Lahaina, the town's galleries open their doors for special shows, demonstrations, and refreshments. There are even strolling musicians wandering the streets.

If you're hungry for Hawaiian music, the **Masters of Hawaiian Slack Key Guitar Series** (☎ **888/669-3858;** www. slackkey.com) features some of the great masters (and some Grammy Award winners) of this guitar style unique to the Hawaiian Islands. Concerts are held every Wednesday night at 7:30pm at the Napili Kai Beach Resort. Tickets are $40; call in advance for reservations.

On the first and third weekends of the month, Hawaiian artists sell and share culture, arts, and crafts under the famous landmark **Banyan Tree** in Lahaina. On the other weekends, the Lahaina Arts Society holds an exhibit and sale of various works of art in the same place.

You don't have to spend a good chunk of change and order two drinks to experience the Hawaiian art of hula. There are **free hula performances** every week. In **Lahaina,** they take place Tuesday and Thursday at 7pm in the Lahaina Cannery Mall. In **Kaanapali,** they're Monday, Wednesday, and Sunday nights, 7 to 8pm at the Whalers Village; and every night at 6:30pm at the Kaanapali Beach Hotel. If you would like to try the hula yourself, there are free hula lessons at Whalers Village every Thursday from 3 to 4pm.

Maui's produce has long been a source of pride for islanders; check out farmers' markets around the island on p. 232.

cocktail party featuring about a dozen of Maui's best chefs. Call ✆ **808/667-9175** or go to www.visitmaui.com. Second weekend in September.

Hana Relays, Hana Highway. Hundreds of runners, in relay teams, crowd the Hana Highway from Kahului to Hana (you might want to avoid the road on this day). Go to www.virr.com. Early September.

Maui Marathon, Kahului to Kaanapali. Runners line up at the Maui Mall before daybreak and head off for Kaanapali. Call ✆ **866/280-5801** or go to www.virr. com or www.mauimarathonhawaii.com. Mid- to late September.

Na Wahine O Ke Kai, Molokai. The top women canoe paddlers from across the state will arrive at Hale Lono Harbor on Molokai and paddle across the ocean to Oahu. Call ✆ **808/259-7112** or go to www.nawahineokekai.com. Mid-September.

Maui County Fair, War Memorial Complex, Wailuku, Maui. The oldest county fair in Hawaii features a parade, amusement rides, live entertainment, and exhibits. Go to **www.mauifair.com**. Last weekend in September.

OCTOBER

Aloha Festivals Hoolaulea, Lahaina. This all-day cultural festival, which marks the end of Maui's Aloha Festivals Week, is held at Banyan Tree Park and features Hawaiian food, music, and dance, along with arts and crafts on display and for sale. Call ✆ **888/310-1117** or 808/667-9194, or go to www.visitlahaina.com. September or October.

Molokai Hoe, Molokai to Oahu. This men's 40-mile outrigger contest starts in Molokai and finishes at Fort DeRussy Beach in Waikiki. Call ✆ **808/259-7112** or go to www.molokaihoe.com.

NOVEMBER

Hawaii International Film Festival, various locations throughout the state. This cinema festival with a cross-cultural spin features filmmakers from Asia, the Pacific

Islands, and the United States. Call ✆ **808/792-1577** or go to www.hiff.org. Late October or early November.

EA Sports Maui Invitational Basketball Tournament, Lahaina Civic Center, Lahaina. Top college teams vie in this annual preseason tournament. Call ✆ **808/667-DUNK** (3865) or go to www. mauiinvitational.com. Mid- to late November.

DECEMBER

Na Mele O Maui, Kaanapali, Maui. A traditional Hawaiian song competition for children in kindergarten through 12th grade, held in the ballroom of one of the Kaanapali Resort hotels. Admission is a $5 donation. Call ✆ **808/242-7469** or go to www.kaanapaliresort.com. First Friday in December.

Hui Noeau Christmas House, Makawao. The festivities in the beautifully decorated Hui mansion include shopping, workshops and art demonstrations, children's activities and visits with Santa, holiday music, fresh-baked goods, and local foods. Call ✆ **808/572-6560** or go to www.huinoeau.com. Late November through Christmas.

Billabong Pro Maui, Honolua Bay at Kapalua Resort, Maui. The final Triple Crown women's surfing contest of the year, bringing together the best of the women's international surfing community. Go to www.billabongpro.com. Early December.

Festival of Trees, Lahaina Cannery Mall, Lahaina. Look for decorated trees as well as entertainment. Call ✆ **808/661-5304.** Early December.

Lighting of the Banyan Tree, Lahaina. At 6:30pm, Lahaina's historic Banyan Tree is lit up with thousands of Christmas lights for the entire holiday season. Santa Claus makes an appearance, and choirs sing Christmas carols accompanied by hula. Kids can join a cookie workshop. Call ✆ **808/667-9194** or 667-9194 or go to www.visitlahaina.com. Early December.

Christmas Light Parade, Kaunakakai, Molokai. This is a light parade with music and holiday arts and crafts. Call ✆ **808/553-3773.** Mid-December.

Festival of Lights, all islands. On Maui, marching bands, floats, and Santa roll down Lahaina's Front Street in an annual parade. Molokai celebrates with a host of activities in Kaunakakai. Call ✆ **808/667-9175** for Maui; ✆ 808/553-4482 for Molokai. Early December.

Banyan Tree Lighting Celebration, Lahaina, Maui. This day of Christmas carolers, Santa Claus, live music and entertainment, a crafts fair, holiday baked goods, and activities for children takes place in the Banyan Tree Park on Front Street. Call ✆ **888/667-9193** or go to www.visitlahaina.com. First weekend in December.

FirstLight; Academy Screening on Maui, Maui Arts & Cultural Center, Kahului, Maui. Major films are screened at this festival; past selections have included *The Lord of the Rings: Return of the King, Mystic River, The Aviator, Hotel Rwanda,* and many others. Not to be missed. Call ✆ **808/579-9244** or 808/242-7469 or go to www.mauifilmfestival.com. Late November and throughout December.

THE LAY OF THE LAND

The first Hawaiian islands were born of violent volcanic eruptions that took place deep beneath the ocean's surface about 70 million years ago—more than 200 million years after the major continental landmasses were formed. As soon as the islands emerged, Mother Nature's fury began to carve beauty from barren rock. Untiring volcanoes spewed forth rivers of fire that cooled into stone. Severe tropical storms, some with hurricane-force winds, battered and blasted the cooling lava rock into a series of shapes. Ferocious earthquakes flattened, shattered, and reshaped the islands into precipitous valleys, jagged cliffs, and recumbent flatlands. Monstrous surf and gigantic tidal waves rearranged and polished the lands above and below the reaches of the tide.

It took millions of years for nature to shape the familiar form of Diamond Head on Oahu, Maui's majestic peak of Haleakala, the waterfalls of Molokai's northern side, the reefs of Hulopoe Bay on Lanai, and the lush rainforests of the Big Island. The result is an island chain like no other—a tropical dreamscape of a landscape rich in flora and fauna, surrounded by a vibrant underwater world.

The Flora of the Islands

Hawaii is filled with sweet-smelling flowers, lush vegetation, and exotic plant life.

AFRICAN TULIP TREES Even from afar, you can see the flaming red flowers on these large trees, which can grow to be more than 50 feet tall. The buds hold water, and Hawaiian children use the flowers as water pistols.

ANGEL'S TRUMPETS These small trees can grow up to 20 feet tall, with an abundance of large (up to 10-in.-diameter) pendants—white or pink flowers that resemble, well, trumpets. The Hawaiians call them *nana-honua,* which means "earth gazing." The flowers, which bloom continually from early spring to late fall, have a musky scent. ***Warning:*** All parts of the plant are poisonous and contain a strong narcotic.

ANTHURIUMS Anthuriums originally came from the tropical Americas and the Caribbean islands. There are more than 550 species, but the most popular are the heart-shaped red, orange, pink, white, and purple flowers with tail-like spathes. Look for the heart-shaped green leaves in shaded areas. These exotic plants have no scent but will last several weeks as cut flowers. Anthuriums are particularly prevalent on the Big Island.

BANYAN TREES   Among the world's largest trees, banyans have branches that grow out and away from the trunk, forming descending roots that grow down to the ground to feed and form additional trunks, making the tree very stable during tropical storms. The banyan in the courtyard next to the old courthouse in Lahaina, Maui, is an excellent example of a spreading banyan—it covers ⅔ acre.

BIRDS OF PARADISE   These natives of Africa have become something of a trademark of Hawaii. They're easily recognizable by the orange and blue flowers nestled in gray-green bracts, looking somewhat like birds in flight.

BOUGAINVILLEA   Originally from Brazil, these vines feature colorful, tissue-thin bracts, ranging in color from majestic purple to fiery orange, that hide tiny white flowers.

BREADFRUIT TREES   A large tree—more than 60 feet tall—with broad, sculpted, dark-green leaves, the famous breadfruit produces a round, head-size green fruit that's a staple in the diets of all Polynesians. When roasted or baked, the whitish-yellow meat tastes somewhat like a sweet potato.

BROMELIADS   There are more than 1,400 species of bromeliads, of which the pineapple plant is the best known. "Bromes," as they're affectionately called, are generally spiky plants ranging in size from a few inches to several feet in diameter. They're popular not only for their unusual foliage, but also for their strange and wonderful flowers. Used widely in landscaping and interior decoration, especially in resort areas, bromeliads are found on every island.

COFFEE   Hawaii is the only state that produces coffee commercially. Coffee is an evergreen shrub with shiny, waxy, dark-green pointed leaves. The flower is a small, fragrant white blossom that develops into ½-inch berries that turn bright red when ripe. Look for coffee at elevations above 1,500 feet on the Kona side of the Big Island and on large coffee plantations on Kauai, Molokai, Oahu, and Maui.

GINGER   White and yellow ginger flowers are perhaps the most fragrant in Hawaii. Usually found in clumps growing 4 to 7 feet tall in areas blessed by rain, these sweet-smelling, 3-inch-wide flowers are composed of three dainty petal-like stamens and three long, thin petals. Ginger was introduced to Hawaii in the 19th century from the Indonesia-Malaysia area. Look for white and yellow ginger from late spring to fall.

Other members of the ginger family frequently seen in Hawaii include red, shell, and torch ginger. Red ginger consists of tall green stalks with foot-long red "flower heads." The red "petals" are actually bracts, which protect the 1-inch-long white flowers. Red ginger, which does not share the heavenly smell of white ginger, lasts a week or longer when cut. Look for red ginger from spring through late fall. Shell ginger, which originated in India and Burma, thrives in cool, wet mountain forests. These plants, with their pearly white, clamshell-like blossoms, bloom from spring to fall.

Perhaps the most exotic ginger is the red or pink torch ginger. Cultivated in Malaysia as seasoning, torch ginger rises directly out of the ground.

ABOVE: **Ripe coffee berries.** RIGHT: **Hibiscus.**

The flower stalks, which are about 5 to 8 inches in length, resemble the fire of a lighted torch. This is one of the few types of ginger that can bloom year-round.

HELICONIA   Some 80 species of the colorful heliconia family came to Hawaii from the Caribbean and Central and South America. The bright yellow, red, green, and orange bracts overlap and appear to unfold like origami birds. The most obvious heliconia to spot is the lobster claw, which resembles a string of boiled crustacean pincers. Another prolific heliconia is the parrot's beak: Growing to about hip height, it's composed of bright-orange flower bracts with black tips. Look for parrot's beaks in spring and summer.

HIBISCUS   The 4- to 6-inch hibiscus flowers bloom year-round and come in a range of colors, from lily white to lipstick red. The flowers resemble crepe paper, with stamens and pistils protruding spirelike from the center. Hibiscus hedges can grow up to 15 feet tall. The yellow hibiscus is Hawaii's official state flower.

JACARANDA   Beginning around March and sometimes lasting until early May, these huge lacy-leaved trees metamorphose into large clusters of spectacular lavender-blue sprays. The bell-shaped flowers drop quickly, leaving a majestic purple carpet beneath the tree.

MACADAMIA   A transplant from Australia, macadamia nuts have become a commercial crop in recent decades in Hawaii, especially on the Big Island and Maui. The large trees—up to 60 feet tall—bear a hard-shelled nut encased in a leathery husk, which splits open and dries when the nut is ripe.

MONKEYPOD TREES   The monkeypod is one of Hawaii's most majestic trees; it grows more than 80 feet tall and 100 feet across, and is often seen near older homes and in parks. The leaves of the monkeypod drop in February and March. Its wood is a favorite of woodworking artisans.

NIGHT-BLOOMING CEREUS   Look along rock walls for this spectacular night-blooming flower. Originally from Central America, this vinelike member of the cactus family has green scalloped edges and produces foot-long white flowers that open as darkness falls and wither as the sun rises. The plant also bears an edible red fruit.

ORCHIDS　To many minds, nothing says Hawaii more than orchids. The most widely grown variety—and the major source of flowers for leis and garnish for tropical libations—is the vanda orchid. The vandas used in Hawaii's commercial flower industry are generally lavender or white, but they grow in a rainbow of colors, shapes, and sizes. The orchids used for corsages are the large, delicate cattleya; the ones used in floral arrangements—you'll probably see them in your hotel lobby—are usually dendrobiums.

PANDANUS　Called *hala* by Hawaiians, pandanus is native to Polynesia. Thanks to its thick trunk, stiltlike supporting roots, and crown of long, swordlike leaves, the *hala* tree is easy to recognize. In what is quickly becoming a dying art, Hawaiians weave the *lau* (leaves) of the *hala* into hats, baskets, mats, bags, and the like.

PLUMERIA　Also known as frangipani, this sweet-smelling, five-petal flower, found in clusters on trees, is the most popular choice of lei makers. The Singapore plumeria has five creamy white petals, with a touch of yellow in the center. Another popular variety, ruba—with flowers from soft pink to flaming red—is also used in leis. When picking plumeria, be careful of the sap from the flower—it's poisonous and can stain clothes.

PROTEA　Originally from South Africa, this unusual oversize shrub comes in more than 40 varieties. The flowers of one species resemble pincushions;

THE lei OF THE LAND

There's nothing like a lei: the stunning tropical beauty of the delicate garland, the deliciously sweet fragrance of the blossoms, the sensual way the flowers curl softly around your neck. There's no doubt about it: Getting lei'd in Hawaii is a sensuous experience. Leis are one of the nicest ways to say hello, goodbye, congratulations, I salute you, my sympathies are with you, or I love you. The custom of giving leis can be traced back to Hawaii's very roots; according to chants, the first lei was given by Hiiaka, the sister of the volcano goddess Pele, who presented Pele with a lei of lehua blossoms on a beach in Puna. The presentation of a kiss with a lei didn't come about until World War II; it's generally attributed to an entertainer who kissed an officer on a dare and then quickly presented him with her lei, saying it was an old Hawaiian custom. Leis are the perfect symbol for the islands: They're given in the moment and their fragrance and beauty are enjoyed in the moment, but even after they fade, their spirit of aloha lives on.

Lei making is a tropical art form. All leis are fashioned by hand in a variety of traditional patterns; some are sewn with hundreds of tiny blooms or shells, or bits of ferns and leaves. Some are twisted, some braided, some strung; all are presented with love. The lei of choice on Maui is the *lokelani*, a small rose. Molokai's specialty lei is the *kukui*, the white blossom of a candlenut tree. On Lanai, it's the *kaunaoa*, a bright yellow moss.

Plumeria.

Protea.

those of another look like a bouquet of feathers. Once dried, proteas will last for years.

SILVERSWORD This very uncommon and unusual plant is seen only on the Big Island and in the Haleakala Crater on Maui. This rare relative of the sunflower family blooms between July and September. The silversword in bloom is a fountain of red-petaled, daisylike flowers that turn silver soon after blooming.

TARO Around pools, near streams, and in neatly planted fields, you'll see these green heart-shaped leaves, whose dense roots are a Polynesian staple. The ancient Hawaiians pounded the roots into poi. Originally from Sri Lanka, taro not only is a food crop, but also is grown for ornamental reasons.

The Fauna of the Islands

When the first Polynesians arrived in Hawaii between A.D. 500 and 800, scientists say they found some 67 varieties of endemic Hawaiian birds, a third of which are now believed to be extinct. They did not find any reptiles, amphibians, mosquitoes, lice, fleas, or even cockroaches.

There were only two endemic mammals: the hoary bat and the monk seal. The **hoary bat** must have accidentally blown to Hawaii at some point, from either North or South America. It can still be seen during its early-evening forays, especially around the Kilauea Crater on the Big Island.

The **Hawaiian monk seal,** a relative of warm-water seals found in the Caribbean and the Mediterranean, was nearly slaughtered into extinction for its skin and oil during the 19th century. These seals have recently experienced a minor population explosion; sometimes they even turn up at various beaches throughout the state. They're protected under federal law by the Marine Mammal Protection Act. If you're fortunate enough to see a monk seal, just look; don't disturb one of Hawaii's living treasures.

The first Polynesians brought a few animals from home: dogs, pigs, and chickens (all were for eating), as well as rats (stowaways). All four species are still found in the Hawaiian wild today.

BIRDS

More species of native birds have become extinct in Hawaii in the past 200 years than anywhere else on the planet. Of 67 native species, 23 are extinct and 30 are endangered. Even the Hawaiian crow, the **alala,** is threatened.

Aeo, or Hawaiian stilt.

Pueo.

The **aeo**, or Hawaiian stilt—a 16-inch-long bird with a black head, black coat, white underside, and long pink legs—can be found in protected wetlands such as the Kanaha Wildlife Sanctuary (where it shares its natural habitat with the Hawaiian coot) and Kealia Pond on Maui.

The **nene** is Hawaii's state bird. It's being brought back from the brink of extinction through strenuous protection laws and captive breeding. A relative of the Canada goose, the nene stands about 2 feet high and has a black head and yellow cheeks. The approximately 500 nene in existence can be seen in only three places: on Maui at Haleakala National Park, on the Big Island at Mauna Kea State Recreation Area bird sanctuary, and on the slopes of Mauna Kea.

The Hawaiian short-eared owl, the **pueo**, which grows to between 12 and 17 inches, can be seen at dawn and dusk. According to legend, spotting a pueo is a good omen.

Leapin' Lizards!

Geckos are harmless, soft-skinned, insect-eating lizards that come equipped with suction pads on their feet, enabling them to climb walls and windows to reach tasty insects such as mosquitoes and cockroaches. You'll see them on windows outside a lighted room at night or hear their cheerful chirp.

SEA LIFE

Approximately 680 species of fish are known to inhabit the waters around the Hawaiian Islands. Of those, approximately 450 species stay close to the reef and inshore areas.

CORAL   The reefs surrounding Hawaii are made up of various corals and algae. The living coral grows through sunlight that feeds specialized algae, which, in turn, allow the development of the coral's calcareous skeleton. The reef, which takes thousands of years to develop, attracts and supports fish and crustaceans, which use it for food and habitat. Mother Nature can batter the reef with a strong storm, but humans have proven far more destructive.

The corals most frequently seen in Hawaii are hard, rocklike formations named for their familiar shapes: antler, cauliflower, finger, plate, and razor coral. Some coral appears soft, such as tube coral; it can be found in the ceilings of caves. Black coral, which resembles winter-bare trees or shrubs, is found at depths of more than 100 feet.

REEF FISH Of the approximately 450 types of reef fish here, about 27% are native to Hawaii and are found nowhere else in the world. During the millions of years it took for the islands to sprout up from the sea, ocean currents—mainly from Southeast Asia—carried thousands of marine animals and plants to Hawaii's reef; of those, approximately 100 species adapted and thrived. You're likely to spot one or more of the following fish while underwater.

○ **Angelfish** can be distinguished by the spine, located low on the gill plate. These fish are very shy; several species live in colonies close to coral.

○ **Blennies** are small, elongated fish, ranging from 2 to 10 inches long, with the majority in the 3- to 4-inch range. Blennies are so small that they can live in tide pools; you might have a hard time spotting one.

○ **Butterflyfish,** among the most colorful of the reef fish, are usually seen in pairs (scientists believe they mate for life) and appear to spend most of their day feeding. There are 22 species of butterflyfish, of which three (bluestripe; lemon, or milletseed; and multiband, or pebbled butterflyfish) are endemic. Most butterflyfish have a dark band through the eye and a spot near the tail resembling an eye, meant to confuse their predators (moray eels love to lunch on them).

○ **Moray and conger eels** are the most common eels seen in Hawaii. Morays are usually docile except when provoked or when there's food around. Unfortunately, some morays have been fed by divers and now associate divers with food; thus, they can become aggressive. But most morays like to keep to themselves. While morays may look menacing, conger eels look downright happy, with big lips and pectoral fins (situated so that they look like big ears) that give them the appearance of a perpetually smiling face. Conger eels have crushing teeth so they can feed on crustaceans; because they're sloppy eaters, they usually live with shrimp and crabs that feed off the crumbs they leave.

○ **Parrotfish,** one of the largest and most colorful of the reef fish, can grow up to 40 inches long. They're easy to spot—their front teeth are fused together, protruding like buck teeth that allow them to feed by scraping algae from rocks and coral. The rocks and coral pass through the parrotfish's system, resulting in fine sand. In fact, most of the white sand found in Hawaii is parrotfish waste; one large parrotfish can produce a ton of sand a year. Native parrotfish species include yellowbar, regal, and spectacled.

○ **Scorpion fish** are what scientists call "ambush predators": They hide under camouflaged exteriors and ambush their prey. Several kinds sport a venomous dorsal spine. These fish don't have a gas bladder, so when they stop swimming, they sink—that's why you usually find them "resting" on ledges and on the ocean bottom. They're not aggressive, but be very careful where you put your hands and feet in the water so as to avoid those venomous spines.

○ **Surgeonfish,** sometimes called tang, get their name from the scalpel-like spines located on each side of the body near the base of the tail. Several surgeonfish,

Parrotfish.

such as the brightly colored yellow tang, are boldly colored; others are adorned in more conservative shades of gray, brown, or black. The only endemic surgeonfish—and the most abundant in Hawaiian waters—is the convict tang, a pale white fish with vertical black stripes (like a convict's uniform).

o **Wrasses** are a very diverse family of fish, ranging in length from 2 to 15 inches. Wrasses can change gender from female to male. Some have brilliant coloration that changes as they age. Several types of wrasse are endemic to Hawaii: Hawaiian cleaner, shortnose, belted, and gray (or old woman).

GAME FISH Hawaii is known around the globe as *the* place for big-game fish—marlin, swordfish, and tuna. Six kinds of **billfish** are found in the offshore waters around the islands: Pacific blue marlin, black marlin, sailfish, broadbill swordfish, striped marlin, and shortbill spearfish. Hawaii billfish range in size from the 20-pound shortbill spearfish and striped marlin to the 1,805-pound Pacific blue marlin, the largest marlin ever caught with rod and reel in the world.

Tuna ranges in size from small (1 lb. or less) mackerel tuna used as bait (Hawaiians call them *oio*) to 250-pound yellowfin ahi tuna. Other local species of tuna are big-eye, albacore, kawakawa, and skipjack.

Other types of fish, also excellent for eating, include **mahimahi** (also known as dolphin fish or dorado), in the 20- to 70-pound range; **rainbow runner,** from 15 to 30 pounds; and **wahoo** (ono), from 15 to 80 pounds. Shoreline fishermen are always on the lookout for **trevally** (the state record for a giant trevally is 191 lb.), **bonefish, ladyfish, threadfin, leatherfish,** and **goatfish.** Bottom fishermen pursue a range of **snapper**—red, pink, gray, and others—as well as **sea bass** (the state record is a whopping 563 lb.) and **amberjack** (which weigh up to 100 lb.).

WHALES Humpback whales are popular visitors that come to Hawaii to mate and calve every year, beginning in November and staying until spring—April or so—when they return to Alaska. On every island, you can take winter whale-watching cruises that will let you observe these magnificent leviathans up close. You can also spot them from shore—humpbacks grow to up to 45 feet long, so when one breaches (jumps out of the water), you can see it for miles.

Humpbacks are among the biggest whales found in Hawaiian waters, but other whales—such as pilot, sperm, false killer, melon-headed, pygmy killer, and beaked—can be seen year-round, especially in the calm waters off the Big Island's Kona Coast.

SHARKS Yes, there *are* sharks in Hawaii, but you more than likely won't see one unless you're specifically looking. About 40 species of sharks inhabit the waters surrounding Hawaii, ranging from the totally harmless whale shark (at 60 ft., the world's largest fish), which has no teeth and is so docile that it frequently lets divers ride on its back, to the not-so-docile, extremely uncommon great white shark. The most common sharks seen in Hawaii are white-tip or gray reef sharks (about 5 ft. long) and black-tip reef sharks (about 6 ft. long).

Hawaii's Ecosystem Problems

Officials at Hawaii Volcanoes National Park on the Big Island saw a potential problem a few decades ago with people taking a few rocks home with them as "souvenirs." To prevent this problem from escalating, the park rangers created a legend that the fiery volcano goddess, Pele, would punish these souvenir seekers with bad luck. There used to be a display case in the park's visitor center filled with letters from people who had taken rocks from the volcano, relating stories of

Humpback whale.

all the bad luck that followed. Most begged Pele's forgiveness and instructed the rangers to please return the rock to the exact location that was its original home.

Unfortunately, Hawaii's other ecosystem problems can't be handled as easily.

MARINE LIFE   Hawaii's beautiful and abundant marine life has attracted so many visitors that they threaten to overwhelm it. A great example of this is **Molokini,** a small crater off the coast of Maui. Twenty-five years ago, one or two small six-passenger boats made the trip once a day to Molokini; today it's not uncommon to sight 20 or more boats, each carrying 20 to 49 passengers, moored inside the tiny crater. One tour operator has claimed that, on some days, it's so crowded that you can actually see a slick of suntan oil floating on the surface of the water.

Hawaii's **reefs** have faced increasing impact over the years as well. Runoff of soil and chemicals from construction, agriculture, and erosion can blanket and choke a reef, which needs sunlight to survive. Human contact with the reef can also upset the ecosystem. Coral, the basis of the reef system, is very fragile; snorkelers and divers grabbing onto it can break off pieces that took decades to form. Feeding the fish can also upset the balance of the ecosystem (not to mention upsetting the digestive systems of the fish). In areas where they're fed, the normally shy reef fish become more aggressive, surrounding divers and demanding food.

FLORA   The rainforests are among Hawaii's most fragile environments. Any intrusion—from hikers carrying seeds on their shoes to the rooting of wild boars—can upset the delicate balance of these complete ecosystems. In recent years, development has moved closer and closer to the rainforests. On the Big Island, people have protested the invasion of bulldozers and the drilling of geothermal wells in the Wao Kele O Puna rainforest for years.

FAUNA   The biggest impact on the fauna in Hawaii is the decimation of native birds by feral animals, which have destroyed the birds' habitats, and by mongooses that have eaten the birds' eggs and young. Government officials are vigilant about snakes because of the potential damage they can do to the remaining bird life.

A recent pest introduced to Hawaii is the coqui frog. That loud noise you hear after dark, especially on the eastern side of the Big Island and various parts of Maui, including the Kapalua Resort area and on the windward side of the island, is the cry of the male coqui frog looking for a mate. A native of Puerto Rico, where the frogs are kept in check by snakes, the coqui frog came to Hawaii in some plant material, found no natural enemies, and has spread across the Big Island and Maui. A chorus of several hundred coqui frogs is deafening (it's been measured at 163 decibels, or the noise level of a jet engine from 100 ft.). In some places, like Akaka Falls, on the Big Island, there are so many frogs that they are now chirping during daylight hours.

RESPONSIBLE TRAVEL

If there is one place on the planet that seems ideally suited for ecotourism and sustainable travel, it's Hawaii, a place people visit because of the ecology—the ocean, the beach, the mountains, and the overall beauty of the place. It seems only natural that the maintenance of its environment would be a concern, both

HAWAII'S MOST DANGEROUS invaders

There's trouble in Paradise—serious trouble. Invasive species not native to Hawaii have destroyed native forests, killed the majority of the native birds, obliterated decades-old indigenous trees, and wiped out endemic fish found nowhere else on the planet.

The flora and fauna in Hawaii, the most isolated chain in the world, never developed defensive properties to warn off predators because there were no predators. Today, there are more endangered species per square mile in Hawaii than any other place on the planet.

- **Rats.** Rats came to Hawaii either on outrigger canoes steered by the Polynesians or on the whaling ships that showed up in the 1800s (or possibly both). Either way, the result was that rats ate birds' eggs and destroyed their habitat in the native forests.

- **Mongooses.** The small Indian mongoose was brought to Hawaii by sugar planters in 1883 as a solution to the rat problem. Unfortunately, no one considered that rats are nocturnal and the mongoose is not. Instead of killing rats, mongooses quickly started feasting on the eggs and chicks of native birds.

- **Pigs.** The Polynesians brought pigs with them to Hawaii. Feral pigs have since had an impact on nearly every native plant community in Hawaii. They root for food, eating native plants; invasive plants then establish themselves in the disturbed soil. The holes they leave behind fill with water, allowing mosquitoes carrying avian malaria to breed. With the destruction of native vegetation comes the destruction of native bird and insect populations as well.

- **Erythrina gall wasp.** This tiny wasp came to Hawaii in recent years. It lays its eggs in the leaves and stems of wiliwili trees, creating an outbreak of tumors (galls) on the leaves. The infected tree dies, and the wind carries diseased leaves off to infect more wiliwili trees.

- **Gorilla seaweed.** In the 1970s, scientists introduced this edible seaweed to Hawaiian waters, thinking it would make a good aquaculture crop. Since then this quickly growing seaweed has taken over several reefs, forming large, thick mats that overgrow and kill coral and other seaweeds, essentially smothering the reefs.

- **Tilapia.** Blame the scientists for this one too. This fish was introduced to Hawaii as an aquaculture crop. The problem is that tilapia can survive in both salt and fresh water, and feeds on almost anything from algae to insects. In particular, tilapia have had damaging effects on Hawaii's native shrimp and gobies.

- **Man.** From clear-cutting land (destroying Hawaii's native forests and all the plant, bird, and insect species found there) to polluting the pristine waters with agricultural and other chemicals, to filling in sand at beaches, to creating harbors, to channeling streams, man's impact on the islands is unequaled.

to the people who live there and to the visitors who come to enjoy all that its ecosystem has to offer.

In fact, Hawaii has a long history of environmental stewardship. The ancient Hawaiians not only knew about sustainability, but also practiced it in their daily lives. They had to! When the ancient Hawaiians occupied the islands, they did not have the luxury of "importing" goods from anywhere else. They had the land under their feet and the ocean to gain subsistence from, and those resources had to last not only for their own lifetime, but also for the lifetimes of generations to come. So these ancient people lived in harmony with the land and sea, and had a complex social structure that managed resources and forbade the taking of various resources during certain times of the year, to allow those resources to replenish themselves.

Now fast-forward to the 21st century. Today we, the current stewards of the islands of Hawaii, are just beginning to appreciate just how wise and advanced the ancient Hawaiians were. In some ways, the state of Hawaii is a pioneer when it comes to the various ways it protects and saves its natural resources. (For example, Hawaii is second only to California in the number of marine reserves in the National System of Marine Protected Areas.) And yet in other ways, modern Hawaii still falls short of the ancient Hawaiians, whose unique system sustained, without imports, the entire population.

Ongoing Environmental Initiatives

The state of Hawaii has several excellent stewardship programs to preserve the ocean environment and its resources, such as Marine Life Conservation Districts (an ocean version of parks—the waters surrounding Molokini is an example), Fishery Management Areas (where what you can take from the ocean is restricted), Fishery Replenishment Areas, and Estuarine Reserves. On land, there are corresponding programs to protect the environment, from the Soil and Water Conservation District to Watershed Reserves.

In the visitor industry, the majority of hotels have adopted green practices, not only to save the environment, but also to save them money. Nearly every hotel in the state will have a card in your room asking you to consider whether you really need a new towel or if you can hang it up and use it one more day. Various statewide organizations have numerous programs recognizing hotels that are helping the environment, such as the Green Business Awards Program, which recently awarded **Ritz-Carlton Kapalua** for its use of coreless toilet paper rolls in bathrooms, the elimination of plastic ware in dining areas, the installation of sustainable bamboo floors in select facilities, and for offering sustainable dining featuring organic heirloom herbs and vegetables as well as local exotic fruit. The hotel also runs a Jacques Cousteau Ambassadors of the Environment program, which teaches guests about natural tide pools, the rainforest, humpback whales, and local ecosystems through interactive activities with trained naturalists. Another Maui hotel, the **Fairmont Kea Lani,** also was recognized for its green practices, specifically for its "Recycling Cents Program," which donates money from recyclables to local charities, raising some $20,000 in 2010; an improved laundry water recycling system, which has saved over 50 million gallons of water since installation in 2005; the use of automatic eco-MODE thermostats, reducing air-conditioning costs by 20%; the use of biodegradable food containers; for using rock salt treating systems in pools; and for serving sustainable cuisine in its restaurants.

Every island has recycling centers (varying from collection of recyclable bottles only to places that take everything); for a list of recycling centers close to where you will be staying, visit the website of the **Hawaii State Department of Health** (http://hi5deposit.com/redcenters.html).

Restaurants across Maui—including **Market Fresh Bistro** in Makawao; **Merriman's** in Kapalua; **I'O, Pacific'O, Mala Ocean Tavern,** and **David Paul's** in Lahaina; and **Beverly Gannon's, Joe's,** and **Mala Wailea** in Wailea—are using more local products and produce than ever. Many proudly tell you that all of their products were grown, grazed, or caught within 100 miles of their restaurant. You can support this effort by ordering local (drink Kona coffee, not a coffee from Central America; eat local fish, not imported seafood). Ask the restaurant which items on its menu are grown or raised on the island, and then order the local items.

Below are some helpful hints travelers to Hawaii might want to keep in mind during their adventure to the islands so that their ecological footprint on Hawaii will be minimal.

WHAT VISITORS CAN DO IN & AROUND THE OCEAN

1. Do not touch anything in the ocean. In fact, unless you are standing on the sandy bottom where the waves roll into shore, try not to walk or stand on the ocean floor. The no-touch rule of thumb is not only for your protection—there are plenty of stinging, stabbing things out there that could turn your vacation into a nightmare—but also for the protection of the marine environment. Coral is composed of living things, which take years to grow, and a careless brush of your hand or foot could destroy them. Fragile habitats for marine critters can be damaged forever by your heavy foot.

2. Do not feed the fish, or any other marine creature. They have their own food and diet, and they can be irreparably harmed by your good intentions if you feed them "people food" or, even worse, some "fish food" you have purchased.

3. Leave the ocean and beach area cleaner than you found it. If you see trash in the ocean (plastic bags, bottles, and so on), remove it. You may save the life of a fish, turtle, marine mammal, or even seabird by removing that trash, which kills hundreds of marine inhabitants every year. The same thing is true of the beach: Pick up trash, even if it's not yours.

4. The beach is not an ashtray. Do not use the sand for your cigarette butts. How would you like someone using your living room carpet as his ashtray?

5. Look at, but don't approach, turtles or Hawaiian monk seals resting on the shoreline. The good news is that the number of turtles and Hawaiian monk seals is increasing. Visitors may not know it, but both are protected by law. You must stay 100 feet away from them. So take photos, but do not attempt to get close to the resting sea creatures (and no, they are not dead or injured, just resting).

6. If you plan to go fishing, practice catch and release. Let the fish live another day. Ask charter boat captains if they practice catch and release; if they say no, book with someone else.

7. If you are environmentally conscious, I do not recommend that you rent jet skis, because they have a significant environmental impact.

WHAT VISITORS CAN DO ON LAND

1. Don't litter (this includes throwing a cigarette butt out of your car).

2. Before you go hiking, in addition to the safety tips outlined on p. 375, scrub your hiking shoes (especially the soles) to get rid of seeds and soil.

3. When hiking, carry a garbage bag so you can carry out everything you carried in, including your litter (and if you see other garbage on the trail, carry it out, too).

4. Stay on the trail. Wandering off a trail is dangerous to you (you can get lost, fall off overgrown cliffs, or get injured by stepping into a hidden hole), and you could possibly carry invasive species into the native forests.

5. Do not pick flowers or plants along your hike. Just leave the environment the way you found it.

TRANSPORTATION CONCERNS

RENTAL CARS Most visitors coming to Hawaii seem to think "convertible" when they think of renting a car, or they think "SUV" for off-road adventures. If you're thinking "hybrid," you'll have to check your budget, because hybrids from car-rental agencies are not only hard to find, but also extremely expensive in Hawaii. Car-rental agencies do have a variety of cars to rent, though, and you can make a point of selecting a car that gets good gas mileage. Also, ask for a white car, as they use less energy to air-condition than a dark-colored car.

INTERISLAND TRANSPORTATION Now that the interisland ferry, Superferry, has declared bankruptcy, the only option for interisland travel between most islands is via air. There are two exceptions, however. If you're traveling between Maui and Lanai, you may want to consider taking the passenger-only Expeditions Maui-Lanai Passenger Ferry (commonly referred to as the Lanai Ferry). If you're traveling between Maui and Molokai, you can take the passenger-only *Molokai Princess.* Not only are these ferries cheaper than air travel, but their impact on the environment is also less, especially when you consider that most airlines will route you from Maui to Honolulu, then from Honolulu on to either Molokai or Lanai.

TOURS

If all you want is a fabulous beach and a perfectly mixed mai tai, then Maui has what you're looking for. But the island's wealth of natural wonders is equally hard

---

Volunteering on Vacation

If you are looking for a different type of experience during your next vacation to Hawaii, you might want to consider becoming a volunteer and leaving the islands a little nicer than when you arrived. People interested in volunteering at beach and ocean cleanups can contact the **University of Hawaii Sea Grant College Program** (✆ **808/956-7031**) or **Hawaii Wildlife Fund** (✆ **808/280-8124;** www.wildhawaii.org). For eco-volunteering on land, contact

Malama Hawaii (www.malamahawaii.org/get_involved/volunteer.php), a statewide organization dedicated to *malama* (taking care) of the culture and environment of Hawaii. With Malama Hawaii you will find a range of opportunities on various islands, such as weeding gardens and potting plants in botanical gardens, restoring taro patches, cleaning up mountain streams, bird-watching, and even hanging out at Waikiki Beach helping with a reef project.

GENERAL RESOURCES FOR green travel

The following websites provide valuable wide-ranging information on sustainable travel. For a list of even more sustainable resources, as well as tips and explanations on how to travel greener, visit Frommers.com/tips.

o **Responsible Travel** (www.responsible travel.com) is a great source of sustainable travel ideas; the site is run by a spokesperson for ethical tourism in the travel industry. **Sustainable Travel International** (www.sustainable travelinternational.org) promotes ethical tourism practices and manages an extensive directory of sustainable properties and tour operators around the world.

o **Carbonfund** (www.carbonfund.org) and **TerraPass** (www.terrapass.org) provide info on "carbon offsetting," or offsetting the greenhouse gas emitted during flights.

o **Greenhotels** (www.greenhotels.com) recommends green-rated member hotels around the world that fulfill the company's stringent environmental requirements. **Environmentally Friendly Hotels** (www.environmentally friendlyhotels.com) offers more green accommodation ratings.

o **Sustain Lane** (www.sustainlane.com) identifies sustainable eating and drinking choices around the U.S.; also visit **www.eatwellguide.org** for tips on eating sustainably in the U.S. and Canada.

o **Tread Lightly** (www.treadlightly.org) provides information on animal-friendly issues throughout the world, and the **Whale and Dolphin Conservation Society** (www.wdcs. org) offers information about the ethics of swimming with dolphins.

to resist; the year-round tropical climate and spectacular scenery tend to inspire almost everyone to get outside and explore.

If you don't have your own snorkel gear or other watersports equipment, or if you just don't feel like packing it, don't fret: Everything you'll need is available for rent. I discuss all kinds of places to rent or buy gear in the chapters that follow.

Setting Out on Your Own vs. Using an Outfitter

There are two ways to go: Plan all the details before you leave and either rent gear or schlep your stuff 2,500 miles across the Pacific, or go with an outfitter or a guide and let someone else worry about the details.

Experienced outdoors enthusiasts may head to coastal campgrounds or even trek to the 10,000-foot-high summit of Haleakala on their own. But in Maui, it's often preferable to go with a local guide who is familiar with the conditions at both sea level and summit peaks, knows the land and its flora and fauna in detail, and has all the gear you'll need. It's also good to go with a guide if time is an issue or if you have specialized interests. If you really want to see native birds, for instance, an experienced guide will take you directly to the best areas for sightings. And many forests and valleys in the interior of the islands are either on private property or in wilderness preserves accessible only on guided tours. The downside? If you go with a guide, plan on spending at least $100 a day per person. I've recommended the best local outfitters and tour-guide operators in the chapters that follow.

But if you have the time, already own the gear, and love doing the research and planning, try exploring on your own. This book discusses the best spots to set out on your own, from the top offshore snorkel and dive spots to great daylong hikes, as well as the federal, state, and county agencies that can help you with hikes on public property; I also list references for spotting birds, plants, and sea life. I recommend that you always use the resources available to inquire about weather, trail, or surf conditions; water availability; and other conditions before you take off on your adventure.

For hikers, a great alternative to hiring a private guide is taking a guided hike offered by the **Nature Conservancy of Hawaii,** 923 Nu'uanu Ave., Honolulu, HI 96817 (© **808/572-7849** on Maui, or 808/553-5236 on Molokai); or the **Hawaii Chapter of the Sierra Club,** P.O. Box 2577, Honolulu, HI 96803 (© **808/538-6616** on Oahu; www.sierraclubhawaii.com). Both organizations offer guided hikes in preserves and special areas during the year, as well as day- to weeklong work trips to restore habitats and trails and to root out invasive plants. It might not sound like a dream vacation to everyone, but it's a chance to see the "real" Hawaii—including wilderness areas that are ordinarily off-limits.

All Nature Conservancy hikes and work trips are free (donations are appreciated). However, you must reserve a spot for yourself, and a deposit is required for guided hikes to ensure that you'll show up; your deposit is refunded when you do. The hikes are generally offered once a month on Maui, Molokai, and Lanai. For all islands, call the Oahu office for reservations. Check their website, www. nature.org, for a schedule of guided hikes and other programs.

The Sierra Club offers weekly hikes on Maui. They are led by certified Sierra Club volunteers and are classified as easy, moderate, or strenuous. These half- or all-day affairs cost (recommended donation) $1 for Sierra Club members and $5 for nonmembers (bring exact change). You can find the latest edition of the club newsletter on their website.

For more information, contact the **Hawaii Ecotourism Association** (© **877/954-2910;** www.hawaiiecotourism.org).

Using Activities Desks to Book Your Island Fun

If you're unsure of which activity or which outfitter or guide is the right one for you and your family, you might want to consider booking through a discount activities center or activities desk. Not only will they save you money, but good activities centers should also be able to help you find, say, the snorkel cruise that's right for you, or the luau that's most suitable for both you *and* the kids.

Outdoor Etiquette

Act locally, think globally, and carry out what you carry in. Find a trash container for all your litter (including cigarette butts; it's *very* bad form to throw them out of your car window or to use the beach as an ashtray). Observe KAPU (taboo) and NO TRESPASSING signs. Don't climb on ancient Hawaiian *heiau* walls or carry home rocks, all of which belong to the Hawaiian volcano goddess, Pele. Some say it's just a silly superstition, but each year the national and state park services get boxes of lava rocks in the mail that have been sent back to Hawaii by visitors who've experienced unusually bad luck.

Remember, however, that it's in the activities agent's best interest to sign you up with outfitters from which they earn the most commission. Some agents have no qualms about booking you into any activity if it means an extra buck for them. If an agent tries to push a particular outfitter or activity too hard, be skeptical. Conversely, they'll try to steer you away from outfitters who don't offer big commissions. For example, **Trilogy** (p. 162), the company that offers Maui's most popular snorkel cruises to Lanai (and the only one with rights to land at Lanai's Hulopoe Beach), offers only minimum commissions to agents and does not allow agents to offer any discounts at all. As a result, most activities desks will automatically try to steer you away from Trilogy.

Another word of warning: Stay away from activities centers that offer discounts as fronts for timeshare sales presentations. Using a free or discounted snorkel cruise or luau tickets as bait, they'll suck you into a 90-minute presentation—and try to get you to buy into a Hawaii timeshare in the process. Because their business is timeshares, not activities, they won't be as interested in, or as knowledgeable about, which activities might be right for you. These shady deals seem to be particularly rampant on Maui.

There are a number of very reliable local activities centers on each of the neighbor islands. On Maui, your best bet is **Tom Barefoot's Cashback Tours,** 250 Alamaha St., Kahului (© **800/779-6305** or 808/661-8889; www.tombarefoot.com). Finally, you can reserve activities yourself and save the commission by booking via the Internet. Most outfitters offer 10% to 25% off their prices if you book online.

Outdoor Activities A to Z

Here's a brief rundown of the many outdoor activities available in Maui. For my recommendations on the best places to go, the best shops for renting equipment, and the best outfitters to use, see chapters 4, 5, 10, and 11.

BIRDING

Many of Hawaii's tropical birds are found nowhere else on Earth. There are curved-bill honeycreepers, black-winged red birds, and the rare o'o, whose yellow feathers Hawaiians once plucked to make royal capes. When you go birding, take along *A Field Guide to the Birds of Hawaii and the Tropical Pacific* (Princeton University Press, 1987), by H. Douglas Pratt, Phillip L. Bruner, and Delwyn G. Berett.

Molokai, in particular, is a great place to go birding. The lush rainforest of Molokai's Kamakou Preserve is home to the Molokai thrush and Molokai creeper, which live only on this 30-mile-long island.

For more on birding, see p. 316 for the discussion of Molokai's Kamakou Preserve.

BOATING

Almost every type of nautical experience is available in the islands, from old-fashioned Polynesian outrigger canoes to America's Cup racing sloops to submarines. You'll find details on all these seafaring experiences in the individual island chapters that follow.

No matter which type of vessel you choose, be sure to see the islands of Maui, Molokai, Lanai, and Kahoolawe from offshore if you can afford it. It's easy to combine multiple activities into one cruise: Lots of snorkel boats double as sightseeing cruises and, in winter, whale-watching cruises. The main harbors for visitor activities are Lahaina and Maalaea, Maui; Kaunakakai, Molokai; and Manele Bay, Lanai.

BODY BOARDING (BOOGIE BOARDING) & BODYSURFING

Bodysurfing—riding the waves without a board, becoming one with the rolling water—is a way of life in Hawaii. Some bodysurfers just rely on hands to ride the waves; others use hand boards (flat, paddlelike gloves). For additional maneuverability, try a boogie board or body board (also known as belly boards or *paipo* boards). These 3-foot-long boards support the upper part of your body and are very maneuverable in the water. Both bodysurfing and body boarding require a pair of open-heeled swim fins to help propel you through the water. The equipment is inexpensive and easy to carry, and both sports can be practiced in the small, gentle waves. See chapter 5 for details on where to rent boards and where to go.

CAMPING

Maui's year-round balmy climate makes camping a breeze. However, tropical campers should always be ready for rain, especially in Hawaii's wet winter season, but in the dry summer season as well. And remember to bring a good mosquito repellent. If you're heading to the top of Hawaii's volcanoes, you'll need a down mummy bag. If you plan to camp on the beach, bring a mosquito net and a rain poncho. Always be prepared to deal with contaminated water (purify it by boiling, through filtration, or by using iodine tablets) and the tropical sun (protect yourself with sunscreen, a hat, and a long-sleeved shirt). Also be sure to check out the "Health" section of "Fast Facts: Maui," in chapter 12, for hiking and camping tips.

There are many established campgrounds at beach parks, Maui's Waianapanapa Beach, and Hulopoe, on Lanai. Campgrounds are also located in the interior at Maui's Haleakala National Park. See "Beaches" and "Hiking & Camping" in the individual island chapters for the best places to camp.

Hawaiian Trail and Mountain Club, P.O. Box 2238, Honolulu, HI 96804, offers an information packet on hiking and camping on its website, www. htmclub.org. Another good source is the *Hiking/Camping Information Packet,* available from **Hawaii Geographic Maps and Books,** P.O. Box 1698 (49 S. Hotel St.), Honolulu, HI 96808 (**hawaiigeographicsociety@gmail.com;** ✆ 800/538-3950 or 808/538-3952), for $7. The **University of Hawaii Press,** 2840 Kolowalu St., Honolulu, HI 96822 (✆ **888/847-7737;** www.uhpress.hawaii.edu), has an excellent selection of hiking, backpacking, and bird-watching guides, especially *The Hiker's Guide to the Hawaiian Islands,* by Stuart M. Ball, Jr.

> ## Travel Tip
>
> When planning sunset activities, be aware that Hawaii, like other places close to the equator, has a very short (5- to 10-min.) twilight period after the sun sets. After that, it's dark. If you hike out to watch the sunset, be sure you can make it back quickly, or else take a flashlight.

GOLF

Nowhere else on Earth can you tee off to whale spouts, putt under rainbows, and play around a live volcano. Hawaii has some of the world's top-rated golf courses. ***But be forewarned:*** Each course features hellish natural hazards, like razor-sharp lava, gusty trade winds, an occasional wild pig, and the tropical heat. And greens fees tend to be very expensive. Still, golfers flock here from around the world and love every minute of it. See the individual island chapters for coverage of the resort courses worth splurging on (with details, where applicable, on money-saving twilight rates), as well as the best budget and municipal courses. Also check out "The Best Golf Courses," in chapter 1.

A few tips on golfing in Hawaii: There's generally wind—10 to 30 mph is not unusual between 10am and 2pm—so you may have to play two to three clubs up or down to compensate. Bring extra balls: The rough is thick, water hazards are everywhere, and the wind wreaks havoc with your game. On the greens, your putt will *always* break toward the ocean. Hit deeper and more aggressively in the sand because the type of sand used on most Hawaii courses is firmer and more compact than that used on mainland courses (lighter sand would blow away in the constant wind). And bring a camera—you'll kick yourself if you don't capture those spectacular views.

HIKING

Hiking in Hawaii is a breathtaking experience. The islands have hundreds of miles of trails, many of which reward you with a hidden beach, a private waterfall, an Eden-like valley, or simply an unforgettable view. However, rock climbers are out of luck: Most of Hawaii's volcanic cliffs are too steep and brittle to scale.

Hawaiian Trail and Mountain Club, P.O. Box 2238, Honolulu, HI 96804, offers an information packet on hiking and camping in Hawaii on its website, www.htmclub.org. **Hawaii Geographic Maps and Books,** P.O. Box 1698 (49 S. Hotel St.), Honolulu, HI 96813 (**hawaiigeographicsociety@gmail. com;** © 800/538-3950 or 808/538-3952), offers the *Hiking/Camping Information Packet* for $7. Also note that the **Hawaii State Department of Land and Natural Resources,** 1151 Punchbowl St., No. 131, Honolulu, HI 96809 (© **808/587-0300;** www.hawaii.gov), will send you free topographic trail maps.

The **Nature Conservancy of Hawaii** (© **808/572-7849** on Maui or 808/553-5236 on Molokai; www.nature.org) and the **Hawaii Chapter of the Sierra Club,** P.O. Box 2577, Honolulu, HI 96803 (© **808/538-6616** on Oahu; www.sierraclubhawaii.com), both offer guided hikes in preserves and special areas during the year. Also see the individual island chapters for complete details on the best hikes for all ability levels.

A couple of terrific books on hiking are *The Hiker's Guide to the Hawaiian Islands* and *The Hiker's Guide to Oahu,* both by Stuart M. Ball, Jr. (both from University of Hawaii Press).

Before you set out on the trail, see "Health," in the "Fast Facts" section of chapter 12, for tips on hiking safety.

HORSEBACK RIDING

One of the best ways to see Hawaii is on horseback; almost all islands offer riding opportunities for just about every age and level of experience. You can ride inside Haleakala's Crater, along cattle country, or through an upcountry forest. See the individual island chapters for details. Be sure to bring a pair of jeans and closed-toe shoes to wear on your ride.

DON'T LEAVE HOME WITHOUT YOUR
gold card

Almost any activity you can think of, from submarine rides to a Polynesian luau, can be purchased at a discount by using the A3H Gold Card offered by **Activities & Attractions Association of Hawaii,** 355 Hukilike St., No. 202, Kahului, HI 96732 (**(** **800/398-9698** or 808/871-7947; fax 808/877-3104; www.hawaiifun.org). The card, accepted by members on all islands, offers a discount of 10% to 25% off activities and meals for up to four people. It's good for a year from the purchase date and costs $30.

Your A3H Gold Card can lower the regular $149 price of a helicopter ride to only $119, saving you a total of $120 for four people. And there are hundreds of activities to choose from: dinner cruises, horseback riding, watersports, and more—plus savings on rental cars, restaurants, and golf.

Contact Activities & Attractions Association of Hawaii to purchase your card. Then contact the outfitter, restaurant, rental-car agency, or other proprietor directly; supply your card number; and receive the discount.

KAYAKING

Maui is one of the world's most popular destinations for ocean kayaking. You can paddle among the turtles off the Makena coast, or along rolling surf off the coast of Hana, and in the summer, experts can take advantage of the usually flat conditions on the north shore of Molokai, where the sea cliffs are the steepest on Earth and the remote valleys can be reached only by sea. See "Watersports" in chapters 6 through 10 for local outfitters and tour guides.

SCUBA DIVING

Some people come to the islands solely to take the plunge into the tropical Pacific and explore the underwater world. Hawaii is one of the world's top-10 dive destinations, according to *Scuba Diving* magazine. Here you can see the great variety of tropical marine life (more than 100 endemic species found nowhere else on the planet), explore sea caves, and swim with sea turtles and monk seals in clear, tropical water. If you're not certified, try to take classes before you come to Hawaii so you don't waste time learning and can dive right in.

If you dive, **go early in the morning.** Trade winds often rough up the seas in the afternoon, especially on Maui, so most operators schedule early-morning dives that end at noon. To organize a dive on your own, order *The O'ahu Snorkelers and Shore Divers Guide,* by Francisco B. de Carvalho, from University of Hawaii Press.

Tip: It's usually worth the extra bucks to go with a good dive operator. Check "Scuba Diving" in the island chapters that follow; I've listed the operators that'll give you the most for your money.

SNORKELING

Snorkeling is one of Hawaii's main attractions, and almost anyone can do it. All you need is a mask, a snorkel, fins, and some basic swimming skills. In many places, all you have to do is wade into the water and look down at the magical underwater world.

If you've never snorkeled before, most resorts and excursion boats offer snorkeling equipment and lessons. You don't really need lessons, however; it's plenty easy to figure out for yourself, especially once you're at the beach, where everybody around you will be doing it. If you don't have your own gear, you can rent it from one of dozens of dive shops and activities booths, discussed in the individual island chapters.

Favorite snorkel spots include Hulopoe Bay on Lanai and Kapalua Bay on Maui, as well as the Molokini Crater just off Maui, which is accessible only by boat. For tips on the islands' top snorkel boats, see "Watersports" in the chapters that follow.

Some snorkeling tips: Always snorkel with a buddy. Look up every once in a while to see where you are and see if there's any boat traffic. Don't touch anything; not only can you damage coral, but camouflaged fish and shells with poisonous spines could also damage you. Always check with a dive shop, lifeguards, or others on the beach about the area in which you plan to snorkel and ask if there are any dangerous conditions you should know about.

SPORT FISHING

Big-game fishing at its best is found in the waters surrounding the islands of Maui, Molokai, and Lanai, where the deep blue waters offshore yield trophy marlin year-round. You can also try for spearfish, swordfish, various tuna, mahimahi (dorado), rainbow runners, wahoo, barracuda, trevallies, bonefish, and bottom fish, like snappers and groupers. Each island offers deep-sea boat charters for good-eating fish, like tuna, wahoo, and mahimahi. Visiting anglers currently need no license.

Charter fishing boats range widely both in size—from small 24-foot open skiffs to luxurious 50-foot-plus yachts—and in price—from about $100 per person to "share" a boat with other anglers for a half day to $900 a day to book an entire luxury sport-fishing yacht on an exclusive basis. Shop around. Prices vary according to the boat, the crowd, and the captain. See chapters 6, 10, and 11 for details. Also, many boat captains tag and release marlin or keep the fish for themselves (sorry, that's Hawaii style). If you want to eat your mahimahi for dinner or have your marlin mounted, tell the captain before you go.

Money-saving tip: Try contacting the charter-boat captain directly and bargaining. Many charter captains pay a 20% to 30% commission to charter-booking agencies and may be willing to give you a discount if you book directly.

SURFING

The ancient Hawaiian practice of *hee nalu* (wave sliding) is probably the sport most people picture when they think of Hawaii. Believe it or not, you too can do some wave sliding—just sign up at any of the numerous surfing schools located throughout the island (listed in chapter 5).

TENNIS

Tennis is a popular sport in Maui. Chapter 5 lists details on free municipal courts, as well as the best deals on private courts. The etiquette at the free county courts is to play only 45 minutes if someone is waiting.

WHALE-WATCHING

Every winter, pods of Pacific humpback whales make the 3,000-mile swim from the chilly waters of Alaska to bask in Hawaii's summery shallows, fluking, spy hopping, spouting, breaching, and having an all-around swell time. About 1,500 to 3,000 humpback whales appear in Hawaiian waters each year.

Humpbacks are one of the world's oldest, most impressive inhabitants. Adults grow to be about 45 feet long and weigh a hefty 40 tons. Humpbacks are officially an endangered species; in 1992, the waters around Maui, Molokai, and Lanai were designated a Humpback Whale National Marine Sanctuary. Despite the world's newfound ecological awareness, humpbacks and their habitats and food resources are still under threat from whalers and pollution.

The season's first whale is usually spotted in November, but the best time to see humpback whales in Hawaii is **between January and April,** from any island. Just look out to sea. Each island also offers a variety of whale-watching cruises, which will bring you up close and personal with the mammoth mammals; see chapter 5 for details.

Money-saving tip: Book a snorkeling cruise during the winter whale-watching months. The captain of the boat will often take you through the best local whale-watching areas on the way, and you'll get two activities for the price of one. It's well worth the money.

WINDSURFING

Maui is Hawaii's top windsurfing destination. World-class windsurfers head for Hookipa Beach, where the wind roars through Maui's isthmus and creates some of the best windsurfing conditions in the world. Funky Paia, a derelict sugar town saved from extinction by surfers, is now the world capital of big-wave board sailing. And along Maui's Hana Highway, there are lookouts where you can watch the pros flip off the lip of 10-foot waves and gain hang time in the air.

See chapter 5 for outfitters and local instructors.

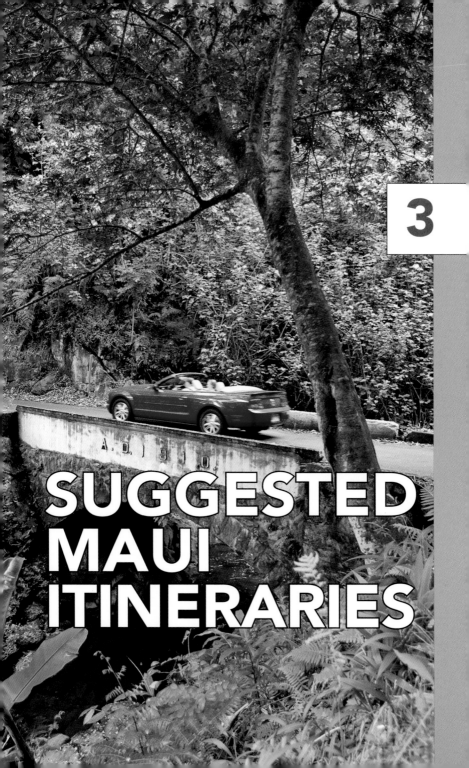

3

SUGGESTED MAUI ITINERARIES

Your vacation time is precious—you have only so many days and you don't want to waste a single one. That's where I come in. Below are several suggestions for what to do and how to spend your time on Maui. I've included ideas if you have 1 week or 2, are traveling with kids, or want a more active vacation. I've also included the best things to see and do on the islands of Molokai and Lanai.

The number-one thing I suggest is this: Don't max out your days. This is Hawaii— allow some time to do nothing but relax. Remember that you most likely will arrive jet-lagged, so it's a good idea to ease into your vacation. In fact, exposure to sunlight can help reset your internal clock, so I include time at the beach on the first day of most of these itineraries.

Also, if this is your first trip to Maui, think of it as a "scouting" trip. Maui is too beautiful, too sensual, too enticing to see just once in a lifetime. You'll be back. You don't need to see and do everything on this trip.

Keep in mind that the following itineraries are designed to appeal to a wide range of travelers. If you're a golf fan or a scuba diver, check out the best golf courses and dive spots in chapter 1 to plan your trip around your passion.

One last thing: You will need a car to get around the island. But plan to get out of the car as much as possible—to smell the sweet perfume of plumeria, to hear the sound of the wind through a bamboo forest, and to plunge into the gentle waters of the Pacific.

THE ISLAND IN BRIEF

See the "Maui" map on p. 82 to locate the following regions.

Central Maui

This flat, often windy corridor between Maui's two volcanoes is where you'll most likely arrive—it's the site of the main airport. It's also home to the majority of the island's population, the heart of the business community, and the local government (courts, cops, and county/state government agencies). You'll find good shopping and dining bargains here but very little in the way of accommodations.

KAHULUI   This is "Dream City," home to thousands of former sugar cane workers whose dream in life was to own their own homes away from the sugar plantations. There's wonderful shopping here (especially at discount stores), and a couple of small hotels near the airport are convenient for 1-night stays if you have a late arrival or early departure; but this is not a place to spend your entire vacation.

WAILUKU   Wailuku is like a time capsule, with its faded wooden storefronts, old plantation homes, shops straight out of the 1940s and 1950s, and relaxed way of life. While most people race through on their way to see the natural

Previous page: **Driving the Hana Highway.**

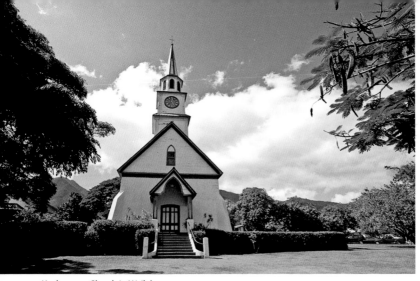

Kaahumanu Church in Wailuku.

beauty of **Iao Valley ★**, this quaint little town is worth a brief visit, if only to see a real place where real people actually appear to be working at something other than a suntan. This is the county seat, so you'll see people in suits on important missions in the tropical heat. Beaches surrounding Wailuku are not great for swimming, but the town has a spectacular view of Haleakala Crater, great budget restaurants, some interesting bungalow architecture, a Frank Lloyd Wright building, a wonderful historic B&B, and the always-endearing Bailey House Museum.

West Maui

This is the fabled Maui you see on postcards. Jagged peaks, green velvet valleys, a wilderness full of native species—the majestic West Maui Mountains are the epitome of earthly paradise. The beaches here are some of Hawaii's best. And it's no secret: This stretch of coastline along Maui's "forehead," from Kapalua to the historic port of Lahaina, is the island's most bustling resort area (with south Maui close behind). Expect a few mainland-style traffic jams.

If you want to book a resort or condo on this coast, first consider what community you'd like to base yourself in. Starting at the southern end of west Maui and moving northward, the coastal communities look like this:

LAHAINA   This old seaport is a tame version of its former self, a raucous whaling town where sailors swaggered ashore in search of women and grog. Today, the vintage village teems with restaurants, T-shirt shops, and a gallery on nearly every block; parts of it are downright tacky, but there's still a lot of real history to be found amid the tourist development. Lahaina makes a great base for visitors: A few old hotels (such as the restored 1901 Pioneer Inn on the harbor), quaint bed-and-breakfasts, and a handful of oceanfront condos offer a variety of choices. This is the place to stay if you want to be in the center of things—restaurants, shops, and nightlife—but parking can be a problem.

KAANAPALI ★   Farther north along the west Maui coast is Hawaii's first master-planned family resort. Pricey midrise hotels line nearly 3 miles of lovely gold-sand beach; they're linked by a landscaped parkway and a walking path along the sand. Golf greens wrap around the slope between beachfront and hillside properties. **Whalers Village**—a seaside mall with 48 shops and restaurants, plus the best little whale museum in Hawaii—and other restaurants are easy to reach on foot along the oceanfront walkway or by resort shuttle, which also serves the small West Maui Airport just to the north. Shuttles also go to Lahaina (see above), 3 miles to the south, for shopping, dining, entertainment, and boat tours. Kaanapali is popular with convention groups and families—especially those with teenagers, who like all the action.

HONOKOWAI, KAHANA & NAPILI   During the building binge of the 1970s, condominiums sprouted along this gorgeous coastline like mushrooms after a rain. Today, these older oceanside units offer excellent bargains for astute travelers. The great location—along sandy beaches, within minutes of both the Kapalua and Kaanapali resort areas, and close enough to the goings-on in Lahaina—makes this area a great place to stay for value-conscious travelers. It feels more peaceful and residential than either Kaanapali or Lahaina.

In **Honokowai** and **Mahinahina,** you'll find mostly older units that tend to be cheaper. There's not much shopping here (mostly convenience stores), but you'll have easy access to the shops and restaurants of Kaanapali.

Kahana is a little more upscale than Honokowai and Mahinahina. Most of its condos are big high-rise types, newer than those immediately to the south. You'll find a nice selection of shops and restaurants (including the Maui branch of Roy's) in the area, and Kapalua–West Maui Airport is nearby.

Napili is a much-sought-after area for condo seekers: It's quiet; has great beaches, restaurants, and shops; and is close to Kapalua. Units are

Wailea.

generally more expensive here (although I've found a few hidden gems at affordable prices; see the Napili Bay listing on p. 277).

KAPALUA ★★   North beyond Kaanapali and the shopping centers of Napili and Kahana, the road starts to climb and the vista opens up to fields of golden-green pineapple and manicured golf fairways. A country lane lined with Pacific pines that leads toward the sea brings you to Kapalua. It's the very exclusive domain of the luxurious Ritz-Carlton Kapalua and expensive condos and villas, set on one of Hawaii's best white-sand beaches, next to two bays that are marine-life preserves (with fabulous surfing in winter).

Even if you don't stay here, you're welcome to come and enjoy Kapalua. The fancy hotel here provides public parking and beach access. The resort has an art school where you can learn local crafts, as well as a golf school, three golf courses, historic features, swanky condos and homes (many available for vacation rental at astronomical prices), and wide-open spaces that include a rainforest preserve—all open to the general public.

Kapalua is a great place to stay put. However, if you plan to "tour" Maui, know that it's a long drive from here to get to many of the island's highlights. You might want to consider a more central place to stay—even Lahaina is a 15-minute drive away.

South Maui

This is the hottest, sunniest, driest, most popular coastline on Maui for sun lovers—Arizona by the sea. Rain rarely falls here, and temperatures stick around 85°F (29°C) year-round. On this former scrubland from Maalaea to Makena, where cactuses once grew wild and cows grazed, there are now four distinctive areas—Maalaea, Kihei, Wailea, and Makena—and a surprising amount of traffic.

MAALAEA   If west Maui is the island's head, Maalaea is just under the chin. This windy oceanfront village centers on a small boat harbor (with a general

store, a couple of restaurants, and a huge new mall) and the **Maui Ocean Center ★★**, an aquarium/ocean complex. This quaint region offers several condominium units to choose from, but visitors staying here should be aware that it's almost always very windy. All the wind from the Pacific is funneled between the West Maui Mountains and Haleakala and comes out in Maalaea.

KIHEI   Kihei is less a proper town than a nearly continuous series of condos and minimalls lining South Kihei Road. This is Maui's best vacation bargain: Budget travelers swarm like sun-seeking geckos over the eight sandy beaches along this scalloped, condo-packed 7-mile stretch of coast. Kihei is neither charming nor quaint; what it lacks in aesthetics, though, it more than makes up for in sunshine, affordability, and convenience. If you want a latte in the morning, fine beaches in the afternoon, and Hawaii Regional Cuisine in the evening—all at reasonable prices—head to Kihei.

WAILEA ★★   Just 4 decades ago, this was wall-to-wall scrub kiawe trees, but now Wailea is a manicured oasis of multimillion-dollar resort hotels along 2 miles of palm-fringed gold coast. It's like Beverly Hills by the sea, except California never had it so good: Wailea has warm, clear water full of tropical fish; year-round golden sunshine and clear blue skies; and hedonistic pleasure palaces on 1,500 acres of black-lava shore indented by five beautiful beaches. It's amazing what a billion dollars can do.

This is the playground of the stretch-limo set. The planned resort development—practically a well-heeled town—has a shopping village, three prized golf courses of its own and three more in close range, and a tennis complex. A growing number of large homes sprawl over the upper hillside, some offering excellent bed-and-breakfast units at reasonable prices. The resorts along this fantasy coast are spectacular, to say the least. Next door to the **Four Seasons,** the most elegant, is the **Grand Wailea Resort,** a public display of ego by Tokyo mogul Takeshi Sekiguchi, who dropped $600 million in 1991 to create his own minicity. Stop in and take a look—it's so gauche, you've gotta see it.

Kayaking is popular along Makenta's gorgeous, pristine beach.

Appealing natural features include the coastal trail, a 3-mile round-trip path along the oceanfront with pleasing views everywhere you look—out to sea and to the neighboring islands, or inland to the broad lawns and gardens of the hotels. The trail's south end borders an extensive garden of native coastal plants, as well as the ruins of ancient lava-rock houses juxtaposed with elegant oceanfront condos. But the chief attractions, of course, are those five outstanding beaches (the best is Wailea Beach).

MAKENA ★★ After passing through well-groomed Wailea, the road suddenly enters raw wilderness. After Wailea's overdone density and overmanicured development, the thorny landscape is a welcome relief. Although beautiful, this is an end-of-the-road kind of place: It's a long drive from Makena to anywhere on Maui. If you're looking for an activities-filled vacation or you want to tour a lot of the island, you might want to try somewhere else, or you'll spend most of your time in the car. But if you crave a quiet, relaxing respite, where the biggest trip of the day is from your bed to the gorgeous, pristine beach, Makena is the place.

Beyond Makena, you'll discover Haleakala's last lava flow, which ran to the sea in 1790; the bay named for French explorer La Pérouse; and a chunky lava trail known as the King's Highway, which leads around Maui's empty south shore past ruins and fish camps. Puu Olai stands like Oahu's Diamond Head on the shore, where a sunken crater shelters tropical fish and empty gold-sand beaches stand at the end of dirt roads.

Upcountry Maui

After a few days at the beach, you'll probably take notice of the 10,000-foot mountain in the middle of Maui. The slopes of Haleakala (House of the Sun) are home to cowboys, growers, and other country people who wave at you as you drive by. They're all up here enjoying the crisp air, emerald pastures, eucalyptus, and flower farms of this tropical Olympus—there's even a misty California red-wood grove. You can see a thousand tropical sunsets reflected in the windows of houses old and new, strung along a road that runs like a loose hound from Makawao, an old cowboy–turned–New Age village, to Kula, where the road leads up to the crater and **Haleakala National Park ★★★**. The rumpled, two-lane blacktop of Hwy. 37 narrows on the other side of Tedeschi Vineyards and Winery, where wine grapes and wild elk flourish on the Ulupalakua Ranch, the biggest on Maui. A stay upcountry is usually affordable, a chance to commune with nature, and a nice contrast to the sizzling beaches and busy resorts below.

MAKAWAO ★★ Until recently, this small, two-street upcountry town consisted of little more than a post office, gas station, feed store, bakery, and restaurant/bar serving the cowboys and farmers living in the surrounding community; the hitching posts outside storefronts were really used to tie up horses. As the population of Maui started expanding in the 1970s, a health-food store sprang up, followed by boutiques, a chiropractic clinic, and a host of health-conscious restaurants. The result is an eclectic amalgam of old *paniolo* (cowboy) Hawaii and the baby boomer trends of transplanted main-landers. **Hui No'eau Visual Arts Center ★**, Hawaii's premier arts collective, is definitely worth a peek. The only accommodations here are reasonably priced bed-and-breakfasts, perfect for those who enjoy great views and don't mind slightly chilly nights.

KULA ★   A feeling of pastoral remoteness prevails in this upcountry community of old flower farms, humble cottages, and newer suburban ranch houses with million-dollar views that take in the ocean, the isthmus, the West Maui Mountains, and, at night, the lights that run along the gold coast like a string of pearls from Maalaea to Puu Olai. Everything flourishes at a cool 3,000 feet (bring a jacket), just below the cloud line, along a winding road on the way up to Haleakala National Park. Everyone here grows something—Maui onions, carnations, orchids, and proteas (those strange-looking blossoms that look like *Star Trek* props). The local B&Bs cater to guests seeking cool tropic nights, panoramic views, and a rural upland escape. Here you'll find the true peace and quiet that only rural farming country can offer—yet you're still just 30 to 40 minutes away from the beach and an hour's drive from Lahaina.

East Maui

ON THE ROAD TO HANA ★★★   When old sugar towns die, they usually fade away in rust and red dirt. Not **Paia** ★★. The tangled spaghetti of electrical, phone, and cable wires hanging overhead symbolizes the town's ability to adapt to the times—it may look messy, but it works. Here, trendy restaurants, eclectic boutiques, and high-tech windsurf shops stand next door to a ma-and-pa grocery, a fish market, and storefronts that have been serving customers since plantation days. Hippies took over in the 1970s; although their macrobiotic restaurants and old-style artists' co-ops have made way for Hawaii Regional Cuisine and galleries featuring the works of renowned international artists, Paia still manages to maintain a pleasant granola vibe. The town's main attraction, though, is **Hookipa Beach Park** ★, where the wind that roars through the isthmus of Maui brings windsurfers from around the world. A few B&Bs are located just outside Paia in the tiny community of **Kuau.**

Ten minutes down the road from Paia and up the hill from the Hana Highway—the connector road to the entire east side of Maui—is **Haiku.** Once a pineapple-plantation village, complete with a cannery (now a shopping complex), Haiku offers vacation rentals and B&Bs in a quiet, pastoral setting: the perfect base for those who want to get off the beaten path and experience the quieter side of Maui, but don't want to feel too removed (the beach is only 10 min. away).

About 15 to 20 minutes past Haiku is the largely unknown community of **Huelo** ★. Every day, thousands of cars whiz by on the road to Hana; most barely glance at the double row of mailboxes overseen by a fading Hawaii Visitors Bureau sign. But if you take the time to head down the road, you'll discover a hidden Hawaii—a Hawaii of an earlier time, where Mother Nature is still sensual and wild, where ocean waves pummel soaring lava cliffs, and where an indescribable sense of serenity prevails. Huelo is not for everyone, but those who hunger for a place still largely untouched by "progress" should check in to a B&B or vacation rental here.

HANA ★★★   Set between an emerald rainforest and the blue Pacific is a village probably best defined by what it lacks: golf courses, shopping malls, and McDonald's. Except for a gas station and a bank with an ATM, you'll find little of what passes for progress here. Instead, you'll discover the simple joys of fragrant tropical flowers, the sweet taste of backyard bananas and papayas, and the easy calm and unabashed small-town aloha spirit of old Hawaii. What saved "Heavenly" Hana from the inevitable march of progress? The 52-mile **Hana Highway,** which winds around 600 curves and crosses more than 50 one-lane bridges on its way from Kahului. You can go to Hana for the day—from Kihei and Lahaina, it's a 3-hour drive (and a half century away)—but spending 3 days is better. The tiny town has one hotel, a handful of great B&Bs, and some spectacular vacation rentals.

MAUI HIGHLIGHTS

I've outlined the highlights of Maui for those who have just 7 days and want to see everything. Two suggestions: First, spend 2 nights in Hana, a decision you will not regret, and second, take the Trilogy boat trip to Lanai for the day. I've designed this itinerary assuming you'll stay in west Maui for 5 days. If you are staying elsewhere (such as Wailea or Kihei), allow extra driving time.

DAY 1: Arriving & Seeing Kapalua Beach ★★★

After checking in to your hotel, head for **Kapalua Beach** (p. 154). Don't overdo the sun on your first day. After an hour or two at the beach, drive to **Lahaina** (p. 104) and spend a couple of hours walking the historic old town. Go to the **Old Lahaina Luau** (p. 247) at sunset to immerse yourself in Hawaiian culture.

DAY 2: Going Up a 10,000-Foot Volcano & Down Again ★★★

You'll likely wake up early on your first day in Hawaii, so take advantage of it and head up to the 10,000-foot dormant volcano, **Haleakala.** You can

Hiking in Haleakala.

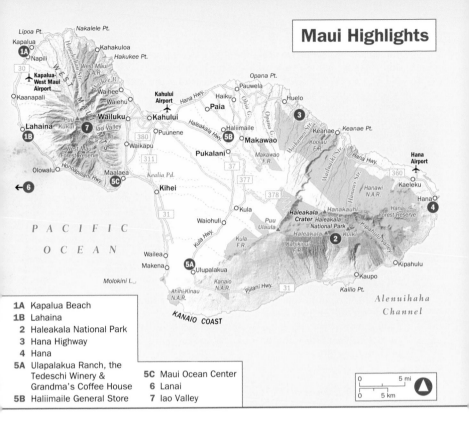

Maui Highlights

Lipoa Pt.
Nakalele Pt.
Kapalua
1A Napili
Kahakuloa
Hakukee Pt.
30
Kapalua-West Maui Airport
Kaanapali
Waihee
Waiehu
Kahului Airport
Hana Hwy.
Haiku
Paia
Opana Pt.
Pauwela
Huelo
3
Wailuku
Iao Valley
7
Kahului
Puunene
380
Waikapu
Haleakala Hwy.
Haliimaile
5B
Makawao
Keanae
Keanae Pt.
Koolau F.R.
Hana Airport
1B Lahaina
West Maui Forest Reserve
311
Pukalani
Makawao F.R.
37
Hanawi N.A.R.
Kaeleku
360
Olowalu
Maalaea
Kealia Pd.
377
378
Haleakala Crater
Hanakauhi
Haleakala National Park
2
Kuiki
Hana Forest Reserve
Hana 4
5C
Kihei
31
Waiohuli
Kula
Puu Ulaula
Haleakala
Kahikinui F.R.
Kipahulu Valley
Waiohuli
Kula Hwy.
Kula F.R.
P A C I F I C
O C E A N
Wailea
Makena
5A
Ulupalakua
Kanaio N.A.R.
Piilani Hwy.
Kaupo
Kipahulu
31
Kailio Pt.
Molokini I.
Ahihi-Kinau N.A.R.
KANAIO COAST
Alenuihaha Channel

1A Kapalua Beach
1B Lahaina
2 Haleakala National Park
3 Hana Highway
4 Hana
5A Ulapalakua Ranch, the Tedeschi Winery & Grandma's Coffee House
5B Haliimaile General Store
5C Maui Ocean Center
6 Lanai
7 Iao Valley

0   5 mi
0   5 km

hike in the crater (p. 175), **speed down the mountain on a bicycle** (p. 186), or just wander about the national park. You don't have to be at the top for sunrise; in fact, it has gotten so congested at sunrise that you may be too busy fighting the crowds to have an awe-inspiring experience. Instead, I suggest heading up anytime during the day. On your way back down, stop and tour **upcountry Maui** (p. 79), particularly the communities of **Kula, Makawao,** and **Paia.** Plan for a sunset dinner in Paia or Kuau.

DAY 3: Driving the Hana Highway ★★★

Pack a lunch and spend the entire day driving the scenic **Hana Highway** (p. 131). Pull over often and get out to take photos, smell the flowers, and jump in the mountain-stream pools. Wave to everyone, move off the road for those speeding by, and breathe in Hawaii. Plan to spend at least 2 nights in Hana (hotel recommendations start on p. 140).

DAY 4: Spending a Day in Heavenly Hana ★★★

You have an entire day in paradise and plenty of things to see. Take an early-morning hike along the black sands of **Waianapanapa State Park** (p. 181); then explore the tiny town of **Hana.** Be sure to see the **Hana Cultural Center & Museum** (p. 143), **Hasegawa General Store** (p. 242), and **Hana Coast Gallery** (p. 240). Get a picnic lunch and drive out to the

Stop in for a tasting at the Tedeschi Vineyards and Winery.

Kipahulu end of Haleakala National Park at **Oheo Gulch** (p. 148). Hike to the waterfalls and swim in the pools. Splurge on dinner in the dining room at the Travaasa Hana (p. 226). Spend another night in Hana.

DAY 5: Enjoying Wine, Food & (Hawaiian) Song

Check to see if the road past Hana is open (roads can be closed due to flooding or debris; call the **Maui Police Department** at ℂ **808/248-8311** for information); if it is, continue driving around the island, past Kaupo and up to the **Tedeschi Vineyards and Winery** (p. 131). Stop at **Grandma's Coffee House** (p. 222) for a cup of java, and then head down the mountain, with a stop for lunch at **Haliimaile General Store** (p. 220). Spend the afternoon at the **Maui Ocean Center,** in Maalaea (p. 78), checking out the sharks and other marine life. Have dinner in Lahaina and see the drama/dance/music show **Ulalena** (p. 248). If the road past Hana is closed, go back along the Hana Highway the way you came, stopping for lunch at Haliimaile, and then follow the rest of the itinerary from there.

Triology offers the best snorkeling and sailing in Hawaii.

DAY 6: Sailing to Lanai ★★★

Trilogy (p. 162) offers the best sailing/snorkeling trip in Hawaii, so don't miss it. You'll spend the day (breakfast and lunch included) sailing to Lanai, snorkeling, touring the island, and sailing back to Lahaina. Plus, you still have the afternoon free to shop or take a nap.

DAY 7: Relaxing & Shopping

Depending on how much time you have on your final day, you can decide to relax on the beach, get pampered in a spa, or shop for souvenirs. Spagoers have a range of terrific spas to choose from, and shopping aficionados should check out some of my favorite stores (recommendations start on p. 231). If you have a late flight, you might want to check out **Iao Valley** (p. 101).

2 WEEKS ON MAUI

Lucky travelers will get 2 weeks to totally relax on the Valley Isle. I recommend adding lots of naps, vegging out on the beach, and stopping to smell all the exotic flowers to the 1-week itinerary above. Below are suggestions for your second week on Maui.

DAYS 1 TO 7

Follow the 1-week itinerary as outlined above.

DAY 8: Flying or Ferrying to Molokai for a Mule Ride ★★★

If you have a spare day or two, head over to the "Friendly Isle" to experience the **Molokai Mule Ride** down into the **Kalaupapa Peninsula** (p. 314). This is an all-day experience that you will remember for the rest of your life. You can either take the ferry over or fly; either way, don't miss this opportunity.

DAY 9: Snorkeling in an Old Volcanic Crater ★★★

Take a day to see the fish inside the **Molokini Crater.** Go in the morning before the wind comes up. If it's whale season and you're lucky, you may spot whales on the way over or back. You'll have to go as part of a tour—my recommendations start on p. 166.

DAY 10: Gliding over the Water in a Kayak ★★★

Kayaking is so easy that you will be paddling away within a few minutes of lessons. One of the best kayak places is **Makena**—it's calm, the water is so clear you can see the fish, and you're protected from the wind. See "Ocean Kayaking" (p. 164) for more suggestions. After a

A sign near Surfing Goat Dairy.

1A Kapalua Beach
1B Lahaina
2 Haleakala National Park
3 Hana Highway
4 Hana
5A Ulapalakua Ranch, the Tedeschi Winery & Grandma's Coffee House
5B Haliimaile General Store
5C Maui Ocean Center
6 Lanai
7 Iao Valley
8 Molokai
9 Molokini Crater
10 Makena
11 O'o Farm tour, Surfing Goat Dairy tour, or Alii Kula Lavender tour
12 Wailuku
13A Lahaina
13B Whalers Village Museum
13C Kahakuloa
13D Halekii and Pihanakalani Heiau

couple hours of kayaking and snorkeling, stop for a picnic lunch at **Makena Landing** and then explore this area. If you still have energy to spare, hike over to **La Pérouse Monument,** along the rugged shoreline. For coverage of Makena, see p. 79.

DAY 11: Taking an Offbeat Tour ★

Plan at least one off-the-beaten-path tour while you're on Maui. If you love good food, book the tour of Chef James McDonald's **O'o Farm** (p. 206), which includes lunch. Cheese aficionados will love visiting **Surfing Goat Dairy** (p. 130) and sampling its cheeses. For a really exotic experience, take the Combo Tour at **Alii Kula Lavender** (p. 130), which includes a tour of the farm and lunch made with lavender products.

DAY 12: Seeing Maui from a Helicopter ★★★

The feeling of suddenly lifting off straight up in the air and then floating over the island of Maui in a helicopter is a memory that will stay with you forever. Of all the helicopter companies, I recommend booking with **Blue Hawaiian Helicopters** (p. 100) for the most comfortable, informative, and fun tour in the air. After the tour, take some time to explore old **Wailuku** town, wander through the shops (p. 100), stop at the **Bailey House Museum** (p. 100), and then take in **Waikapu** (p. 99), **Kahului** (p. 98), and **Puunene** (p. 99).

DAY 13: Walking Back in Time in Lahaina ★★

Plan to arrive in this historic town early, before the crowds. Eat a big breakfast, and then put on your walking shoes and take the self-guided **historic walking tour** (p. 108) of the old town. Plan to do some browsing in the quaint stores (recommendations start on p. 104), watch the surfers skim the waves in front of the library, and pop over to Kaanapali to the **Whalers Village Museum** (p. 116). Then drive around the head of the island on the **Kahekili Highway** (p. 116), stopping to see the ancient Hawaiian village of **Kahakuloa** and the **Halekii** and **Pihanakalani Heiau** on the Wailuku side.

DAY 14: Enjoying Your Last Day

After 13 days of exploring Maui, spend your last day doing what you loved best: beachcombing, snorkeling, hiking, shopping, or whatever your favorite Maui activity is. Pick up a lei before you go to the airport so you will have a little bit of Maui with you as you say aloha.

MAUI WITH KIDS

Your itinerary is going to depend on the ages of your kids. The number-one rule is *don't plan too much*, especially with young children, who will be fighting jet lag, trying to get adjusted to a new bed (and most likely new food), and possibly dealing with excitement to the point of exhaustion. The 7-day itinerary below is a guide to the various family-friendly activities available on Maui. Pick and choose the ones everyone in your family will enjoy.

DAY 1: Arriving & Enjoying Pool Time ★★

If you have young kids who are not used to ocean waves, you might consider taking them to the swimming pool at your hotel. They'll be happy playing in the water, and you won't have to introduce them to ocean safety after that long plane ride. Plan an early dinner, with food your kids are used to. If you're in Lahaina, go to **Cheeseburger in Paradise** (p. 204); if you're in Kihei, consider either **Shaka Sandwich & Pizza** (p. 216) or **Stella Blues Café** (p. 216). Get to bed early.

DAY 2: Going Up a 10,000-Foot Volcano & Down Again ★★★

Your family will likely be up early, so take advantage of it and head up to the 10,000-foot dormant volcano, **Haleakala.** Depending on the age of your children, you can either **hike in the crater** (p. 175), **speed down the**

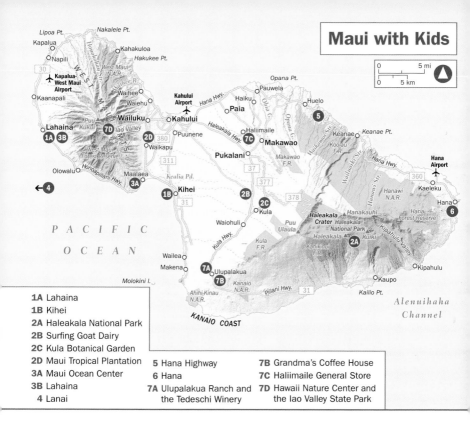

mountain on a bicycle (p. 186), or just wander about the national park. On your way back down, stop and tour the upcountry communities of **Kula, Makawao,** and **Paia.** Plan to visit the **Surfing Goat Dairy** (p. 130), stop and look at the strange flowers at the **Kula Botanical Garden** (p. 130), or take the 40-minute narrated tram tour at **Maui Tropical Plantation** (p. 99). Grab an early dinner—try **A. K.'s Café** in Wailuku (p. 198).

DAY 3: Seeing Sharks, Stingrays & Starfish Without Getting Wet ★★★

After a lazy breakfast, wander over to the **Maui Ocean Center** (p. 78) in Maalaea so your kids can see the fabulous underwater world without having to get wet. Plan to spend the morning immersed in the 5-acre oceanarium. Eat something fishy for lunch. Then head out to **Lahaina,** where you can take the kids underwater in a Jules Verne–type submarine at **Atlantis Adventures** (p. 169); or, if they are too small, hop aboard the **Lahaina/ Kaanapali Sugar Cane Train** (p. 87), or rent some snorkel equipment and hit one of the terrific beaches in west Maui (recommendations start on p. 153). Book ahead for the **Old Lahaina Luau** (p. 247) in the evening.

DAY 4: Sailing to Lanai ★★★

Now that the kids have seen the underwater world, take them sailing to Lanai. **Trilogy** (p. 162) offers the best sailing/snorkeling trip in Hawaii, so

The tide pool at Maui Ocean Center.

don't miss it. In the afternoon, wander around Lahaina and see the giant **Banyan Tree** (p. 111), the old **Lahaina Courthouse** (p. 111), and the **old prison** (p. 114).

DAY 5: Driving the Hana Highway ★★★

Pack a lunch and spend the entire day driving the **Hana Highway** (p. 131), the world's most scenic tropical road. Pull over often and get out to take photos, smell the flowers, and jump in the mountain-stream pools. Wave to everyone, move off the road for those speeding by, and breathe in Hawaii. Plan to spend at least 2 nights in Hana (hotel recommendations start on p. 140).

DAY 6: Spending a Day in Heavenly Hana ★★★

You have an entire day in paradise and plenty of things to see. Take an early-morning hike along the black sands of **Waianapanapa State Park** (p. 181); then explore the tiny town of **Hana.** Be sure to see the **Hana Cultural Center & Museum** (p. 143), **Hasegawa General Store** (p. 242), and

Oheo Gulch.

Hana Coast Gallery (p. 240). Get a picnic lunch and drive out to the Kipahulu end of Haleakala National Park at **Oheo Gulch** (p. 148). Hike to the waterfalls and swim in the pools. Splurge on dinner in the dining room at the Travaasa Hana (p. 226). Spend another night in Hana.

DAY 7: Seeing the World from a Dragonfly's Point of View ★★

Check to see if the road past Hana is open; if it is, continue driving around the island, past Kaupo and up to the **Tedeschi Vineyards and Winery** (p. 131). Stop at **Grandma's Coffee House** (p. 222) for a cup of java and head down the mountain, with a stop for lunch at **Haliimaile General Store** (p. 220). Spend the afternoon at the **Hawaii Nature Center** (p. 103) and the **Iao Valley State Park** (p. 101) next door. If the road past Hana is closed, go back along the Hana Highway the way you came, stopping for lunch at Haliimaile.

Iao Valley State Park.

MAUI FOR THE ADVENTUROUS

If you can't stand the thought of just lazing around the beach all day, and your idea of the perfect vacation is to be up, active, and trying new adventures, then Maui is the place for you. This itinerary covers all the basics of what to see on Maui, with added adventures that active people like you will love.

DAY 1: Arriving in Maui & Hitting the Beach ★★

Your first stop after you get off the plane should be **Snorkel Bob's** (p. 153) to pick up snorkel gear (the staff will even show you how to use it). Check in to your hotel, and then head for the beach. Great snorkeling spots in west Maui include **D.T. Fleming Beach Park, Kapalua Beach, Black Rock on Kaanapali Beach,** and **Wahikuli County Wayside Park.** In south Maui, wonderful snorkeling beaches include the north end of **Oneloa (Big) Beach** in Makena (by the cinder cone), **Ulua Beach** and **Wailea Beach** in Wailea, and **Kamaole III Beach** in Kihei. Beach coverage begins on p. 169. Remember not to overdo the sun on your first day. If you just can't get enough of the underwater world, take a submarine trip with **Atlantis Adventures** (p. 169).

DAY 2: Going Up a 10,000-Foot Volcano & Down Again ★★★

You'll likely wake up early on your first day in Hawaii, so take advantage of it and head up to the 10,000-foot dormant volcano, **Haleakala.** Plan to **hike in the crater** (p. 175), **speed down the mountain on a bicycle**

Experiencing Haleakala's crater on horseback.

(p. 186), see the crater on horseback with **Pony Express Tours** (p. 188), or just wander about the national park. You don't have to be at the top for sunrise; in fact, it has gotten so congested at sunrise that you may be too busy fighting the crowds to have an awe-inspiring experience. Instead, I suggest heading up anytime during the day.

On your way back down, stop and take **Skyline Eco-Adventures'** **Zipline Haleakala Tour** (p. 175)—not for the faint of heart.

DAY 3: Driving the Hana Highway ★★★

Pack a lunch and spend the entire day driving the scenic **Hana Highway** (p. 131). Pull over often and get out to take photos, smell the flowers, and jump in the mountain-stream pools. Wave to everyone, move off the road for those speeding by, and breathe in Hawaii. Plan to spend at least 2 nights in Hana (hotel recommendations start on p. 140).

DAY 4: Spending a Day in Heavenly Hana ★★★

You have an entire day in paradise and plenty of things to see. Take an early-morning hike along the black sands of **Waianapanapa State Park** (p. 181) and explore the **Piilanihale Heiau** in the **Kahanu Garden** (p. 98). Set up a spelunking tour with **Hana Lava Tube** (p. 189). Get a picnic lunch and drive out to the Kipihulu end of Haleakala National Park at **Oheo Gulch** (p. 148). Hike to the waterfalls and swim in the pools. While you're out there, book a horseback tour with **Maui Stables** (p. 188). Spend another night in Hana.

DAY 5: Trying Something New & Exciting

Check to see if the road past Hana is open. If it is, continue driving around the island, past Kaupo and up to the **Ulupalakua Ranch** (p. 131) and the

Lipoa Pt.
Nakalele Pt.
Kapalua
1A ○ Napili
30
✈ **Kapalua-
West Maui
Airport**
○ Kaanapali

Kahakuloa
Hakukee Pt.
West Maui
N.A.R.
Waihee ○
Waiehu ○

Opana Pt.
Pauwela
**Kahului
Airport** Hana Hwy. Haiku ○
✈ **Paia** Huelo ○
3

Lahaina ○ *Puu
Kukui* ○ **Kahului**
Iao Valley ○ Puunene
380
○ Waikapu
West Maui
Forest Reserve
311
Olowalu ○ Honoapiilani Hwy.
Maalaea ○

Wailuku ○
Haleakala Hwy. ○ Haliimaile
5D ○ **Makawao**

Pukalani ○
Makawao
F.R.
37
377
Kula

Keanae ○ Keanae Pt.
Koolau
F.R.

**Hana
Airport**
✈
360 Kaeleku
Hanawi
N.A.R. Hana ○
4

PACIFIC
OCEAN
6

Kealia Pd.
Kihei
31

Waiohuli ○
1B

Wailea ○
Makena ○
Molokini I.
7

Kula
Kula Hwy.
378
2B

**Haleakala
Crater** Hanakauhi
Haleakala
National Park
Haleakala Hwy.
Kahikinui
F.R.

Puu
Ulaula
Kuiki
2A

Kipahulu Valley

Kaupo
5A ○ Kaupo
Kailio Pt.

*Alenuihaha
Channel*

5B ○ Ulupalakua
5C
Kanaio
N.A.R.
Ahihi-Kinau
N.A.R.
KANAIO COAST
Piilani Hwy. **31**

0   5 mi
0   5 km

○ Kipahulu

1A West Maui beaches
1B South Maui beaches
2A Haleakala National Park
2B Skyline Eco-Adventures'
    Zipline Haleakala Tour
3 Hana Highway
4 Hana
5A Kaupo

5B Ulupalakua Ranch and
    the Tedeschi Winery
5C Grandma's Coffee House
5D Haliimaile General Store
6 Lanai
7 Molokini Crater

Tedeschi Vineyards and Winery (p. 131). Stop at **Grandma's Coffee House** (p. 222) for a cup of java and head down the mountain. Plan to do something you've never tried before, such as **learning how to surf** with **Rivers to the Sea** (p. 170), **ocean rafting** with **Capt. Steve's Rafting Excursions** (p. 168), or **windsurfing** (p. 172). If the road past Hana is closed, go back along the Hana Highway the way you came, stopping for lunch at **Haliimaile General Store** (p. 220), and then follow the rest of the itinerary from there.

DAY 6: Sailing to Lanai ★★★

Trilogy (p. 162) offers the best sailing/snorkeling trip in Hawaii, so don't miss it. You'll spend the day (breakfast and lunch included) sailing to Lanai, snorkeling, touring the island, and sailing back to Lahaina. The really adventurous can also try **scuba diving.**

DAY 7: Enjoying Your Last Chance at Adventure

It's your last chance to do something out of the ordinary. My first pick would be to book a helicopter ride with **Blue Hawaiian Helicopters** (p. 100) to discover what Maui looks like from above. Or if you're a fan of the underwater world, sign up for a **sailing/snorkel tour of Molokini** (p. 168). Even a **guided hike into Maui's rainforest** (p. 174) will remain etched in your memory.

A WEEK ON MOLOKAI

The island of Molokai is for people trying to get away from everything or those look-ing for adventure. There are no direct flights from the mainland to Molokai, so you will have to fly into Honolulu and then take a commuter plane to Molokai.

DAY 1: Arriving & Stopping in Kaunakakai

If you're staying in a condo or vacation rental, head into **Kaunakakai** and stock up on groceries. While you're here, wander around the old two-street town and check out the stores. Be sure to stop at the **Kapuaiwa Coconut Grove/Kiowea Park** (p. 309) and watch the sunset.

DAY 2: Riding a Mule to Kalaupapa ★★★

Your internal clock will still be set to mainland time, so you should have no problem waking up early for the **Molokai Mule Ride** (p. 314). This adven-ture will take you through 26 switchbacks on a 1,600-foot cliff and give you a chance to tour the **Kalaupapa Peninsula,** where people suffering from leprosy lived for decades.

DAY 3: Heading for the Beach

Molokai has terrific beaches—and on weekdays they are generally empty! Depending on the time of year and the weather, great beaches for snorkeling are **Murphy Beach Park (Kumimi Beach Park)** and **Sandy Beach** (p. 321) on the East End, and **Kapukahehu (Dixie Maru) Beach** (p. 323) on the West End. Pack a picnic lunch or stop by **Outpost Natural Foods** (p. 330) or the **Sundown Deli** (p. 331), both in Kaunakakai. Stay all day. Relax.

DAY 4: Hiking in a Tropical Valley ★

After a day at the beach, you'll be ready for a hike into the tropical jungle of **Halawa Valley** (p. 309). Bring a picnic lunch for after the hike, and then spend the rest of the day on the beach at Halawa. Stop to see the **fishponds** before you leave the East End.

Descending the switchbacks on a mule ride to Kalaupapa.

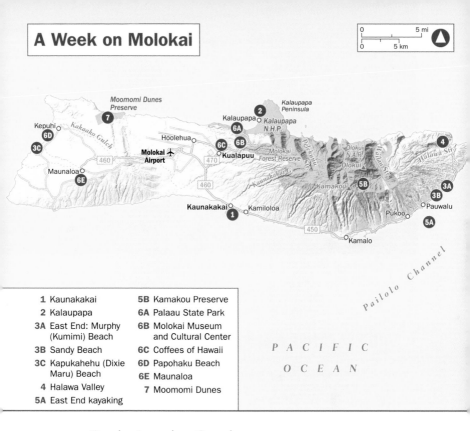

A Week on Molokai

0		5 mi
0		5 km

1 Kaunakakai
2 Kalaupapa
3A East End: Murphy (Kumimi) Beach
3B Sandy Beach
3C Kapukahehu (Dixie Maru) Beach
4 Halawa Valley
5A East End kayaking
5B Kamakou Preserve
6A Palaau State Park
6B Molokai Museum and Cultural Center
6C Coffees of Hawaii
6D Papohaku Beach
6E Maunaloa
7 Moomomi Dunes

P A C I F I C

O C E A N

DAY 5: Exploring the Outdoors ★

Spend a day kayaking, biking, or hiking.

My choice would be kayaking along the shallow waters of the East End. Hikers should check out **Pepeopae Trail** (p. 325) or the **Kamakou Preserve** (p. 316).

DAY 6: Touring the West End ★★

Because you've already seen the East End, spend a day exploring the rest of the island. Start out with a tour of the central part of Molokai by driving out to **Palaau State Park** (p. 312), which overlooks the Kalaupapa Peninsula, and then stop at the **Molokai Museum and Cultural Center** (p. 311) and take a coffee break at **Coffees of Hawaii** (p. 310). Next head to the 3-mile-long, white-sand **Papohaku Beach** (p. 320). After an hour or so at the beach, drive up to the cool air in Maunaloa town to see the best store on the island: the **Big Wind Kite Factory & Plantation Gallery** (p. 334).

DAY 7: Seeing Moomomi Dunes: Archaeology Heaven

Before your flight back, stop by the **Moomomi Dunes** (p. 315), located close to the Hoolehua Airport. This wild, sand-covered coast is a treasure-trove for archaeologists. Buried in the mounds are ancient Hawaiian burial sites, fossils, Hawaiian artifacts, and even the bones of prehistoric birds. If

Molokai's Kalaupapa Peninsula as viewed from Palaau State Park.

you have time, take the 20-minute easy walk west to **Kawaaloa Bay,** the perfect place to say aloha to Molokai.

A WEEK ON LANAI

The smallest of all the Hawaiian Islands, Lanai was once a big pineapple planta-tion and is now home to two exclusive resorts, hundreds of years of history, and just one small town with some of the friendliest people you will ever meet. As with the island of Molokai, there are no direct flights from the mainland to Lanai. You will have to fly into Honolulu and then take a commuter plane to Lanai.

DAY 1: Arriving & Seeing Hulopoe Bay ★★

After you settle into your hotel, head for the best beach on the island: the marine preserve at **Hulopoe Bay** (p. 350). It's generally safe for swimming, the snorkeling is terrific, and the fish are so friendly you practically have to shoo them away.

DAY 2: Touring the Island in a Four-Wheel-Drive Vehicle

Lanai is a fantastic place to go four-wheeling. Generally, you won't need a car if you're staying at one of the two resorts or at the Hotel Lanai (they provide shuttle service), so splurge and rent a four-wheel-drive vehicle for 2 or 3 days. Get a picnic lunch from **Pele's Other Garden** (p. 360) and head out of Lanai City to the **Kanepuu Preserve** (p. 349), a 590-acre dry-land forest. Next stop is **Garden of the Gods** (p. 347) and a picnic lunch at **Polihua Beach** (p. 351), Lanai's largest white-sand beach. The beach generally is not safe for swimming and can be windy, but it will probably be deserted and you'll have a great view of Molokai in the distance. After lunch, reverse direction and head to **Shipwreck Beach** (p. 352) and then on to **Keomoku Village** (p. 350).

DAY 3: Spending a Day at the Beach

Plan a lazy day at **Hulopoe Beach** (p. 350). Grab a book, watch the kids play in the surf, or take a long walk around the crescent-shaped bay. For

lunch, wander over to the **Four Seasons Resort at Manele Bay** and sit poolside at **Fresco** (p. 358), or else head to the resort's **Challenge at Manele Clubhouse** (p. 359). In the afternoon, plan a nap or try your hand at some crafts at the **Lanai Art Center** (p. 362).

DAY 4: Hiking (or Driving) the Munro Trail

If it has not been raining and the ground is dry, do a little exploring. The adventurous can spend the day (plan on at least 7 hr.) climbing to the top of Lanai on the **Munro Trail** (p. 355). The not so adventurous can take a four-wheel-drive vehicle. Soak in a hot tub on your return.

DAY 5: Enjoying a Day on the Water ★★

Ring up **Trilogy Lanai Ocean Sports** (p. 353) and book a sailing/snorkeling, whale-watching, or scuba trip.

Polihua Beach.

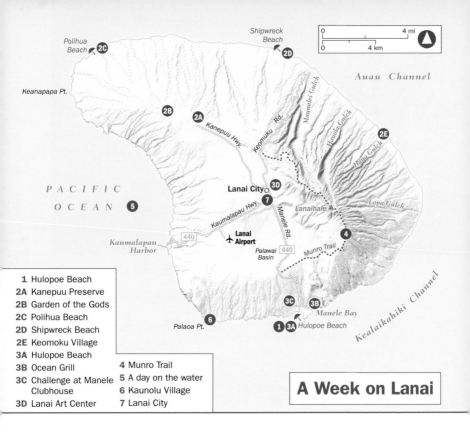

1 Hulopoe Beach
2A Kanepuu Preserve
2B Garden of the Gods
2C Polihua Beach
2D Shipwreck Beach
2E Keomoku Village
3A Hulopoe Beach
3B Ocean Grill
3C Challenge at Manele Clubhouse
3D Lanai Art Center
4 Munro Trail
5 A day on the water
6 Kaunolu Village
7 Lanai City

A Week on Lanai

DAY 6: Kayaking or Horseback Riding, Followed by a Trip Back in Time

If you can't get enough time on the water, plan a morning kayaking tour with **Trilogy Lanai Ocean Sports** (p. 353). A picnic lunch is included. Horse lovers should arrange a tour of Lanai through the **Stables at Koele** (p. 357). In the afternoon, take a four-wheel-drive vehicle to the historic ruins of the old **Kaunolu Village** (p. 349), on the southwestern side of the island.

DAY 7: Biking & Shopping

The best way to get around the tiny village of Lanai City is via bicycle. Rent one from the **Four Seasons Resort Lanai, The Lodge at Koele** (p. 356), and ride (downhill) into town. Lanai City has some terrific boutiques that you'll find nowhere else (descriptions of my favorites start on p. 360).

Garden of the Gods.

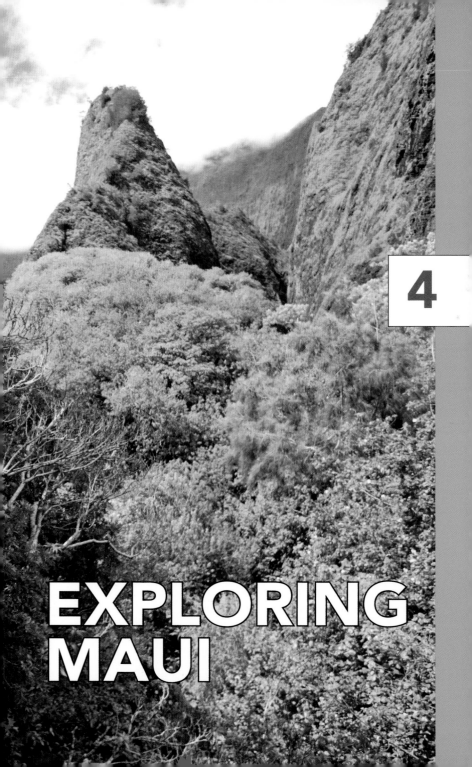

4

EXPLORING MAUI

A fter a few days of just relaxing on the beach, the itch to explore the rest of Maui sets in: What's on top of Haleakala, looming in the distance? Is the road to Hana really the tropical jungle everyone raves about? What does the inside of a 19th-century whaling boat look like?

There is far more to the Valley Isle than just sun, sand, and surf. Get out and see for yourself the otherworldly interior of a 10,000-foot volcanic crater, watch endangered sea turtles make their way to nesting sites in a wildlife sanctuary, wander back in time to the days when whalers and missionaries fought for the soul of Lahaina, and feel the energy of a thundering waterfall cascade into a serene mountain pool.

MAUI'S TOP SIGHTS & ATTRACTIONS

- Ali'i Kula Lavender Farm (p. 150)
- Haleakala National Park (p. 175)
- Hana town (p. 140)
- Iao Valley (p. 101)
- Lahaina Town (p. 232)
- Maui Ocean Center (p. 78)
- National Tropical Botanical Garden (p. 141)
- Surfing Goat Dairy (p. 130)
- Tedeschi Vineyards and Winery (p. 131)

CENTRAL MAUI

Central Maui isn't exactly tourist central; this is where real people live. You'll most likely land here and head directly to the beach. However, there are a few sights worth checking out if you feel like a respite from the sun and surf.

Kahului

Under the airport flight path, next to Maui's busiest intersection and across from Costco and Kmart in Kahului's business park, is a most unlikely place: the **Kanaha Wildlife Sanctuary,** Haleakala Highway Extension and Hana Highway (© **808/984-8100**). Look for the parking area off Haleakala Highway Extension (behind the mall, across the Hana Hwy. from Cutter Automotive), and you'll find a 50-foot trail that meanders along the shore to a shade shelter and lookout. Watch for the sign proclaiming this the permanent home of the endangered black-neck Hawaiian stilt, whose population is now down to about 1,000 to 1,500. Naturalists say this is a good place to see endangered Hawaiian koloa

FACING PAGE: **Iao Valley.**

The Kanaha Wildlife Sanctuary.

ducks, stilts, coots, and other migrating shorebirds. For a quieter, more natural-looking wildlife preserve, visit the **Kealia Pond National Wildlife Preserve,** in Kihei (p. 120).

Puunene

This town, located in the middle of the central Maui plains, is nearly gone. Once a thriving sugar-plantation town with hundreds of homes, a school, a shopping area, and a community center, Puunene is little more than a sugar mill, a post office, and a museum today. The Hawaiian Commercial & Sugar Co., owner of the land, has slowly phased out the rental plantation housing to open up more land to plant sugar.

Alexander & Baldwin Sugar Museum MUSEUM   This former sugar-mill superintendent's home has been converted into a museum that tells the story of sugar in Hawaii. Exhibits explain how sugar is grown, harvested, and milled. An eye-opening display shows how Samuel Alexander and Henry Baldwin managed to acquire huge chunks of land from the Kingdom of Hawaii, then fought to gain access to water on the other side of the island, making sugar cane an economi-cally viable crop. Allow about half an hour to enjoy the museum.

Puunene Ave. (Hwy. 350) and Hansen Rd. www.sugarmuseum.com. (𝒞 **808/871-8058.** Admission $7 adults, $5 seniors, $2 children 6–17, free for children 5 and under. Daily 9:30am–4pm.

Waikapu

Across the sugar cane fields from Puunene, and about 3 miles south of Wailuku on the Honoapiilani Highway, lies the tiny, one-street village of Waikapu, which has two attractions that are worth a peek, especially if you're trying to kill time before your flight out.

Relive Maui's past by taking a 40-minute narrated tram ride around fields of pineapple, sugar cane, and papaya trees at **Maui Tropical Plantation** ☺, 1670 Honoapiilani Hwy. (𝒞 **800/451-6805** or 808/244-7643; www.mauitropical plantation.com), a real working plantation open daily from 9am to 4pm. A shop sells fresh and dried fruit, and a restaurant serves lunch. Admission is free; the

FLYING HIGH: helicopter rides

Only a helicopter can bring you face to face with remote sites like Maui's little-known Wall of Tears, near the summit of Puu Kukui in the West Maui Mountains. You'll glide through canyons etched with 1,000-foot waterfalls and over dense rainforests; you'll climb to 10,000 feet, high enough to glimpse the summit of Haleakala, and fly by the dramatic vistas on Molokai.

The first chopper pilots in Hawaii were good ol' boys on their way back from Vietnam—hard-flying, hard-drinking cowboys who cared more about the ride than the scenery. But not anymore. Today's pilots, like the ones at Blue Hawaiian (see below), are an interesting hybrid: part Hawaiian historian, part DJ, part tour guide, and part amusement-ride operator. As you soar through the clouds, you'll learn about the island's flora, fauna, history, and culture.

Among the many helicopter-tour operators on Maui, the best is **Blue**

Hawaiian Helicopters ★★, at Kahului Airport (© **800/745-BLUE** [2583] or 808/871-1107; www.bluehawaiian.com), which not only takes you on the ride of your life but also entertains, educates, and leaves you with an experience you'll never forget. Blue Hawaiian is also the only helicopter company in the state to have the latest high-tech, environmentally friendly (and quiet) Eco-Star helicopters, specially designed for air-tour operators. Flight times range from 30 to 90 minutes and cost $169 to $437 (if you book on their website, rates start at $149).

tram tours, which start at 10:45am and leave about every 45 minutes, are $15 for adults and $5 for kids 3 to 12.

Wailuku

This historic gateway to **Iao Valley** (see below) is worth a visit, if only for a brief stop at the Bailey House Museum and some terrific shopping (see chapter 7).

Bailey House Museum ★ MUSEUM   Missionary and sugar planter Edward Bailey's 1833 home—an architectural hybrid of stones laid by Hawaiian craftsmen and timbers joined in a display of Yankee ingenuity—is a treasure-trove of Hawaiiana. Inside, you'll find an eclectic collection, from precontact artifacts like

A tram ride through the fields of Maui Tropical Plantation.

scary temple images, dog-tooth necklaces, and a rare lei made of tree-snail shells to latter-day relics like Duke Kahanamoku's 1919 redwood surf board and a koa-wood table given to President Ulysses S. Grant, who had to refuse it because he couldn't accept gifts from foreign countries. There's also a gallery devoted to a few of Bailey's landscapes, painted from 1866 to 1896, which capture on canvas a Maui we can only imagine today.

2375-A Main St. www.mauimuseum.org. ✆ **808/244-3326.** Admission $7 adults, $5 seniors, $2 children 7–12, free for children 6 and under. Mon–Sat 10am–4pm.

Iao Valley ★

A couple of miles north of Wailuku, past the Bailey House Museum, where the little plantation houses stop and the road climbs ever higher, Maui's true nature begins to reveal itself. The transition from suburban sprawl to raw nature is so abrupt that most people who drive up into the valley don't realize they're suddenly in a rainforest. The walls of the canyon begin to close around them, and a 2,250-foot-high needlelike rock pricks gray clouds scudding across the blue sky. The moist, cool air and the shade are a welcome comfort after the hot tropic sun. This is Iao (pronounced *E*-ow) Valley, an eroded volcanic caldera in the West Maui Mountains whose great nature, history, and beauty have been enjoyed by millions of people from around the world for more than a century.

The 1833 home of missionary and sugar planter Edward Bailey is now a museum.

POWERFUL plantations

Coffee, pineapples, and even macadamia nuts are all grown on huge farms in Hawaii. But the biggest of them all were the once-dominant sugar plantations. Sugar was Hawaii's claim to fame long before the tourists arrived, with the first plantation opening in 1835. At one time, more than 240,000 acres of sugar cane were under cultivation. But unfortunately, a little less than a century and a half later, sugar went bust—the victim of cheaper labor and cheaper shipping costs elsewhere. In the late 1970s Hawaii produced nearly 1.2 billion tons of sugar; today it produces less than 200 million. Though most of the plantations are long gone, with fields of cane giving way to resorts and golf courses, their impact on Hawaiian culture should not be underestimated.

Plantation Life   Low wages. Abusive overseers. Poor conditions. For plantation workers, these things were all part of the job. The immigrant laborers who built sugar into Hawaii's primary industry were generally treated like indentured servants. They signed binding contracts that required they pay off the cost of their transportation to the islands and their living expenses. Their paltry wages (41¢ per day in 1841) were quickly eaten up by exorbitant rates charged by the company store. However, from this disparaging past Hawaii's labor unions arose after World War II (some say because Hawaii's boys went out and saw that the rest of the world was not under the iron rule of plantations). Today, more than 6 decades later, Hawaii is still a strong labor union state.

A song popular with sugar plantation laborers at the turn of the 19th century summed up their lot in life.

> **Sure a Poor Man** (Pua Mana No)
>
> *I labored on a sugar plantation*
> *Growing sugarcane*
> *My back ached, my sweat poured,*
> *All for nothing.*
> *I fell in debt at the plantation store.*
> *I fell in debt at the plantation store.*
> *And remained a poor man.*

Plantations & Politics   Many of Hawaii's first white families were missionaries who "came to do good and stayed to do well." Five prominent families (the Big Five) saw in sugar the potential for major profits, and they wasted no time in making sure their stranglehold on the industry was secure. From the beginning, the U.S. was the predominant beneficiary of all that sweetness. Just one problem: Hawaii was independent, which meant there were trade tariffs to be paid. No matter—white businessmen simply banded together to push through "reforms" that gave them more and more power. Sanford Dole, the son of missionaries, was an advisor to Queen Liliuokalani, but he was also interested in promoting the cause of his family's plantations. He helped lead the 1893 U.S. Marine-backed coup that overthrew the monarchy, then got himself named president of Hawaii from 1894 to 1900, and served as provisional governor after the U.S. annexed the islands.

—By Linda Barth

Iao (Supreme Light) Valley is 10 miles long and encompasses 4,000 acres. The head of the valley is a broad circular amphitheater where four major streams converge into Iao Stream. At the back of the amphitheater is rain-drenched Puu Kukui, the West Maui Mountains' highest point. No other Hawaiian valley lets

Iao Valley is an eroded volcanic caldera in the West Maui Mountains that is now home to a rainforest.

you go from seacoast to rainforest so easily. This peaceful valley, full of tropical plants, rainbows, waterfalls, swimming holes, and hiking trails, is a place of solitude, reflection, and escape for residents and visitors alike.

You can take the loop trail into the massive green amphitheater of Iao Valley for free. The public walkway crosses the bridge of Iao Stream and continues along the stream itself. The .35-mile paved loop is an easy walk—you can even take your grandmother on this one. A leisurely stroll will allow you to enjoy lovely views of the Iao Needle and the lush vegetation. Others often proceed beyond the state park border and take two trails deeper into the valley, but the trails enter private land, and NO TRESPASSING signs are posted.

The feature known as **Iao Needle** is an erosional remnant consisting of basalt dikes. This phallic rock juts an impressive 2,250 feet above sea level. Youngsters play in **Iao Stream,** a peaceful brook that belies its bloody history. In 1790, King Kamehameha the Great and his men engaged in the battle of Iao Valley to gain control of Maui. When the battle ended, so many bodies blocked Iao Stream that the battle site was named Kepaniwai, or "damming of the waters." An architectural heritage park of Hawaiian, Japanese, Chinese, Filipino, and New England–style houses stands in harmony by Iao Stream at **Kepaniwai Heritage Garden.** This is a good picnic spot, with plenty of tables and benches. You can see ferns, banana trees, and other native and exotic plants in the **Iao Valley Botanic Garden,** along the stream.

To get here from Wailuku, take Main Street; then turn right on Iao Valley Road to the entrance to the state park. The park is open daily from 7am to 7pm. Go early in the morning or late in the afternoon, when the sun's rays slant into the valley and create a mystical atmosphere. You can bring a picnic and spend the day, but be prepared at any time for a tropical cloudburst, which often soaks the valley and swells both waterfalls and streams. The entrance fee is $5 per car.

For information, contact the **Division of State Parks,** 54 S. High St., Room 101, Wailuku, HI 96793 (℃ **808/984-8109;** www.hawaiistateparks.org/parks/maui). The **Hawaii Nature Center ★**, 875 Iao Valley Rd. (℃ **808/244-6500;** www.hawaiinaturecenter.org), home of the Iao Valley Nature Center, features interactive exhibits and displays relating the story of Hawaiian natural history; it's an important stop for all who want to explore Iao Valley. Hours are Wednesday through Friday from noon to 4pm, and Saturday 11am to 3pm. Admission is $5. Wear closed-toe shoes (no sandals) suitable for an uneven trail. Tours, which include a visit to the museum, are $20 for adults and $15 for children 5 and older (younger children not allowed). Book in advance.

LAHAINA & WEST MAUI

Olowalu

Most people drive right by Olowalu, on the Honoapiilani Highway 5 miles south of Lahaina; there's little to mark the spot but a small general store. Olowalu (Many Hills) was the scene of a bloody massacre in 1790. The Hawaiians stole a skiff from the USS *Eleanora,* took it back to shore here, and burned it for its iron parts. The captain of the ship, Simon Metcalf, was furious and tricked the Hawaiians into sailing out in their canoes to trade with the ship. As the canoes approached, he mowed them down with his cannons, killing 100 people and wounding many others.

Olowalu has great snorkeling around **mile marker 14,** where there is a turtle-cleaning station about 150 to 225 feet out from shore. Turtles line up here to have cleaner wrasses (small bony fish) pick off small parasites.

Historic Lahaina

Located between the West Maui Mountains and the deep azure ocean offshore, Lahaina stands out as one of the few places in Hawaii that has managed to preserve its 19th-century heritage while still accommodating 21st-century guests.

In ancient times, powerful chiefs and kings ruled this hot, dry, oceanside village. At the turn of the 19th century, after King Kamehameha united the Hawaiian Islands, he made Lahaina the royal capital—which it remained until 1845, when Kamehameha III moved the capital to the larger port of Honolulu.

In the 1840s, the whaling industry was at its peak: Hundreds of ships called into Lahaina every year. The streets were filled with sailors 24 hours a day. Even Herman Melville, who later wrote *Moby-Dick,* visited Lahaina.

Just 20 years later, the whaling industry was waning, and sugar had taken over the town. The Pioneer Sugar Mill Co. reigned over Lahaina for the next 100 years.

Lahaina.

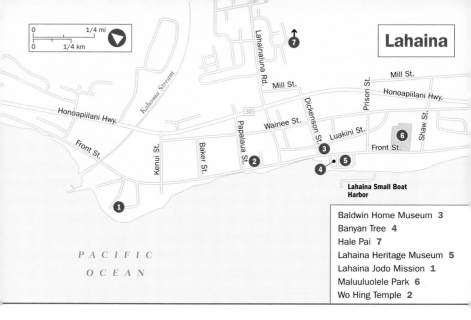

Lahaina

Baldwin Home Museum **3**
Banyan Tree **4**
Hale Pai **7**
Lahaina Heritage Museum **5**
Lahaina Jodo Mission **1**
Maluuluolele Park **6**
Wo Hing Temple **2**

Today, the drunken and derelict whalers who wandered through Lahaina's streets in search of bars, dance halls, and brothels have been replaced by hordes of tourists crowding into the small mile-long main section of town in search of boutiques, art galleries, and chic gourmet eateries. Lahaina's colorful past continues to have a profound influence. This is no quiet seaside village, but a vibrant, cutting-edge kind of place, filled with a sense of history—but definitely with its mind on the future.

See chapter 5 for details on the various cruises and outfitters operating out of Lahaina.

Baldwin Home Museum ★ MUSEUM   The oldest house in Lahaina, this coral-and-rock structure was built in 1834 by Rev. Dwight Baldwin, a doctor with the fourth company of American missionaries to sail to Hawaii. Like many missionaries, he came to Hawaii to do good—and did very well for himself. After 17 years of service, Baldwin was granted 2,600 acres in Kapalua for farming and grazing. His ranch manager experimented with what Hawaiians called *hala-kahiki*, or pineapple, on a 4-acre plot; the rest is history. The house looks as if Baldwin has just stepped out for a minute to tend a sick neighbor down the street.

Next door is the **Master's Reading Room,** Maui's oldest building (included with museum admission). This became visiting sea captains' favorite hangout once the missionaries closed down all of Lahaina's grog shops and banned prostitution. By 1844, when hotels and bars started reopening, it lost its appeal. It's now the headquarters of the **Lahaina Restoration Foundation,** a plucky band of historians who try to keep this town alive and antique at the same time. Stop in and pick up a self-guided walking-tour map, which will take you to Lahaina's most historic sites.

120 Dickenson St. (at Front St.). www.lahainarestoration.org. (C) **808/661-3262.** Admission $3 per person, $5 family, free for children 12 and under. Daily 10am–4pm.

Master's Reading Room.

Banyan Tree ☺ NATURAL ATTRACTION   Of all the banyan trees in Hawaii, this is the greatest—so big that you can't get it all in your camera's view-finder. It was only 8 feet tall when it was planted in 1873 by Maui sheriff William O. Smith to mark the 50th anniversary of Lahaina's first Christian mission. Now it's more than 50 feet tall, has 12 major trunks, and shades ⅔ acre in Courthouse Square.

At the Courthouse, 649 Wharf St.

Hale Pai MUSEUM   When the missionaries arrived in Hawaii to spread the word of God, they found the Hawaiians had no written language. They quickly recti-fied the situation by converting the Hawaiian sounds into a written language. They then built the first printing press in order to print educational materials that would assist them on their mission. Hale Pai was the printing house for the Lahainaluna Seminary, the oldest American school west of the Rockies. Today, Lahainaluna is the public high school for the children of west Maui.

Lahainaluna High School Campus, 980 Lahainaluna Rd. (at the top of the mountain). www.lahaina restoration.org/halepai. ℂ **808/661-3262.** Free admission. Mon–Wed 10am–4pm, or by appointment.

Lahaina Heritage Museum MUSEUM   Located on the second floor of the old Lahaina Courthouse, this museum presents the history and culture of Lahaina. In addition to ever-changing exhibits, there are videos, live demonstra-tions by cultural artisans, "touch and feel" displays, and interactive exhibits.

648 Wharf St. www.lahainarestoration.org. ℂ **808/661-3262.** Free admission. Daily 9am–5pm.

Lahaina Jodo Mission TEMPLE   This site has long been held sacred. The Hawaiians called it Puunoa Point, which means "the hill freed from taboo." Once a small village named Mala (garden), this peaceful place was a haven for Japa-nese immigrants, who came to Hawaii in 1868 as laborers for the sugar cane

WHERE TO park FREE—OR NEXT TO FREE—IN LAHAINA

Lahaina is the worst place on Maui for parking. The town was created and filled with shops, restaurants, and historic sites before the throngs of tourists (and their cars) invaded. Street parking is hit-or-miss. You can either drive around the block for hours looking for a free place to park on the street or park in one of the nearly 20 parking lots. I've identified below the lots that are free for customers and those that offer a discount with validation.

Free for Customers: The three lots on Papalaua Street are all free for customers. The largest is the Lahaina Cannery Mall lot. Next in size is the Lahaina Center, across the street (which allows 2 hr. free, but you must get validation from a store in the Lahaina Center). The smallest is the Lahaina Square lot at Wainee Street, which offers 2 free hours for customers.

Discount with Validation: Customers of the Wharf Cinema Center, located on Front Street, can get a discount by parking at either of the theater's two lots—both are between Dickenson and Prison streets, but one is on Wainee Street and the other on Luakini Street.

plantations. They eventually built a small wooden temple to worship here. In 1968, on the 100th anniversary of Japanese presence in Hawaii, a Great Buddha statue (some 12 ft. high and weighing 3½ tons) was brought here from Japan. The immaculate grounds also contain a replica of the original wooden temple and a 90-foot-tall pagoda.

12 Ala Moana St. (off Front St., near the Mala Wharf). www.lahainajodomission.com. © **808/661-4304.** Free admission. Daily during daylight hours.

Malu Ulu Olele Park PARK   At first glance, this Front Street park appears to be only a hot, dry field. But actually it's sacred ground; a royal compound stood here more than 100 years ago, but is now buried under tons of red dirt and sand. Here, Prince Kauikeaouli, who ascended the throne as King Kamehameha III when he was only 10, lived with the love of his life, his sister, Princess Nahienaena. Missionaries took a dim view of incest, which was acceptable to Hawaiian nobles in order to preserve the royal bloodline. Torn between love for her brother and the new Christian morality, Nahienaena grew despondent and died at the age of 21. King Kamehameha III, who reigned for 29 years—longer than any other Hawaiian monarch—presided over Hawaii as it went from kingdom to constitutional monarchy, and as power over the islands began to shift from island nobles to missionaries, merchants, and sugar planters. Kamehameha died in 1854 at the age of 39. In 1918, his royal compound, containing a mausoleum and artifacts of the kingdom, was demolished and covered with dirt to create a 4.7-acre public park.

Front and Shaw sts.

Wo Hing Temple ★ TEMPLE   The Chinese were among the various immigrants brought to Hawaii to work in the sugar cane fields. In 1909, several Chinese workers formed the Wo Hing society, a chapter of the Chee Kun Tong society, which dates from the 17th century. In 1912, they built this social hall for

The Great Buddha statue was brought to Lahaina Jodo Mission from Japan.

Colorful decorations on the altar at the Wo Hing Temple.

the Chinese community. Completely restored, the Wo Hing Temple contains displays and artifacts on the history of the Chinese in Lahaina. Next door in the old cookhouse is a theater with movies of Hawaii taken by Thomas Edison in 1898 and 1903.

858 Front St. (btw. Wahie Lane and Papalaua St.). www.lahainarestoration.org. ℂ **808/661-3262.** Admission $2 per person, free for children 12 and under. Sat–Thurs 10am–4pm; Fri 1–8pm.

WALKING TOUR: HISTORIC LAHAINA

GETTING THERE: **From Kahului Airport, take the Kuihelani Highway (Hwy. 38) to the intersection of Honoapiilani Highway (Hwy. 30), where you turn left. Follow Honoapiilani Highway to Lahaina and turn left on Lahainaluna Road. When Lahainaluna Road ends, make a left on Front Street. Dickenson Street is a block down (see "Where to Park Free—or Next to Free—in Lahaina," above).**

START: **Front and Dickenson streets.**

FINISH: **Same location.**

TIME: **About an hour.**

BEST TIME: **Monday–Friday, 10am–3pm**

Back when "there was no God west of the Horn," Lahaina was the capital of Hawaii and the Pacific's wildest port. Today it's a milder version of its old self—mostly a hustle bustle of whale art, timeshares, and "Just Got Lei'd" T-shirts. I'm not sure the rowdy whalers would be pleased. But if you look hard, you'll still find the historic port town they loved, filled with the kind of history that inspired James Michener to write his best-selling epic novel *Hawaii*.

Members of the Lahaina Restoration Foundation have worked for 5 decades to preserve Lahaina's past. They have labeled a number of historic sites with

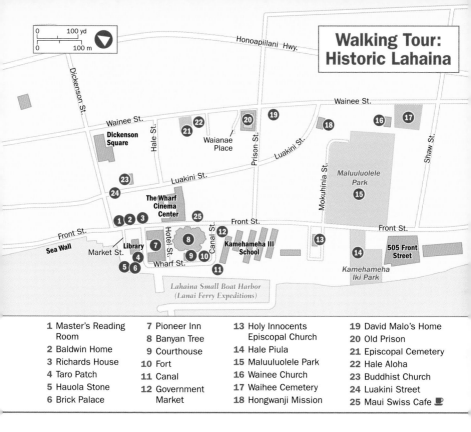

1 Master's Reading Room	**7** Pioneer Inn	**13** Holy Innocents Episcopal Church	**19** David Malo's Home
2 Baldwin Home	**8** Banyan Tree	**14** Hale Piula	**20** Old Prison
3 Richards House	**9** Courthouse	**15** Maluuluolele Park	**21** Episcopal Cemetery
4 Taro Patch	**10** Fort	**16** Wainee Church	**22** Hale Aloha
5 Hauola Stone	**11** Canal	**17** Waihee Cemetery	**23** Buddhist Church
6 Brick Palace	**12** Government Market	**18** Hongwanji Mission	**24** Luakini Street
			25 Maui Swiss Cafe 🍴

brown-and-white markers; below, I provide explanations of the significance of each site as you walk through Lahaina's past.

Begin your tour at the:

1 Master's Reading Room

This coral-and-stone building looks just as it did in 1834, when Rev. William Richards and Rev. E. Spaulding convinced the whaling-ship captains that they needed a place for the ships' masters and captains, many of whom traveled with their families, to stay while they were ashore. The bottom floor was used as a storage area for the mission; the top floor, from which you could see the ships at anchor in the harbor, was for the visiting ships' officers.

Next door is the:

2 Baldwin Home Museum

Harvard-educated physician Rev. Dwight Baldwin, with his wife of just a few weeks, sailed to Hawaii from New England in 1830. Baldwin was first assigned to a church in Waimea, on the Big Island, and then to Lahaina's Wainee Church in 1838. He and his family lived in this house until 1871. The Baldwin Home and the Master's Reading Room are the oldest standing buildings in Lahaina, made from thick walls of coral and hand-milled timber.

Baldwin also ran his medical office and his missionary activities out of this house. (See "Baldwin Home Museum," p. 232, for hours and admission.)

On the other side of the Baldwin Home Museum is the former site of the:

3 Richards House

The open field is empty today, but it was the site of the former home of Lahaina's first Protestant missionary, Rev. William Richards. Richards went on to become the chaplain, teacher, and translator to Kamehameha III. He was also instrumental in drafting Hawaii's constitution and acted as the

The Baldwin Home Museum.

king's envoy to the United States and England, seeking recognition of Hawaii as an independent nation. After his death in 1847, he was buried in the Wainee Churchyard.

From here, cross Front Street and walk toward the ocean, with the Lahaina Public Library on your right and the green Pioneer Inn on your left, until you see the:

4 Taro Patch

The lawn in front of the Lahaina Public Library was once a taro patch stretching back to the Baldwin home. The taro plant was a staple of the Hawaiian diet: The root was used to make poi, and the leaves were used in cooking. At one time Lahaina looked like a Venice of the tropics, with streams, ponds, and waterways flooding the taro fields. As the population of the town grew, the water was siphoned off for drinking.

Walk away from the Lahaina Harbor toward the edge of the lawn, where you'll see the:

5 Hauola Stone

Hawaiians believed that certain stones placed in sacred places had the power to heal. *Kahuna* (priests) of medicine used stones like this to help cure illnesses.

Turn around and walk back toward the Pioneer Inn; look for the concrete depression in the ground, which is all that's left of the:

6 Brick Palace

This structure was begun in 1798 as the first Western-style building in Hawaii. King Kamehameha I had this 20×40-foot, two-story brick structure built for his wife, Queen Kaahumanu (who is said to have preferred a grass-thatched house nearby). Inside, the walls were constructed of wood and the windows were glazed glass. Kamehameha I lived here from 1801 to 1802, when he was building his war canoe, *Peleleu*, and preparing to invade Kauai. A handmade stone sea wall surrounded the palace to protect it from the surf. The building stood for 70 years. In addition to being a royal compound, it was also used as a meetinghouse, storeroom, and warehouse.

7 Pioneer Inn

Lahaina's first hotel was the scene of some wild parties at the start of the 20th century. George Freeland, of the Royal Canadian Mounted Police, tracked a criminal to Lahaina and then fell in love with the town. He built the hotel in 1901 but soon discovered that Lahaina didn't get a lot of visitors. To make ends meet, Freeland built a movie theater, which was wildly successful. The Pioneer Inn remained the only hotel in all of west Maui until the 1950s. You can stay at this restored building today (p. 262).

From the Pioneer Inn, cross Hotel Street and walk along Wharf Street, which borders the harbor. On your left is the:

8 Banyan Tree

This ancient tree has witnessed decades of luau, dances, concerts, private chats, public rallies, and resting sojourners under its mighty boughs. It's hard to believe that this huge tree was only 8 feet tall when it was planted here.

Continue along Wharf Street. Near the edge of the park is the:

9 Courthouse

In 1858, a violent windstorm destroyed about 20 buildings in Lahaina, including Hale Piula, which served as the courthouse and palace of King Kamehameha III. It was rebuilt immediately, using the stones from the previous building. It served not only as courthouse, but also as custom house, post office, tax collector's office, and government offices. Upstairs on the second floor is the **Lahaina Heritage Museum,** with exhibits on the history and culture of Lahaina (free admission; open daily 9am–5pm).

The Pioneer Inn.

The Banyan Tree has been the site for luau, dances, concerts, and more.

Continue down Wharf Street to Canal Street. On the corner are the remains of the:

10 Fort

This structure once covered an acre and had 20-foot-high walls. In 1830, some whalers fired a few cannonballs into Lahaina in protest of Rev. William Richards's meddling in their affairs. (Richards had convinced Gov. Hoapili to create a law forbidding the women of Lahaina from swimming out to greet the whaling ships.) In response to this threat, the fort was constructed from 1831 to 1832 with coral blocks taken from the ocean where the Lahaina Harbor sits today. As a further show of strength, cannons were placed along the waterfront, where they remain today. Historical accounts seem to scoff at the "fort," saying it appeared to be more for show than for force. It was later used as a prison, until it was finally torn down in the 1850s; its stones were used for construction of the new prison, Hale Paahao (see stop 20, below).

Cross Canal Street to the:

11 Canal

Unlike Honolulu with its natural deep-water harbor, Lahaina was merely a roadstead with no easy access to the shore. Whalers would anchor in deep water offshore, then board smaller boats (which they used to chase down and harpoon whales) to make the passage over the reef to shore. If the surf was up, coming ashore could be dangerous. In the 1840s, the U.S. consular representative recommended digging a canal from one of the freshwater streams that ran through Lahaina and charging a fee to the whalers who wanted to obtain fresh water. In 1913, the canal was filled in to construct Canal Street.

Up Canal Street is the:

12 Government Market

A few years after the canal was built, the government built a thatched marketplace with stalls for Hawaiians to sell goods to the sailors. Merchants quickly took advantage of this marketplace and erected drinking establishments, grog shops, and other pastimes of interest nearby. Within a few years, this entire area became known as "Rotten Row."

Make a right onto Front Street and continue down the street, past Kamehameha III Elementary School. Across from the park is:

13 Holy Innocents Episcopal Church

When the Episcopal missionaries first came to Lahaina in 1862, they built a church across the street from the current structure. In 1909, the church moved to its present site, which was once a thatched house built for the daughter of King Kamehameha I. The present structure, built in 1927, features unique paintings of a Hawaiian Madonna and birds and plants endemic to Hawaii, executed by Delos Blackmar in 1940.

Continue down Front Street, and at the next open field, look for the white stones by the ocean, marking the former site of the "iron-roofed house" called:

14 Hale Piula

In the 1830s, a two-story stone building with a large surrounding courtyard was built for King Kamehameha III. However, the king preferred sleeping in a small thatched hut nearby, so the structure was never really completed. In the 1840s, Kamehameha moved his capital to Honolulu and wasn't using Hale Piula, so it became the local courthouse. The windstorm of 1858, which destroyed the courthouse on Wharf Street (see stop 9, above), also destroyed the iron-roofed house. The stones from Hale Piula were used to rebuild the courthouse on Wharf Street.

Continue down Front Street; across from the 505 Front Street complex is:

15 Maluuluolele Park

This spot sacred to Hawaiians is now the site of a park and ball field. This used to be a village, Mokuhinia, with a sacred pond that was the home of a *moo* (a spirit in the form of a lizard), which the royal family honored as their personal guardian spirit. In the middle of the pond was a small island, Mokuula, home to Maui's top chiefs. After conquering Maui, Kamehameha I claimed this sacred spot as his own; he and his two sons, Kamehameha II and III, lived here when they were in Lahaina. In 1918, in the spirit of progress, the pond was drained and the ground leveled for a park.

Make a left onto Shaw Street and then another left onto Wainee Street. On the left side, just past the cemetery, is:

16 Wainee Church

This was the first stone church built in Hawaii (1828–32). At one time the church could seat some 3,000 people, albeit tightly packed together, complete with "calabash spittoons" for the tobacco-chewing Hawaiian chiefs and the ship captains. That structure didn't last long—the 1858 windstorm that destroyed several buildings in Lahaina also blew the roof off the original church, knocked over the belfry, and picked up the church's bell and deposited it 100 feet away. The structure was rebuilt, but that too was destroyed—this time by Hawaiians protesting the 1894 overthrow of the monarchy. Again the church was rebuilt, and again it was destroyed—by fire in 1947. The next incarnation of the church was destroyed by yet another windstorm in 1951. The current church has been standing since 1953. Be sure to walk around to the back of the church: The row of palm trees on the ocean side includes some of the oldest palm trees in Lahaina.

Wander next door to the first Christian cemetery in Hawaii:

17 Waihee Cemetery

Established in 1823, this cemetery tells a fascinating story of old Hawaii, with graves of Hawaiian chiefs, commoners, sailors, and missionaries and their families (infant mortality was high then). Enter this ground with respect, because Hawaiians consider it sacred—many members of the royal family are buried here, including Queen Keopuolani, who was wife of King Kamehameha I, mother of kings Kamehameha II and III, and the first Hawaiian baptized as a Protestant. Among the other graves are those of Rev. William Richards (the first missionary in Lahaina) and Princess Nahien-aena (sister of kings Kamehameha II and III).

Continue down Waihee Street to the corner of Luakini Street and the:

18 Hongwanji Mission

The temple was originally built in 1910 by members of Lahaina's Buddhist sect. The current building was constructed in 1927, housing a temple and language school. The public is welcome to attend the New Year's Eve celebration, Buddha's birthday in April (see "Maui, Molokai & Lanai Calendar of Events," p. 46), and O Bon Memorial Services in August.

Continue down Wainee Street. Just before the intersection with Prison Street, look for the historical marker for:

19 David Malo's Home

Although no longer standing, the house that once stood here was the home of Hawaii's first scholar, philosopher, and well-known author, educated at Lahainaluna School. Malo's book on ancient Hawaiian culture, *Hawaiian Antiquities,* is considered *the* source on Hawaiiana today. His alma mater celebrates David Malo Day every year in April in recognition of his contributions to Hawaii.

Cross Prison Street. On the corner of Prison and Waihee is the:

20 Old Prison

The Hawaiians called the prison Hale Paahao (Stuck in Irons House). Sailors who refused to return to their boats at sunset used to be arrested and taken to the old fort (see stop 10, above). In 1851, however, the fort physician told the government that sleeping on the ground at night made the prisoners ill, costing the government quite a bit of money to treat them—so the Kingdom of Hawaii used the prisoners to build a prison from the coral block of the old fort. Most prisoners here had terms of a year or less (those with longer terms were shipped off to Honolulu) and were convicted of crimes like deserting ship, being drunk, or working on Sunday. Today, the grounds of the prison have a much more congenial atmosphere and are rented out to community groups for parties.

Continue down Waihee Street, just past Waianae Place, to the small:

21 Episcopal Cemetery

This burial ground tells another story in Hawaii's history. During the reign of King Kamehameha IV, his wife, Queen Emma, formed close ties with British royalty. She encouraged Hawaiians to join the Anglican Church after asking the Archbishop of Canterbury to form a church in Hawaii. This cemetery contains the burial sites of many of those early Anglicans.

Next door is:

22 Hale Aloha

This "house of love" was built in 1858 by Hawaiians in "commemoration of God's causing Lahaina to escape the smallpox," while it decimated Oahu in 1853, carrying off 5,000 to 6,000 souls. The building served as a church and school until the turn of the 20th century, when it fell into disrepair. It is no longer standing, but artifacts remain.

Turn left onto Hale Street and then right onto Luakini Street to the:

23 Buddhist Church

This green wooden Shingon Buddhist temple is very typical of myriad Buddhist churches that sprang up all over the island when the Japanese laborers were brought to work in the sugar cane fields. Some of the churches were little more than elaborate false "temple" fronts on existing buildings.

On the side of Village Galleries, on the corner of Luakini and Dickenson streets, is the historical marker for:

24 Luakini Street

"Luakini" translates as a *heiau* (temple) where the ruling chiefs prayed and where human sacrifices were made. This street received its unforgettable name after serving as the route for the funeral procession of Princess Harriet Nahienaena, sister of kings Kamehameha II and III. The princess was a victim of the rapid changes in Hawaiian culture. A convert to Protestantism, she had fallen in love with her brother, Kamehameha III. Just 20 years earlier, their relationship would have been nurtured in order to preserve the purity of the royal bloodlines. The missionaries, however, frowned on brother and sister marrying. In August 1836, the couple had a son, who lived only a few short hours. Nahienaena never recovered and died in December of that same year (the king was said to mourn her death for years, frequently visiting her grave at the Waihee Cemetery; see stop 17, above). The route of her funeral procession through the breadfruit and koa trees to the cemetery became known as "Luakini," in reference to the gods "sacrificing" the beloved princess.

Turn left on Dickenson and walk down to Front Street, where you'll be back at the starting point.

25 Winding Down ☕
Ready for some refreshment after your stroll? Head to **Maui Swiss Cafe,** 640 Front St. (✆ **808/661-6776**), for tropical smoothies, great espresso, and affordable snacks. Sit in the funky garden area, or get your drink to go and wander over to the sea wall to watch the surfers.

A Whale of a Place in Kaanapali

Heading north from Lahaina, the next resort area you'll come to is Kaanapali, which boasts a gorgeous stretch of beach. If you haven't seen a real whale yet, go to **Whalers Village,** 2435 Kaanapali Pkwy., an oceanfront shopping center that has adopted the whale as its mascot. You can't miss it: A huge, almost life-size metal sculpture of a mother whale and two nursing calves greets you. A few more steps, and you're met by the looming, bleached-white skeleton of a 40-foot sperm whale; it's pretty impressive.

On the second floor of the mall is the **Whalers Village Museum** (✆ **808/661-5992;** www.whalersvillage.com/mallinfo.htm), which celebrates the "Golden Era of Whaling" from 1825 to 1860. Harpoons and scrimshaw are on display; the museum has even re-created the cramped quarters of a whaler's seagoing vessel. It's open during mall hours, daily from 10am to 6pm; admission is free.

The Scenic Route from West Maui to Central or Upcountry Maui: The Kahekili Highway

The usual road from west Maui to Wailuku is the Honoapiilani Highway (Hwy. 30), which runs along the coast and then turns inland at Maalaea. But those in search of a back-to-nature driving experience should go the other way, along the **Kahekili Highway (Hwy. 340)** ★. (*Highway* is a bit of a euphemism for this paved but somewhat precarious narrow road; check your rental-car agreement before you head out—some companies don't allow their cars on this road. If it is raining or has been raining, skip this road due to mud and rock slides.) The road is named after the great chief Kahekili, who built houses from the skulls of his enemies.

You'll start out on the Honoapiilani Highway (Hwy. 30), which becomes

Whalers Village has adopted the whale as its mascot.

Kahakuloa village church.

the Kahekili Highway (Hwy. 340) after Honokohau, at the northernmost tip of the island. Around this point are **Honolua Bay** ★ and **Mokuleia Bay** ★, which have been designated as Marine Life Conservation Areas (the taking of fish, shells, or anything else is prohibited).

From this point, the quality of the road deteriorates, and you may share the way with roosters, goats, cows, and dogs. The narrow road weaves along for the next 20 miles, following an ancient Hawaiian coastal footpath and showing you the true wild nature of Maui. These are photo opportunities from heaven: steep ravines, rolling pastoral hills, tumbling waterfalls, exploding blowholes, crashing surf, jagged lava coastlines, and a tiny Hawaiian village straight off a postcard.

Just before **mile marker 20,** look for a small turnoff on the mauka (*mow*-kah, meaning toward the mountain) side of the road, just before the guardrail starts. Park here and walk across the road, and on your left you'll see a spouting **blowhole.** In winter, this is an excellent spot to look for whales.

About 3 miles farther along the road, you'll come to a wide turnoff providing a great photo op: a view of the jagged coastline down to the crashing surf.

Less than half a mile farther along, just before **mile marker 16,** look for the POHAKU KANI sign, marking the huge 6×6-foot **bell-shaped stone.** To "ring" the bell, look on the side facing Kahakuloa for the deep indentations, and strike the stone with another rock.

Along the route, nestled in a crevice between two steep hills, is the picturesque village of **Kahakuloa** ★ (The Tall Hau Tree), with a dozen weatherworn houses, a church with a red-tile roof, and vivid green taro patches. From the northern side of the village, you can look back at the great view of Kahakuloa, the dark boulder beach, and the 636-foot Kahakuloa Head rising in the background.

At various points along the drive are artists' studios nestled into the cliffs and hills. One noteworthy stop is the **Kaukini Gallery,** located on Kahekili Highway (© **808/244-3371;** www.kaukinigallery.com), which features work by more than two dozen local artists, with lots of gifts and crafts to buy in all price ranges. (You may also want to stop here to use one of the few restrooms along the drive.)

When you're approaching Wailuku, stop at the **Halekii and Pihanakalani Heiau** (www.mauimuseum.org/heiau.html), which visitors rarely see. To get here from Wailuku, turn north from Main Street onto Market Street. Turn right onto Mill Street and follow it until it ends; then make a left on Lower Main Street. Follow Lower Main until it ends at Waiehu Beach Road (Hwy. 340) and turn left. Turn left on Kuhio Street and again at the first left onto Hea Place, and drive through the gates and look for the Hawaii Visitors Bureau marker.

These two *heiau,* built in 1240 from stones carried up from the Iao Stream below, sit on a hill with a commanding view of central Maui and Haleakala. Kahekili, the last chief of Maui, lived here. After the bloody battle at Iao Stream, Kamehameha I reportedly came to the temple here to pay homage to the war god, Ku, with a human sacrifice. Halekii (House of Images) is made of stone walls with a flat grassy top, whereas Pihanakalani (Gathering Place of Supernatural Beings) is a pyramid-shaped mount of stones. If you sit quietly nearby (never walk on any *heiau*—it's considered disrespectful), you'll see that the view alone explains why this spot was chosen.

SOUTH MAUI

Maalaea

At the bend in the Honoapiilani Highway (Hwy. 30), Maalaea Bay runs along the south side of the isthmus between the West Maui Mountains and Haleakala. This is the windiest area on Maui: Trade winds blowing between the two mountains are funneled across the isthmus, and by the time they reach Maalaea, gusts of 25 to 30 mph are not uncommon.

This creates ideal conditions for **windsurfers** out in Maalaea Bay. Surfers are also seen just outside the small boat harbor in Maalaea, which has one of the fastest breaks in the state.

Maui Ocean Center ★★ ☺ AQUARIUM   This 5-acre facility houses the largest aquarium in the state and features one of Hawaii's largest predators: the tiger shark. Exhibits are geared toward the residents of Hawaii's ocean waters. As you walk past the three dozen or so tanks and numerous exhibits, you'll slowly

Halekii and Pihanakalani Heiau sit on a hill with a commanding view of central Maui and Haleakala.

The turtle pool at the Maui Ocean Center.

descend from the "beach" to the deepest part of the ocean without ever getting wet. Start at the surge pool, where you'll see shallow-water marine life like spiny urchins and cauliflower coral; then move on to the reef tanks, turtle pool, touch pool (with starfish and urchins), and eagle-ray pool before reaching the star of the show: the 100-foot-long, 600,000-gallon main tank featuring tiger, gray, and white-tip sharks, as well as tuna, surgeonfish, triggerfish, and numerous others. A walkway goes right through the tank, so you'll be surrounded on three sides by marine creatures. A very cool place, and well worth the time. Some new additions are a hammerhead exhibit and the Shark Dive Maui Program (Mon, Wed, and Fri; $199 per certified diver); if you're a certified scuba diver, you can plunge into the aquarium with sharks, stingrays, and tropical fish while friends and family watch from the other side of the glass. ***Helpful hint:*** Buy your tickets online to avoid the long admission lines.

At Maalaea Harbor Village, 192 Maalaea Rd. (the triangle btw. Honoapiilani Hwy. and Maalaea Rd.). www.mauioceancenter.com. ℂ **808/270-7000.** Admission $25 adults, $22 seniors, $18 children 3–12. Daily 9am–5pm (until 6pm July–Aug).

Kihei

Capt. George Vancouver "discovered" Kihei in 1778, when it was only a collection of fishermen's grass shacks on the hot, dry, dusty coast (hard to believe, eh?). A **totem pole** stands today where he's believed to have landed, across from the Aston Maui Lu Resort, 575 S. Kihei Rd. Vancouver sailed on to what later became British Columbia, where a great international city and harbor now bear his name.

West of the junction of Piilani Highway (Hwy. 31) and Mokulele Highway (Hwy. 350) is **Kealia Pond National Wildlife Preserve** (𝄐 808/ 875-1582; www.fws.gov/kealia pond), a 700-acre U.S. Fish and Wildlife wetland preserve where endangered Hawaiian stilts, coots, and ducks hang out and splash. These ponds work two ways: as bird preserves and as sedimentation basins that keep the coral reefs from silting from runoff. You can take a self-guided tour along a boardwalk dotted with interpretive signs and shade shelters, through sand dunes, and around ponds to Maalaea Harbor. The boardwalk starts at the outlet of Kealia Pond on the ocean side of North Kihei Road (near mile marker 2 on Piilani Hwy.). Among the Hawaiian water birds seen here are the black-crowned high

A totem pole marks the spot where Capt. George Vancouver first landed on Maui.

heron, Hawaiian coot, Hawaiian duck, and Hawaiian stilt. There are also shorebirds like sanderling, Pacific golden plover, ruddy turnstone, and wandering tattler. From July to December, the hawksbill turtle comes ashore here to lay her eggs. *Tip:* If you're bypassing Kihei, take the Piilani Highway (Hwy. 31), which parallels strip-mall-laden South Kihei Road, and avoid the hassle of stoplights and traffic.

Wailea

The dividing line between arid Kihei and artificially green Wailea is distinct. Wailea once had the same kiawe-strewn, dusty landscape as Kihei until Alexander & Baldwin Inc. (of sugar cane fame) began developing a resort here in the 1970s (after piping water from the other side of the island to the desert terrain of Wailea). Today, the manicured 1,450 acres of this affluent resort stand out like an oasis along the normally dry leeward coast.

The best way to explore this golden resort coast is to rise with the sun and head for Wailea's 1.5-mile **coastal nature trail** ★, stretching between the Fairmont Kea Lani and the green grass of the Wailea Beach Marriott. It's a great morning walk on a serpentine path that meanders uphill and down past native plants, old Hawaiian habitats, and a billion dollars' worth of luxury hotels. You can pick up the trail at any of the resorts or from clearly marked SHORELINE ACCESS points along the coast. The best time to go is early morning; joggers clog the trail by midmorning and beachgoers take over later on. As the path crosses several bold black-lava points, it affords vistas of islands and ocean. Benches

The Wailea coastal nature trail.   Keawalai Congregational Church.

allow you to pause and contemplate the view across Alalakeiki Channel, where you may see whales in season. Sunset is another good time to hit the trail.

Makena

A few miles south of Wailea, the manicured coast changes over to the wilderness of Makena (abundance). In the 1800s, cattle were driven down the slope from upland ranches and loaded onto boats that waited to take them to market. Now **Makena Landing ★** is a beach park with boat-launching facilities, showers, toilets, and picnic tables. It's great for snorkeling and for launching kayaks bound for La Pérouse Bay and Ahihi-Kinau Natural Preserve.

From the landing, go south on Makena Road; on the right is **Keawalai Congregational Church** (℗ **808/879-5557**), built in 1855 with walls 3 feet thick. Surrounded by ti leaves, which by Hawaiian custom provide protection, and built of lava rock with coral used as mortar, this Protestant church sits on its own cove with a gold-sand beach. It always attracts a Sunday crowd for its 10am Hawaiian-language service. Take time to wander through the cemetery; you'll see some tombstones with a ceramic picture of the deceased on them, which is an old custom.

A little farther south on the coast is **La Pérouse Monument ★**, a pyramid of lava rocks that marks the spot where French explorer Adm. Comte de la Pérouse set foot on Maui in 1786. The first Westerner to "discover" the island, he described the "burning climate" of the leeward coast, observed several fishing villages near Kihei, and sailed on into oblivion, never to be seen again; some believe he may have been eaten by cannibals in what is now Vanuatu. To get here, drive south past Puu Olai to Ahihi Bay, where the road turns to gravel. Go another 2 miles along the coast to La Pérouse Bay; the monument sits amid a clearing in black lava at the end of the dirt road.

The rocky coastline and some-times rough seas contribute to the lack of appeal for water activities here; **hiking** opportunities, however, are excellent. Bring plenty of water and sun protection, and wear hiking boots that can withstand walking on lava. From La Pérouse Bay, you can pick up the old King's Highway trail, which at one time circled the island. Walk along the sandy beach at La Pérouse and look for the trail indentation in the lava, which leads down to the lighthouse at the tip of Cape Hanamanioa, about a .75-mile round-trip. Or you can continue on the trail as it climbs up the hill for 2 miles, then ventures back toward the ocean, where there are quite a few old Hawaiian home foundations and rocky coral beaches.

La Pérouse Monument.

HALEAKALA NATIONAL PARK ★★★

At once forbidding and compelling, Haleakala (House of the Sun) National Park is Maui's main natural attraction. More than 1.3 million people a year ascend the 10,023-foot-high mountain to peer down into the crater of the world's largest dormant volcano. (Haleakala is officially considered active, even though it has not rumbled since 1790.) That hole would hold Manhattan: 3,000 feet deep, 7½ miles long by 2½ miles wide, and encompassing 19 square miles.

The Hawaiians recognize the mountain as a sacred site. Ancient chants tell of Pele, the volcano goddess, and one of her siblings doing battle on the crater floor where Kawilinau (Bottomless Pit) now stands. Commoners in ancient Hawaii didn't spend much time here, though. The only people allowed into this sacred area were the *kahuna* (priests), who took their apprentices to live for periods of time in this intensely spiritual place. Today, New Agers also revere Haleakala as one of the earth's powerful energy points, and even the U.S. Air Force has a not-very-well-explained presence here.

But there's more to do here than simply stare into a big black hole: Just going up the mountain is an experience in itself. Where else on the planet can you climb from sea level to 10,000 feet in just 37 miles, or a 2-hour drive? The snaky road passes through big, puffy cumulus clouds to offer magnificent views of the isthmus of Maui, the West Maui Mountains, and the Pacific Ocean.

Many drive up to the summit in predawn darkness to watch the **sunrise over Haleakala;** writer Mark Twain called it "the sublimest spectacle" of his life. Others take a trail ride inside the bleak lunar landscape of the wilderness inside the crater or coast down the 37-mile road from the summit on a bicycle with special brakes (see "Biking" and "Horseback Riding," in chapter 5).

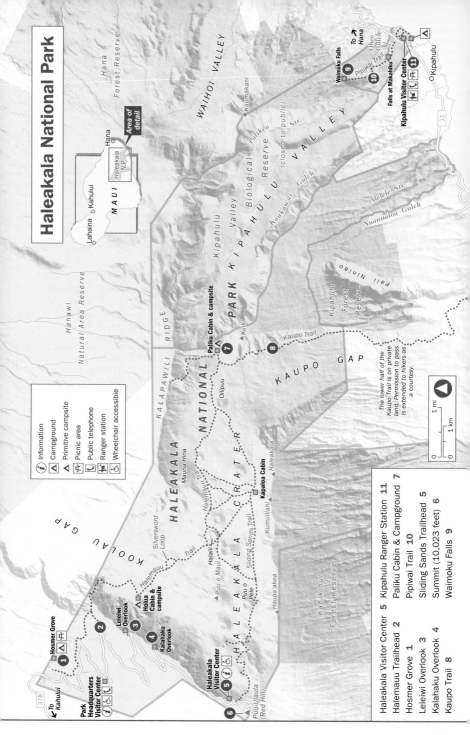

Haleakala National Park

Legend:
- (i) Information
- ▲ Campground
- ▲ Primitive campsite
- 🌲 Picnic area
- 📞 Public telephone
- 🧍 Ranger station
- ♿ Wheelchair accessible

Haleakala Visitor Center **5**
Halemauu Trailhead **2**
Hosmer Grove **1**
Leleiwi Overlook **3**
Kalahaku Overlook **4**
Kaupo Trail **8**

Kipahulu Visitor Center **5**
Paliku Cabin & Campground **7**
Pipiwai Trail **10**
Sliding Sands Trailhead **5**
Summit (10,023 feet) **6**
Waimoku Falls **9**

Kipahulu Ranger Station **11**

The lower half of the Kaupo Trail is on private land. Permission to pass is extended to hikers as a courtesy.

Hardy adventurers hike and camp inside the crater's wilderness (see "Hiking & Camping," in chapter 5). Those bound for the interior should bring their survival gear, for the terrain is raw, rugged, and punishing—not unlike the moon. However, if you choose to experience Haleakala National Park, it will prove memorable—guaranteed.

Just the Facts

Haleakala National Park extends from the summit of Mount Haleakala into the crater, down the volcano's southeast flank to Maui's eastern coast, beyond Hana. There are actually two separate and distinct destinations within the park: **Haleakala Summit** and the **Kipahulu** coast (see "Tropical Haleakala: Oheo Gulch at Kipahulu," p. 148). The summit gets all the publicity, but Kipahulu draws crowds, too—it's lush, green, and tropical, and home to Oheo Gulch (also known as Seven Sacred Pools). No road links the summit and the coast; you have to approach them separately, and you need at least a day to see each place.

WHEN TO GO At the 10,023-foot summit, weather changes fast. With wind-chill, temperatures can be freezing any time of year. Summer can be dry and warm; winter can be wet, windy, and cold. Before you go, get current weather conditions from the park (© **808/572-4400**) or the **National Weather Service** (© **866/944-5025**, option 4; www.prh.noaa.gov/hnl).

From sunrise to noon, the light is weak, but the view is usually free of clouds. The best time for photos is in the afternoon, when the sun lights the crater and clouds are few. Go on full-moon nights for spectacular viewing. However, even when the forecast is promising, the weather at Haleakala can change in an instant—be prepared.

ACCESS POINTS **Haleakala Summit** is 37 miles, or a 1½- to 2-hour drive, from Kahului. To get here, take Hwy. 37 to Hwy. 377 to Hwy. 378. For details on the drive, see "The Drive to the Summit," below. Pukalani is the last town for water, food, and gas.

The **Kipahulu** section of Haleakala National Park is on Maui's east end near Hana, 60 miles from Kahului on Hwy. 36 (Hana Hwy.). Due to traffic and rough road conditions, plan on 4 hours for the one-way drive from Kahului. For complete information, see "Driving the Road to Hana," later in this chapter. Hana is the only nearby town for services,

Nene, a Hawaiian goose.

A horseback ride in Haleakala's crater.

water, gas, food, and overnight lodging; some facilities may not be open after dark.

At both entrances to the park, the admission fee is $5 per person or $10 per car, good for 3 days of unlimited entry.

INFORMATION, VISITOR CENTERS, & RANGER PROGRAMS   For information before you go, contact **Haleakala National Park,** P.O. Box 369, Makawao, HI 96768 (✆ **808/572-4400;** www.nps.gov/hale).

One mile from the park entrance, at 7,000 feet, is **Haleakala National Park Headquarters** (✆ **808/572-4400**), open daily from 7am to 3:45pm. Stop here to pick up information on park programs and activities, get camping permits, and, occasionally, see a nene (Hawaiian goose)—one or more are often here to greet visitors. Restrooms, a pay phone, and drinking water are also available.

The **Haleakala Visitor Center,** open daily from sunrise to 3pm, is near the summit, 11 miles past the park entrance. It offers a panoramic view of the volcanic landscape, with photos identifying the various features, and exhibits that explain the area's history, ecology, geology, and volcanology. Park staff members are often on hand to answer questions. Restrooms and water are available.

Rangers offer excellent, informative, and free Citizen Scientists talks from 9am to 2pm daily in the summit building. For information on hiking (including guided hikes) and camping, including cabins and campgrounds in the wilderness itself, see "Hiking & Camping," p. 173.

The Drive to the Summit

If you look on a Maui map, almost in the middle of the part that resembles a torso, you'll see a black wiggly line. That's **Hwy. 378,** also known as **Haleakala Crater Road**—one of the fastest-ascending roads in the world. This grand corniche has at least 33 switchbacks; passes through numerous climate zones; goes under, in, and out of clouds; takes you past rare silversword plants and

Dominating the east side of Maui is the 10,000-foot summit of Mount Haleakala, long recognized by Hawaiians as a sacred site. The volcano and its surrounding wilderness, extending down the volcano's southeast flank to Maui's eastern coast, offer spectacular treats for the senses. At the summit, you'll encounter dry alpine air, multihued volcanic landscapes, dramatic mists and clouds, and views of three other islands on a clear day; near the sea, the lush green of a subtropical rainforest takes over. You'll find freshwater pools, towering ohia and koa trees, ginger and ti plants, *kukui*, mango, guava, and bamboo.

The "House of the Sun"

According to ancient legend, Haleakala got its name from a clever trick that the demigod Maui pulled on the sun. Maui's mother, the goddess Hina, complained one day that the sun sped across the sky so quickly that her tapa cloth couldn't dry. Maui, known as a trickster, devised a plan. The next morning he went to the top of the great mountain and waited for the sun to poke its head above the horizon. Quickly, Maui lassoed the sun, bringing its path across the sky to an abrupt halt. The sun begged Maui to let go, and Maui said he would on one condition: that the sun slow its trip across the sky to give the island more sunlight. The sun assented. In honor of this agreement, the Hawaiians call the mountain Haleakala, or "House of the Sun." To this day, the top of Haleakala has about 15 minutes more sunlight than the communities on the coastline below.

The Lay of the Land

Scientists believe that the Haleakala volcano began its growth on the ocean floor about 2 million years ago, as magma from below the Pacific Ocean floor erupted through cracks in the Pacific Plate. The volcano has erupted numerous times over the past 10,000 years. Though the most

recent eruption is thought to have occurred about 1790, Haleakala is still considered an active volcano. You'll pass through as many ecological zones on a 2-hour drive from the humid coast to the harsh summit of the mountain as you would on a journey from Mexico to Canada, and the temperature can vary 30 degrees from sea level to summit. Haleakala is home to more endangered species than any other national park in the U.S., and the park was designated an International Biosphere Reserve in 1980. Among the rare birds and animals you may see here:

Nene (Hawaiian goose) *[Branta sandwichensis]:* A relative of the Canada goose, the nene is Hawaii's state bird, standing about 2 feet high with a black head and yellow cheeks. The wild nene on Haleakala number fewer than 250, and the species remains endangered.

'U'au (Hawaiian petrel) *[Pterodroma sandwichensis]:* These large, dark-grey-brown and white birds travel as far as Alaska and Japan on 2-week feeding trips. Their status is listed as vulnerable; it's estimated that fewer than 1,000 birds are nesting on the Haleakala crater.

Kike koa (Maui parrotbill) *[Pseudonestor xanthophrys]:* One of Hawaii's rarest birds, currently listed on the endangered list, has an olive green body and yellow chest. Its strong, hooked, parrotlike bill is used to pry chunks of koa bark as it searches for food.

'Akohekohe (Crested honeycreeper) *[Palmeria dolei]:* Listed as a critically endangered species, this bird is native only to a 22-square-mile area on the northeastern slope of Haleakala. It has primarily black plumage, with bright-orange surrounding the eyes and nape, and a furl of white feathers sprouting over the beak.

endangered Hawaiian geese sailing through the clear, thin air; and offers a view that extends for more than 100 miles.

Going to the summit takes 1½ to 2 hours from Kahului. No matter where you start out, you'll follow Hwy. 37 (Haleakala Hwy.) to Pukalani, where you'll pick up Hwy. 377 (which is also Haleakala Hwy.), which you'll take to Hwy. 378. Along the way, expect fog, rain, and wind. You may encounter stray cattle and downhill bicyclists. Fill up your gas tank before you go—the only gas available is 27 miles below the summit at Pukalani. There are no facilities beyond the ranger stations, so bring your own food and water.

Remember, you're entering a high-altitude wilderness area. Some people get dizzy due to the lack of oxygen; you might also suffer lightheadedness, shortness of breath, nausea, severe headaches, flatulence, or dehydration. People with asthma, pregnant women, heavy smokers, and those with heart conditions should be especially careful in the rarefied air. Bring water and a jacket or a blanket, especially if you go up for sunrise. Or you might want to go up to the summit for sunset, which is also spectacular.

As you go up the slopes, the temperature drops about 3° every 1,000 feet, so the temperature at the top can be 30° cooler than it was at sea level. Come prepared with sweaters, jackets, and rain gear.

At the **park entrance,** you'll pay an entrance fee of $10 per car (or $5 per person without a vehicle). About a mile from the entrance is **park headquarters,** where an endangered **nene,** or Hawaiian goose, may greet you with its unique call. With its black face, buff cheeks, and partially webbed feet, the gray-brown bird looks like a small Canada goose with zebra stripes; it brays out "nay-nay" (thus its name), doesn't migrate, and prefers lava beds to lakes. The unusual goose clings to a precarious existence on these alpine slopes. Vast populations of more than 25,000 once inhabited Hawaii, but hunters, pigs, feral cats and dogs, and mongooses preyed on the nene; coupled with habitat destruction, these

EXPLORING MAUI

Haleakala National Park

The Leleiwi Overlook affords a panoramic view of the lunarlike crater of Haleakala.

Silverswords only grow in Hawaii and take from 4 to 50 years to bloom.

predators nearly caused its extinction. By 1951, there were only 30 left. Now protected as Hawaii's state bird, the wild nene on Haleakala number fewer than 250—and the species remains endangered.

Beyond headquarters are **two scenic overlooks** on the way to the summit; stop at Leleiwi on the way up and Kalahaku on the way back down, if only to get out, stretch, and get accustomed to the heights. Take a deep breath, look around, and pop your ears. If you feel dizzy or drowsy, or get a sudden headache, consider turning around and going back down.

Leleiwi Overlook ★ is just beyond mile marker 17. From the parking area, a short trail leads you to a panoramic view of the lunarlike crater. When the clouds are low and the sun is in the right place, usually around sunset, you may experience a phenomenon known as the "Specter of the Brocken"—you can see a reflection of your shadow, ringed by a rainbow, in the clouds below. It's an optical illusion caused by a rare combination of sun, shadow, and fog that occurs in only two other places on the planet: Scotland and Germany.

Two miles farther along is **Kalahaku Overlook ★**, the best place to see a rare **silversword.** You can turn into this overlook only when you are descending from the top. The silversword is the punk of the plant world, its silvery bayonets displaying tiny purple bouquets—like a spacey artichoke with attitude. This botanical wonder proved irresistible to humans, who gathered them in gunnysacks for Chinese potions and British specimen collections, and just for the sheer thrill of having something so rare. Silverswords grow only in Hawaii, take from 4 to 50 years to bloom, and then, usually between May and October, send up a 1- to 6-foot stalk with a purple bouquet of sunflower-like blooms. They're very rare, so don't even think about taking one home.

Continue on, and you'll quickly reach the **Haleakala Visitor Center ★**, which offers spectacular views. You'll feel as if you're at the edge of the earth. But don't turn around here: The actual summit's a little farther on, at **Puu Ulaula Overlook ★** (also known as Red Hill), the volcano's highest point, where you'll

STOP & SMELL THE lavender

While in the upcountry Kula region, stop by **Ali'i Kula Lavender,** 1100 Waipoli Rd., Kula (© **808/878-3004;** www.aliikula lavender.com), which grows several varieties of lavender, so there's usually at least one type in bloom. There are great tours to take while you're here. On the 30-minute **Lavender Garden Walking Tour** (daily at 9:30, 10:30, and 11:30am and 1 and 2:30pm for $12 per person, $10 with advance reservations), you're served lavender herb tea with a lavender scone and given a garden and studio tour. My favorite, the **Combo Tour** ($28 per person, 24-hr. advance reservation) combines the walking tour with a lunch basket, which includes a choice of lavender beverage, a delicious lavender-seasoned chicken wrap, lavender gourmet chips, fresh fruit, and a decadent lavender brownie. Seasonal events range from a fabulous Valentine's Day luncheon to a woven-lavender-wand-making workshop in the summer. Be sure to stop by the store and look over the culinary products

(lavender seasonings, dressings, scones, honey, jelly, and teas), bath and body goodies (lotions, soaps, bubble baths, bath gels), aromatherapy (oil, candles, eye pillows), and other items (T-shirts, gift baskets, and dried lavender).

find a mysterious cluster of buildings officially known as Haleakala Observatories, but unofficially called **Science City.** If you go up for sunrise, the building at Puu Ulaula Overlook, a triangle of glass that serves as a windbreak, is the best viewing spot. After the daily miracle of sunrise—the sun seems to rise out of the vast crater (hence the name "House of the Sun")—you can see all the way across Alenuihaha Channel to the often-snowcapped summit of Mauna Kea on the Big Island.

When driving back down the mountain on the Haleakala Crater Road, be sure to put your car in low gear. That way, you won't destroy your brakes by riding them the whole way down.

MORE IN UPCOUNTRY MAUI

Come upcountry and discover a different side of Maui: On the slopes of Haleakala, cowboys, planters, and other country people make their homes in serene, neighborly communities like **Makawao** and **Kula,** a world away from the bustling beach resorts. Even if you can't spare a day or two in the cool upcountry air, there are some sights that are worth a look on your way to or from the crater. Shoppers and gallery hoppers might want to spend more time here; see chapter 7 for details. For a map of this area, turn to the "Restaurants in Upcountry & East Maui" map on p. 221.

Just beyond the sugar cane fields, on the slopes of Haleakala, lies the **Surfing Goat Dairy,** 3661 Omaopio Rd., Kula (*(©* **808/878-2870;** www.surfinggoat dairy.com). Some 140 dairy goats blissfully graze the 42 acres and contribute the milk for 24 different cheeses, which are made every day. If you have kids in tow, they will love the 2-hour **Grand Dairy Tour** ($25, but call for reservations; they do it every Sat at 9am)—they get to be a goat herder for a day and even get to try to milk a goat. They can also play with the kids—goat kids, that is. Meanwhile, Mom and Dad can learn how to make cheese and sample the different varieties made on the premises. If you don't have a lot of time, drop by for the 20-minute casual dairy tour (Mon–Sat 10am–3pm; Sun 10am–1pm) for just $10 per adult and $7 for children. Or check out the Evening Chores and Milking Tour (Mon–Sat 3:15pm) for $15 adults, $12 children. Be sure to sample the goat cheeses (off-the-charts terrific) and buy a bar or two of goat-milk soap.

On the slopes of Haleakala, Maui's farmers have been producing vegetables since the 1800s. In fact, during the gold rush in California, the Hawaiian farmers in Kula shipped so many potatoes that it was nicknamed Nu Kaleponi, a sort of pidgin Hawaiian pronunciation of "New California." In the late 1800s, Portuguese and Chinese immigrants, who had fulfilled their labor contracts with the sugar cane companies, moved to this area, drawn by the rural agricultural lifestyle. That lifestyle continues today, among the fancy gentlemen's farms that have sprung up in the past 3 decades. Kula continues to grow its well-known onions, lettuce, tomatoes, carrots, cauliflower, and cabbage. It is also a major source of cut flowers for the state: Most of Hawaii's proteas, as well as nearly all the carnations used in leis, come from Kula.

To experience a bit of the history of Kula, turn off the Kula Highway (Hwy. 37) onto Lower Kula Road. Well before the turnoff, you'll see a white octagonal building with a silver roof, the **Holy Ghost Catholic Church** (*(©* **808/878-1091**). Hawaii's only eight-sided church, it was built between 1884 and 1897 by Portuguese immigrants. It's worth a stop to see the hand-carved altar and works of art for the Stations of the Cross, with inscriptions in Portuguese.

Kula Botanical Garden ★ PARK/ GARDEN You can take a self-guided, informative, leisurely stroll through more than 700 native and

Kula Botanical Garden.

A sign points the way to Tedeschi Vineyards and Winery.

exotic plants—including three unique collections of orchids, proteas, and bromeliads—at this 5-acre garden. It offers a good overview of Hawaii's exotic flora in one small, cool place.

Hwy. 377, south of Haleakala Crater Rd. (Hwy. 378), ½ mile from Hwy. 37. www.kulabotanical garden.com. *C* **808/878-1715.** Admission $10 adults, $3 children 6–12, free for children 5 and under. Daily 9am–4pm.

Tedeschi Vineyards and Winery ★ WINERY On the southern shoulder of Haleakala is **Ulupalakua Ranch,** a 20,000-acre spread once owned by legendary sea captain James Makee, celebrated in the Hawaiian song and dance "Hula O Makee." Wounded in a Honolulu waterfront brawl in 1843, Makee moved to Maui and bought Ulupalakua. He renamed it Rose Ranch, planted sugar as a cash crop, and grew rich. Still in operation, the ranch is now home to Maui's only winery, established in 1974 by Napa vintner Emil Tedeschi, who began growing California and European grapes here and producing serious still and sparkling wines, plus a silly wine made of pineapple juice. The rustic grounds are the perfect place for a picnic. Pack a basket before you go, and enjoy it with a bottle of Tedeschi wine.

Across from the winery are the remains of the three smokestacks of the **Makee Sugar Mill,** built in 1878. You may do a double take at the people lounging on the front porch. On closer inspection you'll see that they are not "people," but the work of Maui artist Reems Mitchell, who carved the mannequins on the front porch of the Ulupalakua Ranch Store: a Filipino with his fighting cock, a cowboy, a farmhand, and a sea captain, all representing the people of Maui's history.

Off Hwy. 37 (Kula Hwy.). www.mauiwine.com. *C* **877/878-6058** or 808/878-6058. Daily 10am–5pm. Free tastings daily 10am–5pm. Free tours at 10:30am and 1:30pm.

DRIVING THE ROAD TO HANA ★★★

Top down, sunscreen on, radio tuned to a little Hawaiian music on a Maui morning: It's time to head out to Hana along the Hana Highway (Hwy. 36), a wiggle of a road that runs along Maui's northeastern shore. The drive takes at least 3 hours from Lahaina or Kihei—but plan to take all day. Going to Hana is about the journey, not the destination.

There are wilder roads, steeper roads, and more dangerous roads, but in all of Hawaii, no road is more celebrated than this one. It winds 50 miles past taro patches, magnificent seascapes, waterfall pools, botanical gardens, and verdant rainforests, and ends at one of Hawaii's most beautiful tropical places.

The outside world discovered the little village of Hana in 1926, when the narrow coastal road, carved by pickax-wielding convicts, opened. The mud-and-gravel road, often subject to landslides and washouts, was paved in 1962, when tourist traffic began to increase; now more than 1,000 cars traverse the road each day, according to Hana storekeeper Harry Hasegawa. That equals about 500,000

The Hana Highway runs along Maui's north-eastern shore.

people a year, which is way too many. Go at the wrong time, and you'll be stuck in a bumper-to-bumper rental-car parade—peak traffic hours are mid-morning and midafternoon year-round, especially on weekends.

In the rush to "do" Hana in a day, most visitors spin around town in 10 minutes flat and wonder what all the fuss is about. It takes time to take in Hana, play in the waterfalls, sniff the tropical flowers, hike to bamboo forests, and marvel at the spectacular scenery; stay overnight if you can.

However, if you really must do the Hana Highway in a day, go just before sunrise and return after sunset: On a full-moon night, the sea and the waterfalls glow in soft white light, with mysterious shadows appearing in the jungle. And you'll have the road almost to yourself on the way back.

Tips: Forget your mainland road manners. Practice aloha. Give way at one-lane bridges, wave at oncoming motorists, and let the big guys in 4×4s have the right-of-way—it's just common sense, brah. If the guy behind you blinks his lights, let him pass. And don't honk your horn—in Hawaii, it's considered rude.

THE JOURNEY BEGINS IN PAIA   Before you even start out, fill up your gas tank. Gas in Paia is expensive (even by Maui standards), and it's the last place for gas until you get to Hana, some 42 miles, 54 bridges, and 600 hairpin turns down the road.

The former plantation village of Paia was once a thriving sugar-mill town. The mill is still here, but the population shifted to Kahului in the 1950s when subdivisions opened there, leaving Paia to shrivel up and die. But the town refused to give up and has proven its ability to adapt to the times. Now chic eateries and trendy shops stand next door to the mom-and-pop establishments that have been serving generations of Paia customers.

Plan to be here early, around 7am, when **Charley's ★★** (p. 223), 142 Hana Hwy. (© **808/579-9453**), opens. Enjoy a big, hearty breakfast for a reasonable price.

After you leave Paia, just before the bend in the road, you'll pass the Kuau Mart on your left. This small general store is the only reminder of the sugar-plantation community of **Kuau.** The road then bends into an S-turn; in the middle of the S is the entrance to **Mama's Fish House,** marked by a restored boat with Mama's logo on the side. Just past the truck on the ocean side is the entrance to Mama's parking lot and adjacent small sandy cove in front of the restaurant. It's not good for swimming—ocean access is over very slippery rocks into strong surf—but the beach is a great place to sit and soak up some sun.

WINDSURFING MECCA   A mile from Mama's, just before mile marker 9, is a place known around the world as one of the greatest windsurfing spots on the planet: **Hookipa Beach Park ★**. Hookipa (Hospitality) is where the top-ranked windsurfers come to test themselves against thunderous surf and forceful wind. World-championship contests are held here, but on nearly every windy afternoon (the board surfers have the waves in the morning), you can watch dozens of windsurfers twirling and dancing in the wind like colorful butterflies. To watch the windsurfers, do not stop on the highway, but go past the park and turn left at the entrance on the far side of the beach. You can either park on the high grassy bluff or drive down to the sandy beach and park alongside the pavilion. Facilities include restrooms, a shower, picnic tables, and a barbecue area.

A surfer takes a walk in Paia, a once-thriving sugar-mill town.

INTO THE COUNTRY Past Hookipa Beach, the road winds down into **Maliko (Budding) Gulch** at mile marker 10. At the bottom of the gulch, look for the road on your right, which will take you out to **Maliko Bay.** Take the first right, which goes under the bridge and past a rodeo arena (scene of competitions by the Maliko Roping Club in summer) and on to the rocky beach. There are no facilities here except a boat-launch ramp. In the 1940s, Maliko had a thriving community at the mouth of the bay, but its residents rebuilt farther inland after a tsunami wiped it out. The bay may not look that special, but if the surf is up, it's a great place to watch the waves.

Back on the Hana Highway, as you leave Maliko Gulch, around mile marker 11, you'll pass through the rural area of **Haiku,** where you'll see banana patches, cane grass blowing in the wind, and forests of guava trees, avocados, *kukui* trees, palms, and Christmas berry. Just before mile marker 15 is the **Maui-Grown Market and Deli (© 808/572-1693)**, a good stop for drinks or snacks for the ride.

JAWS If it's winter and the waves are up, here's your chance to watch some serious surfing off **Pauwela Point** at an area known as Jaws (because the waves will chew you up). Expert tow-in surfers (who use a personal watercraft to pull a surfer into waves that are bigger than what could be caught by traditional paddling) battle the mammoth waves, which can get up to around 60 feet tall. To get here, make a small detour off the Hana Highway by turning left at Hahana Road, between mile markers 13 and 14. After the paved road ends, the dirt road is private property (Maui Land & Pine), so you may have to hike in about a mile and a half to get close to the ocean. Practice aloha, do not park in the pineapple fields, and do not pick or even touch the pineapples. Be very careful along the oceanside cliffs.

Back on the Hana Highway, at mile marker 16, the curves begin, one right after another. Slow down and enjoy the view of bucolic rolling hills, mango trees, and vibrant ferns. After mile marker 16, the road is still called the Hana Highway, but the number changes from Hwy. 36 to Hwy. 360, and the mile markers go back to 0.

AN ILLEGAL PLUNGE ALONG THE WAY A couple of miles later, we used to recommend a dip in the **Twin Falls** waterfall pool, but besides being illegal (you have to trespass to get there—past a NO TRESPASSING sign posted on the gate), the increased number of visitors hiking from the road to the falls has become such a crowded scene that we no longer recommend it. You'll see plenty of other waterfalls along the road during your trip.

HIDDEN HUELO Just before mile marker 4 on a blind curve, look for a double row of mailboxes on the left side by a pay phone. Down the road lies a hidden Hawaii of an earlier time, where an indescribable sense of serenity prevails. Hemmed in by Waipo and Hoalua bays is the remote community of **Huelo ★**, which means "tail end, last." This fertile area once supported a population of 75,000; today only a few hundred live among the scattered homes here, where a handful of B&Bs and exquisite vacation rentals cater to a trickle of travelers (see p. 297 for my recommendation).

The only reason Huelo is even marked is the historic 1853 **Kaula-napueo Church.** Reminiscent of New England architecture, this coral-and-cement church, topped with a plantation-green steeple and a gray tin roof, is still in use, although services are held just once or twice a month. It

Surfers battle the mammoth waves at Jaws.

still has the same austere interior of 1853: straight-backed benches, a no-nonsense platform for the minister, and no distractions on the walls to tempt you from paying attention to the sermon. Next to the church is a small graveyard, a personal history of this village in concrete and stone.

KOOLAU FOREST RESERVE After Huelo, the vegetation seems more lush, as though Mother Nature had poured Miracle-Gro on everything. This is the edge of the **Koolau Forest Reserve.** *Koolau* means "windward," and this certainly is one of the greatest examples of a lush windward area: The coastline here gets about 60 to 80 inches of rain a year, as well as runoff from the 200 to 300 inches that falls from farther up the mountain. You'll see trees laden with guavas, as well as mangoes, java plums, and avocados the size of softballs. The spiny, long-leafed plants are *hala* trees, which the Hawaiians used for weaving baskets, mats, and even canoe sails.

From here on out, there's a waterfall (and a one-lane bridge) around nearly every turn in the road, so drive slowly and be prepared to stop and yield to oncoming cars.

DANGEROUS CURVES About ½ mile after mile marker 6, there's a sharp U-curve in the road, going uphill. The road is practically one lane here, with a brick wall on one side and virtually no maneuvering room. Sound your horn at the start of the U-curve to let approaching cars know you're coming. Take this curve, as well as the few more coming up in the next several miles, very slowly.

Just before mile marker 7 is a forest of waving **bamboo.** The sight is so spectacular that drivers are often tempted to take their eyes off the road. Be very cautious. Wait until just after mile marker 7, at the **Kaaiea (Breath-taking View) Bridge,** to pull over and take a closer look at the hand-hewn stone walls. Then turn around to see the vista of bamboo.

A GREAT FAMILY HIKE   At mile marker 9, there's a small state wayside area with restrooms, picnic tables, and a barbecue area. The sign says KOOLAU FOREST RESERVE, but the real attraction here is the **Waikamoi Ridge Trail ★,** a great family hike that wanders on a clearly marked path, has a very gentle slope (easy enough for toddlers and grandparents) and scenic vistas, and has lots of interesting vegetation (which is marked with signs). The .75-mile loop is just the right amount of time to stretch your legs and be ready to get back in the car and head to Hana.

SAFETY WARNING   I used to recommend seeing **Puohokamoa Falls** at mile marker 11, but not anymore. Unfortunately, what was once a great thing has been overrun by hordes of not-so-polite tourists. You will see cars parking on the already dangerous, barely-two-lane Hana Highway ½ mile before the waterfall. Slow down after mile marker 10. As you get close to mile marker 11, the highway becomes a congested one-lane road due to visitors parking on this narrow stretch. Don't add to the congestion by trying to park: You'll see plenty of other great waterfalls along the road during your drive; just drive slowly and safely through this area.

CAN'T-MISS PHOTO OPS   Just past mile marker 12 is the **Kaumahina State Wayside Park ★** (*kaumahina* means "moon rise"). This is not only a good pit stop (restrooms are available) and a wonderful place for a picnic (with

Kaulanapueo Church, from 1853, is notable for its New England-style architecture.

tables and a barbecue area), but also a great vista point. The view of the rugged coastline makes an excellent shot—you can see all the way down to the jutting Keanae Peninsula.

Another mile and a couple of bends in the road, and you'll enter the Honomanu Valley, with its beautiful bay. To get to the **Honomanu Bay County Beach Park ★**, look for the turnoff on your left, just after mile marker 14, located at a point in the road where you begin your ascent up the other side of the valley. The rutted dirt-and-cinder road takes you down to the rocky black-sand beach. There are no facilities here. Because of the strong rip currents offshore, swimming is best in the stream inland from the ocean. You'll consider the drive down worthwhile as you stand on the beach, well away from the ocean, and turn to look back on the steep cliffs covered with vegetation.

MAUI'S BOTANICAL WORLD   Farther along the winding road, between mile markers 16 and 17, is a cluster of bunkhouses composing the YMCA Camp Keanae. A quarter-mile down is the **Keanae Arboretum ★★**, where the region's botany is divided into three parts: native forest, introduced forest, and traditional Hawaiian plants, food, and medicine. You can swim in the pools of Pinaau Stream, or press on along a mile-long trail into Keanae Valley, where a lovely tropical rainforest waits at the end (see "Hiking & Camping," in chapter 5).

KEANAE PENINSULA   The old Hawaiian village of **Keanae ★★** (The Mullet) stands out against the Pacific like a place time forgot. Here, on an old lava flow graced by an 1860 stone church and swaying palms, is one of the last coastal enclaves of native Hawaiians. They still grow taro in patches and pound it into poi, the staple of the old Hawaiian diet. And they still pluck opihi (limpet) from tide pools along the jagged coast and cast throw nets at schools of fish.

The turnoff to the Keanae Peninsula is on the left, just after the arboretum. The road passes by farms as it hugs the peninsula. Where the road bends, there's a small beach where fishermen gather to catch dinner. A quarter-mile farther is the **Keanae Congregational Church (✆ 808/248-8040)**, built in 1860 of lava rocks and coral mortar, standing in stark contrast to the green fields surrounding it. Beside the church is a small beachfront park, with false *kamani* trees against a backdrop of black lava and a roiling turquoise sea.

To experience untouched Hawaii, follow the road until it ends. Park by the white fence and take the short 5-minute walk along the shoreline over the black lava. Continue along the footpath through the tall California grass to the black rocky beach, separating the freshwater stream, **Pinaau,** which winds back into the Keanae Peninsula, nearly cutting it off from the rest of Maui. This is an excellent place for a picnic and a swim in the cool waters of the stream. There are no facilities here, so be sure you carry everything out with you and use restrooms before you arrive. As you make your way back, notice the white PVC pipes sticking out of the rocks—they're fishing pole holders for fishermen, usually hoping to catch ulua.

ANOTHER PHOTO OP: KEANAE LOOKOUT   Just past mile marker 17 is a wide spot on the ocean side of the road, where you can see the entire Keanae Peninsula's checkerboard pattern of green taro fields and its ocean boundary

The Keanae lookout.

etched in black lava. Keanae was the result of a postscript eruption of Haleakala, which flowed through the Koolau Gap and down Keanae Valley and added this geological punctuation to the rugged coastline.

FRUIT & FLOWER STANDS   Around mile marker 18, the road widens; you'll start to see numerous small stands selling fruit or flowers. Many of these stands work on the honor system: You leave your money in the basket and select your purchase. I recommend stopping at **Uncle Harry's** (© **808/633-3129),** which you'll find just after the Keanae School around mile marker 18. His family sells a variety of fruits and juices here Monday through Saturday from 10am to 3pm.

WAILUA   Just after Uncle Harry's, look for Wailua Road on the left. This will take you through the hamlet of homes and churches of Wailua, which also contains a shrine depicting what the community calls a "miracle." Behind the pink **St. Gabriel's Church** is the smaller, blue-and-white **Coral Miracle Church,** home of the **Our Lady of Fatima Shrine.** According to legend, in 1860 the men of this village were building a church by diving for coral to make the stone. But the coral offshore was in deep water and the men could only come up with a few pieces at a time, making the construction of the church an arduous project. A freak storm hit the area and deposited the coral from the deep on a nearby beach. The Hawaiians gathered what they needed and completed the church. After the church was completed, another freak storm hit the area and swept all the remaining coral on the beach back out to sea.

If you look back at Haleakala from here, on your left you can see the spectacular, near-vertical **Waikani Falls.** On the remainder of the dead-end road is an eclectic collection of old and modern homes. Turning around at the road's end is very difficult, so I suggest you just turn around at the church and head back for the Hana Highway.

Back on the Hana Highway, just before mile marker 19, is the **Wailua Valley State Wayside Park ★** (*wailua* means "two waters"), on the right

side of the road. Climb up the stairs for a view of the Keanae Valley, waterfalls, and Wailua Peninsula. On a really clear day, you can see up the mountain to the Koolau Gap.

For a better view of the Wailua Peninsula, continue down the road
about ¼ mile. There's a pull-off area with parking on the ocean side.

PUAA KAA STATE WAYSIDE PARK You'll hear this park long before you see it,
about halfway between mile markers 22 and 23. The sound of waterfalls
provides the background music for this small park area with restrooms, a

Fruit and flower stands dot the roadside on the way to Hana.

phone, and a picnic area. In fact, *puaa kaa* translates as "open laughter." There's a well-marked path to the falls and to a swimming hole.

OLD NAHIKU   Just after mile marker 25 is a narrow 3-mile road leading from the highway, at about 1,000 feet elevation, down to sea level—and to the remains of the old Hawaiian community of **Nahiku.** At one time this was a thriving village of thousands; today, the population has dwindled to fewer than 100—including a few Hawaiian families, but mostly extremely wealthy mainland residents who jet in for a few weeks at a time to their luxurious vacation homes. At the turn of the 20th century, this site saw brief commercial activity as the home of the Nahiku Rubber Co., the only commercial rubber plantation in the United States. You can still see rubber trees along Nahiku Road. However, the amount of rainfall, coupled with the damp conditions, could not support the commercial crop; the plantation closed in 1912, and Nahiku was forgotten until the 1980s, when multimillionaires "discovered" the remote and stunningly beautiful area.

At the end of the road, you can see the remains of the old wharf from the rubber-plantation days. Local residents come down here to shoreline fish; there's a small picnic area off to the side. Dolphins are frequently seen in the bay.

HANA AIRPORT   After mile marker 31, a small sign points to the Hana Airport, down Alalele Road on the left. Commuter airline **Pacific Wings** (© 888/ **575-4546;** www.pacificwings.com) offers four flights daily to and from Hana (from Kahului), with connecting flights from Kahului and traveling on to Honolulu. ***Be warned:*** There is no public transportation in Hana. Car rentals are available through **Kihei Rent A Car** (© **800/251-5288** or 808/879-7257; www.KiheiRentACar.com).

WAIANAPANAPA STATE PARK ★★   At mile marker 32, just on the outskirts of Hana, shiny black-sand Waianapanapa Beach appears like a vivid dream, with bright-green jungle foliage on three sides and cobalt-blue water lapping at its feet. The 120-acre park on an ancient lava flow includes sea cliffs, lava tubes, arches, and the beach, plus 12 cabins, tent camping, picnic pavilions, restrooms, showers, drinking water, and hiking trails. If you're interested in staying here, see p. 300 for a review of the cabins; also see "Beaches" and "Hiking & Camping," in chapter 5.

THE END OF THE ROAD: HEAVENLY HANA ★★

Green, tropical Hana is a destination all its own, a small coastal village that's probably what you came to Maui in search of. Here you'll find a rainforest dotted with cascading waterfalls and sparkling blue pools, skirted by red- and black-sand beaches.

Beautiful Hana enjoys more than 90 inches of rain a year—more than enough to keep the scenery lush. Banyans, bamboo, breadfruit trees—everything seems larger than life in this small town, especially the flowers, such as wild ginger and plumeria. Several roadside stands offer exotic blooms for a couple of bucks a bunch. Just "put money in box." It's the Hana honor system.

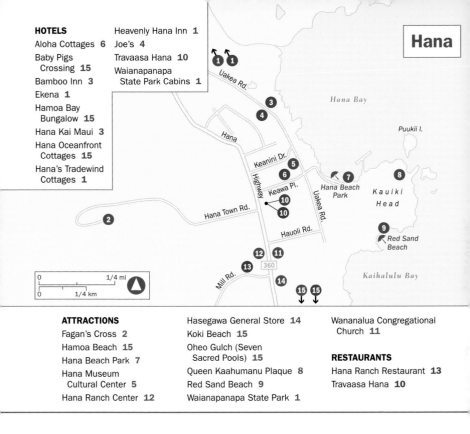

HOTELS

Aloha Cottages **6**
Baby Pigs
  Crossing **15**
Bamboo Inn **3**
Ekena **1**
Hamoa Bay
  Bungalow **15**
Hana Kai Maui **3**
Hana Oceanfront
  Cottages **15**
Hana's Tradewind
  Cottages **1**

Heavenly Hana Inn **1**
Joe's **4**
Travaasa Hana **10**
Waianapanapa
  State Park Cabins **1**

Hana

Hana Bay

Puukii I.

Hana Beach Park

Kauiki Head

Red Sand Beach

Kaihalulu Bay

Uakea Rd.

Hana

Keanini Dr.

Highway

Keawa Pl.

Hana Town Rd.

Hauoli Rd.

Uakea Rd.

Mill Rd.

360

0   1/4 mi
0   1/4 km

ATTRACTIONS

Fagan's Cross **2**
Hamoa Beach **15**
Hana Beach Park **7**
Hana Museum
  Cultural Center **5**
Hana Ranch Center **12**

Hasegawa General Store **14**
Koki Beach **15**
Oheo Gulch (Seven
  Sacred Pools) **15**
Queen Kaahumanu Plaque **8**
Red Sand Beach **9**
Waianapanapa State Park **1**

Wananalua Congregational
  Church **11**

RESTAURANTS

Hana Ranch Restaurant **13**
Travaasa Hana **10**

A Look at the Past

The Hana coast is rich in Hawaiian history and the scene of many turning points in Hawaiian culture. The ancient chants tell of rulers like the 15th-century **Piilani,** who united the island of Maui and built fishponds, irrigation fields, paved roads, and the massive **Piilanihale Heiau,** which still stands today in **Kahanu Garden,** part of the **National Tropical Botanical Garden** (© 808/248-8912; www.ntbg.org/gardens/kahanu.php). It was Piilani's sons and grandson who finished the *heiau* and built the first road to Hana from west Maui, not only along the coast, but also up the Kaupo Gap and through the Haleakala Crater. For information on visiting the garden, see "Hiking" under "Outdoor Activities," below.

In 1849, the cantankerous sea captain **George Wilfong** brought commerce to this isolated village when he started the first sugar plantation on some 60 acres. Because his harsh personality and set demands for plantation work did not sit well with the Hawaiians, Wilfong brought in the first Chinese immigrants to work his fields.

In 1864, two Danish brothers, **August** and **Oscar Unna,** contributed to the growth of the local sugar industry when they established the Hana Plantation. Four years later they brought in Japanese immigrants to labor in the fields.

By the turn of the 20th century, sugar wasn't the only crop booming in Hana (there were some six plantations in the area): Rubber was being commercially

grown in Nahiku, wheat in Kaupo, pineapple in Kipahulu, and tobacco in Ulupalakua.

In the 1920s and 1930s, several self-sufficient towns lined the coast, each with its own general store, school, and churches; some had movie theaters as well. Hana has all of the above plus some 15 stores, a pool hall, and several restaurants.

One can only guess what those towns would have been like today if not for the huge tsunami that hit the state on April 1, 1946. The damage along the Hana coast was catastrophic: The Keanae Peninsula was swept clear (only the stone church remained), Hamoa was totally wiped out, and entire villages completely disappeared.

After World War II, the labor movement became a powerful force in Hawaii. **C. Brewer,** owner of the largest sugar plantation in Hana, decided to shut down his operation instead of fighting the labor union. The closure of the plantation meant not only the loss of thousands of jobs, but also the loss of plantation-supplied homes and the entire plantation lifestyle. Thankfully, **Paul I. Fagan,** an entrepreneur from San Francisco who had purchased the Hana Sugar Co. from the Unna brothers in the 1930s, became the town's guardian angel.

Fagan wanted to retire here, so he focused his business acumen on the tiny town with big problems. Recognizing that sugar was no longer economically feasible, he looked at the community and saw other opportunities. He bought 14,000 acres of land in Hana, stripped it of sugar cane, planted grass, and shipped in cattle from his ranch on Molokai.

Next he did something that was years ahead of his time: He thought tourism might have a future in Hana, so he established an inn in 1946 that later became the **Hotel Hana Maui,** now called the **Travaasa Hana** (p. 226). Fagan also pulled off a public relations coup: He brought the entire San Francisco Seals baseball team (which he happened to own) to Hana for spring training, and, more important, he brought out the sportswriters as well. The writers loved Hana and wrote glowing reports about the town; one even gave the town a nickname that stuck: "Heavenly Hana."

In 1962, the state paved Hana Highway. By the 1970s, tourists not only had "discovered" Maui, but also were willing to make the long trek out to Hana.

The biggest change to the local lifestyle came in December 1977, when television finally arrived—after a local cable operator spent 6 months laying cable

FROM TOP: Travaasa Hana (formerly the Hotel Hana-Maui); The base of Fagan's Cross, in memory of Paul Fagan, the founder of Hotel Hana-Maui.

over cinder cones, mountain streams, and cavernous gulches from one side of the island to the other. Some 125 homes tuned in to the tube—and the rural Hawaiian community was never the same. Today, Hana is inhabited by 2,500 people, many part Hawaiian.

Seeing the Sights

Most visitors zip through Hana, perhaps taking a quick look out their car windows at a few sights before buzzing on down the road. They might think they've seen Hana, but they definitely haven't experienced Hana. Allow at least 2 or 3 days to really let this land of legends show you its beauty and serenity.

Another recommendation: See Hana's attractions, especially the pools, ponds, waterfalls, and hikes, early in the day. You'll have them all to yourself. The day-trippers arrive in Hana around 11am and stay until about 4pm; that's when the area is overrun with hundreds of people in a hurry, who want to see everything in just a few hours.

As you enter Hana, the road splits about ½ mile past mile marker 33, at the police station. Both roads will take you to Hana, but the lower road, Uakea Road, is more scenic. Just before you get to Hana Bay, you'll see the old wood-frame **Hana District Police Station and Courthouse.** Next door is the **Hana Cultural Center & Museum ★**, 4974 Uakea Rd. (© **808/248-8622;** www.hana culturalcenter.org), usually open Monday through Friday from 10am to 4pm. This small building has an excellent collection of Hawaiian quilts, artifacts, books, and photos. Also on the grounds are Kauhala O Hana, composed of four *hale* (houses) for living, meeting, cooking, and canoe building or canoe storage.

Cater-cornered from the cultural center is the entrance to **Hana Bay ★**. You can drive right down to the pier and park. There are restrooms, showers, picnic tables, barbecue areas, and even a snack bar here. The 386-foot, red-faced cinder cone beside the bay is **Kauiki Hill,** the scene of numerous fierce battles in ancient Hawaii and the birthplace of Queen Kaahumanu in 1768. A short 5-minute walk will take you to the spot. Look for the trail along the hill on the wharf side, and follow the path through the ironwood trees; the lighthouse on the point will come into view, and you'll see pocket beaches of red cinder below. Grab onto the ironwood trees for support, as the trail has eroded in some areas. This is a perfect place for a secluded picnic, or you can continue on the path out to the lighthouse. To get to the lighthouse, which sits on a small island, watch the water for about 10 minutes to get a sense of how often and from which direction the waves are coming. Between wave sets, either swim or wade in the shallow, sandy bottom channel or hop across the rocks to the island.

To get to the center of town, leave Hana Bay, cross Uakea Road, and drive up Keawa Place; turn left on Hana Highway, and on the corner will be the hotel **Travaasa Hana** (formerly the Hotel Hana Maui), the now-luxurious hotel established by Paul Fagan in 1946. On the green hills above Travaasa Hana stands a 30-foot-high white cross made of lava rock. Citizens erected the cross in memory of Paul Fagan, who founded the Hana Ranch as well as the hotel and helped keep the town alive. The hike up to **Fagan's Cross** provides a gorgeous view of the Hana coast, especially at sunset, when Fagan himself liked to climb this hill (see p. 182 for details).

Back on the Hana Highway, just past Hauoli Road, is the majestic **Wananalua Congregational Church.** It's listed on the National Register of Historic Places not only because of its age (it was built in 1838–42 using coral stones), but also because of its location, atop an old Hawaiian *heiau.*

Just past the church, on the right side of Hana Highway, is the turnoff to the **Hana Ranch Center,** the commercial center for Hana, with a post office, bank, general store, the Hana Ranch Stables, and a restaurant and snack bar (see "Hana Ranch Restaurant," p. 226). But the real shopping experience is across the Hana Highway at the **Hasegawa General Store ★** (p. 242), a Maui institution, which carries oodles of merchandise from soda and fine French wines to fishing line and name-brand clothing, plus everything you need for a picnic or a gourmet meal. This is also the place to find out what's going on in Hana: The bulletin board at the entrance has fliers and handwritten notes advertising everything from fundraising activities to classes to community-wide events. Don't miss this unique store.

Outdoor Activities

Hana is one of the best areas on Maui for ocean activities; it also boasts a wealth of nature hikes, remote places to explore on horseback, waterfalls to discover, and even lava tubes to investigate.

For more information on the lava tubes, see **"Hana Lava Tube"** on p. 189; for details on horseback riding, see **"Maui Horseback Tours at Maui Stables"** on p. 188. If you're a tennis player, you can take advantage of the free public courts located next to the Travaasa Hana, available on a first-come, first-served basis.

BEACHES & OCEAN ACTIVITIES

Hana's beaches come in numerous varieties—white, black, gray, or red sand; perfectly shaped coves, crescents, or long stretches—and they're excellent for just about every kind of ocean activity you can think of. My favorites are these:

HANA BAY   The waters in Hana Bay are calm most of the time and great for swimming. There's excellent snorkeling and diving by the lighthouse. Strong

Hana Bay.

currents can run through here, so don't venture farther than the lighthouse. See "Seeing the Sights," above, for more details on the facilities and hikes here.

RED SAND BEACH The Hawaiian name for this beach is Kaihalulu (Roaring Sea). It's truly a sight to see. The beach is on the ocean side of Kauiki Hill, just south of Hana Bay, in a wild, natural setting on a pocket cove, where the volcanic cinder cone lost its seaward wall to erosion and spilled red cinders everywhere to create the red sands. Before you put on your bathing suit, there are three things to know about this beach: You have to trespass to get here (which is against the law); due to recent heavy rains, there have been several serious injuries on the muddy, slippery terrain (enter at your own risk; it can be extremely dangerous); and nudity (also illegal in Hawaii— arrests have been made) is common here.

If you are determined to go, ask for permission at the Travaasa Hana. And ask about conditions on the trail (which drops several stories down to the ocean rocks). To reach the beach, put on solid walking shoes (no flip-flops) and walk south on Uakea Road, past Haoli Street and the Travaasa Hana, to the parking lot for the hotel's Sea Ranch Cottages. Turn left and cross the open field next to the Hana Community Center. Look for the dirt trail and follow it to the huge ironwood tree, where you turn right (do not go ahead to the old Japanese cemetery). Use the ironwood trees to maintain your balance as you follow the ever-eroding cinder footpath a short distance along the shoreline, down the narrow cliff trail (do not attempt this if it's wet). The trail suddenly turns the corner, and into view comes the burnt-red beach, set off by the turquoise waters, black lava, and vivid green ironwood trees.

The lava outcropping protects the bay and makes it safe for swimming. Snorkeling is excellent, and there's a natural whirlpool area on the Hana Bay side of the cove. Stay away from the surge area where the ocean enters the cove.

KOKI BEACH ★ One of the best surfing and boogie-boarding beaches on the Hana coast lies just a couple of miles from the Hasegawa General Store in the Oheo Gulch direction. There is a very strong rip current here, so unless it is dead calm and you are a strong swimmer, do not attempt to swim here. However, it's a great place to sit on the white sand and watch the surfers. The only facility is a big parking area. To get here, drive toward Oheo Gulch from Hana, where Hwy. 36 changes to Hwy. 31. About 1½ miles outside of Hana, turn left at Haneoo Road.

HAMOA BEACH ★★ For one of Hana's best beaches—great for swimming, boogie boarding, and sunbathing—continue another ½ mile down the Haneoo Road loop to Hamoa Beach. There is easy access from the road down to the sandy beach, and facilities include a small restroom and an outdoor shower. The large pavilion and beach accessories are for Travaasa Hana guests.

WAIOKA POND Locally, this swimming hole in a series of waterfalls and pools is called Venus Pool. Unfortunately, it has become overrun with impolite tourists who park on the narrow highway, tear down the fence, and aren't very considerate about cleaning up their trash. The land owner, Hana Ranch, has put up NO TRESPASSING signs and is enforcing trespassing laws. (Getting arrested is not a great way to spend your vacation.) I recommend you skip this pond and keep driving to Haleakala National Park down the road. The park has adequate parking as well as restrooms. If you hike just 10 to 15 minutes upstream from the national park's parking lot, you will find much better pools and most likely have them to yourself.

Red Sand Beach.

HIKING

Hana is woven with hiking trails along the shoreline, through the rainforest, and up in the mountains. See p. 182 for a discussion of hiking in Waianapanapa and up to Fagan's Cross.

Another excellent hike that takes you back in time is through Kahanu Garden and to **Piilanihale Heiau ★★**, one of the largest ancient Hawaiian temples in the state. To get here, look for mile marker 31 on Hana Highway, make a left onto Ulaino Road, and drive a little over a mile down the paved road (which turns into a dirt road but is still drivable) to the first streambed (about 1½ miles). If the stream is running with water, do not cross it, as you most likely will get stuck; turn around and go back. If you can forge the stream, cross it and park on the right side of the road by the huge breadfruit trees. The trees are part of the **Kahanu Garden ★★** (✆ **808/248-8912**), owned and operated by the **National Tropical Botanical Garden** (www.ntbg.org). Admission is $10 for adults and free for children 12 and under. The garden is open Monday through Friday from 10am to 2pm. Allow an hour and a half for the self-guided tour. Be sure to wear comfortable walking shoes and long pants, and bring mosquito repellent, a hat for shade, and water. The guided tours are Saturday at 10am and cost $25 per person (free for children 12 and under). Reserve in advance at ✆ **808/248-8912** or www.ntbg.org/gardens/kahanu-tours.php.

Kahanu Garden.

The 122 acres here encompass plant collections from the Pacific Islands, concentrating on plants of value to the people of Polynesia, Micronesia, and Melanesia. Kahanu Garden contains the largest known collection of breadfruit cultivars from more than 17 Pacific Island groups and Indonesia, the Philippines, and the Seychelles.

The real draw here is the Piilanihale Heiau (see "A Look at the Past," earlier in this chapter). Believed to be the largest in the state, it measures 340×415 feet, and it was built in a unique terrace design not seen anywhere else in Hawaii. The walls are some 50 feet tall and 8 to 10 feet thick. Historians believe that Piilani's two sons and his grandson built the mammoth temple, which was dedicated to war, sometime in the 1500s.

Just Beyond Hana

TROPICAL HALEAKALA: OHEO GULCH AT KIPAHULU ★★

If you're thinking about heading out to the so-called Seven Sacred Pools, out past Hana at the Kipahulu end of Haleakala National Park, let's clear this up right now: There are more than seven pools—about 24, actually—and *all* water in Hawaii is considered sacred. It's all a PR campaign that has spun out of control into contemporary myth. Folks here call the attraction by its rightful name, **Oheo Gulch ★★★**, and visitors sometimes refer to it as Kipahulu, which is actually the name of the area where Oheo Gulch is located. No matter what you call it, it's a beautiful sight. The dazzling series of pools and cataracts cascading into the sea is so popular that it has its own roadside parking lot.

Even though Oheo is part of Haleakala National Park, you cannot drive here from the summit. Even hiking from Haleakala to Oheo is tricky: The access trail out of Haleakala is down Kaupo Gap, which ends at the ocean, a good 6 miles down the coast from Oheo. To drive to Oheo, head for Hana, some 60 miles from Kahului on the Hana Highway (Hwy. 36). Oheo is about a 30- to 50-minute drive beyond

Oheo Gulch is a dazzling series of pools and cataracts cascading into the sea.

Charles Lindbergh's gravesite.

Hana, along Hwy. 31. The Hwy. 31 bridge passes over pools near the ocean; the other pools, plus magnificent 400-foot Waimoku Falls, are reachable via an often-muddy, but rewarding, hour-long uphill hike (see "Hiking & Camping at Kipahulu (Near Hana)," p. 179). Expect showers on the Kipahulu coast. The admission fee is $5 per person or $10 per car.

The **Kipahulu Ranger Station** (✆ **808/248-7375**) is staffed from 8:30am to 5pm daily. Restrooms are available, but there's no drinking water. Kipahulu rangers offer safety information, exhibits, books, and a variety of walks and hikes year-round. Check with the park rangers before hiking up to or swimming in the pools, and always keep one eye on the water in the streams; the sky can be sunny near the coast, but floodwaters from Kipahulu Valley can cause the pools to rise 4 feet in less than 10 minutes.

There are a number of hikes in the park, and tent camping is allowed. See "Hiking & Camping at Kipahulu (Near Hana)," on p. 179, for details.

LINDBERGH'S GRAVE

A mile past Oheo Gulch on the ocean side of the road is **Lindbergh's Grave.** First to fly across the Atlantic Ocean, Charles A. Lindbergh (1902–74) found peace in the Pacific; he settled in Hana, where he died of cancer in 1974. The famous aviator is buried under river stones in a seaside graveyard behind the 1857 **Palapala Hoomau Congregational Church,** where his tombstone is engraved with his favorite words from the 139th Psalm: "If I take the wings of the morning and dwell in the uttermost parts of the sea."

EVEN FARTHER AROUND THE BEND

Be careful, as the road here is unpaved all the way to the fishing village of **Kaupo.** It narrows to one lane at times, wandering in and out of valleys with sharp rock walls and blind bends hugging the ocean cliffs. You may encounter wild pigs and stray cows. About 6 miles and 60 minutes from Oheo Gulch, you'll see the restored **Huialoha Congregationalist "Circuit" Church,** originally constructed in 1859. Across from the church and down the road a bit is the **Kaupo Store** (✆ **808/248-8054**), which marks the center of the ranching community of Kaupo. Store hours are officially Monday through Saturday from 10am to 5pm, but in this arid cattle country, posted hours often prove meaningless. The Kaupo Store is the last of the Soon family stores, which at one time stretched from Kaupo to Keanae.

From the Kaupo Store, the landscape turns into barren, dry desert. In the lee of Haleakala, this area gets little rain. There are no phones or services until you reach **Ulupalakua Ranch** (p. 131), where there is a winery and a general store. The gas station is no longer there; however, just 5.5 miles past Ulupalakua is Ching's Store, which sells gas.

Between mile markers 29 and 30, look for the ancient lava flow that created an arch as it rolled down Haleakala. Keep an eye peeled for cattle—this is open-range country. Eventually the road will wind uphill, and suddenly the forest and greenery of Ulupalakua will come into sight. From here, you're about 45 minutes from Kahului.

SIGHTS & ATTRACTIONS BY THEME INDEX

HISTORIC SITES

Hasegawa General Store (p. 242)
Hauola Stone (p. 110)
Lahaina Courthouse (p. 110)
Lahaina Fort (p. 112)
Luakini Street (p. 115)
Kauiki Hill (p. 143)
Old Prison (p. 114)
Pioneer Inn (p. 111)
Taro Patch (p. 110)

MONUMENTS

Fagan's Cross (p. 182)
La Pérouse Monument (p. 121)
Totem Pole (p. 119)

MUSEUMS

Alexander & Baldwin Sugar Museum
(p. 99)
Baldwin Home Museum (p. 232)
Bailey House Museum (p. 100)
Hale Pai (p. 106)
Hana Cultural Center & Museum
(p. 143)
Hawaii Nature Center (p. 103)
Lahaina Heritage Museum (p. 111)
Master's Reading Room (p. 109)
Richards House (p. 110)
Whalers Village Museum (p. 116)

NATIONAL PARKS

Haleakala National Park (p. 122)

NATURAL ATTRACTIONS

Banyan Tree (p. 109)
Iao Needle (p. 103)
Iao Stream (p. 103)
Iao Valley (p. 101)
Kaaiea Bridge (p. 136)
Keanae Lookout (p. 137)
Keanae Peninsula (p. 137)
Oheo Gulch (p. 148)
Puohokamoa Falls (p. 136)
Twin Falls (p. 134)
Waikani Falls (p. 138)

NATURAL RESERVES

Kanaha Wildlife Sanctuary (p. 98)
Kealia Pond National Wildlife Pre-
serve (p. 120)
Koolau Forest Reserve (p. 135)

PARKS/GARDENS

Iao Valley Botanic Garden (p. 103)
Kahanu Garden (p. 141)
Kaumahina State Wayside Park
(p. 138)
Keanae Arboretum (p. 182)
Kepaniwai Heritage Garden (p. 103)
Kula Botanical Garden (p. 130)
Maluuluolele Park (p. 113)
National Tropical Botanical Garden
(p. 147)
Puaa Kaa State Wayside Park (p. 139)
Waianapanapa State Park (p. 181)
Wailua Valley State Wayside Park
(p. 138)

RELIGIOUS SITES

Our Lady of Fatima Shrine (p. 138)

RUINS

Brick Palace (p. 110)
Canal (p. 112)
David Malo's Home (p. 114)
Hale Aloha (p. 115)
Hale Piula (p. 114)
Halekii Heiau (p. 86)
Government Market (p. 113)
Pihanakalani Heiau (p. 86)
Piilanihale Heiau (p. 141)

TEMPLES

Lahaina Jodo Mission (p. 106)
Wo Hing Temple (p. 107)

WINERIES

Tedeschi Vineyards and Winery
(p. 131)

4

EXPLORING MAUI

Sights & Attractions by Theme Index

5

FUN ON &
OFF THE
BEACH

T his is why you've come to Maui—the sun, the sand, and the surf. In this chapter, I'll tell you about the best beaches, from where to soak up the rays to where to plunge beneath the waves. I've covered a range of ocean activities on Maui, as well as my favorite places and outfitters for these marine adventures. Also in this chapter are things to do on dry land, including the best spots for hiking and camping and the greatest golf courses.

BEACHES

Maui has more than 80 accessible beaches of every conceivable description, from rocky black-sand beaches to powdery golden ones; there's even a rare red-sand beach. What follows is a personal selection of the finest of Maui's beaches, carefully chosen to suit a variety of needs and interests.

Hawaii's beaches belong to the people. All beaches, even those in front of exclusive resorts, are public property, and you are welcome to visit. Hawaii state law requires all resorts and hotels to offer public right-of-way access to the beach, along with public parking. So just because a beach fronts a hotel doesn't mean that you can't enjoy the water. Generally, hotels welcome nonguests to their facilities. They frown on nonguests using the beach chairs reserved for guests, but if a nonguest has money and wants to rent gear, buy a drink, or eat a sandwich, well, money is money, and they will gladly accept it from anyone.

For snorkel gear, boogie boards, and other ocean toys, head to one of **Snorkel Bob's** (www.snorkelbob.com) five locations: 1217 Front St., Lahaina (✆ **808/ 661-4421**); Napili Village, 5425 C Lower Honoapiilani Hwy., Lahaina (✆ **808/669-9603**); Honokowai Market Place, 3350 Lower Honoapiilani Hwy., Lahaina (✆ **808/667-9999**); Azeka Place II, 1279 S. Kihei Rd., #310, Kihei (✆ **808/875-6188**); and Kamaole Beach Center, 2411 S. Kihei Rd., Kihei (✆ **808/879-7449**). All locations are open daily from 8am to 5pm. If you're island hopping, you can rent from a Snorkel Bob's location on one island and return equipment to a location on another.

West Maui

D.T. FLEMING BEACH PARK ★★

This quiet, out-of-the-way beach cove, named after the man who started the commercial growing of pineapples on the Valley Isle, is a great place to take the family. The crescent-shaped beach, located north of the Ritz-Carlton hotel, starts at the 16th hole of the Kapalua golf course (Makaluapuna Point) and rolls around to the sea cliffs at the other side. Ironwood trees provide shade on the land side. Offshore, a shallow sandbar extends to the edge of the surf. The waters are generally good for swimming and snorkeling; sometimes, off on the right side near the sea cliffs, the waves build enough for body boarders and surfers to get a few good rides in. This park has lots of facilities: restrooms, showers, picnic tables, barbecue grills, and a paved parking lot.

PREVIOUS PAGE: **The beach at Waianapanapa State Park.**

KAPALUA BEACH ★★★

The beach cove that fronts the Coconut Grove Villas and the former Kapalua Bay hotel (now in the process of being replaced by condos) is the stuff of dreams: a golden crescent bordered by two palm-studded points. The sandy bottom slopes gently to deep water at the bay mouth; the water's so clear that you can see it turn to green and then deep blue. Protected from strong winds and currents by the lava-rock promontories, Kapalua's calm waters are ideal for swimmers of all ages and abilities, and the bay is big enough to paddle a kayak around in without getting into the more challenging channel that separates Maui from Molokai. Waves come in just right for riding, and fish hang out by the rocks, making it great for snorkeling.

Kapalua Beach.

The sandy beach isn't so wide that you'll burn your feet getting in or out of the water, and the inland side is edged by a shady path and cool lawns. Facilities include outdoor showers, restrooms, lifeguards, a rental shack, and plenty of shade. Parking is limited to about 30 spaces in a small lot off Lower Honoapiilani Road, by Napili Kai Beach Resort, so arrive early. Next door is a nice but pricey oceanfront restaurant, Merriman's.

KAANAPALI BEACH ★★

Four-mile-long Kaanapali is one of Maui's best beaches, with grainy gold sand as far as the eye can see. The beach parallels the sea channel along most of its length, and a paved beach walk links hotels and condos, open-air restaurants, and Whalers Village shopping center. Because Kaanapali is so long, and because most hotels have adjacent swimming pools, the beach is crowded only in pockets—there's plenty of room to find seclusion. Summertime swimming is excellent. There's fabulous snorkeling around **Black Rock,** in front of the Sheraton. The water is clear, calm, and populated with clouds of tropical fish. You might even spot a turtle or two.

Facilities include outdoor showers; you can use the restrooms at the

Kaanapali Beach.

HIKES

Fagan's Cross **21**
Halemauu Trail **16**
Hana-Waianapanapa
  Coast Trail **22**
Hosmer Grove
  Nature Trail **14**
Kaupo Gap **19**
Keanae Arboretum **24**
Polipoli Loop **10**
Skyline Trail **12**
Sliding Sands Trail **13**
Waihee Ridge **3**

CABINS & CAMPGROUNDS

Holua Cabin &
  Campground **15**
Hosmer Grove
  Campground **14**
Kanaha Beach Park **5**
Kapalaoa Cabin **17**
Oheo Campground **20**
Paliku Cabin &
  Campground **18**
Polipoli Spring State
  Recreation Area
  Campground **11**
Polipoli State Park Cabin
  & Campground **11**
Waianapanapa State Park
  Cabins & Campground **23**

GOLF COURSES

Elleair Maui Golf Club **6**
Kaanapali Golf Resort **2**
Kapalua Resort **1**
Makena Golf Courses **8**
Pukalani Country Club **9**
Waiehu Municipal
  Golf Course **4**
Wailea Golf Club **7**

Beaches & Outdoor Activities

155

hotel pools. Various beach-activity vendors line up in front of the hotels, offering nearly every type of water activity and equipment. Parking is a problem, though. There are two public entrances: At the south end, turn off Honoapiilani Highway into the Kaanapali Resort and pay for parking there, or continue on Honoapiilani Highway, turn off at the last Kaanapali exit at the stoplight near the Maui Kaanapali Villas, and park next to the beach signs indicating public access (this is a little tricky to find and limited to only a few cars, so to save time, you might want to just head to the Sheraton or Whalers Village and plunk down your money).

WAHIKULI COUNTY WAYSIDE PARK

This small stretch of beach, adjacent to Honoapiilani Highway between Lahaina and Kaanapali, is one of Lahaina's most popular beach parks. It's packed on weekends, but during the week it's a great place for swimming, snorkeling, sunbathing, and picnics. Facilities include paved parking, restrooms, showers, and small covered pavilions with picnic tables and barbecue grills.

LAUNIUPOKO STATE WAYSIDE PARK

Families with children will love this small park off Honoapiilani Highway, just south of Lahaina. A large wading pool for kids fronts the shady park, with giant boulders protecting the wading area from the surf outside. Just to the left is a small sandy beach with good swimming when conditions are right. Offshore, the waves are occasionally big enough for surfing. The view from the park is one of the best: You can see the islands of Kahoolawe, Lanai, and Molokai in the distance. Facilities include a paved parking lot, restrooms, showers, picnic tables, and barbecue grills. It's crowded on weekends.

South Maui

KAMAOLE III BEACH PARK ★

Three beach parks—Kamaole I, II, and III—stand like golden jewels in the front yard of the funky seaside town of Kihei, which is exploding with suburban sprawl. The beaches are the best thing about Kihei; these three are popular with local residents and visitors alike because they're easily accessible. On weekends, they're jampacked with fishermen, picnickers, swimmers, and snorkelers.

The most popular is Kamaole III, or "Kam-3," as locals say. The biggest of the three beaches, with wide pockets of gold sand, it's the only one with a children's playground and a grassy lawn that meets the sand. Swimming is safe here, but scattered lava rocks are toe stubbers at the waterline, and parents should make sure kids don't venture too far out, as the bottom slopes off

Kamaole III Beach Park.

quickly. Both the north and the south shores are rocky fingers with a surge big enough to attract fish and snorkelers; the winter waves appeal to bodysurfers. Kam-3 is also a wonderful place to watch the sunset. Facilities include restrooms, showers, picnic tables, barbecue grills, and lifeguards. There's plenty of parking on South Kihei Road, across from the Maui Parkshore condos.

ULUA BEACH ★

One of the most popular beaches in Wailea, Ulua is a long, wide, crescent-shaped gold-sand beach between two rocky points. When the ocean's calm, Ulua offers Wailea's best snorkeling; when it's rough, the waves are excellent for bodysurfing. The ocean bottom is shallow and gently slopes down to deeper waters, making swimming generally safe. The beach is usually occupied by guests of nearby resorts; in high season (Christmas–Mar and June–Aug), it's carpeted with beach towels and packed with sunbathers like sardines in cocoa butter.

Ulua Beach.

Facilities include showers and restrooms. Beach equipment is available for rent at the nearby Wailea Ocean Activity Center. To find Ulua, look for the blue SHORELINE ACCESS sign on South Kihei Road, near the Wailea Beach Marriott Resort and Spa. There's a tiny parking lot nearby.

WAILEA BEACH ★★

Wailea is the best gold-sand crescent on Maui's sunbaked southwestern coast. One of five beaches within Wailea Resort, Wailea is big, wide, and protected on both sides by black-lava points. It's the front yard of the Four Seasons Resort and the Grand Wailea Resort, Maui's most elegant and outrageous beach hotels, respectively. From the beach, the view out to sea is magnificent, framed by neighboring Kahoolawe and Lanai and the tiny crescent of Molokini, probably the most popular diving and snorkeling spot in these parts. The clear waters tumble to shore in waves just the right size for gentle riding, with or without a board. From shore, you can see Pacific humpback whales in season (Dec–Apr) and unreal sunsets nightly. Facilities include restrooms, outdoor showers, and limited free parking at the blue SHORELINE ACCESS sign, on Wailea Alanui Drive, the main drag of this resort.

MALUAKA BEACH (MAKENA BEACH) ★★

On the southern end of Maui's resort coast, development falls off dramatically, leaving a wild, dry countryside of green kiawe trees. The Makena Beach and Golf Resort sits in isolated splendor, sharing Makena Resort's 1,800 acres with only a

Maluaka Beach.

couple of first-rate golf courses and a necklace of perfect beaches. The strand nearest the hotel is Maluaka Beach, often called Makena, notable for its beauty and its views of Molokini Crater, the offshore islet, and Kahoolawe, the so-called target island (it was used as a bombing target from 1945 until the early 1990s). This is a short, wide, palm-fringed crescent of golden, grainy sand set between two black-lava points and bounded by big sand dunes topped by a grassy knoll. The swimming in this mostly calm bay is considered the best on Makena Bay, which is bordered on the south by Puu Olai cinder cone and historic Keawalai Congregational Church. The waters around Makena Landing, at the north end of the bay, are particularly good for snorkeling. Facilities include restrooms, showers, a landscaped park, lifeguards, and roadside parking. Along Makena Alanui, look for the SHORELINE ACCESS sign near the hotel, turn right, and head down to the shore.

ONELOA BEACH (BIG BEACH) ★★

Oneloa, meaning "Long Sand" in Hawaiian, is one of the most popular beaches on Maui. Locals call it Big Beach—it's 3,300 feet long and more than 100 feet wide. Mauians come here to swim, fish, sunbathe, surf, and enjoy the view of Kahoolawe and Lanai. Snorkeling is good around the north end, at the foot of Puu Olai, a 360-foot cinder cone. During storms, however, big waves lash the shore and a strong rip current sweeps the sharp drop-off, posing a danger for inexperienced open-ocean swimmers. There are no facilities except for portable toilets, but there's plenty of parking. To get here, drive past the Maui Prince Hotel to the second dirt road, which leads through a kiawe thicket to the beach.

On the other side of Puu Olai is **Little Beach,** a small pocket beach where assorted nudists work on their all-over tans, to the chagrin of uptight authorities. You can get a nasty sunburn and a lewd-conduct ticket too.

East Maui

BALDWIN PARK

Located off the Hana Highway between Sprecklesville and Paia, this beach park draws lots of Maui residents, especially body-board enthusiasts. It's easy to see why this place is so popular: The surf breaks along the entire length of the white-sand beach, creating perfect conditions for body boarding. On occasion, the waves get big enough for surfing. A couple of swimming areas are safe enough for children: one in the lee of the beach rocks near the large pavilion, and another at the opposite end of the beach, where beach rocks protect a small swimming area. There's a large pavilion with picnic tables and kitchen facilities, barbecue grills, additional picnic tables on the grassy area, restrooms, showers, a semipaved parking area, a baseball diamond, and a soccer field. The park is well used on weekends; weekdays are much quieter.

HOOKIPA BEACH PARK ★

Two miles past Paia, on the Hana Highway, is one of the most famous windsurfing sites in the world. Due to its constant winds and endless waves, Hookipa attracts top windsurfers and wave jumpers from around the globe. Surfers and fishermen also enjoy this small gold-sand beach at the foot of a grassy cliff, which provides a natural amphitheater for spectators. Except when competitions are being held, weekdays after noon are the best time to watch the daredevils fly over the waves (the board surfers have access to the waves before noon). When the water is flat, snorkelers and divers explore the reef. Facilities include restrooms, showers, pavilions, picnic tables, barbecue grills, and a parking lot.

Hookipa Beach.

WAIANAPANAPA STATE PARK ★

Four miles before Hana, off the Hana Highway, is this beach park, which takes its name from the legend of the Waianapanapa Cave. Chief Kaakea, a jealous and cruel man, suspected his wife, Popoalaea, of having an affair. Popoalaea left her husband and hid herself in a chamber of the Waianapanapa Cave. A few days later, when Kaakea was passing by the cave, the shadow of a servant gave away Popoalaea's hiding place, and Kaakea killed her. During certain times of the year, the water in the tide pool turns red, commemorating Popoalaea's

Safety Tip

Be sure to see the "Health & Safety" section in chapter 12 before setting out on your Maui adventures. You'll find useful information on hiking, camping, and ocean safety, plus how to avoid seasickness and sunburn, and what to do should you get stung by a jellyfish.

5

FUN ON & OFF THE BEACH

Beaches

Waianapanapa State Park.

Hamoa Beach.

death. (Scientists claim, less imaginatively, that the water turns red due to the presence of small red shrimp.)

Waianapanapa State Park's 120 acres contain 12 cabins (p. 300), a caretaker's residence, a beach park, picnic tables, barbecue grills, restrooms, showers, a parking lot, a shoreline hiking trail, and a black-sand beach (it's actually small black pebbles). This is a wonderful area for shoreline hikes (mosquitoes are plentiful, so bring insect repellent) and picnicking. Swimming is generally unsafe due to strong waves and rip currents. Waianapanapa is crowded on weekends; weekdays are generally a better bet.

HAMOA BEACH ★★

This half-moon-shaped, gray-sand beach (a mix of coral and lava) in a truly tropical setting is a favorite among sunbathers seeking rest and refuge. The Travaasa Hana Resort maintains the beach and acts as though it's private, which it isn't—so just march down the lava-rock steps and grab a spot on the sand. James Michener called it "a beach so perfectly formed that I wonder at its comparative obscurity." The 100-foot-wide beach is three football fields long and sits below 30-foot black-lava sea cliffs. Surf on this unprotected beach breaks offshore and rolls in, making it a popular surfing and bodysurfing area. Hamoa is often swept by powerful rip currents, so be careful. The calm left side is best for snorkeling in summer. The hotel has numerous facilities for guests; there are outdoor showers and restrooms for nonguests. Parking is limited. Look for the Hamoa Beach turnoff from Hana Highway.

WATERSPORTS

Snorkel Bob's (www.snorkelbob.com) rents snorkel gear, boogie boards, and other ocean toys; see p. 153 for five locations. If you're island hopping, you can rent from a Snorkel Bob's location on one island and return the equipment to a location on another.

Boss Frog's Dive and Surf Shops (www.bossfrog.com) has nine locations for rental and other gear: 5059 Napilihau St., Lahaina (© **808/669-4949**); Kahana Manor Shopping Center, 4310 Lower Honoapiilani Rd., Lahaina

(© **808/669-6700**); 3636 Lower Honoapiilani Rd., Lahaina (© **808/665-1200**); Lahaina Cannery Mall, 1221 Honoapiilani Hwy., Lahaina (© **808/661-5995**); 150 Lahainaluna Rd., Lahaina (© **808/661-3333**); Longs Drugs Shopping Center, 1215 S. Kihei Rd., Kihei (© **808/891-0077**); Dolphin Plaza, 2395 S. Kihei Rd., Kihei (© **808/875-4477**); 1770 S. Kihei Rd., Kihei (© **808/874-5225**); and 3636 Lower Honoapiilani Rd., in Kaanapali (© **808/665-1200**).

Boating & Sailing

To really appreciate Maui, you need to get off the land and get on the sea. Trade winds off the Lahaina coast and the strong wind that rips through Maui's isthmus make sailing around the island exciting. Many different boats, from a three-masted schooner to spacious trimarans, offer day cruises from Maui.

Later in this chapter, you can find information on snorkel cruises to Molokini under "Snorkeling," fishing charters under "Sport Fishing," and trips that combine snorkeling with whale-watching under "Whale-Watching Cruises."

Scotch Mist Sailing Charters　Scotch Mist's 50-foot *Santa Cruz* sailboat offers 4-hour **snorkel cruises**. Rates include a fruit platter and beverages, gear, and instruction. Other options include an afternoon sail or a whale-watching trip, and an evening champagne sunset cruise.

Note: Scotch Mist doesn't allow children 4 and under unless you charter the whole boat.

Lahaina Harbor, slip 2. © **808/661-0386.** www.scotchmistsailingcharters.com. Afternoon sail or whale-watching cruise $50 ages 13 and up, $25 children 5–12; 4-hr. snorkel cruise $99 ages 13 and up, $50 children 5–12; champagne sunset cruise $60 ages 13 and up, $30 children 5–12.

DAY CRUISES TO MOLOKAI

You can travel across the seas by ferry from Maui's Lahaina Harbor to Molokai's Kaunakakai Wharf on the ***Molokai Princess*** (© **877/500-6284** or

Molokai Princess.

808/667-6165; www.mauiprincess.com). The 100-foot yacht, certified for 149 passengers, is fitted with the latest generation of gyroscopic stabilizers, making the ride smoother. The ferry makes the 90-minute journey from Lahaina to Kaunakakai daily; the round-trip cost is $127 for adults and $64 for children 3 to 12. Or you can choose to tour the island on one of two package options: **Cruise-Drive,** which includes round-trip passage and a rental car for $245 for the driver, $115 per additional adult passenger, and $55 for children; or the **Alii Tour,** which is a guided tour in an air-conditioned van plus lunch for $230 per adult and $160 per child.

DAY CRUISES TO LANAI

Expeditions Maui-Lanai Passenger Ferry 🐾   The cheapest way to get to Lanai is this ferry, which runs five times a day, 365 days a year. It leaves Lahaina at 6:45am, 9:15am, 12:45pm, 3:15pm, and 5:45pm; the return ferry from Lanai's Manele Bay leaves at 8am, 10:30am, 2pm, 4:30pm, and 6:45pm. The 9-mile channel crossing takes between 45 minutes and an hour, depending on sea conditions. Reservations are strongly recommended. Baggage is limited to two checked bags and one carry-on. Call **Lanai City Service** (⌀ **800/800-4000** or 808/565-7227) or **Dollar Rent A Car** (⌀ **800/800-4000**) to arrange a car rental or bus ride when you arrive.

Ferries depart from Lahaina Harbor; office: 658 Front St., Ste. 127, Lahaina. ⌀ **800/695-2624** or 808/661-3756. www.go-lanai.com. Round-trip fares from Maui to Lanai $60 adults, $40 children 2–11.

Trilogy ★★★ ☺   Trilogy offers my favorite **snorkel-sail trips.** Hop aboard one of the fleet's custom-built catamarans, from 54 to 64 feet long, for a 9-mile sail from Lahaina Harbor to **Lanai's Hulopoe Beach,** a terrific marine preserve, for a fun-filled day of sailing, snorkeling, swimming, and **whale-watching** (in season, of course). This is the only cruise that offers a personalized ground

Trilogy snorkel-sail trips are expensive, but worth every penny.

tour of the island and the only one with rights to take you to Hulopoe Beach. The full-day trip costs $159 for adults, $142 for teenagers (ages 13–18), and $95 for children (ages 3–12). Ask about overnights to Lanai, too.

Trilogy also offers snorkel-sail trips to **Molokini,** one of Hawaii's best snorkel spots. This half-day trip leaves from Maalaea Harbor and costs $89 for adults, $83 for teenagers, and $55 for children 3 to 12, including breakfast and a barbecue lunch. Other options include a late-morning, half-day snorkel-sail off Kaanapali Beach for the same price, plus a host of other trips.

These are the most-expensive snorkel-sail cruises on Maui, but they're worth every penny. The crews are fun and knowledgeable, and the boats comfortable and well equipped. All trips include breakfast (homemade cinnamon buns) and a very good barbecue lunch (onboard on the half-day trip, on land on the Lanai trip). Note, however, that you will be required to wear a flotation device no matter how good your swimming skills are; if this bothers you, go with another outfitter.

© **888/225-MAUI** (6284) or 808/TRILOGY (874-5649). www.sailtrilogy.com. Prices and departure points vary depending on cruise.

Body Boarding (Boogie Boarding) & Bodysurfing

Bodysurfing—riding the waves without a board, becoming one with the rolling water—is a way of life in Hawaii. Some bodysurfers just rely on their hands to ride the waves; others use hand boards (flat, paddlelike gloves). For additional maneuverability, try a boogie board or body board (also known as belly boards or *paipo* boards). These 3-foot-long boards support the upper part of your body and are easy to carry and very maneuverable in the water. Both bodysurfing and body boarding require a pair of open-heeled swim fins to help propel you through the water.

Baldwin Beach, just outside of Paia, has great bodysurfing waves nearly year-round. In winter, Maui's best bodysurfing spot is **Mokuleia Beach,** known

Maui offers excellent waves for boogie boarding.

Kayaking is a great way to see Maui the way early Hawaiians did, from the sea.

locally as Slaughterhouse because of the cattle slaughterhouse that once stood here, not because of the waves—although they are definitely for expert bodysurfers only. To get to Mokuleia, take Honoapiilani Highway just past Kapalua Resort; various hiking trails will take you down to the pocket beach. Storms from the south bring fair body-surfing conditions and great boogie boarding to the lee side of Maui: **Oneloa Beach (Big Beach)** in Makena, **Ulua Beach** and **Kamaole III Beach Park** in Kihei, and **Kapalua Beach** are all good choices.

Ocean Kayaking

Gliding silently over the water, propelled by a paddle, seeing Maui from the sea the way the early Hawaiians did—that's what ocean kayaking is all about. One of Maui's best kayak routes is along the **Kihei Coast,** where there's easy access to calm water. Early mornings are always best, as the wind comes up around 11am, making seas choppy and paddling difficult.

For beginners, my favorite kayak-tour operator is **Makena Kayak & Tours ★** (✆ **808/879-8426**). Professional guide Dino Ventura leads a 2½-hour trip from Makena Landing for $55, and loves taking first timers over the secluded coral reefs and into remote coves. His wonderful tour will be a highlight of your vacation. The 4-hour tour (with lunch) costs $85. Prices include refreshments and snorkel and kayak equipment. Check the website for discounts.

South Pacific Kayaks, 95 Halekauai St., Kihei (✆ **800/776-2326** or 808/875-4848; www.southpacifickayaks.com), is Maui's oldest kayak-tour company. Its experts lead ocean-kayak trips that include lessons, a guided tour, and snorkeling. Tours run from 3 to 5 hours and range in price from $65 to $99.

Ocean Rafting

If you're semiadventurous and looking for a more intimate experience with the sea, try ocean rafting. The inflatable rafts hold 6 to 24 passengers. Tours usually include snorkeling and coastal cruising. One of the best (and most reasonable) outfitters is **Hawaii Ocean Rafting** (✆ **888/677-RAFT** [7238] or 808/667-7238; www. hawaiioceanrafting.com), which operates out of Lahaina Harbor. The best deal is the 5-hour morning tour, which is $79 for adults and $56 for children 5 to 12. It includes three snorkeling stops and time spent searching for dolphins, plus continental breakfast and midmorning snacks. Check the website for discounts.

Parasailing

Soar high above the crowds (at around 400 ft.) for a bird's-eye view of Maui. This ocean adventure sport, which is something of a cross between sky diving and water-skiing, involves sailing through the air, suspended under a large parachute attached by a towline to a speedboat. Keep in mind, though, that parasailing tours don't run during whale season, which is roughly December through May.

I recommend **UFO Parasailing** (✆ **800/FLY-4-UFO** [359-4836] or 808/661-7-UFO [7836]; www.ufoparasail.net), which picks you up at Kaanapali Beach. UFO offers parasail rides daily from 8am to 4pm. The cost is $65 for the standard flight of 7 minutes of airtime at 600 feet, $75 for a 10-minute ride at 800 feet. (Save $5 on each ride by booking on the website at least 2 days in advance.) You can go up alone or with a friend; no experience is necessary. Operating in Maui only from May 16 to December 14.

Scuba Diving

Some people come to Maui for the sole purpose of plunging into the tropical Pacific and exploring the underwater world. You can see the great variety of tropical marine life (more than 100 endemic species found nowhere else on the planet), explore sea caves, and swim with sea turtles and monk seals in the clear tropical waters off the island. I recommend going early in the morning. Trade winds often rough up the seas in the afternoon, so most dive operators schedule early-morning dives that end at noon, and then take the rest of the day off.

Unsure about scuba diving? Take an introductory dive: Most operators offer no-experience-necessary dives, ranging from $119 to $150. You can learn from this glimpse into the sea world whether diving is for you.

Everyone dives **Molokini,** a marine-life park and one of Hawaii's top dive spots. This crescent-shaped crater has three tiers of diving: a 35-foot plateau inside the crater basin (used by beginner divers and snorkelers), a wall sloping to 70 feet just beyond the inside plateau, and a sheer wall on the outside and backside of the crater that plunges 350 feet. This underwater park is very popular, thanks to calm, clear, protected waters and an abundance of marine life, from manta rays to clouds of yellow butterflyfish.

For personalized diving, **Ed Robinson's Diving Adventures** ★ (✆ **800/ 635-1273** or 808/879-3584; www.mauiscuba.com) is the only Maui company rated one of *Scuba Diver* magazine's top-five best dive operators for 7 years straight. Ed, a widely published underwater photographer, offers specialized charters for small groups. Two-tank dives are $130; check in at their new store in the Kukui Mall, 1819 S. Kihei Rd.; boats depart from Kehei Boat Ramp.

The best time for scuba diving is early in the morning, before trade winds rough up the seas.

If Ed is booked, call **Mike Severns Diving** (✆ **808/879-6596;** www.mikesevernsdiving.com) for small (maximum 12 people, divided into two groups of six), personal diving tours on a 38-foot Munson/Hammerhead boat with freshwater shower, a rare amenity that makes your post-dive experience much more pleasant. Mike and his wife, Pauline Fiene-Severns, are both biologists who make diving in Hawaii educational as well as fun. (They have a spectacular underwater photography

AN EXPERT SHARES HIS SECRETS:
maui's best dives

Ed Robinson, of **Ed Robinson's Diving Adventures** (see above), knows Maui's best dives. Here are some of his favorites:

Hawaiian Reef   This area off the Kihei-Wailea Coast is so named because it hosts a good cross section of Hawaiian topography and marine life. Diving to depths of 85 feet, you'll see everything from lava formations and coral reef to sand and rubble, plus a diverse range of both shallow- and deepwater creatures. It's clear why this area was so popular with ancient Hawaiian fishermen: Large helmet shells, a healthy garden of antler coral heads, and big schools of snapper are common.

Third Tank   Located off Makena Beach at 80 feet, this World War II tank is one of the most picturesque artificial reefs you're likely to see around Maui. It acts like a fish magnet: Because it's the only large solid object in the area, any fish or invertebrate looking for a safe home comes here. Surrounding the tank is a cloak of schooling snappers and goatfish just waiting for a photographer with a wide-angle lens. Despite its small size, Third Tank is loaded with more marine life per square inch than any site off Maui.

Molokini Crater   The backside of the crater is always done as a live boat-drift dive. The vertical wall plummets from more than 150 feet above sea level to around 250 feet below. Looking down to unseen depths gives you a feeling for the vastness of the open ocean. Pelagic fish and sharks are often sighted, and living coral perches on the wall, which is home to lobsters, crabs, and a number of photogenic black-coral trees at 50 feet.

There are actually two great dive sites around Molokini Crater. Named after common chub or rudderfish, **Enenue Side** gently slopes from the surface to about 60 feet and then drops rapidly to deeper waters. The shallower area is an easy dive, with lots of tame butterflyfish. It's also the home of Morgan Bentjaw, one of the friendliest moray eels. Enenue Side is often done as a live boat-drift dive to extend the range of the tour. Diving depths vary. Divers usually do a 50-foot dive, but on occasion advanced divers drop to the 130-foot level to visit the rare boarfish and the shark condos.

Almost every kind of fish found in Hawaii can be seen in the crystalline waters of **Reef's End.** It's an extension of the rim of the crater, which runs for about 600 feet underwater, barely breaking the surface. Reef's End is shallow enough for novice snorkelers and exciting enough for experienced divers. The end and outside of this shoal drop off in dramatic terraces to beyond diving range. In deeper waters, there are shark ledges at varying depths and dozens of eels, including moray, dragon, snowflake, and garden eels. The shallower inner side is home to Garbanzo, one of the largest and first eels to be tamed. The reef is covered with cauliflower coral; in bright sunlight, it's one of the most dramatic underwater scenes in Hawaii.

La Pérouse Pinnacle   In the middle of scenic La Pérouse Bay, site of Haleakala's most recent lava flow, is a pinnacle rising from the 60-foot bottom to about 10 feet below the surface. Getting to the dive site is half the fun: The scenery above water is as exciting as that below the surface. Underwater, you'll enjoy a very diversified dive. Clouds of damselfish and triggerfish will greet you on the surface. Divers can approach even the timid bird wrasse. There are more porcupine puffers here than anywhere else, as well as schools of goatfish and fields of healthy finger coral. La Pérouse is good for snorkeling and long, shallow second dives.

book called *Molokini Island,* Island Heritage 2002.) In their 30 years of operation, they have been accident free. Two-tank dives are $145, including equipment, or $130 if you have your own equipment.

Stop by any location of **Maui Dive Shop ★** (www.mauidiveshop.com), Maui's largest diving retailer, with everything from rentals to scuba-diving instruction to dive-boat charters, for a free copy of the 40-page *Maui Dive & Surf Magazine* (you can also order a copy from the website). Inside are maps of and details on the 20 best shoreline and offshore dives and snorkel sites, each ranked for beginner, intermediate, or advanced snorkelers/divers. Maui Dive Shop has branches in Kihei at Azeka Place II Shopping Center, 1455 S. Kihei Rd. (© **808/879-3388**); Kamaole Shopping Center (© **808/879-1533**); and Shops at Wailea (© **808/875-9904**). In Lahaina, there is a shop at Lahaina Gateway Mall (© **808/661-5388**). In Maalaea, there are shops at Maalaea Village (© **808/244-5514**); Whalers Village, Kaanapali (© **808/661-5117**); and Kahana Gateway (© **808/669-3800**).

Snorkeling

Snorkeling is the main attraction in Maui—and almost anyone can do it. All you need are fins, a mask, a snorkel, and some basic swimming skills. Floating over underwater worlds through colorful clouds of tropical fish is like a dream. In many places all you have to do is wade into the water and look down. If you've never snorkeled before, most resorts and excursion boats offer instruction, but it's plenty easy to figure out for yourself.

Some snorkeling tips: Always go with a buddy. Look up every once in a while to see where you are, how far offshore you are, and whether there's any boat traffic. Don't touch anything; not only can you damage coral, but camouflaged fish and shells with poisonous spines can also damage you. Always check with a dive shop, lifeguards, and others on the beach about the area in which you plan to snorkel: Are there any dangerous conditions you should know about? What are the current surf, tide, and weather conditions? If you're not a good swimmer, wear a life jacket or another flotation device, which you can rent at most places offering watersports gear.

Snorkel Bob's ★ (www.snorkelbob.com) or **Boss Frog's Dive and Surf Shops** (www.bossfrog.com) will rent you everything you need; see p. 153 and 160 for their locations. Also see "Maui Dive Shop," above, for a free booklet on great snorkeling sites.

Maui's best snorkeling spots include **Kapalua Beach;** at **Black Rock at Kaanapali Beach,** in front of the Sheraton; along the Kihei coastline, especially at **Kamaole III Beach Park;** and along the Wailea coastline, particularly at **Ulua Beach.** Mornings are best because local winds don't kick in until around noon. **Olowalu** has great snorkeling around **mile marker 14,** where there is a turtle-cleaning station about 150 to 225 feet out from shore. Turtles line up here to have cleaner wrasses pick off small parasites.

Ahihi-Kinau Natural Preserve is another terrific place. I recommend it, even though it requires more effort to get there, but it's worth it because it's home to Maui's tropical marine life at its best. *Note:* Portions of the reserve have been closed to protect resources, but the most frequently used areas remain open to the public. You will need to follow signs at the site for more information. You can't miss in Ahihi Bay, a 2,000-acre state natural area reserve in the lee of Cape Kinau, on Maui's rugged south coast, where Haleakala spilled red-hot lava that ran to the sea around 400 years ago. Fishing is strictly *kapu* (forbidden) here, and the fish know it; they're everywhere in this series of rocky coves and black-lava tide pools. The black, barren, lunarlike land stands in stark contrast to the green-blue water. After you snorkel, check out La Pérouse Bay on the south side of Cape Kinau, where the French admiral La Pérouse became the first European to set foot on Maui. A lava-rock pyramid known as Pérouse Monument marks the spot. To get here, drive south of Makena past Puu Olai to Ahihi Bay. At Cape Kinau take the shortest trail, nearest La Pérouse Bay. If you have a

There are plenty of great snorkeling spots on Maui that are just offshore.

standard car, drive as far as you can, park, and walk the remainder of the way. For information on the preserve, go to http://hawaii.gov/dlnr/dofaw/nars/reserves/maui/ahihikinau. The **Department of Land and Natural Resources** (✆ **808/984-8100**) has a free printed brochure available by mail.

When the whales aren't around, **Capt. Steve's Rafting Excursions** (✆ **808/667-5565;** www.captainsteves.com) conducts 5½-hour snorkel trips from Mala Wharf in Lahaina to the waters around **Lanai** (you don't actually land on the island). Discounted website rates of $139 for adults and $99 for children 12 and under include breakfast, lunch, snorkel gear, and wet suits.

If you'd like to head over to Lanai for a day of snorkeling in its pristine waters, see "Day Cruises to Lanai," earlier in this chapter.

SNORKEL CRUISES TO MOLOKINI

Like a crescent moon fallen from the sky, the crater of **Molokini** ★ sits almost midway between Maui and the uninhabited island of Kahoolawe. Tilted so that only the thin rim of its southern side shows above water in a perfect semicircle, Molokini stands like a scoop against the tide, and it serves, on its concave side, as a natural sanctuary for tropical fish and snorkelers, who commute daily in a fleet of dive boats to this marine-life preserve. *Note:* In high season, Molokini can be crowded with dozens of boats, each carrying scores of snorkelers.

Maui Classic Charters ★★ Maui Classic Charters offers morning and afternoon **snorkel-sail cruises to Molokini** on *Four Winds II,* a 55-foot glass-bottom catamaran. Rates for the morning sail are $89 for adults and $59 for children 3 to 12; in the afternoon, the rates are $42 for adults and $30 for children (book on the website and save 15%). *Four Winds II* trips include continental breakfast and a hot lunch (lunch is optional on the afternoon cruise); complimentary beer, wine, and soda; snorkeling gear and instruction; and sport fishing along the way. Those looking for speed should book a trip on the state-of-the-art catamaran *Maui Magic.* A 5-hour snorkel journey to both Molokini and La Pérouse costs $112 for adults and $92 for children 5 to 12, including continental breakfast; barbecue lunch; beer, wine, and soda; snorkel gear; and instruction. During whale season (Dec 22–Apr 22), the *Four Winds II* has a 3½-hour **whale-watching cruise** that costs $42 for adults and $30 for children 3 to 12 (including beverages).

Maalaea Harbor, slip 55 and slip 80. © **800/736-5740** or 808/879-8188. www.mauicharters.com. Prices vary depending on cruise.

Pacific Whale Foundation This not-for-profit foundation supports its whale research, public education, and conservation programs by offering **whale-watching cruises, wild dolphin encounters,** and **snorkel tours,** some to Molokini and Lanai. There are 17 daily trips to choose from, offered December through May, out of both Lahaina and Maalaea harbors.

300 Maalaea Rd., Ste. 211, Wailuku. © **800/942-5311** or 808/879-8811. www.pacificwhale.org. Trips from $39 adults, from $23 children 7–12, free for children 6 and under.

Pride of Maui For a high-speed, action-packed snorkel-sail experience, consider the *Pride of Maui*. It offers 5-hour **snorkel cruises to Molokini** with stops at Turtle Bay and Makena; the cost is $96 for ages 13 and up and $62 for children 3 to 12. Rates include continental breakfast, barbecue lunch, beverages and open bar, gear, and instruction. Other options include an afternoon Molokini cruise ($42 for ages 13 and up, $30 for children 3–12), an evening sunset cruise ($70 for ages 13 and up, $56 for children 3–12), and, during whale season, a whale-watching cruise ($42 for ages 13 and up, $30 for children 3–12). *Tip:* Discounts are available if you book your cruise on the website.

Maalaea Harbor. © **877/TO-PRIDE** (867-7433) or 808/875-0955. www.prideofmaui.com. Prices vary depending on cruise.

Sport Fishing

Marlin (as big as 1,200 lb.), tuna, ono, and mahimahi await the baited hook in Maui's coastal and channel waters. No license is required; just book a sport-fishing vessel out of Lahaina or Maalaea harbor. Most charter boats that troll for big-game fish carry a maximum of six passengers. You can walk the docks, inspect boats, and talk to captains and crews, or book through your hotel's activities desk or one of the outfitters recommended below.

Shop around: Prices vary widely depending on the boat, the crowd, and the captain. A shared boat for a half-day of fishing starts at $139; a shared full day of fishing starts at around $250. A half-day exclusive (you get the entire boat) starts at $600; a full-day exclusive starts at $1,000. Also, many boat captains tag and release marlin or keep the fish for themselves (sorry, that's Hawaii style). If you want to eat your mahimahi for dinner or have your marlin mounted, tell the captain before you go.

The best way to book a sport-fishing charter is through the experts; the top booking desk in the state is **Sportfish Hawaii ★** (© **877/388-1376** or 808/396-2607; www.sportfishhawaii.com), which books boats on all the islands. These fishing vessels are inspected and must meet rigorous criteria to guarantee that you'll have a great time. Prices range from $999 to $1,100 for a full-day exclusive charter (you, plus five friends, get the entire boat to yourself); a half-day exclusive charter starts at $599.

Submarine Dives

Plunging 100 feet below the surface of the sea in a state-of-the-art, high-tech submarine is a great way to experience Maui's magnificent underwater world, especially if you're not a swimmer. **Atlantis Adventures ★**, 658 Front St., Lahaina (© **800/548-6262** or 808/667-2224; www.atlantisadventures.com),

The submarine *Atlantis.*

offers trips out of Lahaina Harbor every hour on the hour from 9am to 2pm; prices are $99 for adults and $45 for children 11 and under (children must be at least 3 ft. tall). Book on the website and save 10%. Allow 2 hours for this underwater adventure. **Warning:** This is not a good choice if you're claustrophobic.

Surfing

The ancient Hawaiian sport of *hee nalu* (wave sliding) is probably the sport most people picture when they think of the islands. If you'd like to give it a shot, just sign up at any one of the recommended surfing schools listed below.

Tide and Kiva Rivers, two local boys (actually twins) who have been surfing since they could walk, operate **Rivers to the Sea ★★** (© **808/280-8795** or 280-6236; www.riverstothesea.com), one of the best surfing schools on Maui. Rates are $75 per person for a 1½-hour class for a group of three or more, $220 for a 1½-hour class for a couple, and $160 for a 1½-hour private lesson. All lessons include equipment. The instructor decides where the lesson will take place based on the client's ability and where the surf is on that day. Tide, who has been surfing for over 25 years, says he has beginners standing up in their first lesson.

Well-known surfer Nancy Emerson can also teach you how to surf—just call the **Nancy Emerson School of Surfing,** 505 Front St., Ste. 201, Lahaina (© **808/244-SURF** [7873]; www.mauisurfclinics.com). Nancy has been surfing since 1961 and has even been a stunt performer for various movies, such as *Waterworld.* She's pioneered a new instructional technique called "Learn to Surf in One Lesson" (you can, really). It's $78 per person for a 2-hour group lesson; private 2-hour classes are $165. All instructors are certified lifeguards.

Whale-Watching

Every winter, pods of Pacific humpback whales make the 3,000-mile swim from the chilly waters of Alaska to bask in Maui's summery shallows, fluking, spyhopping, spouting, and having an all-around swell time.

Maui has some great surfing instructors who can get you up and riding the waves.

The humpback is the star of the annual whale-watching season, which usually begins in December or January and lasts until April or sometimes May. About 1,500 to 3,000 humpback whales appear in Hawaii waters each year. Adults grow to be about 45 feet long and weigh a hefty 40 tons. Humpbacks are officially an endangered species: In 1997, some of the waters around the state were designated the Hawaiian Islands Humpback Whale National Marine Sanctuary, the country's only federal single-species sanctuary.

WHALE-WATCHING FROM SHORE

Between mid-December and April, you can just look out to sea. There's no best time of day for whale-watching, but the whales seem to appear when the sea is glassy and the wind calm. Once you see one, keep watching in the same vicinity; they might stay down for 20 minutes. Bring a book—and binoculars, if you can. Some good whale-watching points on Maui include these:

MCGREGOR POINT   On the way to Lahaina, on the Honoapiilani Highway, there's a scenic lookout at mile marker 9 (just before you get to the Lahaina Tunnel); it's a good viewpoint to scan for whales.

OLOWALU REEF   Along the straight part of Honoapiilani Highway, between McGregor Point and Olowalu, you'll sometimes see whales leap out of the water. Their appearance can bring traffic to a screeching halt: People abandon their cars and run down to the sea to watch, causing a major traffic jam. If you stop, pull off the road so others may pass.

WAILEA BEACH MARRIOTT RESORT & SPA   On the Wailea coastal walk, stop at this resort to look for whales through the telescope installed as a public service by the Hawaiian Islands Humpback Whale National Marine Sanctuary.

PUU OLAI   It's a tough climb up this coastal landmark near the Maui Prince Hotel, but you're likely to be well rewarded: This is the island's best spot for offshore whale-watching. On the 360-foot cinder cone overlooking Makena

A whale watching cruise can let you get a close look at these gentle giants.

Beach, you'll be at the right elevation to see Pacific humpbacks as they dodge Molokini and cruise up Alalakeiki Channel between Maui and Kahoolawe. If you don't see one, you'll at least have a whale of a view.

WHALE-WATCHING CRUISES

For a closer look, take a whale-watching cruise. The **Pacific Whale Foundation,** 101 N. Kihei Rd., Kihei (📞 **800/942-5311** or 808/879-8811; www.pacific whale.org), is a nonprofit foundation in Kihei that supports its whale research by offering cruises and snorkel tours, some to Molokini and Lanai. It operates a 65-foot power catamaran called the *Ocean Explorer,* a 50-foot sailing catamaran called the *Manute'a,* and other boats. There are 15 daily trips from which to choose, and the rates for a 2-hour whale-watching cruise would make Captain Ahab smile (starting at $25 for adults, $17 for children). Cruises are offered from December to May, out of both Lahaina and Maalaea harbors.

If you want to combine ocean activities, then a snorkel or dive cruise to Molokini, the sunken crater off Maui's south coast, might be just the ticket. You can see whales on the way there, at no extra charge. See "Scuba Diving" and "Boating & Sailing," earlier in this chapter.

WHALE-WATCHING BY KAYAK & RAFT

Seeing a humpback whale from an ocean kayak or raft is awesome. **Capt. Steve's Rafting Excursions** (📞 **808/667-5565;** www.captainsteves.com) offers 2-hour whale-watching excursions out of Lahaina Harbor from $49 for adults and from $35 for children 5 to 12.

Windsurfing

Maui has Hawaii's best windsurfing beaches. In winter, windsurfers from around the world flock to the town of **Paia** to ride the waves. **Hookipa Beach,** known all over the globe for its brisk winds and excellent waves, is the site of several world-championship contests. Go in the afternoon—board surfers have access to the waves in the morning and the windsurfers take over after noon. **Kanaha**

Maui has Hawaii's best windsurfing beaches.

Beach, west of Kahului Airport, also has dependable winds. When the winds turn northerly, **Kihei** is the spot to be; some days, you can spot whales in the distance behind the windsurfers. The northern end of Kihei is best: **Ohukai Park,** the first beach as you enter South Kihei Road from the northern end, has not only good winds, but also parking, a long strip of grass to assemble your gear, and good access to the water. Experienced windsurfers here are found in front of the **Maui Sunset** condo, 1032 S. Kihei Rd., near Waipuilani Street (a block north of McDonald's), which has great windsurfing conditions but a very shallow reef (not good for beginners).

    Hawaiian Island Surf & Sport, 415 Dairy Rd., Kahului (© **800/231-6958** or 808/871-4981; www.hawaiianisland.com), offers lessons (from $89), rentals, and repairs. Other shops that offer rentals and lessons are **Hawaiian Sailboarding Techniques,** 425 Koloa St., Kahului (© **800/968-5423** or 808/871-5423; www.hstwindsurfing.com), with 2½-hour lessons from $79; and **Maui Windsurf Co.,** 22 Hana Hwy., Kahului (© **800/872-0999** or 808/877-4816; www.maui-windsurf.com), which has complete equipment rental (board, sail, rig harness, and roof rack) from $54, plus 2½-hour lessons from $89.

    For daily reports on wind and surf conditions, call the **Wind and Surf Report** at © **808/877-3611.**

HIKING & CAMPING

In the past 3 decades, Maui has grown from a rural island to a fast-paced resort destination, but its natural beauty remains largely inviolate; there are still many places that can be explored only on foot. Those interested in seeing the backcountry—complete with virgin waterfalls; remote wilderness trails; and quiet, meditative settings—should head for Haleakala's upcountry or the tropical Hana Coast.

    Camping on Maui can be extreme (inside a volcano) or benign (by the sea in Hana). It can be wet, cold, and rainy, or hot, dry, and windy—often all on the same day. If you're heading for Haleakala, remember that U.S. astronauts trained for the moon inside the volcano: Bring survival gear. Don't forget both your swimsuit and your rain gear if you're bound for Waianapanapa. No matter where you are headed, bring your own gear, as there are no places to rent camping equipment on Maui.

For more information on Maui camping and hiking trails, and to obtain free maps, contact **Haleakala National Park,** P.O. Box 369, Makawao, HI 96768 (✆ **808/572-4400;** www.nps.gov/hale); or the **State Division of Forestry and Wildlife,** 54 S. High St., Wailuku, HI 96793 (✆ **808/984-8100;** www.hawaiistateparks.org). For information on trails, hikes, camping, and permits for state parks, contact the **Hawaii State Department of Land and Natural Resources,** State Parks Division, 54 S. High St., Wailuku, HI 96793 (✆ **808/984-8109;** www.hawaiistateparks.org/camping/fees.cfm). *Note:* You can get information from the state's website as well as obtain permits there. For Maui County Parks, contact the **Maui County Department of Parks and Recreation,** 700 Halia Nakoa St., Wailuku, HI 96793 (✆ **808/270-7230;** www.co.maui.hi.us/departments/parks).

TIPS ON SAFE HIKING & CAMPING Water might be everywhere in Hawaii, but it more than likely isn't safe to drink. Most stream water must be treated because cattle, pigs, and goats have probably contaminated the water upstream. The Department of Health continually warns campers of bacterium leptospirosis, which is found in freshwater streams throughout the state and enters the body through breaks in the skin or through the mucous membranes. It produces flulike symptoms and can be fatal. Make sure that your drinking water is safe by vigorously boiling it, or if boiling is not an option, use tablets with hydroperiodide; portable water filters will not screen out bacterium leptospirosis. Firewood isn't always available, so it's a good idea to carry a small, light backpacking stove, which you can use both to boil water and to cook meals.

Remember, the island is not crime free: Never leave your valuables (wallet, airline ticket, and so on) unprotected. Carry a day pack if you have a campsite, and never camp alone. Some more do's and don'ts: Do bury personal waste away from streams. Don't eat unknown fruit. Do carry your trash out. And don't forget there is very little twilight in Maui when the sun sets—it gets dark quickly.

See "Health & Safety" in chapter 12 for more hiking and camping tips.

GUIDED HIKES If you'd like a knowledgeable guide to accompany you on a hike, call **Maui Hiking Safaris** ★ (✆ **888/445-3963** or 808/573-0168; www.mauihikingsafaris.com). Owner Randy Warner takes visitors on half- and full-day hikes into valleys, rainforests, and coastal areas. Randy's been hiking around Maui for more than 3 decades and is wise in the ways of Hawaiian history, native flora and fauna, and volcanology. His rates are $69 to $99 for a half-day and $120 to $159 for a full day, which include day packs, rain parkas, snacks, water, and, on full-day hikes, sandwiches.

Maui's oldest hiking-guide company is **Hike Maui** ★ (✆ **866/324-6284** or 808/879-5270; www.hikemaui.com), headed by Ken Schmitt, who pioneered guided hikes on the Valley Isle. Hike Maui offers five different hikes a day, ranging in length and difficulty. There are also numerous hikes offered by **Eco Adventures with Hike Maui** (same phone as

For those looking for a different perspective of Haleakala, try **Skyline Eco-Adventures' Zipline Haleakala Tour** ((*✆* **808/878-8400;** www.zipline.com/locations/haleakala), which blends a short hike through a eucalyptus forest with four zipline crossings. During the zipline crossing, you'll be outfitted with a seat harness and connected to a cable, then launched from a 70-foot-high platform to "zip" along the cable suspended over the slopes of Haleakala. From this viewpoint, you fly over treetops, valleys, gulches, and waterfalls at 10 to 35 mph. These bird's-eye tours operate daily and take riders from ages 10 and up, weighing between 80 and 260 pounds. The cost is $86, if you book on the company's website.

above; www.ecomaui.com). You'll hike by streams and waterfalls, through native trees and plants, and on to breathtaking vistas. The tour includes a stop for a picnic lunch, a swim in secluded pools, and memorable photo ops. The 7-hour excursion costs $140 per person, including hotel pickup, a fanny pack with bottled water, and rain gear if necessary. There's also a shorter, less-strenuous jaunt for $75. **Note:** Book online for a 10% discount.

Haleakala National Park ★★★

For complete coverage of the national park, see "Haleakala National Park," p. 122.

HIKING INTO THE WILDERNESS: SLIDING SANDS & HALEMAUU TRAILS

Hiking into Maui's dormant volcano is the best way to see it. The terrain inside the wilderness area of the volcano, which ranges from burnt-red cinder cones to

Hiking into Haleakala's crater is the best way to experience it.

ebony-black lava flows, is simply spectacular. Inside the crater there are some 27 miles of hiking trails, two camping sites, and three cabins.

Try to arrange to stay at least 1 night in the park; 2 or 3 nights will allow you more time to explore the fascinating interior of the volcano (see "Camping Near the Main Entrance," below, for details on the cabins and campgrounds in the wilderness area of the valley). If you want to venture out on your own, the best route includes two trails: into the crater along **Sliding Sands Trail ★**, which begins on the rim at 9,800 feet and descends into the belly of the beast, to the valley floor at 6,600 feet; and back out along **Halemauu Trail ★**. Hardy hikers can consider making the 11-mile one-way descent, which takes 9 hours, and the equally long return ascent in a day. The rest of us will need to extend this steep but wonderful hike to 2 days. The descending and ascending trails aren't loops; the trail heads are miles (and several thousand feet in elevation) apart, so you'll need to make advance transportation arrangements to get back to your car, which you'll leave at the beginning of the hike, about a 30- to 45-minute drive from where the Halemauu Trail ends. You either arrange with someone to pick you up, hitchhike back up to your car, or hook up with other people doing the same thing and drop off one car at each trail head. Before you set out, stop at park headquarters to get camping and hiking updates. There is no registration for day hikers.

The trail head for Sliding Sands is well marked, and the trail is easy to follow over lava flows

> ## 📎 A Word of Warning About the Weather
>
> The weather at nearly 10,000 feet can change suddenly and without warning. Come prepared for cold, high winds, rain, and even snow in winter. Temperatures can range from 77°F (25°C) down to 26°F (−3°C), and high winds (which make it feel even colder) are frequent. Rainfall varies from 40 inches a year on the west end of the crater to more than 200 inches on the eastern side. Bring boots, waterproof gear, warm clothes, extra layers, and lots of sunscreen—the sun shines very brightly up here.

and cinders. As you descend, look around: The view is breathtaking. In the afternoon, waves of clouds flow into the Kaupo and Koolau gaps. Vegetation is sparse to nonexistent at the top, but the closer you get to the crater floor, the more growth you'll see: bracken ferns, pili grass, shrubs, even flowers. On the floor, the trail travels across rough lava flows, passing by rare silversword plants, volcanic vents, and multicolored cinder cones.

The Halemauu Trail goes over red and black lava and past vegetation such as evening primrose as it begins its ascent up the crater wall. Occasionally, riders on horseback use this trail as an entry and exit from the park. The proper etiquette is to step aside and stand quietly next to the trail as the horses pass.

DAY HIKES FROM THE MAIN ENTRANCE

In addition to the difficult hike into the crater, the park has a few shorter and easier options. Anyone can take a .5-mile walk down the **Hosmer Grove Nature Trail ★**, or you can start down **Sliding Sands Trail** for a mile or two to get a hint of what lies ahead (even this short hike can be exhausting at the high altitude). A good day hike is **Halemauu Trail** to Holua Cabin and back, an 8-mile, half-day trip.

A 20-minute orientation presentation is given daily in the Summit Building at 9:30, 10:30, and 11:30am. The park rangers offer a 3-hour, 3-mile **Waikamoi Cloud Forest Hike** that leaves every Monday and Thursday at 8:45am; it starts at the Hosmer Grove, just inside the park entrance, and traverses through the Nature Conservancy's Waikamoi Preserve. *Always call in advance:* The hikes and briefing sessions may be canceled, so check first. For details, call the park at ☎ **808/572-4400** or visit www.nps.gov/hale.

CAMPING NEAR THE MAIN ENTRANCE

Most people stay at one of two tent campgrounds; for more information, contact **Haleakala National Park,** P.O. Box 369, Makawao, HI 96768 (☎ **808/572-4400;** www.nps.gov/hale).

If you want to stay in one of Haleakala's cabins, be sure to book way in advance.

CABINS It can get really cold and windy down in the valley (see "A Word of Warning About the Weather," above), so try for a cabin. They're warm, provide protection from the elements, and are reasonably priced. Each has 12 padded bunks (but no bedding; bring your own), a table, chairs, cooking utensils, a two-burner propane stove, and a wood-burning stove with firewood (you might also have a few cockroaches). The cabins are spaced so that each one is an easy walk from the other: Holua Cabin is on the Halemauu Trail, Kapalaoa Cabin on Sliding Sands Trail, and Paliku Cabin on the eastern end by the Kaupo Gap. The rates are $75 a night if you book more than 3 weeks in advance or $60 a night if you book less than 3 weeks in advance (though you run the risk of the cabins selling out).

The cabins are so popular, requests for cabins must be made 3 months in advance (be sure to request alternate dates). You can request all three cabins at once; you're limited to 2 nights in one cabin and 3 nights total within the wilderness per month. Visit **www.fhnp.org/wcr** for complete rules and regulations, as well as an online application.

CAMPGROUNDS If you can't get a cabin for the dates you want, all is not lost—there are three tent-camping sites that can accommodate you: two in the wilderness area, and one just outside at Hosmer Grove. There is no charge for tent camping.

Hosmer Grove, located at 6,800 feet, is a small, open, grassy area surrounded by a forest. Trees protect campers from the winds, but nights still get quite cold—sometimes there's ice on the ground up here. This is the best place to spend the night in a tent if you want to see the Haleakala sunrise. Come up the day before, enjoy the park, take a day hike, and then turn in early. The enclosed-glass Summit Building opens at sunrise for those who come to greet the dawn—a welcome windbreak. Facilities at Hosmer Grove include a covered pavilion with picnic tables and grills, chemical toilets, and

Camping at Kipahulu.

drinking water. No permits are needed, and there's no charge—but you can stay for only 3 nights in a 30-day period.

The two tent-camping areas inside the volcano are **Holua,** just off Halemauu at 6,920 feet; and **Paliku,** just before the Kaupo Gap at the eastern end of the valley, at 6,380 feet. Facilities at both campgrounds are limited to pit toilets and nonpotable catchment water. Water at Holua is limited, especially in summer. No open fires are allowed inside the volcano, so bring a stove if you plan to cook. Tent camping is restricted to the signed area. No camping is allowed in the horse pasture. The inviting grassy lawn in front of the cabin is off-limits. Camping is free but limited to 2 consecutive nights, and no more than 3 nights a month inside the volcano. Permits are issued at park headquarters daily from 8am to 3pm on a first-come, first-served basis on the day you plan to camp. Occupancy is limited to 25 people in each campground.

HIKING & CAMPING AT KIPAHULU (NEAR HANA)

In the east Maui section of Haleakala National Park, you can set up at **Oheo Campground,** a first-come, first-served, drive-in campground with tent sites for 100 near the ocean. It has a few tables, barbecue grills, and chemical toilets. No permit is required, but there's a 3-night limit. No food or drinking water is available, so bring your own. Bring a tent as well—it rains 75 inches a year here. Contact **Kipahulu Ranger Station,** Haleakala National Park, HI 96713 (✆ **808/248-7375;** www.nps.gov/hale/planyourvisit/wilderness-camping.htm), for information.

HIKING FROM THE SUMMIT   If you hike from the crater rim down **Kaupo Gap** to the ocean, more than 20 miles away, you'll pass through climate zones ranging from arctic to tropical. On a clear day, you can see every island except Kauai on the trip down.

APPROACHING KIPAHULU FROM HANA   If you drive to Kipahulu, you'll have to approach it from the Hana Highway—it's not accessible from the summit. Always check in at the ranger station before you begin your hike; the staff can inform you of current conditions and share their wonderful stories about the history, culture, flora, and fauna of the area. The entry fee is $10 a car, the same as for the summit atop Haleakala.

There are two hikes you can take here. The first is a short, easy .5-mile loop along the **Kaloa Point Trail** (Kaloa Point is a windy bluff overlooking **Oheo Gulch**), which leads toward the ocean along pools and waterfalls and back to the ranger station. The clearly marked path leaves the parking area and rambles along the flat, grassy peninsula. Along the way you'll see the remnants of an ancient fishing shrine, a house site, and a lauhala-thatched building depicting an earlier time. The pools are above and below the bridge; the best for swimming are usually above the bridge.

The second hike is for the hardier. Although just a 4-mile round-trip, the trail is steep and you'll want to stop and swim in the pools, so allow 3 hours. You'll be climbing over rocks and up steep trails, so wear hiking boots. Take water, snacks, swim gear, and insect repellent. Always be on the lookout for flash-flood conditions. This walk will pass two magnificent waterfalls, the 181-foot **Makahiku Falls** and the even bigger 400-foot **Waimoku Falls ★**. The trail starts at the ranger station, where you'll walk uphill for .5 mile to a fence overlook at the thundering Makahiku Falls. If you're tired, you can turn around here; true adventurers should press on. Behind the lookout, the well-worn trail picks up again and goes directly to a pool on the top of the Makahiku Falls. The pool is safe to swim in as long as the waters aren't rising; if they are, get out and head back to the ranger station. The rest of the trail takes you through a meadow and bamboo forest to Waimoku Falls.

GUIDED HIKES The rangers at Kipahulu conduct a 1-mile hike to the **Bamboo Forest ★** at 9:30am daily and a 4-mile round-trip hike to **Waimoku Falls** on Saturday at 9:30am. All programs and hikes begin at the ranger station; they may be canceled, so check in advance by contacting the **Kipahulu Ranger Station,** Haleakala National Park, HI 96713 (*C* **808/248-7375;** www.nps.gov/hale).

Skyline Trail, Polipoli Spring State Recreation Area ★

This is some hike—strenuous but worth every step. It's 8 miles, all downhill, with a dazzling 100-mile view of the islands dotting the blue Pacific, plus the West Maui Mountains, which seem like a separate island.

The trail is located just outside Haleakala National Park at Polipoli Spring State Recreation Area; however, you access it by going through the national park to the summit. The Skyline Trail starts just beyond the Puu Ulaula summit building on the south side of Science City and follows the southwest rift zone of Haleakala from its lunarlike cinder cones to a cool redwood grove. The trail drops 3,800 feet on a 4-hour hike to the recreation area in the 12,000-acre Kahikinui Forest Reserve. If you'd rather drive, you'll need a four-wheel-drive vehicle.

There's a **campground** at the recreation area, at 6,300 feet. Permits and reservations are required. Fees are $18 for the first camper and $3 for each additional camper to a maximum of $30 per campsite per night, and your stay must be limited to 5 nights. One eight-bunk cabin is available for $90 per cabin per night; it has a cold shower and a gas stove, but no electricity or drinking water (bring your own). To reserve, go to their website or contact the **State Parks Division,** 54 S. High St., Room 101, Wailuku, HI 96793 (*C* **808/984-8109;** www.hawaiistateparks.org/camping/fees.cfm).

Polipoli State Park ★

You'll find one of the most unusual hiking experiences in the state at Polipoli State Park, part of the 21,000-acre Kula and Kahikinui Forest Reserve on the slope of Haleakala. At Polipoli, it's hard to believe that you're in Hawaii. First of all, it's cold, even in summer, because the loop is up at 5,300 to 6,200 feet. Second, this former forest of native koa, ohia, and mamane trees, which was overlogged in the 1800s, was reforested in the 1930s with introduced species: pine, Monterey cypress, ash, sugi, red alder, redwood, and several varieties of eucalyptus.

The **Polipoli Loop ★** is an easy 3.5-mile hike that takes about 3 hours; dress warmly for it. To get here, take the Haleakala Highway (Hwy. 37) to Keokea and turn right onto Hwy. 337; after less than ½ mile, turn on Waipoli Road, which climbs swiftly. After 10 miles, Waipoli Road ends at the Polipoli State Park campground. The well-marked trail head is next to the parking lot, near a stand of Monterey cypress; the tree-lined trail offers the best view of the island.

The Polipoli Loop is really a network of three trails: Haleakala Ridge Trail, Plum Trail, and Redwood Trail. After .5 mile of meandering through groves of eucalyptus, blackwood, swamp mahogany, and hybrid cypress, you'll join the

Haleakala Ridge Trail, which, about a mile in, joins with the Plum Trail (named for the plums that ripen in June–July). This trail passes through massive redwoods and by an old Conservation Corps bunkhouse and a run-down cabin before joining up with the Redwood Trail, which climbs through Mexican pine, tropical ash, Port Orford cedar, and, of course, redwood.

Camping is allowed in the park with an $18-per-night permit from the **State Parks Division,** 54 S. High St., Room 101, Wailuku, HI 96793 (*©* **808/ 984-8109;** www.hawaiistateparks.org/camping/fees.cfm). There's one cabin, which is available by reservation.

Kanaha Beach Park Camping

One of the few Maui County camping facilities on the island is at Kanaha Beach Park, located next to the Kahului Airport. The county has two separate areas for camping: 7 tent sites on the beach and an additional 10 tent sites inland. This well-used park is a favorite of windsurfers, who take advantage of the strong winds that roar across this end of the island. Facilities include a paved parking lot, portable toilets, outdoor showers, barbecue grills, and picnic tables. Camping is open 5 days a week (closed Mon–Tues) and limited to no more than 3 consecutive days. Per-night permit fees are Wednesday and Thursday $5 per adult and $2 per child ages 17 and under; and Friday through Sunday $8 adults and $3 children ages 17 and under. Permits can be obtained from the **Maui County Parks and Recreation Department,** 700 Halia Nakoa St., Unit 2, Wailuku, HI 96793 (*©* **808/ 270-7389;** www.mauimapp.com/information/campingcounty.htm). The 17 sites book up quickly; reserve your dates far in advance (the county will accept reservations a year in advance).

Waianapanapa State Park ★★

Tucked in a tropical jungle on the outskirts of the little coastal town of Hana is Waianapanapa State Park, a black-sand beach set in an emerald forest.

Hana-Waianapanapa Coast Trail ★   This is an easy 6-mile hike that takes you back in time. Allow 4 hours to walk along this relatively flat trail, which parallels the sea, along lava cliffs and a forest of lauhala trees. The best time to take the hike is either early morning or late afternoon, when the light on the lava and surf makes for great photos. Midday is the worst time; not only is it hot (lava intensifies the heat), but there's also no shade or potable water available. There's no formal trail head; join the route at any point along the Waianapanapa Campground and go in either direction.

Along the trail, you'll see remains of an ancient *heiau* (temple), stands of lauhala trees, caves, a blowhole, and a remarkable plant, Naupaka, that flourishes along the beach. Upon close inspection, you'll see that the Naupaka only half blossoms; according to Hawaiian legend, a similar plant living in the mountains has the other half of the blossoms. One ancient explanation is that the two plants represent never-to-be-reunited lovers: As the story goes, the couple bickered so much that the gods, fed up with their incessant quarreling, banished one lover to the mountain and the other to the sea.

Camping   Waianapanapa has 12 cabins and a tent campground. Go for the cabins (reviewed on p. 300), as it rains torrentially here, sometimes turning the campground into a mud-wrestling arena. Cabins are $90 per night; tent camping is $18 per night for the first 6 campers, $3 per person after that up to $30, but

Paul Fagan used to enjoy hiking up the hill where this cross now stands in his memory.

limited to 5 nights in a 30-day period. Permits are available from the **State Parks Division,** 54 S. High St., Room 101, Wailuku, HI 96793 (© **808/984-8109;** www.hawaiistateparks.org/camping/fees.cfm). Facilities include restrooms, outdoor showers, drinking water, and picnic tables.

Hana: The Hike to Fagan's Cross

This 3-mile hike to the cross erected in memory of Paul Fagan, the founder of Hana Ranch and Hotel Hana Maui (now the Travaasa Hana Resort), offers spectacular views of the Hana Coast, particularly at sunset. The uphill trail starts across Hana Highway from the Travaasa Hana resort. Enter the pastures at your own risk; they're often occupied by glaring bulls and cows with new calves. Watch your step as you ascend this steep hill on a jeep trail across open pastures to the cross and the breathtaking view.

Keanae Arboretum ★

About 47 miles from Kahului, along the Hana Highway and just after the Keanae YMCA Camp (and just before the turnoff to the Keanae Peninsula), is an easy walk through the Keanae Arboretum, which is maintained by the Hawaii Department of Land and Natural Resources. The walk, which is just over 2 miles, passes through a forest with both native and introduced plants. Allow 1 to 2 hours, longer if you take time out to swim. Take rain gear and mosquito repellent.

Park at the Keanae Arboretum and pass through the turnstile. Walk along the fairly flat jeep road to the entrance. For .5 mile, you will pass by plants introduced to Hawaii (ornamental timber, pomelo, banana, papaya, hibiscus, and more), all with identifying tags. Next is a taro patch showing the different varieties that Hawaiians used as their staple crop. After the taro, a 1-mile trail leads through a Hawaiian rainforest. The trail crisscrosses a stream as it meanders

Keanae Arboretum is an ideal spot for an easy walk.

through the forest. My favorite swimming hole is just to the left of the first stream crossing, at about 300 feet.

Waihee Ridge ★

This strenuous 3- to 4-mile hike, with a 1,500-foot climb, offers spectacular views of the valleys of the West Maui Mountains. Allow 3 to 4 hours for the round-trip hike. Pack a lunch, carry water, and pick a dry day, as this area is very wet. There's a picnic table at the summit with great views.

To get here from Wailuku, turn north on Market Street, which becomes the Kahekili Highway (Hwy. 340) and passes through Waihee. Go just over 2½ miles from the Waihee Elementary School and look for the turnoff to the Boy Scouts' Camp Maluhia on the left. Turn into the camp and drive nearly a mile to the trail head on the jeep road. About ⅓ mile in, there will be another gate, marking the entrance to the West Maui Forest Reserve. A foot trail, kept in good shape by the Department of Land and Natural Resources, begins here. The trail climbs to the top of the ridge, offering great views of the various valleys. The trail is marked by a number of switchbacks and can be extremely muddy and wet. In some areas, it's so steep that you have to grab onto the trees and bushes for support. The trail takes you through a swampy area, then up to **Lanilili Peak,** where a picnic table and magnificent views await.

GREAT GOLF

In some circles, Maui is synonymous with golf. The island's world-famous golf courses start at the very northern tip of the island and roll right around to Kaana-pali, jumping down to Kihei and Wailea in the south. There are also some lesser-known municipal courses that offer challenging play for less than $100.

Golfers new to Maui should know that it's windy here, especially between 10am and 2pm, when winds of 10 to 15 mph are the norm. Play two to three clubs up or down to compensate for the wind factor. I also recommend bringing extra balls—the rough is thicker here and the wind will pick your ball up and drop it in very unappealing places (like water hazards).

If your heart is set on playing on a resort course, book at least a week in advance. For the ardent golfer on a tight budget, consider playing in the afternoon, when discounted twilight rates are in effect. There's no guarantee you'll get 18 holes in, especially in winter when it's dark by 6pm, but you'll have an opportunity to experience these world-famous courses at half the usual fee.

For last-minute and discount tee times, call **Hawaii Stand by Golf** (✆ **888/645-2665;** www.hawaiistandbygolf.com), which offers savings on greens fees, plus guaranteed tee times for same-day or future golfing.

Golf Club Rentals (✆ **808/665-0800;** www.mauiclubrentals.com) has custom-built clubs for men, women, and juniors (both right- and left-handed), which can be delivered islandwide; steel clubs are $25 a day, and a full graphite set is $30 a day, plus free delivery and pickup.

Central Maui

Waiehu Municipal Golf Course ✦   This public, oceanside par-72 golf course is like playing two different courses: The first 9 holes, built in 1930, are set along the dramatic coastline, while the back 9 holes, added in 1966, head toward the mountains. It's a fun course that probably won't challenge your handicap. The only hazard here is the wind, which can rip off the ocean and play havoc with your ball. The only hole that can raise your blood pressure is the 511-yard, par-5 4th hole, which is very narrow and very long. Facilities include a snack bar, a driving range, practice greens, club rentals, and a clubhouse. Because this is a public course, the greens fees are low—but getting a tee time is tough.

Lower Waiehu Beach Rd., Wailuku. ✆ **808/244-5934.** www.co.maui.hi.us/parks/maui/central/ waiehugolfcourse.htm. Greens fees $55, $20 for a cart. From the Kahului Airport, turn right on the Hana Hwy. (Hwy. 36), which becomes Kaahumanu Ave. (Hwy. 32). Turn right at the stoplight at the junction with Waiehu Beach Rd. (Hwy. 340). Go another 1½ miles and you'll see the entrance on your right.

West Maui

Kaanapali Golf Resort ★   Both courses at Kaanapali offer a challenge to all golfers, from high handicappers to near pros. The par-71, nearly 6,700-yard **Royal Kaanapali Course** is a true Robert Trent Jones, Sr., design: an abundance of wide bunkers; several long, stretched-out tees; and the largest, most contoured greens on Maui. The par-70, 6,400-yard **Kaanapali Kai** is an Arthur Jack Snyder design; although shorter than the Royal Kaanapali Course, it requires more accuracy on the narrow, hilly fairways. Facilities include a driving range, putting course, and clubhouse with dining. You'll have a better chance of getting a tee time on weekdays.

Off Hwy. 30, Kaanapali. ✆ **808/661-3691.** www.kaanapali-golf.com. Greens fees Royal Kaanapali Course $235 nonguests, $189 resort guests, $129 twilight; Kaanapali Kai Course $195 nonguests, $149 resort guests, $109 twilight. At the 1st stoplight in Kaanapali, turn onto Kaanapali Pkwy.; the 1st building on your right is the clubhouse.

Kapalua Resort ★★★   The views alone from these two championship courses are worth the greens fees. The par-72, 6,761-yard **Bay Course** (✆ **808/669-8820**) was designed by Arnold Palmer and Ed Seay. This course is a bit forgiving, with its wide fairways; the greens, however, are difficult to read. The often-photographed 5th overlooks a small ocean cove; even the pros have trouble with this rocky par-3, 205-yard hole. The **Plantation Course** (✆ **808/669-8877**), site of the PGA championship, is a Ben Crenshaw/Bill Coore design. This par-73, 6,547-yard course, set on a rolling hillside, is excellent for developing your low shots and precise chipping. Facilities for both courses include locker rooms, a driving range, and excellent dining. Weekdays are your best bet for tee times.

Off Hwy. 30, Kapalua. ✆ **877/KAPALUA** (527-2582). www.kapaluamaui.com. Greens fees Bay Course $208 nonguests, $183 resort guests, $178 midday, $138 twilight; Plantation Course $268 nonguests, $218 resort guests, $218 midday, $158 twilight.

South Maui

Elleair Maui Golf Club   Sitting in the foothills of Haleakala, just high enough to afford spectacular ocean vistas from every hole, Elleair (formerly Silversword Golf Club) is a course for golfers who love the views as much as the fairways and greens. It's very forgiving. ***Just one caveat:*** Go in the morning. Not only is it cooler, but, more important, it's also less windy. In the afternoon, the winds bluster down Haleakala with great gusto. This is a fun course to play, with some challenging holes: The par-5 2nd hole is a virtual minefield of bunkers, and the par-5 8th hole shoots over a swale and then uphill. Facilities include a clubhouse, driving range, putting green, pro shop, and lessons.

1345 Piilani Hwy. (near Lipoa St. turnoff), Kihei. ✆ **808/874-0777.** www.elleairmauigolfclub.com. Greens fees $120, $70 twilight.

Makena Golf Courses ★★   Here you'll find 36 holes of "Mr. Hawaii Golf"—Robert Trent Jones, Jr.—at its best. Add to that spectacular views: Molokini islet looms in the background, humpback whales gambol offshore in winter, and the tropical sunsets are spectacular. The par-72, 6,876-yard **South Course** has a couple of holes you'll never forget. The view from the par-4 15th, which shoots from an elevated tee 183 yards downhill to the Pacific, is magnificent. The 16th hole has a two-tiered green that's blind from the tee 383 yards away (that is, if you make it past the gully off the fairway). The par-72, 6,823-yard **North Course** is more difficult and more spectacular. The 13th hole, located partway up the mountain, has a view that makes most golfers stop and stare. The next hole is even more memorable: a 200-foot drop between tee and green. Facilities at Makena include a clubhouse, a driving range, two putting greens, a pro shop, lockers, and lessons. Beware of weekend crowds.

On Makena Alanui Dr., just past the Makena Beach and Golf Resort. ✆ **808/891-4000.** www.makenagolf.com. Greens fees $179 nonguests, $139 resort guests, $125 afternoon nonguests, $99 afternoon guests, $99 twilight nonguests, $79 twilight guests. Check website for seasonal rates.

Wailea Golf Club ★★   There are three courses to choose from at Wailea. The **Blue Course,** a par-72, 6,758-yard course designed by Arthur Jack Snyder and dotted with bunkers and water hazards, is for duffers and pros alike. The wide fairways appeal to beginners, while the undulating terrain makes it a course everyone can enjoy. A little more difficult is the par-72, 7,078-yard championship **Gold Course,** with narrow fairways, several tricky dogleg holes, and the classic Robert Trent Jones, Jr., challenges: natural hazards, like lava-rock walls, and native Hawaiian grasses. The **Emerald Course,** also designed by Robert Trent

Jones, Jr., is Wailea's newest, with tropical landscaping and a player-friendly design. With 54 holes to play, getting a tee time is slightly easier on weekends than at other resorts, but weekdays are still best (the Emerald Course is usually the toughest to book). Facilities include two pro shops, restaurants, locker rooms, and a complete training facility.

Wailea Alanui Dr. (off Wailea Iki Dr.), Wailea. ℂ **888/328-MAUI** (6284) or 808/875-7450. www.waileagolf.com. Greens fees Gold Course and Emerald Course $225 nonguests, $190–$199 resort guests; Blue Course $190 nonguests, $140 guests, $110 after noon. Check website for seasonal rates.

Upcountry Maui

Pukalani Country Club   This cool par-72, 6,962-yard course at 1,100 feet offers a break from the resorts' high greens fees, and it's really fun to play. The 3rd hole offers golfers two different options: a tough (especially into the wind) iron shot from the tee, across a gully (yuck!) to the green; or a shot down the side of the gully across a second green into sand traps below. (Most people choose to shoot down the side of the gully; it's actually easier than shooting across a ravine.) High handicappers will love this course, and more experienced players can make it more challenging by playing from the back tees. Facilities include club and shoe rentals, practice areas, lockers, a pro shop, and a restaurant.

360 Pukalani St., Pukalani. ℂ **808/572-1314.** www.pukalanigolf.com. Greens fees $88 before noon, $61 noon–2:30pm, $27 after 2:30pm. Take the Hana Hwy. (Hwy. 36) to Haleakala Hwy. (Hwy. 37) to the Pukalani exit; turn right onto Pukalani St. and go 2 blocks.

BIKING, HORSEBACK RIDING & OTHER OUTDOOR ACTIVITIES

Biking

It's not even close to dawn, but here you are, rubbing your eyes awake, riding in a van up the long, dark road to the top of Maui's dormant volcano. It's colder than you ever thought possible for a tropical island. The air is thin. The place is crowded, packed with people. You stomp your chilly feet while you wait, sipping hot coffee. Then comes the sun, exploding over the yawning Haleakala Crater, which is big enough to swallow Manhattan whole—it's a mystical moment you won't soon forget. Now you know why Hawaiians named the crater the House of the Sun. But there's no time to linger: Decked out in your screaming-yellow parka, you mount your mechanical steed and test its most important feature, the brakes—because you're about to coast 37 miles down a 10,000-foot volcano.

Cruising down Haleakala, from the lunarlike landscape at the top past flower farms, pineapple fields, and eucalyptus groves, is quite an experience—and you don't have to be an expert cyclist to do it. This is a safe trip that requires some stamina in the colder, wetter winter months but is fun for everyone in the warmer months—the key word being *warmer*. In winter and the rainy season, conditions can be harsh, especially on the top, with below-freezing temperatures and 40 mph winds.

Maui's oldest downhill company is **Maui Downhill** ★ (ℂ **800/535-BIKE** [2453] or 808/871-2155; www.mauidownhill.com), which offers a sunrise safari bike tour, including continental breakfast and a stop for lunch (not

Gliding down Haleakala by bike.

hosted), starting at $169 ($149 if booked on their website). If it's all booked up, try **Mountain Riders Bike Tours** (✆ **800/706-7700** or 808/242-9739; www.mountainriders.com), which offers sunrise rides for $150 ($120 if booked on the website) and midday trips for $130 ($104 on their website). All rates include hotel pickup, transport to the top, bicycle, safety equipment, and coffee and pastries (there is a stop for food down the mountain that guests pay for themselves). Wear layers of warm clothing—there may be a 30° change in temperature from the top of the mountain to the ocean. Generally, tour groups will not take riders 11 and under, but younger children can ride along in the van that accompanies the groups, as can pregnant women.

If you want to avoid the crowds and go down the mountain at your own pace, call **Haleakala Bike Company** (✆ **888/922-2453**; www.bikemaui.com), which will outfit you with the latest gear and take you up Haleakala.

Note: Not all tours go to the summit. If you want to start your bike ride at the summit, be sure to confirm. The cheapest trip starts at around the 6,500-foot level (about two-thirds of the way up the mountain). After making sure you are secure on the bike, the staff will let you ride down by yourself at your own pace.

5

MORATORIUM ON bike tours IN HALEAKALA NATIONAL PARK

At press time, a National Park Service moratorium on commercial bicycle tours inside Haleakala National Park was in effect due to the September 26, 2007, death of a tourist who lost control of her bicycle and struck a van inside the park.

Some bike-tour operators circumvent this moratorium by staging their bicycle tours outside the park's boundaries. There are also a handful of companies that have "road-based" tour permits, which allows them to transport their clients within the park boundaries by van, but does not allow their clients to bike inside the park. This way you can still see the sunrise from Haleakala Crater, then you'll travel by van to the start of your bike tour, outside park boundaries.

The moratorium does not affect private citizens riding their bikes inside the park boundaries. For information on bikeways and maps, get a copy of the *Maui County Bicycle Map,* which has details on road suitability, climate, trade winds, mileage, elevation changes, bike shops, safety tips, and various bicycling routes. The map is available from **www.southmauibicycles.com;** click on the link to "Maui County Bicycle Map." A great book for mountain bikers who want to venture out on their own is John Alford's *Mountain Biking the Hawaiian Islands,* published by Ohana Publishing, 2010. Buy the book at www.bikehawaii.com.

Trips range from $70 to $115; bicycle rentals (from $35 a day) are also available if you'd like to tour other parts of Maui on your own.

Horseback Riding

Maui offers spectacular adventure rides through rugged ranch lands, into tropical forests, and to remote swimming holes. I recommend riding with **Mendes Ranch & Trail Rides ★**, 3530 Kahekili Hwy., Wailuku (© **808/244-7320;** www.mendesranch.com). The 300-acre Mendes Ranch is a real-life working cowboy ranch that has the essential elements of an earthly paradise—rainbows, waterfalls, palm trees, coral-sand beaches, lagoons, tide pools, a rainforest, and its own volcanic peak (more than a mile high). Allan Mendes, a third-generation wrangler, will take you from the edge of the rainforest out to the sea. On the way, you'll cross tree-studded meadows where Texas longhorns sit in the shade and pass a dusty corral. Allan keeps close watch, turning often in his saddle to make sure everyone is happy. He points out flora and fauna and fields questions, but generally just lets you soak up Maui's natural splendor in golden silence. A 2-hour morning or afternoon ride costs $110; add on a barbecue lunch at the corral for an additional $20.

Another one of my favorites is **Piiholo Ranch,** in Makawao (© **866/572-5544** or 808/357-5544; www.piiholo.com). A working cattle ranch owned by the *kamaaina* (longtime resident) Baldwin family, it offers horseback-riding adventures with a variety of options to suit your ability. Rates start at $120 for a 2-hour country ride through a working cattle ranch.

If you're out in Hana, don't pass up **Maui Horseback Tours at Maui Stables ★★**, a mile past Oheo Gulch between mile markers 40 and 41 in Kipahulu (© **808/248-7799;** www.mauistables.com). It offers a daily ride (9:45am–1:30pm) through the mountains above Kipahulu Valley—and you get a fantastic historical and cultural tour through the unspoiled landscape, to boot. It is an experience you will not forget. The ride is $160 ($150 if you book from their website). If you enjoy your ride, remember to kiss your horse and tip your guide.

For horse lovers looking for the ultimate, check out Frank Levinson's **Maui Horse Whisperer Experience** (© **808/572-6211;** www.mauihorses.com), which includes a seminar on the language of the horse. Prices are $200 for half-day and $300 for full-day workshops. No horse aficionado should pass it up.

HALEAKALA ON HORSEBACK   If you'd like to ride down into Haleakala's crater, contact **Pony Express Tours ★** (© **808/667-2200** or 878-6698; www.ponyexpresstours.com), which leads a variety of rides down to the crater floor and back up, from $182 per person. Shorter 1- and 2-hour rides are also offered at Haleakala Ranch, located on the beautiful lower slopes of the volcano, for $95 to $110. If you book via the website, you get 10% off. Pony

Maui offers spectacular adventure rides through ranch lands and tropical forests.

Express provides well-trained horses and experienced guides and accommodates all riding levels. You must be at least 10 years old, weigh no more than 230 pounds, and wear long pants and closed-toe shoes.

Spelunking

Don't miss the opportunity to see how the Hawaiian Islands were made by exploring a million-year-old underground lava tube/cave. Chuck Thorne, of **Hana Lava Tube ★** (**ℂ 808/248-7308;** www.mauicave.com), offers several tours of this unique geological feature. After more than 10 years of leading scuba tours through underwater caves around Hawaii, Chuck discovered some caves on land that he wanted to show visitors. When the land surrounding the largest cave on Maui went on the market in 1996, Chuck snapped it up and started his own tour company. Daily, between 10:30am and 4pm, you can take a self-guided 30- to 45-minute tour for just $12 (free for kids 5 and under).

If you want to combine caving with a tour of Hana, contact **Temptation Tours** (**ℂ 808/877-8888;** www.temptationtours.com). Its Cave Quest option costs $219, which covers a 1¼-hour cave tour, an air-conditioned van tour from your hotel to Hana, continental breakfast, a beachside picnic lunch, and a stop for a swim.

Tennis

Maui has excellent public tennis courts; all are free and available from daylight to sunset (a few are even lit for night play until 10pm). The courts are available on a first-come, first-served basis; when someone's waiting, limit your play to 45 minutes. For a complete list of public courts, call **Maui County Parks and Recreation** (**ℂ 808/270-7383;** www.co.maui.hi.us/facilities.aspx). Because most public courts require a wait and are not conveniently located near the major resort areas, most visitors are likely to pay a fee to play at their own hotels. The exceptions to this are in Kihei (which has courts in Kalama Park on South Kihei Rd., and in Waipualani Park on West Waipualani Rd., behind the Maui Sunset condo), in Lahaina (which has courts in Malu'uou o lele Park, at Front and Shaw sts.), and in Hana (which has courts in Hana Park, on the Hana Hwy.).

Private tennis courts are available at most resorts and hotels on the island. The **Kapalua Tennis Garden and Village Tennis Center,** Kapalua Resort (**ℂ 808/662-7730;** www.kapaluamaui.com), is home to the Kapalua Open, which features the largest purse in the state, on Labor Day weekend. Court rentals are $10 per person before noon and $8 per person after noon. The staff will match you up with a partner if you need one. In Wailea, try the **Wailea Tennis Club,** 131 Wailea Iki Place (**ℂ 808/879-1958;** www.waileatennis.com), with 11 Plexipave courts. Court fees are $15 per player.

6

WHERE TO EAT

With soaring visitor statistics and a glamorous image, the Valley Isle is fertile ground not only for an international name or two (Wolfgang Puck of Spago) but also for Hawaii's famous enterprising chefs, such as Roy Yamaguchi of Roy's; Gerard Reversade of Gerard's; James McDonald of I'O and Pacific'O; Peter Merriman of Peter Merriman Kapalua; Mark Elman of Maui Tacos, Mala Ocean Tavern, and Mala Wailea; D. K. Kodama of Sansei Seafood Restaurant; and Beverly Gannon of Haliimaile General Store, Joe's, and Gannon's. There are also a few newcomers who are cooking up a storm and getting a well-deserved following, including Ryan Luckey of Pineapple Grill, Dana Pastula of the Cafe O'Lei restaurants, and Don Ritchey of Moana Bakery & Cafe.

In this dizzying scenario, some things haven't changed: You can still dine well at Lahaina's open-air waterfront watering holes, where the view counts for 50% of the experience. There are still budget eateries, but not many; Maui's old-fashioned, multigenerational mom-and-pop diners are disappearing, eclipsed by the flashy newcomers, or clinging to the edge of existence in the older neighborhoods of central Maui, such as lovable Wailuku. Although you'll have to work harder to find them in the resort areas, you won't have to go far to find creative cuisine, pleasing style, and stellar dining experiences.

Reservations are not necessary unless otherwise noted in the reviews below.

BEST RESTAURANT BETS

- **Best Bang for Your Buck:** With locations all over the island, **Maui Tacos** (p. 210) delivers gourmet Mexican on paper plates at affordable prices. Barely more than a takeout counter with a few tables, this Hawaii chain is popular with hungry surfers, discerning diners, burrito buffs, and Hollywood glitterati. Another great "value" venue is **A. K.'s Café** (p. 198), hidden in the industrial district of Wailuku. It may be slightly off the tourist path, but the creative cuisine coming out of the kitchen makes it well worth the effort to find this delicious eatery. Prices are so eye-poppingly cheap, you might find yourself wandering back here during your vacation.

- **Best for Families:** If you are coming with kids, they will love **Cheeseburger in Paradise** (p. 204), located on the water in Lahaina. Prices are family-friendly and the food is great! For a little more upscale dinner, make reservations for sunset at **Gannon's** (p. 219), overlooking the ocean and the island of Kahoolawe from its perch in the Wailea Golf Course. Mom and dad will love award-winning chef Bev Gannon's creative American home cooking with a Hawaiian twist, and the kids will love the Keiki (kids') menu.

PREVIOUS PAGE: **Grilled seafood is popular islandwide.**

PRICE CATEGORIES

The restaurant reviews below are listed according to geographic areas and pricing. Pricing is based on the cost of the majority of the entrees (generally a dinner entree, unless noted).

Very Expensive	$45 and up
Expensive	$30–$45
Moderate	$15–$30
Inexpensive	under $20

○ **Most Hawaiian Atmosphere:** Nothing can match the Hawaiian decor of **Duke's Beach House** (p. 207), perched on the side of the ocean, facing the beautiful Kaanapali Beach and housed in what appears to be an open-air plantation home. In addition to the fabulous beachfront location and great decor, the food is fabulous.

○ **Best Luau:** Maui's best choice is indisputably the nightly **Old Lahaina Luau** (p. 247), on its 1-acre site just oceanside of the Lahaina Cannery. There's no fire dancing in the program, but you won't miss it. For that, go to the **Feast at Lele** (p. 199), where dances from Hawaii, New Zealand, Tahiti, and Samoa are presented, up close and personal, in full-costumed splendor.

○ **Best Splurge:** For that "special" night out on your vacation, go to **Ko** (p. 217), nestled in Wailea's Fairmont Kea Lani. This open-air restaurant features various ethnic cuisines from Maui's old plantation days (Hawaiian, Filipino, Portuguese, Korean, Puerto Rican, and European) cooked up in a gourmet fashion. At the other end of the island, overlooking the Kapalua Golf Course, the **Pineapple Grill** (p. 212) offers creative Pacific Regional Cuisine with items ranging from ahi steak crusted with pistachios and wasabi peas to a paella.

○ **Most Romantic:** On a point jetting out into the ocean, overlooking Kapalua Bay on one side and the island of Molokai in the distance, well-known local chef Peter Merriman, who is a James Beard award winner, opened **Merriman's** restaurant (p. 212) in 2008. For a romantic evening, book your reservation for sunset to really experience this incredible vista. If sunset tables are booked, come for sunset anyway and sit on the large open-air patio and enjoy a cocktail and an appetizer. Another romantic venue, located just down the highway in Kaanapali's Hyatt Regency Maui, is **Son'z Maui at Swan Court** (p. 205), which overlooks a man-made lagoon and the rolling surf of the Pacific in the distance, and has to be one of the most romantic experiences you will get.

○ **Best Service:** As you would expect, the service at the Ritz-Carlton Kapalua's **The Banyan Tree** (p. 212) is outstanding, matching the high quality of the food and the romantic atmosphere (with a view of the ocean and the island of Molokai in the distance—be sure to get reservations for sunset). At the other end of the island, in the Wailea Resort, **Nick's Fishmarket Maui** (p. 218) also features top-notch service, matching the level of their cuisine. You won't be disappointed, from the moment you step onto the open-air terrace overlooking Maui's south shore, to the last bit of dessert. Service is professional and prompt, but not cloying.

○ **Best Brunch:** You won't forget your brunch at **Mala Ocean Tavern** (p. 202). Hanging over the ocean, this tiny "tavern" offers healthy, organically grown food and fresh fish. Brunch is very popular; make reservations and try the "killer" French toast. For a more traditional buffet brunch try **Tiki Terrace Restaurant** (p. 208) at the Kaanapali Beach Hotel. Their Hawaiian Sunday Champagne Brunch features more than 50 items on the buffet, plus stir-fry, carving, and omelet stations, along with Belgian waffles and great desserts, all accompanied by Hawaiian music.

○ **Most Trendy:** Maui Chef D.K. Kodama's two restaurants top the list of Maui's most trendy. **Cane & Taro** (p. 207), located ocean side of the Whalers Shopping Center in the Kaanapali Resort, features an eclectic menu ranging from shrimp dynamite (crispy tempura rock shrimp with a *masago* aioli and *unagi* glaze) to Kona coffee baby back ribs. His other "trendy" place is his first Maui restaurant, in the Kapalua Resort, **Sansei Seafood Restaurant & Sushi Bar** (p. 213), where he offers an extensive menu of Japanese and East-West delicacies that are part fusion, part Hawaii Regional Cuisine. Desserts are not to be missed.

family-FRIENDLY RESTAURANTS

You don't have to mortgage the kids' college fund, nor do you have to survive on peanut-butter-and-jelly sandwiches to keep the kids happy during your Maui vacation. Below is a list of restaurants that actually cater to families. Not just with kids' menus, but with a real appreciation and understanding of what kids want to eat and how to make them happy while on Maui.

Charley's Restaurant Located in Paia, on the road to Hana, this is a great place to stop for breakfast or lunch. The staff bends over backward to make your little one happy. See p. 223.

Cheeseburger in Paradise The kids will love the burgers, you'll love the ocean view, everyone will be happy (for a few minutes). See p. 204.

Cilantro: Fresh Mexican Grill Take the kids to this fresh-food takeout where fabulous Mexican food is served at frugal prices. See p. 204.

CJ's Deli & Diner You can eat in, take out, or even arrange for your own personal chef at this Kaanapali diner where the kids' menu is even cheaper than the already budget-priced menu. See p. 209.

Lahaina Coolers Breakfast, lunch, and dinner at this outdoor restaurant feature burgers, sandwiches, and pastas that kids adore. See p. 204.

Maui Tacos You'll get good food at great prices at this take-out restaurant with several branches all over the island. See p. 210.

Nikki's Pizza Pizzas, pasta, and desserts: Nikki's gives you everything kids love in a casual atmosphere at the Whaler's Village in the Kaanapali Resort. See p. 209.

Peggy Sue's This 1950s diner will thrill the kids, and the burgers and fries will fill them up. See p. 216.

Shaka Sandwich & Pizza If you are staying in South Maui, this Kihei pizzeria (with sandwiches) is the perfect solution for cranky, hungry kids. See p. 216.

o **Off the Beaten Path:** Real foodies will happily make the drive to these two noteworthy restaurants for the sheer pleasure of their outstanding cuisine. Chef Bev Gannon, one of the original Hawaii Regional Cuisine chefs, has been going strong at her well-known **Haliimaile General Store** (p. 220). The food, a blend of eclectic American with ethnic touches, puts an innovative spin on Hawaii Regional Cuisine. **Market Fresh Bistro** (p. 220), located in Makawao, is a long drive from a resort area, but Chef Justin Pardo (formerly of the Union Square Café in New York City and the Wailea Grand on Maui) is a culinary genius who uses 90% local products. The menu changes daily.

PLATE LUNCHES & MORE: LOCAL FOOD

Hawaii has a classification of food seen nowhere else on the planet. I affectionately call it "local food." By that, I mean plate lunches and poke, shave ice and saimin, bento lunches and *manapua*—cultural hybrids all.

Reflecting a polyglot population of many styles and ethnicities, Hawaii's idiosyncratic dining scene is eminently inclusive. Consider surfer chic: Barefoot in the sand, in a swimsuit, you chow down on a **plate lunch** ordered from a lunch wagon, consisting of fried mahimahi (or teriyaki beef or shoyu chicken), "two scoops rice," macaroni salad, and a few leaves of green, typically julienned cabbage. Heavy gravy is often the condiment of choice, accompanied by a soft drink in a paper cup or straight out of the can. Like **saimin**—the local version of noodles in broth topped with scrambled eggs, green onions, and sometimes pork—the plate lunch is Hawaii's version of high camp.

But it was only a matter of time before the humble plate lunch became a culinary icon in Hawaii. These days, even the most chichi restaurant has a version of this modest island symbol (not at plate-lunch prices, of course), while vendors selling the real thing—carb-driven meals served from wagons—have queues that never end.

Because this is Hawaii, at least a few licks of poi—cooked, pounded taro (the traditional Hawaiian staple crop)—are a must. Other **native foods** include those from before and after Western contact, such as laulau (pork, chicken, or fish steamed in ti leaves), kalua pork (pork cooked in a Polynesian underground oven known here as an *imu*), lomi salmon (salted salmon with tomatoes and green onions), squid luau (cooked in coconut milk and taro tops), poke (cubed raw fish seasoned with onions and seaweed and the occasional sprinkling of roasted *kukui* nuts), haupia (creamy coconut pudding), and *kulolo* (steamed pudding of coconut, brown sugar, and taro).

Bento, another popular quick meal available throughout Hawaii, is a compact, boxed assortment of picnic fare usually consisting of neatly arranged sections of rice, pickled vegetables, and fried chicken, beef, or pork. Increasingly, however, the bento is becoming more health-conscious, as in macrobiotic or vegetarian brown rice bentos. A derivative of the modest box lunch for Japanese immigrants who once labored in the sugar and pineapple fields, bentos are dispensed everywhere, from department stores to corner delis and supermarkets.

Also from the plantations comes *manapua,* a bready, doughy sphere filled with tasty fillings of sweetened pork or sweet beans. In the old days, the

Chinese *"manapua* man" would make his rounds with bamboo containers balanced on a rod over his shoulders. Today you'll find white or whole-wheat *manapua* containing chicken, vegetables, curry, and other savory fillings.

The daintier Chinese delicacy **dim sum** is made of translucent wrappers filled with fresh seafood, pork hash, and vegetables, served for breakfast and lunch in Chinese restaurants. The Hong Kong–style dumplings are ordered fresh and hot from bamboo steamers rolled on carts from table to table. Much like hailing a taxi in Manhattan, you have to be quick and loud for dim sum.

For dessert or a snack, the prevailing choice is **shave ice,** Hawaii's version of a snow cone. Particularly on hot, humid days, long lines of shave-ice lovers gather for heaps of finely shaved ice topped with sweet tropical syrups. (The sweet-sour *li hing mui* flavor is a current favorite.) The fast-melting mounds, which require prompt, efficient consumption, are quite the local summer ritual for sweet tooths. Aficionados order shave ice with ice cream and sweetened adzuki beans plopped in the middle.

CENTRAL MAUI

Kahului and Wailuku is where the majority of Maui's resident population lives. So this is the area catering to the locals. Restaurants here are generally cheaper than in resort areas and offer more ethnic foods. Deals can be had here and you also get to see a slice of life on how local people live and eat.

Kahului

MODERATE

Bistro Casanova ★ 👤 MEDITERRANEAN   This cosmopolitan bistro in the heart of Kahului serves tapas, pastas, steaks, and seafood for lunch and dinner. The space—located in a Kahului office complex formerly housing the restaurant the Manana Garage—has been totally renovated and now sports a nautical theme (everything is blue) with a great outdoor dining area. Packed with a business crowd at lunch and a more relaxed atmosphere at dinner (when mainly local residents dine), Bistro Casanova has some interesting items, such as sweet and savory crepes, quinoa salads, and Maui-raised beef, in addition to traditional Italian pastas, a tasty *osso buco,* and fresh fish.

33 Lono Ave., Kahului. www.casanovamaui.com. ✆ **808/873-3650.** Main courses $9–$18 lunch, $14–$38 dinner. AE, DISC, MC, V. Mon–Sat 11am–9:30pm.

Ichiban 👤 JAPANESE/SUSHI   What a find: an informal neighborhood restaurant that serves inexpensive, home-cooked Japanese food *and* good sushi at realistic prices. Local residents consider Ichiban a staple for breakfast, lunch, or dinner and a haven of comforts: egg-white omelets; great saimin; combination plates of teriyaki chicken, teriyaki meat, *tonkatsu* (pork cutlet), rice, and pickled cabbage; chicken yakitori; and sushi—everything from *unagi* and scallop to California roll. The sushi items may not be cheap, but like the specials, such as steamed opakapaka, they're a good value. I love the tempura, miso soup, and spicy ahi hand roll.

At the Kahului Shopping Center, 47 Kaahumanu Ave., Kahului. ℂ **808/871-6977.** Main courses $7–$9 breakfast, $10–$13 lunch, $10–$35 dinner; combination plates $17 lunch, $13 dinner; dinner specials from $12. AE, DC, MC, V. Mon–Fri 7am–2pm and 5–9pm; Sat 10:30am–2pm and 5–9pm. Closed 1–2 weeks around Christmas and New Year's.

Marco's Grill & Deli ITALIAN   Located in the thick of central Maui, where the roads to upcountry, west, and south Maui converge, Marco's is popular among area residents for its homemade Italian fare and friendly informality. Everything—from the meatballs, sausages, and burgers to the sauces, salad dressings, and raviolis—is made in-house. The 35 choices of hot and cold sandwiches and entrees are served all day; some favorites include vodka rigatoni with imported prosciutto and simple pasta with marinara sauce. The antipasto salad and roasted peppers are taste treats, but the meatballs and Italian sausage are famous in central Maui. This is one of those comfortable neighborhood fixtures favored by all generations. It also has a full bar.

At the Dairy Center, 444 Hana Hwy., Kahului. ℂ **808/877-4446.** Main courses $12–$39. AE, DISC, MC, V. Daily 7:30am–10pm (Sat–Sun till 1am).

INEXPENSIVE

The **Queen Kaahumanu Center** (www.queenkaahumanucenter.com)—the structure that looks like a white *Star Wars* umbrella in Kahului at 275 Kaahumanu Ave. (a 10-min. drive from Kahului Airport on Hwy. 32)—has a very popular food court. Favorites include **Ramen Ya** for a steaming bowl of noodles, and **Panda Express,** which serves tasty Chinese food. Outside of the food court, but still in the shopping center, are **Ruby's,** dishing out burgers, fries, and shakes; and **Starbucks.** There's also a branch of **Maui Tacos** (p. 223). When you leave Kaahumanu Center, take a moment to gaze at the West Maui Mountains to your left from the parking lot.

Down to Earth 🍃 HEALTH FOOD   If you are looking for a healthy alternative to fast food, here's your place. Healthful organic ingredients, 90% vegan, appear in scrumptious salads, lasagna, chili, curries, and dozens of tasty dishes, presented at hot and cold self-serve stations. Stools line the counters in the simple dining area, where a few tables are available for those who don't want takeout. The food is great: millet cakes, mock tofu chicken, curried tofu, and Greek salad, nearly everything organic and tasty, with herb-tamari marinades and pleasing condiments such as currants or raisins, apples, and cashews. (The fabulous tofu curry has apples, raw cashews, and raisins.) The food is sold by the pound, but you can buy a hearty, wholesome plate for $7.

305 Dairy Rd., Kahului. www.downtoearth.org. ℂ **808/877-2661.** Sandwiches $5–$8; plates by the pound usually around $7–$10. AE, MC, V. Mon–Sat 7am–7:45pm; Sun 8am–6pm (store hours Mon–Sat 7am–9pm; Sun 8am–8pm).

Restaurant Matsu JAPANESE/HAWAIIAN   Customers have come from Hana (more than 50 miles away) just for Matsu's California rolls, while regulars line up for the cold saimin (julienned cucumber, egg, Chinese-style sweet pork, and red ginger on noodles) and for the bento plates (various assemblages of chicken, teriyaki beef, fish, and rice). The *nigiri* sushi items are popular, especially among the don't-dally lunch crowd. The *katsu* pork and chicken, breaded

ROSELANI: MAUI'S best ICE CREAM

For the culinary highlight of your trip to Maui, try **Roselani Ice Cream,** Maui's only made-from-scratch, old-fashioned ice cream. In fact, be sure to try it early in your trip so you can eat your way through this little bit of heaven at restaurants and scooping parlors, or get your own stash at grocery stores. There are more than 40 flavors, divided into two brands under the Roselani label: the Premium Parlour Flavors (ranging from the traditional vanilla to the unique black cherry, cappuccino chip, fresh-brewed coffee, and choco-cookie crunch) and the Tropics (with delicious varieties like the best-selling haupia, made from coconut and macadamia nut, or the popular chocolate macadamia nut, Kona mud pie, mango and cream, coconut pineapple, and luau fudge pie). Each rich, creamy flavor contains 12% to 16% butterfat. For a list of hotels, restaurants, ice-cream parlors, and grocery stores that carry Roselani, either call Roselani Ice Cream at ✆ **808/244-4108** or check online at www.roselani.com.

and deep fried, are other specialties of this casual Formica-style diner. I love the tempura *udon,* steaming mounds of wide noodles swimming in homemade broths and topped with condiments. The daily specials are a changing lineup of home-cooked classics: oxtail soup, roast pork with gravy, teriyaki ahi, miso butterfish, and breaded mahimahi.

161 Alamaha St., Kahului. ✆ **808/871-0822.** Most items under $14. DISC, MC, V. Mon–Fri 9am–3pm and 5–8pm; Sat–Sun 9:30am–2pm.

Wailuku

MODERATE

Class Act ★ 🎁 INTERNATIONAL   Part of a program run by the distinguished Food Service Department of Maui Community College, now housed in a state-of-the-art culinary facility (with floor-to-ceiling windows at one end and an exhibition kitchen at the other end), Class Act is a "classroom" restaurant with a huge following. Student chefs show their stuff with a flourish and pull out all the stops to give you a dining experience you will long remember. The appetizer, soup, salad, and dessert are set, but you can choose between the regular entrees and a heart-healthy main course prepared in the culinary tradition of the week. The menu roams the globe, with highlights of Italy, Mexico, Maui, Napa Valley, France, and New Orleans. The filet mignon of French Week is popular, as are the New Orleans gumbo and Cajun shrimp, the sesame-crusted mahimahi on taro-leaf pasta, the polenta flan with eggplant, and the bean and green-chile *chilaquile.*

At Maui Community College, 310 Kaahumanu Ave., Wailuku. http://mauiculinary-campusdining.com/dining/classact.html. ✆ **808/984-3280.** Reservations recommended. 4-course lunch $30. MC, V. Wed and Fri 11am–12:30pm (last seating). Closed June–Aug and parts of Dec and Jan.

A Saigon Cafe ★★ 🛍 VIETNAMESE   Fans drive from all over the island for owner/chef Jennifer Nguyen's crisp spiced Dungeness crab, steamed opakapaka (a Hawaiian fish that feeds on lobster) with ginger and garlic, and wok-cooked Vietnamese specials tangy with spices, herbs, and lemongrass. There are a dozen different soups, cold and hot noodles (including the popular beef noodle soup called pho), and chicken and shrimp cooked in a clay pot. You can create your own Vietnamese "burritos" from a platter of tofu, noodles, and vegetables that you wrap in rice paper and dip in garlic sauce. Among my favorites are the shrimp lemon grass, savory and refreshing, and the tofu curry, swimming in herbs and vegetables straight from the garden. The *Nhung Dam*—a hearty spread of basil, cucumbers, mint, romaine, bean sprouts, pickled carrots, turnips, and vermicelli, wrapped in rice paper and dipped in a legendary sauce—is cooked at your table.

1792 Main St., Wailuku. ℂ **808/243-9560.** Main courses $9–$27. MC, V. Mon–Sat 10am–9:30pm; Sun 10am–8:30pm. Heading into Wailuku from Kahului, go over the bridge and take the 1st right onto Central Ave.; then take the 1st right on Nani St. At the next stop sign, look for the building with the neon sign that says OPEN.

INEXPENSIVE

A. K.'s Café ★★ 🍴 HEALTH FOOD/HAWAIIAN   Chef Elaine Rothermel has a winner with this tiny cafe in the industrial district of Wailuku. It may be slightly off the tourist path, but the creative cuisine coming out of the kitchen makes it well worth the effort to find this delicious eatery. Prices are so eye-poppingly cheap, you might find yourself wandering back here during your vacation. The menu features everything from hamburger steak to blackened ono with mango sauce. Dinner specials include pot roast with mushroom gravy, crab cakes with papaya beurre blanc, or sometimes a tofu Napoleon with ginger-basil sauce or Hunan lamb chops. There are plenty of heart-healthy options to choose from.

1237 Lower Main St., Wailuku. www.akscafe.com. ℂ **808/244-8774.** Main courses $8–$18. MC, V. Mon–Fri 11am–1:30pm and 5–8:30pm. Live Hawaiian music Fri nights.

Main Street Bistro 🍴 AMERICAN   Formerly Who's the Boss restaurant and, before that, Iao Café, this popular eatery, located on the main street of Wailuku, is now owned by Chef Tom Selman, well-known in culinary circles on Maui. Main Street Bistro is open for lunch, and a *pau hana* (after-work) menu (offered 3–7pm) includes tapas like crispy crab and shrimp *gau gee,* mini hamburgers, and barbecued ribs. He calls his cuisine "refined comfort food," with signature items that include onion rings with house-made smoky ketchup, roasted Chinese chicken salad, "Mother's Roast Beef Sandwich" (served open-faced on a French roll), Southern-fried chicken, Maryland-style crab cake, and a roasted-veggie sandwich. The chef will happily customize any menu item for those who prefer low-calorie, low-fat, or low-carbohydrate options. Daily specials range from grilled steak to Asian risotto with shrimp, crab, and veggies. Live music is offered Friday evenings.

2051 Main St., Wailuku. www.msbmaui.com. ℂ **808/244-6816.** Main courses $7–$14 lunch, tapas $5–$23; daily specials $8–$17. MC, V. Mon–Fri 11am–7pm. Live music 1st Fri of the month.

Sam Sato's NOODLES/PLATE LUNCH   Sam Sato's is a Maui institution, not only for its noodles (saimin, dry noodles, chow fun), but also for its flaky baked *manju,* a pastry filled with sweetened lima beans or adzuki beans. Sam opened his family eatery in 1933, and his daughter, Lynne Toma, makes the broth from scratch. The noodles, with broth that comes in a separate bowl, are big sellers. Eat at the counter, with well-worn wooden stools and homemade salt and pepper shakers. Try the plate lunch with two barbecued meat sticks, two scoops of rice, and macaroni salad. The peach, apple, coconut, and pineapple turnovers fly out the door, as do takeout noodles. *Tip:* If you want them to hold the MSG, be sure to make your request early.

At the Millyard, 1750 Wili Pa Loop, Wailuku. ℂ **808/244-7124.** Plate lunches $7.50–$9. No credit cards. Mon–Sat 7am–2pm. Bakery and preordered takeout items 7am–4pm.

WEST MAUI

The West and South Coasts of Maui are where most of the island's visitors stay, so these oceanside communities offer a range of restaurants, from Maui's well-known chefs to small mom-and-pop cafes. You will find eateries with romantic atmosphere, breathtaking views, and yummy food. You will also find an increase in prices.

Lahaina

There's a **Maui Tacos** (p. 223) in Lahaina Square (ℂ **808/661-8883**). Maui's branch of the **Hard Rock Cafe** is at 900 Front St., in Lahaina (ℂ **808/667-7400**).

VERY EXPENSIVE

The Feast at Lele ★★ POLYNESIAN   The owners of the **Old Lahaina Luau** (p. 247) have recruited the culinary prowess of chef James McDonald (I'O and Pacific'O), found the perfect outdoor oceanfront setting, and added the exquisite dancers of the Old Lahaina Luau. The result: a culinary and cultural experience that sizzles. As if the sunset weren't heady enough, dances from Hawaii, New Zealand, Tahiti, and Samoa are presented, up close and personal, in full-costumed splendor. Chanting, singing, drumming, dancing, the swish of ti-leaf skirts, the scent of plumeria—it's an adventure, even for the most jaded luau aficionado. Guests sit at white-clothed, candlelit tables set on the sand (unlike the luau, where seating is en masse) and dine on entrees: *imu*-roasted kalua pig and island fish with mango sauce from Hawaii, or Maori fishcake. Particularly mesmerizing is the evening's opening: A softly lit canoe carries three people ashore to the sound of conch shells.

505 Front St., Lahaina. www.feastatlele.com. ℂ **866/244-5353** or 808/667-5353. Reservations required. Set 5-course menu (including all beverages) $112 adults, $82 children 2–12. AE, DISC, MC, V. Apr–Sept daily 6:30–9:30pm; Oct–Mar daily 5:30–8:30pm.

Lahaina Grill ★★ AMERICAN   Despite Chef David Paul Johnson's departure, this Lahaina hot spot has maintained its popularity. It's still filled with chic, tanned diners in stylish aloha shirts, and there's still attitude aplenty at the entrance. The signature items remain: tequila shrimp and firecracker rice, Kona coffee–roasted rack of lamb, Maui onion–crusted seared ahi, and Pommery mustard–crusted veal chop. A custom-designed chef's table can be arranged with 72 hours' notice for larger parties. The ambience—black-and-white tile floors, pressed-tin ceilings, eclectic 1890s decor—is striking, and the bar, despite not having an ocean view, is the busiest spot in Lahaina.

127 Lahainaluna Rd., Lahaina. www.lahainagrill.com. ℂ **808/667-5117.** Reservations required. Main courses $40–$60. AE, DC, DISC, MC, V. Daily 6–9 or 10pm. Bar daily 6–10pm (earlier if it's slow).

EXPENSIVE

David Paul's Island Grill ★★ HAWAII REGIONAL   One of Hawaii's top chefs, David Paul, opened yet another restaurant in Lahaina in 2008 introducing his "new island cooking," a combination of his latest American cuisine and island products—such as slow-braised roasts, seared fresh fish, macadamia nut–smoked and fire-grilled meals, brick-pressed chicken, and olive oil–poached Keahole lobster. Although his menu changes weekly, my picks are the roasted island snapper with sautéed upcountry field greens and house-cured pork shoulder; the pot roast scented with five Chinese spices; and the grilled pork chops with shiitake reduction and lobster cream. Chef David has an exhibit kitchen, so you can watch all the action. The Sky Lounge has tapas, cocktails, and wines by the glass, starting at $8.

At Lahaina Center, 900 Front St., Ste. A-101, Lahaina. www.davidpaulsislandgrill.com. ✆ **808/ 662-3000.** Main courses $29–$40; tasting menu $150, $225 with wine pairings. AE, DC, DISC, MC, V. Restaurant daily 5:30–9:30pm. Lounge daily 5pm–midnight.

Gerard's ★★★ 🎁 FRENCH   The charm of Gerard's—soft lighting, excellent service, Edith Piaf on the sound system—is matched by a menu of uncompromising standards. After more than 3 decades in Lahaina, Gerard Reversade never runs out of creative offerings, yet stays true to his French roots. Roasted opakapaka with star anise, fennel fondue, and hints of orange and ginger is a stellar entree on a menu of winners. Quail pie with foie gras promises ecstasy, and the spinach salad with scallops is among the finest I've tasted. Gerard's has an excellent appetizer menu, with oyster mushrooms and prosciutto ham in puff pastry, fresh ahi and smoked salmon carpaccio, and a very rich, highly touted escargot ragout with burgundy butter and garlic cream. The restaurant is a frequent winner of the Wine Spectator Award of Excellence.

At the Plantation Inn, 174 Lahainaluna Rd., Lahaina. www.gerardsmaui.com. ✆ **808/661-8939.** Reservations recommended. Main courses $36–$56. AE, DC, DISC, MC, V. Daily 6–9pm.

I'O ★ PACIFIC RIM   I'O is a fantasy of sleek curves and etched glass, co-owned by chef James McDonald. He offers an impressive selection of appetizers (his strong suit) and some lavish Asian-Polynesian interpretations of seafood, such as his "Rainbow catch"—fresh fish of the day topped with lemon grass pesto, tomatoes, truffle oil, and goat-cheese fondue sauce—or his "scallops ala bondage"—scallops wrapped in sage and jalapeño bacon, served with roasted Japanese eggplant and a ponzu-cream sauce. McDonald also owns **Pacific'O Restaurant** (reviewed below) and is the chef for **Feast at Lele** (reviewed above).

🎁 The Ultimate Cookies

Looking for the ultimate taste treat to take to the folks back home? Try mouth-watering **Broke da Mouth Cookies,** 190 Alamaha St., Kahului (✆ **808/873-9255**), open Monday through Friday from 6am to 7:30pm and Saturday from 7am to 5pm (get here early before the locals buy everything up). These terrific cookies range from chocolate mac-nut, oatmeal raisin, and shortbread to almond, peanut butter, and coconut crunch. While you're here, take a look at the other goodies—the sweet potato–haupia pie is to die for, and the *lilikoi* (passion fruit) cake will make your taste buds stand up and applaud.

Restaurants in Lahaina & Kaanapali

505 Front St., Lahaina. www.iomaui.com. ℂ **808/661-8422.** Reservations recommended. Main courses $34–$44. AE, DC, MC, V. Daily 5:30–10pm.

Pacific'O Restaurant ★ PACIFIC RIM   You can't get any closer to the ocean than the tables here, which are literally on the beach. With good food complementing this sensational setting, both foodies and aesthetes have much to enjoy. The split-level dining starts near the entrance, with a long bar (where you can also order lunch or dinner) and a few tables along the railing. Steps lead down to the outdoor tables, where the award-winning seafood dishes come to you with the backdrop of Lanai across the channel. Favorites include the fresh island catch crusted in Indian spices topped with a warm avocado and Maui onion salsa, or the *hapa hapa* tempura with white miso dressing and lime basil sauce. If you like seafood, sunsets, and touches of India and Indonesia in your fresh-from-the-sea dining choices, you will be happy here.

505 Front St., Lahaina. www.pacificomaui.com. ℂ **808/667-4341.** Reservations recommended. Main courses $13–$16 lunch, $30–$40 dinner. AE, MC, V. Daily 11:30am–4pm and 5:30–9:30pm.

MODERATE

Kimo's STEAK/SEAFOOD   Kimo's has a loyal following that keeps it from falling into the faceless morass of waterfront restaurants serving surf and turf with great sunset views. It's a formula restaurant that works not only because of its oceanfront patio and upstairs dining room, but also because, for the price, there are some satisfying choices. It's always crowded, buzzing with people on a deck offering views of Molokai, Lanai, and Kahoolawe. Burgers and sandwiches are affordable and consistent, and the fresh catch in an orange-ginger glaze is a top seller. The waistline-defying hula pie—macadamia nut ice cream in a chocolate-wafer crust with fudge and whipped cream—originated here.

845 Front St., Lahaina. www.kimosmaui.com. ℂ **808/661-4811.** Reservations recommended for dinner. Main courses $11–$16 lunch, $23–$36 dinner. AE, DC, DISC, MC, V. Restaurant daily 11am–3:30pm and 5–10pm. Bar daily 11am–midnight.

Lahaina Fish Company SEAFOOD   The open-air dining room is literally over the water, with flickering torches after sunset and an affordable menu that covers the seafood-pasta basics. Head to an oceanside table and order a cheeseburger, turkey burger, ahi sandwich, generous basket of peel-and-eat shrimp, or sashimi—lingering is highly recommended. The light lunch/grill menu offers appetizers (sashimi, seared ahi, spring rolls, and pot stickers), salads, sandwiches, and soups. The restaurant has spiffed up its dinner selections to include hand-carved steaks, several pasta choices, and local fare, such as stir-fry dishes, teriyaki chicken, and luau-style ribs. The specialty, though, remains the fresh seafood: Four types of fresh fish are offered nightly, in three preparations. Pacific Rim specials include fresh ahi, seared spicy or cooked in a sweet ginger-soy sauce.

831 Front St., Lahaina. www.lahainafishcompany.com. ℂ **808/661-3472.** Main courses $10–$17 lunch, $16–$36 dinner. AE, MC, V. Daily 11am–9:30pm.

Mala Ocean Tavern ★★ ✦ SEAFOOD   Perched right on the ocean, this tiny "tavern" is the brainchild of Mark and Judy Ellman, owners of **Maui Tacos** (p. 205) and **Penne Pasta Café** (p. 223). They use healthy, organically grown food and fresh fish to make intriguing dishes. The atmosphere could not be more enticing, with just a handful of tables out on the oceanfront lanai and several more tables in the warmly decorated interior. The staff is helpful and efficient, and the food is outstanding. If you're in the mood, ask for the exotic martini menu. You can opt for "tavern food" like an ahi burger or a cheeseburger, one of the tempting salads (the beet and Kula goat cheese is divine), or something off the "big plate" menu (like wok-fried fresh catch or hoisin-glazed baby back ribs). Don't miss the weekend brunches (I recommend the "killer" French toast). This is a popular place, so try to avoid prime lunch and dinner hours.

1307 Front St. (across from the Lahaina Cannery Mall's Safeway grocery store), Lahaina. www. malaoceantavern.com. ©️ **808/667-9394.** Main courses $15–$26 lunch, $18–$43 dinner; $8–$16 brunch. AE, DISC, MC, V. Mon–Fri 11am–9:30pm; Sat 9am–9pm; Sun 4:30–9pm.

INEXPENSIVE

Aloha Mixed Plate ★ 🍴 PLATE LUNCH   Look for the festive turquoise-and-yellow, plantation-style front with the red corrugated-iron roof and adorable bar directly across from the Lahaina Cannery Mall. Grab a picnic table at ocean's edge, in the shade of large kiawe and milo trees, where you can watch the bobbing sailboats and the two islands on the near horizon. (On the upper level, there are umbrellas and plumeria trees—just as charming.) Then tuck into inexpensive

🎁 EAT LIKE A local

Are you the type of visitor who feels you haven't "experienced" a destination unless you've hit the restaurants where the local residents eat? Do you enjoy National Public Radio's *Road Food,* or any of the Food Network's on-the-road culinary shows? Then sign up for **Tour da Food ★★★** (©️ **808/242-8383;** www. tourdafood.com). Pastry chef (and food writer, restaurant publicist, and cookbook author) Bonnie Friedman takes foodies off the tourist path to discover the

culinary treasures—from snack shacks to restaurants to markets and manufacturers—that make up Maui's unique cuisine. You will laugh your way across the island with Bonnie's wonderful commentary about Maui's multicultural food options and its colorful history—and you'll also eat some of the island's most yummy food (which you never would have discovered on your own). Check out her website to read about the different tours (from breakfast at an old inn to "lunch like a local"); prices begin at $280 per couple, which includes transportation, a main meal, snacks, an island traditional dessert, a bag of goodies to take home, and Bonnie's personal list of under-the-radar eating places. *Tip:* Book this tour early in your trip, so you have time to follow Bonnie's terrific suggestions of places to eat on Maui. (Best to book at least 1 week in advance.) Bonnie's latest great idea is a personal restaurant guide, created from your food preferences (after you complete an online questionnaire), of 20 Maui restaurants for only $10!

breakfast, lunch, or dinner, featuring "local style" menu items like mahimahi, kalua pig and cabbage, shoyu chicken, teriyaki beef, and other plate-lunch specials, all at budget-friendly prices, served with macaroni salad and rice. The shoyu chicken is the best I've had, fork tender and tasty, and the spicy chicken drumettes come from a fabled family recipe. (The bestsellers are the coconut prawns and the Aloha Mixed Plate of shoyu chicken, teriyaki beef, and mahimahi.) I don't know of anywhere else where you can order a mai tai with a plate lunch and enjoy table service with an ocean view.

1285 Front St., Lahaina. www.alohamixedplate.com. © **808/661-3322.** Main courses breakfast $8–$12, lunch and dinner $6–$14. MC, V. Daily 8am–10pm.

Cheeseburger in Paradise ☺ AMERICAN   Wildly successful, always crowded, highly visible, and very noisy (especially when live music plays in the evenings), Cheeseburger is a shrine to the American classic. The home of three-napkin cheeseburgers with attitude, this is burger country, tropical-style, with everything from tofu and veggie burgers to the biggest, juiciest beef and chicken burgers, served on whole-wheat and sesame buns baked fresh daily. There are good reasons why the two-story green-and-white building next to the sea wall is always packed: good value, good grinds, and a great ocean view. The Cheeseburger in Paradise—a hefty hunk with jack and cheddar cheeses, sautéed onions, lettuce, fresh tomatoes, and Thousand Island dressing—is a paean to the basics. Onion rings, chili-cheese fries, and cold beer complete the carefree fantasy.

811 Front St., Lahaina. www.cheeseburgerland.com. © **808/661-4855.** Burgers $10–$16. AE, DISC, MC, V. Daily 8am–10pm.

Cilantro: Fresh Mexican Grill ★ 🍴 ☺ MEXICAN   This is Maui's best bet for fabulous Mexican food at frugal prices. And, believe it or not, this fast-food restaurant serves fresh, healthy food. The chef and owner is Paris Nabavi, creator of Maui's **Pizza Paradiso Italian Kitchen** (p. 210). He wanted the "challenge of something different," so he took off to Mexico to find out how the Mexicans used to cook in "the old days." Even the corn tortillas are handmade daily. Signature dishes include the citrus-and-herb-marinated chipotle rotisserie chicken, the veggie Mariposa salad, the popular Mother-Clucker flautas, and lip-smacking "al pastor"-style adobo pork. All this at budget-pleasing prices. It's a great place to take the kids; Los Niños menu items are under $5.

170 Papalaua Ave., Lahaina. www.cilantrogrill.com. © **808/667-5444.** Main courses $9–$14. MC, V. Daily 11am–9pm.

Lahaina Coolers ★ ☺ AMERICAN/INTERNATIONAL   A huge marlin hangs above the bar, epic wave shots and wall sconces made of surfboard fins fill the walls, and open windows line three sides of this ultracasual indoor/outdoor restaurant. This is a great breakfast joint, with feta-cheese Mediterranean omelets; huevos rancheros; and fried rice made with jasmine rice, Kula vegetables, and Portuguese sausage. There are three types of eggs Benedict: the classic, a vegetarian version (with Kula vegetables—excellent), and the local, with kalua pork and sweetbread. At lunch, burgers rule and the sandwiches, from grilled fresh fish to the Cajun wrap, are ideal for casual Lahaina. The pasta, made fresh daily, is prepared Asian-style (with chicken and spicy Thai peanut sauce), with pesto, or vegetarian (in a spicy Creole sauce). Pizzas, fresh catch, steak, and enchiladas round out the entrees. Everything can be vegetarian upon request.

180 Dickenson St., Lahaina. www.lahainacoolers.com. ✆ **808/661-7082.** Main courses $10–$15 breakfast, $10–$16 lunch, $15–$26 dinner. AE, DC, DISC, MC, V. Daily 8am–1am.

Maui Sunrise Café 🍴 DELI   If you want to know where to find the best breakfasts or the most filling lunches on a budget, follow the surfers to this teeny-tiny cafe located on Front Street, next door to the library. Eat in the patio garden out back or take your lunch to the beach. You'll find huge breakfasts, delicious gourmet sandwiches, and filling lunch plates all at bargain prices. It's tough to find a parking spot nearby (and you can't park at the library), but you'll probably want a brisk walk after eating here anyway.

693A Front St., Lahaina. ✆ **808/661-8558.** Breakfast items under $11; lunch items $7–$12. No credit cards. Daily 6am–4pm.

Maui Swiss Cafe SANDWICHES/PIZZA   Recently renovated and double its original size (which was tiny), Swiss Cafe continues to serve excellent sandwiches and continental breakfast. It still serves $7.50 lunch specials and two scoops of Roselani ice cream for $4 (and sometimes the ice cream is free with the lunch special). Top-quality breads baked fresh daily, Dijon mustard, good Swiss cheese, and keen attention to sandwich fillings and pizza toppings make this a very special sandwich shop. The Swiss owner, Rolf Egli, maintains the European flavor in this corner of Lahaina, down to the Swiss breakfast of sliced ham, cheese, hard-boiled egg, and freshly baked muffins. *Tip:* The "signature melt" sandwiches, with imported Emmenthal cheese baked on an Italian Parmesan crust, are something to watch for, and there are excellent vegetarian and turkey sandwiches as well.

640 Front St., Lahaina. www.swisscafe.net. ✆ **808/661-6776.** Sandwiches and crepes $8–$12. AE, DISC, MC, V. Daily 8am–8pm.

Penne Pasta Café ★ 🍴 ITALIAN/MEDITERRANEAN   Bargain hunters head for this neighborhood cafe, under the helm of chef Juan Gomez, Mark Ellman's (of Maui Tacos and Mala fame) partner until he recently bought the cafe. It features delicious Italian and Mediterranean cuisine. You'll get a sit-down meal at takeout prices, and *mamma mia!*—those are big plates of pasta, pizzas, salads, and sandwiches. So, what's the catch? No waitstaff. You order at the counter, and the manager delivers your order to your table. Favorites include the *molto bene* linguine pesto, baked penne, and pizza with olives, capers, basil, and roasted pepper. Wine (from $8 a glass) and beer are available, too.

180 Dickenson St., Lahaina. www.pennepastacafe.com. ✆ **808/661-6633.** Main courses $9–$15; specials up to $18. AE, DISC, MC, V. Daily 11am–9:30pm.

Kaanapali

EXPENSIVE

Son'z Maui at Swan Court ★★★ HAWAII REGIONAL   This iconic restaurant already had perhaps the most romantic location in Maui, overlooking a man-made lagoon and the rolling surf of the Pacific in the distance. Under its new ownership, the combination of the chef Geno Sarmiento's creative dishes, fresh local ingredients (Kula corn and strawberries, Ono Farms avocados, Hana hearts of palm, Maui Cattle Company beef, fresh Hawaiian fish, and sweet Maui onions), top-notch service, and relaxing atmosphere makes this one of Maui's best restaurants. My personal picks from the very tempting menu are the

Chef McDonald Has a Farm, E-I-E-I-O

Here's your chance to see where those delicious greens, sweet basil, and wonderful tropical fruits that make up your dinner at **Pacific'O** and **I'O** restaurants (p. 202) come from. James McDonald was the first chef in the state to own and operate a farm for the purpose of supplying his own restaurants. Your visit to **O'o Farm** begins with hot apple cider and pastries. The tour is led by a culinary specialist who helps you handpick items for your lunch. At the end of the tour, lunch is served. The cost is $50 per person. For more information, call © **808/667-4341** or go to www. oofarm.com.

escargot profiterole appetizer (with baby spinach, alii oyster mushrooms, and Gorgonzola foam) and, for a main course, either the Hawaiian opakapaka piccata (with artichokes, caperberries, Lisbon lemon, sweet-potato hash browns, and tomato purée) or the seared scallops BLT (with bacon and poached cherry tomatoes in a Caesar-salad emulsion, served with truffled potato chips).

At the Hyatt Regency Maui Resort, 200 Nohea Kai Dr., Kaanapali. www.tristarrestaurants.com. © **808/667-4506.** Reservations required for dinner. Main courses $24–$50. AE, DC, DISC, MC, V. Daily 5:30–10pm.

MODERATE

Beachside Grill/Leilani's on the Beach STEAK/SEAFOOD The Beachside Grill is the informal, less-expensive room downstairs on the beach, where folks wander in off the sand for a frothy beer and a beachside burger. Leilani's is the dinner-only room, with more expensive but still not outrageously priced steak and seafood offerings. At Leilani's, you can order everything from fresh fish to filet mignon to fried coconut prawns. All of this, of course, comes with an ocean view. There's live music Tuesday, Thursday, Friday, and Saturday from 3 to 5pm.

At Whalers Village, 2435 Kaanapali Pkwy., Kaanapali. www.leilanis.com. © **808/661-4495.** Reservations suggested for dinner. Main courses $10–$20 Beachside Grill, $20–$40 Leilani's. AE, DC, DISC, MC, V. Beachside Grill daily 11am–11pm. Leilani's daily 5–9:30pm.

Cane & Taro ★ ASIAN FUSION   Another winner in Chef D.K. Kodama's growing list of fabulous restaurants (Sansei Seafood Restaurant & Sushi Bar on Maui, Oahu, and the Big Island; and d.k Steakhouse, Hiroshi, and Vino on Oahu), Cane & Taro marks a departure from the chef's creative sushi, steaks, and tapas. Located oceanside in the former Rusty Harpoon Restaurant, it has fantastic panoramic views that quickly become secondary when the meal arrives. Breakfast includes five kinds of eggs Benedict; lunch and dinner feature award-winning items such as rock-shrimp dynamite (crispy tempura rock shrimp with a *masago* aioli and *unagi* glaze), crunchy noodle crab and shrimp cake (with ginger-lime-chili and cilantro pesto), and Kona-coffee baby back ribs (roasted with cof-fee-mango barbecue sauce and served with a smoked tomato slaw). The restaurant is always packed. ***Tip:*** Tuesday and Wednesday, if you are seated between 5 and 5:30pm, your meal is 50% off (25% off Thurs–Mon).

At Whaler's Village, 2435 Kaanapali Pkwy., Kaanapali. www.dkrestaurants.com. © **808/662-0668.** Reservations recommended for dinner. Main courses $10–$16 lunch, $23–$40 dinner. AE, DC, DISC, MC, V. Daily 8am–11am, 11:30am–4:30pm, and 5–10pm.

Duke's Beach House ★★ PACIFIC RIM   Perched on the side of the ocean, facing the beautiful Kaanapali Beach and housed in what appears to be an open-air plantation home, the latest of TS Restaurants (which include Kimo's and Leilani's on Maui) opened in late 2009. It was a winner from the start, with a fabulous beachfront location and great decor, but more important, the food is fabulous. Following the new locavore tradition, the staff is committed to a "farm to fork" dining experience and stresses that ingredients are obtained on Maui. Breakfast features a host of omelets, eggs, pancakes, and even a "beach boy bur-rito" (with eggs, sausage, bacon, potatoes, chipotle cream, and avocado salsa); the lunch menu features creative salads, sandwiches, burgers, and fresh fish. Dinner adds steaks, chicken, and a seafood risotto. Leave room for the hula pie—Oreo cookie crust topped with macadamia-nut ice cream, hot fudge, and whipped cream—for dessert.

At Honua Kai Resort & Spa, 130 Kai Malina Pkwy., Kaanapali. www.dukesmaui.com. © **808/662-2900.** Main courses $10–$15 breakfast, $10–$15 lunch, $20–$35 dinner; 3-course tasting menu $26 5–6pm. AE, MC, V. Daily 7:30am–9:30pm.

Umalu ★ PACIFIC RIM   This is the kind of restaurant that visitors dream about. Located oceanside with a great view of the islands of Molokai and Lanai in the distance, you will be happy way before you get your first exotic cocktail. Umalu translates into "the shade cast by a cliff," and that is an apt description of the relaxed, casual atmosphere of this outdoor restaurant. Casual menu options include the Maui Waui–style fish tacos (beer-battered mahimahi on warm flour tortillas), the ahi poke nachos with Surfing goat cheese and lomi salsa, angus burgers, and pizzas (from a sausage and pepperoni pie to a ham-pineapple and Maui-onion pie).

At the Hyatt Regency Maui Resort & Spa, 200 Nohea Kai Dr., Kaanapali. www.maui.hyatt.com. © **808/661-1234.** Main courses $16–$20. AE, DC, MC, V. Daily 11am–10pm.

INEXPENSIVE

Whalers Village, 2435 Kaanapali Pkwy. in Kaanapali (www.whalersvillage.com/restaurants.htm), has a food court where you can buy pizza, Chinese food, ice cream, sandwiches, wraps, and burgers at self-serve counters and courtyard

☆ THE tiki TERRACE

Bravo to the Kaanapali Beach Hotel for the low-salt, employee-tested Native Hawaiian diet served in its **Tiki Terrace Restaurant,** 2525 Kaanapali Pkwy. (✆ **808/667-0124**). The Native Hawaiian Combination features the healthy, traditional diet of fresh fish (you can also order it with chicken breast) and taro greens and tomato, flavored with ginger and herbs. Fresh mild *limu* (seaweed) adds some natural saltiness, and you can always add your own salt and pepper to taste. The Native Hawaiian menu also includes a salad made from *pohole* fern shoots and ogo marinated with sweet Maui onions and tomatoes tossed with a lime-soy vinaigrette and served with papaya. (With their freshness, pleasing crunch, and mild flavor, fern shoots are one of the most underused greens of Hawaii.) Entree choices are accompanied by steamed purple sweet potato, taro, and fresh poi made on the premises. The dessert is half a chilled Hana papaya with lemon, grilled bananas, and pineapple slices. The cost for the Native Hawaiian Combination is $23.

The use of fresh local ingredients is a noteworthy touch in the a la carte menu as well. My favorites are the baked crab and shrimp with artichoke hearts and the coconut shrimp. Try Chef Muromoto's signature sesame shoyu dressing on the Kula greens salad—it's a house favorite. The a la carte menu entrees are headed up by the Huki Hukilau, a combination of fresh catch, jumbo prawn, and baby lobster tail. The menu also includes steak, ribs, teriyaki grilled chicken, and rack of lamb.

The dining room is old-fashioned Hawaii, not fancy, with tables on a terrace

ringed with plumeria and palm trees. Nightly entertainment is a hula show from 6:30 to 7:30pm and music for dancing under the stars until 9pm.

The regular Tiki Terrace breakfast menu presents all the old favorites along with the opportunity to sample Hawaiian food in a familiar context: taro hash browns; three-egg lomi salmon omelet with sweet-potato home fries; a fruit plate of banana baked in ti leaf with lehua honey and macadamia nuts, served with yogurt; and French toast made with taro bread. There are even Hawaiian taro pancakes, and they're wonderful. The Hawaiian **Sunday Champagne Brunch** ($37) features more than 50 items on the buffet, plus stir-fry, carving, and omelet stations, along with Belgian waffles and great desserts, all accompanied by Hawaiian music (9am–1pm).

The hotel also serves guests a complimentary **Ohana Welcome Breakfast** on their first morning at 8am Monday through Saturday, with live music, hula, a buffet breakfast, and advice on how to make the most of a Maui vacation. The hotel's staff greets guests, then takes to the stage for one of their specialties—singing and dancing hulas. Then they are off to work while guests enjoy a tour of hotel events and island activities.

The emphasis on Hawaiian food is only one part of a pervasive spirit of aloha that distinguishes this hotel. Reservations are recommended for dining in the **Tiki Terrace** (✆ **808/667-0124**). Dinner is served daily from 6 to 9pm.

tables. It's an inexpensive alternative and a quick, handy stop for shoppers and Kaanapali beachgoers.

CJ's Deli & Diner ★ 🍴 ☺ AMERICAN/DELI   If you're staying in Kaanapali, this restaurant is within walking distance of your resort; if you're not, it's worth the drive to sample the "comfort food" (as they call it) at this hip, happening eatery with prices so low you won't believe you're still on Maui. A huge billboard menu hangs from the yellow-and-gold textured wall, and highly polished wooden floors give the roadside eatery a homey feeling. You can eat in or take out (you can even get a "chef-to-go" to come to your accommodations and cook for you). Huge, delicious breakfasts are served from 7 to 11am (check out the $6.95 early-bird special of two eggs, bacon or sausage, rice, and coffee). There's a wide selection of egg dishes, plus pancakes and waffles, and don't forget the tempting delights from the bakery. Lunch ranges from deli sandwiches and burgers to pot roast, ribs, and fish dishes. If you are on your way to Hana or up to the top of Haleakala, stop by and get a box lunch. CJ's even has a menu for the kids.

At the Fairway Shops at Kaanapali, 2580 Kekaa Dr. (just off the Honoapiilani Hwy.), Kaanapali. www.cjsmaui.com. ✆ **808/667-0968.** Main courses $5–$10 breakfast; $8.50–$19 lunch; Hana Lunch Box $12; Air Travel Lunch Box $12. AE, MC, V. Daily 7am–8pm.

Nikki's Pizza ☺ PIZZA   Formerly Pizza Paradiso, Nikki's has a full menu of pastas, pizzas, and desserts, including smoothies, coffee, and ice cream. This is a welcome addition to the Kaanapali scene, where casual is king and good food doesn't have to be fancy. The pizzas reflect a simple and effective formula that has won acclaim through the years: good crust, true-blue sauces, and toppings loyal to tradition but with just enough edge for those who want it. Create your own pizza with roasted eggplant, mushrooms, anchovies, artichoke hearts, sausage, and a slew of other toppings. Nikki's offers some heroic choices, from the Hawaiian (ham and Maui pineapple) to the Sopranos (roasted chicken, artichoke hearts, and sun-dried tomatoes).

At Whalers Village, 2435 Kaanapali Pkwy., Kaanapali. www.nikkispizzamaui.com. ✆ **808/667-0333.** Pizza by the slice $4–$5, whole pizzas $17–$22. AE, DISC, MC, V. Daily 8am–9pm.

Honokowai, Kahana & Napili

Note: You'll find the following restaurants on the "Restaurants from Kapalua to Honokowai" map on p. 211.

EXPENSIVE

Roy's Kahana Bar & Grill ★★★ HAWAII REGIONAL   Despite the lack of dramatic view and an upstairs location in a shopping mall, Roy's remains crowded and extremely popular for one reason: fabulous food. It bustles with young, hip, impeccably trained servers delivering Szechuan barbecue–grilled ahi steak, basil-seared opakapaka with wild mushroom and asparagus risotto, and glazed honey-mustard short ribs. You could make a meal of the incredibly creative appetizers, such as Roy's original Kai-style ahi, crab cakes, lobster and shrimp potstickers, crispy shrimp and pork *lumpia*, or lemon grass–poached pear salad. Don't get your heart set on anything, as Roy changes his menu frequently.

At Kahana Gateway Shopping Center, 4405 Honoapiilani Hwy., Lahaina. www.roysrestaurant. com. ✆ **808/669-6999.** Reservations strongly recommended. Main courses $27–$50. AE, DC, DISC, MC, V. Daily 5:30–10pm.

Sea House Restaurant PACIFIC RIM   The Sea House is not glamorous, famous, or hip, but it's worth mentioning for its spectacular view of Napili Bay. The **Napili Kai Beach Resort** (p. 272), where the Sea House is located, is a charming throwback to the days when hotels blended in with their surroundings, had lush tropical foliage, and were sprawling rather than vertical. Dinner entrees range from taro-crusted sea bass with green papaya salad to seafood cioppino to coffee-crusted lamb loin. There's even a menu for the *keiki* (kids), with items such as hamburgers and chicken nuggets. *Tip:* From 5:30 to 6pm each evening, Sea House offers a three-course dinner for $30.

At Napili Kai Beach Resort, 5900 Honoapiilani Hwy., Lahaina. www.napilikai.com. © **808/669-1500.** Reservations required for dinner. Main courses $7–$15 breakfast, $10–$16 lunch, $24–$39 dinner; appetizers $3–$6. AE, DISC, MC, V. Daily 7am–9pm.

MODERATE

Maui Brewing Co. SEAFOOD/STEAK   The menu here covers basic tastes: salads, fish and chips, fresh-fish sandwiches, cheeseburgers, and pizza, as well as heavier fare of beef stew, jambalaya, and a kalua pig plate lunch. And, of course, beer—lots of it. The late-night menu offers sliders, pizza slices, and lighter fare.

At Kahana Gateway Shopping Center, 4405 Honoapiilani Hwy., Lahaina. www.mauibrewingco.com. © **808/669-3474.** Reservations recommended for dinner. Main courses $12–$25. AE, DC, DISC, MC, V. Daily 11am–midnight. Sun brunch 7am–3pm during football season (Sept–Jan).

INEXPENSIVE

Maui Tacos ☺ MEXICAN   Mark Ellman's Maui Tacos chain has grown faster than you can say, "Haleakala." Ellman put gourmet Mexican on paper plates and on the island's culinary map long before Maui became known as Hawaii's center for salsa and chimichangas. Barely more than a takeout counter with a few tables, this and the six other Maui Tacos in Hawaii (five on Maui alone) are popular with hungry surfers, discerning diners, burrito buffs, and Hollywood glitterati like Sharon Stone, whose picture adorns a wall or two. Choices include excellent fresh-fish tacos (garlicky and flavorful), chimichangas, and mouth-breaking compositions such as the Hookipa: a "surf burrito" of fresh fish, black beans, and salsa. The Haiku burrito contains greens, black beans, rice, cheese, and potatoes—it's a knockout, requiring a siesta afterward. Expect good food but not very fast service.

At Napili Plaza, 5095 Napilihau St., Lahaina. www.mauitacos.com. © **808/665-0222.** All items $5–$10. AE, DISC, MC, V. Mon–Sat 9am–9pm; Sun 9am–8pm. Additional locations at Lahaina Sq., Lahaina, © 808/661-8883; Kamaole Beach Center, Kihei, © 808/879-5005; Piilani Village Shopping Center, Kihei, © 808/875-9340; and Kaahumanu Center, Kahului, © 808/871-7726.

Pizza Paradiso Italian Kitchen PIZZA/ITALIAN   Order at the counter (pastas, gourmet pizza whole or by the slice, panini, salads, and desserts) and find a seat at one of the few tables. The pasta sauces—marinara, pescatore, Alfredo, Florentine, and pesto, with options and add-ons—are as popular as the pizzas (which took "best pizza" in a recent *Maui News'* reader poll for the third year in a row). The Massimo, a pesto sauce with artichoke hearts, sun-dried tomatoes, and capers, comes with a choice of chicken, shrimp, or clams, and is so good it was a Taste of Lahaina Festival winner. Recent additions to the menu include gyros, souvlakia, hummus, and cheesesteak sandwiches. Takeout, dine in, or delivery, this is a hot spot in the neighborhood.

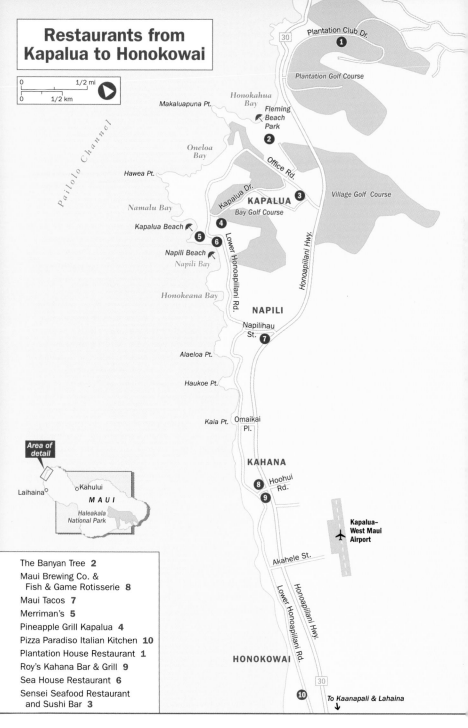

Restaurants from Kapalua to Honokowai

0 1/2 mi
0 1/2 km

Plantation Club Dr.
Plantation Golf Course
Honokahua Bay
Makaluapuna Pt.
Fleming Beach Park
Oneloa Bay
Office Rd.
Hawea Pt.
Kapalua Dr.
KAPALUA
Bay Golf Course
Village Golf Course
Namalu Bay
Kapalua Beach
Napili Beach
Napili Bay
Lower Honoapiilani Rd.
Honokeana Bay
NAPILI
Napilihau St.
Alaeloa Pt.
Haukoe Pt.
Kaia Pt.
Omaikai Pl.
KAHANA
Hoohui Rd.
Kapalua–West Maui Airport
Akahele St.
Honoapiilani Hwy.
Lower Honoapiilani Rd.
HONOKOWAI
To Kaanapali & Lahaina

Paiolo Channel

Area of detail
Laihaina
Kahului
MAUI
Haleakala National Park

The Banyan Tree **2**
Maui Brewing Co. & Fish & Game Rotisserie **8**
Maui Tacos **7**
Merriman's **5**
Pineapple Grill Kapalua **4**
Pizza Paradiso Italian Kitchen **10**
Plantation House Restaurant **1**
Roy's Kahana Bar & Grill **9**
Sea House Restaurant **6**
Sensei Seafood Restaurant and Sushi Bar **3**

At the Honokowai Marketplace, 3350 Lower Honoapiilani Rd., Lahaina. www.pizzaparadiso.com. © **808/667-2929.** Pastas $9–$11; pizzas $19–$28. MC, V. Daily 10am–9pm.

Kapalua

Note: You'll find the following restaurants on the "Restaurants from Kapalua to Honokowai" map on p. 211.

VERY EXPENSIVE

The Banyan Tree ★★ ASIAN   The most recent *chef de cuisine,* in a long line of outstanding chefs chosen from the stables of the Ritz-Carlton resorts around the globe, is JoJo Vasquez. His distinctive seasonal menus might include Kona lobster with vegetable succotash and tobiko caviar glace; seared ahi with zinfandel gastrique to which you can add a seared foie gras pairing; or rack of lamb with chickpea cake. The atmosphere is extremely romantic, overlooking the ocean with the island of Molokai in the distance—get reservations for sunset. At press time the restaurant was offering a tasting menu of four courses with wine for $120.

At the Ritz-Carlton Kapalua, 1 Ritz-Carlton Dr., Kapalua. www.ritzcarlton.com. © **808/669-6200.** Reservations recommended. Main courses $38–$48. AE, DC, DISC, MC, V. Tues–Sat 5:30–9:30pm.

Merriman's ★★★ PACIFIC RIM   This is probably the most beautiful location for a restaurant in the state. On a point jetting out into the ocean, overlooking Kapalua Bay on one side and the island of Molokai in the distance, in the former location of the Kapalua Bay Club, well-known local chef Peter Merriman, who is a James Beard award winner, opened this spectacular restaurant in 2008. His fantastic menu, in which he pioneered the "farm to table" concept of serving only fresh products from local farmers, fishermen, and ranchers, is on display here with Haleakala Ranch–raised lamb, his well-known wok-charred ahi (served with pumpkin purée and tangerine-green peppercorn jus), and even locally grown fresh taro for his pan-sautéed taro cakes for the vegetarians. To really experience Merriman's culinary genius, order the "Mix Plate" tasting entree. The night I dined, it included crispy mahimahi with citrus ponzu, Maui Beef filet with pesto, and the fabulous wok-charred ahi. **Tip:** Book your reservation for sunset to really experience this incredible vista. If sunset tables are booked, come for sunset anyway and sit on the large open-air patio and enjoy a cocktail and an appetizer.

At Kapalua Resort, One Bay Club Place, Kapalua. www.merrimanshawaii.com. © **808/669-6400.** Reservations recommended. Main courses $29–$65. AE, MC, V. Daily 5:30–9pm. Point Bar menu 3–9pm.

EXPENSIVE

Pineapple Grill ★★★ PACIFIC RIM   If you had only a single night to eat on the island of Maui, this would be the place to go. Up-and-coming young chef Ryan Luckey (a local Lahaina boy) has taken the helm and is winning high praise from both critics and the local residents who flock here nightly. My picks on this creative menu are ahi steak crusted with pistachios and wasabi peas (served with coconut-scented "forbidden" rice, Hamakua mushrooms, and wasabi-ginger butter), candied macadamia–crusted roast mahimahi (in a poha berry beurre blanc), and the wonderful Maui-style paella. An excellent list of wine pairings by the glass is available. Save room for the Maui gold-pineapple upside-down cake (with Hana Bay dark-rum sauce and Maui-made Roselani gourmet mac-nut ice cream). There are lots of tasty sandwiches and salads at lunch. Plus, it's all served in a very Maui-like atmosphere, overlooking the rolling hills of the Kapalua golf course out to the Pacific Ocean.

At the Kapalua Golf Club Bay Course, 200 Kapalua Dr., Kapalua. www.pineapplekapalua.com. ℂ **808/669-9600.** Reservations recommended for dinner. Main courses $9–$18 breakfast and lunch, $27–$50 dinner. AE, MC, V. Daily 8am–2:30pm and 5:30–9pm; bar menu daily 2:30–5:30pm.

Plantation House Restaurant ★★ SEAFOOD/MEDITERRANEAN With its teak tables, fireplace, and open sides, Plantation House gets stellar marks for atmosphere. *Maui News* has deemed it as having the island's "Best Ambience"—a big honor on an island of wonderful views. It's the best place for breakfast in west Maui, hands down, and one of my top choices for dinner. The eggs Mediterranean makes a superb start to your day, and at lunch, sandwiches (open-faced smoked turkey, roasted vegetable, and goat-cheese wrap) and salads rule. When the sun sets, the menu expands to marvelous starters, such as polenta and scampi-style shrimp, crab cakes, and Kula and Mediterranean salads. The menu changes constantly but may include fresh fish prepared several ways—among them, Mediterranean (on roasted Maui onions with couscous), Venice (pressed in *panko,* with a golden-raisin/pine nut butter), Maui (pistachio crusted), and Italy (pepper dusted with olives and caper-berry salsa). Don't forget the numerous vegetarian entrees and wonderful Australian lamb, New Zealand lobster, and a roast pork tenderloin you'll long remember.

At the Kapalua Golf Club Plantation Course, 2000 Plantation Club Dr., Kapalua. www.theplantation house.com. ℂ **808/669-6299.** Reservations recommended. Main courses $8–$17 breakfast, $12–$18 lunch, $27–$42 dinner. AE, DC, MC, V. Daily 8am–3pm and 5:30–9pm (6–9pm Apr 16–Sept 14); Cafe menu in lounge 3–5:30pm.

MODERATE

Sansei Seafood Restaurant & Sushi Bar ★★★ PACIFIC RIM/SUSHI Perpetual award winner Sansei offers an extensive menu of Japanese and East-West delicacies. Part fusion, part Hawaii Regional Cuisine, Sansei is tirelessly creative, with a menu that scores higher with adventurous palates than with purists. If you don't like cilantro, watch out for those complex mango/crab-salad rolls. Other choices include *panko*-crusted ahi sashimi, sashimi trio, ahi carpaccio, noodle dishes, lobster, Asian shrimp cakes, and sauces that surprise, in creative combinations, such as ginger-lime chile butter and cilantro pesto. But there's simpler fare as well, such as shrimp tempura, noodles, and wok-tossed upcountry vegetables. Desserts are not to be missed. If it's autumn, don't pass up the Granny Smith apple tart with vanilla ice cream and homemade caramel sauce. There's karaoke Thursday nights from 10pm to 1am. *Tip:* Eat early; all food is 25% off between 5:30 and 6pm—but be aware that the line for this budget deal starts forming before 5pm.

At the Kapalua Resort, 600 Office Rd., Lahaina. www.sanseihawaii.com. ℂ **808/669-6286.** Reservations recommended. Main courses $16–$43. AE, DISC, MC, V. Daily 5:30–10pm. A 2nd location is at Kihei Town Center, Kihei. ℂ 808/879-0004.

SOUTH MAUI

South Maui, like West Maui, is a popular visitor area, offering a range of restaurants. Starting in Kihei, the prices are more frugal than in the affluent Wailea Resort. But some of Maui's top chefs and dining experiences can be found here, as well as affordable delis and diners.

Kihei/Maalaea

There's a **Maui Tacos** at Kamaole Beach Center, in Kihei (*C* **808/879-5005**).

EXPENSIVE

Buzz's Wharf AMERICAN   Buzz's is another formula restaurant that offers a superb view, substantial sandwiches, meaty french fries, and surf-and-turf fare—in a word, satisfying but not sensational. Still, this bright, airy dining room makes a fine way station for whale-watching over a cold beer and an ahi sandwich. Consider opting for several appetizers (stuffed mushrooms, steamer clams, clam chowder, onion soup) and a salad, and then splurge on dessert—try the bananas wrapped in pastry and fried, topped with vanilla ice cream, cinnamon, macadamia nuts, and raspberry and caramel syrups.

At Maalaea Bay Harbor, 960 Front St., Lahaina. www.buzzswharf.com. *C* **808/244-5426.** Reservations recommended. Main courses $11–$25 lunch, $18–$51 dinner. AE, DC, DISC, MC, V. Daily 11am–9pm.

Five Palms ★ PACIFIC RIM   This is the best lunch spot in Kihei—open air, with tables a few feet from the beach and up-close-and-personal views of Kahoolawe and Molokini. You'll have to walk through a nondescript parking area and the modest entrance of the Mana Kai Maui Resort to reach this unpretentious place. It features a menu of breakfast and lunch items served from 8am to 2:30pm, so if you're jet-lagged and your stomach isn't on Hawaiian time, you can get a crab omelet at two in the afternoon or a juicy Kobe beef hamburger at eight in the morning. At dinner, with the torches lit on the beach and the main dining room open, the ambience shifts to evening romantic, but still casual. Just-caught fish is the star of the dinner menu. From 5 to 5:30pm, Five Palms offers the Sunset Special: a three-course meal for $30.

At Mana Kai Maui Resort, 2960 S. Kihei Rd., Kihei. www.fivepalmsrestaurant.com. *C* **808/879-2607.** Reservations recommended for dinner. Main courses $8–$20 breakfast and lunch, $24–$58 dinner. AE, MC, V. Daily 8am–2:30pm and 5–9pm.

The Maalaea Waterfront Restaurant ★★ SEAFOOD   As we went to press, this well-established, family-owned restaurant (winner of many prestigious awards for wine excellence, service, and seafood) was sold and was in the process of moving from their old location in the Milowai condominium to a new location, just 300 yards away in the Maalaea Harbor Shops and Restaurants. The new location triples the space they previously had (from 1,700 sq. ft. to 5,200 sq. ft.). The new owners plan to keep the same menu and also add lunch. Be sure to call to make sure they are finished with renovations by the time you make it to Maui.

At Maalaea Harbor Shops and Restaurants, 300 Maalaea Rd., Maalaea. www.waterfrontrestaurant. net. *C* **808/244-9028.** Reservations recommended. Main courses $21–$46. AE, DC, DISC, MC, V. Daily 5pm–closing (last seating at 8pm).

MODERATE

Cafe O'Lei Kihei ★★ STEAK/SEAFOOD   Chefs Michael and Dana Pastula have had a host of Cafe O'Lei restaurants on Maui, and I've loved every one of them. Their latest is in an out-of-the-way location, the not-very-attractive Rainbow Mall. Nevermind—you come here for the food, not the view. Inside, the open and airy room has floor-to-ceiling windows, hardwood floors, a big circular bar in the middle, and an exhibition kitchen. The atmosphere is relaxing and

Restaurants in South Maui

inviting. The food is, as usual, not only outstanding, but also a real bargain. You can't beat the daily plate lunch for under $8 (arrive early, as the locals will book tables in advance). Dinners range from fresh fish to prime rib, mac-nut-crusted chicken breast to roast duck, and even a mushroom-asparagus-pine-nut linguine for the vegetarians. Save room for dessert, such as pineapple upside-down cake or a fudge brownie sundae (yum).

2439 S. Kihei Rd., Kihei. © **808/891-1368.** Reservations recommended. Main courses $7–$13 lunch, $17–$35 dinner. AE, DC, DISC, MC, V. Daily 10:30am–3:30pm and 4:30–9:30pm.

Stella Blues Café ★ AMERICAN   Stella Blues gets going at breakfast and continues through to dinner with something for everyone—vegetarians, kids, pasta and sandwich lovers, hefty steak eaters, and sensible diners who go for the inexpensive salad of fresh Maui greens. Grateful Dead posters line the walls, and a covey of gleaming motorcycles is invariably parked outside. It's loud and lively, irreverent and unpretentious. Sandwiches are the highlight, ranging from the half-pound Maui Beef Company Blues burger to grilled chicken to the kalua pork and cabbage plate lunch. Mountain-size salads are popular, as are large coffee shakes with mounds of whipped cream. Daily specials include fresh seafood and other surprises—all home-style cooking, made from scratch, down to the pesto mayonnaise and herb bread. At dinner, selections are geared toward good-value family dining, from affordable full dinners to pastas and burgers. There's live music every evening. Starting times vary, so check the website for times.

At Azeka Place II Shopping Center, 1279 S. Kihei Rd., Kihei. www.stellablues.com. © **808/874-3779.** Main courses $6–$13 breakfast, $9–$20 lunch, $12–$28 dinner. AE, DC, MC, V. Daily 7:30am–10pm. Bar until 11pm.

INEXPENSIVE

Joy's Place 🖋 HEALTH FOOD/DELI/SANDWICHES   If you're in Kihei and looking for a healthy, delicious breakfast or lunch at a rock-bottom price, it's worth hunting around for Joy's Place. This tiny hole in the wall has humongous sandwiches (turkey and avocado, tuna salad), wheat-free wraps, fresh salads, hot items (falafel burger, veggie burger), soups, and desserts. Most items are organic. There are a few places to sit inside, but the beach is just a couple minutes' walk away.

In the Island Surf Building, 1993 S. Kihei Rd. (entrance on Auhana St.), Kihei. © **808/879-9258.** All items under $12. AE, MC, V. Mon–Sat 8am–3pm.

Peggy Sue's ☺ AMERICAN   Just for a moment, forget that diet and take a leap. This 1950s-style diner has oodles of charm and is a swell place to spring for the best chocolate malt on the island. You'll also find sodas, shakes, floats, egg creams, milkshakes, and made-on-Maui Roselani-brand gourmet ice cream. Old-fashioned soda-shop stools, an ELVIS PRESLEY BOULEVARD sign, and jukeboxes on every Formica table serve as a backdrop for the famous burgers (and gardenburgers), brushed with teriyaki sauce and served with all the goodies. The fries are great, too.

At Azeka Place II Shopping Center, 1279 S. Kihei Rd., Kihei. www.peggysues-maui.com. © **808/875-8944.** Burgers $10–$12; plate lunches $7–$17. DISC, MC, V. Sun–Thurs 11am–9pm; Fri–Sat 11am–10pm.

Shaka Sandwich & Pizza ☺ PIZZA   How many "best pizzas" are there on Maui? It depends on which shore you're on, the west or the south. This south-shore old-timer recently moved to a new (and much larger) location, but the award-winning pizzas, New York–style heroes, Philly cheesesteaks, calzones, salads, and homemade garlic bread haven't changed. Shaka uses fresh Maui produce, long-simmered sauces, and homemade Italian bread. Choose thin or Sicilian-thick crust with gourmet toppings: Maui onions, spinach, anchovies, jalapeños, and a spate of other vegetables. Try the white pizza; with the perfectly balanced flavors of olive oil, garlic, and cheese, you won't even miss the tomato sauce. My favorite, the spinach pizza (with olive oil, spinach, garlic, and mozzarella), is a real treat.

1770 S. Kihei Rd., Kihei. www.shakapizza.com. ⓒ **808/874-0331.** Sandwiches $7–$16; pizzas $18–$28. MC, V. Sun–Thurs 10:30am–9pm; Fri–Sat 10:30am–10pm.

Wailea

The **Shops at Wailea** (www.shopsatwailea.com), with a sprawling location between the Grand Wailea Resort and Outrigger Wailea Resort, has added a spate of shops and restaurants to this stretch of south Maui. Five restaurants and dozens of shops, most of them upscale, are among the new tenants of this complex. Ruth's Chris Steak House is here, as well as Tommy Bahama's Tropical Cafe & Emporium, Honolulu Coffee Company, Kai Wailea, **Longhi's** (reviewed below), Cheeseburger Island Style, and Lappert's Ice Cream. Next door at the Wailea Beach Marriott Resort is **Mala Wailea** (reviewed below). *Note:* You'll find the restaurants in this section on the "Restaurants in South Maui" map (p. 215).

VERY EXPENSIVE

Ko ★★★ HAWAII REGIONAL   The concept behind this successful restaurant in the Fairmont Kea Lani is pure genius: taking the various ethnic cuisines from Maui's old plantation days (Hawaiian, Filipino, Portuguese, Korean, Puerto Rican, and European) and cooking them up in a gourmet fashion. Quicker than you can say, "humuhumukununukuapua'a" (Hawaii's state fish), you have a culinary success. Many of the recipes Ko uses come from old family recipes. The word *ko* means "cane," as in sugar cane, and references the days when the sugar cane plantations had "camp" housing for each ethnic group. Among the wonderful taste treats you won't want to miss is ahi "on the rocks," in which the server brings you chunks of fresh ahi to cook on a hot *ishiyaki* stone to your desired doneness and then dip into an orange-ginger-miso sauce. Other options include Filipino *lumpia* (a sort of spring roll with green papaya, shrimp, and pork [or chicken and mushroom], accompanied by a spicy sauce); *paniolo* (cowboy) ribeye steak with fern shoots; Korean-style spicy chicken served with Maui lavender honey; and a wonderful Portuguese bean soup. ***Budget tip:*** Ko offers a three-course dinner from 5:30 to 6:30pm for $39.

At the Fairmont Kea Lani, 4100 Wailea Alanui Dr., Wailea. www.fairmont.com. ⓒ **808/875-4100.** Reservations recommended. Main courses $21–$50. AE, DC, DISC, MC, V. Daily 5:30–9pm.

Longhi's ★ ITALIAN   Unfortunately, the ocean view is now blocked by yet another high-rise, but Longhi's open-air room and its trademark black-and-white checkered floor still make a great backdrop to start the day. Breakfasts here are worth waking up for: perfect baguettes, fresh-baked cinnamon rolls (one is enough for two people), and eggs Benedict or Florentine. Lunch is either an Italian banquet (ahi *torino,* prawns amaretto, and a wide variety of pastas) or fresh salads and sandwiches. Dinner is where Longhi's shines, with a long list of fresh-made pasta dishes, seafood platters, and beef and chicken dishes (filet mignon with basil, veal scaloppine). Leave room for the daily dessert specials.

At the Shops at Wailea, 3750 Wailea Alanui Dr., Wailea. www.longhis.com. (C) **808/891-8883.** Reservations recommended for dinner. Main courses $9.50–$21 breakfast, $9–$38 lunch, $17–$120 dinner. AE, DC, DISC, MC, V. Mon–Fri 8am–10pm; Sat–Sun 7:30am–10pm.

Mala Wailea ★★★ HAWAIIAN REGIONAL/SEAFOOD   This upscale version of **Mala Ocean Tavern** in Lahaina (p. 202) occupies the prime restaurant location at the Wailea Beach Marriott Resort & Spa. Created by Chef Mark Ellman, one of the original founders of the Hawaii Regional Cuisine movement (his other restaurants on Maui include Maui Tacos, Penne Pasta Café, and Mala Ocean Tavern), this is a great place to enjoy island food in a casual atmosphere. Chef Ellman has created a menu that rivals the spectacular ocean view for your attention: Balinese stir-fry with fresh island fish, ginger-garlic black bean sauce over a whole wok-fried fish, and hoisin-glazed baby back ribs. Or you can choose from the lighter "tavern" menu of ahi burger, fresh island fish sandwich, or Kobe beef cheeseburger. Breakfast features both a la carte items (such as the "killer" French toast or the *chilaquiles*—salsa, corn tortillas, eggs, sour cream, and feta cheese) and a full buffet.

At the Wailea Beach Marriott Resort & Spa, 3700 Wailea Alanui Dr., Wailea. www.malaoceantavern.com. (C) **808/875-9394.** Reservations recommended. Breakfast buffet $28; main courses $26–$45. AE, DC, DISC, MC, V. Daily 6:30–11am and 5:30–9:30pm. Bar until 10pm.

Nick's Fishmarket Maui ★★ SEAFOOD   Here's the place to bring your sweetie to enjoy the moon rise and the sweet smell of the stephanotis growing on the terrace. Fans love this classic seafood restaurant that sticks to the tried and true. The few detractors complain that the food is too old-style (circa 1970s, before anyone was worried about cholesterol); but most agree that there is a high degree of professionalism in both service and preparation, and it's hard to beat the fantasy setting on the south Maui shoreline. The Greek Maui Wowie salad gets my vote as one of the top salads in Hawaii. The rest of the menu features great fresh fish like opakapaka (one of the signature dishes), grilled opah, and Hawaiian spiny lobster. There are ample choices for those who don't eat fish as well, including rack of lamb, roasted chicken, and dry-aged New York steak.

At the Fairmont Kea Lani Maui, 4100 Wailea Alanui Dr., Wailea. www.tristarrestaurants.com. (C) **808/879-7224.** Reservations recommended. Main courses $32–$120. AE, DC, DISC, MC, V. Daily 5:30–9:45pm.

Spago ★★ HAWAII REGIONAL/PACIFIC RIM   California meets Hawaii in this contemporary eatery featuring fresh, local Hawaii ingredients prepared under the culinary watch of master chef Wolfgang Puck. Formerly Seasons Dining Room, the space, located in the Four Seasons Resort Maui, has been stunningly transformed into a sleek, modern layout using stone and wood in the open-air setting overlooking the Pacific. The cuisine lives up to Puck's reputation of tweaking traditional Hawaiian dishes with his own brand of cutting-edge innovations. The menu changes daily and can feature Hawaiian moi steamed Hong Kong–style; pineapple grilled mahi; grilled Chinois-style lamb chops; and roast Cantonese duck with pineapple and papaya. The wine and beverage list is well thought out and extensive. Make reservations as soon as you land on the island (if not before); this place is popular. And bring plenty of cash or your platinum card. ***Budget tip:*** A three-course prix-fixe dinner for $49 is served from 5:30 to 6pm and again from 8:45 to 9:30pm.

At the Four Seasons Resort Maui at Wailea, 3900 Wailea Alanui Dr., Wailea. www.fourseasons. com/maui. © **808/879-2999.** Reservations required. Main courses $39–$116. AE, DC, DISC, MC, V. Daily 6–9:30pm. Bar with pupu daily 6–11pm.

EXPENSIVE

Ferraro's Bar e Ristorante ★ ITALIAN   This was a master stroke for the Four Seasons—authentic Italian fare in a casual outdoor tropical setting, with a drop-dead-gorgeous view of the ocean and the West Maui Mountains. Ferraro's is not inexpensive, but the food is first-rate. Lunch in the open-air restaurant features fabulous salads (my pick is the seared Hawaiian tuna and niçoise salad), sandwiches (get the lobster salad sandwich), and some Hawaiian classics (try the kalua egg rolls). The fish selection is noteworthy; try the olive oil–poached ahi with potato gnocchi, green beans, capers, and olives; or roasted sea bass, with potatoes and Haiku cherry tomatoes. Save room for dessert. My favorite is the warm hazelnut cake with cabernet grapes. At dinner, the romantic setting, complete with the sound of the ocean waves, adds to a memorable evening.

At the Four Seasons Resort Maui at Wailea, 3900 Wailea Alanui Dr. © **808/874-8000.** www. fourseasons.com/maui. Reservations recommended. Main courses $19–$28 lunch, $29–$50 dinner. AE, DC, DISC, MC, V. Daily 11:30am–9pm (beverages served from 11am).

MODERATE

Gannon's ★★ AMERICAN   Award-winning chef Bev Gannon has taken over the former Sea Watch restaurant, perched high on a hill above the Wailea Golf Course with a spectacular ocean view and Molokini in the distance. Chef Gannon (of Haliimaile General Store and Joe's on Maui plus Lanai City Grille on Lanai) is known for her American home cooking with a regional twist—in this case a Hawaiian twist, such as miso-glazed black cod with Asian slaw and wasabi mashed potatoes; Kurobuta pork chop, Portuguese sausage, and corn bread stuffing with pineapple chutney; or Tandoori loin of lamb, Israeli couscous, and tamarind sauce. The restaurant serves breakfast, lunch, and dinner. Some highlights: Gannon's version of loco moco, a local dish consisting of a couple scoops of white rice with a hamburger patty on top and generous amounts of gravy; and the ahi *panzanella* salad with *kalamata* olives, haricot vert, and white beans with truffle oil and balsamic syrup vinaigrette. ***Insider's tip:*** Get reservations to watch the sunset for dinner.

At the Wailea Golf Course, 100 Wailea Golf Club Dr., Wailea. www.bevgannonrestaurants.com. © **808/875-8080.** Reservations recommended for dinner. Main courses $10–$14 breakfast, $9–$18 lunch, $24–$46 dinner. AE, DC, DISC, MC, V. Mon–Fri 10am–3pm and 5:30–9:30pm; Sat–Sun 8am–3pm and 5:30–9:30pm.

Joe's ★★ AMERICAN   The 270-degree view spans the golf course, tennis courts, ocean, and Haleakala—a worthy setting for Beverly Gannon's hearty staples, which include excellent mashed potatoes, Kobe hamburger, fresh fish, and prime rib, but the meatloaf (a whole loaf, like Mom used to make) seems to upstage them all. The Tuscan white-bean soup is superb, and the roasted pork shank with goat-cheese grits and dried fruit compote is American home cooking at its best. Daily specials could be grilled ahi with white-truffle, Yukon-gold mashed potatoes or sautéed mahimahi with shrimp bisque and sautéed spinach. If chocolate cake is on the menu, you should definitely spring for it.

At the Wailea Tennis Club, 131 Wailea Ike Place, Wailea. www.bevgannonrestaurants.com. © **808/875-7767.** Reservations recommended. Main courses $19–$38. AE, DC, DISC, MC, V. Daily 5:30–9:30pm.

Haliimaile (on the Way to Upcountry Maui)

Away from the beaches, the Upcountry Maui area is generally a residential area that offers excellent dining opportunities, from Chef Bev Gannon's award-winning Haliimaile General Store to Chef Justin Pardo's Market Fresh Bistro in the cowboy town of Makawao. Here's your chance to sample Maui's top food without the resort areas' marked-up prices.

EXPENSIVE

Haliimaile General Store ★★★ HAWAII REGIONAL/AMERICAN   For more than 2 decades, Bev Gannon, one of the original Hawaii Regional Cuisine chefs, has been going strong at her foodie haven in the pineapple fields. You'll dine at tables set on old wood floors under high ceilings (sound ricochets fiercely here), in a peach-colored room emblazoned with works by local artists. The food, a blend of eclectic American with ethnic touches, puts an innovative spin on Hawaii Regional Cuisine. Even the fresh-catch sandwich on the lunch menu is anything but prosaic. Sip the *lilikoi* lemonade and nibble the sashimi napoleon or the house salad (island greens with mandarin oranges, onions, toasted walnuts, and blue-cheese crumble)—all are notable items on a menu that bridges Hawaii and Gannon's Texas roots. Wednesday and Thursday nights are "Tapas Nights" with live music, wine specials, and tapas under $9, as well as the regular menu.

900 Haliimaile Rd., Haliimaile. www.haliimailegeneralstore.com. © **808/572-2666.** Reservations recommended. Main courses $10–$18 lunch, $26–$42 dinner. AE, DC, MC, V. Mon–Fri 11am–2:30pm and 5:30–9:30pm; Sat–Sun 5:30–9pm.

Makawao & Pukalani

MODERATE

Casanova Italian Restaurant & Deli ★ ITALIAN/DELI   Look for the tiny veranda with a few stools, always full, in front of a deli at Makawao's busiest intersection—that's the most visible part of the Casanova restaurant and lounge. Makawao's nightlife center contains a stage, dance floor, restaurant, and bar—and food to love and remember. This is pasta heaven; try the spaghetti *fra diavolo* or the spinach gnocchi in a Gorgonzola sauce. Other options include a huge pizza selection, grilled lamb chops in an Italian mushroom marinade, lots more pasta dishes, and luscious desserts. My personal picks on a stellar menu: garlic spinach topped with Parmesan and pine nuts, and for dessert, the best tiramisu on the island. Check the website for a schedule of top entertainment, such as Willie K and his band.

1188 Makawao Ave., Makawao. www.casanovamaui.com. © **808/572-0220.** Reservations recommended for dinner. Main courses $9–$18 lunch, $24–$36 dinner; 12-in. pizzas $12–$20; pastas $12–$18. AE, DC, DISC, MC, V. Mon–Sat 11:30am–2pm and 5:30–9:30pm; Sun 5:30–9:30pm. Lounge daily 5:30pm–1:30am (closing time varies depending on entertainment). Deli Mon–Sat 7:30am–5:30pm; Sun 8:30am–5:30pm.

Market Fresh Bistro ★★ 🎒 MEDITERRANEAN   Attention foodies: Plan to eat dinner here at least once during your stay on Maui. Yes, it's a long drive from a resort area, but Chef Justin Pardo (formerly of the Union Square Café in

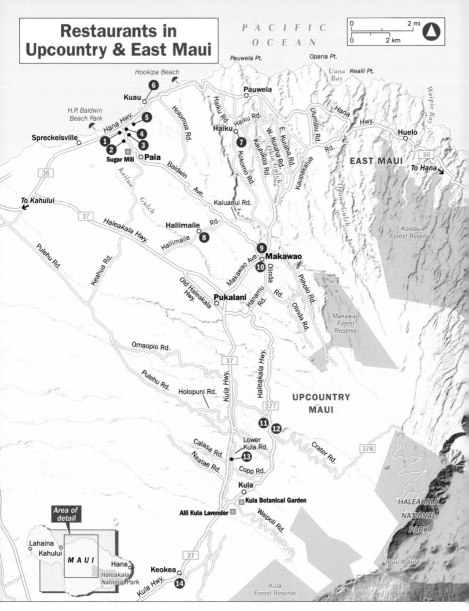

Restaurants in Upcountry & East Maui

PACIFIC OCEAN

New York City and the Wailea Grand on Maui) is a culinary genius who uses 90% local products at this off-the-beaten-path restaurant, hidden in a minimall complex. The menu changes daily; the chef's creations include an appetizer of pan-seared sea scallops with a watermelon curried gazpacho or a spice-crusted duck breast in a port-wine marinade with local figs and micro-greens. Entrees range from taro-crusted fish with roasted carrots and asparagus in a fennel-saffron tomato jus to a pork loin wrapped in applewood-smoked bacon. Every Thursday night they serve their prix-fixe farm dinners, featuring the best from local farmers in a seven-course dinner for $60 (wine pairing add $48).

3620 Baldwin Ave., Makawao. www.marketfreshbistromaui.com. © **808/572-4877.** Reservations recommended for dinner. Breakfast $10–$13; lunch $10–$15; dinner $28–$34. AE, MC, V. Tues–Sat 9–11am; Sun 9am–2pm; Tues–Wed 11:30am–4pm; Thurs–Sat 11:30am–3pm; Thurs–Sat 6–8:30pm.

Kula (at the Base of Haleakala National Park)

MODERATE

Kula Lodge ★ HAWAII REGIONAL/AMERICAN   Don't let the dinner prices scare you: The Kula Lodge is equally enjoyable, if not more so, at breakfast and lunch, when the prices are lower and the views through the picture windows are eye-popping. The vista spans the flanks of Haleakala, the ocean, and the West Maui Mountains. The Kula Lodge has always been known for its breakfasts: fabulous eggs Benedict, including a vegetarian version with spinach, tomatoes, and feta cheese; legendary mac-nut pancakes; and a highly recommended Loco Moco, a classic of hamburger, rice, brown gravy, and fried egg. Go for sunset cocktails and watch the colors change into deep end-of-day hues. When darkness descends, a roaring fire adds to the coziness of the room. The dinner menu features "small plates" of Thai summer rolls, seared ahi, and other starters. Fresh catch with a choice of preparations is a good bet, but there's also pasta, roast beef, baby-back ribs, and Cornish game hen.

15200 Haleakala Hwy. (Hwy. 377), Kula. www.kulalodge.com. © **808/878-2517.** Reservations recommended for dinner. Main courses $10–$18 breakfast, $12–$26 lunch, $12–$35 dinner. AE, DC, DISC, MC, V. Daily 7am–9pm.

INEXPENSIVE

Cafe 808 AMERICAN   Despite its out-of-the-way location (or perhaps because of it), Cafe 808 has become the universal favorite among upcountry residents of all ages. The breakfast coffee group, the lunchtime crowd, and dinner regulars all know it's the place for tasty home-style cooking with no pretensions: beloved burgers (teriyaki, hamburger, cheeseburger, gardenburger, mahimahi, taro), roast pork, smoked turkey, and a huge selection of local-style specials. Regulars rave about the chicken *katsu*, saimin, and beef stew. The few tables are sprinkled around a room with linoleum floors, hardwood benches, plastic patio chairs, and old-fashioned booths—rough around the edges in a pleasing way, and very camp.

4566 Lower Kula Rd. (past Holy Ghost Church, across from Morihara Store), Kula. © **808/878-6874.** Main courses $8–$12; burgers from $5. MC. Daily 6am–8pm.

Grandma's Coffee House COFFEEHOUSE/AMERICAN   Alfred Franco's grandmother started what is now a fifth-generation coffee business back in 1918, when she was 16 years old. Today, this tiny wooden coffeehouse, still fueled by homegrown Haleakala coffee beans, is the quintessential roadside oasis. Grandma's offers espresso, hot and cold coffees, home-baked pastries, inexpensive pasta, sandwiches (including sensational avocado veggie burgers), homemade soups, fresh juices, and local plate-lunch specials that change daily. Rotating specials include Hawaiian beef stew, ginger chicken, chicken curry, lentil soup, and sandwiches piled high with Kula vegetables. The coffee is legendary, but the real standouts are the lemon squares and the pumpkin bread.

9232 Kula Hwy. (at the end of Hwy. 37, about 6 miles before the Tedeschi Winery and Vineyards in Ulupalakua), Keokea. www.grandmascoffee.com. ☏ **808/878-2140.** Most items under $10. DISC, MC, V. Daily 7am–5pm.

Kula Sandalwoods Cafe ★ AMERICAN   Chef Eleanor Loui, a graduate of the Culinary Institute of America, makes hollandaise sauce every morning from fresh upcountry egg yolks, sweet butter, and Meyer lemons, which her family grows in the yard above the cafe. This is Kula cuisine, with produce from the backyard and everything made from scratch, including French toast with home-baked Portuguese sweet bread, hotcakes with fresh fruit, open-faced country omelets, hamburgers drenched in a special cheese sauce made with grated sharp cheddar, a killer kalua-pork sandwich, a grilled ono sandwich, and an outstanding veggie burger. Dine in the gazebo or on the terrace, with dazzling views in all directions—including, in the spring, a yard dusted with lavender jacaranda flowers and a hillside ablaze with fields of orange *akulikuli* blossoms.

15427 Haleakala Hwy. (Hwy. 377), Kula. www.kulasandalwoods.com. ☏ **808/878-3523.** Main courses $9–$15 breakfast, $8–$15 lunch. MC, V. Mon–Fri 7:30am–3pm; Sun 7:30–11:30am.

EAST MAUI: ON THE ROAD TO HANA

The residential areas on the road to Hana range from the eclectic eateries in Paia to the gourmet cuisine at Colleen's in the Haiku Cannery to Mama's excellent fresh fish (at astronomical prices) in the oceanside community of Kuau.

Paia

MODERATE

Charley's Restaurant ★★ ☺ AMERICAN/MEXICAN   Although Charley's (named after Charley P. Woofer, a Great Dane) serves three meals a day, breakfast is really the time to come here. Located in downtown Paia, Charley's is a cross between a 1960s hippie hangout, a windsurfers' power-breakfast spot, and a honky-tonk bar that gets going after dark. Before you head out to Hana, stop at Charley's for a larger-than-life breakfast (eggs, potatoes, toast, and coffee will set you back about $9.50). There are plenty of espresso drinks, but the regular coffee is excellent. Lunch is burgers, sandwiches, calzones, and pizza (after 2pm). Dinner is grilled fish and steak. The current chef is featuring a menu with stir-fry, a variety of pasta dishes, a meatloaf, and fresh fish. You'll see all walks of life here, from visitors on their way to Hana at 7am to buff windsurfers chowing down at noon to Willie Nelson on his way to the bar to play a tune.

142 Hana Hwy., Paia. www.charleysmaui.com. ☏ **808/579-8085.** Main courses $10–$16 breakfast, $11–$12 lunch, $11–$22 dinner. AE, DISC, MC, V. Daily 7am–10pm.

Milagros Food Company ★ SOUTHWESTERN/SEAFOOD   Milagros has gained a following with its great home-style cooking, upbeat atmosphere, and highly touted margaritas. Sit outdoors and watch the parade of Willie Nelson look-alikes ambling by as you tuck into the ahi creation of the evening, a combination of Southwestern and Pacific Rim styles and flavors accompanied by fresh veggies and Kula greens. Lunch ranges from ahi burgers to honey and mac-nut grilled-salmon salad. For dinner, options include blackened ahi tacos, seafood enchiladas, steak fajitas, shrimp tostada, and sometimes Chesapeake Bay crab cakes. I love Paia's tie-dyes, beads, and hippie flavor, and this is the front-row seat for it all. Watch for happy hour, with cheap and fabulous margaritas.

3 Baldwin Ave., Paia. ☎ **808/579-8755.** Main courses $8–$13 lunch, $13–$19 dinner. AE, MC, V. Daily 10:45am–10pm.

Moana Bakery & Cafe ★★ CAFE/ASIAN   Moana gets high marks for its stylish concrete floors, high ceilings, booths and cafe tables, and fabulous food. Don Ritchey, formerly a chef at Haliimaile General Store, has created the perfect Paia eatery, a casual bakery/cafe that highlights his stellar skills. The lemon grass–grilled prawns with green-papaya salad is an explosion of flavors and textures, and the Thai red curry with coconut milk, served over vegetables, seafood, or tofu, comes atop jasmine rice with crisp rice noodles and fresh sprouts to cool the fire. I also vouch for Ritchey's special gift with fish: The nori-sesame-crusted mahimahi with miso-garlic tapioca pearls is cooked, like the curry, to perfection. There's open mic and $7 spaghetti on Tuesday nights, and live music Wednesday, Friday, and Saturday nights from 6:30 to 8:30pm. Sushi is available after 4pm Tuesday through Sunday.

71 Baldwin Ave., Paia. www.moanacafe.com. ☎ **808/579-9999.** Reservations recommended for dinner. Main courses $8–$15 breakfast, $9–$17 lunch, $10–$44 dinner. MC, V. Mon 8am–3pm; Tues–Sun 8am–9pm.

INEXPENSIVE

Café des Amis ★★ 💼 CREPES/MEDITERRANEAN/INDIAN   This tiny eatery is a hidden delight: healthy and tasty breakfasts, lunches, and dinners that are easy on the wallet. Crepes are the star here, and they are popular: spinach with feta cheese, shrimp curry with coconut milk, and dozens more choices, including breakfast crepes and dessert crepes (like banana and chocolate or strawberries and cream). Equally popular are the Greek salads and smoothies. Dinners feature authentic Indian curries (served with rice, mango chutney, and tomato chutney), such as a vegetable curry with spinach, carrots, cauliflower, and potato with Tamil spices and tomato. You'll also find the best coffee in Paia here.

42 Baldwin Ave., Paia. ☎ **808/579-6323.** Crepes $9–$12; entrees $15–$20. MC, V. Daily 8:30am–8:30pm.

Paia Fish Market SEAFOOD   When you step inside this former fish market, you expect to see filets of just-caught fish in the deli case. What you do find is cooked seafood, salads, pastas, fajitas, and quesadillas to take out or enjoy at the few picnic tables inside the restaurant. It's an appealing selection: Cajun-style fresh catch, fresh-fish specials (usually ahi or salmon), fresh-fish tacos and quesadillas, and seafood and chicken pastas. You can also order hamburgers, cheeseburgers, fish and chips (or shrimp and chips), and wonderful lunch and dinner plates that are cheap and tasty. Photos of the number-one sport here, windsurfing, adorn the walls.

110 Hana Hwy., Paia. www.paiafishmarket.com. ℂ **808/579-8030.** Lunch and dinner plates $11–$16. DISC, MC, V. Daily 11am–9:30pm.

Haiku

MODERATE

Colleen's at the Cannery ★★ 🎁 INTERNATIONAL Way, way, way off the beaten path lies this fabulous find in the rural Haiku Cannery Marketplace. Once through the doors, you'll swear you've dropped down in the middle of a hot, chic boutique restaurant in SoHo in Manhattan (only, when you look around at the patrons, they are pure Haiku upcountry residents). It's worth the drive to enjoy Colleen's fabulous culinary creations, like a wild-mushroom ravioli with sautéed portobello mushrooms, tomatoes, herbs, and a roasted-pepper *coulis* for $17 (not New York City prices); pan-seared ahi for $21; or filet mignon for $30. Colleen also serves up smaller meals, such as burgers and fish and chips. Breakfast includes wonderful omelets and mouthwatering French toast made with Colleen's own homemade bread. Lunch stars baguette sandwiches, wraps, salads, and burgers and fries. I only wish Colleen's would take reservations.

At Haiku Cannery Marketplace, 810 Haiku Rd., Haiku. www.colleensinhaiku.com. ℂ **808/575-9211.** Reservations not accepted. Main courses $6.50–$14 breakfast, $8–$15 lunch, $9–$30 dinner. AE, DISC, MC, V. Daily 6am–10pm.

Elsewhere on the Road to Hana

VERY EXPENSIVE

Mama's Fish House ★★★ SEAFOOD Okay, it's expensive (maybe the most expensive seafood house on Maui), but if you love fish, this is the place for you. The restaurant's entrance, a cove with windsurfers, tide pools, and white sand, is a South Seas fantasy worthy of Gauguin. The interior features curved lauhala-lined ceilings, walls of split bamboo, and picture windows to let in the view. Mama's mood is hard to beat. The fish is fresh (the fishermen are even credited by name on the menu) and prepared either Hawaiian-style (with tropical fruit or baked in a crust of macadamia nuts and vanilla beans) or in a number of dishes involving ferns, seaweed, Maui onions, and roasted *kukui* nut. My favorite is mahimahi laulau with luau leaves (taro greens) and Maui onions, baked in ti leaves and served with kalua pig and Hanalei poi. Other special touches include the use of Molokai sweet potato, organic lettuces, Haiku bananas, and fresh coconut.

799 Poho Place (just off the Hana Hwy.), Kuau. www.mamasfishhouse.com. ℂ **808/579-8488.** Reservations recommended for lunch, required for dinner. Main courses $26–$48 lunch, $27–$58 dinner. AE, DC, DISC, MC, V. Daily 11am–3pm and 4:15–9pm (last seating).

AT THE END OF THE ROAD IN EAST MAUI: HANA

The quaint Hawaiian village of Hana offers visitors a trip back to Maui's yesteryear. Unfortunately, the town does not offer very many dining options—just Travaasa Hana, the very expensive dining room at the town's only resort hotel, and the moderately priced takeout food at the Hana Ranch Hotel.

Expensive

Ka'uiki at Travaasa Hana ★★ INTERNATIONAL   The focus at the main dining room of the former Hotel Hana Maui is on fresh fish caught by local fishermen, produce brought in by nearby farmers, and seasonal fruits. The result is true Hawaiian food, grown right on the island. Breakfast features Maui egg dishes, macadamia-nut pancakes, Longhi's famous French toast, and local papaya. Lunch ranges from free-range beef burgers and hand-cut fries to a just-caught-fish sandwich. The dinner menu, which changes twice a week, can include fresh local lettuce for a baby wedge salad with Gorgonzola dressing, and entrees like *lilikoi* glazed opah, purple sweet-potato mash, and coconut-lime sauce; or baked Hana mahi with vegetable stir-fry and ginger soy glaze. Live Hawaiian music Sunday, Monday, and Thursday nights from 7 to 9pm.

At the Travaasa Hana, 5031 Hana Hwy., Hana. www.travaasa.com/hana. © **808/248-8212.** Reservations recommended for Fri–Sat dinner. Main courses $12–$25 breakfast, $8–$18 lunch, $28–$40 dinner. AE, DISC, MC, V. Daily 7:30am–11am and 11:30am–8pm.

Moderate

Hana Ranch Restaurant AMERICAN   Owned and operated by Travaasa Hana, the Hana Ranch Restaurant is the informal, in-town alternative to the hotel's dining room for lunch or dinner. The menu is burgers, chicken, and fish, with the addition of steaks, ribs, and grilled fish for dinner. There are indoor tables as well as two outdoor pavilions that offer distant ocean views. At the adjoining takeout stand, fast-food classics prevail: teriyaki plate lunch, mahimahi sandwiches, cheeseburgers, hot dogs, and ice cream.

Mill Place, Hana. www.travaasa.com/hana. © **808/270-5280.** Main courses $13–$16 lunch, $22–$30 dinner. AE, DISC, MC, V. Daily 11am–8:30pm. Takeout counter daily 11am–2:30pm. Live music Tues and Sat 7–10pm.

RESTAURANTS BY CUISINE

AMERICAN

Buzz's Wharf (**$$$,** p. 214)
Cafe 808 (**$,** p. 222)
Charley's Restaurant ★★ (**$$,** p. 223)
Cheeseburger in Paradise (**$,** p. 204)
CJ's Deli & Diner ★ (**$,** p. 209)
Gannon's ★★ (**$$,** p. 219)
Grandma's Coffee House (**$,** p. 222)
Haliimaile General Store ★★★ (**$$$,** p. 220)
Hana Ranch Restaurant (**$$,** p. 226)
Joe's ★★ (**$$,** p. 219)
Kula Lodge ★ (**$$,** p. 222)
Kula Sandalwoods Cafe ★ (**$,** p. 223)
Lahaina Coolers ★ (**$,** p. 204)

Lahaina Grill ★★ (**$$$$,** p. 199)
Main Street Bistro (**$,** p. 198)
Peggy Sue's (**$,** p. 216)
Stella Blues Café ★ (**$$,** p. 216)

ASIAN

The Banyan Tree ★★ (**$$$$,** p. 212)
Moana Bakery & Cafe ★★ (**$$,** p. 224)

ASIAN FUSION

Cane & Taro ★ (**$$,** p. 207)

CAFE/COFFEEHOUSE

Grandma's Coffee House (**$,** p. 222)
Moana Bakery & Cafe ★★ (**$$,** p. 224)

KEY TO ABBREVIATIONS:
$$$$** = Very Expensive   **$$$** = Expensive   **$$** = Moderate   **$ = Inexpensive

CREPES

Café des Amis ★★ (**$,** p. 224)

DELI

Casanova Italian Restaurant & Deli ★
(**$$,** p. 220)
CJ's Deli & Diner ★ (**$,** p. 209)
Joy's Place (**$,** p. 216)
Maui Sunrise Café (**$,** p. 205)

FRENCH

Gerard's ★★★ (**$$$,** p. 200)

HAWAII REGIONAL & HAWAIIAN

A.K.'s Café ★★ (**$,** p. 198)
David Paul's Island Grill ★★
(**$$$,** p. 200)
Haliimaile General Store ★★★
(**$$$,** p. 220)
Ko ★★★ (**$$$$,** p. 217)
Kula Lodge ★ (**$$,** p. 222)
Mala Wailea ★★★ (**$$$$,** p. 218)
Roy's Kahana Bar & Grill ★★★
(**$$$,** p. 209)
Tiki Terrace (**$$,** p. 208)
Son'z Maui at Swan Court ★★★
(**$$$,** p. 205)
Spago ★★ (**$$$$,** p. 218)

HEALTH FOOD

A. K.'s Café ★★ (**$,** p. 198)
Down to Earth (**$,** p. 240)
Joy's Place (**$,** p. 216)

INDIAN

Café des Amis ★★ (**$,** p. 224)

INTERNATIONAL

Class Act ★ (**$,** p. 197)
Colleen's at the Cannery ★★
(**$$,** p. 225)
Ka'uiki at Travaasa Hana ★★
(**$$$,** p. 226)
Lahaina Coolers ★ (**$,** p. 204)

ITALIAN

Casanova Italian Restaurant & Deli ★
(**$$,** p. 220)
Ferraro's Bar e Ristorante ★
(**$$$,** p. 219)

Longhi's ★ (**$$$$,** p. 217)
Marco's Grill & Deli (**$$,** p. 196)
Penne Pasta Café ★ (**$,** p. 205)
Pizza Paradiso Italian Kitchen
(**$,** p. 210)

JAPANESE/SUSHI

Ichiban (**$$,** p. 195)

MEDITERRANEAN

Bistro Casanova ★ (**$$,** p. 195)
Café des Amis ★★ (**$,** p. 224)
Market Fresh Bistro ★★ (**$$,** p. 220)
Penne Pasta Café ★ (**$,** p. 205)
Plantation House Restaurant ★★
(**$$$,** p. 213)

MEXICAN

Charley's Restaurant ★★ (**$$,** p. 223)
Cilantro: Fresh Mexican Grill ★
(**$,** p. 204)
Maui Tacos (**$,** p. 210)

NOODLES

Sam Sato's (**$,** p. 198)

PACIFIC RIM

Duke's Beach House ★★ (**$$,** p. 207)
Five Palms ★ (**$$$,** p. 214)
I'O ★ (**$$$,** p. 200)
Merriman's ★★★ (**$$$$,** p. 212)
Pacific'O Restaurant ★ (**$$$,** p. 202)
Pineapple Grill ★★★ (**$$$,** p. 212)
Sea House Restaurant (**$$$,** p. 210)
Sansei Seafood Restaurant & Sushi
Bar ★★★ (**$$,** p. 213)
Spago ★★ (**$$$$,** p. 218)
Umalu ★ (**$$,** p. 207)

PIZZA

Maui Swiss Cafe (**$,** p. 205)
Nikki's Pizza (**$,** p. 209)
Pizza Paradiso Italian Kitchen (**$,** p. 210)
Shaka Sandwich & Pizza (**$,** p. 216)

PLATE LUNCH

Aloha Mixed Plate ★ (**$,** p. 203)
Sam Sato's (**$,** p. 198)

POLYNESIAN

The Feast at Lele ★★ (**$$$$,** p. 199)

SANDWICHES

Joy's Place (**$**, p. 216)
Maui Swiss Cafe (**$**, p. 205)

SEAFOOD

Lahaina Fish Company (**$$**, p. 202)
The Maalaea Waterfront
    Restaurant ★★ (**$$$**, p. 214)
Mala Wailea ★★★ (**$$$$**, p. 218)
Mama's Fish House ★★★
    (**$$$$**, p. 225)
Paia Fish Market (**$**, p. 224)
Plantation House Restaurant ★★
    (**$$$**, p. 213)

SOUTHWESTERN

Milagros Food Company ★
    (**$$**, p. 224)

STEAK/SEAFOOD

Beachside Grill/Leilani's on the Beach
    (**$$**, p. 206)
Cafe O'Lei Kihei ★★ (**$$**, p. 214)
Kimo's (**$$**, p. 202)
Mala Ocean Tavern ★★ (**$$**, p. 202)
Maui Brewing Co. (**$$**, p. 210)
Milagros Food Company ★
    (**$$**, p. 224)
Nick's Fishmarket Maui ★★
    (**$$$$**, p. 218)

SUSHI

Sansei Seafood Restaurant & Sushi
    Bar ★★★ (**$$**, p. 213)

VIETNAMESE

A Saigon Cafe ★ (**$**, p. 198)

PRACTICAL MATTERS: MAUI'S RESTAURANT SCENE

Dining on Maui tends to be casual—don't wear your bathing suit, but an aloha shirt with nice shorts and shoes will do in most restaurants.

Hours

People eat early on Maui. Many local residents get up before the sun, and tend to eat around 6 or 7pm. Visitors generally are jet-lagged and happy to go to dinner around sunset. Most restaurants on Maui close early and don't take reservations after 8:30pm unless noted. Late dining on Maui is 8:30pm.

Prices, Taxes & Tipping

Prices in Maui are higher than you are probably used to paying at home. But remember, you are on an isolated island—things just are more expensive here. Budget a little more money for your meals.

You can get more for your money by visiting the more expensive restaurants at lunch, when menu prices are generally cheaper. Most price ranges listed in this chapter are just the cost of the entree; obviously, if you also order an appetizer, salad, or dessert, the bill will be higher.

Expect to see Hawaii's general excise tax (4%) to be added to your bill. Tipping is the standard custom in Hawaii (just like the mainland United States), and good service is rewarded with a 15% to 20% tip, based on your total bill (minus the tax).

Ordering Fresh Fish

If you are looking forward to enjoying Hawaii's fresh tropical fish, see our "Ahi, Ono, & Opakapaka: A Hawaiian Seafood Primer," on p. 42, for descriptions of our local fish. The Monterey Bay Aquarium website (www.montereybayaquarium.org) offers lots of information on sustainable fish choices, plus free downloadable pocket guides and smartphone apps. Click on "Save the Oceans" to get started.

Most restaurants on Maui are honest and want to give you the freshest of the daily catch, but some are not so honest. Be sure to ask your server:

- When was the fresh catch caught?
- Where was it caught? (If it was not caught in Hawaii waters, it is not fresh.)
- Has the fish ever been frozen? (Some restaurants think "fresh frozen" is the same thing as "fresh fish." Do not eat at restaurants that think this way.)

Reservations

If you want to get a good seat at sunset, be sure to make reservations. Restaurants fill up for sunset, which varies from 5:30 to 6:30pm, depending on the time of year. During the Christmas season and winter, when Maui is full of tourists, you might want to make reservations for dinner so you won't have to wait for a seat.

SHOPS & GALLERIES

M aui is a shopaholic's dream as well as an arts center, with a large number of resident artists who show their works in dozens of galleries and countless gift shops. Maui is also the queen of specialty products, thanks to an agricultural cornucopia that includes Kula onions, upcountry protea, Kaanapali coffee, and many other tasty treats that are shipped worldwide.

As with any popular visitor destination, you'll have to wade through bad art and mountains of trinkets, particularly in Lahaina and Kihei, where touristy boutiques line the streets between rare pockets of treasures. If you shop in south or west Maui, expect to pay resort prices, clear down to a bottle of Evian or sunscreen.

The **Shops at Wailea,** an upscale shopping-and-restaurant complex, features more than 50 shops and five restaurants, including Louis Vuitton, Tiffany, Gap, Banana Republic, and a few locally well-known stores like Ki'i Gallery. This is resort shopping in the vein of **Whalers Village** in Kaanapali, where shopping and restaurant activity is concentrated in a single oceanfront complex.

Don't ignore central Maui, home to some first-rate boutiques. Watch the quaint town of **Wailuku,** which is poised for a resurgence. It has its own antiques alleys, and a major promenade on Main Street is in the works. The **Kaahumanu Center,** in neighboring Kahului, is becoming more fashionable by the month.

Upcountry, the boutiques of **Makawao** are worth seeking out, despite some attitude and high prices. The charm of shopping on Maui has always rested in the small, independent shops and galleries that crop up in surprising places.

CENTRAL MAUI

Kahului

Maui's residential population lives in these expansive suburbs. You're not going to find designer clothing, but down-to-earth items that people on Maui need to live, with shops like Foodland, Safeway and Longs Drugs. You can also hunt for treasure at the quirky **Maui Swap Meet** (p. 235). You'll find the best prices on essentials in this area.

Wailuku

Located at the gateway to Iao Valley, Wailuku is the county seat, the part of Maui where people live and work. Wailuku's attractive vintage architecture, smattering of antiques shops, and mom-and-pop eateries imbue the town with a down-home charm noticeably absent from Maui's resort areas. The community spirit fuels festivals throughout the year and is slowly attracting new businesses, but Wailuku is still a work in progress. It's a mixed bag—of course, there's junk, but a stroll along Main and Market streets usually turns up a treasure or two.

PREVIOUS PAGE: **Traditional Hawaiian leis.**

FARM FRESH: MAUI'S farmers MARKETS

Maui's produce has long been a source of pride for islanders. Check out the following farmers markets around the island (http://hawaii.gov/hdoa/add/farmers-market-in-hawaii/Maui.pdf):

○ **Maui's Fresh Produce Farmers Market,** at the Queen Kaahumanu Center, Kahului (© **808/877-4325**), on Tuesday, Wednesday, and Friday from 8am to 4pm, is the place to find a fresh, inexpensive selection of Maui-grown fruit, vegetables, flowers, and plants. They do have baked goods.

○ **Maui Mall Farmers Market & Craft Fair** is at the Maui Mall, Kahului (© **808/871-1307**), on Tuesday,

Wednesday, and Friday from 7am to 4pm.

○ **Farmers Market of Maui– Honokowai,** on lower Honoapiilani Road, across from the Honokowai Park (near Haku Hale Place; © **808/669-7004**), is every Monday, Wednesday, and Friday from 7 to 11am.

○ **Kihei Farmers Market** at Suda Store on Kihei Road in Kihei, is Monday through Friday from 8am to 4pm.

Worthwhile stops include the **Bailey House Museum Shop** (p. 237), **Bird of Paradise Unique Antiques** (p. 323), **Brown-Kobayashi** (p. 236), **Sandell** (p. 243), and **Takamiya Market** (p. 240).

WEST MAUI
Lahaina

Lahaina has something for everyone. Just walking along the variety of shops on Front Street is a fun activity. Lahaina's merchants and art galleries go all out from 7 to 10pm every Friday, when **Art Night** brings an extra measure of hospitality and community spirit. The Art Night openings are usually marked with live entertainment and refreshments, plus a livelier-than-usual street scene.

If you're in Lahaina on the second or last Thursday of the month, stroll by the front lawn of the **Baldwin Home Museum** for a splendid look at the craft of lei making (p. 237).

Mall lovers will be thrilled with the **Lahaina Center,** 900 Front St. (© **808/667-9216**), formerly a big, belching pineapple cannery, now a maze of more than 30 shops, a salon, restaurants, a nightclub, and a four-plex movie-theater complex. **Ruth's Chris Steak House** has opened its doors here, and **Hard Rock Cafe** serves lunch and dinner and offers

Lahaina Art Night.

nighttime live music on weekdays. Among the shopping stops are **Hilo Hattie** (a dizzying emporium of aloha wear) and **ABC Discount Store** (a chain of convenience stores located throughout Hawaii selling groceries, souvenirs, drugs, and cosmetics).

Hale Kahiko is a re-creation of a traditional Hawaiian village.

Even nonshoppers will be fascinated with the re-creation of a traditional Hawaiian village, called **Hale Kahiko,** at the Lahaina Center. With the commercialization of modern Lahaina, it's easy to forget that it was once the capital of the Hawaiian kingdom and a significant historic site. Hale Kahiko features three main houses *(hale):* a sleeping house; the men's dining house; and the crafts house, where women pounded *hala* (pandanus) strips to weave into mats and baskets. Construction of the houses consumed 10,000 square feet of ohia wood from the island, 20 tons of pili grass, and more than 4 miles of hand-woven coconut sennit for the lashings. Artifacts, weapons, a canoe,

Maui's Own: Ocean Vodka

If you're looking for a souvenir of your fabulous Maui trip to take home, or a unique gift for friends, consider Ocean Vodka. Produced by Hawaii Sea Spirits, this ultrapremium brand is not only USDA certified to contain organic ingredients, but also the water comes from 3,000 feet beneath the ocean off the Kona coast of the Big Island. The deep-sea water is harvested by KOYO USA, producers of MaHaLo Hawaii Deep Sea Water. The desalinated water has become widely popular in Japan, where people swear it has provided beneficial health effects (so far, no scientific studies have backed up this claim). The MaHaLo water is shipped to Maui, where it is blended with organic corn and rye to produce this one-of-a-kind vodka. It's available at restaurants, bars, hotels, and retail shops (for a complete list, see www.oceanvodka.com).

and indigenous trees are among the authentic touches in this village; you can take a free guided tour daily between 9am and 6pm.

Kaanapali

The Kaanapali Resort has its own upscale shopping complex, **Whalers Village,** 2435 Kaanapali Pkwy. (© **808/661-4567;** www.whalersvillage.com). Although it offers everything from whale blubber to Tommy Bahama and Sephora, it's short on local shops, and parking at the nearby lot is expensive. The complex is home to the **Whalers Village Museum** (p. 116), with its interactive exhibits, 40-foot sperm whale skeleton, and sand castles on perpetual display, but shoppers come for the designer thrills and beachfront dining. Budget shoppers take note: You can find most of the items featured here in the shops in Lahaina.

Honokowai, Kahana & Napili

North of Kaanapali on the Lower Honoapiilani Road is a small shopping mall, **Honokowai Marketplace,** only minutes before the Kapalua Airport. It houses restaurants, a handful of shops, a grocery store, and a dry cleaner. Not a lot of shopping opportunities, but convenient for the nearby condominium owners.

Nearby **Kahana Gateway** is another small mall built to serve the condominium community that has sprawled along the coastline between Honokowai and Kapalua.

Kapalua

The Kapalua Resort has a few upscale shops at the Ritz-Carlton. There's not much else, other than the **Honolua Store** (p. 242) and **Village Galleries** (p. 242).

SOUTH MAUI

Kihei

Kihei is one long strip of strip malls. Most of the shopping here is concentrated in the **Azeka Place Shopping Center** on South Kihei Road. Fast food abounds at the Azeka center. Across the street, there's another Azeka, called **Azeka Place II,** which houses the Coffee Store and a cluster of specialty shops with everything from children's clothes to shoes, sunglasses, and swimwear. Also on South Kihei Road is the **Kukui Mall,** with movie theaters, fast eats, and a few other visitor-oriented stores.

Wailea

Shopping fans will love the high-end mall, the Shops at Wailea, with a range of shops and restaurants. Other shopping opportunities abound at the string of luxury hotels which line the coast in this resort area.

UPCOUNTRY MAUI

Makawao

Bargain hunters should plan to spend a day checking out the unique boutique shops in Makawao, with one-of-a-kind gifts, clothing, and art, all at bargain prices. On the third Friday of every month, Makawao celebrates with live entertainment on the street and various festivities (10-min. chair massages, pony rides for the kids, and cheese and wine receptions at various shops and galleries), and all the shops stay open to 9pm.

Besides being a shopper's paradise, Makawao is the home of the island's most prominent arts organization, the **Hui No'eau Visual Arts Center ★**, 2841 Baldwin Ave. (© **808/572-6560;** www.huinoeau.com). Designed in 1917 by C. W. Dickey, one of Hawaii's most prominent architects, the two-story, Mediterranean-style stucco home that houses the center is located on a sprawling 9-acre estate called Kaluanui. A legacy of Maui's prominent *kamaaina* (old-timers) Harry and Ethel Baldwin, the estate became an arts center in 1976. Visiting artists offer lectures, classes, and demonstrations, all at reasonable prices, in basketry, jewelry making, ceramics, painting, and other media. Classes on Hawaiian art, culture, and history are also available. Call ahead for schedules and details. The exhibits here are drawn from a wide range of disciplines and multicultural sources and include both contemporary and traditional art from established and emerging artists. The gift shop, featuring many one-of-a-kind works by local artists and artisans, is worth a stop. Hours are Monday through Saturday from 10am to 4pm.

Kula

Kula isn't really a shopping destination unless you're looking for exotic cut flowers. Like anthuriums on the Big Island, proteas are a Maui trademark and an abundant crop on Haleakala's rich volcanic slopes. They also travel well, dry beautifully, and can be shipped worldwide with ease. **Proteas of Hawaii** (© **808/878-2533;** www.proteasofhawaii.com), a great source for these unusual flowers, is located across the street from the University of Hawaii Extension Service in Kula. Its gardens are open to the public.

EAST MAUI
On the Road to Hana: Paia

The tiny, two-street town of Paia is a "find" for serious shoppers and bargain hunters. Boutique stores line the street, offering everything from art (made on Maui) to vintage clothing.

Where the Deals Are: Maui Swap Meet

Every Saturday from 7am to 1pm, vendors spread out their wares in booths and under tarps, in a festival-like atmosphere that is pure Maui with a touch of kitsch. The colorful Maui specialties include vegetables from Kula and Keanae, fresh taro, plants, proteas, crafts, household items, homemade ethnic foods, and baked goods, including some fabulous fruit breads. Now students at the community college sell artwork and ceramics; the culinary-arts program has prepared food for sale. Between the cheap Balinese imports and New Age crystals and incense, you may find some vintage John Kelly prints and 1930s collectibles. Admission is 50¢, and if you go early while the vendors are setting up, no one will turn you away. At Maui Community College, in an area bounded by Kahului Beach Road and Wahine Pio Avenue (access via Wahine Pio Ave.). Call © 808/244-3100 for more information.

Hana

Hana is not a shopping destination, but definitely stop in at **Hana Coast Gallery** (p. 240) and **Hasegawa General Store** (p. 242) if you're here.

SHOPPING A TO Z

Aloha Wear

Hurricane   This boutique carries clothing, gifts, accessories, and books that are two steps ahead of the competition. Tommy Bahama aloha shirts and aloha print dresses; the Nick & Zoe line; work by local artists; a notable selection of fragrances for men and women; and hard-to-find, eccentric books and home accessories are part of the Hurricane appeal. Open 10am to 6pm Monday to Saturday and 11am to 5pm Sunday. 3639 Baldwin Ave. www.hurricanemaui.com. © **808/572-5076.**

Moonbow Tropics   If you're looking for a tasteful aloha shirt, go to Moonbow. The selection consists of a few carefully culled racks of the top labels in aloha wear, in fabrics ranging from the finest silks and linens to Egyptian cotton and spun rayons. Some of the finds: aloha shirts by Tori Richard, Reyn Spooner, Kamehameha, Paradise Found, Kahala, and other top brands. Silk pants, silk shorts, vintage-print neckwear, and an upgraded women's selection hang on colorful racks. The jewelry pieces, ranging from tanzanite to topaz, rubies, and moonstones, are mounted in unique settings made on-site. Open daily 10am to 6pm. 20 Baldwin Ave. www.moonbowtropics.com. © **808/579-8775.** Additional locations: 612 Front St., Lahaina, © 808/667-7998; and Shops at Wailea, © 808/874-1170.

Antiques, Collectibles & Vintage

Bird of Paradise Unique Antiques   Owner Joe Myhand loves furniture, old Matson liner menus, blue willow china, and anything nostalgic that happens to be Hawaiian. The furniture ranges from 1940s rattan to wicker and old koa—items tailor-made for informal island living and leisurely moments on the lanai. The collection ebbs and flows depending on his finds, keeping buyers waiting for his Depression glass, California pottery from the 1930s and 1940s, old dinnerware, perfume bottles, vintage aloha shirts, and vintage Hawaiian music on cassettes. Hours vary; please call first. 56 N. Market St. © **808/242-7699.**

Brown-Kobayashi   Graceful living is the theme here. Prices range from a few dollars to the thousands in this 1,700-square-foot treasure-trove. The owners have added a fabulous selection of antique stone garden pieces that mingle quietly with Asian antiques and old and new French, European, and Hawaiian objects. Although the collection is eclectic, there is a strong cohesive aesthetic that sets Brown-Kobayashi apart from other Maui antiques stores. Exotic and precious Chinese woods (purple sandalwood and *huanghuali*) glow discreetly from quiet corners, and an occasional monarchy-style lidded milo bowl comes in and flies out. Hours vary, so please call first. 38 N. Market St. © **808/242-0804.**

Duck Soup   Way, way off the beaten path lies this warehouse full of Asian and Indonesian treasures. Owners Judy Bruder and Sandi Stoner definitely have an eye for spotting the unusual and chic. Most of their buying trips to Indonesia are for interior designers, homeowners, and hotels, but they also bring back some incredible jewelry, handbags, and art, all at prices that will put a smile on your face. The location is a bit tricky; call first for directions and note that it is open only Wednesday through Saturday, 10am to 3pm. Off Mokulele Hwy. (Hwy. 311), about a mile from Puunene, near the Maui Animal Shelter and the Central Maui Baseyard. www.ducksoupmaui.com. © **808/871-7875.**

Lahaina Printsellers Specializes in a selection of antique prints, maps, paintings, and engravings, including 18th- to 20th-century cartography, all of which offer great browsing and gift potential. Open 10am to 5pm Monday through Friday. 1013 Limahana Place, Lahaina. www.printsellers.com. © **808/667-7843.**

Arts, Crafts & Museum Stores

Bailey House Museum Shop For made-in-Hawaii items, Bailey House is a must stop. It offers a thoroughly enjoyable browse through authoritative Hawaiiana, in a museum that's one of the finest examples of missionary architecture, dating from 1833. The shop, a small space of discriminating taste, packs a wallop with its selection of remarkable gift items, from Hawaiian music to exquisite woods, traditional Hawaiian games to pareu and books. Prints by the legendary Hawaii artist Joelle Purse, lauhala hats, hand-sewn pheasant hatbands, jams and jellies, Maui cookbooks, and an occasional Hawaiian quilt are some of the treasures to be found here. Open Monday to Saturday from 10am to 4pm. At the Bailey House Museum, 2375-A Main St. www.mauimuseum.org. © **808/244-3326.**

Baldwin Home Museum If you are in Lahaina on the second or last Thursday of the month, stop by the front lawn for a splendid look at the craft of lei making and an opportunity to meet the gregarious seniors of Lahaina. In a program sponsored by AARP, they gather from 10am to 4pm to demonstrate lei making, to sell their floral creations, and, equally important, to socialize. During some winter months when flowers aren't blooming, the event is not held, so call first. 120 Dickenson St., Lahaina. www.mauimuseum.org. © **808/661-3262.**

Banana Wind Tucked into the Lahaina Cannery, this whimsical store has everything from T-shirts to woven baskets, candles, pareu, shells, and even carved wooden banana trees (just $6,000 and very tricky to transport in your luggage). This is the place to find some great souvenirs to take back home. Open 9:30am to 9pm Monday to Saturday and 9am to 7pm on Sunday. At the Lahaina Cannery Mall, 1221 Honoapiilani Hwy. www.lahainacannerymall.com. © **808/661-1600.**

Hui No'eau Visual Arts Center ★ Designed in 1917 by C. W. Dickey, one of Hawaii's most prominent architects, the two-story, Mediterranean-style stucco home that houses the center is located on a sprawling 9-acre estate called Kaluanui. A legacy of Maui's prominent *kamaaina* Harry and Ethel Baldwin, the estate became an arts center in 1976. Visiting artists offer lectures, classes, and demonstrations, all at reasonable prices, in basketry, jewelry making, ceramics, painting, and other media. Classes on Hawaiian art, culture, and history are also available. Call ahead for schedules and details. The exhibits here are drawn from a wide range of disciplines and multicultural sources and include both contemporary and traditional art from established and emerging artists. The gift shop, featuring many one-of-a-kind works by local artists and artisans, is worth a stop. Hours are Monday through Saturday from 10am to 4pm. 2841 Baldwin Ave. www.huinoeau.com. © **808/572-6560.**

Find one-of-a-kind word at Hui No'eau Visual Arts Center.

Lahaina Arts Society Galleries   With its membership of more than 185 Maui artists, the nonprofit Lahaina Arts Society is an excellent community resource. Changing monthly exhibits in the Banyan Tree and Old Jail galleries offer a good look at the island's artistic well: two-dimensional art, fiber art, ceramics, sculpture, prints, jewelry, and more. In the shade of the humongous banyan tree in the square across from Pioneer Inn, "Art in the Park" fairs are offered several times month. (Check the calendar on the society's website for dates and times.) 648 Wharf St., Ste. 103. www.lahaina-arts.com. © **808/661-3228.**

Maui Crafts Guild   The old wooden storefront at the gateway to Paia houses crafts of high quality and in all price ranges, from pit-fired raku to bowls of Norfolk pine and other Maui woods, fashioned by Maui hands. Artist owned and operated, the guild claims 25 members who live and work on Maui. Basketry, hand-painted fabrics, jewelry, beadwork, traditional Hawaiian stonework, pressed flowers, fused glass, stained glass, copper sculpture, banana-bark paintings, and pottery of all styles are displayed in the two-story gift gallery. Upstairs, sculptor Arthur Dennis Williams shows his breathtaking work in wood, bronze, and stone. Everything can be shipped. Open daily 10am to 6pm. **Aloha Bead Co.** (© **808/ 579-9709**), in the back of the gallery, is a treasure-trove for bead workers. 69 Hana Hwy. www.mauicraftsguild.com. © **808/579-9697.**

Maui Hands   Maui hands have made 90% of the items in this shop/gallery. Because it's a consignment shop, you'll find Hawaii-made handicrafts and prices that aren't inflated. The selection includes paintings, prints, jewelry, glass marbles, native-wood bowls, and tchotchkes for every budget. This is an ideal stop for made-on-Maui products and crafts of good quality. Open daily from 9:30am to 6:30pm. 84 Hana Hwy. www.mauihands.com. © **808/579-9245.** Additional locations: Hyatt Regency, 200 Nohea Kai Dr., Kaanapali, © 808/667-7997; and Lahaina Old Town, 612 Front St., © 808/667-9898.

Sherri Reeve Gallery & Gifts   If you want to take a little bit of the beauty of Maui home with you, stop by this open-air gallery. Artist Sherri Reeve grew up in Hawaii (the local phone book featured her art on the cover one year), and she has captured the vibrant color and feel of the islands. You can find everything from inexpensive cards, hand-painted tiles, and T-shirts to original works and limited editions. Open daily 10am to 6pm. 3669 Baldwin Ave. www.sreeve.com. ✆ **808/ 572-8931.**

Fashion

Collections Gecko Trading Co. Boutique   The selection in this tiny boutique is eclectic and always changing: One day it's mesh T-shirts in a dragon motif, the next it's Provence soaps and antique lapis jewelry. I've seen everything from handmade crocheted bags from New York to hammered-tin candle holders from Mexico, plus clothing from Spain and France, collectible bottles, toys, and shawls. The prices are reasonable, the service is friendly, and it's more homey than glammy—not as self-conscious as some of the other local boutiques. Open daily from 10am to 6pm. 3621 Baldwin Ave. www.gtcboutique.com. ✆ **808/572-0249.**

CY Maui   Women who like flowing clothing in silks, rayons, and natural fibers will love this shop, formerly the popular Manikin in Kahului. If you don't find what you want on the racks of simple bias-cut designs, you can have it made from the bolts of stupendous fabrics lining the store. Except for a few hand-painted silks, everything here is washable. Open daily from 9:30am to 9pm. At the Shops at Wailea, 3750 Wailea Alanui Dr. www.cymaui.com. ✆ **808/891-0782.**

Fairmont Store   This chic boutique in the Fairmont Kea Lani stands out due to the careful eye of buyer Lennette Clark, who has an excellent sense of fashion. Here you'll find Michael Stars and Glima T-shirts, Yellow Box and Matisse sandals, Sophia and Chloe jewelry, Hobo handbags, and a range of locally-made-on-Maui gifts. It's definitely worth your time to browse this airy and well-lit shop, with a truly helpful staff. Open 8am to 9pm Monday through Friday and 9am to 5pm Saturday. At the Fairmont Kea Lani Maui, 4100 Wailea Alanui Dr. ✆ **808/875-4100,** ext. 810.

Hemp House   Clothing and accessories made of hemp, a sturdy, eco-friendly fiber, are finally making their way into the mainstream. The Hemp House has as complete a selection as you can expect to see in Hawaii, with "denim" hemp jeans, lightweight linenlike trousers, dresses, shirts, and a full range of sensible, easy-care wear. Open 9:30am to 7pm daily. 16 Baldwin Ave. www.hemphousemaui. com. ✆ **808/579-8880.**

Holiday & Co.   Attractive women's clothing in natural fibers hangs from racks, while jewelry to go with it beckons from the counter. Recent finds include elegant fiber evening bags, luxurious bath gels, easygoing dresses and separates, Dansko clogs, shawls, soaps, aloha shirts, books, picture frames, and jewelry. Open from 10am to 6pm daily. 3681 Baldwin Ave. ✆ **808/572-1470.**

Maggie Coulombe 🎁   You'll find this high-fashion store with the unique designs of Maggie Coulombe in the midst of Lahaina. You'll find Maggie's latest couture, jersey, linen, pareu, and shoes, plus accessories, jewelry, purses, and a few surprises. Open daily from 9:30am to 10pm. 2535 Kaanapali Pkwy., Whalers Village. www.maggiecoulombe.com. ✆ **808/344-6672.**

Flowers

Proteas of Hawaii This is a great source for these unusual flowers. It's open to the public, so you can just view the exotic proteas for free. But beware: They are so captivating that it is hard to resist the temptation to send a few bouquets back home. Open Monday to Friday, 8am to 3pm. Located next to Kula Lodge and across the street from the University of Hawaii Extension Service in Kula. 417 Mauna Place, Kula. www.proteasofhawaii.com. ℂ **808/878-2533.**

Food & Drink

Down to Earth Natural Foods For those looking after their waistlines or for fans of health food, this is your pace. Make a healthy meal out of the fresh organic produce, bountiful salads, sandwiches, and smoothies, or shop from several aisles packed with vitamins and supplements, fresh-baked goods, snacks, whole grains, and other vegetarian and health foods. Open 7am to 9pm Monday to Saturday, 8am to 8pm Sunday. 305 Dairy Rd. www.downtoearth.org. ℂ **808/ 877-2661.**

Rodeo General Store In addition to the precooked spaghetti and lasagna to take home, this well-stocked convenience store in Makawao also has sandwiches, salads, and changing specials At the far end of the store is the oenophile's bonanza, a superior wine selection housed in its own temperature-controlled cave. Open 6:30am to 10pm Monday to Saturday and 6:30am to 9pm Sunday. 3661 Baldwin Ave. ℂ **808/572-7841.**

Takamiya Market To experience the cuisine eaten by local residents, check out the unpretentious home-cooked foods, prepared daily and served on plastic-foam plates, at this grocery store in Wailuku. This is a great place to pick up a picnic, an exotic picnic: from the chilled-fish counter come fresh sashimi and poke, and among the renowned assortment of prepared foods are mounds of shoyu chicken, tender fried squid, roast pork, kalua pork, laulau, Chinese noodles, fiddlehead ferns, and Western comfort foods, such as corn bread and potato salad. Fresh produce and paper products are also available, but it's the prepared foods and fresh-fish counter that have made Takamiya a household name in central Maui. Open 5:15am to 6:30pm Monday to Saturday. 359 N. Market St., Wailuku. http://takamiyamarket.com. ℂ **808/244-3404.**

T. Komoda Store and Bakery This is the place to get Komoda's famous cream puffs. Old-timers know to come early, before they're sold out. Then the cinnamon rolls, doughnuts, pies, and chocolate cake take over. Pastries are just the beginning: Poi, macadamia nut candies and cookies, and small bunches of local fruit keep the customers coming. Open 7am to 5pm Monday, Tuesday, Thursday, and Friday; 7am to 2pm Saturday. 3674 Baldwin Ave., Makawao. ℂ **808/ 572-7261.**

Galleries

Hana Coast Gallery 🎁 This gallery is a good reason to go to Hana: It's an aesthetic and cultural experience that informs as it enlightens. Tucked away in the posh Travaasa Hana, the gallery is known for its high level of curatorship and commitment to the cultural art of Hawaii. There are no jumping whales or dolphins here, and except for a section of European and Asian masters, the 3,000-square-foot gallery is devoted entirely to Hawaii artists, whose sculptures, paintings, prints, feather work, stonework, and carvings are featured in displays that are so natural, they could well exist in someone's home. In response to the ongoing revival of the American crafts movement, the gallery has expanded its selection of koa-wood furniture with a Hawaiian/Japanese influence. Stellar artists, like Ricardo Vasquez and Robert Lippoth from Maui, are among those represented. Connoisseurs will find the crème de la crème of the crafts here: Susan Jenson's Maui baskets, Randall Watkins's rocking chairs, and pieces by Tom Calhoun, master artisan-woodworker. You won't find a better selection elsewhere under one roof. The award-winning gallery has won accolades from the top travel and arts magazines in the country *(Travel + Leisure, Arts & Antiques)* and has steered clear of trendiness. Open 9am to 5pm. At the Travaasa Hana, 5031 Hana Hwy. www.hanacoast.com. **© 808/248-8636.**

Hot Island Glassblowing Studio & Gallery   You can watch the artist transform molten glass into works of art and utility in this studio at the Makawao Courtyard, where an award-winning family of glass blowers built its own furnaces. It's fascinating to watch the shapes emerge from glass melted at 2,300°F (1,260°C). The colorful works range from small paperweights to large vessels. Four to five artists participate in the demonstrations, which begin when the furnace is heated, about a half-hour before the studio opens daily at 9am; it closes at 5pm. 3620 Baldwin Ave. www.hotislandglass.com. **© 808/572-4527.**

Ki'i Gallery   Some of the works are large and lavish, such as the Toland Sand prisms for just under $5,000 and the John Stokes handblown glass. Those who love glass in all forms, from handblown vessels to jewelry, will love a browse through Ki'i. I found Pat Kazi's work in porcelain and other objects, such as a mermaid in a teacup, inspired by fairy tales and mythology, both fantastic and compelling. The gallery is devoted to glass and original paintings and drawings; roughly half of the artists are from Hawaii. Open daily from 9am to 8pm. At the Grand Wailea Resort, 3860 Wailea Alanui Dr. www.kiigallery.com. **© 808/874-3059.** A 2nd location is at the Shops at Wailea, 3750 Wailea Alanui Dr. © 808/874-1181.

Martin Lawrence Galleries   The front is garish, with pop art, kinetic sculptures, and bright, carnivalesque glass objects. Toward the back of the gallery, however, there's a sizable inventory of two-dimensional art and some plausible choices for collectors of Keith Haring, Andy Warhol, and other pop artists. The originals, limited-edition graphics, and sculptures also include works by Marc Chagall, Pablo Picasso, Joan Miró, Roy Lichtenstein, and other noted artists. Open daily from 10am to 10pm. At the Market Place at Lahaina, 790 Front St. www.martinlawrence.com. **© 808/661-1788.**

Peter Lik Gallery   Australian photographer Peter Lik is known for his spectacular panoramic photos, and his gallery is a lot like his art: spacious, eye-catching, and full of surprises. Stop by just to see his incredible vistas. Even if you can't afford one of his photos, there are posters, cards, books, and other items for sale. Open daily from 9am to 10pm. 712 Front St. www.peterlik.com. **© 808/661-6623.**

Viewpoints Gallery   Maui's only fine-arts cooperative showcases the work of 20 established artists in an airy, attractive gallery located in a restored theater with a courtyard, glass blowing studio, and restaurants. The gallery features two-dimensional art, jewelry, fiber art, stained glass, paper, sculpture, and other media. This is a fine example of what can happen in a collectively supportive artistic environment. Open daily 10am to 6pm. 3620 Baldwin Ave. www.viewpointsgallerymaui.com. **© 808/572-5979.**

Village Galleries   The nearly 30-year-old Village Galleries is the oldest continuously running gallery on Maui, and it's esteemed as one of the few galleries with consistently high standards. Art collectors know this as a respectable showcase for regional artists; the selection of mostly original two- and three-dimensional art offers a good look at the quality of work originating on the island. The newer contemporary gallery at the Ritz-Carlton offers colorful gift items and jewelry. Open daily from 9am to 9pm. 120 Dickenson St. www.villagegalleriesmaui.com. © **808/661-4402.** Additional locations: Master's Reading Room, 120 Dickenson St., © 808/661-5519; and Ritz-Carlton Kapalua, 1 Ritz-Carlton Dr., © 808/669-1800.

General Store

Hasegawa General Store   Established in 1910, immortalized in song since 1961, burned to the ground in 1990, and back in business in 1991, this legendary store is indefatigable and more colorful than ever in its fourth generation in business. The aisles are choked with merchandise: coffee specially roasted and blended for the store, Ono Farms organic dried fruit, fishing equipment, every tape and CD that mentions Hana, the best books on Hana to be found, T-shirts, beach and garden essentials, baseball caps, film, baby food, napkins, and other necessities for the Hana life. Open 7am to 7pm Monday to Saturday and 8am to 6pm on Sunday. Hana Hwy. © **808/248-8231.**

Honolua Store   Walk on the old wood floors peppered with holes from golf shoes and find your everyday essentials: bottled water, stationery, mailing tape, jackets, chips, wine, soft drinks, paper products, fresh fruit and produce, and aisles of notions and necessities. With picnic tables on the veranda and a takeout counter offering deli items—more than a dozen types of sandwiches, salads, and budget-friendly breakfasts—there are always long lines of customers. Golfers and surfers love to come here for the morning paper and coffee. Open daily 6am to 8pm. 502 Office Rd. (next to the Ritz-Carlton Kapalua). www.kapalua.com. © **808/665-9105.**

Gifts & Souvenirs

Collections   This longtime Makawao attraction is showing renewed vigor after more than 2 decades on Baldwin Avenue. It's one of my favorite Makawao stops, full of gift items and spirited clothing reflecting the ease and color of island living. Its selection of sportswear, soaps, jewelry, candles, and tasteful, marvelous miscellany reflects good sense and style. Dresses (including up-to-the-moment Citron in cross-cultural and vintage-looking prints), separates, home and bath accessories, sweaters, and other good things make this a Makawao must. Open Monday to Saturday from 9am to 6pm and 11am to 5pm on Sunday. 3677 Baldwin Ave. © **808/572-0781.**

Lei Spa Maui   Expanded to include two massage rooms and shower facilities, this day spa offers facials and other therapies. About 95% of the beauty and bath products sold here are made on Maui, and that includes Hawaiian Botanical Pikake shower gel, *kukui* and macadamia-nut oils, Hawaiian potpourris, mud masks with Hawaiian seaweed, and a spate of rejuvenating potions for hair and skin. Aromatherapy body oils and perfumes are popular, as are the handmade soaps and fragrances of torch ginger, plumeria, coconut, tuberose, and sandalwood. Scented candles in coconut shells, inexpensive and fragrant, make great gifts. Open 9:30am to 10pm Monday to Saturday and noon to 10pm on Sunday. 505 Front St. www.leispa.com. © **808/661-1178.**

Totally Hawaiian Gift Gallery   This gallery makes for a good browse with its selection of Niihau shell jewelry, excellent Hawaiian CDs, Norfolk pine bowls, and Hawaiian quilt kits. Hawaiian quilt patterns sewn in Asia (at least they're honest about it) are labor-intensive, less expensive, and attractive, although not totally Hawaiian. Hawaiian-quilt-pattern gift wraps and tiles, perfumes and soaps, handcrafted dolls, and koa accessories are of good quality, and the artists, such as Kelly Dunn (Norfolk wood bowls), Jerry Kermode (wood), and Pat Coito (wood), are among the tops in their fields. Open 9:30am to 10pm daily. At Whalers Village, 2435 Kaanapali Pkwy. www.totallyhawaiian.com. © **808/667-4070.**

Home Design, Furnishings & Housewares

Martin & MacArthur   For the discriminating buyer looking for unusual gifts and furniture, this store features Hawaii's top artists and craftsmen. Open daily from 9:30am to 9pm. Shops at Wailea, 3750 Wailea Alanui Dr. www.shopsatwailea.com. © **808/891-6770.** Also at Whaler's Village, 2435 Kaanapali Pkwy., Kaanapali, © 808/677-7422; and Westin Maui, 2365 Kaanapali Pkwy., Kaanapali, © 808/270-0888.

The Mercantile   The jewelry, home accessories (especially the Tiffany-style glass-and-shell lamps), dinnerware, Italian linens, plantation-style furniture, and clothing here are a salute to the good life. There's exquisite bedding, rugs, hand-carved armoires, slipcovers, and a large selection of Kiehl's products. The clothing—comfortable cottons and upscale European linens—is for men and women, as are the soaps, which include Maui Herbal Soap products and some unusual finds from France. Maui-made jams, honey, soaps, ceramics, and Jurlique organic facial and body products are among the new winners. 3673 Baldwin Ave. © **808/572-1407.**

Shoes, Slippers & Sandals

Sandal Tree   It's unusual for a resort shop to draw local customers on a regular basis, but the Sandal Tree attracts a flock of footwear fanatics who come here from throughout the islands for rubber thongs and Top-Siders, sandals and dressy pumps, athletic shoes and hats, designer footwear, and much more. Sandal Tree also carries a generous selection of Mephisto and Arche comfort sandals, Donald J Pliner, Anne Klein, Charles Jourdan, and beachwear and casual footwear for all tastes. Accessories range from fashionable knapsacks to avant-garde geometrical handbags—for town and country, day and evening, kids, women, and men. Prices are realistic, too. Open 9:30am to 10pm daily. At Whalers Village, 2435 Kaanapali Pkwy., Kaanapali. sandaltree.com. © **808/667-5330.** Additional location: Shops at Wailea, 3750 Wailea Alanui Dr., Wailea. © 808/874-9006.

T-Shirts

Sandell 🎁   Since the early 1970s, artist, illustrator, and cartoonist David Sandell has been commenting on Maui through his artwork. Don't miss the opportunity to stop by this shop and "talk story" with the talented artist, who watched Maui go from undiscovered to discovered. His work—from original oils to prints to T-shirts—makes excellent souvenirs to take home. Hours vary; please call in advance. 133 Market St. www.sandellmaui.com. © **808/249-0234.**

PRACTICAL MATTERS: THE SHOPPING SCENE

Business Hours

Usual shopping hours vary. Generally, most shops are open by 9am and those in shopping centers remain open to 9pm. But in Maui's small towns (like Makawao) many shops don't open until 10am and several close at 6pm. See the individual reviews above, and keep your sense of humor: This is Maui, so even if the posted hours say 9am, that could mean 9:30 or 9:45.

Shipping

Most stores will happily ship your purchases back home for you. They probably will charge you shipping, but at least you don't have to worry about trying to fit everything into your suitcase.

Taxes

Hawaii state tax of 4% will be added to everything your purchase on Maui.

8

ENTERTAINMENT
& NIGHTLIFE

I n addition to the performing arts, alive and well at the Maui Arts & Cultural Center (see below), nightlife and entertainment on Maui also means enjoying the hula at a luau, listening to Hawaiian music as the sun drops into the Pacific, watching first-run movies under the stars, or sipping a liquid libation as you enjoy a tropical sunset.

THE PERFORMING ARTS

Concert & Theater Venues

Iao Theater   It's not Broadway, but if you're in the mood for a night at the theater, head to Wailuku. Shows range from locally written productions to well-known plays and musicals. 68 N. Market St. ✆ **808/242-6969** for box office and program information; 808/244-8680 for dinner theater options. www.mauionstage.com.

Maui Arts & Cultural Center   Maui's Performing Arts scene is centered around this $32-million venue in Kahului. Bonnie Raitt has performed here, as have Hiroshima, Pearl Jam, Ziggy Marley, Tony Bennett, the American Indian Dance Theatre, the Maui Symphony Orchestra, and Jonny Lang, not to mention the finest in local talent. The center boasts a visual-arts gallery, an outdoor amphitheater, offices, rehearsal space, a 300-seat theater for experimental performances, and a 1,200-seat main theater. The center's activities are well publicized locally, so check the *Maui News* or ask your hotel concierge what's going on during your visit. 1 Cameron Way, Kahului. www.mauiarts.org. ✆ **808/242-7469.**

ABOVE: **The historic Iao Theater hosts Maui's rich community theater tradition.**
PREVIOUS PAGE: **Luau, Maui style.**

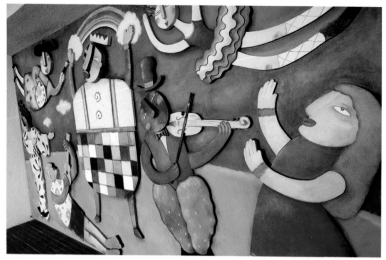

A display at the Maui Arts & Cultural Center.

Luau

Most of the larger hotels in Maui's major resorts offer luau on a regular basis. You'll pay about $60 to $112 to attend one. The best luau in Maui are the ones held in someone's backyard celebrating a birthday or graduation. But since you probably won't be invited to one of these private affairs, there are commercial luau that capture the romance and spirit of the luau with quality food and entertainment in outdoor settings. For information on all of Maui's luau, go to www.mauihawaiiluau.com.

See also Feast at Lele, p. 199.

Old Lahaina Luau Maui's best choice is indisputably this nightly luau on a 1-acre site just oceanside of the Lahaina Cannery. The Old Lahaina Luau maintains its high standards in food and entertainment in a peerless oceanfront setting. Local craftspeople display their wares only a few feet from the water. Seating is provided on lauhala mats for those who wish to dine as the traditional Hawaiians did, but there are tables for everyone else. There's no fire dancing in the program, but you won't miss it. This luau offers a healthy balance of entertainment, showmanship, authentic high-quality food, educational value, and sheer romantic beauty. (No watered-down mai tais, either; these are the real thing.)

The luau begins at sunset and features Tahitian and Hawaiian entertainment, including various forms of hula and an intelligent narrative on the dance's rocky course of survival into modern times. The entertainment is riveting, even for jaded locals. The food, served from an open-air thatched structure, is as much Pacific Rim as authentically Hawaiian: *imu*-roasted kalua pig, baked mahimahi in Maui-onion cream sauce, guava chicken, teriyaki sirloin steak, lomi salmon, poi, dried fish, poke, Hawaiian sweet potato, sautéed vegetables, seafood salad, and the ultimate taste treat, taro leaves with coconut milk. 1251 Front St., Lahaina. www.oldlahainaluau.com. ⓒ **800/248-5828** or 808/667-1998. Shows nightly. $95 adults, $65 children 12 and under.

Other Shows

Kupanaha This wonderful show is perfect for the entire family. It features the renowned magicians Jody and Kathleen Baran and their entire family, including child-prodigy magician Crystal. The dinner show includes magic, illusions, and the story of the Hawaii fire goddess, Pele, presented through hula and chant performed by the children of the Kano'eau Dance Academy. Show prices include dinner (entree choices include island fish, roasted stuffed chicken, steak and shrimp, and a vegetarian dish, with a children's menu available). 2525 Kaanapali Pkwy., Lahaina (at the Kaanapali Beach Hotel). www.kupanaha.com. ✆ **808/661-0011.** Shows Tues–Sat. Tickets $79–$89 adults, $55–$89 youth 13–20, $39–$89 children 6–12.

Ulalena ★ This riveting evening of entertainment weaves Hawaiian mythology with drama, dance, and state-of-the-art multimedia capabilities in a multi-million-dollar theater. Polynesian dance, original music, acrobatics, and chant, performed by a local and international cast, combine to create an evocative experience that often leaves the audience speechless. It's interactive, with dancers coming down the aisles, drummers and musicians in surprising corners, and mind-boggling stage and lighting effects that draw the audience in. Some special moments: the goddesses dancing on the moon, the white sail of the first Europeans, the wrath of the volcano goddess Pele, the labors of the field-worker immigrants. The story unfolds seamlessly; at the end, you'll be shocked to realize that not a single word of dialogue was spoken. Maui Theatre, 878 Front St., Lahaina. www.ulalena.com. ✆ **877/688-4800** or 808/661-9913. Tickets $60–$80 adults, $25–$45 children 12 and under. Performances Tues–Sat at 6:30pm.

A traditional performance at the Old Lahaina Luau.

Ulalena weaves Hawaiian mythology with drama and dance.

Warren & Annabelle's This magic/comedy cocktail show stars illusionist Warren Gibson and "Annabelle," a ghost from the 1800s who plays the grand piano (even taking requests from the audience), as Warren dazzles you with his sleight-of-hand magic. Appetizers, desserts, and cocktails are available (either as a package or a la carte). You must be 21 or older to attend. 900 Front St., Lahaina. www.warrenandannabelles.com. © **808/667-6244.** Tickets $59 show only; $100 for show, appetizers, and dessert. Shows Mon–Sat; check-in is at 5pm (also 7:30pm if the 1st show sells out).

THE BAR SCENE

Nightlife in Maui begins at sunset, when all eyes turn westward to see how the day will end. And what better way to take it all in than over cocktails? With its view of Molokai to the northwest and Lanai to the west, Kaanapali and west Maui boast panoramic vistas unique to this island. In south Maui's resort areas of Wailea and Makena, the island of Kahoolawe and the crescent-shaped atoll of Molokini islet are visible on the horizon, and the West Maui Mountains look like an entirely separate island. No matter what your vantage point, you are likely to be treated to an astonishing view.

In Kaanapali, park at Whalers Village and head for **Leilani's on the Beach** (© 808/661-4495; www.leilanis.com) or **Hula Grill** (© 808/667-6636; www.hulagrill.com), next to each other on the beach. Both have busy, upbeat bars and tables bordering the sand. These are happy places for great people-watching, gazing over at Lanai, and enjoying mai tais and margaritas. Hula Grill's Barefoot Bar appetizer menu is a cut above. Leilani's has live music Tuesday and Thursday through Sunday from 3 to 5pm, while at Hula Grill the happy hour starts at 3pm, with live music from 11am to 9pm.

Now, Lahaina: It's a sunset lover's nirvana, lined with restaurants that have elevated mai tais to an art form. If you love loud rock, head for **Cheeseburger in Paradise** (© 808/661-4855; www.cheeseburgerland.com). A few doors away, the **Lahaina Prime Rib & Fish Co.** (© 808/661-3472; www.lahainafish company.com) and **Kimo's** (© 808/661-4811; www.kimosmaui.com) are magnets all day long and especially at sunset, when their open decks fill up with revelers.

At the southern end of Lahaina, in the 505 Front St. complex, **Pacific'O** (© 808/667-4341; www.pacificomaui.com) is a solid hit, with a raised bar, seating on the ocean, and a backdrop of Lanai across the channel. A few steps away, sister restaurant **I'O**, 505 Front St., Lahaina (© 808/661-8422; www.iomaui. com), shares the same vista, with an appetizer menu and a curved bar that will wow you as much as the drop-dead-gorgeous view.

In Wailea, the restaurants at the Shops at Wailea, including the highly successful **Tommy Bahama** (© 808/875-9983; www.tommybahama.com) and **Longhi's** (© 808/891-8883; www.longhis.com), are noteworthy additions to the beachfront retail-and-dining scene. **Ferraro's** and **Spago** (© 808/874-8000; www.fourseasons.com/maui/dining), both at the neighboring Four Seasons Resort Wailea, have great sunset views to go with their Italian and Pacific Rim menus. Farther south, in Makena, you can't beat the Makena Resort's **Molokini Bar & Grill** (© 808/874-1111; www.makenaresortmaui.com/ Dining/Dining.asp), with its casual elegance and unequaled vista of Molokini islet on the ocean side and, on the mauka side, a graceful, serene courtyard with ponds, rock gardens, and lush foliage. From 6 to 9pm nightly, the *pupu* menu features poke of the day, truffle fries, or a grilled petite fillet.

Don't forget the upcountry view: **Kula Lodge** (© **808/878-2517**; www. kulalodge.com) has a phenomenal one that takes in central Maui, the West Maui Mountains (looking like Shangri-La in the distance), and the coastline. Dinner begins at 4pm, so you can take in the sunset over lavender rack of lamb, New York steak, and other country-comfort fare.

THE CLUB & MUSIC SCENE

Nightlife options on Maui are limited—there are very few clubs on the island; most clubs and bars with entertainment or dancing tend to be located close to resort areas. Because Maui is so spread out, you may find yourself driving a great distance to get to a club that is providing the kind of entertainment you want. *Here's a tip:* First check out the nightlife and entertainment options in the major hotels near you. Hotels generally have lobby lounges offering Hawaiian music, soft jazz, or hula shows beginning at sunset. Other music venues are listed below. Also check out the local daily newspaper, The Maui News (www. mauinews.com).

The best of Hawaiian music can be heard every Wednesday night at 7:30pm at the Napili Kai Beach Resort's indoor amphitheater, thanks to the Grammy-winning **Masters of Hawaiian Slack Key Guitar Concert Series** (© **888/ 669-3858**; www.slackkey.com). The weekly shows present a side of Hawaii that few visitors ever get to see. Host George Kahumoku, Jr., introduces a new slack-key master every week. Not only is there incredible Hawaiian music and singing, but George and his guest also "talk story" about old Hawaii, music, and Hawaiian culture. Not to be missed. Ticket price varies but generally is around $45 for the show and $82 for the show and dinner.

West Maui: Lahaina, Kaanapali & Kapalua

The **Hard Rock Cafe,** 900 Front St., Lahaina (© **808/667-7400**), offers live music every night, so it wouldn't hurt to call to see if something's up. Usually it features mainland bands but check the website (www.hardrock.com) for the schedule. Tickets range from $20 to $50.

You won't have to ask what's going on at **Cheeseburger in Paradise,** 811 Front St., Lahaina (© **808/661-4855;** www.cheeseburgerland.com), the two-story green-and-white building at the corner of Front and Lahainaluna streets. Just go outside and you'll hear it. Loud, live, tropical rock blasts into the streets and out to sea nightly from 4:30 to 10pm (no cover).

Other venues for music in west Maui include the following:

- **Hula Grill,** in Whalers Village, Kaanapali (© **808/667-6636;** www.hulagrill. com), has live music (usually Hawaiian) from 11:30am to 9pm nightly.

- **Kimo's,** 845 Front St., Lahaina (© **808/661-481;** www.kimosmaui.com), has live musicians nightly; call for details.

- **Lahaina Pizza,** 730 Front St., Lahaina (© **808/661-0700**), offers live music from 6:30 to 8:30pm Thursday through Saturday nights.

- **Leilani's on the Beach,** in Whalers Village, Kaanapali (© **808/661-4495;** www.leilanis.com), has live music from 3 to 5pm Tuesday and Friday through Sunday; the styles range from contemporary Hawaiian to rock.
- **Moose McGillycuddy's,** 844 Front St., Lahaina (© **808/667-7758;** www.moosemcgillycuddys.com), offers live and DJ music, but the schedule varies, so call for details.
- **Pineapple Grill,** 200 Kapalua Dr., Kapalua (© **808/669-9600;** www.pineapplekapalua.com), features live music on Thursday and Friday, and jazz on Saturday from 7 to 10pm.
- **Pioneer Inn,** 658 Wharf St., Lahaina (© **808/661-3636;** www.pioneerinnmaui.com), offers a variety of live music Tuesday through Thursday nights starting at 5:30pm.
- **Sansei Seafood Restaurant & Sushi Bar,** 600 Office Rd., Kapalua (© **808/669-6286;** www.sanseihawaii.com), has karaoke Thursday through Saturday from 10pm to 1am.
- **Sea House Restaurant,** at the Napili Kai Beach Resort, Napili (© **808/669-1500**), has live music from 7 to 9pm nightly.

South Maui: Kihei-Wailea

- **Kahale's Beach Club,** 36 Keala Place, Kihei (© **808/875-7711**), offers a potpourri of live music nightly; call for details.
- **Life's a Beach,** 1913 S. Kihei Rd., Kihei (© **808/891-8010;** www.mauibars.com), has live music Tuesday through Saturday; call for times.
- **Lobby Lounge,** at the Four Seasons Resort Maui at Wailea (© **808/874-8000;** www.fourseasons.com/Maui), features nightly live music from 5:30 to 6:30pm and 8 to 10:30pm.
- **LuLu's,** 1945 S. Kihei Rd., Kihei (© **808/879-9944;** www.lulusmaui.com), offers entertainment Thursday and Saturday starting at 8pm, and karaoke on Wednesday and Sunday 7:30 to 11pm. Call for schedule and cover charges.
- **Mulligan's on the Blue,** 100 Kaukahi St., Wailea (© **808/874-1131;** www.mulligansontheblue.com), has live music nightly. Call or check the website for times and cover charges.
- **Sansei Seafood Restaurant & Sushi Bar,** in Kihei Town Center (© **808/879-0004;** www.sanseihawaii.com), has karaoke Thursday through Saturday from 10pm to 1am.
- **South Shore Tiki Lounge,** 1913 S. Kihei Rd., Kihei (© **808/874-6444;** www.southshoretikilounge.com), has dancing nightly from 10pm to 1:30am.
- **Sports Page Bar,** 2411 S. Kihei Rd., Kihei (© **808/879-0602**), has live music nightly starting at 6:30pm except on Saturday nights, when it starts at 9pm.

Upcountry Maui

Upcountry in Makawao, the party never ends at **Casanova,** 1188 Makawao Ave. (© **808/572-0220;** www.casanovamaui.com), the popular Italian ristorante where the good times roll with the pasta. The newly renovated bar area has large booths, all the better for socializing around the stage and dance floor. If a big-name mainland band is resting up on Maui following a sold-out concert on Oahu, you may find its members setting up for an impromptu night here. DJs take over on Wednesday (ladies' night); on Friday and Saturday, live entertainment or a DJ draws fun lovers from even the most remote reaches of the island. Entertainment starts at 9 or 10pm and continues to 1:30am. (Check the website for schedules and cover charges.) Expect good blues, rock 'n' roll, reggae, jazz, Hawaiian, and the top names in local and visiting entertainment. Elvin Bishop, the local duo Hapa, Los Lobos, and many others have taken Casanova's stage. The cover is usually $7 to $10. Some Sunday afternoons, from 2:30 to 5:30pm, they have excellent live jazz, but call ahead to make sure.

Paia & Central Maui

In central Maui, The **Kahului Ale House,** 355 E. Kamehameha Ave., Kahului (© **808/877-9001**), features live music or a DJ most nights. Times vary; call for the schedule and cover charges.

In Paia, **Charley's Restaurant,** 142 Hana Hwy. (© **808/579-8085;** www.charleysmaui.com), features an eclectic selection of music from country and western (Willie Nelson has been seen sitting in) to fusion/reggae to rock 'n' roll; call or check the website for details. Also in Paia, the **Moana Bakery & Cafe,** 71 Baldwin Ave. (© **808/579-9999;** www.moanacafe.com), has everything from Hawaiian music to cool jazz to sizzling Latin to swing; call or check the website for details.

AT THE MOVIES

The 12-screen movie megaplex at the **Maui Mall,** 70 E. Kaahumanu Ave. (© **808/249-2222**), in Kahului, features current releases. In June, the not-to-be-missed **Maui Film Festival ★★★** (© **808/579-9244;** www.mauifilm festival.com) puts on nights of cinema under the stars in Wailea (see "The Best Place in the World to See a Movie," below). The Maui Film Festival also presents "Firstlight: Academy Screenings" films for the avant-garde, ultrahip movie buff in December at the **Maui Arts & Cultural Center,** 1 Cameron Way (just off Kahului Beach Rd.), Kahului, usually followed by local catering (with bar) and live music and poetry readings.

Film buffs can check the local newspapers to see what's playing at the other theaters around the island: the **Kaahumanu Theatres,** at the Kaahumanu Center, in Kahului (© **808/873-3137**); the **Kukui Mall Theater,** 1819 S. Kihei Rd., in Kihei (© **808/874-8624**); the Wallace Theaters at the **Wharf Cinema Center,** 658 Front St., in Lahaina (© **808/249-2222**); and the **Front Street Theatres** at the Lahaina Center, 900 Front St. (© **808/249-2222**).

SPECTATOR SPORTS

In addition to the information below, check the "Calendar of Events," p. 46, for information on major sporting tournaments, such as surfing and golf championships.

THE BEST PLACE IN THE WORLD TO SEE A movie

Imagine lounging on a comfy beach chair on the island of Maui watching the stars come out in the night sky. As soon as it gets dark enough, the biggest outdoor screen you've ever seen comes to life with a film premiere. This has to be the best place in the entire world to watch movies.

If you're headed to Maui in June, plan your travel dates around the **Maui Film Festival** (© 808/ 579-9244; www.mauifilmfestival.com), which always starts the Wednesday before Father's Day. This is an event you won't want to miss. The 5-day festival features nightly films in the "Celestial Cinema," an under-the-stars, open-air "outdoor theater" on the Wailea Golf Course, lit by the moon and powered by the sun (thanks to its capture of solar energy). The event features premieres and special advance screenings on a 50-foot-wide screen in Dolby Digital Surround Sound, as well as live (in person) appearances of A-list film luminaries. The festival organizer, director and film producer Barry Rivers, selects "life-affirming" films that often become box office hits.

In addition to the 5 days and nights of films and filmmaker panels, there are many other events: a Taste of Chocolate night, a Taste of Wailea (with Maui's top chefs creating exquisite culinary masterpieces), a Starry Night dance party, and a host of other foodie events. For the family, there's a Father's Day concert of contemporary Hawaiian music, a sand-sculpture contest, and picnics. And for those interested in Hawaii culture, the festival presents TheStarShow, where live images of celestial objects are projected onto the screen, as experts in Polynesian astronomy and cultural history take the audience on a tour of the night sky and Polynesian navigational lore.

As Rivers puts it, "rising stars, shooting stars, movie stars, all under the stars."

Hawaiian Canoe Paddling

Nearly every weekend, from early February to late November, various Canoe Clubs around the island meet for a regatta. The daylong events are free and open to the public. It's a great opportunity to experience an uniquely Hawaiian event. For information on the paddling schedule, contact the **Lae'Ula O Kai Canoe Club,** www.luok.org, or the club's coaches, Sharon and Rick Balidoy, © **808/ 879-5644.**

Polo

Along with the *paniolo* (Hawaiian cowboys) came the sport of Polo. The **Maui Polo Club** (© 808/877-7744; www.mauipoloclub.com) has been playing the "sport of kings" for more than 100 years. What started as an informal group of guys trying to improve their horse-riding skills is recognized today as one of the most respected polo teams in the Pacific. Matches are nearly every weekend

WATCH FOR THE green flash

If you're gathered in a crowd on Maui watching a sunset, you may hear someone call out: "Green flash!" If you're lucky, you may get to see it yourself.

The romantic version of the story is the green flash happens when the sun kisses the ocean good night (honeymooners love this version). The scientific version is not quite as dreamy: Light bends as it goes around the curve of the earth. When the sun dips beneath the horizon, it is at the far end of the spectrum. So this refraction of the sun's light, coupled with the atmosphere on the extreme angle of the sunset on the horizon, causes only the color green to be seen in the color spectrum just before the light disappears.

Here's how to view the green flash: First, it has to be a clear day, with no clouds or haze on the horizon. Second, the sun has to set on the ocean (if it sets behind an island, you won't see the flash). Keep checking the sun as it drops (try not to look directly into the sun; just glance at it to assess its position). If the conditions are ideal, just as the sun drops into the blue water, a "flash" or laserlike beam of green will appear to shoot out for an instant.

(usually Sun) from early April to late June, and then again from September to November. You can catch a match at either the **Manduke Baldwin Polo Arena,** 1 mile above the King Kekaulike School on Haleakala Highway (Apr–June), or the **Olinda Field,** at the Kaonoulu Ranch, 1 mile above Makawao on Olinda Road (Sept–Nov). Gates generally open at 12:30pm and the match begins at 1:30pm; after the match there is usually a party with food and music. Admission is $5; kids 11 and under enter free.

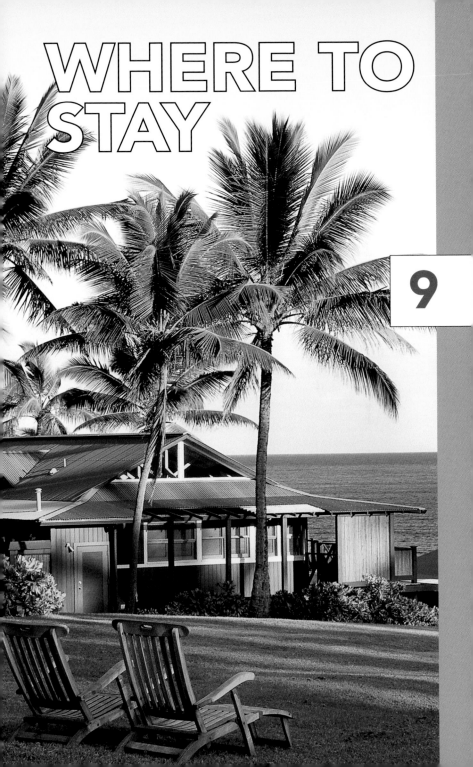

WHERE TO STAY

9

Maui has accommodations to fit every taste and budget, from luxury oceanfront suites and historic bed-and-breakfasts to reasonably priced condos that will sleep a family of four.

When planning your trip to Maui, remember: The high season, during which rooms are always booked and rates are at the top end, runs from mid-December to March. A second high season, when rates are high but reservations are somewhat easier to get, is summer (late June to early Sept). The off seasons, with fewer tourists and cheaper rates, are April to early June and late September to mid-December.

Remember to add Hawaii's 17.5% accommodations tax to your final bill. Parking is free unless otherwise noted.

Important note: Before you book, be sure to read "Tips on Accommodations" (p. 371).

BEST BETS

- **Best Bang for Your Buck:** Located on Maui's breathtaking Kaanapali Beach, the **Kaanapali Beach Hotel** (p. 271) offers great value (with rooms starting at $143). If you are looking for a smaller, more intimate accommodation, the **Pineapple Inn Maui** (p. 284), in Kihei, has panoramic ocean views, sound-proof rooms, and your own private lanai (rooms start at $139). From the gourmet breakfast to the comfy rooms in a historic plantation manager's house, one of the best deals on Maui is the **Old Wailuku Inn at Ulupono** (p. 260). Although the location (in Wailuku) is off the beaten path for visitors, you are still within driving distance to the beach and Maui's numerous activities.

- **Best Bed & Breakfast:** Hostess Eva Tantillo runs her wonderful bed & breakfast, **What a Wonderful World** (p. 287) like a top resort, from well-appointed units to the delicious breakfast. Another great B&B, just a 10-minute walk from the beach in Kihei, is **Tutu Mermaids on Maui B&B** (p. 286), where continental breakfast is placed on your doorstep every morning so you can sleep as late as you like. In Lahaina, located just 50 feet from the water, **Penny's Place Inn Paradise** (p. 267), a small B&B with expertly decorated rooms and a yummy breakfast, offers a terrific deal (starting at $88 a night).

PRICE CATEGORIES

Very Expensive	$300 and up
Expensive	$200–$300
Moderate	$125–$200
Inexpensive	Under $125

PREVIOUS PAGE: **Travaasa Hana.**

WHAT YOU'LL really PAY

The prices quoted here are for each hotel's rack rates, the maximum that it charges. Be sure to check the hotel's website, as frequently deals are offered that are way below the rack rate. Also keep in mind the time of the year you are booking; during Christmas or high season, there generally is high demand and rack rates are the only rates available, as hotels book up quickly. During the off season (Sept to early Dec and Mar–June), you will find the best deals.

When comparing rates, expect to pay more for a one-bedroom condo apartment than you would for just a hotel room.

Note: Quoted discount rates almost never include breakfast, hotel tax, or any applicable resort fees.

○ **Best for Families:** Kids love the terrific children's program at the **Four Seasons Resort Maui at Wailea** (p. 288). Parents love such family-friendly options as kids' menus in the restaurants and the opportunity to prepurchase infant necessities like diapers and baby food and have them waiting for you at the hotel when you arrive. If your kids are older and more active, they will love the Environment Educational Center (created by Jean-Michel Cousteau) at the **Ritz-Carlton Kapalua** (p. 277), which offers myriad activities to keep them occupied. For a more relaxed vacation, venture away from the resort areas and head into the country at the **Haiku Cannery Inn** (p. 295), where the kids have 3 acres to play among the topical fruit trees.

○ **Most Hawaiian Accommodations:** Picture this: a romantic, intimate cottage, overlooking a stream with a waterfall, the air is filled with the sweet fragrance of ginger and the wind is whispering as it blows through the bamboo. Book fast, the **Wild Ginger Falls** (p. 292) is very, very popular. For more of a resort setting, the **Honua Kai Resort & Spa** (p. 270) has 38 units (from studios to three-bedrooms) on the North Kaanapali Beach, where the stars glisten at night and the warm breezes beckon you to the white-sand beach during the day.

○ **Best Hostels:** Located in the town of Wailuku, the two best hostels on the island are **Banana Bungalow Maui** (p. 260) and **Northshore**

Old Wailuku Inn.

Four Seasons Resort Maui.

Hostel (p. 260). Both offer dorm-style accommodations (at $27–$30) and amenities not usually seen at hostels, like low-priced tours of the island, high-speed Internet, and even a hot-tub whirlpool.

- **Best Moderately Priced Accommodations:** You don't have to be a 1 per-center to enjoy Maui. You can stay in an intimate cottage, across the street from a white-sand beach, tucked among the palm and fruit trees at the **Nona Lani Cottages** (p. 260) in Kihei (starting at $120 a night). Or stay in the antique-filled, historic old **Lahaina Inn** (p. 264), where rooms start at $112 a night and well-known and highly praised David Paul's Lahaina Grill is located downstairs. **Hale Ho'okipa Inn Makawao** (p. 291) offers not only a bargain ($140 a night, including breakfast) but charm as well at this off-the-beaten-path, 1924 plantation-style home, which is totally restored and on the National Register of Historic Places.

- **Most Romantic:** Imagine a secluded cottage, surrounded by a 1-acre "fra-grance" garden (carefully planted with Hawaii's best-smelling flowers), located within driving distance of Hana, but in a remote, secluded area. This is the separate guest house at **Baby Pigs Crossing Bed & Breakfast** (p. 298), where romance is in the air. If you want the amenities of a resort, the **Fairmont Kea Lani Maui** (p. 287) looks like something out of a fairy tale, but this all-suite hotel offers a relaxing atmosphere on one of Wailea's best stretches of beach. For those wanting more nightlife, head to Lahaina, where the decor of the Victorian-style **Plantation Inn** (p. 265) takes advantage of this historic period with four-poster canopy beds, hardwood floors, and Tif-fany-style lamps.

- **Best Resorts with Spas:** There is no spa in the island more grand than the one at the **Grand Wailea** (p. 289). It's Hawaii's largest spa, with 50,000 square feet of baths, hot tubs, mineral pools, saunas, steam rooms, and a huge menu of treatments. The **Hyatt Regency Maui Resort & Spa** (p. 267) is Hawaii's first oceanfront spa, with exercise rooms overlooking Kaanapali Beach and a wide range of pampering services. At the northern end of the island, the **Ritz-Carlton Kapalua** (p. 277) recently renovated their 17,500-square-foot Waihua Spa, which features 15 treatment rooms, saunas, a whirlpool with lava-stone walls, and a fitness center, all of which make even the most jaded spa connoisseurs very happy.

- **Best Service:** It's hard to beat the incredible proficient service at the **Four Seasons Resort Maui at Wailea** (p. 288), where you get service with aloha. It seems as soon as you check in, everyone at the hotel, from the bell desk to the housekeeping staff, knows your name and greets you. Want a different kind of pillow, and it's whisked to your room; ask for the location of a Maui restaurant, and the bell staff whips out a map and highlighter and gives you precise directions. We wish the Four Seasons would give other hotels and resorts lessons in service.

- **Best Splurge:** If money is no object, head out to the remote village of Hana to vacation in the lap of luxury at the incredible **Travaasa Hana** (formerly the Hotel Hana Maui). The resort sits on 66 rolling seaside acres, with a wellness center, spa, two pools, and great dining. Rates start at $325 a night, but if you can swing it, go for the oceanside Sea Ranch Cottages ($525–$625): These luxury duplex bungalows with cathedral ceilings, comfy beds, and giant soaking tubs overlook the craggy shoreline and rolling surf. You'll remember this trip long after your tan has faded.

Grand Wailea.

CENTRAL MAUI

Wailuku

Wailuku is like a time capsule, with its faded wooden storefronts, old plantation homes, shops straight out of the 1940s and 1950s, and relaxed way of life. The town has a spectacular view of Haleakala Crater, great budget restaurants, some interesting bungalow architecture, a Frank Lloyd Wright building, a wonderful historic B&B, and the always-endearing Bailey House Museum.

Best for: Architecture buffs; interacting with locals.

Drawbacks: Beaches surrounding Wailuku are not great for swimming.

MODERATE

Old Wailuku Inn at Ulupono ★ ★ 🎁   This 1924 former plantation manager's home, lovingly restored by innkeepers Janice and Thomas Fairbanks, offers a genuine old-Hawaii experience. The theme is Hawaii of the 1920s and 1930s, with decor, design, and landscaping to match. The spacious rooms are gorgeously outfitted with ohia-wood floors, high ceilings, and traditional Hawaiian quilts. The owners recently added the Vagabond House, a modern three-room complex in the inn's lavishly landscaped backyard. These rooms are decorated in island designer Sig Zane's floral prints, plus plenty of modern amenities (including an ultraluxurious multihead shower). You'll feel right at home lounging on the living room sofa or in an old wicker chair on the enclosed lanai (a balcony or porch), where a full gourmet breakfast is served in the morning. The inn is located in the historic area of Wailuku, just a few minutes' walk from the Maui County Seat Government Building, the courthouse, and a wonderful stretch of antiques shops.

2199 Kahookele St. (at High St., across from the Wailuku School), Wailuku, HI 96732. www.maui inn.com. ℂ **800/305-4899** or 808/244-5897. Fax 808/242-9600. 10 units. $165–$195 double. Rates include full breakfast. 2-night minimum. MC, V. **Amenities:** Jacuzzi. *In room:* A/C, TV/VCR, high-speed Internet access (free).

INEXPENSIVE

Backpackers should head to **Banana Bungalow Maui,** a funky Happy Valley hostel at 310 N. Market St., Wailuku, HI 96793 (www.mauihostel.com; ℂ **800/846-7835** or 808/244-5090), with $30 dorm rooms and some private rooms ($70 single, $79 double). It provides many free amenities not often found in hostel-type accommodations, such as tours of Maui, high-speed Internet access, and a Jacuzzi out back. Dorm-style accommodations ($27) and private rooms ($69–$79 single or double) are also available in old Wailuku at the **Northshore Hostel,** 2080 W. Vineyard St., Wailuku, HI 96793 (www.northshore hostel.com; ℂ **866/946-7835** or ℂ/fax 808/986-8095). **Note:** Women traveling alone might not feel safe here after dark.

Happy Valley Hale 🦅   The Kong family, owners of **Nona Lani Cottages** in Kihei (p. 260), have with loving care turned this old plantation home into a tiny oasis in the midst of an economically challenged area. Keep in mind this is basic accommodation for the frugal—think of it as an alternative to a youth hostel. However, the place is immaculately clean, and the Kongs have made extensive renovations. The four bedrooms—each with twin beds, small fridge, dresser, and closet—share two bathrooms. It's like staying in a family home, with a shared kitchen (no stove, but microwave, griddle, coffeemaker, and so on) and common room with TV. The front yard sports a barbecue and picnic area. The only drawback is that Happy Valley is not exactly a resort area—public housing is just across the street. But for those on extremely tight budgets, it's a good option.

332 N. Market St., Wailuku, HI 96793. www.bestmauihostel.com. © **808/870-9100.** 4 units. $33 per bed in shared room; $65 double private room; $99 triple private room. MC, V. **Amenities:** Shared kitchen. *In room:* Small fridge, no phone.

WEST MAUI

Lahaina

Once upon a time, this old seaport swarmed with sailors in search of women and grog. Today, the vintage village teems with restaurants, T-shirt shops, and a gallery on nearly every block.

Best for: Travelers who want to be in the midst of a historic town, with shopping, restaurants, and activities.

Drawbacks: Pricey accommodations, pricey shopping, pricey dining.

VERY EXPENSIVE

Ho'oilo House ★ Located just outside Lahaina, about a mile up the West Maui Mountains from Launiupoko Wayside Park, this six-bedroom house is constructed and furnished with materials and furniture from Bali, but the view is all Maui. The atmosphere is relaxing, the rooms are decorated with traditional Bali doors and custom beds, there's a private lanai, and the big bathrooms have huge tubs and outdoor showers. My favorite rooms are the Kohola and the Nalu (great ocean views). There's also a small swimming pool on the property. My only complaint is that $229 to $369 a night seems a bit high for a double room with no hot tub and no fridge.

138 Awaiku St., Lahaina, HI 96761. www.hooilohouse.com. © **808/667-6669.** Fax 808/661-7857. 6 units. $229–$369 double. Rates include continental breakfast. 3-night minimum. AE, MC, V. **Amenities:** Pool. *In room:* A/C, TV/VCR, Wi-Fi (free).

📎 B&B Etiquette

In Hawaii, it is traditional and customary to remove your shoes before entering anyone's home. The same is true for most bed-and-breakfast facilities. Most hosts post signs or will politely ask you to remove your shoes before entering the B&B. Not only does this keep the place clean, but you'll also be amazed at how relaxing it is to walk around barefoot. If this custom is unpleasant to you, a B&B may not be for you.

If you've never stayed at a B&B before, here are a few other hints:

Generally the hosts live on the property, and their part of the house is off-limits to guests (you do not have the "run of the house"). Most likely there will be a common area that you can use. Don't expect daily maid service. Your host may tidy up, but will not do complete maid service. Also don't expect amenities like little bottles of shampoo and conditioner—this is a B&B, not a resort. Remember you are sharing your accommodations with other guests, so be considerate when you come in late at night.

Puunoa Beach Estates ★★ ☺ If you're taking a family to Maui, consider these 10 gorgeous town houses in an exclusive 3-acre enclave on a white-sand beach. The individually owned and decorated two-bedroom units (1,700 sq. ft. and up) all have private beachfront lanai, hardwood floors, marble bathrooms, and modern kitchens. Prices are high, but the amenity list has everything you should want for a first-class vacation rental in a dream location. It's within walking distance of the center of Lahaina, but the residential location makes you feel miles away.

45 Kai Pali Place, Lahaina, HI 96761. www.puunoabeachestates.com. ⓒ **866/504-9465** or 808/661-3339. Fax 808/667-5631. 10 units. $640–$1,100 2-bedroom (sleeps 4). 3- to 7-night minimum. AE, MC, V. **Amenities:** Concierge; fitness center; free Internet; outdoor pool; sauna; complimentary snorkeling equipment; video library; whirlpool. *In room:* A/C, TV/VCR/DVD, hair dryer, Internet access (free), full kitchen.

MODERATE

Best Western Pioneer Inn This once-rowdy home away from home for sailors now seems respectable—even charming. The historic hotel is a two-story plantation-style structure with big verandas that overlook the streets of Lahaina and the harbor, which is just 50 feet away. All rooms have been totally remodeled, with vintage bathrooms and new curtains and carpets. The quietest units face either the garden courtyard—devoted to refined outdoor dining accompanied by live (but quiet) music—or the square-block-size banyan tree next door. I recommend room no. 31, over the banyan court, with a view of the ocean and the harbor. If you want a front-row seat for all the Front Street action, book no. 36 or 49.

658 Wharf St. (in front of Lahaina Pier), Lahaina, HI 96761. www.pioneerinnmaui.com. ⓒ **800/457-5457** or 808/661-3636. Fax 808/667-5708. 34 units. $145–$205 double; from $185 suite. AE, DC, DISC, MC, V. **Amenities:** Restaurant (good for breakfast); bar w/live music; outdoor pool. *In room:* A/C, TV, fridge, hair dryer, high-speed Internet access (free).

Garden Gate Bed & Breakfast This oasis of a B&B, located on a quiet residential street just outside Lahaina town, is 5 minutes from the beach by car. The six units all have private entrances and a garden or ocean view; the deluxe suites have a deck and a separate pullout sofa for kids. Continental breakfast is served in the garden (Mon–Sat), and hosts Jamie and Bill Mosley are available to answer any questions about things to do or places to eat. Bicycles, boogie boards, beach chairs, and mats are available at no charge. The barbecue area and adjacent laundry facilities are available for guests' use.

67 Kaniau Rd., Lahaina, HI 96761. www.gardengatebb.com. ⓒ **800/939-3217** or 808/661-8800. Fax 808/748-0001. 6 units. $119–$169 double. Extra person $15. Rates include continental breakfast. 3-night minimum preferred. AE, DC, DISC, MC, V. *In room:* A/C, TV, VCR (on request), fridge, hair dryer, microwave, Wi-Fi.

House of Fountains Bed & Breakfast 📇 This 7,000-square-foot contemporary home, in a quiet residential subdivision at the north end of town, is popular with visitors from around the world. Hostess Daniela Atay keeps the place immaculate; in 2002, she won the prestigious "Most Hawaiian Accommodation" award from the Hawaii Visitors & Convention Bureau. The oversize rooms are fresh and quiet, with white ceramic-tile floors, handmade koa furniture, Hawaiian quilt bedspreads, and a Hawaiian theme; the four downstairs rooms all open onto flower-filled private patios. Guests share a fully equipped kitchen and

Hotels in Lahaina & Kaanapali

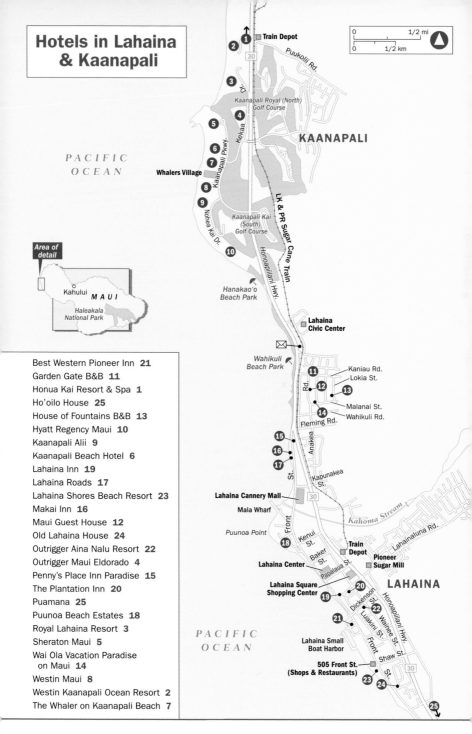

barbecue area and are welcome to curl up on the living room sofa with a book from the library. The nearest beach is about a 5-minute drive away; tennis courts are nearby. Around the pool is a Hawaiian *hale* (a thatched-roof Hawaiian hut). There is even an *imu* (which is a hole in the ground used as an underground oven to cook a pig) for a luau, and an area that's perfect for Hawaiian weddings (arrangements available).

1579 Lokia St. (off Fleming Rd., north of Lahaina town), Lahaina, HI 96761. www.alohahouse.com. ✆ **800/789-6865** or 808/667-2121. Fax 808/667-2120. 6 units, with shower only. $150–$170 double. Rates include continental breakfast. AE, MC, V. From Hwy. 30, take the Fleming Rd. exit; turn left on Ainakea; after 2 blocks, turn right on Malanai St.; go 3 blocks, and turn left onto Lokia St. **Amenities:** Jacuzzi; outdoor pool. *In room:* A/C, TV/DVD, fridge, hair dryer, Wi-Fi (free).

Lahaina Inn ★ If you like old hotels that have genuine historic touches, you'll love this place. As in many older hotels, some of these antiques-stuffed rooms are small; if that's a problem for you, ask for a larger unit. All come with private bathrooms and lanai. The best room in the house is no. 7, which overlooks the beach, the town, and the island of Lanai. There's an excellent, though unaffiliated, restaurant in the same building (**David Paul's Lahaina Grill,** p. 258) and a bar downstairs.

127 Lahainaluna Rd. (near Front St.), Lahaina, HI 96761. www.lahainainn.com. ✆ **800/222-5642** or 808/661-0577. Fax 808/667-9480. 12 units, most with shower only. $112–$221 double; from $195 suite. AE, MC, V. Next-door parking $10 per day. **Amenities:** Bar; concierge; Wi-Fi ($10 per day). *In room:* A/C, hair dryer, Wi-Fi ($10 per day).

Lahaina Roads ✦ If you dream of an oceanfront condo but your budget is on the slim side, here's your place. This condominium complex offers small, reasonably priced units in an older building located in the quiet part of Lahaina, away from the noisy, crowded downtown area, overlooking the boats in the Mala Wharf roadstead (a protected place to anchor near the shore). The compact units have full kitchens and soundproof walls—a real plus. The bedrooms face the road, while the living rooms and lanai overlook the ocean and the island of Lanai. The building is nearly 40 years old but well maintained. The only drawbacks are no air-conditioning (it can be boiling hot in the summer in Lahaina) and no laundry facilities.

1403 Front St. (1 block north of Lahaina Cannery Mall), Lahaina, HI 96761. Reservations c/o Klahani Travel, 159 Halelo St., Lahaina, HI 96761. www.klahani.com. ✆ **800/669-MAUI** (6284) or 808/667-2712. Fax 808/661-5875. 5 units. $150 1-bedroom (sleeps up to 4). 3-night minimum. AE, DISC, MC, V. **Amenities:** Oceanside outdoor pool. *In room:* TV, hair dryer, kitchen.

Lahaina Shores Beach Resort ★ First there's the location, right on the beach; second there's the location, away from the hustle and bustle of downtown Lahaina; and third there's the location, next door to the 505 Front St. restaurants and shops. This recently upgraded condominium project (of studios and one-bedroom units) resembles an old plantation home, with arched colonnades at the entry and an open-air, beachfront lobby. From the moment you step into the airy units (ranging in size from 550 to 1,430 sq. ft.), you'll feel like you are home. The units all have full kitchens, large lanai, and ocean or mountain views. Ask for an oceanfront unit for that terrific view of the water with the island of Lanai in the distance.

475 Front St., Lahaina, HI 96761. www.lahainashores.com. ✆ **866/750-2812** or 808/661-4835. 199 units. $158–$232 studio double; $305–$355 1-bedroom double; from $355 1-bedroom penthouse double. Rollaway bed $20. AE, MC, V. Parking $8. **Amenities:** Concierge; outdoor pool; tennis courts (across the street); whirlpool. *In room:* A/C, TV, hair dryer, high-speed Internet access ($10), kitchen.

Maui Guest House ★★ 🎁

This is one of Lahaina's great bed-and-breakfast deals: a charming house with more amenities than the expensive Kaanapali hotels just down the road. The roomy home features parquet floors and floor-to-ceiling windows; its swimming pool—surrounded by a deck and comfortable lounge chairs—is larger than some at high-priced condos. Every unit has a quiet lanai and a romantic Jacuzzi. Guests share the large, well-equipped kitchen, barbecue, and computers with high-speed Internet access. Scuba divers are welcome here (and provided with places to wash and store their gear). The Maui Guest House also operates **Trinity Tours** and offers discounts on car rentals and other island activities. Tennis courts are nearby, and the nearest beach is about a block away.

1620 Ainakea Rd. (off Fleming Rd., north of Lahaina town), Lahaina, HI 96761. www.mauiguest house.com. ✆ **800/621-8942** or 808/661-8085. Fax 808/661-1896. 4 units. $169 single; $189 double. Extra person $15. Rates include continental breakfast. MC, V. Take Fleming Rd. off Hwy. 30; turn left on Ainakea; it's 2 blocks down. **Amenities:** Concierge; shared kitchen; huge outdoor pool; free use of watersports equipment. *In room:* A/C, TV/VCR/DVD, fridge, Jacuzzi, Wi-Fi (free).

Outrigger Aina Nalu ★

Set on 9 acres in the middle of Lahaina, this collection of apartments offers a different type of accommodation in a quieter, more residential part of Lahaina. The units in this first-class property are owned privately and put in a rental pool, but all have the latest appliances, new furniture, and 21st-century conveniences. The property is on a quiet side street (a rarity in Lahaina) and within walking distance of restaurants, shops, attractions, and the beach (just 3 blocks away). All of the good-size rooms, decorated in tropical-island style, are comfortable and quiet. The complex includes a sun deck and pool, a barbecue, and a picnic area. The friendly staff will take the time to answer all of your questions.

660 Wainee St. (btw. Dickenson and Prison sts.), Lahaina, HI 96761. www.outrigger.com. ✆ **866/956-4262** or 808/667-9766. Fax 808/661-3733. 197 units. $145–$175 studio; $175–$315 1-bedroom (sleeps up to 4); $189–$365 2-bedroom with 1 bathroom (sleeps 6); $199–$395 2-bedroom with 2 bathrooms (sleeps 6). AE, DC, DISC, MC, V. Parking $15. **Amenities:** Outdoor pool; whirlpool. *In room:* A/C, TV/DVD, hair dryer, high-speed Internet access (free), kitchenette (in studio), full kitchen (in 1- and 2-bedroom units).

The Plantation Inn ★★ 🎁

Attention, romance-seeking couples: Look no further. This charming Victorian-style inn, located a couple of blocks from the water, looks like it's been here 100 years or more, but it's actually of 1990s vintage—an artful deception. The rooms are romantic to the max, tastefully done with period furniture, hardwood floors, stained glass, and ceiling fans. There are four-poster canopy beds in some rooms, brass beds and wicker beds in others. All units are soundproof (a plus in Lahaina) and come with a private lanai; the suites have kitchenettes. The rooms wrap around the large pool and deck. Breakfast is served around the pool and in an elegant pavilion lounge. Also on the property is an outstanding French restaurant, **Gerard's** (p. 200).

174 Lahainaluna Rd. (btw. Wainee and Luakini sts., 1 block from Hwy. 30), Lahaina, HI 96761. www.theplantationinn.com. ⓒ **800/433-6815** or 808/667-9225. Fax 808/667-9293. 19 units, some with shower only. $159–$219 double; $265–$290 suite. Extra person $30. Check the website for package deals. Rates include full breakfast. AE, DC, DISC, MC, V. **Amenities:** Acclaimed restaurant and bar; concierge; Jacuzzi; large outdoor pool. *In room:* A/C, TV/DVD, fridge, hair dryer, kitchenette (in suites), Wi-Fi (free).

Puamana These 28 acres of town houses set right on the water are ideal for those who want to be able to retreat from the crowds and cacophony of downtown Lahaina into the serene quiet of an elegant neighborhood. Private and peaceful are apt descriptions for this complex: Each unit is a privately owned individual home, with no neighbors above or below. Most are exquisitely decorated, and all come with full kitchen, lanai, barbecue, and at least two bathrooms. Puamana was once a private estate in the 1920s, part of the sugar plantations that dominated Lahaina; the plantation manager's house has been converted into a clubhouse with an oceanfront lanai, library, card room, sauna, table-tennis tables, and office. I've found the best rates by booking through Klahani Travel (see below for contact information), but its office is not on-site, which has caused some problems with guests getting assistance. If you'd rather book directly with the Puamana association office, contact Puamana Community Association, 34 Puailima Place, Lahaina, HI 96761 (ⓒ **808/661-3423;** fax 808/667-0398; info@puamana.info).

Front St. (at the extreme southern end of Lahaina, ½ mile from downtown), Lahaina, HI 96761. Reservations c/o Klahani Travel, 159 Halelo St., Lahaina, HI 96761. www.klahani.com. ⓒ **800/669-6284** or 808/667-2712. Fax 808/661-5875. 40 units. $140–$250 1-bedroom; $180–$200 2-bedroom; $350–$400 3-bedroom. Resort fee $10 per day. 3-night minimum. AE, DISC, MC, V. **Amenities:** Jacuzzi; 3 pools (1 for adults only); tennis court. *In room:* TV, hair dryer, Internet access in some units (free), kitchen.

Wai Ola Vacation Paradise on Maui ★ Just 2 blocks from the beach, in a quiet residential development behind a tall concrete wall, lies this lovely retreat, with shade trees, sitting areas, gardens, a pool, an ocean mural, and a range of accommodations. You can book a small studio, a couple of suites inside the home, a separate honeymoon cottage, a one-bedroom apartment, or the entire 5,000-square-foot house. Hosts Kim and Jim Wicker will gladly provide any information you need to make your vacation fabulous. Every unit has a welcome fruit basket when you arrive, plus coffee beans for the coffeemaker. Kim often surprises her guests with "a little something" from her kitchen, like cheesecake or heavenly brownies. You'll also find a deck, barbecue facilities, and an outdoor wet bar on the property; a great beach and tennis courts are nearby. This is an adults-only property.

1565 Kuuipo St. (P.O. Box 12580), Lahaina, HI 96761. www.waiola.com. ⓒ **800/492-4652** or 808/661-7901. Fax 808/661-1119. 4 units. $169–$235 studio; from $179 suite; from $209 1-bedroom honeymoon cottage. MC, V. No children allowed. **Amenities:** Jacuzzi; outdoor pool; free use of watersports equipment. *In room:* A/C, TV/DVD/VCR, fridge, hair dryer, kitchenette (some rooms), Wi-Fi (free).

INEXPENSIVE

In addition to the following choices, consider value-priced **Old Lahaina House** (www.oldlahaina.com; ✆ **800/847-0761** or 808/667-4663; fax 808/669-9199), which features comfy twin- and king-bedded doubles for just $89 to $139. It's about a 2-minute walk to the water just across Front Street.

Makai Inn 🏄 *Budget travelers, take note:* Here's a small apartment complex located right on the water (okay, no white-sand beach out front, but what do you want at these eye-popping prices?). You can take a 10-minute stroll from this quiet neighborhood to the closest white-sand beach, or walk 20 minutes to the center of Lahaina town. The units are small (400 sq. ft.) but clean and have full kitchens, views of the ocean (from most units), and separate bedrooms. There are no phones or TVs, but there's a public phone by the office. In the middle of the complex is a tropical garden. I recommend the Paradise Found unit, which has windows on two sides overlooking the ocean, for just $180. Families will like the Pineapple "Sweet," the only two-bedroom unit (800 sq. ft.), also priced at $180.

1415 Front St., Lahaina, HI 96761. www.makaiinn.net. ✆ **808/662-3200.** Fax 808/661-9027. 18 units. $105–$180 double. Extra person $15. AE, MC, V. *In room:* Kitchen, no phone, Wi-Fi.

Penny's Place Inn Paradise ★ 🎁 No attention to detail has been spared in this Victorian-style bed-and-breakfast, just 50 feet from the water with a fabulous view from the front porch of Molokai and Lanai. Each of the four rooms is uniquely decorated, with themes ranging from contemporary Hawaiian to formal Victorian. Guests are welcome to use the balcony kitchenette (fridge, microwave, toaster, coffeemaker, and ice machine). The only problem is the location—a small island bounded by Honoapiilani Highway on one side and busy Front Street on the other. The house is soundproof, and air-conditioning in each room drowns out the noise inside. Penny recently enclosed the outdoor lanai area, so you can enjoy your breakfast without the highway noise.

1440 Front St., Lahaina, HI 96761. www.pennysplace.net. ✆ **888/329-0777** or 808/661-1068. Fax 808/667-7102. 4 units. $88–$134 double. Rates include continental breakfast Mon–Sat. 3-night minimum. DISC, MC, V. *In room:* A/C, TV/DVD, Wi-Fi (free).

Kaanapali

This master-planned family resort features nearly 3 miles of lovely gold-sand beach. Walking paths link hotels, shops, and restaurants. It's a quick shuttle ride to Lahaina, 3 miles to the south.

Best for: Travelers who want a high-end resort experience, with the incredible white-sand beach nearby, close to golf, tennis, dining, and shopping.

Drawbacks: You won't find any budget accommodations here.

VERY EXPENSIVE

Hyatt Regency Maui Resort & Spa ★★ ☺ Spagoers will love this resort. Hawaii's first oceanfront spa, the Spa Moana, boasts 20,000 square feet of facilities, including an exercise floor with an ocean view, 15 treatment rooms, sauna and steam rooms, and a huge menu of massages, body treatments, and therapies. Book your treatment before you leave home—this place is popular.

This fantasy resort has lots of imaginative touches: a collection of exotic species (pink flamingos, unhappy-looking penguins, and an assortment of loud parrots and macaws in the lobby), nine waterfalls, and an eclectic Asian and Pacific art collection. It covers some 40 acres; even if you don't stay here, you might want to walk through the expansive tree-filled atrium and the parklike grounds, which contain a ½-acre outdoor pool with a 150-foot lava-tube slide, a cocktail bar under the falls, a "honeymooners' cave," and a swinging rope bridge. There's even a kids-only pool with its own beach, tidal pools, and fountains.

The rooms, spread out among three towers, are pleasantly outfitted with an array of amenities and have very comfortable separate sitting areas and private lanai with eye-popping views. The latest, most comfortable bedding (including fluffy feather beds) is now standard in every room. Two Regency Club floors offer a private concierge, complimentary breakfast, sunset cocktails, and snacks.

Families will appreciate Camp Hyatt, a year-round program offering young guests a range of activities, from "Olympic Games" to a scavenger hunt. There's also a game room for kids with video games, pool, Ping-Pong, and air hockey.

200 Nohea Kai Dr., Lahaina, HI 96761. www.maui.hyatt.com. ⓒ **800/233-1234** or 808/661-1234. Fax 808/667-4498. 806 units. $289–$534 double; $439–$609 Regency Club double; from $955 suite. Extra person $75 ($125 in Regency Club rooms). Children 18 and under stay free in parent's room using existing bedding. Packages available. Daily $25 resort fee for access to Moana Athletic Club, local newspaper delivery, local and toll-free calls, Internet access, and 1-hr. tennis-court time per day. AE, DC, DISC, MC, V. Valet parking $20; free self-parking. **Amenities:** 5 restaurants; 3 bars; babysitting; year-round children's program ($80 full day, $45 half-day per child); concierge; concierge-level rooms; 36-hole golf course; health club w/weight room; Jacuzzi; ½-acre outdoor pool; room service; state-of-the-art spa; 6 tennis courts; watersports equipment rentals. In room: A/C, TV, fridge, hair dryer, high-speed Internet access (included in resort fee), minibar, 2-line phone.

Kaanapali Alii ★★ ☺ These luxurious oceanfront condominiums sit on 8 landscaped acres right on Kaanapali Beach. Kaanapali Alii combines the amenities of a luxury hotel (including a 24-hr. front desk) with the conveniences of a condominium. Each of the one-bedroom (1,500 sq. ft.) and two-bedroom (1,900 sq. ft.) units is impeccably decorated and comes with all the comforts of home (fully equipped kitchen, washer/dryer, lanai, two full bathrooms) and then some (room service from the Westin next door, daily maid service, complimentary local newspaper). The beachside recreation area includes a swimming pool, a separate children's pool, a whirlpool, gas barbecue grills and picnic areas, exercise rooms, saunas, and tennis courts. You can even take yoga classes on the lawn.

50 Nohea Kai Dr., Lahaina, HI 96761. www.kaanapali-alii.com. ⓒ **866/664-6410** or 808/661-3124. Fax 808/661-5686. 264 units. $460–$645 1-bedroom (sleeps 4); $650–$975 2-bedroom (sleeps 6). **Amenities:** Babysitting; children's program (seasonally at the Westin next door for a fee); concierge; fitness center; nearby golf course; Jacuzzi; room service; 3 lighted tennis courts; watersports equipment rentals. In room: A/C, TV/DVD, hair dryer, high-speed Internet (free), kitchen.

Sheraton Maui Resort and Spa ★★ ☺ Terrific facilities for families and fitness buffs and a premier beach location make this beautiful resort an all-around great place to stay. The grande dame of Kaanapali Beach is built into the side of a cliff on the curving, white-sand cove next to Black Rock (a lava formation that rises 80 ft. above the beach), where there's excellent snorkeling. The resort comprises six buildings of six stories or fewer set in well-established tropical gardens. The elevated lobby has panoramic views, and a lagoonlike pool features lava-rock waterways, wooden bridges, and an open-air whirlpool. Watch cliff divers swan dive off the torch-lit lava-rock headland in a traditional sunset ceremony—a sight to see. And the views of Kaanapali Beach, with Lanai and Molokai in the distance, are some of the best around.

Every unit is outfitted with amenities galore, right down to toothbrushes and toothpaste. Other pluses include a private balcony, and a "no-hassle" check-in policy: The valet takes you and your luggage straight to your room. There's also a new emphasis on family appeal, with a class of rooms dedicated to those traveling with kids. These "family suites" have three beds, a sitting room with full-size couch, and two TVs, both equipped with Nintendo. In addition, there's the Keiki Aloha program, with fun activities ranging from Hawaiian games to visits to nearby attractions. Children 12 and younger eat free when dining with one adult.

2605 Kaanapali Pkwy., Lahaina, HI 96761. www.sheraton-maui.com. © **866/716-8109** or 808/661-0031. Fax 808/661-0458. 510 units. $369–$569 double; from $699 suite. Extra person $89. Children 17 and under stay free in parent's room using existing bedding. Daily $26 resort fee for in-room Internet access, self-parking, local calls, and credit card calls up to 60 min. AE, DC, DISC, MC, V. Valet parking $5. **Amenities:** 3 restaurants; poolside bar; indoor lounge; babysitting; children's program (at the Westin); lobby and poolside concierge; fitness center; 36-hole golf course; Jacuzzi; lagoon-style pool; room service; day spa; 3 tennis courts; watersports equipment rentals. *In room:* A/C, TV, fridge, hair dryer, high-speed Internet access (free), PlayStation.

The Westin Ka'anapali Ocean Resort Villas ★ ★ ☺

Not to be confused with the other Westin in Kaanapali (see "Westin Maui Resort & Spa," below), this oceanfront condominium project, located at the very serene north end of Kaanapali, features full kitchens with marble counters in the kitchen and bathrooms, big living rooms, spacious bedrooms, and whirlpool tubs in all guest rooms. The individually owned units are all managed by the Westin Resort people, who maintain top standards, from the kitchen appliances to the comfy beds. The units range from 440-square-foot studios with a complete kitchen to 960-square-foot one-bedroom units (with a pullout couch for the kids). In addition to all the amenities of the Kaanapali Resort (golf course, tennis courts, restaurants, and shops), the Westin also has three restaurants on the property, plus a general store, a fresh food market, and the terrific Spa Helani (not to be missed).

6 Kai Ala Dr., Kaanapali Resort, HI 96761. www.westinkaanapali.com. © **866/716-8112** or 808/667-3200. Fax 808/667-3201. 1,021 units. $389–$469 double studio; $549–$889 double 1-bedroom; $789–$900 double 2-bedroom. Extra person $89. AE, DC, DISC, MC, V. Self-parking $9. **Amenities:** 3 restaurants; 2 bars; babysitting; body treatments; children's program; concierge; 36-hole golf course; health club; Jacuzzi; 3 outdoor pools; separate children's pool; room service; sauna; shuttle services to Lahaina; tennis courts. *In room:* A/C, TV, hair dryer, high-speed Internet access (free), complete kitchen.

Westin Maui Resort & Spa ★ ★ ☺

The 758-room Westin Maui has added a $5-million spa and gym, and in the spirit of having a healthy environment, smoking is no longer allowed in guest rooms. I love the fabulous pillow-top Westin Heavenly Beds, with your choice of five different pillows. If that doesn't give you sweet dreams, nothing will. Once you get up, head to the aquatic playground—an 87,000-square-foot pool area with five free-form heated pools joined by swim-through grottoes, waterfalls, and a 128-foot-long water slide. This is the Disney World of water-park resorts, and your kids will be in water-hog heaven. The fantasy theme extends from the estatelike grounds into the interior's public spaces, which are filled with the shriek of tropical birds and the splash of waterfalls. Most of the rooms in the two 11-story towers overlook the aquatic playground, the ocean, and the island of Lanai in the distance.

2365 Kaanapali Pkwy., Lahaina, HI 96761. www.westinmaui.com. © **866/716-8112** or 808/667-2525. Fax 808/661-5764. 758 units. $339–$639 double; from $759 suite. Extra person $89. Starwood members receive a discount. Daily $26 resort fee for local calls, use of fitness center and spa, a souvenir shopping bag, a 4x6-in. photo, shuttle services to golf and tennis facilities, in-room high-speed Internet access, self-parking, and local newspaper delivery. AE, DC, DISC, MC, V. Valet parking $15. **Amenities:** 4 restaurants; 3 bars; babysitting; bike rentals; children's program; concierge; 36-hole golf course; health club; Jacuzzi; 5 free-form outdoor pools; room service; spa; tennis courts; watersports equipment rentals. *In room:* A/C, TV, fridge, hair dryer, high-speed Internet access (included in resort fee), minibar.

EXPENSIVE

Another option to consider, in addition to those below, is the **Royal Lahaina Resort** (www.hawaiianhotelsandresorts.com; © **800/222-5642** or 808/661-3611; fax 808/661-6150). But skip the overpriced hotel rooms: Stay here only if you can get one of the 132 cottages tucked among the well-manicured grounds. Book on the website, where rates are $180 to $522.

Honua Kai Resort & Spa ★★

Opened in 2009, this North Kaanapali Beach resort, on 38 acres facing the ocean, features luxury condominium units, ranging from 590-square-foot studios to 2,800-square-foot three-bedroom units, with top-of-the-line appliances, lanai, and ocean views. The property has a full-service restaurant (Duke's Beach House), plus a deli with takeout. Every unit is fully furnished and has daily housekeeping. If you are looking for a relaxing vacation for your family, this is the place.

130 Kai Malina Pkwy., North Kaanapali Beach, HI 96761. www.honuakaimaui.com. © **855/718-5789** or 808/662-2800. Fax 808/662-2871. 628 units. $269–$299 studio double; $249–$399 1-bedroom (sleeps up to 4); $399–$499 2-bedroom (sleeps up to 6); $719–$1,199 3-bedroom (sleeps up to 8). $25 daily resort fee for unlimited local calls, fitness center, pool and beach services, resort charging privileges, in-room and resortwide Internet access, daily housekeeping, and parking. AE, DC, DISC, MC, V. **Amenities:** 1 restaurant; 1 deli; 1 bar; nearby 36-hole golf course; 5 outdoor pools; nearby tennis courts; whirlpool. *In room:* A/C, TV/DVD, Internet access (included in resort fee) , full kitchen.

The Whaler on Kaanapali Beach ★

In the heart of Kaanapali, right on the world-famous beach, lies this oasis of elegance, privacy, and luxury. The relaxing atmosphere strikes you as soon as you enter the open-air lobby, where light reflects off the dazzling koi in the meditative lily pond. No expense has been spared on these gorgeous accommodations; every unit has a full kitchen, marble bathroom, 10-foot beamed ceilings, and blue-tiled lanai—and spectacular views of Kaanapali's gentle waves or the humpback peaks of the West Maui Mountains. Next door is Whalers Village, with numerous restaurants, bars, and shops; Kaanapali Golf Club's 36 holes are across the street.

2481 Kaanapali Pkwy. (next to Whalers Village), Lahaina, HI 96761. www.astonhotels.com. © **877/997-6667** or 808/661-4861. Fax 808/661-8315. 360 units. $260–$345 studio double;

$334–$430 1-bedroom (sleeps up to 4); $575–$899 2-bedroom (sleeps up to 6). Check website for specials. AE, DC, DISC, MC, V. Parking $12 per day. **Amenities:** Concierge; refurbished fitness room; Jacuzzi; outdoor pool; Hina Mana Salon & Spa; tennis courts. *In room:* A/C, TV/VCR/DVD, hair dryer, free high-speed Internet access, kitchen.

MODERATE

Kaanapali Beach Hotel ★ ⚑ ☺   It's older and less high-tech than its upscale neighbors, but the Kaanapali Beach Hotel has an irresistible local style and a real Hawaiian warmth that's missing from many other Maui properties. Three low-rise wings, bordering a fabulous stretch of beach, are set around a wide, grassy lawn with coco palms and a whale-shaped pool. The spacious, spotless motel-like rooms are done in wicker and rattan, with Hawaiian-style bedspreads and a lanai facing the courtyard and the beach. The beachfront rooms are separated from the water only by Kaanapali's landscaped walking trail.

Old Hawaii values and customs are always close at hand, and the service is some of the friendliest around. Tiki torches, hula, and Hawaiian music create a festive atmosphere every night in the expansive courtyard. As part of the hotel's extensive Hawaiiana program, you can learn to cut pineapple, weave lauhala, and even dance the hula. The children's program is complimentary. There's also an arts-and-crafts fair every day, a morning welcome reception and orientation Monday through Saturday, and a farewell lei ceremony when you depart.

2525 Kaanapali Pkwy., Lahaina, HI 96761. www.kbhmaui.com. ℂ **800/262-8450** or 808/661-0011. Fax 808/667-5978. 430 units. $143–$272 double; from $288 suite. Extra person $30. Packages and senior discounts available. AE, DC, DISC, MC, V. Valet parking $11; self-parking $9. **Amenities:** 2 restaurants; poolside bar (where you can get a mean piña colada); babysitting; children's program; concierge/guest services; 36-hole golf course nearby; outdoor pool; access to tennis courts; watersports equipment rentals. *In room:* A/C, TV, fridge, high-speed Internet ($10 per day).

Outrigger Maui Eldorado ★ ☺   These spacious condominium units—each with full kitchen, washer/dryer, and daily maid service—were built at a time when land in Kaanapali was cheap, contractors took pride in their work, and visitors expected spacious units with views from every window. You'll find it hard to believe that this was one of Kaanapali's first properties in the late 1960s; this first-class choice still looks like new. The Outrigger chain has managed to keep prices reasonable, especially in spring and fall. This is a great choice for families, with its big units, grassy areas that are perfect for running off excess energy, and a beachfront (with beach cabanas and a barbecue area) that's usually safe for swimming. Tennis courts are nearby.

2661 Kekaa Dr., Lahaina, HI 96761. www.outrigger.com. ℂ **888/339-8585** or 808/661-0021. Fax 808/667-7039. 204 units. $155–$305 studio double; $195–$345 1-bedroom (sleeps up to 4); $295–$509 2-bedroom (sleeps up to 6). Packages available. AE, DC, DISC, MC, V. Parking $7. **Amenities:** Concierge; 36-hole golf course; 3 outdoor pools. *In room:* A/C, TV, hair dryer, high-speed Internet access (free), kitchen.

Honokowai, Kahana & Napili

This is condominium row. Units tend to be older here, but it's a great location on sandy beaches, just minutes from Kapalua and Kaanapala, and convenient to Lahaina as well.

Best for: Travelers with families or those looking for the extras that a condo unit will provide. If you want a quiet, restful vacation, this is your place.

Drawbacks: Because this is a residential area, there is virtually no nightlife, and limited shopping. Thanks to the location, this area tends to be pricey.

EXPENSIVE

Napili Kai Beach Resort ★★ 🍴   This comfortable oceanfront complex lies just south of the Kapalua Resort, nestled in a small white-sand cove. The one- and two-story units, with double-hipped Hawaii-style roofs, face a gold-sand beach that's safe for swimming. Many units have a view of the Pacific, with Molokai and Lanai in the distance. Those who prefer air-conditioning should book into the Honolua Building, where you'll get a room set back from the shore around a grassy, parklike lawn and pool. Every unit (except eight hotel rooms) has a fully stocked kitchenette with full-size fridge, cooktop, microwave, toaster oven, washer/dryer, and coffeemaker; some have dishwashers. On-site pluses include daily maid service, even in the condo units; two shuffleboard courts; barbecue areas; complimentary morning coffee and afternoon tea; weekly lei making, hula lessons, and horticultural tours; and a free weekly mai tai party. There are three nearby championship golf courses and excellent tennis courts at the adjacent Kapalua Resort.

5900 Honoapiilani Rd. (at the extreme north end of Napili, next to Kapalua), Lahaina, HI 96761. www.napilikai.com. ✆ **800/367-5030** or 808/669-6271. Fax 808/669-5740. 162 units. $250–$365 double; $320–$510 studio double (sleeps up to 4); $495–$710 1-bedroom suite (sleeps up to 5); $760–$1,055 2-bedroom suite (sleeps up to 7). Packages available. AE, DISC, MC, V. **Amenities:** Restaurant; bar; babysitting; free children's activities at Easter, June 15–Aug 31, Thanksgiving, and Christmas; concierge; good-size fitness room; 2 18-hole putting greens (w/free use of golf putters); Jacuzzi; 4 outdoor pools; tennis courts nearby (and complimentary use of tennis rackets); complimentary watersports equipment. *In room:* A/C (in most units), TV/DVD, fridge, hair dryer, high-speed Internet access (free), kitchenette (in most units).

MODERATE

In addition to the choices below, consider **Polynesian Shores,** 3975 Lower Honoapiilani Rd. (near Kahana and just 2 min. from the Kapalua–West Maui Airport), Lahaina, HI 96761 (www.polynesianshores.com; ✆ **800/433-6284** or 808/669-6065; fax 808/669-0909). Every unit (one to three bedrooms, $125–$325) has floor-to-ceiling sliding-glass doors that open onto a private lanai with an ocean view. There's great snorkeling off the beach out front.

Aston at Papakea Resort 🌿   Just a mile down the beach from Kaanapali lie these low-rise buildings, surrounded by manicured, landscaped grounds and ocean views galore. Palm trees and tropical plants dot the property, a putting green wraps around two kidney-shaped pools, and a footbridge arches over a lily pond brimming with carp. Each pool has its own private cabana with sauna, Jacuzzi, and barbecue grills; a poolside shop rents snorkel gear for exploring the offshore reefs. All units have dishwashers, big lanai, and washer/dryers. The studios have pull-down beds to save space during the day. Definitely a good value.

3543 Lower Honoapiilani Rd. (in Honokowai), Lahaina, HI 96761. www.astonhotels.com. ✆ **877/ 997-6667** or 808/669-4848. Fax 808/665-0662. 364 units. $157–$329 studio double; $184–$320 1-bedroom (sleeps up to 4); $239–$415 2-bedroom (sleeps up to 6). AE, DISC, MC, V. **Amenities:**

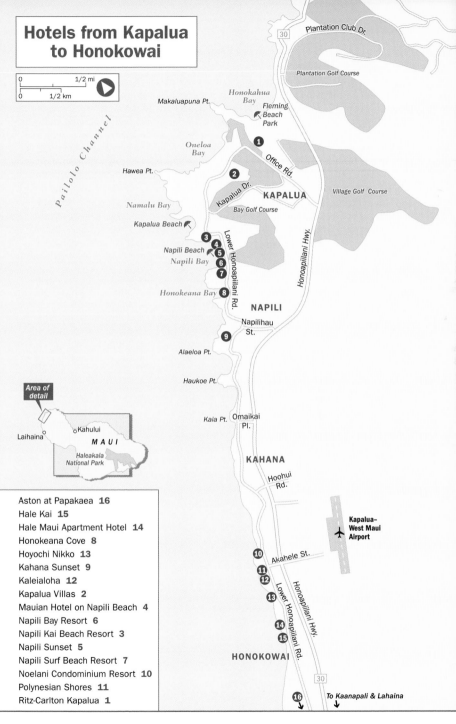

Hotels from Kapalua to Honokowai

0 — 1/2 mi
0 — 1/2 km

Pailolo Channel

30
Plantation Club Dr.
Plantation Golf Course

Makaluapuna Pt.
Honokahua Bay
Fleming Beach Park

Office Rd.
1

Oneloa Bay

Hawea Pt.
2
Kapalua Dr.
KAPALUA
Village Golf Course

Namalu Bay
Bay Golf Course

Kapalua Beach
3

Napili Beach
4
5
Napili Bay
6
7

Honokeana Bay
8

Lower Honoapiilani Rd.

Honoapiilani Hwy.

NAPILI

Napilihau St.
9

Alaeloa Pt.

Haukoe Pt.

Kaia Pt. Omaikai Pl.

KAHANA

Hoohui Rd.

Kapalua–West Maui Airport

10 Akahele St.
11
12
13
Lower Honoapiilani Rd.
Honoapiilani Hwy.
14
15

HONOKOWAI

30

16 To Kaanapali & Lahaina

Area of detail
Laihaina
Kahului
M A U I
Haleakala National Park

Aston at Papakaea **16**
Hale Kai **15**
Hale Maui Apartment Hotel **14**
Honokeana Cove **8**
Hoyochi Nikko **13**
Kahana Sunset **9**
Kaleialoha **12**
Kapalua Villas **2**
Mauian Hotel on Napili Beach **4**
Napili Bay Resort **6**
Napili Kai Beach Resort **3**
Napili Sunset **5**
Napili Surf Beach Resort **7**
Noelani Condominium Resort **10**
Polynesian Shores **11**
Ritz-Carlton Kapalua **1**

2 Jacuzzis; 2 outdoor pools; 3 tennis courts; watersports equipment rentals. *In room:* A/C, TV/VCR, wireless Internet access (free), kitchen.

Hale Kai ★ ☺   This small two-story condo complex is ideally located, right on the beach and next door to a county park—a great location for those traveling with kids. Shops, restaurants, and ocean activities are all within a 6-mile radius. The units are older but in excellent shape; they come with well-equipped kitchens (with dishwasher, disposal, microwave, and blender) and louvered windows that open to the trade winds. Lots of guests clamor for the oceanfront pool units, but I find the parkview units cooler, and they still have ocean views (upstairs units also have cathedral ceilings). This place fills up fast, so book early; repeat guests make up most of the clientele.

3691 Lower Honoapiilani Rd. (in Honokowai), Lahaina, HI 96761. www.halekai.com. ✆ **800/446-7307** or 808/669-6333. Fax 888/831-0122. 40 units. $160 1-bedroom double; $210 2-bedroom (sleeps up to 4); $350 3-bedroom (sleeps up to 6). Extra person $10. 5-night minimum. MC, V. **Amenities:** Concierge; outdoor pool. *In room:* TV/VCR, hair dryer, high-speed Internet access (free), kitchen.

Honokeana Cove 🐾   These large, secluded units—cozily set around a pool in a lush tropical setting—have fabulous views of Honokeana Cove. The beach here isn't sandy (it's composed of smooth round rocks), but the water just offshore is excellent for snorkeling (turtles have been spotted here) and for whale-watching in winter. The well-appointed units all come with full kitchens and lanai. Amenities include barbecues and deck chairs. The management holds weekly *pupu* (appetizers) parties so you can meet the other guests. All in all, a well-priced option in an expensive neighborhood.

5255 Lower Honoapiilani Rd. (in Napili), Lahaina, HI 96761. www.honokeana-cove.com. ✆ **800/237-4948** or 808/669-6441. Fax 808/669-8777. 33 units. $189–$205 1-bedroom; $218–$305 2-bedroom (sleeps up to 4); $310 3-bedroom (sleeps up to 6). Extra person $10–$15. 3- to 5-night minimum; 7- to 14-night minimum over Christmas/New Year's. MC, V. **Amenities:** Concierge; outdoor pool. *In room:* TV/VCR, kitchen, Wi-Fi (free).

Kahana Sunset ★★ ☺   Lying in the crook of a sharp horseshoe curve on Lower Honoapiilani Road is this series of wooden condo units, stair stepping down the side of a hill to a postcard-perfect white-sand beach. The unique location, nestled between the coastline and the road above, makes this a very private place to stay. In the midst of the buildings sits a grassy lawn with a small pool and Jacuzzi; down by the sandy beach are gazebos and picnic areas. The units feature full kitchens (complete with dishwashers), washer/dryers, large lanai with terrific views, and sleeper sofas. This is a great complex for families: The beach is safe for swimming, the grassy area is away from traffic, and the units are roomy. There is daily maid service.

4909 Lower Honoapiilani Hwy. (at the northern end of Kahana, almost in Napili), Lahaina, HI 96761. www.kahanasunset.com. ✆ **800/669-1488** or 808/669-8700. Fax 808/669-4466. 79 units. $170–$300 1-bedroom (sleeps up to 4); $295–$550 2-bedroom (sleeps up to 6). 3- to 5-night minimum. AE, DISC, MC, V. From Hwy. 30, turn makai (toward the ocean) at the Napili Plaza (Napilihau St.), and then left on Lower Honoapiilani Rd. **Amenities:** Concierge; 2 outdoor pools (1 for children). *In room:* TV/DVD/VCR, high-speed Internet access (free), kitchen,

Kaleialoha   This condo complex for the budget minded has recently been upgraded, with new paint, bedspreads, and drapes in each apartment.

Each one-bedroom unit has a sofa bed in the living room, which allows you to comfortably sleep four. All of the island-style units feature fully equipped kitchens, with everything from dishwashers to washer/dryers. There's great ocean swimming just off the rock wall (no sandy beach); a protective reef mows waves down and allows even timid swimmers to relax.

3785 Lower Honoapiilani Rd. (in Honokowai), Lahaina, HI 96761. www.mauicondosoceanfront. com. ☎ **800/222-8688** or 808/669-8197. Fax 808/669-2502. 18 units. $124–$250 1-bedroom double. Extra person $10. Children 4 and under stay free in parent's room. Cleaning fee $95 for less than 7-night stay. 3- to 5-night minimum. DISC, MC, V. **Amenities:** Concierge; outdoor pool. *In room:* TV/DVD, high-speed Internet access (free), kitchen.

Mauian Hotel on Napili Beach ★ The Mauian is perched above a beautiful ½-mile-long white-sand beach with great swimming and snorkeling; there's a pool with lounges, umbrellas, and tables on the sun deck; and the verdant grounds burst with tropical color. The rooms feature Indonesian-style furniture, and big lanai with great views. The floorings and furnishings were redone in 2008. Thoughtful touches include fresh flowers, plus chilled champagne for guests celebrating a special occasion. There are no phones or TVs in the rooms, but the large *ohana* (family) room does have a TV with a VCR and an extensive library if you need entertainment. There's a barbecue area, great restaurants are just a 5-minute walk away, and Kapalua Resort is up the street. The nightly sunsets off the beach are spectacular.

5441 Lower Honoapiilani Rd. (in Napili), Lahaina, HI 96761. www.mauian.com. ☎ **800/367-5034** or 808/669-6205. Fax 808/669-0129. 44 units. $179 double; $199–$299 double studio (sleeps up to 4). Extra person $10. Children 5 and under stay free in parent's room. AE, DISC, MC, V. **Amenities:** Golf course nearby; outdoor pool; tennis courts nearby; free Wi-Fi in family room. *In room:* Fridge, kitchen (most units), no phone.

Napili Sunset 🌊 Housed in three buildings just down the street from **Napili Bay Resort** (see below), these older, well-maintained units offer good value. At first glance, the plain two-story structures don't look like much, but the location, the moderate prices, and the friendly staff are the real hidden treasures here. In addition to daily maid service, the units all have full kitchens (with dishwashers), ceiling fans (no air-conditioning), sofa beds, small dining rooms, and small bedrooms. The studio units are located in the building off the beach and a few steps up a slight hill; they're a good size, with a full kitchen and either a sofa bed or a Murphy bed, and they overlook the small pool and garden. The one- and two-bedroom units are all on the beach (the downstairs units have lanai that lead right to the sand). The staff makes sure each unit has the basics (paper towels, dishwasher soap, coffee filters, condiments) to get your stay off to a good start. There are restaurants within walking distance. The beach—one of Maui's best—can get a little crowded because the public beach access is through this property.

46 Hui Rd. (in Napili), Lahaina, HI 96761. www.napilisunset.com. ☎ **800/447-9229** or 808/669-8083. Fax 808/669-2730. 42 units. $135 studio double; $239–$259 1-bedroom double (sleeps up to 6); $399 2-bedroom (sleeps up to 7). Extra person $15. Children 2 and under stay free in parent's room. Check the website for specials. MC, V. **Amenities:** Small outdoor pool. *In room:* TV, kitchen, Wi-Fi (free).

Napili Surf Beach Resort ★ 📠 This well-maintained, superbly landscaped condo complex has a great location on Napili Beach. The well-furnished, recently renovated units (all with full kitchens) offer free daily maid service, a rarity in condo properties. Management encourages socializing: In addition to weekly mai tai parties and coffee socials, the resort hosts annual shuffleboard and golf tournaments, as well as get-togethers on July 4th, Thanksgiving, Christmas, and New Year's. Facilities include three shuffleboard courts and three gas barbecue grills.

50 Napili Place (off Lower Honoapiilani Rd., in Napili), Lahaina, HI 96761. www.napilisurf.com. ✆ **888/627-4547** or 808/669-8002. Fax 808/669-8004. 53 units, some with shower only. $125–$249 studio double (sleeps up to 3); $250–$353 1-bedroom double (sleeps up to 4). Extra person $15. No credit cards. **Amenities:** 2 outdoor pools. *In room:* TV/VCR, kitchen, Wi-Fi (free).

Noelani Condominium Resort ★★ ☺   This oceanfront condo is a great value, whether you stay in a studio or a three-bedroom unit (ideal for large families). Everything is first-class, from the furnishings to the oceanfront location. Though it's on the water, there's no sandy beach here (despite the photos posted on the website)—but right next door is a sandy cove at the county park. There's good snorkeling off the cove, which is frequented by spinner dolphins and turtles in summer and humpback whales in winter. All units feature complete kitchens, entertainment centers, and spectacular views (all except the studio units also have their own washer/dryers and dishwashers). My favorites are in the Anthurium Building, where the condos have oceanfront lanai just 20 feet from the water. Frugal travelers will love the cheaper deluxe studios in the Orchid Building, with great ocean views. Guests are invited to a continental breakfast orientation on their first day and mai tai parties at night; there are also oceanfront barbecue grills for guest use.

4095 Lower Honoapiilani Rd. (in Kahana), Lahaina, HI 96761. www.noelani-condo-resort.com. ✆ **800/367-6030** or 808/669-8374. Fax 808/669-7904. 45 units. $125–$193 studio double; $175–$217 1-bedroom (sleeps up to 4); $245–$319 2-bedroom (sleeps up to 6); $330–$393 3-bedroom (sleeps up to 8). Extra person $20. Children 17 and under stay free in parent's room. Packages available. Rates include continental breakfast on 1st morning. 3-night minimum. AE, MC, V. **Amenities:** Concierge; fitness center; oceanfront Jacuzzi; 2 freshwater pools (1 heated for night swimming). *In room:* TV/VCR, hair dryer, high-speed Internet access (free), kitchen.

INEXPENSIVE

In addition to the choices below, consider **Hale Maui Apartment Hotel** (www.halemaui.com; ✆ **808/669-6312;** fax 808/669-1302), a wonderful, tiny place run by Hans and Eva Zimmerman and daughter Marika, whose spirit is 100% aloha. The one-bedroom suites, which start at around $115 for a double, come with ceiling fans, private lanai, and complete kitchens (the kitchens were remodeled and new furniture was added in 2008). There's no pool, but a private path leads to a great swimming beach.

Another option is **Hoyochi Nikko,** 3901 Lower Honoapiilani Rd. (in Honokowai), Lahaina, HI 96761 (www.mauilodging.com; ✆ **800/487-6002,** ext. 1, or 808/669-0089, ext. 1; fax 808/669-3937), which has 17 older (but well-maintained) one-bedroom units (and a few one-bedrooms with a separate loft) sharing 180 feet of oceanfront ($130–$190 one-bedroom double). There's a surcharge for stays of fewer than 10 nights.

Napili Bay Resort ★ ⛱   One of Maui's best bargains is this small two-story complex right on Napili's beautiful ½-mile white-sand beach. It's perfect for a romantic getaway: The atmosphere is comfortable and relaxing, the ocean lulls

Nickel-and-Dime Charges at High-Priced Hotels

Several upscale resorts in Hawaii engage in a practice that I find distasteful, dishonest, and downright discouraging: charging a so-called resort fee. This daily fee (generally $15–$26 a day) is added to your bill for such "complimentary" items as a daily newspaper, local phone calls, and use of the fitness facilities—amenities that the resort used to happily provide its guests free. In most cases, you do not have an option to decline the resort fee—in other words, this is a sneaky way to further increase the nightly rate without telling you. I oppose this practice and urge you to voice your complaints to the resort management. Otherwise, what'll be next—a charge for using the tiny bars of soap or miniature shampoo bottles?

you to sleep at night, and bird song wakes you in the morning. The beach here is one of the best on the coast, with great swimming and snorkeling—in fact, it's so beautiful that people staying at much more expensive resorts down the road frequently come here. The studio apartments are definitely small, but they pack in everything you need to feel at home, from a full kitchen to a comfortable queen-size bed, plus a roomy lanai that's great for watching the sun set over the Pacific. There's no air-conditioning, but louvered windows and ceiling fans keep the units fairly cool during the day. There are lots of restaurants and a convenience store within walking distance, and you're about 10 to 15 minutes away from Lahaina and some great golf courses.

33 Hui Dr. (off Lower Honoapiilani Hwy., in Napili), Lahaina, HI 96761. www.alohacondos.com. ℂ **877/877-5758** or 808/930-1830. 28 units. $89–$269 double. Cleaning fee $100–$110. 1- to 3-night minimum. MC, V. *In room:* TV, high-speed Internet access (most units, free), kitchen.

Kapalua

This luxury resort area features exquisite white-sand beaches bordered by waving palm trees. It's probably the most expensive place to stay on Maui.

Best for: Relaxing in sumptuous surroundings; close to golf, tennis, and ocean activities; great dining and shopping.

Drawbacks: Pricey and located at the extreme northern end of Maui, which means long drives for exploring the island.

VERY EXPENSIVE

Ritz-Carlton Kapalua ★★★ ☺ This Ritz is a complete universe, one of those resorts where you can happily sit by the ocean with a book for 2 whole weeks and never leave the grounds. It rises proudly on a knoll, in a singularly spectacular setting between the rainforest and the sea. During construction, the burial sites of hundreds of ancient Hawaiians were discovered in the sand, so the hotel was moved inland to avoid disrupting the graves. The setback gives the hotel a commanding view of Molokai.

In 2008, the Ritz reopened after an extensive $160-million renovation that transformed the place into an even more elegant property, with a focus on a Hawaiian (vs. the former European) theme. All guest rooms now have the latest technology. The penthouse floor has been converted into Residential Suites (with kitchens, living rooms, and separate bedrooms), available for guests. If you can afford it, stay on the **Club Level ★★★**—it offers the best amenities in the state, from French-roast coffee in the morning to a buffet at lunch, from cookies in the afternoon to *pupu* and drinks at sunset.

Other transformations include upgrades to the signature 10,000-square-foot, three-tiered pool; a new children's pool; an Ambassadors of the Environment Education Center (by Jean-Michel Cousteau); and a new 17,500-square-foot Waihua Spa, with 15 treatment rooms, saunas, whirlpool with lava-stone walls, and fitness center. Your children will enjoy the Ritz Kids program's wide variety of activities, plus the weekly "Ritz Kids Night Out" that allows parents to spend a quiet evening alone.

1 Ritz-Carlton Dr., Kapalua, HI 96761. www.ritzcarlton.com. ⓒ **800/262-8440** or 808/669-6200. Fax 808/669-1566. 463 units. $299–$719 double; $549–$969 Club Level double; from $599 suite; from $899 Club Level suite; from $595 1–bedroom residential suite; from $975 2-bedroom residential suite. Extra person $50. Packages available. Daily $25 resort fee for use of fitness center, steam room, sauna, selected wellness classes, Aloha Friday festivities, cultural-history tours, in-room wireless Internet access, self-parking, resort shuttle service, morning coffee at the Lobby Lounge, preferred tee times, 9-hole putting green, tennis and basketball courts, and games of boccie ball on the lawn. AE, DC, DISC, MC, V. Valet parking $18; free self-parking. **Amenities:** 5 restaurants; 4 bars (including 1 serving drinks and light fare next to the beach); babysitting; bike rentals; children's program; concierge; concierge-level rooms (some of Hawaii's best); fitness room; access to the Kapalua Resort's 3 championship golf courses (each w/ a pro shop), golf academy, and deluxe tennis complex; 2 outdoor hot tubs; outdoor pool; room service; spa; watersports equipment rentals. *In room:* A/C, TV, hair dryer, wireless Internet access (free).

EXPENSIVE

If you're interested in a luxurious condo or town house, consider **Kapalua Villas** (www.kapaluavillas.com; ⓒ **800/545-0018** or 808/669-8088). The palatial units dotting the oceanfront cliffs and fairways of this idyllic coast are a (relative) bargain, especially if you're traveling with a group. In 2009 the locally respected Outrigger chain of resorts took over the management of this property. The one-bedroom condos go for $249 to $349; two-bedrooms go for $339 to $574; three-bedrooms start at $559, plus a $25 daily recreation fee (which covers parking, unlimited local and national calls, high-speed Internet access, use of in-villa safe; delivery of newspaper Mon–Fri to the Gold villas, use of computer at Kapalua Resort Center, access to Ritz-Carlton pools and pool towels, access to Ritz-Carlton Spa, preferred guest rates at the Kapalua Golf Courses and tennis courts, and resortwide charging privileges). Numerous package deals (which include golf, tennis, honeymoon amenities, and car) can save you even more money.

SOUTH MAUI

Kihei

This stretch of condos and minimalls may lack charm, but it offers plenty of sunshine and some of the best hotel bargains on Maui.

Best for: Budget-minded travelers looking for condos. Golf, tennis, and ocean activities abound.

Hotels in South Maui

KIHEI

Uwapo Rd.

Piilani Hwy.

Kihei Beach

Kulanihakoi St.

S.

Kihei Rd.

Keonoulu Beach

Waipuilani Rd.

Kulanihakoi Gulch

Lipoa St.

Elleair Maui Golf Club

South Maui Community Park

Halama St.

PACIFIC

OCEAN

Lahaina   Kahului

MAUI

Area of detail

Haleakala National Park

0   1 mi
0   1 km

Kalama Beach Park

Kamaole Beach Park I

KAMAOLE

Piilani Hwy.

Kamaole Beach Park II

Keonekai Rd.

Kamaole Beach Park III

S. Kihei Rd.

Kilohana Dr.

Keawakapu Beach

Kihei Rd.

WAILEA

Mokapu Beach

Ulua Beach

Wailea Beach

Polo Beach

Palauea Beach

Poolenalena Beach

Maluaka Beach

MAUI MEADOWS

Wailea Alanui Dr.

Wailea Old Blue Golf Course

Wailea Ike Dr.

Kaukahi St.

Makena Rd.

Wailea Emerald Golf Course

Wailea Gold Golf Course

MAKENA

Makena Rd.

Makena Alanui

Makena Golf Course

Makena State Park

Makena South Golf Course (closed for renovation)

Makena Rd.

Aston at the Maui Banyan **15**
Aston Maui Hill **19**
Dreams Come True **22**
Eva Villa **23**
Fairmont Kea Lani Maui **28**
Four Seasons Resort Maui at Wailea **27**
Grand Wailea Resort Hotel & Spa **26**
Hale Alana **24**
Hale Pau Hana Resort **14**
Kamanole Nalu Resort **13**
Kealia Resort **1**
Kihei Beach Resort **3**
Kihei Kai Resort **2**
Koa Resort **8**
Leinaala **10**
Luana Kai Resort **9**
Maalaea Surf Resort **1**
Makena Beach & Golf Resort **29**
Mana Kai Maui Resort **20**
Maui Coast Hotel **12**
Maui Kamaole **18**
Maui Sunseeker Resort **6**
Menehune Shores **7**
Nona Lani Cottages **4**
Pineapple Inn **21**
Puahoa Beach Apts. **11**
Two Mermaids on Maui B&B **17**
Wailana Kai **5**
Wailea Beach Marriott Resort and Spa **25**
What a Wonderful World B&B **16**

Drawbacks: Some people find Kihei a little too developed—as you drive down Kihei Road, the main drag, it's one condo after another, occasionally punctuated with a minimall.

EXPENSIVE

Aston Maui Hill ★ If you can't decide between the privacy of a condo and the conveniences of a hotel, try this place. Maui Hill gives you the best of both worlds. Located on a hill above the heat of Kihei town, this large Spanish-style resort combines all the amenities and activities of a hotel—pool, hot tub, tennis courts, Hawaiiana classes, maid service, and more—with large luxury condos that have full kitchens and plenty of privacy. Nearly all units have ocean views, dishwashers, washer/dryers, queen-size sofa beds, and big lanai. Beaches, restaurants, and shops are within easy walking distance; a golf course is nearby; and barbecue grills are provided for guests' use. The management here goes out of its way to make sure your stay is perfect. **Note:** Some of the units have converted to timeshares, but I wasn't bothered by any timeshare salespeople during my stay.

2881 S. Kihei Rd. (across from Kamaole Park III, btw. Keonekai St. and Kilohana Dr.), Kihei, HI 96753. www.astonhotels.com. (C) **877/997-6667** or 808/879-6321. Fax 808/879-8945. 140 units. $253–$280 1-bedroom ($223–$246 if you book on the website); $305–$337 2-bedroom (from $268 on the website); from $459 3-bedroom (from $431 on the website). AE, DC, DISC, MC, V. **Amenities:** Concierge; Jacuzzi; putting green; outdoor pool; tennis courts. *In room:* A/C, TV/VCR, hair dryer, high-speed Internet access (free), kitchen.

Hale Pau Hana Resort ★ ☺ Located on the sandy shores of Kamaole Beach Park, but separated from the white-sand beach by a velvet-green manicured lawn, this is a great condo resort for families. Each of the large units has a private lanai, a terrific ocean view, and a complete kitchen. The management goes above and beyond, personally greeting each guest and acting as your own concierge service. Guests can mingle at the free morning coffee hour Monday through Saturday, or at the bring-your-own *pupu* parties held twice a week at sunset. The location is in the heart of Kihei, close to shopping, restaurants, and activities.

2480 S. Kihei Rd., Kihei, HI 96753. www.hphresort.com. (C) **800/367-6036** or 808/879-2715. Fax 808/875-0238. 79 units. $195–$255 1-bedroom; $280–$375 2-bedroom. Extra person $15–$25.

4- to 7-night minimum. DISC, MC, V. **Amenities:** Concierge; outdoor pool. *In room:* A/C in bedrooms, TV, hair dryer, high-speed Internet access (free), full kitchen.

Maalaea Surf Resort ★   Enjoy a quiet, relaxing vacation on this well-land-scaped property, with a beautiful white-sand beach right outside. Located at the quiet end of Kihei Road, this two-story complex sprawls across 5 acres of lush tropical gardens. The luxury town houses all have ocean views, big kitchens (with dishwashers), cable TV, and VCRs. Amenities include maid service three times per week (Mon–Sat), shuffleboard, barbecue grills, and discounts on tee times at nearby golf courses; restaurants and shops are within a 5-minute drive.

12 S. Kihei Rd. (at S. Kihei Rd. and Hwy. 350), Kihei, HI 96753. www.maalaeasurfresort.com. ✆ **800/ 423-7953** or 808/879-1267. Fax 808/874-2884. 34 units. $285–$335 1-bedroom (sleeps up to 4); $380–$450 2-bedroom (sleeps up to 6). MC, V. **Amenities:** Concierge; 2 outdoor pools; 2 tennis courts. *In room:* A/C, TV/VCR/DVD, hair dryer, high-speed Internet access (free), kitchen.

Maui Coast Hotel ★   This place stands out as one of the few hotels in Kihei (which is largely full of affordable condo complexes rather than traditional hotels or resorts). The Extra Value Package gives you a rental car for just a few dollars more than your room rate. The other chief advantage of this hotel is its location, about a block from **Kamaole Beach Park I** (p. 156), with plenty of bars, restau-rants, and shopping within walking distance, plus a golf course nearby. Guest rooms offer extras such as sitting areas, whirlpool tubs, ceiling fans, and private lanai.

2259 S. Kihei Rd. (1 block from Kamaole Beach Park I), Kihei, HI 96753. www.mauicoasthotel. com. ✆ **800/895-6284** or 808/874-6284. Fax 808/875-4731. 265 units. $215 double; from $235 suite; $255 1-bedroom (sleeps up to 4). Extra person $20. Children 17 and under stay free in parent's room using existing bedding. Packages available. Daily resort fee $18. AE, DC, DISC, MC, V. **Amenities:** Restaurant; pool bar w/nightly entertainment; concierge; fitness room; outdoor pool (plus children's wading pool); room service; 2 lighted tennis courts. *In room:* A/C, TV, fridge, hair dryer, high-speed Internet access (free).

MODERATE

The **Kihei Beach Resorts,** 36 S. Kihei Rd., Kihei, HI 96753 (www.kihei beachresort.com; ✆ **800/367-6034** or 808/879-2744; fax 808/875-0306), has spacious condos right on the beach. The downside is the constant traffic noise from Kihei Road. Rates are $165 to $200 for a one-bedroom double, $270 to $295 for a two-bedroom (sleeps 4); there's a 4- to 10-night minimum and a $10 charge per extra person.

Also, there's the **Aston at the Maui Banyan** (www.astonhawaii.com; ✆ **877/997-6667** or 808/924-2924), a condo property across the street from Kamaole Beach Park II. The large one- to three-bedroom units are very nicely done and feature full kitchens, air-conditioning, and washer/dryers. Rates start at $195 for hotel rooms ($117 if you book on the website), $230 for one-bedroom units ($138 on the website), and $289 for two-bedroom units—be sure to ask about packages.

Eva Villa ★★ 🎒   This three-unit bed-and-breakfast is located on ½ acre of lushly landscaped property at the top of the Maui Meadows subdivision. Hosts Rick and Dale Pounds have done everything to make this one of Maui's classiest vacation rentals. From the continental breakfast stocked in the unit's kitchen (fresh fruit, juice, bread, muffins, jam, coffee, and tea) to the decor of the suites, from the heated pool and Jacuzzi to the individual barbecue facilities, this is a great place to stay. The location couldn't be better—just a few minutes' drive to Kihei's sunny beaches, restaurants in Kihei and Wailea, golf courses, and plenty of tennis and shopping. Each unit is a roomy 600 square feet. The separate cottage has a living room, full kitchen, bedroom, and washer/dryer; the poolside studio is a one-room unit with a huge kitchen; and the poolside suite has two bedrooms and a kitchenette. You can't go wrong booking here.

815 Kumulani Dr., Kihei, HI 96753. www.mauibnb.com. © **800/884-1845** or 808/874-6407. Fax 808/874-6407. 3 units. $135–$175 double. Extra person $20. 4-night minimum. No credit cards. **Amenities:** Jacuzzi; heated outdoor pool (summer only). *In room:* AC, TV/DVD, CD player, kitchen or kitchenette, Wi-Fi (free).

Kamaole Nalu Resort This six-story condominium complex is located between two beach parks, **Kamaole I and Kamaole II** (p. 156), and right across the street from a shopping complex. Units have fabulous ocean views, large living rooms, and private lanai; the kitchens are a bit small but come fully equipped. I recommend no. 306 for its wonderful bird's-eye view. The property also has an oceanside pool and great barbecue facilities. Restaurants, bars, a golf course, and tennis courts are nearby. *Warning:* Because the building is right on Kihei Road, it can be noisy.

2450 S. Kihei Rd. (btw. Kanani and Keonekai roads, next to Kamaole Beach Park II), Kihei, HI 96753. www.kamaolenalu.com. © **800/767-1497** or 808/879-1006. Fax 808/879-8693. 28 units. High season $250–$350 double; low season $190–$275 double. Extra person $20. Children 12 and under stay free in parent's room using existing bedding. Booking fee $30. 5-night minimum; 2-week minimum over Christmas and New Year's. MC, V. **Amenities:** Outdoor pool. *In room:* TV, hair dryer, high-speed Internet access (free), kitchen.

Kealia Resort 🏄 This oceanfront property at the northern end of Kihei is well maintained and nicely furnished—and the prices are excellent. But as tempting as the lower-priced units may sound, don't give in: They face noisy Kihei Road and are near a major junction, so you'll be listening to big trucks downshifting all night. Instead, go for one of the oceanview units, which all have full kitchens and private lanai. The grounds face a 5-mile stretch of white-sand beach. Social gatherings include free coffee-and-doughnut get-togethers every Friday morning and *pupu* parties on Wednesday.

191 N. Kihei Rd. (north of Hwy. 31, at the Maalaea end of Kihei), Kihei, HI 96753. www.kealia resort.com. © **800/265-0686** or 808/280-1192. Fax 808/875-1540. 51 units. $115–$130 studio double; $150–$190 1-bedroom double; $215–$250 2-bedroom (sleeps up to 4). Children 12 and under stay free in parent's room. Booking fee $25. 4-night minimum; 10-night minimum Dec 15–Jan 10. AE, MC, V. **Amenities:** Outdoor pool. *In room:* TV, hair dryer, high-speed Internet access (some units, free), kitchen.

Leinaala ★ From Kihei Road, you can't see Leinaala amid the jumble of buildings, but this oceanfront boutique condo offers excellent accommodations at moderate prices. The building is set back from the water, with a county park—an oasis of green grass and tennis courts—in between. A golf course is nearby. The units are compact but filled with everything you need: a full kitchen, sofa bed, and oceanview lanai. (Hideaway beds are available if you need one.)

998 S. Kihei Rd., Kihei, HI 96753. www.mauicondo.com. © **800/822-4409.** Fax 808/874-6144. 24 units. $190–$220 1-bedroom double; $243–$264 2-bedroom (sleeps up to 4). Check the website

for specials. Booking fee $40. 4-night minimum. AE, MC, V. **Amenities:** Outdoor pool. *In room:* A/C, TV, wireless Internet access ($10 per day), kitchen.

Mana Kai Maui Resort ★ ☺ This eight-story complex, situated on a beautiful white-sand cove, is an unusual combination of hotel and condominium. The hotel rooms, which account for half of the total number of units, are small but nicely furnished. Families should consider the condo units, which feature full kitchens and open living rooms with sliding-glass doors that lead to small lanai overlooking the sandy beach and ocean. Some units are beginning to show their age (the building is more than 35 years old), but they're all clean and comfortable. One of the best snorkeling beaches on the coast is just steps away; a golf course and tennis courts are nearby.

2960 S. Kihei Rd. (btw. Kilohana and Keonekai roads, at the Wailea end of Kihei), Kihei, HI 96753. www.manakaimaui.com. ⓒ **800/525-2025** or 808/879-1561. Fax 808/874-5042. 105 units. Hotel: $163–$195 double. Condo: $252–$387 1-bedroom (sleeps up to 4); $304–$448 2-bedroom (sleeps up to 6). Booking fee $35. 4- to 7-night minimum. AE, MC, V. **Amenities:** Restaurant; bar; concierge; outdoor pool. *In room:* A/C (in hotel rooms only), TV, fridge, complimentary high-speed Internet access, kitchen (in condo units).

Maui Kamaole You'll find this condo complex right across the street from the Kihei Public Boat Ramp and beautiful Kamaole Beach Park III, which is great for swimming, snorkeling, and beachcombing. Each roomy, fully furnished unit comes with a private lanai, two bathrooms (even in the one-bedroom units), and an all-electric kitchen. The one-bedroom units—which can comfortably accommodate four—are quite a deal, especially if you're traveling in low season. The grounds are nicely landscaped and offer barbecues. Restaurants and bars are within walking distance; a golf course and tennis courts are also nearby.

2777 S. Kihei Rd. (btw. Keonekai and Kilohana roads, at the Wailea end of Kihei), Kihei, HI 96753. www.mauikamaole.com. ⓒ **800/822-4409** or 808/879-5445. Fax 808/874-6144. 62 units. $190–$308 1-bedroom (sleeps up to 4); $268–$386 2-bedroom (sleeps up to 6). Cleaning fee $100 for less than 4 nights. Booking fee $40. AE, MC, V. **Amenities:** Jacuzzi; 2 outdoor pools; tennis courts. *In room:* A/C, TV, high-speed Internet access (some units, $10 per day), kitchen.

Menehune Shores ✦ Though this property is showing its age in some places, all units are well maintained and have ocean views and lanai. The kitchens are fully equipped, all units have washer/dryers, and the oceanfront location guarantees a steady breeze that keeps the rooms cool (there's no air-conditioning). The building sits in front of the ancient Hawaiian fishponds of Kalepolepo. Some Hawaiians still fish them using traditional throw nets, but generally the pond serves as protection from the ocean waves, making it safe for children (and those unsure of their ability) to swim in the relatively calm waters. There's also a heated pool, shuffleboard courts, and a whale-watching platform on the roof garden. Don't expect the Ritz, but this budget option offers oceanfront units at affordable prices in the heart of Kihei.

760 S. Kihei Rd. (btw. Kaonoulu and Hoonani sts.), P.O. Box 1327, Kihei, HI 96753. www.menehune reservations.com. ⓒ **800/558-9117** or 808/879-3428. Fax 808/879-5218. 64 units. $150–$200 1-bedroom double; $190–$230 2-bedroom for up to 4; $275–$310 3-bedroom for up to 6. Extra person $7.50. Booking fee $20. 3-night minimum. No credit cards. **Amenities:** Restaurant; bar; gas grills; outdoor pool. *In room:* TV/VCR, kitchen, Internet access (some units, free).

Pineapple Inn Maui ★★ 🎁 This charming inn (four rooms, plus a two-bedroom cottage) is not only an exquisite find, but also a terrific value. Located in the residential Maui Meadows area, with panoramic ocean views, the two-story inn is expertly landscaped, with a lily pond in the front and a giant saltwater pool and Jacuzzi overlooking the ocean. Each of the expertly decorated, sound-proof rooms (you won't hear the traffic from nearby Piilani Highway) has a private lanai with an incredible view, plus a small kitchenette stocked with juice, pastries, and drinks on your arrival. There's also a two-bedroom, one-bathroom cottage (wood floors, beautiful artwork) that's landscaped for maximum privacy, and it has a full kitchen, separate bedrooms, phone and answering machine, and private lanai. There's a barbecue area and an outdoor kitchen for guests.

3170 Akala Dr., Kihei, HI 96753. www.pineappleinnmaui.com. © **877/212-MAUI** (6284) or 808/298-4403. 5 units. $139–$169 double (3-night minimum); from $215 cottage for 4 (6-night minimum). No credit cards. **Amenities:** Jacuzzi; large saltwater pool. *In room:* A/C, TV/VCR, hair dryer, kitchenette or kitchen, no phone (in rooms), Wi-Fi (free).

Punahoa Beach Apartments ★ 🗡 Book this place! I can't put it any more simply than that. The location—off noisy, traffic-ridden Kihei Road, on a quiet side street with ocean frontage—is fabulous. A grassy lawn rolls about 50 feet down to the beach, where there's great snorkeling just offshore and a popular surfing spot next door; shopping and restaurants are all within walking distance. All of the beautifully decorated units in this small four-story building have fully equipped kitchens and lanai with great ocean views. Rooms go quickly in winter, so reserve early.

2142 Ililili Rd. (off S. Kihei Rd., 300 ft. from Kamaole Beach I), Kihei, HI 96753. www.punahoa beach.com. © **800/564-4380** or 808/879-2720. Fax 808/875-9147. 13 units. $139–$179 studio double; $174–$254 1-bedroom double; $214–$284 2-bedroom double; $209–$279 1-bedroom penthouse. Extra person $15. Booking fee $35. 5-night minimum. AE, MC, V. *In room:* A/C (some units), TV, Internet access (free), kitchen.

INEXPENSIVE

In addition to the choices below, also check out **Luana Kai Resort,** 940 S. Kihei Rd., Kihei, HI 96753 (www.luanakai.com; © **800/669-1127** or 808/879-1268; fax 808/879-1455). This older condo complex has 113 units ($109–$179 one-bedroom, $129–$229 two-bedroom, $249–$299 three-bedroom; 4- to 7-night minimum).

Kihei Kai Resort, 61 N. Kihei Rd., Kihei, HI 96753 (www.kiheikai.com; © **888/778-7717** or 808/891-0780; fax 808/891-9403), has one-bedroom apartments ($125–$190 double; 4-night minimum) that are ideal for families.

Dreams Come True on Maui 🗡 This bed-and-breakfast (where "you are never just renting a room") was a dream come true for hosts Tom Croly and Denise McKinnon, who, after several years of vacationing in Maui, opened this three-unit property in 2002. It's centrally located in the Maui Meadows subdivision, just a few minutes' drive to golf courses, tennis courts, white-sand beaches, shopping, and restaurants in Kihei and Wailea. The one-bedroom oceanview cottage has its own gourmet kitchen, two TVs, a washer/dryer, a computer with high-speed Internet access, and wraparound decks. Also available are two rooms in the house (one with a king-size bed, one with queen-size), each with TV, private entrance, kitchenette, use of washer/dryer, and lots of other amenities not usually found in B&Bs. Guests are invited to use the centrally located oceanview deck; the house living room, which has a computer with high-speed Internet connection; and an outdoor cooking area with barbecue grill, sink, and microwave. Every guest is given personal concierge treatment, from the lowdown on good snorkeling to a tour of the property. In the evenings, Tom shows movies on an 8-foot-wide movie screen. The owners recently acquired some condo units across the street from the beach, which they rent for $875 to $1,095 per week.

3259 Akala Dr., Kihei, HI 96753. www.dreamscometrueonmaui.com. © **877/782-9628** or 808/879-7099. Fax 808/879-7099. 3 units. $89–$119 double (4-night minimum); $149–$179 cottage double (6-night minimum; extra person $15). Rooms in the house include continental breakfast. MC, V. **Amenities:** Concierge, computer. *In room:* A/C (optional, $3–$5 per day), TV/VCR, CD player, hair dryer, Internet access (free), kitchen or kitchenette.

Hale Alana ★ 🏠 In 2010, this three-bedroom, three-bathroom Polynesian-style home received $30,000 in upgrades, including new furniture, new beds (and linens), all new appliances in the kitchen, and refurbished hot tub and barbecue grill, which makes this large vacation home in the residential neighborhood of Maui Meadows (and a 5-min. drive from the nearest good beach) a great value. It's a terrific deal for a large family or three couples traveling together. The master bedrooms have California-king-size beds, walk-in closets, and dual sinks and showerheads; the third bedroom has two double beds and a large closet. Skylights, ceiling fans, and an interior lava-rock wall add to the tropical environment. The deck has outdoor tables and chairs, and the recently refurbished hot tub and a barbecue grill.

490 Mikioi Place (in Maui Meadows), Kihei, HI 96753. www.halealana.com or www.beachbreeze. com. © **855/283-2231** or 808/283-2231. Fax 808/442-1015. 1 unit. $400–$550 3-bedroom (sleeps up to 6). Extra person $35–$40. Cleaning fee $250. 7-night minimum. MC, V. **Amenities:** Jacuzzi; pool. *In room:* A/C, TV/VCR/DVD, hair dryer, Internet access (free), kitchen.

Koa Resort ★ ☺ Located just across the street from the ocean, Koa Resort comprises five two-story wooden buildings on more than 5½ acres of landscaped grounds. There's plenty of room for families, who can enjoy the tennis courts, pool, and putting green. The spacious, privately owned one-, two-, and three-bedroom units are decorated with care and come fully equipped, right down to the dishwasher and disposal in the kitchens. All feature large lanai, ceiling fans, and washer/dryers. For maximum peace and quiet, ask for a unit far from Kihei Road. Bars, restaurants, and a golf course are nearby.

811 S. Kihei Rd. (btw. Kulanihakoi St. and Namauu Place), Kihei, HI 96753. Reservations c/o Bello Realty, P.O. Box 1776, Kihei, HI 96753. www.bellomaui.com. © **800/541-3060** or 808/879-3328. Fax 808/875-1483. 54 units, some with shower only. $99–$125 1-bedroom; $100–$150 2-bedroom; $195–$295 3-bedroom. MC, V. **Amenities:** 18-hole putting green; Jacuzzi; outdoor pool; 2 tennis courts. *In room:* TV, high-speed Internet access (most units, free), kitchen.

Maui Sunseeker 🏠 This former budget property, located just across the street from a terrific white-sand beach, has a new management team that has spiffed up the studio and one-bedroom units by adding custom furniture, air-conditioning, and other amenities not usually seen at small properties (like high-speed Internet access and concierge services). This property is geared for adults, so families with children, this is not the place for you. The redone units have been tastefully decorated. The one-bedrooms, which have a pullout sofa in the living room and new appliances in the kitchen, are a deal during low season. All units have private oceanview lanai and the beach just a few steps away, plus there's a gas barbecue for guests' use. The new owners also bought the apartment complex next door, where they've put slate in the bathrooms and new tile on the floor, bought new furniture, and repainted. The units are small, but the lanai are large and the price is right—and there's even a rooftop lanai where you can sit in the hot tub and enjoy great ocean views. They now cater to the gay and lesbian market, but welcome all adults.

551 S. Kihei Rd. (P.O. Box 276), Kihei, HI 96753. www.mauisunseeker.com. 📞 **800/532-6284** or 808/879-1261. Fax 808/874-3877. 23 units. $99–$175 double; $135–$175 studio double; $165–$205 junior suite double; $175–$235 premium junior suite double; $179–$249 1-bedroom double; $229–$519 penthouse apt. Extra person $45. AE, DISC, MC, V. No children allowed. **Amenities:** Concierge; hot tub. *In room:* A/C, TV/VCR, hair dryer, kitchen or kitchenette, Wi-Fi (free).

Nona Lani Cottages ★ 🎁   Picture this: a grassy expanse dotted with eight cottages tucked among palm, fruit, and sweet-smelling flower trees, right across the street from a white-sand beach. This is one of the great hidden deals in Kihei. The cottages are tiny but contain everything you'll need: a complete kitchen, twin beds that double as couches in the living room, a separate bedroom with a queen-size bed, and a lanai with table and chairs. The real attraction, however, is the garden setting next to the beach. There are no phones in the cabins, but there's a public one by the check-in area. There's also a barbecue area and a charming *hale* for weddings. Your hosts, the industrious Kong family, also run **Happy Valley Hale** (p. 260), hostel accommodations on the other side of the island in Happy Valley, next to Wailuku.

455 S. Kihei Rd. (just south of Hwy. 31), P.O. Box 655, Kihei, HI 96753. www.nonalanicottages.com. 📞 **800/733-2688** or 808/879-2497. 12 units. $105–$150 studio double; $120–$165 cottage double. Extra person $15. 4- to 7-night minimum. No credit cards. *In room:* A/C, TV, kitchen, no phone.

Tutu Mermaids on Maui B&B ★ 🎁   The two mermaids, Juddee and Miranda, both avid scuba divers, offer a friendly B&B, professionally decorated with brilliant colors and hand-painted art of the island. It sits in a quiet neighborhood just a 10-minute walk from the beach. My favorite unit is the Ocean Ohana, a large one-bedroom apartment (with the option of a separate connecting bedroom), complete with kitchenette, huge private deck, private entry, and your own giant hot tub. Equally cute is the Poolside Suite, with private entry next to the outdoor pool. This studio (with the option of a separate connecting bedroom) is a living room during the day; at night it converts to a bedroom with a pull-down bed. Continental breakfast, with some of the best homemade bread on the island, is placed on your doorstep every morning (so you can sleep in). Amenities include guitars in every unit, a range of complimentary beach equipment, microwave popcorn, and a barbecue area. If the spirit moves you, Juddee is a licensed minister who can perform weddings.

2840 Umalu Place, Kihei, HI 96753. www.twomermaids.com. 📞 **800/598-9550** or 808/874-8687. Fax 808/875-1833. 2 units. $115–$140 studio double; $140–$170 1-bedroom double; $140–$200 2-bedroom double. Rates include continental breakfast. 3-night minimum. No credit cards, but will do credit cards through PayPal. **Amenities:** Babysitting; golf nearby; hot tub; outdoor pool; tennis courts nearby. *In room:* TV, DVD (on request), hair dryer, kitchenette, Wi-Fi (free).

Wailana Kai ★ 🐚 Bello Realty has added this renovated two-story apartment building to its collection. Located at the end of a cul-de-sac, and just a 1-minute walk to the beach, the property was totally renovated several years ago. All units have full kitchens and concrete soundproof walls, and the second floor has ocean views. There's also a barbecue area for guests.

34 Wailana Place, Kihei, HI 96753. Reservations c/o Bello Realty, P.O. Box 1776, Kihei, HI 96753. www.bellomaui.com. ℂ **800/541-3060** or 808/879-3328. Fax 808/875-1483. 10 units. $110–$120 1-bedroom; $125–$150 2-bedroom. 5-night minimum. MC, V. **Amenities:** Outdoor pool. *In room:* TV/VCR, high-speed Internet access (in some units, free), kitchen.

What a Wonderful World B&B ★ 🐚 This impeccably done B&B has a great location, excellent rates, and thought and care put into every room. Hostess Eva Tantillo has not only a full-service travel agency, but also a master's degree—along with several years of experience—in hotel management. The result? One of Maui's finest bed-and-breakfasts, centrally located in Kihei (½ mile to Kamaole II Beach Park, 5 min. from Wailea golf courses, and convenient to shopping and restaurants). Choose from one of four units: the master suite, the studio apartment, or two one-bedroom apartments. Eva serves a gourmet expanded continental breakfast on her lanai, which boasts views of white-sand beaches, the West Maui Mountains, and Haleakala. You're also welcome to use the communal barbecue.

2828 Umalu Place (near Keonekai St. and Hwy. 31), Kihei, HI 96753. www.amauibedandbreakfast. com. ℂ **800/943-5804** or 808/879-9103. Fax 808/879-5340. 4 units. $89–$150 double. Children 11 and under stay free in parent's room. Rates include breakfast. AE, MC, V. **Amenities:** Computer, hot tub. *In room:* TV, fridge, hair dryer, kitchen (in apartment units), Wi-Fi (free).

Wailea

Great weather, lush landscaping, multimillion-dollar resort hotels, golf courses, luxury homes, 2 miles of golden shoreline—Wailea has it all. Expect to pay accordingly.

Best for: Travelers who want to make sure it will not rain on their vacation (no guarantee, but this area is very low in rainfall) and want sumptuous accommodations. Great for ocean activities, golf, and tennis.

Drawbacks: Pricey. The location, at the extreme southern end of Maui, means you will have to do a lot of driving when touring the island.

VERY EXPENSIVE

The Fairmont Kea Lani Maui ★★★ At first glance, this blinding-white complex of arches and turrets may look a bit out of place in tropical Hawaii (it's a close architectural cousin of Las Hadas, the *Arabian Nights* fantasy resort in Manzanillo, Mexico). But once you enter the flower-filled lobby and see the big blue Pacific outside, there's no doubt you're in Hawaii.

It's not cheap, but for the price of a hotel room in other luxury resorts, you get an entire suite here—plus a few extras. In 2011 all the "soft goods" (bedspreads, drapes, and so on) were updated. Each unit in the all-suite hotel has a kitchenette, a living room with entertainment center and sofa bed (great if you have the kids in tow), a wet bar, an oversize marble bathroom, a spacious bedroom, and a large lanai that overlooks the pools, lawns, and white-sand beach.

The small boutique spa offers the latest in body work in intimate, relaxing surroundings—not to be missed, even if you're staying elsewhere.

The rich and famous stay in the villas—2,000-square-foot two- and three-bedroom fantasy beach bungalows, each with its own plunge pool and gourmet kitchen (and includes a luxury car rental).

4100 Wailea Alanui Dr., Wailea, HI 96753. www.fairmont.com/kealani. © **866/540-4456** or 808/875-4100. Fax 808/875-1200. 450 units. $459–$1,049 suite (sleeps up to 4); from $1,750 villa. Valet parking $20. AE, DC, DISC, MC, V. **Amenities:** 4 restaurants, plus gourmet bakery and deli; 3 bars; babysitting; year-round children's program; concierge; fine 24-hr. fitness center; nearby Wailea Golf Club's 3 18-hole championship golf courses, as well as the Makena and Elleair golf courses; 2 large swimming lagoons connected by a 140-ft. water slide and swim-up bar, plus an adults-only pool; room service; excellent full-service spa; use of Wailea Tennis Center's 11 courts (3 lit for night play) and pro shop; watersports equipment rentals; 2 whirlpools. *In room:* A/C, TV/DVD/VCR, CD player, hair dryer, high-speed Internet access ($15 per day), kitchenette, microwave. (*Tip:* If you join the President's Club, which is free, there is no charge for the Internet access.)

Four Seasons Resort Maui at Wailea ★★★ ☺ If money's no object, this is the place to spend it. It's hard to beat this modern version of a Hawaiian palace by the sea, with a relaxing, casual atmosphere. Although it sits on a glorious beach between two other hotels, you won't feel like you're on resort row: The Four Seasons inhabits its own world, thanks to an open courtyard of pools and gardens. Amenities are first-rate here, including outstanding restaurants and an excellent spa. This may also be the most kid-friendly resort on the island: There's a complete activities program for *keiki* (children), plus other perks like milk and cookies on arrival, kids' menus in all restaurants, infant gear, and a game room. You can even prepurchase necessities like diapers and baby food; the hotel will have them waiting for you when you arrive.

The spacious (about 600-sq.-ft.) guest rooms feature furnished lanai, nearly all with ocean views, that are great for watching whales in winter and sunsets year-round. The grand bathrooms contain deep marble tubs and showers for two. Service is attentive but not cloying. At the pool, guests lounge in casbahlike tents, pampered with iced Evian and chilled towels.

The fabulous spa—which is smaller than the one at the Grand Wailea but has more intimate service—features an incredible menu of treatments ranging from traditional Hawaiian to craniosacral to ayurvedic massage, offered in 13 treatment rooms and three oceanside *hale.*

The ritzy neighborhood surrounding the hotel is home to great restaurants and shopping, the Wailea Tennis Center (known as Wimbledon West), and six golf courses—not to mention that great beach, with gentle waves and islands framing the view on either side.

3900 Wailea Alanui Dr., Wailea, HI 96753. www.fourseasons.com/maui. © **800/311-0630** or 808/874-8000. Fax 808/874-2244. 380 units. $485–$985 double; $1,195–$1,295 Club Floor double; from $1,295 suite. Extra person $100 ($150 in Club Floor rooms). Children 17 and under stay free in parent's room. Packages available. AE, DC, MC, V. Valet parking $20. **Amenities:** 3 restaurants; 3 bars (w/nightly entertainment); babysitting; free use of bikes; fabulous year-round children's program; one of Maui's best concierge desks; concierge-level rooms; putting green; use of Wailea Golf Club's 3 18-hole championship golf courses, as well as the nearby Makena and Elleair golf courses; health club featuring outdoor cardiovascular equipment (w/individual TV/VCRs); 3 fabulous outdoor pools; room service; excellent spa; 2 on-site tennis courts; use of

Wailea Condos

For a complete selection of condo units throughout Wailea and Makena, contact **Destination Resorts** (www.drhmaui.com; ℰ **866/384-1366** or 808/891-6200; fax 808/874-3554). Its luxury units include studio doubles starting at $265, one-bedroom doubles from $285, two bedrooms from $395, and three bedrooms from $575. At most properties, those rates include free long-distance calls, high-speed Internet access, and parking; all properties are smoke free. Children 11 and under stay free; minimum stays vary by property.

Wailea Tennis Center's 11 courts; beach pavilion w/watersports equipment rentals and 1-hr. free use of snorkel equipment; 2 whirlpools (1 for adults only). *In room:* A/C, TV, fridge, hair dryer, minibar, Wi-Fi ($10–$18 per day except Club Level).

Grand Wailea ★★★ *Spa aficionados, take note:* Hawaii's largest (50,000-sq.-ft.) and most elaborate spa is located here, with every kind of body treatment you can imagine. Treatments include use of the numerous baths, hot tubs, mineral pools, saunas, steam rooms, and other relaxation amenities in the his-and-hers spa area.

Built at the pinnacle of Hawaii's brief fling with fantasy megaresorts, the Grand Wailea (now a Waldorf=Astoria resort) is extremely popular with families, conventions, and honeymooners. Some features include an intricate pool system with slides, waterfalls, rapids, and a water-powered elevator to take you up to the top of the building; a restaurant in a man-made tide pool; a floating New England–style wedding chapel; and nothing but oceanview, amenity-filled guest rooms. It's all crowned with a $30-million collection of original art, much of it created expressly for the hotel by Hawaii artists and sculptors. Though minimalists may be put off, there's no denying that the Grand Wailea is plush, professional, and pampering, with all the diversions you could imagine. Oh, and did I mention the fantastic beach out front?

Those looking for more room can try the Villas at Ho'olei, adjoining the Grand Wailea Resort. The 3,200- to 4,000-square-foot, three-bedroom, three-and-a-half-bath, two-story villas have it all: elevators, gourmet kitchens, two-level covered lanai with gas grill and refrigerator, and access to all of the services and amenities of the resort.

3850 Wailea Alanui Dr., Wailea, HI 96753. www.grandwailea.com. ℰ **800/888-6100** or 808/875-1234. Fax 808/874-2442. 780 units. $489–$1,130 double; from $1,300 suite; from $869 Napua Club Room (in Napua Tower); from $1,036 Ho'olei Villa. Extra person $50 ($100 in Napua Tower). Daily $25 resort fee for lei greeting on arrival, welcome drink, local calls, use of spa, admission to scuba diving clinics and water aerobics, art and garden tours, nightly turndown service, in-room high-speed Internet access, self-parking, and shuttle service to Wailea area. AE, DC, DISC, MC, V. Valet parking $25. **Amenities:** 4 restaurants; 4 bars; babysitting; children's program; concierge; concierge-level rooms; complete fitness center; use of Wailea Golf Club's 3 18-hole championship golf courses, as well as the nearby Makena and Elleair golf courses; Jacuzzi; 2,000-ft.-long Activity Pool, featuring a swim/ride through mountains and grottoes; room service; Hawaii's largest spa; use of Wailea Tennis Center's 11 courts and pro shop; watersports equipment rentals; windsurfing and diving lessons. *In room:* A/C, TV, hair dryer, high-speed Internet access (included in the resort fee), kitchenette, minibar.

EXPENSIVE

Wailea Beach Marriott Resort & Spa ★★   This classic, open-air, 1970s-style hotel in a tropical garden by the sea gives you a sense of what Maui was like before the big resort boom. It was the first resort built in Wailea (in 1976), and it remains the most Hawaiian of them all. Airy and comfortable, with touches of Hawaiian art throughout and a terrific aquarium that stretches forever behind the front desk, it just feels right. What's truly special about this hotel is how it fits into its environment without overwhelming it. Eight buildings, all low-rise except for an eight-story tower, are spread along 22 gracious acres of lawns and gardens spiked by coco palms, with lots of open space and a half-mile of oceanfront property on a point between Wailea and Ulua beaches. The vast, parklike expanses are a luxury on this now-crowded coast.

The small Mandara Spa offers a long list of treatments, from relaxing massages to aromatherapy wraps to rejuvenating facials in a very Zen atmosphere.

3700 Wailea Alanui Dr., Wailea, HI 96753. www.waileamarriott.com. 📞 **800/367-2960** or 808/ 879-1922. Fax 808/874-8331. 545 units. $249–$825 double; from $485 suite. Extra person $40. Packages available. Daily $30 resort fee for local and long distance calls, Internet access, self-parking, discounts on spa services, luau and snorkel-gear rentals, and free kids' meals with purchase of adult entree. AE, DC, DISC, MC, V. Valet parking $30. **Amenities:** 2 restaurants; 2 bars; babysitting; concierge; fitness center; use of Wailea Golf Club's 3 18-hole championship golf courses; outdoor pools (including 1 for kids only); recreation center; room service; full-service Mandara Spa w/steam rooms and whirlpools; use of Wailea Tennis Center's 11 courts (3 lit for night play) and pro shop; watersports equipment rentals. *In room:* A/C, TV, hair dryer, high-speed Internet access (free), 4-outlet technology console, wet bar.

Makena

Makena's raw wilderness is quite a contrast to well-groomed Wailea. If you're looking for peace and quiet and lots of time on a pristine beach, Makena might be the place for you.

Best for: Travelers who want to spend most of their time on the beach.

Drawbacks: You'll do a lot of driving if you want to explore the rest of the island.

VERY EXPENSIVE

Makena Beach and Golf Resort ★★   If you're looking for a vacation in a beautiful, tranquil spot with a gold-sand beach, here's your place. In early 2012, the Makena completed a "to the walls" make-over of all of its rooms and suites as well as a transformation of its public spaces. Recently, Benchmark Hospitality took over the management, and you can expect a standard of luxury. The location, on one of Maui's best beaches, is beautiful; the interior atrium, filled with tropical plants and a koi-filled waterfall stream, is gorgeous.

5400 Makena Alanui, Makena, HI 96753. www.makenaresortmaui.com. 📞 **800/321-6284** or 808/874-1111. Fax 808/879-8763. 310 units. $349–$659 double; from $609 suite. Extra person $15. Packages available. Daily $25 resort fee for local and long distance calls, parking, Internet access, use of computers in the lobby. AE, DC, MC, V. **Amenities:** 4 restaurants; 2 bars; babysitting; concierge; fitness room; Jacuzzi; 2 outdoor 36-hole golf course (designed by Robert Trent Jones, Jr.); pools (1 for adults, 1 for children); room service; 6 Plexipave tennis courts (2 lit for night play); watersports equipment rentals. *In room:* A/C, TV, fridge, hair dryer, high-speed Internet access ($15 per day).

UPCOUNTRY MAUI
Makawao

This charming little upcountry town serves the cowboys and farmers in the surrounding community as well as visitors and transplanted mainlanders, which results in an eclectic mix of shops and restaurants.

Best for: Travelers looking for a reasonably priced bed-and-breakfast, off the beaten path.

Drawbacks: Very limited nightlife, a 20- to 30-minute drive to the beach, and the weather in the winter can be rainy and chilly.

EXPENSIVE

Aloha Cottage ★★ 📷 Hidden in the secluded rolling hills of Olinda on a 5-acre parcel of manicured, landscaped tropical foliage is this tropical cottage, designed and decorated by hosts Ron and Ranjana Serle. The Thai Tree House resembles an upscale Thai home with high vaulted ceilings, teak floors, a complete kitchen and dining area, and a king-size cherrywood bed in the center of the room. The private deck and private soaking tub make this a very romantic lodging.

1879 Olinda Rd., Makawao, HI 96765. www.alohacottage.com. (✆) **888/328-3330** or 808/573-8555. Fax 808/573-2551. 1 unit. $299 double. $100 cleaning fee. 3-night minimum preferred. MC, V. Not suitable for children 9 and under. *In room:* TV/VCR, CD player, hair dryer, wireless Internet (free), kitchen.

MODERATE

Banyan Tree House ★ 📷 Huge monkeypod trees (complete with swing and hammock) extend their branches over this 2½-acre property like a giant green canopy. The restored 1920s plantation manager's house can accommodate a big family or a group of friends; it has three spacious bedrooms and three private marble bathrooms. A fireplace stands at one end of the huge living room, a large lanai runs the entire length of the house, and the hardwood floors shine throughout. The four smaller guest cottages have been totally renovated to match. The quiet neighborhood and old Hawaii ambience give this place a comfortable, easygoing atmosphere. Restaurants and shops are just minutes away in Makawao, and the beach is a 15-minute drive—but this place is so relaxing that you may want to do nothing but lie in a hammock and watch the clouds float by. Recently they've added a yoga and meditation center.

3265 Baldwin Ave. (next to Veterans' Cemetery, less than a mile below Makawao), Makawao, HI 96768. www.banyantreehouse.com. (✆) **808/572-9021.** Fax 808/573-5072. 7 units. $155–$175 double room in house; $155–$190 cottage for 2. Extra person $30. Children 12 and under stay in parent's room for $15. Cleaning fee $30–$40. Rates include continental breakfast. AE, DC, DISC, MC, V. **Amenities:** Babysitting; Jacuzzi; outdoor pool *In room:* TV (in some cottages), kitchen or kitchenette, Wi-Fi (free).

Hale Ho'okipa Inn Makawao ★ 📷 Step back in time at this 1924 plantation-style home, rescued by owner Cherie Attix in 1996 and restored to its original charm (and listed on the Hawaii Register of Historic Places and the National Register of Historic Places). Cherie lovingly refurbished the old wooden floors, filled the rooms with furniture from the 1920s, and hung works by local artists on the walls. The result is a serene place to stay, just a 5-minute walk from the shops and restaurants of Makawao, 15-minute drive to beaches, and an hour's drive from the top of Haleakala. The guest rooms have separate outside entrances and private bathrooms. The house's front and back porches are wonderful spots for sipping tea and watching the sun set. The Kona Wing is a two-bedroom suite with a private bathroom and use of the kitchen.

32 Pakani Place, Makawao, HI 96768. www.maui-bed-and-breakfast.com. © **877/572-6698** or ©/fax 808/572-6698. 4 units, 2 with shower only. $140–$180 double. Extra person $20. Rates include continental breakfast. MC, V. From Haleakala Hwy., turn left on Makawao Ave., and turn right on the 5th street on the right off Makawao Ave. (Pakani Place); it's the 2nd-to-last house on the right (green house with white picket fence and water tower). No children 8 and under. *In room:* A/C, TV, hair dryer, Wi-Fi (free).

Wild Ginger Falls ★ 🎁   This cozy, romantic, intimate cottage, hidden in Miliko Gulch, overlooks a stream with a waterfall, bamboo, sweet-smelling ginger, and banana trees. It's perfect for honeymooners, lovers, and fans of Hawaiiana art. The moment you step into this 400-square-foot, artistically decorated Hawaiian cottage (with an additional 156-sq.-ft. screened deck), you will be delighted at the carefully placed memorabilia (ukulele tile, canoe paddle, and the like) found throughout. The cottage has a full kitchen with everything you could possibly want to cook with. The Hawaiian theme carries into the living room, where a cabinet painted with a tropical design houses a VCR and stereo. The comfy queen bed opens to the living area. The screened porch has a table, chairs, and a couch—perfect for curling up with a good book. To boot, there's a barbecue outside, plus all the beach toys you could want to borrow. Host Bob is a ceramic artist (with his creations throughout the cottage), and his wife, Sonny, manages Dolphin Galleries, from where she has selected the best of the best artwork for the cottage.

355 Kaluanui Rd., Makawao, HI 96768. www.wildgingerfalls.com. © **808/573-1173.** 1 unit. $155–$170 double. 3- to 5-night minimum. Credit cards via PayPal. **Amenities:** Outdoor hot tub. *In room:* TV/DVD/VCR, hair dryer, kitchen, Wi-Fi (free).

Kula

This cool, remote, upcountry community offers million-dollar views and a location convenient to Haleakala National Park. Here you'll find true peace and quiet about a 30- to 40-minute drive away from the beach.

Best for: Travelers looking to get away from it all, looking for lower-priced options, or wanting to be close to Haleakala National Park.

Drawbacks: Residential, few amenities for visitors, limited dining experiences, accommodations limited to B&Bs. Can be chilly at 3,000 feet and rainy in the winter.

INEXPENSIVE

In addition to the options below, consider **Gildersleeve's,** formerly known as Elaine's Upcountry Guest Rooms (© **808/878-6623**), where the warm and welcoming hosts rent three rooms in their spacious pole house ($85 double; 3-night minimum).

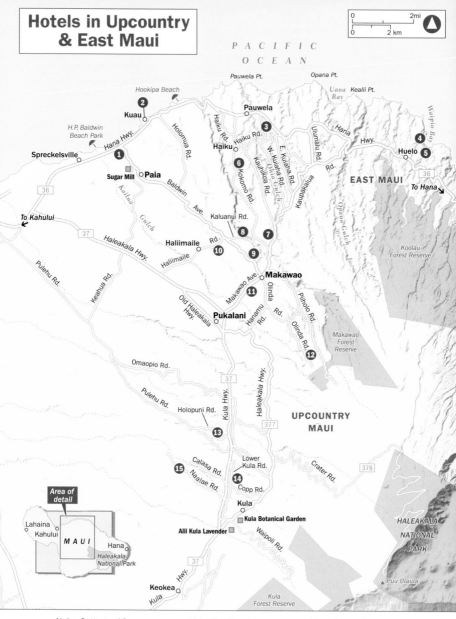

Hotels in Upcountry & East Maui

PACIFIC OCEAN

Aloha Cottage **12**
Banyan Tree House **9**
Cliff's Edge **4**
Gildersleeve's Vacation Rentals **15**
Haiku Cannery Inn **6**

Hale Ho'okipa Inn Makawao **11**
The Inn at Mama's Fish House **2**
Kula Cottage **14**
Kula View B&B **13**

Maui Dream Cottage **3**
Paia Inn **1**
Peace of Maui **10**
Piialoha B&B Cottage **7**
Tea House Cottage **5**
Wild Ginger Falls **8**

A Private Cottage

If you'd like your own private cottage, consider **Peace of Maui,** 1290 Haliimaile Rd. (just outside Haliimaile town), Haliimaile, HI 96768 (www.peaceofmaui.com; © **888/475-5045** or 808/572-5045), which has a full kitchen, two bedrooms, a daybed, and a large deck. The cottage goes for $165 (plus a $75 cleaning fee), and children are welcome. The owners also have rooms in the main house (with shared bathroom and kitchen facilities) from $65 single and $75 double.

Kula Cottage ★ 🎁 I can't imagine having a less-than-fantastic vacation here. Tucked away on a quiet street amid a large grove of blooming papaya and banana trees, Cecilia and Larry Gilbert's romantic honeymoon cottage is very private—it even has its own driveway and carport. The 700-square-foot cottage has a full kitchen (complete with dishwasher) and three huge closets that offer enough storage space for you to move in permanently. The lanai is outfitted with a gas barbecue and an umbrella-covered table and chairs. Cecilia stocks the cottage for breakfasts during your stay. Groceries and a small takeout lunch counter are within walking distance; it's a 30-minute drive to the beach.

40 Puakea Place (off Lower Kula Rd.), Kula, HI 96790. www.kulacottage.com. © **808/878-2043** or 808/871-6230. Fax 808/871-9187. 1 unit. $110 double. Extra person $15. Rate includes continental breakfast supplies. 3-night minimum. No credit cards. *In room:* TV, kitchen, Wi-Fi (free).

Kula View Bed & Breakfast 🎁 This cute private suite has a huge deck with a panoramic view of Haleakala and a private bathroom, which hostess Susan Kauai renovated in 2009. Inside, there's a reading area with a comfy lounge chair and an eating area with table and chairs, toaster oven, coffeemaker, and electric teakettle. Susan serves breakfast in your suite (or will pack a picnic breakfast if you are out early) of tasty breads or muffins, fruit, juice, and tea and coffee. She has plenty of warm jackets, sweaters, and blankets you can borrow if you plan to make the trip to the top of Haleakala. Be sure to take a stroll through her magical garden.

P.O. Box 322, Kula, HI 96790. sue@kulaview.com. © **808/878-6736.** 1 unit. $125 double suite. Rate includes continental breakfast. 2-night minimum. No credit cards. *In room:* Fridge.

EAST MAUI

Paia & Kuau

This former sugar town was reborn as a haven for hippies. Today the vibe is more sophisticated and artsy, but still pleasantly "granola."

Best for: Windsurfers wanting to be close to the waves at legendary Hookipa Beach Park, or travelers wanting to experience a different side of Maui.

Drawbacks: Limited accommodations, just one small inn in Paia and another oceanside in Kuau. Limited nightlife.

EXPENSIVE

Paia Inn I really wanted to love this boutique inn, which opened in 2009 in the tiny, funky town of Paia. But the main problems here are that the rooms are tiny (almost claustrophobic) and noisy (not only from the street outside, but also from other guest rooms), and given the very expensive rack rates and virtually no parking, you can find better deals in this area; it's included here because lodging options in this area are so limited. The inn features bamboo wood floors and a common living room where guests can gather (which contributes to the noise). Each of the guest rooms has 500-thread-count sheets, tiny travertine bathrooms, high-definition flatscreen televisions, iPod docking stations, and very limited space to unpack your clothes. There is complimentary coffee and tea with muffins and scones every morning.

93 Hana Hwy., Paia, HI 96779. www.paiainn.com. ℂ **800/721-4000** or 808/579-6000. 9 units. $189–$249 double, $259–$469 suites, from $999 3-bedroom beach house. AE, MC, V. **Amenities:** Bike, surfboard, and stand-up paddle-board rentals; concierge; room service. *In room:* A/C, fridge, free Wi-Fi.

MODERATE

The Inn at Mama's Fish House ★★
The fabulous location (nestled in a coconut grove on secluded Kuau Beach), beautifully decorated interior (with rattan furniture and works by Hawaiian artists), and extras (gas barbecue, 27-in. TVs, and beach toys) make this place a gem for those seeking a centrally located vacation rental. All this, and the fabulous **Mama's Fish House** (p. 225) restaurant is just next door. The one-bedrooms are nestled in a tropical jungle (red ginger surrounds the garden patio), while the two-bedrooms face the beach. All have wood or terra-cotta floors, kitchenettes or complete kitchens, sofa beds, and laundry facilities.

799 Poho Place (off the Hana Hwy. in Kuau), Paia, HI 96779. www.mamasfishhouse.com. ℂ **800/860-HULA** (4852) or 808/579-9764. Fax 808/579-8594. 12 units. $175 garden studio double; $250 1-bedroom (sleeps up to 4); $275–$575 2-bedroom (sleeps up to 6); from $325 junior suite; $575 beachfront cottage. 3-night minimum in Dec and Jan. AE, DISC, MC, V. **Amenities:** Restaurant. *In room:* A/C, TV/VCR, hair dryer, kitchen, Wi-Fi (free).

Haiku

This former pineapple-plantation village offers vacation rentals and B&Bs in a quiet, pastoral setting about 10 minutes from the beach.

Best for: Travelers who want a quiet, residential setting at moderate rates. Those looking to experience how Maui residents live.

Drawbacks: This is a residential area geared more to residents than visitors. There are limited dining and shopping opportunities, and no nightlife.

MODERATE

Haiku Cannery Inn ★★ ☺
If you are looking for an off-the-beaten-path vacation, I recommend staying here. This historic plantation manager's home has been converted into a pastoral country inn. Located on 3 acres filled with tropical fruit trees, bamboo, and ginger, the inn is 5 minutes from a wonderful restaurant (**Colleen's at the Cannery,** p. 225). Best of all, the innkeeper, Benni Denbeau, is a longtime Maui resident who is great at suggesting where to eat, what to do, and where to get the best deals. The guest rooms are spacious, and several rooms have full-size pull-out couches. Rates for the rooms in the inn include a continental breakfast (laid out in the old-fashioned pantry, allowing you to sleep in as

long as you want). In addition, the property has a separate stand-alone two-bedroom cottage with mango hardwood floors, lychee wood cabinets, and a fully equipped kitchen. The cottage is perfect for families or for adventure travelers, who can store their equipment (windsurfing boards, scuba gear, and so forth) in the two-car garage. *Note:* Rates for cottages do *not* include continental breakfast.

1061 Kokomo Rd., HI 96708. www.haikucanneryinn.com. *C* **808/283-1274.** 4 units. $95–$125 double room, rates include continental breakfast, 3-night minimum; $150–$250 cottage, rates include starter package for breakfast for the 1st day, 5-night minimum. DISC, MC, V. **Amenities:** Complimentary beach towels; hair dryer; big-screen TV w/DVD in Inn; complimentary Wi-Fi and guest computer in Inn. *In room:* Hair dryer, high-speed Internet access (free).

Pilialoha B&B Cottage ★ The minute you arrive at this split-level country cottage, set on a large lot with half-century-old eucalyptus trees, you'll see owner Machiko Heyde's artistry at work. In front of the quaint cottage, a garden blooms with some 200 varieties of roses. There's a queen-size bed in the master bedroom, from which a large lanai extends. There's a great movie collection for rainy days or cool country nights, plus a garage. If you plan on an early-morning ride to the top of Haleakala, Machiko will make sure you go with a Thermos of coffee and her homemade bread. The property is not appropriate for children.

2512 Kaupakalua Rd. (½ mile from Kokomo intersection), Haiku, HI 96708. www.pilialoha.com. *C* **808/572-1440.** 1 unit. $145 double. 3-night minimum. No credit cards. No children. **Amenities:** Complimentary use of beach toys (including snorkel equipment). *In room:* TV, kitchenette, Wi-Fi (free).

INEXPENSIVE

Maui Dream Cottage 🏄 Essentially a vacation rental, this country estate is located atop a hill overlooking the ocean. The grounds are dotted with fruit trees (bananas, papayas, and avocados, all free for the picking), and the front lawn is comfortably equipped with a double hammock, chaise longues, and table and chairs. The cottage has one bedroom, a full kitchen, and washer/dryer, and is very well maintained and comfortably outfitted with furniture that's attractive but casual. The Haiku location is quiet and restful, offering the opportunity to see how real islanders live. However, you'll have to drive a good 20 to 25 minutes to restaurants in Makawao or Paia. Hookipa Beach is about a 20-minute drive, and Baldwin Beach (good swimming) is 25 minutes away.

265 W. Kuiaha Rd. (1 block from Pauwela Cafe), Haiku, HI 96708. www.mauidreamcottage.com. *C* **808/575-9079.** Fax 808/575-9477. 1 unit, with shower only. $880 per week double. Extra person $10. 7-night minimum. MC, V. *In room:* TV, kitchen, Wi-Fi (free).

Huelo

About 15 to 20 minutes past Haiku, the largely unknown community of Huelo appeals to those who appreciate places still largely untouched by "progress."

Best for: Visitors looking for a quiet, relaxing vacation, way, way off the beaten path in a remote, peaceful, serene location.

Drawbacks: Way, way, way off the beaten bath. It's a drive to dining, shopping, and activities. No nightlife.

EXPENSIVE

Cliff's Edge ★ 🎁   This B&B and vacation rental couldn't be much closer to the ocean without being underwater. The saltwater swimming pool perches on the edge of a 300-foot cliff in Huelo. The tropically landscaped 2-acre property also has a hot tub and 600-square-foot sun deck. Accommodations include two bedrooms in the main house, a two-bedroom 900-square-foot guesthouse, and a 600-square-foot cottage. The rooms in the B&B range in size from 300 to 600 square feet, all with awesome ocean views, private entries, private lanai, private bathrooms, small kitchenettes (with microwave, coffeemaker, and refrigerator), and ceiling fans. Restaurants and shopping are about 30 minutes away in Paia.

P.O. Box 1095, Haiku, HI 96708. www.cliffsedge.com. © **866/262-6284** or 808/268-4530. 4 units. $185–$225 double room; $350 cottage. Extra person $25. Rates include continental breakfast. 3-night minimum. No credit cards. No children under 13. **Amenities:** Hot tub; pool; Wi-Fi (free). *In room:* TV (in cottages), stereo/CD player, kitchenette or kitchen, microwave.

INEXPENSIVE

Tea House Cottage   Hidden in a secluded jungle, powered by alternative energy (no utility poles!), this place gives you the chance to get away from it all while staying connected. Your private cottage has two decks, a screened lanai, a bedroom, a small kitchen, and a unique bathhouse. Rates include taxes and complimentary breakfast the first morning. Owners Cameron and Megan are on the property and can provide any helpful tips you need during your vacation.

Haiku Rd. www.mauiteahouse.com. © **800/215-6130** or 808/572-8596. 1 unit. $150 double. Discounts available for 4 or more nights. 2-night minimum. No credit cards. *In room:* CD player, kitchen, Wi-Fi (free).

AT THE END OF THE ROAD IN EAST MAUI: HANA

Most visitors make Hana a day trip, but if you spend a few days you can explore the beautiful tropical surroundings and really get a sense of the small-town aloha spirit of old Hawaii.

Best for: Travelers looking for "old Hawaii," in a remote location, where enjoying the outdoors (swimming in the ocean, hiking in the rainforest) is the main attraction.

Drawbacks: A very remote location, a long drive to "civilization." Very little nightlife, dining options, and shopping are found here. No golf, and the only tennis courts are the public courts in Hana. Not a good location to tour the island.

Note: To locate the following accommodations, see the "Hana" map on p. 141.

Very Expensive

Travaasa Hana ★★★ ☺   This hotel sits on 66 rolling seaside acres and offers a wellness center, two pools, and access to one of the best beaches in Hana. This is the atmosphere, the landscape, and the culture of old Hawaii set in 21st-century accommodations. Every unit is excellent, but my favorites are the Sea Ranch Cottages (especially unit nos. 215–218 for the best views), where individual duplex bungalows look out over the craggy shoreline to the rolling surf.

You step out of the oversize, airy units (with floor-to-ceiling sliding doors) onto a huge lanai with views that will stay with you long after your tan has faded. These comfy units have been totally redecorated with every amenity you can think of, and you won't be nickel-and-dimed for things like coffee and water—everything provided, from the homemade banana bread to the bottled water, is complimentary. Cathedral ceilings, a plush feather bed, a giant soaking tub, Hawaiian artwork, bamboo floors—this is luxury. The white-sand beach (just a 5-min. shuttle away), top-notch wellness center with some of the best massage therapists in Hawaii, and numerous activities (horseback riding, mountain biking, tennis, pitch-and-putt golf) make this one of the top resorts in the state. I highly recommend this little slice of paradise.

5031 Hana Hwy. (P.O. Box 9), Hana, HI 96713. www.travaasa.com/hana. ✆ **800/321-HANA** (4262) or 808/248-8211. Fax 808/248-7202. 66 units. $325 Bay Cottage double; $525–$625 Sea Ranch Cottage double; $1,100 2-bedroom suite for 6; from $4,000 Plantation House 2-bedroom. Extra person $140. AE, DC, DISC, MC, V. **Amenities:** Restaurant (w/Hawaiian entertainment Sun evenings); bar (entertainment nightly); babysitting; concierge; fitness center; complimentary use of the 3-hole practice golf courses (and complimentary use of clubs); 2 outdoor pools; room service; full-service spa; tennis courts. *In room:* Hair dryer, kitchenette.

Expensive

Baby Pigs Crossing Bed & Breakfast ★ 🏠   If you're looking for a quiet, romantic little cottage, nestled away from it all in old Hawaii but close enough to Hana to drive in for dinner, this is your place. International artist Arabella Gail Ark (formerly known as Gail Bakutis) has created a lovely retreat on her 1-acre parcel of land, which is landscaped in a "fragrance" garden carefully planted with Hawaii's best sweet-smelling plants. The separate guesthouse, with an ocean view from the lanai, is professionally decorated with comfort in mind, from the very cozy rattan furniture to the king-size sofa bed. There's a separate bedroom with a queen-size bed and a utilitarian kitchenette. The surprise is the unique bathroom with glass ceiling and walls (with privacy curtains), which opens onto a garden area. Even if you are not staying here, stop by and see the Ark Ceramics Gallery (daily 11am–4pm).

P.O. Box 667, Hana, HI 96713. www.mauibandb.com. ✆ **808/248-8890.** Fax 808/248-4865. 1 unit. Double $250 for 1 night, $225 per night for 2 nights, $200 per night for 3 nights. AE, MC, V. *In room:* TV/VCR, kitchenette.

Ekena ★   Just one glance at the 360-degree view, and you can see why hosts Robin and Gaylord gave up their careers on the mainland and moved here. This 8½-acre piece of paradise in rural Hana boasts ocean and rainforest vistas; the floor-to-ceiling glass doors in the spacious Hawaiian-style pole house bring the outside in. The elegant two-story vacation rental is exquisitely furnished, from the comfortable U-shaped couch that invites you to relax and take in the view to the top-of-the-line mattress on the king-size bed. The fully equipped kitchen has everything you should need to cook a gourmet meal. Only one floor (and one two-bedroom unit) is rented at any given time to ensure privacy. The grounds are impeccably groomed and dotted with tropical plants and fruit trees. Hiking trails into the rainforest start right on the property, and beaches and waterfalls are just minutes away. Robin places fresh flowers in every room and makes sure you're comfortable; after that, she's available to answer questions, but she also respects your privacy.

P.O. Box 728 (off Hana Hwy., above Hana Airport), Hana, HI 96713. www.ekenamaui.com. ☏ **808/248-7047.** Fax 808/248-7853. 2 units. $225 1-bedroom (sleeps 2); $295–$400 2-bedroom (sleeps 4). 3-night minimum. MC, V. No children 13 and under. *In room:* TV/DVD, CD player, kitchen, free Wi-Fi.

Hamoa Bay House & Bungalow ★ 👔   Down a country lane guarded by two Balinese statues stands a little bit of Indonesia in Hawaii: a carefully crafted bungalow and an Asian-inspired two-bedroom house overlooking Hamoa Bay. This enchanting retreat is just 2 miles beyond Hasegawa General Store on the way to Kipahulu. It sits on 4 verdant acres within walking distance of Hamoa Beach. The 600-square-foot Balinese-style cottage is distinctly tropical, with elephant-bamboo furniture from Indonesia, batik prints, a king-size bed, a full kitchen, and a screened porch with hot tub and shower. Hidden from the cottage is a 1,300-square-foot home with a soaking tub and private outdoor stone shower. It offers an elephant-bamboo king-size bed in one room, a queen-size bed in another, a screened-in sleeping porch, a full kitchen, and wonderful ocean views.

P.O. Box 773, Hana, HI 96713. hamoabay@maui.net. ☏ **808/248-7884.** Fax 808/248-7853. 2 units. $225 cottage (sleeps 2); $285 house for 2; $395 house for 4. 3-night minimum. MC, V. No children 13 and under. **Amenities:** Hot tub. *In room:* TV/DVD, CD player, wireless Internet access (free), kitchen.

Hana Oceanfront Cottages ★★   Just across the street from Hamoa Bay, Hana's premier white-sand beach, lie these two plantation-style units, impeccably decorated in old Hawaii decor. My favorite unit is the romantic cottage, complete with front porch where you can sit and watch the ocean; a separate bedroom; top-notch kitchen appliances; and a comfy living room. The 1,000-square-foot vacation suite, located downstairs from hosts Dan and Sandi's home (but totally soundproof—you'll never hear them), has an elegant master bedroom with polished bamboo flooring, a spacious bathroom with custom hand-painted tile, and a fully appointed kitchen. Outside is a 320-square-foot lanai. The units sit on the road facing Hana's most popular beach, so there is traffic during the day. At night the traffic disappears, the stars come out, and the sound of the ocean lulls you to sleep.

P.O. Box 843, Hana, HI 96713. www.hanabythesea.com. ☏ **808/248-7558.** Fax 808/248-8034. 2 units. $250–$275 double. 3- to 5-night minimum. MC, V. *In room:* TV/VCR/DVD, stereo/CD player, hair dryer, wireless Internet, kitchen.

Moderate

Bamboo Inn   This inn sits on a historic site with ancient fishponds and a cave. There's access to a nearby rocky beach, which isn't good for swimming but makes a wonderful place to watch the sunset. All accommodations include fully equipped kitchens, bathrooms, bedrooms, living/dining areas, and private lanai. The oceanfront Bamboo Inn contains three units (two studios and a convertible one- or two-bedroom unit).

P.O. Box 374, Hana, HI 96713. www.bambooinn.com. ☏ **808/248-7718.** 3 units. $185–$250 double. Extra person $15. Rates include continental breakfast. 2-night minimum. MC, V. **Amenities:** Jacuzzi. *In room:* TV/DVD, Jacuzzi, kitchen.

Hana Kai Maui Resort   Hana's only vacation condo complex, Hana Kai offers studio and one-bedroom units overlooking Hana Bay. All units have large kitchens and private lanai. Each of the one-bedroom units has a sliding door that separates the bedroom from the living room, plus a sofa bed that sleeps two additional guests. Ask for a corner unit with wraparound ocean views.

1533 Uakea Rd. (P.O. Box 38), Hana, HI 96713. www.hanakaimaui.com. ℂ **800/346-2772** or 808/248-8426. Fax 808/248-7482. 17 units. $195–$260 studio double; $205–$275 1-bedroom (sleeps up to 4); $425 2-bedroom (sleeps 4–6). Extra person $15. Children 6 and under stay free in parent's room. Service fee for less than 2 nights $15. MC, V. *In room:* Kitchen, Wi-Fi (free).

Hana's Tradewind Cottages ★ 🗡 ☺

Nestled among the ginger and heliconias on a 5-acre flower farm are two separate cottages, each with a carport, barbecue, private hot tub, sofa bed, and ceiling fans. The studio cottage sleeps up to four; a bamboo shoji blind separates the sleeping area (with queen-size bed) from the sofa bed in the living room. The Tradewinds Cottage has two bedrooms (with a queen-size bed in one room and two twins in the other), one bathroom (shower only), and a huge front porch. The atmosphere is quiet and relaxing, and hostess Rebecca Buckley, who has been in business for more than a decade, welcomes families. You can use the laundry facilities if staying 3 or more nights.

135 Alalele Place (the airport road), P.O. Box 385, Hana, HI 96713. www.hanamaui.net. ℂ **800/327-8097** or 808/248-8980. Fax 808/248-7735. 2 units. $175 studio double; $175 2-bedroom double. Extra person $25. 2-night minimum. AE, DISC, MC, V. *In room:* TV, kitchen, no phone, Wi-Fi (free).

Inexpensive

Mrs. Nakamura has been renting her **Aloha Cottages** (ℂ **808/248-8420**) since the 1970s. Located in residential areas near Hana Bay, these five budget rentals are simply but adequately furnished, varying in size from a roomy studio with kitchenette to a three-bedroom, two-bathroom unit. They're all fully equipped, clean, and fairly well kept. Rates run from $80 to $105 double (rate includes taxes). Not all units have TVs, and none have phones, but Mrs. N is happy to take messages.

Joe's Rentals 🗡

This is as close to a hostel as you can get in Hana. Joe's is a large, rambling house located just spitting distance from Hana Bay. Seven spartan but immaculately clean bedrooms share showers and a bathroom; one has private facilities. All guests are welcome to use the large living room with TV and adjoining communal kitchen (free coffee available all day). Other amenities include a rec room, barbecue, and owner Ed Hill himself. He'll tell you the long story about the name if you ask, and he can also talk about what to do and see in Hana all day if you let him.

4870 Uakea Rd. (P.O. Box 746), Hana, HI 96713. www.joesrentals.com. ℂ **808/248-7033.** 8 units, 7 with shared bathroom. $50 double with shared bathroom; $60 double with private bathroom. Extra person $10. MC, V. *In room:* No phone.

Waianapanapa State Park Cabins 🗡

These 12 rustic cabins are the best lodging deal on Maui. Everyone knows it, too—so make your reservations early (up to 6 months in advance). The cabins are warm and dry, and come complete with kitchen, living room, bedroom, and bathroom with hot shower; furnishings include linens, towels, dishes, and very basic cooking and eating utensils. Don't expect luxury—this is a step above camping, albeit in a beautiful tropical jungle setting. The key attraction at this 120-acre state beach park is the unusual horseshoe-shaped black-sand beach on Pailoa Bay, popular for shore fishing, snorkeling, and swimming. There's an on-site caretaker, along with restrooms, showers, picnic tables, shoreline hiking trails, and historic sites. Bring mosquito protection—this is the jungle, after all.

Off Hana Hwy. Reservations c/o State Parks Division, 54 S. High St., Room 101, Wailuku, HI 96793. © **808/984-8109.** 10 units. $90 for 4 people. 5-night maximum. No credit cards. *In room:* Kitchen, no phone.

10

MOLOKAI, THE MOST HAWAIIAN ISLE

Born of volcanic eruptions 1.5 million years ago, Molokai remains a time capsule on the dawn of the 21st century. It has no deluxe resorts, no stoplights, and no buildings taller than a coconut tree. Molokai is the least developed of all the islands, making it especially attractive to adventure travelers and peace seekers.

Molokai lives up to its reputation as the most Hawaiian place chiefly through its lineage; there are more people here of Hawaiian blood than anywhere else. This slipper-shaped island is the birthplace of hula and the ancient science of aqua-culture. An aura of ancient mysticism clings to the land here, and the old ways still govern life. The residents survive by fishing and hunting wild pigs and axis deer on the range. Some folks still catch fish for dinner by throwing nets and trolling the reef.

Modern Hawaii's high-rise hotels, shopping centers, and other trappings of tourism haven't been able to gain a foothold here. The lone low-rise resort on the island, Kaluakoi, was Molokai's token attempt at contemporary tourism (it opened in 1977, closed in 2000, and is empty now).

Not everyone will love Molokai. The slow-paced, simple life of the people and the absence of contemporary landmarks attract those in search of the "real" Hawaii. I once received a letter from a New York City resident who claimed that any "big city resident" would "blanche" at the lack of "sophistication." This is a place where Mother Nature is wild and uninhibited, with very little intrusion by man. Forget sophistication; this is one of the few spots on the planet where one can stand in awe of the island's diverse natural wonders: Hawaii's highest waterfall and greatest collection of fishponds; the world's tallest sea cliffs; sand dunes, coral reefs, rainforests, and hidden coves; and gloriously empty beaches.

ABOVE: **A little friendly advice for Molokai's visitors.**
PREVIOUS PAGE: **The cliffs of Molokai's north shore.**

WHAT A VISIT TO MOLOKAI IS REALLY LIKE There's plenty of aloha on Molokai, but the so-called friendly island remains ambivalent about vacationers. One of the least-visited Hawaiian islands, Molokai welcomes about 50,000 to 70,000 visitors annually on its own take-it-or-leave-it terms; it never wanted to attract too big of a crowd, anyway. A sign at the airport offers the first clue: SLOW DOWN THIS IS MOLOKAI—wisdom to heed on this island, where life proceeds at its own pace.

Rugged, red-dirt Molokai isn't for everyone, but those who like to explore remote places and seek their own adventures will love it. The best of the island can be seen only on foot, bicycle, mule, horseback, kayak, or boat. The sea cliffs are accessible by sea in summer (when the Pacific is calm) or via a 10-mile trek through the Wailau Valley—an adventure only a handful of hardy hikers attempt each year. The great **Kamakou Preserve** is open just once a month, by special arrangement with the Nature Conservancy. Even **Moomomi** (p. 315), which holds bony relics of prehistoric flightless birds and other creatures, requires a guide to divulge the secrets of the dunes.

Those in search of nightlife have come to the wrong place; Molokai shuts down after sunset. The only public diversions are softball games under the lights of Mitchell Pauole Field, movies at Maunaloa, and the few restaurants that stay open after dark, often serving local brew and pizza.

The "friendly" island may enchant you as the "real" Hawaii of your dreams. On the other hand, you may leave shaking your head, never to return. Regardless of how you approach Molokai, remember my advice: Take it slow.

FROMMER'S FAVORITE MOLOKAI EXPERIENCES

o **Riding a Mule into a Leper Colony:** Don't pass up the opportunity to see this hauntingly beautiful peninsula. Buzzy Sproat's mules (p. 314) go up and down the 3-mile Kalaupapa Trail to Molokai's famous leper colony. The views are breathtaking: You'll see the world's highest sea cliffs (over 300 stories tall) and waterfalls plunging thousands of feet into the ocean. If you're afraid of heights, catch the views from the Kalaupapa Lookout.

o **Venturing into the Garden of Eden:** Drive the 30 miles along Molokai's East End (p. 338). Take your time. Stop to smell the flowers and pick guavas by the side of the road. Pull over for a swim. Wave at every car you pass and every person you see. At the end of the road, stand on the beach at Halawa Valley and see Hawaii as it must have looked in A.D. 650, when the first people arrived on the islands.

o **Celebrating the Ancient Hula:** Hula is the heartbeat of Hawaiian culture, and Molokai is its birthplace. Although most visitors to Hawaii never get to experience the real thing, it's possible to see it here—once a year, on the second or third Saturday in May, when Molokai celebrates the birth of the hula at its Ka Hula Piko Festival. The daylong affair includes dance, music, food, and crafts. For details, contact the Moloka`i Visitor Association (② 800/800-6367 or 808/553-3876; www.molokai-hawaii.com).

o **Strolling the Sands at Papohaku:** Go early, when the tropical sun isn't so fierce, and stroll this 3-mile stretch of unspoiled golden sand on Molokai's West End. It's one of the longest beaches in Hawaii. The big surf and riptides make swimming somewhat risky, but Papohaku is perfect for walking, beach-combing, and, in the evening, picnicking and sunset watching.

o **Traveling Back in Time on the Pepeopae Trail:** This awesome hike takes you through the Molokai Forest Reserve (p. 325) and back a few million years in time. Along the misty trail (actually a boardwalk across the bog), expect close encounters of the botanical kind: mosses, sedges, violets, lichens, and knee-high ancient ohia.

Molokai

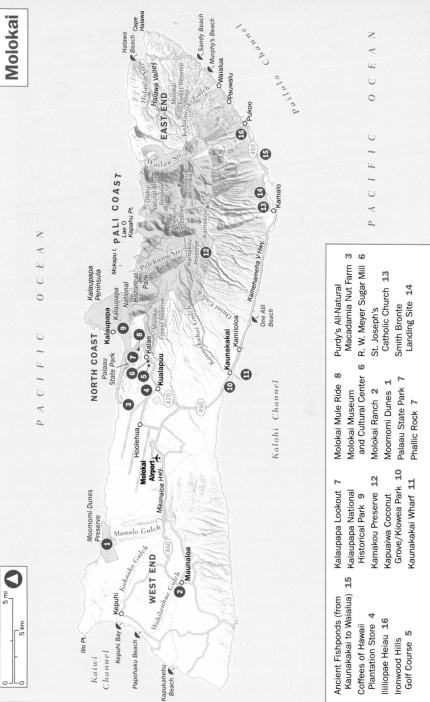

Ancient Fishponds (from Kaunakakai to Waialua) **15**
Coffees of Hawaii Plantation Store **4**
Ililiopae Heiau **16**
Ironwood Hills Golf Course **5**

Kalaupapa Lookout **7**
Kalaupapa National Historical Park **9**
Kamakou Preserve **12**
Kapuaiwa Coconut Grove/Kiowea Park **10**
Kaunakakai Wharf **11**

Molokai Mule Ride **8**
Molokai Museum and Cultural Center **6**
Molokai Ranch **2**
Moomomi Dunes **1**
Palaau State Park **7**
Phallic Rock **7**

Purdy's All-Natural Macadamia Nut Farm **3**
R. W. Meyer Sugar Mill **6**
St. Joseph's Catholic Church **13**
Smith Bronte Landing Site **14**

- **Soaking in the Warm Waters off Sandy Beach:** On the East End, about 20 miles outside Kaunakakai—just before the road starts to climb to Halawa Valley—lies a small pocket of white sand known as Sandy Beach (p. 321). Submerging yourself here in the warm, calm waters (an outer reef protects the cove) is a sensuous experience par excellence.

- **Snorkeling Among Clouds of Butterfly Fish:** The calm waters off Murphy (Kumimi) Beach (p. 321), on the East End, are perfect for snorkelers. Just don your gear and head to the reef, where you'll find lots of exotic tropical fish, including long-nosed butterfly fish, saddle wrasses, and convict tangs.

Kapuaiwa Coconut Grove.

- **Kayaking Along the North Shore:** This is the Hawaii of your dreams: waterfalls thundering down sheer cliffs, remote sand beaches, miles of tropical vegetation, and the wind whispering in your ear. The best times to go are late March and early April, or in summer, especially August to September, when the normally galloping ocean lies down flat.

- **Watching the Sunset from a Coconut Grove:** Kapuaiwa Coconut Grove/Kiowea Park (p. 309), off Maunaloa Highway (Hwy. 460), is a perfect place to watch the sunset. The sky behind the coconut trees fills with a kaleidoscope of colors as the sun sinks into the Pacific. Be careful where you sit, though: Falling coconuts could have you seeing stars well before dusk.

- **Sampling the Local Brew:** Saunter up to the Espresso Bar at the Coffees of Hawaii (p. 310), in Kualapuu, for a fresh cup of java made from beans that were grown, processed, and packed on this 450-acre plantation. While you sip, walk next door to the Blue Monkey Store, where you can survey the vast collection of Made-on-Molokai crafts.

- **Tasting Aloha at a Macadamia Nut Farm:** It could be the owner, Tuddie Purdy, and his friendly disposition that make the macadamia nuts here taste so good. Or it could be his years of practice in growing, harvesting, and shelling them on his 1½-acre farm. Either way, Purdy produces a perfect crop. See how he does it on a short, free tour of Purdy's All-Natural Macadamia Nut Farm (www.molokai.com/eatnuts) (p. 310), in Hoolehua, just a nut's throw from the airport.

- **Talking Story with the Locals:** The number-one favorite pastime of most islanders is "talking story," or exchanging experiences and knowledge. You can probably find residents more than willing to share their wisdom with you while fishing from the wharf at Kaunakakai, hanging out at Molokai Fish & Dive (p. 322), or having coffee at any of the island's restaurants.

○ **Posting a Nut:** Why send a picturesque postcard to your friends and family back home when you can send a coconut? The Hoolehua Post Office (p. 310) will supply the coconuts if you'll supply the postage fee of $10 to $15, weight dependent.

ESSENTIALS
Arriving

BY PLANE   Molokai has two airports, but you'll most likely fly into **Hoolehua Airport,** which everyone calls "the Molokai Airport." It's on a dusty plain about 6 miles from Kaunakakai town. Twin-engine planes offer daily service. Commuter airlines **Pacific Wings** serves Molokai (✆ **888/575-4546** or 808/873-0877; www.pacificwings.com) with two daily nonstop flights between Molokai and Honolulu and one daily flight between Kahului, Maui, and Molokai (all flights to Kalaupapa stop first at the Molokai airport). Another inexpensive air carrier is **go! Express** (✆ **888/I-FLY-GO-2** [435-9462]; www.iflygo.com), which has five to eight direct flights a day from Honolulu to Molokai and three to five flights a day from Maui to Molokai. Another interisland carrier is **Island Air** (✆ **800/323-3345** from the mainland or 800/652-6541 interisland; www.islandair.com), with 5 to 10 direct flights a day from Honolulu. I must tell you that I have gotten less than sterling service from Island Air; their reservations system (or customer service, depending on who is blaming whom) has left me stranded in midroute, not once, but twice!

George's Aviation (✆ **866/834-2120** or 808/834-2120; www.georges aviation.com) will provide charter flights from any island to Molokai.

BY BOAT   You can travel across the seas by ferry from Maui's Lahaina Harbor to Molokai's Kaunakakai Wharf on the *Molokai Princess* (✆ **877/500-6284** or 808/667-6165; www.mauiprincess.com). The 100-foot yacht, certified for 149 passengers, is fitted with the latest generation of gyroscopic stabilizers, making the ride smoother. The ferry makes the 1-hour-and-45-minute journey from Lahaina to Kaunakakai daily; as we went to press, a round-trip ticket cost $115, including a fuel surcharge for adults (half-price for kids 3–12, free for kids 2 and under). Be sure to check what the current fuel charge is before you go.

Visitor Information

Contact the **Molokai Visitors Association,** P.O. Box 960, Kaunakakai, HI 96748 (✆ **800/800-6367** from the U.S. mainland and Canada, or 808/553-3876; www.gohawaii.com/molokai), or stop by their office Monday through Friday from 9am to noon, in the Moore Center, 2 Kamoi St., Ste. 2, Kaunakakai. The staff can give you all the information you need on what to see and do while you're on Molokai.

The Island in Brief

Only 38 miles from end to end and just 10 miles wide, Molokai stands like a big green wedge in the blue Pacific. It has an east side, a west side, a back side, and a top side. This long, narrow island is like yin and yang: One side is a flat, austere, arid desert; the other is a lush, green, tropical Eden. Three volcanic eruptions formed Molokai; the last produced the island's "thumb"—a peninsula jutting out of the steep cliffs of the north shore, like a punctuation mark on the island's geological story.

KAUNAKAKAI ★

On the red-dirt southern plain, where most of the island's 7,000 residents live, the rustic village of **Kaunakakai ★** looks like the set of an old Hollywood Western, with sun-faded clapboard houses and horses tethered on the side of the road. Mile marker 0, in the center of town, divides the island into east and west. Kaunakakai is the closest thing Molokai has to a business district. **Friendly Isle Realty** and **Friendly Isle Travel** offer islanders dream homes and vacations; **Rabang's Filipino Food** posts bad checks in the window; antlered deer-head trophies guard the grocery aisles at **Misaki's Market;** and **Kanemitsu's,** the town's legendary bakery, churns out fresh loaves of onion-cheese bread daily. At the end of Wharf Road is Molokai Wharf, a picturesque place to fish, photograph, and just hang out.

Kaunakakai is the dividing point between the lush, green East End and the dry, arid West End. On the west side of town stands a cactus, and on the east side of town there's thick, green vegetation.

THE NORTH COAST ★★

Upland from Kaunakakai, the land tilts skyward and turns green, with scented plumeria in yards and glossy coffee trees all in a row, until it blooms into a true forest—and then abruptly ends at a great precipice, falling 3,250 feet to the sea. The green sea cliffs are creased with five V-shaped crevices so deep that light is seldom seen (to paraphrase a Hawaiian poet). The north coast is a remote, forbidding place, with a solitary peninsula—**Kalaupapa ★★★**—that was once the home for exiled lepers (it's now a National Historical Park). This region is easy on the eyes but difficult to visit. It lies at a cool elevation, and frequent rain squalls blow in from the ocean. In summer the ocean is calm, providing great opportunities for kayaking, fishing, and swimming, but during the rest of the year, giant waves come rolling onto the shores.

THE WEST END ★

This end of the island, once home to **Molokai Ranch,** is miles of stark desert terrain, bordered by the most beautiful white-sand beaches in Hawaii. The rugged rolling land slopes down to Molokai's only destination resort, **Kaluakoi,** a cul-de-sac of condos clustered around a 1977 seafront hotel (closed in 2000) near 3-mile-long Papohaku, the island's biggest beach. On the way to Kaluakoi, you'll find **Maunaloa,** a 1920s-era pineapple-plantation town that's been a ghost town since the Molokai Ranch closed all its operations in 2008. The West End is dry, dry, dry. It hardly ever rains, but when it does (usually in the winter), expect a downpour and lots of red mud.

THE EAST END ★★★

The area east of Kaunakakai is lush, green, and tropical, with golden pocket beaches and a handful of cottages and condos that are popular with thrifty travelers. With this voluptuous landscape comes rain. However, most storms are brief (15-min.) affairs. Winter is Hawaii's rainy season, so expect more rain from January to March, but even then, the storms usually are brief, and the sun comes back out.

Beyond Kaunakakai, the two-lane road curves along the coast past piggeries, palm groves, and a 20-mile string of fishponds as well as an ancient *heiau* (temple), Damien-built churches, and a few contemporary condos by the sea. The road ends in the glorious **Halawa Valley ★**, one of Hawaii's most beautiful valleys.

GETTING AROUND

Getting around Molokai isn't easy if you don't have a rental car, and rental cars are often hard to find here. On holiday weekends (see "When to Go," in chapter 2), car-rental agencies simply run out of cars. Book before you go. There's no municipal transit or shuttle service, but a 24-hour taxi service is available (see "**TAXI & TOUR SERVICES,**" below).

CAR-RENTAL AGENCIES　Car-rental options on Molokai include the privately owned **Island Kine Auto Rental** (☎ **877/553-5242** or 808/553-5242; www.molokai-hawaii.com); **Alamo Rent a Car** (☎ **877/222-9075** or 808/ 567-6381; www.alamo.com), located at the Molokai airport; and **National Car Rental** (☎ **877/222-9058** or 808/553-3596; www.nationalcar.com), which has a rental desk at the Aqua Hotel Molokai.

TAXI & TOUR SERVICES　**Molokai Outdoors Activities** (☎ **877/553-4477** or 808/553-4477; www.molokai-outdoors.com) can shuttle you from the airport to Kaunakakai (for $14 per person), and it offers a full range of island tours. **Midnight Taxi** (☎ 808/658-1410) also offers transportation from the airport to Kaunakakai for $30 per taxi.

[FastFACTS] MOLOKAI

ATMs　The **Bank of Hawaii** (☎ **808/553-3273**), in downtown Kaunakakai, has a 24-hour ATM.

Emergencies　For local emergencies, call ☎ **911.**

Hospitals　**Molokai General Hospital** (☎ **808/553-5331**) is in Kaunakakai.

Police　For nonemergencies, call the police at ☎ **808/553-5355.**

Post Office　The number for the downtown Kaunakakai post office is ☎ **808/553-5845.**

EXPLORING MOLOKAI

Note: You'll find the following attractions on the "Molokai" map (p. 305).

In & Around Kaunakakai

Kapuaiwa Coconut Grove/Kiowea Park ★ ☺ HISTORIC SITE/PARK
This royal grove—1,000 coconut trees on 10 acres planted in 1863 by the island's high chief Kapuaiwa (later King Kamehameha V)—is a major roadside attraction. The shoreline park is a favorite subject of sunset photographers and visitors, who delight in a hand-lettered sign that warns: DANGER: FALLING COCONUTS. In its backyard, across the highway, stands Church Row: seven churches, each a different denomination—clear evidence of the missionary impact on Hawaii.
Along Maunaloa Hwy. (Hwy. 460), 2 miles west of Kaunakakai.

Flying a Kite (p. 334) You can get a guaranteed-to-fly kite at the **Big Wind Kite Factory** (✆ **808/552-2364;** www.bigwindkites.com) in Maunaloa, where kite designer Jonathan Socher offers free kite-flying classes to kids, who'll learn how to make their kites soar, swoop, and, most important, stay in the air for more than 5 minutes.

Spending the Day at Murphy (Kumimi) Beach Park (p. 321) Just beyond Waialua on the East End is this small wayside park that's perfect for kids. You'll find safe swimming conditions, plenty of shade from the ironwood trees, and small pavilions with picnic tables and barbecue grills.

Post-A-Nut ★ ICON The postmaster, Gary Lam, will help you say "Aloha" to friends back home with a Molokai coconut. Just write a message on the coconut with a felt-tip pen, and he'll send it via U.S. mail. Coconuts are free, but postage averages $10 to $15 for a mainland-bound coconut. Gary mails out about 3,000 per year and likes to decorate them with colorful stamps.

Hoolehua Post Office, Puu Peelua Ave. (Hwy. 480), near Maunaloa Hwy. (Hwy. 460). ✆ **808/567-6144.** Mon–Fri 8:30am–noon and 12:30–4:30pm.

Purdy's All-Natural Macadamia Nut Farm (Na Hua O'Ka Aina) ★ 🎒 FARM The Purdys have made buying macadamia nuts an entertainment event, offering tours of the homestead and giving lively demonstrations of nutshell cracking in the shade of their towering trees. The tour of the 70-year-old nut farm explains the growth, bearing, harvesting, and shelling processes.

Lihi Pali Ave. (behind Molokai High School), Hoolehua. ✆ **808/567-6601.** www.molokai-aloha.com/macnuts. Free admission. Tues–Fri 9:30am–3:30pm; Sat 10am–2pm. Closed on holidays.

The North Coast

Even if you don't get a chance to see Hawaii's most dramatic coast in its entirety—not many people do—you shouldn't miss the opportunity to glimpse it from the **Kalaupapa Lookout** at Palaau State Park. On the way, there are a few diversions (arranged here in geographical order).

EN ROUTE TO THE NORTH COAST

Coffees of Hawaii FARM The defunct Del Monte pineapple town of Kualapuu is rising again—only this time, coffee is the catch, not pineapple. Located in the cool foothills, Coffees of Hawaii has planted coffee beans on 600 acres of former pineapple land. The plantation irrigates the

A sign at Kapuaiwa Coconut Grove.

Molokai's north coast.

plants with a high-tech, continuous water-and-fertilizer drip system. You can see it all on the self-guided walking tour or the guided Morning Espresso Tour, which shows visitors the sorting facility and processing procedures. Next door, the Blue Monkey (formerly the Plantation Store) sells arts and crafts from Molokai. Stop by the Espresso Bar for a Mocha Mama, an intoxicating blend of coffee, ice cream, and chocolate that will keep you going all day—maybe even all night.

1630 Farrington Ave. (near the junction of Hwy. 470), Kualapuu. www.coffeesofhawaii.com/plantations/molokai. © **877/322-FARM** (3276) or 808/567-9490, ext. 26. Self-guided tour free. Mon–Fri 6am–5pm, Sat 8am–8pm, Sun 8am–5pm. Morning Espresso Tour Mon–Fri 11am ($20 adults, $10 kids 6–12, $2.50 kids 2–5). Espresso Bar Mon–Sat 7am–4:30pm, Sun 10am–6pm. Store Mon–Sat 10am–4pm, Sun 1am–5pm. Hawaiian song and dance Sun 3–5pm.

Molokai Museum and Cultural Center MUSEUM/HISTORIC SITE
En route to the California Gold Rush in 1849, Rudolph W. Meyer (a German

Coffee plants.

professor) came to Molokai, married the high chieftess Kalama, and began to operate a small sugar plantation near his home. Now on the National Register of Historic Places, this restored 1878 sugar mill, with its century-old steam engine, mule-driven cane crusher, copper clarifiers, and redwood evaporating pan (all in working order), is the last of its kind in Hawaii. The mill also houses a museum that traces the history of sugar growing on Molokai and has special events, such as wine tastings, taro festivals, an annual music festival, and occasional classes in ukulele making, loom weaving, and sewing. Call for a schedule.

Phallic Rock.

Meyer Sugar Mill, Hwy. 470 (just after the turnoff for the Ironwood Hills Golf Course and 2 miles below Kalaupapa Overlook), Kalae. ✆ **808/567-6436.** Admission $2.50 adults, $1 children and students. Mon–Sat 10am–2pm.

Palaau State Park ★ PARK   This 234-acre piney-woods park, 8 miles out of Kaunakakai, doesn't look like much until you get out of the car and take a hike, which literally puts you between a rock and a hard place. Go right, and you end up on the edge of Molokai's magnificent sea cliffs, with its panoramic view of the well-known Kalaupapa leper colony; go left, and you come face to face with a stone phallus.

If you have no plans to scale the cliffs by mule or on foot (see "Hiking & Camping," later in this chapter), the **Kalaupapa Lookout ★★★** is the only place from which to see the former place of exile. The trail is marked, and historic photos and interpretive signs will explain what you're seeing.

It's airy and cool in the ironwood forest, where camping is free at the designated state campground. You'll need a permit from the **State Division of Parks** (✆ **808/984-8109;** www.hawaiistateparks.org/camping/maui.cfm). Not many people seem to camp here, probably because of the legend associated with the **Phallic Rock ★.** Six feet high and pointed at an angle that means business, Molokai's famous Phallic Rock is a legendary fertility tool: According to Hawaiian legend, a woman who wishes to become pregnant need only spend the night near the rock and, *voilà!*

Phallic Rock is at the end of a well-worn uphill path that passes an ironwood grove and several other rocks that vaguely resemble sexual body parts. No mistaking the big guy, though. Supposedly, it belonged to Nanahoa, a demigod who quarreled with his wife, Kawahuna, over a pretty girl. In the tussle, Kawahuna was thrown over the cliff, and both husband and wife were turned to stone. Of all the phallic rocks in Hawaii and the Pacific, this is the one to see. It's featured on a postcard with a tiny, awestruck Japanese woman standing next to it.

THE LEGACY OF FATHER DAMIEN: KALAUPAPA NATIONAL HISTORICAL PARK ★★★

Kalaupapa, an old tongue of lava that sticks out to form a peninsula, became infamous because of man's inhumanity to victims of a formerly incurable contagious disease.

Ruins of the leper colony at Kalaupapa.

King Kamehameha V sent the first lepers—nine men and three women—into exile on this lonely shore, at the base of ramparts that rise like temples against the Pacific, on January 6, 1866. By 1874, more than 11,000 lepers had been dispatched to die in one of the world's most beautiful—and lonely—places. They called Kalaupapa "The Place of the Living Dead."

Leprosy is actually one of the world's least contagious diseases, transmitted only by direct, repetitive contact over a long period of time. It's caused by a germ, *Mycobacterium leprae,* that attacks the nerves, skin, and eyes, and is found mainly, but not exclusively, in tropical regions. American scientists found a cure for the disease in the 1940s.

Before science intervened, there was Father Damien. Born to wealth in Belgium, Joseph de Veuster traded a life of excess for exile among lepers; he devoted himself to caring for the afflicted at Kalaupapa. Horrified by the conditions in the leper colony, Father Damien worked at Kalaupapa for 11 years, building houses, schools, and churches and giving hope to his patients. He died on April 15, 1889, in Kalaupapa, of leprosy. He was 49.

Father Damien, who was canonized as a Catholic saint in 2009, is buried not in his tomb next to Molokai's St. Philomena Church but in his native Belgium. Well, most of him anyway. His hand was recently returned to Molokai and was reinterred at Kalaupapa as a relic of his martyrdom.

This small peninsula is probably the final resting place of more than 11,000 souls. The sand dunes are littered with grave markers, sorted by the religious affiliations—Catholic, Protestant, Buddhist—of those who died here. But so many are buried in unmarked graves that no accurate census of the dead exists.

Kalaupapa is now a National Historical Park (© **808/567-6802;** www.nps. gov/kala) and one of Hawaii's richest archaeological preserves, with sites that date from A.D. 1000. About 60 former patients chose to remain in the tidy village, where statues of angels stand in the yards of whitewashed houses. The original name for their former affliction, leprosy, was officially banned in Hawaii by the state legislature in 1981. The name used now is "Hansen's disease," for Dr. Gerhard Hansen of Norway, who discovered the germ in 1873.

Kalaupapa welcomes visitors who arrive on foot, by mule, or by small plane. Father Damien's St. Philomena Church, built in 1872, is open to visitors, who can see it from a yellow school bus. You won't be able to roam freely, and you'll be allowed to enter only the museum, the crafts shop, and the church.

If you have no plans to scale the cliffs by mule (see below) or on foot (see "Hiking & Camping," on p. 355), the **Kalaupapa Lookout** ★★★ is the only place from which to see the former place of exile. The trail is marked, and historic photos and interpretive signs will explain what you're seeing.

KALAUPAPA RARE ADVENTURE ★★★

The first turn's a gasp, and it's all downhill from there. You can close your eyes and hold on for dear life, or slip the reins over the pommel and sit back, letting the mule do the walking down the precipitous path to Kalaupapa National Historical Park.

Even if you have only a day to spend on Molokai, spend it on a mule. This is a once-in-a-lifetime ride. The cliffs are taller than a 300-story skyscraper, but Buzzy Sproat's mules go safely up and down the narrow 3-mile trail daily, rain or shine. Starting at the top of the nearly perpendicular ridge (1,600 ft. high), the sure-footed mules step down the muddy trail,

If you have only 1 day to spend on Molokai, spend it on a mule.

pausing often on the 26 switchbacks to calculate their next move—and always, it seems to me, veering a little too close to the edge. Each switchback is numbered; by the time you get to number four, you'll catch your breath, put the mule on cruise control, and begin to enjoy Hawaii's most awesome trail ride.

The mule tours are offered once a day Monday through Saturday; the park is closed on Sunday. Tours start at 8am and last until about 3pm. It costs $199 per person for the all-day adventure, which includes the round-trip mule ride, a guided bus tour of the settlement, a visit to Father Damien's church and tomb, lunch at Kalawao, and souvenirs. Book in advance, as these tours often fill up. To go, you must be at least 16 years old and physically fit, and weigh less than 250 pounds. Contact **Molokai Mule Ride ★★★**, 100 Kalae Hwy., Suite 104, on Hwy. 470, 5 miles north of Hwy. 460 (© **800/567-7550** or 808/567-6088, 8am–3pm; www.muleride.com). Advance reservations (at least 2 weeks ahead) are required.

The West End

MAUNALOA

The 1920s-era pineapple-plantation town of Maunaloa has become a ghost town ever since the Molokai Ranch closed all of its operations in 2008 (including the movie theater, restaurant, lodge, and some shops).

The Moomoni Dunes.

ON THE NORTHWEST SHORE: MOOMOMI DUNES

Undisturbed for centuries, the Moomomi Dunes, on Molokai's northwest shore, are a unique treasure chest of great scientific value. The area may look like just a pile of sand as you fly over on the final approach to Hoolehua Airport, but Moomomi Dunes is much more than that. Archaeologists have found adz quarries, ancient Hawaiian burial sites, and shelter caves; botanists have identified five endangered plant species; and marine biologists are finding evidence that endangered green sea turtles are coming out from the waters once again to lay eggs here. The greatest discovery, however, belongs to Smithsonian Institute ornithologists, who have found bones of prehistoric birds—some of them flightless—that existed nowhere else on earth.

Accessible by jeep trails that thread downhill to the shore, this wild coast is buffeted by strong afternoon breezes. It's hot, dry, and windy, so take water, sunscreen, and a Windbreaker. At Kawaaloa Bay, a 20-minute walk to the west, there's a broad golden beach that you can have all to yourself. (**Warning:** Due to the rough seas, stay out of the water.) Within the dunes, there's a 920-acre preserve accessible via monthly guided nature tours led by the **Nature Conservancy of Hawaii;** call ✆ **808/553-5236,** ext. 6581, or e-mail hike_molokai@ tnc.org for an exact schedule and details. Hikes are $25 per person.

To get here, take Hwy. 460 (Maunaloa Hwy.) from Kaunakakai; turn right onto Hwy. 470, and follow it to Kualapuu. At Kualapuu, turn left on Hwy. 480 and go through Hoolehua Village; it's 3 miles to the bay.

The East End

The East End is a cool and inviting green place that's worth a drive to the end of King Kamehameha V Highway (Hwy. 450). Unfortunately, the trail that leads into the area's greatest natural attraction, Halawa Valley, is now off-limits.

ILIILIOPAE HEIAU

Out on the East End, you bump along a dirt trail through an incredible mango grove, bound for an ancient temple of human sacrifice. This temple of doom, which looks like something right out of *Indiana Jones,* is Iliiliopae, a huge rectangle of stone made of 90 million rocks, overlooking the once-important village of Mapulehu and four ancient fishponds. You trek under the perfumed mangoes, then head uphill through a kiawe forest filled with Java plums to the *heiau,* which stands across a dry streambed under cloud-spiked Kaunolu, the 4,970-foot island summit.

As one of Hawaii's most powerful *heiau,* this ancient temple attracted *kahuna* (priests) from all over the islands. They came to learn the rules of human sacrifice at this university of sacred rites. Contrary to Hollywood's version, historians say that the victims here were always men, not young virgins, and that they were strangled, not thrown into a volcano, while priests sat on lauhala mats watching silently. Spooky, eh?

This is the biggest, oldest, and most famous *heiau* on Molokai. The massive 22-foot-high stone altar is dedicated to Lono, the Hawaiian god of fertility. The *heiau* resonates with *mana* (power) strong enough to lean on. Legend says Iliiliopae was built in a single night by a thousand men who passed rocks hand over hand through the Wailau Valley from the other side of the island; in exchange for the *ili'ili* (rock), each received a *'opae* (shrimp). Others say it was built by *menehune,* mythic elves who accomplished Herculean feats. It's off King Kamehameha V Highway (Hwy. 450), near mile marker 15.

KAMAKOU PRESERVE

It's hard to believe, but close to the nearly mile-high summit here, it rains more than 80 inches a year—enough to qualify as a rainforest. The Molokai Forest, as it was historically known, is the source of 60% of Molokai's water. Nearly 3,000 acres, from the summit to the lowland forests of eucalyptus and pine, are now held by the Nature Conservancy, which has identified 219 Hawaiian plants that grow here exclusively. The preserve is also the last stand of the endangered *olomao* (Molokai thrush) and *kawawahie* (Molokai creeper).

To get to the preserve, take the Molokai Forest Reserve Road from Kaunakakai. It's a 45-minute four-wheel-drive trip on a dirt trail to Waikolu Lookout Campground; from here, you can venture into the wilderness preserve on foot across a boardwalk on a 1½-hour hike (see "The Pepeopae Trail," p. 325). For more information, or to sign up for one of their monthly guided hikes ($25 per person), contact the **Nature Conservancy** (© **808/553-5236,** ext. 6581; www.nature.org or e-mail hike_molokai@tnc.org).

EN ROUTE TO HALAWA VALLEY

No visit to Molokai is complete without at least a passing glance at the island's **ancient fishponds,** a singular achievement in Pacific aquaculture. With their hunger for fresh fish and lack of ice and refrigeration, Hawaiians perfected aquaculture in A.D. 1400, before Christopher Columbus "discovered" America. They built gated, U-shaped stone and coral walls on the shore to catch fish on the incoming tide; they would then raise them in captivity. The result: a constant, ready supply of fresh fish.

The ponds, which stretch for 20 miles along Molokai's south shore and are visible from Kamehameha V Highway (Hwy. 450), offer insight into the island's

Alii Fish Pond.

ancient population. It took something like a thousand people to tend a single fishpond, and more than 60 ponds once existed on this coast. Some are silted in by red-dirt runoff from south-coast gulches; others are in use by folks who raise fish and seaweed.

The largest, 54-acre **Keawa Nui Pond,** is surrounded by a 3-foot-high, 2,000-foot-long stone wall. **Alii Fish Pond,** reserved for kings, is visible through the coconut groves at One Alii Beach Park (p. 319). From the road, you can see **Kalokoeli Pond,** 6 miles east of Kaunakakai on the highway.

Our Lady of Sorrows Catholic Church, one of five built by Father Damien on Molokai and the first outside Kalaupapa, sits across the highway from a fishpond. Park in the church lot (except on Sun) for a closer look.

St. Joseph's Catholic Church CHURCH The afternoon sun strikes St. Joseph's Church with such a bold ray of light that it looks as if God is about to perform a miracle. This little 1876 wood-frame church is one of four Father Damien built "topside" on Molokai. Restored in 1971, the church stands beside a seaside cemetery, where feral cats play under the gaze of a Damien statue amid gravestones decorated with flower leis.

King Kamehameha V Hwy. (Hwy. 450), just after mile marker 10.

This statue of Father Damien stands outside St. Joseph's Catholic Church.

Smith Bronte Landing Site MONUMENT   In 1927, Charles Lindbergh soloed across the Atlantic Ocean in a plane called *The Spirit of St. Louis* and became an American hero. That same year, Ernie Smith and Emory B. Bronte took off from Oakland, CA, on July 14, in a single-engine Travel Air aircraft named *The City of Oakland,* and headed across the Pacific Ocean for Honolulu, 2,397 miles away. The next day, after running out of fuel, they crash-landed upside down in a kiawe thicket on Molokai, but emerged unhurt to become the first civilians to fly to Hawaii from the U.S. mainland. The 25-hour, 2-minute flight landed Smith and Bronte a place in aviation history—and on a roadside marker on Molokai.

King Kamehameha V Hwy. (Hwy. 450), at mile marker 11, on the makai (ocean) side.

HALAWA VALLEY ★

Of the five great valleys of Molokai, only Halawa—with its two waterfalls, golden beach, sleepy lagoon, great surf, and offshore island—is easily accessible. Unfortunately, the trail through fertile Halawa Valley, which was inhabited for centuries, and on to the 250-foot Moaula Falls has been closed for some time. There is one operator who conducts hikes to the falls (see "Halawa Valley: A Hike Back in History," on p. 319).

You can spend a day at the county beach park (described under "Beaches," below), but do not venture into the valley on your own. In a kind of 21st-century *kapu,* the private landowners in the valley, worried about slip-and-fall lawsuits, have posted no-trespassing signs on their properties.

To get to Halawa Valley, drive north from Kaunakakai on Hwy. 450 for 30 miles along the coast to the end of the road, which descends into the valley past Jersalema Hou Church. If you'd just like a glimpse of the valley on your way to the beach, there's a scenic overlook along the road: After Pu'u O Hoku Ranch at mile marker 25, the narrow two-lane road widens at a hairpin curve, and you'll find the overlook on your right; it's 2 miles more to the valley floor.

Halawa Valley.

Halawa Falls.

HALAWA VALLEY: A hike BACK IN HISTORY

"There are things on Molokai, sacred things, that you may not be able to see or may not hear, but they are there," says Pilipo Solotario, who was born and raised in Halawa Valley and survived the 1946 tsunami that barreled into the ancient valley. "As Hawaiians, we respect these things."

If people are going to "like Molokai," Solotario feels it is important that they learn about the history and culture; they are part of the secret of appreciating the island.

"I see my role, and I'm nearly 70 years old, as educating people, outsiders, on our culture, our history," he said at the beginning of his cultural hike into his family property in Halawa Valley. "To really appreciate Molokai, you need to understand and know things so that you are *pono*, you are right with the land and don't disrespect the culture. Then, then you see the real Molokai."

Solotario and his family, who own the land in the valley, are the only people allowed to hike into Halawa. They begin daily tours, which start at the County Park

pavilion, with a history of the valley, a discussion of the Hawaiian culture, and a display of the fruits, trees, and other flora you will be seeing in the valley. Along the hike, Solotario stops to point out historical and cultural aspects, including chanting in Hawaiian before entering a sacred *heiau*. At the waterfalls visitors can swim in the brisk pool water. Cost for the 4-hour tour is $75. Contact **Molokai Fish & Dive** for more information, or to make reservations (© **808/553-5926;** www.molokaifishanddive.com). Bring insect repellent, water, a snack, and a swimsuit. Don't forget your camera.

Note: If you venture away from the county park and into the valley on your own, you are trespassing and can be prosecuted.

BEACHES

With imposing sea cliffs on one side and lazy fishponds on the other, Molokai has little room for beaches along its 106-mile coast. Still, a big gold-sand beach flourishes on the West End, and you'll find tiny pocket beaches on the East End. The emptiness of Molokai's beaches is both a blessing and a curse: The seclusion means no lifeguards on any of the beaches. To locate them, see the "Molokai" map (p. 305).

Kaunakakai

ONE ALII BEACH PARK

This thin strip of sand, once reserved for the *alii* (chiefs), is the oldest public beach park on Molokai. You'll find One Alii Beach Park (*One* is pronounced "O-nay," not "*Won*") by a coconut grove on the outskirts of Kaunakakai. Safe for swimmers of all ages and abilities, it's often crowded with families on weekends, but it can be all yours on weekdays. Facilities include outdoor showers, restrooms, and free parking.

One Alii Beach Park.

Kepuhi Beach.

The West End

KEPUHI BEACH

Sunbathers like this picturesque golden strand's semiprivate grassy dunes—they're seldom, if ever, crowded. Beachcombers often find what they're looking for here, but swimmers have to dodge lava rocks and risk riptides. There are no facilities or lifeguards, but cold drinks and restrooms are handy at the resort.

PAPOHAKU BEACH ★★

Nearly 3 miles long and 300 feet wide, gold-sand Papohaku Beach is one of the biggest in Hawaii (17-mile-long Polihale Beach on Kauai is the biggest). It's great for walking, beachcombing, picnics, and sunset watching year-round. The big surf and riptides make swimming risky except in summer, when the waters are

Papohaku Beach.

Halawa Beach Park.

calmer. Go early in the day, when the tropic sun is less fierce and the winds are calm. The beach is so vast that you may never see another soul. Facilities include outdoor showers, restrooms, picnic grounds, and free parking.

The East End

HALAWA BEACH PARK ★

At the foot of scenic Halawa Valley is this beautiful black-sand beach with a palm-fringed lagoon, a wave-lashed island offshore, and a distant view of the West Maui Mountains across the Pailolo Channel. The swimming is safe in the shallows close to shore, but where the waterfall stream meets the sea, the ocean is often murky and unnerving. A winter swell creases the mouth of Halawa Valley on the north side of the bay and attracts a crowd of local surfers. Facilities are minimal; bring your own water. To get here, take King Kamehameha V Highway (Hwy. 450) east to the end.

MURPHY BEACH PARK (KUMIMI BEACH PARK)

In 1970, the Molokai Jaycees wanted to create a sandy beach park with a good swimming area for the children of the East End. They chose a section known as Kumimi Beach, which was owned by the Pu'u O Hoku Ranch. The beach was a dump—literally. The ranch owner, George Murphy, gave his permission to use the site as a park, and the Jaycees cleaned it up and built three small pavilions, with picnic tables and barbecue grills. Officially, the park is called the George Murphy Beach Park (or just Murphy Beach Park), but some old-timers still call it Kumimi Beach, and, just to make things really confusing, some people call it Jaycees Park.

It's a small park shaded by ironwood trees that line a white-sand beach. This is generally a very safe swimming area, and on calm days snorkeling and diving are great outside the reef. Fishermen also come here to look for papio and other island fish.

SANDY BEACH ★

Molokai's most popular swimming beach—ideal for families with small kids—is a roadside pocket of gold sand protected by a reef, with a great view of Maui and Lanai. You'll find it off the King Kamehameha V Highway (Hwy. 450) at mile marker 20. There are no facilities—just you, the sun, the sand, and the surf.

Murphy Beach Park.

Sandy Beach.

WATERSPORTS

The best place to rent beach toys is **Molokai Fish & Dive,** Kaunakakai (℡ **808/553-5926;** www.molokaifishanddive.com), where you can rent snorkeling gear, fishing gear, even umbrellas and beach chairs. This is also a hot spot for fishing news and tips on what's running where.

Body Boarding (Boogie Boarding) & Bodysurfing

Molokai has only three beaches that offer good waves for body boarding and bodysurfing: Papohaku, Kepuhi, and Halawa. Even these beaches are only for experienced bodysurfers, due to the strength of the rip currents and undertows. You can rent boogie boards with fins for just $5 a day or $20 a week at **Molokai Outdoors Activities** (℡ **877/553-4477** or 808/553-4477; www.molokai-outdoors.com).

Ocean Kayaking

During the summer months, when the waters on the north shore are calm, Molokai offers some of the most spectacular kayaking in Hawaii. However, most of Molokai is for the experienced kayaker only—you must be adept in paddling through open ocean swells and rough waves.

Most of Molokai is for experienced kayakers only.

MOLOKAI'S BEST snorkel SPOTS

Most Molokai beaches are too dangerous for snorkeling in winter, when storms that sweep down from Alaska generate big waves and strong currents. From mid-September to April, stick to Murphy Beach Park (also known as Kumimi Beach Park) on the East End. In summer, roughly May to mid-September, the Pacific Ocean turns into a flat lake, and the whole west coast of Molokai opens up for snorkeling. Mike Holmes, of Molokai Ranch & Fun Hogs Hawaii, says the best spots are as follows:

Kawaikiunui, Ilio Point, and Pohaku Moiliili (West End)   These are all special places seldom seen by even those who live on Molokai. You can reach Kawaikiunui and Pohaku Moiliili on foot after a long, hot, dusty ride in a four-wheel-drive vehicle, but it's much easier and quicker to go by sea. See "Snorkeling,"

above, for places to rent a kayak and get advice. It's about 2 miles as the crow flies from Pohaku Moiliili to Ilio Point.

Kapukahehu (Dixie Maru) Beach (West End)   This gold-sand family beach is well protected, and the reef is close and shallow. The name *Dixie Maru* comes from a 1920s Japanese fishing boat stranded off the rocky shore. One of the Molokai Ranch cowboys hung the wrecked boat's nameplate on a gate by Kapukahehu Beach, and the name stuck. To get here, take Kaluakoi Road to the end of the pavement, and then take the footpath 300 feet to the beach.

Murphy (Kumimi) Beach Park ★ (East End)   This beach is located between mile markers 20 and 21, off Kamehameha V Highway. The reef here is easily reachable, and the waters are calm year-round.

Molokai Outdoors Activities (✆ **877/553-4477** or 808/553-4477; www.molokai-outdoors.com) has a "downwinder" tour: 6 miles of Molokai's reef as you paddle downwind. The cost is $75, plus $10 for lunch, per person. See the website for additional kayak tours. They also rent kayaks; rates start at $26 a day.

Scuba Diving

Want to see turtles or manta rays up close? How about sharks? Molokai resident Tim Forsberg has been diving around these waters for 12 years; he'll be happy to show you whatever you're brave enough to encounter. You can book him through **Molokai Fish & Dive** (✆ **808/553-5926**; www.molokaifishanddive.com), which offers scuba diving trips from $135 (two-tank dive) to $275 (three-tank dive).

Snorkeling

When the waters are calm, Molokai offers excellent snorkeling (see "Molokai's Best Snorkel Spots," below); you'll see a wide range of butterflyfish, tangs, and angelfish. Good snorkeling can be found—when conditions are right—at many of Molokai's beaches. **Molokai Fish & Dive** (℃ **808/553-5926;** www.molokaifishanddive.com) rents mask, snorkel, and fins for $10 for 24 hours.

Sport Fishing

Molokai's waters can provide prime sporting opportunities, whether you're looking for big-game sport fishing or bottom fishing. The number-one person I recommend is Captain Clay, of **Hallelujah Hou Fishing** (℃ **808/336-1870;** www.hallelujahhoufishing.com). Captain Clay, who is also a minister and the nicest guy you may ever meet, leads light-tackle guided fishing trips on his 24-foot power catamaran. The price is $395 to $495 for the first angler and $150 for the second for a 4- to 6-hour trip. He provides all tackle and bottled water; you bring the sunscreen. If you catch something, he'll even filet your fish for dinner. *Note:* There's no "head" (toilet) on the boat.

When customers are scarce, Capt. Joe Reich goes commercial fishing, so he always knows where the fish are biting. He runs **Alyce C Sportfishing** out of Kaunakakai Harbor (℃ **808/558-8377;** ace@aloha.net). A full day of fishing for up to six people is $550, three-quarters of a day is $500, and a half-day is $450. You can usually persuade him to do a whale-watching cruise during the winter months.

For fly-fishing or light-tackle reef-fish trolling, contact Captain Clay of **Hallelujah Hou Fishing** (℃ **808/336-1870;** www.hallelujahhoufishing.com). A 4- to 6-hour trip is $550 for the first angler and an additional $150 per person, up to a total of six.

Molokai Fish & Dive (℃ **808/553-5926;** www.molokaifishanddive.com) has fishing tours for $550 for a half-day, and $125 per hour after that for up to six passengers.

For deep-sea fishing, contact **Fun Hogs Hawaii,** which books through Molokai Outdoors Activities (℃ **877/553-4477** or 808/553-4477; www.molokaioutdoors.com), for fishing excursions on a 27-foot, fully equipped sport-fishing vessel. Prices are $400 for six passengers for 4 hours, $417 for 6 hours, and $521 for 8 hours.

Surfing

Depending on the time of year and the wave conditions, Molokai can offer some great surfing for the beginner, as well as the expert. **Molokai Outdoors Activities** (℃ **877/553-4477** or 808/553-4477; www.molokai-outdoors.com) will not only know where the waves are, but it also rents gear: soft surfboards for $13 a day. Good surfing spots include Kaunakakai Wharf in town, Hale O Lono Beach and Papohaku Beach on the West End, and Halawa Beach on the East End.

Molokai is an excellent place for body surfing.

HIKING & CAMPING
Hiking Molokai's Pepeopae Trail

Molokai's most awesome hike is the **Pepeopae Trail ★★**, which takes you back a few million years. On the cloud-draped trail (actually a boardwalk across the bog), you'll see mosses, sedges, native violets, knee-high ancient ohia, and lichens that evolved in total isolation over eons. Eerie intermittent mists blowing in and out will give you an idea of this island at its creation.

The narrow boardwalk, built by volunteers, protects the bog and keeps you out of the primal ooze. Don't venture off it; you could damage this fragile environment or get lost. The 3-mile round-trip takes about 90 minutes to hike—but first you have to drive about 20 miles from Kaunakakai, deep into the Molokai Forest Reserve on a four-wheel-drive road. **Warning:** Don't try this with a regular car. Plan a full day for this outing. Better yet, go on a guided nature hike with **Nature Conservancy,** which guards this unusual ecosystem. For information, write to the Nature Conservancy at 1116 Smith St., Ste. 201, Honolulu, HI 96817. No permit is required for this easy hike. Call ahead (✆ **808/553-5236;** www.nature.org) to

check on the condition of the ungraded, four-wheel-drive, red-dirt road that leads to the trail head and to let people know that you'll be up there. To get here, take Hwy. 460 west from Kaunakakai for 3½ miles and turn right before the Maunawainui Bridge onto the unmarked Molokai Forest Reserve Road (sorry, there aren't any road signs). The pavement ends at the cemetery; continue on the dirt road. After about 2 to 2½ miles, you'll see a sign telling you that you are now in the Molokai Forest Reserve. At the Waikolu Lookout and picnic area, which is just over 9 miles on the Molokai Forest Reserve Road, sign in at the box near the entrance. Continue on the road for another 5 miles to a fork in the road with the sign PUU KOLEKOLE pointing to the right side of the fork. Do not turn right; instead, continue straight at the fork, which leads to the clearly marked trail head. The drive will take about 45 minutes.

A tree carving in the Molokai Forest Preserve.

Hiking to Kalaupapa ★★

This hike to the site of Molokai's famous leper colony is like going down a switchback staircase with what seems like a million steps. You don't always see the breathtaking view because you're too busy watching your step. It's easier going down (surprise!)—in about an hour, you'll go 2½ miles, from 2,000 feet to sea level. The trip up sometimes takes twice as long. The trail head starts on the mauka (inland) side of Hwy. 470, just past the Mule Barn. Check in here at

7:30am, get a permit, and go before the mule train departs. You must be 16 or older (it's an old state law that kept kids out of the leper colony) and should be in good shape. Wear good hiking boots or sneakers.

Hiking the West End

Molokai Outdoors Activities (℗ **877/553-4477** or 808/553-4477; www. molokai-outdoors.com) offers an all-day (6- to 8-hr.) Halawa Cultural Hike full of historical information on East Molokai. The hike is rated intermediate to advanced, with a distance of 2.2 miles. It has two river crossings, and some rocky areas along the trails, with possible fallen trees after a storm. The cost is $75 per person.

   Molokai Fish & Dive (℗ **808/553-5926;** www.molokaifishanddive.com) offers a hike back into Halawa Valley for $75 (p. 322).

Camping

Bring your own camping equipment, as none is available for rent on the island.

AT THE BEACH

One of the best year-round places to camp on Molokai is **Papohaku Beach Park ★**, on the island's West End. This drive-up seaside site makes a great get-away. Facilities include restrooms, drinking water, outdoor showers, barbecue grills, and picnic tables. Groceries and gas are available in Maunaloa, 6 miles away. Kaluakoi Resort is a mile away. Get camping permits by contacting **Maui County Parks Department,** 700 Halia Nakoa St., Wailuku, HI 96793 (℗ **808/ 553-3204;** www.co.maui.hi.us). Camping is limited to 3 days, but if nobody else has applied, the time limit is waived. The cost is $5 per person per night Monday through Thursday and $8 Friday through Sunday.

A sign points the way to the Kalaupapa Lookout.

IN AN IRONWOOD FOREST

At the end of Hwy. 470 is the 234-acre piney woods known as **Palaau State Park ★★**, home to the Kalaupapa Lookout (the best vantage point for seeing the historic leper colony if you're not hiking or riding a mule in). It's airy and cool in the park's ironwood forest, where many love to camp at the designated state campground. The camping fee for Hawaii state parks is $18 per campsite per night, and you'll need a permit from the **State Division of Parks** (© **808/984-8109;** or online at www.hawaiistateparks.org/camping/maui.cfm). Your best bet is to call the number above—at press time the State Division of Parks was in the process of converting their permit system to its website, so it's possible that the process may take place online instead in the coming year. For more on the park, see p. 312.

GOLF & OTHER OUTDOOR ACTIVITIES

Bicycling

Molokai is a great place to see by bicycle. The roads are not very busy and there are great places to pull off the road and take a quick dip.

Molokai Bicycle, 80 Mohala St., Kaunakakai (© **808/553-3931;** www.bikehawaii.com/molokaibicycle), offers bike rentals for $15 to $24 a day, or $70 to $100 a week, including a complimentary helmet and lock. Owner Phillip Kikukawa is schoolteacher, so call him in late afternoon or on the weekend when he's in the shop.

Golf

Golf is one of Molokai's best-kept secrets: It's challenging and fun, tee times are open, and the rates are lower than your score will be. **Ironwood Hills Golf Course,** off Kalae Highway (© **808/567-6000**), is located just before the Molokai Mule Ride Mule Barn, on the road to the Lookout. Built in 1929 by Del Monte Plantation for its executives, it's one of the oldest courses in the state. This unusual course, which sits in the cool air at 1,200 feet, delights with its rich foliage, open fairways, and spectacular views of the rest of the island. *Tip:* After teeing off on the 6th hole, just take whatever clubs you need to finish playing the hole and a driver for the 7th hole, and park your bag under a tree. The climb to the 7th hole is steep—you'll be glad that you're carrying only a few clubs. Greens fees are $24 for 9 holes, including cart.

Tennis

The only two tennis courts on Molokai are located at the **Mitchell Pauole Center,** in Kaunakakai (© **808/553-3204**). Both are lit for night play and are available free on a first-come, first-served basis, with a 45-minute time limit if someone is waiting. You can also rent tennis rackets ($5 a day, $24 a week) and balls ($3 a day, $12 a week) from **Molokai Outdoors Activities** (© **877/553-4477** or 808/553-4477; www.molokai-outdoors.com).

WHERE TO EAT
Restaurants & Hotels on Molokai

The good news is that you won't find long lines at overbooked, self-important restaurants. But when it comes to dining, Molokai is not nirvana.

A lot of people like it that way and acknowledge that the island's character is unchangeably rugged and natural. Molokai has retained its glacial pace of change. Its culinary offerings are dominated by mom-and-pop eateries, most of them fast-food or takeout places, and many of them with a home-cooked touch. Personally, I like the unpretentiousness of Molokai; it's an oasis in a state where plastic aloha abounds. But sybarites, foodies, and pampered oenophiles had best lower their expectations upon arrival, or turn around and leave the island's natural beauty to nature lovers.

You'll even find a certain defiant stance against the trappings of modernity. Although some of the best produce in Hawaii is grown on this island, you're not likely to find much of it served in its restaurants, other than in the takeout items at Outpost Natural Foods, or at the Molokai Pizza Cafe (one of the most pleasing eateries on the island) and the Aqua Hotel Molokai. The rest of the time, content yourself with ethnic or diner fare—or by cooking for yourself. The many visitors who stay in condos find that it doesn't take long to sniff out the best sources of produce, groceries, and fresh fish to fire up at home when the island's other dining options are exhausted. The "Edibles" section under "Shopping" (below) will point you to the places where you can pick up foodstuffs for your own Island-style feast.

Molokai's restaurants are inexpensive or moderately priced, and several of them do not accept credit cards. Regardless of where you eat, you certainly won't have to dress up. In most cases, I've listed just the town rather than the street address because, as you'll see, street addresses are as meaningless on this island as fancy cars and sequins. Reservations are not accepted unless otherwise noted. Also see the box "Your Own Personal Chef—on Molokai," below).

Kaunakakai
INEXPENSIVE

Aqua Hotel Molokai Hula Shores ★ AMERICAN/ISLAND   On the ocean with a view of Lanai, with torches flickering under palm trees and tiny fairy lights lining the room and the neighboring pool area, the Hotel Molokai's dining room evokes the romance of a South Seas fantasy. It's a casual room that provides the only nightlife in Kaunakakai (see "Entertainment & Nightlife," later in this chapter), and it has the most pleasing ambience on the island. Lunch choices consist of the basics; most promising are salads (Big Island organic greens) and sandwiches, from kalua pig to grilled mahimahi. As the sun sets and the torches are lit for dinner, the menu turns to heavier meats, ribs, fish, and pasta. Try the fresh catch, *kalbi* ribs, barbecued pork ribs, New York steak, or the lip-smacking coconut shrimp. Temper your expectations of culinary excellence, and you're sure to enjoy a pleasing dinner in an atmosphere that's unequaled on the island.

At Hotel Molokai, on Kamehameha V Hwy. ✆ **808/553-5347.** Reservations recommended for dinner. Main courses $7–$17 breakfast, $9.50–$16 lunch, $16–$30 dinner. AE, DC, MC, V. Restaurant daily 7am–2pm and 6–9pm. Bar daily until 10:30pm.

Restaurants & Hotels on Molokai

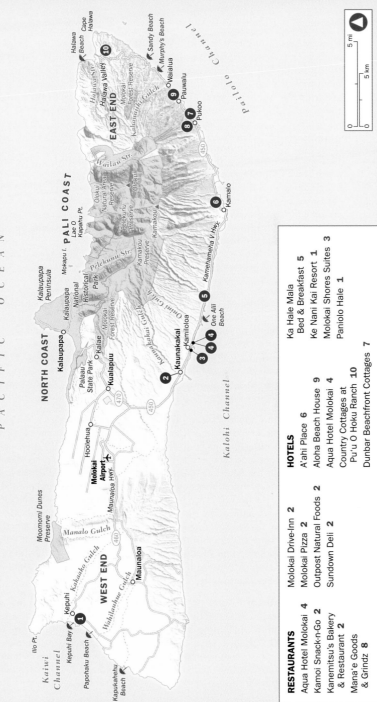

PACIFIC OCEAN

Kaiwi Channel

Illo Pt.
Kepuhi
Kepuhi Bay
Papohaku Beach
Kapukahehu Beach
Moomomi Dunes Preserve

WEST END

Kakaako Gulch
Wahiluhue Gulch
Manalo Gulch
Maunaloa HWY.

Maunaloa

Hoolehua
Molokai Airport
Maunaloa HWY.
470
460
450

NORTH COAST

Kalaupapa Peninsula

Palaau State Park
Kualapuu
Kalae

Kalaupapa
Kalaupapa National Historical Park
Molokai Forest Reserve

Mokapu I.
Lae O Kapahu Pt.

PALI COAST

Okulu Natural Area Reserve
Pelekunu Str.
Pelekunu Preserve

Wailau Str.

Okulu

Kamakou Preserve
Kamakou

Kaunakakai
Kamiloloa
2
3
4 4
One Alii Beach
5
Kamehameha V Hwy.
6
Kamalo

Kaunakakai Gulch
Kawela Gulch

Kaloh Channel

450

Kalunuku Gulch

EAST END

Halawa Valley
Halawa Str.
Halawa Beach
Cape Halawa
10

Sandy Beach
Murphy's Beach
9
Wailaua
Pauwalu
8 7
Pukoo

Pailolo Channel

N

0   5 mi
0   5 km

329

RESTAURANTS

Aqua Hotel Molokai **4**
Kamoi Snack-n-Go **2**
Kanemitsu's Bakery
& Restaurant **2**
Mana'e Goods
& Grindz **8**

Molokai Drive-Inn **2**
Molokai Pizza **2**
Outpost Natural Foods **2**
Sundown Deli **2**

HOTELS

A'ahi Place **6**
Aloha Beach House **9**
Aqua Hotel Molokai **4**
Country Cottages at
Pu'u O Hoku Ranch **10**
Dunbar Beachfront Cottages **7**

Ka Hale Mala
Bed & Breakfast **5**
Ke Nani Kai Resort **1**
Molokai Shores Suites **3**
Paniolo Hale **1**

Kamoi Snack-N-Go ICE CREAM/SNACKS   The Kamoi specialty: sweets and icy treats. Ice cream made by Dave's on Oahu comes in flavors such as green tea, litchi sherbet, *ube* (made from Okinawan sweet potato), haupia, mango, and many others. Lines form for the cones, shakes, sundaes, and popular Icee floats served at this tiny snack shop. If the ice cream doesn't tempt you, maybe something in the aisles full of candies will. It's takeout only; no tables.

In Kamoi Professional Center. ℂ **808/553-3742.** Ice cream $2.80–$3.80; sundaes $4.50–$7. MC, V. Mon–Fri 11am–9pm; Sat 9am–9pm; Sun noon–9pm.

Kanemitsu's Bakery & Restaurant ★ BAKERY/DELI   Morning, noon, and night, this local legend fills the Kaunakakai air with the sweet smells of baking. Taro *lavosh* is the hot seller, joining Molokai bread—developed in 1935 in a cast-iron, kiawe-fired oven—as a Kanemitsu signature. Flavors range from apricot pineapple to coconut or strawberry, but the white, wheat, cheese, sweet, and onion-cheese breads are classics. In the adjoining coffee shop/deli, the hamburgers and egg-salad sandwiches are popular and cheap.

Kanemitsu's has a life after dark, too. See the box "The Hot-Bread Run," p. 336.

79 Ala Malama St. ℂ **808/553-5855.** Most items less than $10. AE, MC, V. Restaurant Wed–Mon 7am–2pm. Bakery Wed–Sat 5:30am–6pm; Sun 5:30am–4pm.

Molokai Drive-Inn AMERICAN/TAKEOUT   It's a greasy spoon, but it's one of the rare drive-up places with fresh akule (mackerel) and ahi (when available), plus fried saimin at budget-friendly prices. The honey-dipped fried chicken is a favorite among residents, who also come here for the floats, shakes, and other artery-clogging choices. But don't expect much in terms of ambience: This is a fast-food takeout counter, and it doesn't pretend to be otherwise.

Kaunakakai. ℂ **808/553-5655.** Most items less than $11. No credit cards. Sun–Thurs 6am–10pm; Fri–Sat 6:30am–10:30pm.

Molokai Pizza Cafe ★ PIZZA   This gathering place serves excellent pizzas and sandwiches that have made it a Kaunakakai staple as well as one of my favorite eateries on the island. The best-selling pies are the Molokai (pepperoni and cheese), the Big Island (pepperoni, ham, mushroom, Italian sausage, bacon, and vegetables), and the Molokini (plain cheese slices). Pasta, sandwiches, and the new addition of "gourmet" hamburgers on homemade buns round out the menu. My personal fave is the vegetarian Maui pizza, but others tout the fresh-baked submarine and pocket sandwiches and the gyro pocket with spinach pie. Saturday and Sunday is prime-rib day and Wednesday is Mexican. Coin-operated cars and a toy airplane follow the children's theme, but adults should feel equally at home with the very popular barbecued baby back rib plate and the fresh-fish dinners.

In Kahua Center, on the old Wharf Rd. ℂ **808/553-3288.** Large pizzas $16–$32. No credit cards. Sun 11am–10pm; Mon–Sat 10am–10pm.

Outpost Natural Foods ★ VEGETARIAN   The healthiest and freshest food on the island is served at the lunch counter of this health food store, around the corner from the main drag on the ocean side of Kaunakakai town. The tiny store abounds in Molokai papayas, bananas, herbs, potatoes, watermelon, and other local produce, complementing its selection of vitamins, cosmetics, and health aids, as well as bulk and shelf items. The salads, burritos, tempeh sandwiches, tofu-spinach lasagna, and mock chicken, turkey, and meatloaf served at the lunch counter are testament to the fact that vegetarian food need not be boring. A must for health-conscious diners and shoppers.

70 Makaena Place. ⓒ **808/553-3377.** Main courses $7–$11. AE, DISC, MC, V. Store Mon–Fri 9am–6pm; Sun 10am–6pm; closed Sat. Cafe Mon–Fri 10am–2:30pm; closed Sat–Sun.

Sundown Deli ★ DELI   From "gourmet saimin" to spinach pie, Sundown's offerings are home cooked and healthful, with daily specials that include vegetarian quiche, vegetarian lasagna, and club sandwiches. The sandwiches (like smoked turkey and chicken salad) and several salads (Caesar, Oriental, stuffed tomato) are served daily, with a soup that changes by the day (clam chowder, Portuguese bean, cream of broccoli). Vitamins, T-shirts, and snacks are sold in this tiny cafe, but most of the business is takeout.

145 Puali St. (across the street from Veteran's Memorial Park). ⓒ **808/553-3713.** Main courses $5–$12. AE, MC, V. Tues–Fri 10am–2pm.

The East End
INEXPENSIVE

Mana'e Goods and Grindz ★ AMERICAN   Formerly the Neighborhood Store, this place has a new name, but it's still the same quick-stop market/lunch counter. It's nothing fancy, and that's what I love about it. Near mile marker 16 in the Pukoo area en route to the East End, this tiny store appears like a mirage, complete with a large parking area and picnic tables. The place serves omelets, Portuguese sausage, and other breakfast specials (brunch is very popular), then segues into sandwiches, salads, mahimahi plates, and varied over-the-counter lunch offerings, served on paper plates with plastic utensils. Favorites include the mahimahi plate lunch, the chicken *katsu,* and the Mexican plate, each one with a tried-and-true home-cooked flavor. There are daily specials, ethnic dishes, and some vegetarian options, as well as burgers (including a killer veggie burger), saimin, and legendary desserts. Made-on-Maui Roselani ice cream is a featured attraction. A Molokai treasure, this is the only grocery store on the East End (see "Shopping," below).

Pukoo. ⓒ **808/558-8498.** Most items less than $11. MC, V. Store Mon–Fri 6:30am–6pm; Sat–Sun 7:30am–4:30pm. Lunch counter Mon and Thurs–Fri 9:30am–4pm; Sat–Sun 7:30am–4:30pm.

Your Own Personal Chef—on Molokai!

The biggest complaint I get about Molokai is the lack of good restaurants. But now personal chef Don Hill (http://molokaichef.com) will help you plan a custom menu, do the grocery shopping, and then cook it and present a fabulous dinner at your accommodation. (He'll even clean everything up!) Chef Don will help design menus for you (he's an expert in various cuisines and is quite knowledgeable in helping you plan a "healthy" diet that still tastes delicious). He's also available for cooking classes. The price? About the cost of a great dinner at a gourmet restaurant, only it's served in the privacy of your vacation accommodation and you don't have to dress up.

SHOPPING
Kaunakakai

Molokai Surf, Molokai Island Creations, and **Lourdes** are clothing and gift shops close to one another in downtown Kaunakakai, where most of the retail shops sell T-shirts, muumuu, surf wear, and informal apparel. For food shopping, there are several good options. Because many visitors stay in condos, knowing the grocery stores is especially important. Other than that, serious shoppers will be disappointed, unless they love kites or native wood vessels. The following are Kaunakakai's notable stores.

Imamura Store   Wilfred Imamura, whose mother founded this store, recalls the old railroad track that stretched from the pier to a spot across the street. "We brought our household things from the pier on a hand-pumped vehicle," he recalls. His store, appropriately, is a leap into the past, a marvelous amalgam of precious old-fashioned things. Rubber boots, Hawaiian-print tablecloths, Japanese tea plates, ukulele cases, plastic slippers, and even coconut bikini tops line the shelves. But it's not all nostalgia: The Molokai T-shirts, jeans, and palaka shorts are of good quality and inexpensive, and the pareu fabrics are a find. In Kaunakakai. ✆ **808/553-5615.**

Kalele Bookstore & Devine Expressions ★★★   Make this your first stop in Kaunakakai, and take a few minutes to have a complimentary cup of coffee and "talk story" with Auntie Teri Waros, who was born and raised on Oahu and came to Molokai several years ago as the General Manager of the Molokai Lodge. After the Lodge closed, Terri decided she loved Molokai and the lifestyle so much that she was determined to stay. So she created the kind of bookstore (with various wonderful things like works of art, jewelry, handmade hats, etc.) that she would love to "hang out" in. Terri seems to know everybody and everything to do on Molokai, and she loves to help visitors explore her favorite island. 64 Ala Malama, Kaunakakai. www.molokaispirit.com. ✆ **808/553-5112.**

Molokai Drugs   David Mikami, whose father-in-law founded this pharmacy in 1935, has made this more than a drugstore. It's a gleaming, friendly stop full of life's basic necessities, with generous amenities such as a phone and a restroom for passersby. Here you'll find the best selection of guidebooks, books about Molokai, and maps, as well as greeting cards, paperbacks, flip-flops, and other essentials. The Mikamis are a household name on the island, not only because of their pharmacy, but also because the family has shown exceptional kindness to the often economically strapped Molokaians. In Kamoi Professional Center. ✆ **808/553-5790.**

Molokai Fish & Dive   Here you'll find the island's largest selection of T-shirts and souvenirs, crammed in among fishing, snorkeling, and outdoor gear that you can rent or buy. Find your way among the fishnets, boogie boards, diving equipment, bamboo rakes, beach towels, postcards, juices and soft drinks, and staggering miscellany of this store. One entire wall is lined with T-shirts, and the selection of Molokai books and souvenirs is extensive. The staff is happy to point out the best snorkeling spots of the day. In Kaunakakai. www.molokaifishanddive.com. ✆ **808/553-5926.**

Molokai Surf   This wooden building houses a selection of skateboards, surf shorts, sweatshirts, sunglasses, T-shirts, footwear, boogie boards, backpacks, and a broad range of clothing and accessories for life in the surf and sun. 130 Kamehameha V Hwy. ✆ **808/553-5093.**

Take's Variety Store   If you need luggage tags, buzz saws, toys, candy, cloth dolls, canned goods, canteens, camping equipment, hardware, batteries, candles, pipe fittings, fishing supplies—whew!—and other products for work and play, this 55-year-old variety store is the answer. You may suffer from claustrophobia in the crowded, dusty aisles, but Take's carries everything. In Kaunakakai. © **808/553-5499.**

EDIBLES

For fresh-baked goods, see "Kanemitsu's Bakery & Restaurant," above.

Friendly Market Center   You can't miss this salmon-colored wooden store-front on the main drag of "downtown" Kaunakakai, where people of all generations can be found just talking story in the Molokai way. Friendly has an especially good selection of produce and healthy foods—from local poi to Glenlivet. Blue-corn tortilla chips, soy milk, organic brown rice, a good selection of pasta sauces, and Kumu Farms macadamia nut pesto, the island's stellar gourmet food, are among the items that surpass standard grocery-store fare. In Kaunakakai. © **808/553-5595.**

Misaki's Grocery and Dry Goods   Established in 1922, this third-generation local legend is one of Kaunakakai's two grocery stores. Some of its notable items: chopped garlic from California, fresh luau leaves (taro greens), fresh okra, Boca Burgers, large Korean chestnuts in season, and gorgeous bananas. The fish section includes akule and ahi, fresh and dried, but the stock consists mostly of meats, produce, baking products, and a humongous array of soft drinks. Liquor, stationery, candies, and paper products round out the selection of this full-service grocery. In Kaunakakai. © **808/553-5505.**

Molokai Wines & Spirits   This is your best bet on the island for a decent bottle of wine. The shop offers 200 labels, including Caymus, Silver Oak, Joseph Phelps, Heitz, Bonny Doon, and a carefully culled European selection. *Wine Spectator* reviews are tacked to some of the selections, and the snack options include imported gourmet cheeses, salami, and Carr's biscuits. In Kaunakakai. © **808/553-5009.**

En Route to the North Coast

Blue Monkey and the Espresso Bar   This is a fairly slick—for Molokai—combination coffee bar, store, and gallery for more than 30 artists and crafts-people from Hawaii. Sold here are the Malulani Estate and Muleskinner coffees that are grown, processed, and packed on the 560-acre plantation surrounding the shop. (See p. 311 for details on plantation tours.) The gift items are worth a look: pikake and plumeria soaps from Kauai, perfumes and pure beeswax candles from Maui, koa bookmarks and hair sticks, pottery, woods, and baskets. Hwy. 480 (near the junction of Hwy. 470), Kualapuu. www.coffeesofhawaii.com. © **800/709-BEAN** (2326) or 808/567-9023.

Kualapuu Market   This market, in its third generation, is a stone's throw from the Coffees of Hawaii store. It's a scaled-down, one-stop shop with wine, food, and necessities—and a surprisingly presentable, albeit small, assortment of produce, from Molokai sweet potatoes to Ka'u navel oranges in season. The shelves are filled with canned goods, propane, rope, hoses, paper products, and baking goods, reflecting the uncomplicated, rural lifestyle of the area. In Kualapuu. © **808/567-6243.**

THE perfect MOLOKAI SOUVENIR

It's small, it's easy to pack and take back home, and it's made only on Molokai. It's Molokai salt. The Hawaii Kai Corporation (www.hawaiikaico.com) has two product lines featuring Molokai salt: the gourmet **Soul of the Sea** and the **Palm Island Premium.** Soul of the Sea salt is hand-harvested from some of the cleanest ocean water in the state, hand-processed and hand-packed on Molokai. It comes in three varietals: Papohaku White, Kilauea Black, and Haleakala Red. While making Soul of the Sea salt, Hawaii Kai Corporation got a byproduct they call Ocean Essence, which they blend with Molokai salt to restore trace minerals lost in the heating process. The result is Palm Island Gourmet, which comes in White Silver, Red Gold, or Black Lava. You can find the salt at Friendly Market, Molokai Drug, and Coffees of Hawaii.

Molokai Museum Gift Shop   This shop is located in a restored 1878 sugar mill that sits 1,500 feet above the town of Kualapuu. It's a considerable drive from town, but a good cause for those who'd like to support the museum and the handful of local artisans who sell their crafts, fabrics, cookbooks, quilt sets, and other gift items in the tiny shop. There's also a modest selection of cards, T-shirts, coloring books, and, at Christmas, handmade ornaments made of lauhala and koa. Meyer Sugar Mill, Hwy. 470 (just after the turnoff for the Ironwood Hills Golf Course and 2 miles below Kalaupapa Overlook), Kalae. www.hawaiimuseums. org/mc/ismolokai_Mmuseum.htm. ℂ **808/567-6436.**

The West End

Big Wind Kite Factory & Plantation Gallery ★★ ☺   Jonathan and Daphne Socher, kite designers and inveterate Bali-philes, have combined their interests in a kite factory/import shop that dominates the commercial landscape of Maunaloa, the reconstituted plantation town. Maunaloa's naturally windy conditions make it ideal for kite-flying classes, which are offered free when conditions are right—you can purchase kites on-site. The adjoining Plantation Gallery features local handicrafts, such as milo-wood bowls, locally made T-shirts, Hawaii-themed sandblasted glassware, baskets of lauhala and other fibers, and Hawaiian-music CDs. There are also many Balinese handicrafts, from jewelry to clothing and fabrics. In Maunaloa. www.bigwindkites.com. ℂ **808/552-2364.**

A Touch of Molokai ★   Even though the Kaluakoi Hotel is closed, this fabulous shop remains open. It is well worth the drive. The surf shorts and aloha shirts sold here are better than the norm, with attractive, up-to-date choices by Jams, Quiksilver, and other name brands. Tencel dresses, South Pacific shell necklaces (up to $400), and a magnificent, hand-turned milo bowl also caught my attention. Most impressive is the handsome array of lauhala bags, all made on Molokai. Since there have been so many stores closing in this area, this place now carries some groceries as well. At Kaluakoi Hotel & Golf Club. © **808/552-0133.**

The East End

Mana'e Goods and Grindz Formerly the Neighborhood Store 'N Counter, the only grocery on the East End sells batteries, aspirin, cookies, beer, Molokai produce, candies, paper products, and other sundries. There's good food pouring out of the kitchen

Some of the colorful wares at Big Wind Kite Factory.

for the breakfast and lunch counter, too. See "Where to Eat," earlier in this chapter, for the restaurant review. In Pukoo. © **808/558-8498.**

ENTERTAINMENT & NIGHTLIFE

Aqua Hotel Molokai, in Kaunakakai (© **808/553-5347;** www.hotelmolokai. com), offers live entertainment by local musicians poolside and in the dining room every night. On Friday from 4 to 10:30pm is Aloha Fridays night, when the musicians of Molokai who have been performing here for decades show you why people love their music and hula. With its South Seas ambience and poolside setting, it has become the island's premier venue for local and visiting entertainers.

WHERE TO STAY

Molokai is Hawaii's most affordable island, especially for hotels. And because the island's restaurants are few, most hotel rooms and condo units come with kitchens, which can save you a bundle on dining costs.

The downside is that there aren't too many accommodations options on Molokai—mostly B&Bs, condos, a few quaint oceanfront vacation rentals, and a motel-like hotel. For camping on Molokai, hardy souls can pitch their own tent at the beach or in the cool upland forest (see "Hiking & Camping," earlier in this chapter). I've listed my top picks below; for additional options, contact **Molokai Vacation Properties,** P.O. Box 1979, Kaunakakai, HI 96748 (www.molokai-vacation-rental.com; © **800/367-2984** or 808/553-8334; fax 808/553-3783). **Note:** Taxes of 13.41% will be added to your hotel bill. Parking is free.

See the map "Restaurants & Hotels on Molokai" for locations of the following accommodations.

Whenever anyone on Molokai mentions "hot bread," he's talking about the hot-bread run at **Kanemitsu's Bakery and Restaurant** (see p. 330), the surreal late-night ritual for die-hard bread lovers. Those in the know line up at the bakery's back door (79 Ala Malama St.; look for the sign that says HOT BREAD in the alley behind the bakery) beginning at 8pm, when the bread is whisked hot out of the oven and into waiting hands. You can order your fresh bread with butter, jelly, cinnamon, or cream cheese, and the bakers will cut the hot loaves down the middle and slather on the works so it melts in the bread. The cream cheese and jelly bread makes a fine substitute for dessert.

Kaunakakai

A'ahi Place 🌿 Just outside of the main town of Kaunakakai and up a small hill lies this dream vacation cottage, complete with a wicker-filled sitting area, a kitchen, and two full-size beds in the bedroom. Two lanai make great places to just sit and enjoy the stars at night. The entire property is surrounded by tropical plants, flowers, and fruit trees. For $10 more per night (for two), you can get all the fixings for a continental breakfast (homegrown Molokai coffee, fresh-baked goods, and fruit from the property) placed in the kitchen. For those who seek a quiet vacation with no phone or TV to distract you, this is the place. And for those who wish to explore Molokai, the central location is perfect.

P.O. Box 2006, Kaunakakai, HI 96748. www.molokai.com/aahi. ☎ **808/553-8033.** 1 unit. $75 double. Extra person $20. Continental breakfast $10. 3-night minimum. No credit cards. *In room:* Kitchen, no phone.

Aqua Hotel Molokai ★ ☺ Since the closing of the Lodge at Molokai Ranch, this nostalgic Hawaiian motel-like complex is the only hotel on the island. The modest hotel is composed of a series of modified A-frame units, nestled under coco palms along a gray-sand beach that has a great view of Lanai but isn't good for swimming. During the most recent renovation, in late 2010, Aqua replaced mattresses and upgraded linens and towels. This is a modest budget hotel—the rooms have all the necessities but aren't fancy. Be sure to ask for a room with a ceiling fan; most rooms have a lanai. The kitchenettes have coffeemakers, toasters, pots, and a two-burner stove.

Kamehameha V Hwy. (P.O. Box 1020), Kaunakakai, HI 96748. www.hotelmolokai.com or www.aquaresorts.com. ☎ **877/553-5347** or 808/553-5347. Fax 800/477-2329. 53 units. $159–$219 double; $229 double with kitchenette; from $249 suite. Extra bed/crib $25. AE, DISC, MC, V. **Amenities:** Restaurant and bar; babysitting; outdoor pool; watersports equipment rentals. *In room:* A/C, TV, fridge, hair dryer, high-speed Internet access (free), kitchenette (in some units).

Ka Hale Mala Bed & Breakfast 🌿 In a subdivision just outside town is this large four-room unit, with a private entrance through the garden and a Jacuzzi just outside. Inside, you'll find white rattan furnishings, room enough to sleep four, and a full kitchen. The helpful owners, Jack and Cheryl, meet all guests at the airport like long-lost relatives. They'll happily share their homegrown, organic produce; I recommend paying the extra $5 each for breakfast here. The owners can also supply snorkel and picnic gear.

7 Kamakana Place (P.O. Box 1582), Kaunakakai (off Kamehameha V Hwy., before mile marker 5), HI 96748. www.molokai-bnb.com. *(C)*/fax **808/553-9009.** 1 unit. $80 double without breakfast; $90 double with breakfast. Extra person $15 without breakfast, $20 with breakfast. No credit cards. **Amenities:** Jacuzzi. *In room:* TV, kitchen, computer and Wi-Fi (free).

Molokai Shores Suites ☺   Basic units with kitchens and large lanai face a small gold-sand beach in this quiet complex of three-story Polynesian-style buildings, less than a mile from Kaunakakai. Alas, the beach is mostly for show (offshore, it's shallow mud flats underfoot), fishing, or launching kayaks, but the swimming pool and barbecue come with an ocean view, and the spacious units make this a good choice for families. Well-tended gardens, spreading lawns, and palms frame a restful view of fishponds, offshore reefs, and neighbor islands. The central location is a plus. There's no daily maid service. I have received some letters complaining about the lack of maintenance and cleanliness; the management swears that they are taking steps to correct these deficiencies. On my most recent visit, the grounds and units I saw were clean and well maintained. However, keep in mind that these units are individually owned (as well as managed by various management companies).

Kamehameha V Hwy. (P.O. Box 1037), Kaunakakai, HI 96748. www.castleresorts.com. *(C)* **800/367-5004** or 808/553-5954. Fax 808/553-3421. 102 units. $179–$418 1-bedroom apt (sleeps up to 4); $269 2-bedroom apt (sleeps up to 6). Corporate, military, senior, weekly stay, and extended stay discounts. Check the website for specials. AE, DISC, MC, V. **Amenities:** Putting green. *In room:* TV, wireless Internet, kitchen.

The West End

Ke Nani Kai Resort ★ ☺   This place is great for families, who will appreciate the space. The large apartments are set up for full-time living with real kitchens, washer/dryers, attractive furnishings, and breezy lanai. There's a huge pool, a volleyball court, and tennis courts. These condos are farther from the sea than other local accommodations but are still just a brief walk from the beach. The two-story buildings are surrounded by parking and garden areas.

In the Kaluakoi Resort development, Kaluakoi Rd., off Hwy. 460 (P.O. Box 289), Maunaloa, HI 96770. Reservations c/o Molokai Vacation Properties, P.O. Box 1979, Kaunakakai, HI 96748. www.molokai-vacation-rental.com. *(C)* **800/367-2984** or 808/553-8334. Fax 808/553-3783. 100 units. $105–$135 1-bedroom apt (sleeps up to 4); $125–$175 2-bedroom apt (sleeps up to 6). Cleaning fee $75–$100. 3- to 7-night minimum. AE, DC, DISC, MC, V. **Amenities:** Nearby golf course; Jacuzzi; outdoor pool; 2 tennis courts. *In room:* TV, high-speed Internet (free), kitchen.

Paniolo Hale ★ 🏠   Tucked into a verdant garden on the dry West End, this condo complex has the advantage of being next door to a white-sand beach and a golf course. The two-story, old Hawaii ranch-house design is airy and homey, with oak floors and walls of folding-glass doors that open to huge screened verandas, doubling your living space. All are spacious and well equipped, with full kitchens and washer/dryers.

The whole place overlooks the Kaluakoi Golf Course, a green barrier that separates these condos from the rest of the rapidly fading Kaluakoi Resort. Out front, Kepuhi Beach is a scenic place for walkers and beachcombers, but the seas are too hazardous for most swimmers. A pool, paddle tennis, and barbecue facilities are on the property, which adjoins open grassland countryside.

As with most condominiums in a rental pool, the quality and upkeep of the individually owned units can vary widely. When booking, spend some time talking with the friendly people at Molokai Vacation Properties so that you can get a top-quality condo that has been renovated recently.

Lio Place (next door to Kaluakoi Resort), Kaluakoi, HI 96770. Reservations c/o Molokai Vacation Properties, P.O. Box 1979, Kaunakakai, HI 96748. www.molokai-vacation-rental.com. ℰ **800/ 367-2984** or 808/553-8334. Fax 808/553-3783. 77 units. $125–$150 studio double; $135–$195 1-bedroom apt (sleeps up to 4); $200 2-bedroom apt (sleeps up to 6). 10% discount for stays of a week or more. Cleaning fee $65–$150. 3-to 7-night minimum. AE, MC, V. **Amenities:** Outdoor pool. *In room:* TV, Internet (free), kitchen.

The East End

Aloha Beach House ★★ 🎒   Book this place! Here is the "Hawaii" of your dreams. This Hawaiian-style beach house sits right on the white-sand beach of Waialua on the lush East End. Perfect for families, this impeccably decorated, two-bedroom, 1,600-square-foot beach house has a huge open living/dining/ kitchen area that opens to an old-fashioned porch for meals or just sitting in the comfy chairs and watching the clouds roll by. It's fully equipped, from the complete kitchen (including a dishwasher) to a library of videos to all the beach toys you can think of. It's close to **Mana'e Goods and Grindz** (p. 335).

Located just after mile marker 19. Reservations c/o Cool Waves, Inc., 4-1191 Kuhio Hwy., Ste. D #24, Kapaa, HI 96746. www.molokaivacation.com. ℰ **888/828-1008** or 808/828-1100. Fax 808/828-2199. 1 unit. $250–$290 double. Extra person $20–$25. Cleaning fee $175–$225 per stay. 3-night minimum. No credit cards. *In room:* TV, high-speed Internet access (free), kitchen.

Country Cottage at Pu'u O Hoku Ranch ★ ☺   Pu'u o Hoku (Star Hill) Ranch, which spreads across 14,000 acres of pasture and forests, is the last place to stay before Halawa Valley—it's at least an hour's drive from Kaunakakai along the shoreline. Two acres of tropically landscaped property circle the ranch's rustic cottage, which boasts breathtaking views of rolling hills and the Pacific Ocean. The wooden cottage features comfortable country furniture, a full kitchen, two bedrooms (one with a double bed, one with two twins), two bathrooms, and a separate dining room on the enclosed lanai. TVs and video players are available on request. Stargaze at night, watch the sunrise in the morning, and hike, swim, or play croquet in the afternoon. For larger parties, there's an 11-bedroom, nine-bathroom lodge (sleeps up to 22) on the property. Kids will have plenty of room to run around and explore.

Kamehameha V Hwy., at mile marker 25. Reservations P.O. Box 1889, Kaunakakai, HI 96748. www.puuohoku.com. ℰ **808/558-8109.** Fax 808/558-8100. 2 units. $225–$300 double. Extra person $30. Cleaning fee $125–$175. 2-night minimum. DISC, MC, V. *In room:* TV/video player (available on request), kitchen, Wi-Fi (free).

Dunbar Beachfront Cottages ★★ ☺   This is one of the most peaceful, comfortable, and elegant properties on Molokai's East End, and the setting is simply stunning. Each of these two green-and-white plantation-style cottages sits on its own secluded beach (good for swimming)—you'll feel like you're on your own private island. Each cottage sleeps up to four (great for a family), and comes with a full kitchen, ceiling fans, tropical furniture, a large furnished deck (perfect for whale-watching in winter), and views of Maui, Lanai, and Kahoolawe across the channel.

Kamehameha V Hwy., past mile marker 18. Reservations c/o Matt and Genesis Dunbar, HC01 Box 738, Kaunakakai, HI 96748. www.molokai-beachfront-cottages.com. ℂ **800/673-0520** or 808/558-8153. 2 units. $175 cottage (sleeps up to 4). Cleaning fee $75. 3-night minimum. No credit cards. *In room:* TV/DVD, kitchen, Wi-Fi (free).

10

MOLOKAI | Where to Stay

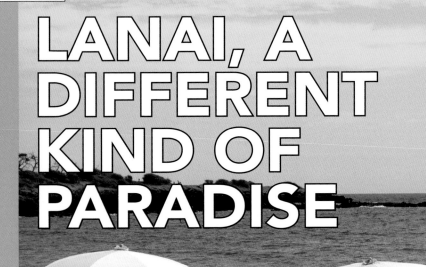

LANAI, A DIFFERENT KIND OF PARADISE

Lanai is not an easy place to reach. There are no direct flights from the mainland. It's almost as if this quiet, gentle oasis—known, paradoxically, for both its small-town feel and its celebrity appeal—demands that its visitors go to great lengths to get here in order to ensure that they will appreciate it.

Lanai (pronounced "Lah-*nigh*-ee"), the nation's biggest defunct pineapple patch, now claims to be one of the world's top tropical destinations. It's a bold claim because so little is here; Lanai has even fewer dining and accommodations choices than Molokai. There are no stoplights and barely 30 miles of paved road. This almost-virgin island is unspoiled by what passes for progress, except for a tiny 1920s-era plantation village—and, of course, the village's fancy new arrivals: two first-class luxury hotels where room rates average $450-plus a night.

As soon as you arrive on Lanai, you'll feel the small-town coziness. People wave to every car, residents stop to "talk story" with their friends, fishing and working in the garden are considered priorities in life, and leaving the keys in your car's ignition is standard practice.

For generations, Lanai was little more than a small village, owned and operated by the pineapple company, surrounded by acres of pineapple fields. The few visitors to the island were either relatives of the residents or occasional weekend hunters. Life in the 1960s was pretty much the same as in the 1930s. But all that changed in 1990, when the Lodge at Koele, a 102-room hotel resembling an opulent English Tudor mansion, opened its doors, followed a year later by the 250-room Manele Bay, a Mediterranean-style luxury resort overlooking Hulopoe Bay. Overnight the isolated island was transformed: Corporate jets streamed into tiny Lanai Airport, former plantation workers were retrained in the art of serving gourmet meals, and the population of 2,500 swelled with transient visitors and outsiders coming to work in the island's new hospitality industry. Microsoft billionaire Bill Gates chose the island for his lavish wedding, booking all of its hotel rooms to fend off the press—and uncomplicated Lanai went on the map as a vacation spot for the rich and powerful.

But this island is also a place where people come looking for beauty, quiet, solitude, and an experience with nature. The sojourners who find their way to Lanai seek out the dramatic views, the tropical fusion of stars at night, and the chance to be alone with the elements.

They also come for the wealth of activities: snorkeling and swimming in the marine preserve known as Hulopoe Bay, hiking on 100 miles of remote trails, talking story with the friendly locals, and beachcombing and whale-watching along stretches of otherwise deserted sand. For the adventurous, there's horseback riding in the forest, scuba diving in caves, playing golf on courses with stunning ocean views, or renting a four-wheel-drive vehicle for the day and discovering wild plains where spotted deer run free.

In a single decade, a plain red-dirt pineapple patch has become one of Hawaii's top fantasy destinations. But the real Lanai is a multifaceted place that's so much more than a luxury resort—and it's the traveler who comes to discover the island's natural wonders, local lifestyle, and other inherent joys who's bound to have the most genuine island experience.

The Pineapple Island's Unusual Past

This old shield volcano in the rain shadow of Maui has a history of resisting change in a big way. Early Polynesians, fierce Hawaiian kings, European explorers, 20th-century farmers—the island has seen them all and sent most of them packing, empty-handed and broken. The ancient Hawaiians believed that the island was haunted by spirits so wily and vicious that no human could survive here. People didn't settle here until around A.D. 1400.

But those spirits never really went away, it seems. In 1778, the king of the Big Island, Kalaniopuu, invaded Lanai in what was called "the war of loose bowels." His men slaughtered every warrior, cut down trees, and set fire to all that was left except a bitter fern whose roots gave them all dysentery.

In 1802, Wu Tsin made the first attempt to harvest a crop on the island, but he ultimately abandoned his cane fields and went away. Charles Gay acquired 600 acres at public auction to experiment with pineapple as a crop, but a 3-year drought left him bankrupt. Others tried in vain to grow cotton, sisal, and sugar beets; they started a dairy and a piggery and raised sheep for wool. But all enterprises failed, mostly for lack of water.

Harry Baldwin, a missionary's grandson, was the first to succeed on Lanai. He bought Lanai for $588,000 in 1917, developed a 20-mile water pipeline between Koele and Manele, and sold the island 5 years later to Jim Dole for $1.1 million.

Dole planted and irrigated 18,000 acres of pineapple, built Lanai City, blasted out a harbor, and turned the island into a fancy fruit plantation. For a half century, he enjoyed great success. Even Dole was ultimately vanquished, however: Cheaper pineapple production in Asia brought an end to Lanai's heyday.

The island still resembles old photographs taken in the glory days of Dole. Any minute now, you half expect to look up and see old Jim Dole himself rattling up the road in a Model-T truck with a load of fresh-picked pineapples. Only now, there's a new lord of the manor, and his name is David Murdock.

Of all who have looked at Lanai with a gleam in their eye, nobody has succeeded quite like Murdock, a self-made billionaire who acquired the island in a merger in 2000. About 97% of it is now his private holding.

Murdock spent $400 million to build two grand hotels on the island: the Lodge at Koele, which resembles an English country retreat, and the Four Seasons Resort Lanai at Manele Bay, a green-tile-roofed Mediterranean palazzo by the sea. Murdock recycled the former field hands into waitstaff, even summoning a London butler to school the natives in the fine art of service, and carved a pair of daunting golf courses, one in the island's interior and the other along the wave-lashed coast. He then set out to attract tourists by touting Lanai as "the private island."

Murdock is now trying to make all this pay for itself by selling vacation homes and condos, all in the million-dollar range, next door to the two resorts.

The redevelopment of this tiny rock should have been a pushover for the big-time tycoon, but island-style politics have continually thwarted his schemes. GO SLOW, a sun-faded sign at Dole's old maintenance shed once said. Murdock might have heeded the warning because his grandiose plans are taking twice as long to accomplish as he had expected. Lanai is under the political thumb of many who believe that the island's precious water supply shouldn't all be diverted to championship golf courses and Jacuzzis, and there remains opposition from Lanaians for Sensible Growth, who advocate affordable housing, alternative water systems, and civic improvements that benefit residents.

Lanai residents might live in a rural setting, but they certainly aren't isolated. Having watched the other islands in Hawaii attempt the balancing act of economic growth and the maintenance of an island lifestyle, the residents of Lanai are cautiously welcoming visitors, but at a pace that is still easy for this former plantation community to digest.

FROMMER'S FAVORITE LANAI EXPERIENCES

- **Snorkeling Hulopoe Beach:** Crystal-clear waters teem with brilliant tropical fish off one of Hawaii's best beaches. There are tide pools to explore, waves to play in, and other surprises—like a pod of spinner dolphins that often makes a splashy entrance.

- **Exploring the Garden of the Gods:** Eroded by wind, rain, and time, these geologic badlands are worth visiting at sunrise or sunset, when the low light plays tricks on the land—and your mind. See p. 347.

- **Hiking the Munro Trail:** The 11-mile Munro Trail is a lofty, rigorous hike along the rim of an old volcano. You'll get great views of the nearby islands. Take a four-wheel-drive vehicle if you want to spend more time on top of the island. See p. 355.

- **Four-Wheeling It:** Four-wheeling is a way of life on Lanai because there are only 30 miles of pavement on the whole island. Plenty of rugged trails lead to deserted beaches, abandoned villages, and valleys filled with wild game.

- **Camping Under the Stars:** The campsites at Hulopoe Beach Park are about as close to the heavens as you can get. The crashing surf will lull you to sleep at night, and chirping birds will wake you in the morning. If you're into roughing it, this is a great way to experience Lanai. See p. 356.

- **Watching the Whales at Polihua Beach:** Located on the north shore, this beach—which gets its name from the turtles that nest here—is a great place to watch for whales during the winter months. See p. 351.

ORIENTATION
Arriving

BY PLANE   No matter where you're coming from, you'll have to make a connection in Honolulu (on Oahu) or Kahului (on Maui), where you can catch a plane for the 25-minute flight to Lanai's airport. You'll touch down in Puuwai Basin, once the world's largest pineapple plantation; it's about 10 minutes by car to Lanai City and 25 minutes to Manele Bay.

Commuter airlines offering service to Lanai are **go!Mokulele Airlines** (© **888/435-9462;** www.iflygo.com) and **Island Air** (© **800/323-3345** from the mainland, 800/652-6541 interisland, or 808/565-6744; www.islandair.com), with daily flights from Honolulu. **Note:** Island Air has left me stranded midroute twice. **George's Aviation** (℃ **866/834-2120,** 808/834-2120 from Honolulu, or 808/893-2120 from Maui; www.georgesaviation.com) will provide charter flights from any island to Molokai.

BY BOAT A round-trip on **Expeditions Maui-Lanai Passenger Ferry** (℃ **800/695-2624** or 808/661-3756; www.go-lanai.com) takes you between Maui and Lanai for $30 for adults and $20 for children, each way. The ferry runs

A signpost in Lanai helps orient visitors.

five times a day, 365 days a year, between Maui (Lahaina) and Lanai's Manele Bay harbor. The 9-mile channel crossing takes 45 minutes to an hour, depending on sea conditions. Reservations are strongly recommended; call or book on the website. Baggage is limited to two checked bags and one carry-on.

Visitor Information

Lanai Visitors Bureau, 1727 Wili Pa Loop, Wailuku, Maui 96793 (℃ **800/947-4774** or 808/565-7600; fax 808/565-9316; www.gohawaii.com/lanai), and the **Hawaii Visitors & Convention Bureau** (℃ **800/GO-HAWAII** [464-2924] or 808/923-1811; www.gohawaii.com) provide brochures, maps, and island guides.

The Island in Brief

Inhabited Lanai is divided into three parts—Lanai City, Koele, and Manele—and two distinct climate zones: hot and dry and cool and misty.

Lanai City (pop. 3,200) sits at the heart of the island at 1,645 feet above sea level. It's the only place on the island where you'll find services. Built in 1924, this plantation village is a tidy grid of quaint tin-roofed cottages in bright pastels, with tropical gardens of banana, *lilikoi,* and papaya. Many of the residents are Filipino immigrants who once worked the pineapple fields. Their clapboard homes, now worth $500,000 or more (for a 1,300-sq.-ft. home, built in 1935, on a tiny 11,000-sq.-ft. lot), are excellent examples of historic preservation; the whole town looks like it's been kept under a bell jar.

Around Dole Park, a charming village square lined with towering Norfolk and Cook Island pines, plantation buildings house general stores selling basic necessities, a post office (where people stop to chat), two banks, three restaurants, an art gallery, an art center, a whimsical shop, and a coffee shop that outshines any Starbucks. A victim of "progress" was the local one-room police station with a jail that consisted of three blue-and-white wooden outhouse-size cells with padlocks. It's now a block from the square with "modern facilities," including regulation-size jail cells.

In the nearby cool upland district of **Koele** is the **Lodge at Koele** (now managed by the Four Seasons Resort), standing alone on a knoll overlooking pastures and the sea at the edge of a pine forest, like a grand European manor.

The Maui-Lanai ferry shuttles visitors between Maui and Lanai five times a day, 365 days a year.

The other bastion of indulgence, the Four Seasons Resort Lanai at Manele Bay, is on the sunny southwestern tip of the island at **Manele.** You'll get more of what you expect from Hawaii here—beaches, swaying palms, mai tais, and the like.

[FastFACTS] LANAI

Emergencies In case of **emergency,** call the police, fire department, or ambulance services at ℂ 911, or the **Poison Control Center** at ℂ 800/222-1222.

Dentists For emergency dental care, call **Dr. Nora Harmsen** (ℂ 808/565-6418).

Doctors If you need a doctor, contact the **Straub Lanai Family Health Center** (ℂ 808/565-6423).

Hospitals You can reach the **Lanai Community Hospital** at ℂ 808/565-8450.

Police For nonemergencies, call the **police** at ℂ 808/565-6428.

Weather For a weather report, call the **National Weather Service** at ℂ 808/565-6033.

GETTING AROUND

With so few paved roads here, you'll need a four-wheel-drive vehicle if you plan to explore the island's remote shores, its interior, or the summit of Mount Lanai-hale. Even if you have only a day on Lanai, rent one and see the island. Both standard cars and four-wheel-drive vehicles are available at the **Dollar Rent A**

Car desk at **Lanai City Service/Lanai Plantation Store,** 1036 Lanai Ave. (𝄐 **800/533-7808** or 800/800-3665). Expect to pay about $139 to $169 a day for a four-wheel-drive jeep.

Warning: Gas is expensive on Lanai, and those four-wheel-drive vehicles get terrible mileage. Because everything in Lanai City is within walking distance, it makes sense to rent a jeep only for the days you want to explore the island.

Though it's fun to rent a car, it is possible to stay here and get to the beach without one. Both Four Seasons Resorts operate shuttles to Hulopoe Beach. When you want to return, you just catch the hourly shuttle (it may run on the half-hour from Four Seasons Resort Lanai at Manele Bay) back to Lanai City. The shuttle picks up at Hotel Lanai as well and will take guests to town, the airport, and the golf courses. There is a one-time charge of $48 per person (for unlimited rides) for Four Seasons guests and $35 per person for Hotel Lanai guests.

If you're staying elsewhere, you can walk to everything in Lanai City. Or you can most likely get a ride back up to Lanai City with a local resident from the airport. Whether or not you rent a car, sooner or later you'll find yourself at Lanai City Service/Lanai Plantation Store. This all-in-one grocery store, gas station, rental-car agency, and souvenir shop serves as the island's Grand Central Terminal—you can pick up information, directions, maps, and all the local gossip here.

EXPLORING LANAI

You'll need a four-wheel-drive vehicle to reach all the sights listed below. Renting a jeep is an expensive proposition on Lanai—from $139 to $179 a day—so I

😊 ESPECIALLY FOR KIDS

Exploring Hulopoe Tide Pools (p. 356)   An entire world of marine life lives in the tide pools on the eastern side of Hulopoe Bay. Everything in the water, including the tiny fish, is small—kid size. After examining the wonders of the tide pool, check out the larger swimming holes in the lava rock, perfect for children.

Hunting for Petroglyphs (p. 348)   The Luahiwa Petroglyph Field, located just outside Lanai City, is spread out over a 3-acre site. Make it a game: Whoever finds the most petroglyphs gets ice cream from the Pine Isle Market.

Listening to Storytellers   Check with the **Lanai Library,** on Fraser Avenue near Fifth Street, in Lanai City (𝄐 **808/ 565-7920;** www.librarieshawaii.org/ locations/lanai/index.htm), to see if any storytelling or other children's activities are scheduled. The events are usually free and open to everyone. Storytelling is usually held on Friday at 10am with Aunty Chelsea, but call ahead.

suggest renting one just for the day (or days) you plan on sightseeing; otherwise, it's easy enough to get to the beach and around Lanai City without your own wheels. For details on vehicle rentals, see "Getting Around," p. 368.

Note: You'll find the following attractions on the map on p. 96.

Garden of the Gods ★

A dirt four-wheel-drive road leads out of Lanai City, through the now uncultivated pineapple fields, past the Kanepuu Preserve (a dry-land forest preserve teeming with rare plant and animal life) to the so-called Garden of the Gods, out on Lanai's north shore. This rugged, barren, beautiful place is full of rocks strewn by volcanic forces and shaped by the elements into a variety of shapes and colors—brilliant reds, oranges, ochers, and yellows.

The Garden of the Gods, on Lanai's north shore.

Ancient Hawaiians considered this desolate, wind-swept place an entirely supernatural phenomenon. Scientists, however, have other, less-colorful explanations. Some call the area an "ongoing posterosional event"; others say it's just "plain and simple badlands." Take a four-wheel-drive ride out here and decide for yourself.

Go early in the morning or just before sunset, when the light casts eerie shadows on the mysterious lava formations. Drive west from the lodge on Polihua Road; in about 2 miles, you'll see a hand-painted sign that points left down a one-lane, red-dirt road through a kiawe forest to the site.

Mount Lanaihale's Summit ★

In the first golden rays of dawn, when lone owls swoop over abandoned pineapple fields, hop into a four-wheel-drive and head out on the two-lane blacktop toward Mount Lanaihale, the 3,370-foot summit of Lanai. Your destination is the Munro Trail, the narrow, winding ridge trail that runs across Lanai's razorback spine to the summit. From here, you may get a rare Hawaii treat: On a clear day, you can see all of the main islands in the Hawaiian chain except Kauai.

When it rains, the Munro Trail becomes slick and boggy, with major washouts. Rainy-day excursions often end with a rental jeep on the hook of the island's lone tow truck—and a $250 tow charge. You could even slide off into a major gulch and never be found, so don't try it. But in late August and September, when trade winds stop and the air over the islands stalls in what's called a *kona* condition, Mount Lanaihale's suddenly visible peak becomes an irresistible attraction.

If it's clear enough to see Mount Lanaihale's summit, rent a four-wheel-drive vehicle and take the Munro Trail to the top. Look for a red-dirt road off Manele Road (Hwy. 440), about 5 miles south of Lanai City; turn left and head

Along the Munro Trail.

up the ridgeline. No sign marks the peak, so you'll have to keep an eye out. Look for a wide spot in the road and a clearing that falls sharply to the sea.

From here you can see Kahoolawe, Maui, the Big Island of Hawaii, and Molokini's tiny crescent. Even the summits show. You can also see the silver domes of Space City on Haleakala in Maui; Puu Moaulanui, the tongue-twisting summit of Kahoolawe; and, looming above the clouds, Mauna Kea on the Big Island. At another clearing farther along the thickly forested ridge, all of Molokai, including the 4,961-foot summit of Kamakou and the faint outline of Oahu (more than 30 miles across the sea), are visible. For details on hiking the trail, see "Hiking & Camping," below.

Luahiwa Petroglyph Field

Lanai is second only to the Big Island in its wealth of prehistoric rock art, but you'll have to search a little to find it. Some of the best examples are on the outskirts of Lanai City, on a hillside site known as Luahiwa Petroglyph Field. The

---

Perfect for a Rainy Day: Lanai Art Center

A perfect activity for a rainy day in Lanai City is the **Lanai Art Center,** 339 Seventh St., located in the heart of the small town. Top artists from across Hawaii frequently visit this homegrown art program and teach a variety of classes, ranging from raku (Japanese pottery), silk printing, silk screening, pareu making (creating your own design on this islanders' wrap), *gyotaku* (printing a real fish on your own T-shirt), and watercolor drawing to a variety of other island crafts. The cost for the 2- to 3-hour classes is usually in the $15-to-$70 range (materials are extra). For information, call © **808/565-7503** or visit www.lanaiart.org.

characters you'll see incised on 13 boulders in this grassy 3-acre knoll include a running man, a deer, a turtle, a bird, a goat, and even a rare curly-tailed Polynesian dog (a latter-day wag has put a leash on him—some joke).

To get here, take the road to Hulopoe Beach. About 2 miles out of Lanai City, look to the left, up on the slopes of the crater, for a cluster of reddish-tan boulders (believed to form a rain *heiau,* or shrine, where people called up the gods Ku and Hina to nourish their crops). A cluster of spiky century plants marks the spot. Look for the Norfolk pines on the left side of the highway, turn left on the dirt road that veers across the abandoned pineapple fields, and after about 1 mile, take a sharp left by the water tanks. Drive for another ½ mile and then veer to the right at the V in the road. Stay on this upper road for about ¼ mile; you'll come to a large cluster of boulders on the right side. It's just a short walk up the cliffs (wear walking or hiking shoes) to the petroglyphs. Exit the same way you came. Go between 3pm and sunset for ideal viewing and photo ops.

Kaunolu Village

Out on Lanai's nearly vertical, Gibraltar-like sea cliffs is an old royal compound and fishing village. Now a National Historic Landmark and one of Hawaii's most treasured ruins, it's believed to have been inhabited by King Kamehameha the Great and hundreds of his closest followers about 200 years ago. It's a hot, dry, dusty, slow-going, 3-mile four-wheel-drive from Lanai City to Kaunolu, but the miniexpedition is worth it. Take plenty of water, don a hat for protection against the sun, and wear sturdy shoes.

Ruins of 86 house platforms and 35 stone shelters have been identified on both sides of Kaunolu Gulch. The residential complex also includes the Halulu Heiau temple, named after a mythical man-eating bird. The king's royal retreat is thought to have stood on the eastern edge of Kaunolu Gulch, overlooking the rocky shore facing Kahekili's Leap, a 62-foot-high bluff named for the mighty Maui chief who leaped off cliffs as a show of bravado. Nearby are burial caves, a fishing shrine, a lookout tower, and many warrior-like stick figures carved on boulders. Just offshore stands the telltale fin of little Shark Island, a popular dive spot that teems with bright tropical fish and, frequently, sharks.

Excavations are underway to discover more about how ancient Hawaiians lived, worked, and worshiped on Lanai's leeward coast. Who knows? The royal fishing village may yet yield the bones of King Kamehameha. His burial site, according to legend, is known only to the moon and the stars.

Kanepuu Preserve

On the west side of the island lies the Kanepuu Preserve, 590 acres riddled with some 48 species of Hawaii native plants. The guardian of this Preserve is the Nature Conservancy, which is especially interested in protecting the rare plants of a dry native Hawaii forest, which once covered much of the dry low-lands of the Hawaiian Islands. Due to recent drought conditions, the Nature Conservancy has temporarily closed access to this native forest; check to see whether it is open. It is a great opportunity to see rare, endemic plant species and trees like the lama, a native ebony, and aiea (which was once used for canoe building).

Off the Tourist Trail: Keomoku Village

If you're sunburned lobster red, have read all the books you packed, and are starting to get island fever, take a little drive to Keomoku Village, on Lanai's east coast. You'll really be off the tourist path here. All that's in Keomoku, a ghost town since the mid-1950s, is a 1903 clapboard church in disrepair, an overgrown graveyard, an excellent view across the 9-mile Auau Channel to Maui's crowded Kaanapali Beach, and some very empty beaches that are perfect for a picnic or a snorkel. This former ranching and fishing village of 2,000 was the first non-Hawaiian settlement on Lanai, but it dried up after droughts killed off the Maunalei Sugar Company. The village, such as it is, is a

A 1903 clapboard church in Keomoku Village.

great little escape from Lanai City. Follow Keomoku Road for 8 miles to the coast, turn right on the sandy road, and keep going for 5¼ miles.

BEACHES

If you like big, wide, empty, gold-sand beaches and crystal-clear, cobalt-blue water full of bright tropical fish—and who doesn't?—go to Lanai. With 18 miles of sandy shoreline, Lanai has some of Hawaii's least crowded and most interesting beaches.

Hulopoe Beach ★★★

In 1997, Dr. Stephen Leatherman of the University of Maryland (a professional beach surveyor who's also known as "Dr. Beach") ranked Hulopoe the best beach in the United States. It's easy to see why. This palm-fringed, gold-sand beach is bordered by black-lava fingers, protecting swimmers from ocean currents. In summer, Hulopoe is perfect for swimming, snorkeling, or just lolling about; the water temperature is usually in the mid-70s (mid-20s Celsius). Swimming is usually safe, except when swells kick up in winter. The bay at the foot of the Four Seasons Resort Lanai at Manele Bay is a protected marine preserve, with schools of colorful fish and spinner dolphins. Humpback whales cruise by here in winter. Hulopoe is also Lanai's premier beach park, with a grassy lawn, picnic tables, barbecue grills, restrooms, showers, and ample parking. You can camp here, too.

Some of the best **lava-rock tide pools** in Hawaii are found along the south shore of Hulopoe Bay. These miniature SeaWorlds are full of strange creatures, such as asteroids (sea stars) and holothurians (sea cucumbers), not to mention spaghetti worms, barber pole shrimp, and Hawaii's favorite local delicacy, the opihi, a tasty morsel also known as the limpet. Youngsters enjoy swimming in the enlarged tide pool at the eastern edge of the bay. When you explore tide pools, do so at low tide. Never turn your back on the waves. Wear tennis shoes or reef

Hulopoe Beach.

walkers, as wet rocks are slippery. Collecting specimens in this marine preserve is forbidden, so don't take any souvenirs home.

Polihua Beach ★

So many sea turtles once hauled themselves out of the water to lay their eggs in the sunbaked sand on Lanai's northwestern shore that Hawaiians named the beach here Polihua, or "egg nest." Although the endangered green sea turtles are

Polihua Beach.

Shipwreck Beach.

making a comeback, they're seldom seen here now. You're more likely to spot an offshore whale (in season) or the perennial litter that washes up onto this deserted beach at the end of Polihua Road, a 4-mile jeep trail. This strand is ideal for beachcombing (those little green-glass Japanese fishing-net floats often show up here), fishing, or just being alone. There are no facilities except fishermen's huts and driftwood shelters. Bring water and sunscreen. Beware of the strong currents, which make the water unsafe for swimming.

Shipwreck Beach ★

This 8-mile-long wind-swept strand on Lanai's northeastern shore—named for the rusty ship *Liberty* stuck on the coral reef—is a sailor's nightmare and a beach-comber's dream. The strong currents yield all sorts of flotsam, from Japanese

The rusty ship *Liberty* is stuck on the coral reef.

hand-blown-glass fish floats and rare pelagic paper nautilus shells to lots of junk. This is also a great place to spot whales from December to April, when the Pacific humpbacks cruise in from Alaska. The road to the beach is paved most of the way, but you really need a four-wheel-drive to get down here.

WATERSPORTS

Lanai has Hawaii's best water clarity because it lacks major development, it has low rainfall and runoff, and its coast is washed clean daily by the sea current (known as "The Way to Tahiti"). But the strong sea currents pose a threat to swimmers, and there are few good surf breaks. Most of the aquatic adventures—swimming, snorkeling, scuba diving—are centered on the somewhat protected south shore, around Hulopoe Bay.

The only outfitter for watersports is **Trilogy Lanai Ocean Sports ★★★** (✆ **888/MAUI-800** [628-4800]; www.visitlanai.com).

Sailing & Snorkeling

Trilogy Lanai Ocean Sports (see above), which has built a well-deserved reputation as the leader in sailing/snorkeling cruises in Hawaii, offers both a morning and an afternoon **snorkel-sailing trip** onboard its luxury custom sailing catamarans or its 32-foot jet-drive rigid aluminum-inflatable vessel. The trips along Lanai's protected coastline sail past hundreds of spinner dolphins and into some of the best snorkeling sites in the world for $181 (half-price for children 3–15) and include lunch, sodas, snorkel gear, and instruction. **Budget tip:** Check the Trilogy website for discounts.

If you just want to snorkel on your own, Hulopoe is Lanai's best snorkeling spot. Fish are abundant in the marine-life conservation area. Try the lava-rock points at either end of the beach and around the lava pools.

Fun in the surf at Hulopoe Bay.

Scuba Diving

Two of Hawaii's best-known dive spots are found in Lanai's clear waters, just off the south shore: **Cathedrals I** and **II,** so named because the sun lights up an underwater grotto like a magnificent church. **Trilogy Lanai Ocean Sports** (see above for contact information) offers several kinds of sailing, diving, and snorkeling trips on catamarans and from its new 32-foot high-tech jet-drive ocean raft. It has its own version of "sunrise services" at the Cathedrals—not only is this the best time of day to dive this incredible area, but there are virtually no other dive boats in the water at this time. Cost is $214 for a two-tank dive, $107 for nondivers. Beach dives are available for $95 (one-tank dive) for certified divers and $102 for an introductory dive for noncertified divers.

A scuba diver explores the waters off Lanai.

Sport Fishing

Spinning Dolphin Charters of Lanai (© 808/565-7676; www.sportfishing lanai.com) offers sport fishing on a 36-foot Twin-V. It will take up to six passengers for $700 for 4 hours ($110 for each additional hour), or you can share a boat for $150 each for 4 hours.

Surfing

If you've ever wanted to learn how to surf, let instructor Nick Palumbo, a surfing champion, take you on a four-wheel-drive surfing safari to a secluded surf spot. He'll have you up and riding the waves in no time. His **Lanai Surf School & Surf Safari** (© 808/306-9837; www.lanaisurfsafari.com) offers a package that includes a 2-hour lesson with surfboard, four-wheel-drive transportation, refreshments, and "a really good time" for $200 per person.

Whale-Watching

During whale season, from December to April, **Trilogy Lanai Ocean Sports** (see above for contact information) takes passengers out on its 26-passenger, rigid-hulled inflatable boat, a 32-foot jet-drive Zodiac named *Manele Kai,* for a 2-hour ocean adventure that explores some of the remote and unspoiled sites in Hawaii. Lanai is also home to one of Hawaii's largest schools of spinner dolphins and a haven for North Pacific humpback whales. The captains and crew are certified island naturalists, who make each trip educational as well as entertaining, and they can usually find these wonderful and playful mammals. The cost is $81 (half-price for children 3–15), which includes soft drinks.

HIKING & CAMPING
Hiking

A LEISURELY MORNING HIKE

The 3-hour self-guided **Koele Nature Hike** starts by the reflecting pool in the backyard of the Lodge at Koele and takes you on a 5-mile loop through Norfolk Island pines, into Hulopoe Valley, past wild ginger, and up to Koloiki Ridge, with its panoramic view of Maunalei Valley and of Molokai and Maui in the distance. You're welcome to take the hike even if you're not a guest at the lodge. The path isn't clearly marked, so ask the concierge for a free map. Do this hike in the morning; by afternoon, the clouds usually roll in, marring visibility at the top and increasing your chance of being caught in a downpour.

THE CHALLENGING MUNRO TRAIL

This tough, 11-mile (round-trip) uphill climb through the groves of Norfolk pines is a lung buster, but if you reach the top, you'll be rewarded with a breathtaking view of Molokai, Maui, Kahoolawe, the peaks of the Big Island, and—on a really clear day—Oahu in the distance. Plan on 7 hours. The trail begins at Lanai Cemetery along Keomoku Road (Hwy. 44) and follows Lanai's ancient caldera rim, ending up at the island's highest point, Lanaihale. Go in the morning for the best visibility. After 4 miles, you'll get a view of Lanai City. The weary retrace their steps from here, while the more determined go the last 1.25 miles to the top. Diehards head down Lanai's steep south-crater rim to join the highway to Manele Bay, though you'll need to be picked up if you take the south-crater rim and hike to the highway. As an alternative, you can skip this steep hike and retrace the route you came in on. For more details on the Munro Trail—including information on four-wheel-driving it to the top—see "Mount Lanaihale's Summit," above.

The Munro Trail leads to a spectacular view of Molokai, Maui, Kahoolawe, the peaks of the Big Island, and, ona a clear day. Oahu.

A SELF-GUIDED NATURE TRAIL

This self-guided nature trail in the Kanepuu Preserve (described above) is about a 10- to 15-minute walk through eight stations, or interpretive signs explaining the natural or cultural significance of what you're seeing. The trail head is clearly marked on Polihua Road on the way to the Garden of the Gods. Kanepuu is one of the last remaining examples of the type of forest that once covered the dry lowlands throughout the state. There are some 49 plant species here that are found only in Hawaii. At press time, the Kanepuu Preserve was closed but had plans for reopening, with guided hikes soon. There are also plans to reconstruct the self-guided trails and signage, which have fallen into serious disrepair, but no dates or projections were available at press time.

GUIDED HIKES

The **Lodge at Koele** (© 808/565-4000; www.fourseasons.com/lanai) offers a 2-hour Koloiki Ridge nature hike through 5 miles of the upland forests of Koele at 10am daily. The fee is $30. It's considered moderate, with some uphill and downhill hiking.

Camping at Hulopoe Beach Park

There is only one legal place to camp on Lanai: **Hulopoe Beach Park,** which is owned by Castle and Cooke Resorts. To camp in this exquisite beach park, with its crescent-shaped white-sand beach bordered by kiawe trees, contact Doug Stevenson, Castle and Cooke Resorts, P.O. Box 630310, Lanai City, HI 96763 (© 808/565-3000, ext. 3315). There's a $25 registration fee, plus a charge of $10 per person, per night. Hulopoe has eight campsites; each can accommodate up to five people. Facilities include restrooms, running water, showers, barbecue areas, and picnic tables.

GOLF & OTHER OUTDOOR ACTIVITIES

Golf

Cavendish Golf Course 🎁 This quirky, par-36, 9-hole public course lacks not only a clubhouse and club pros, but also tee times, score cards, and club rentals. To play, just show up, put a donation into the little wooden box next to the first tee, and hit away. The 3,071-yard, E. B. Cavendish–designed course was built by the Dole plantation in 1947 for its employees. The greens are a bit bumpy, but the views of Lanai are great and the temperatures usually quite mild.

Next to the Lodge at Koele in Lanai City. No phone. Suggested donation $5–$10.

The Challenge at Manele ★★ This target-style, desert-links course, designed by Jack Nicklaus, is one of the most challenging courses in the state. Check out the local rules: "No retrieving golf balls from the 150-foot cliffs on the ocean holes 12, 13, or 17," and "All whales, axis deer, and other wild animals are considered immovable obstructions." That's just a hint of the unique experience you'll have on this course, which is routed among lava outcroppings, archaeological sites, kiawe groves, and *ilima* trees. The five sets of staggered tees pose a challenge to everyone from the casual golfer to the pro. Facilities include a clubhouse, pro shop, rentals, practice area, lockers, and showers.

Next to the Four Seasons Resort Lanai at Manele Bay. www.golfonlanai.com/manele. ☏ **808/ 565-2222.** Greens fees $225 nonguests, $210 resort guests.

The Experience at Koele ★★   This traditional par-72 course, designed by Greg Norman with fairway architecture by Ted Robinson, has very different front and back 9 holes. Mother Nature reigns throughout: You'll see Cook Island and Norfolk pines, indigenous plants, and lots of water—seven lakes, flowing streams, cascading waterfalls, and one green (the 17th) completely surrounded by a lake. All goes well until you hit the signature hole, number 8, where you tee off from a 250-foot elevated tee to a fairway bordered by a lake on the right and trees and dense shrubs on the left. After that, the back 9 holes drop dramatically through ravines filled with pine, koa, and eucalyptus trees. The grand finale, the par-5 18th, features a green rimmed by waterfalls that flow into a lake on the left side. To level the playing field, there are four different sets of tees. Facilities include a clubhouse, a pro shop, rentals, a practice area, lockers, and showers.

Next to the Lodge at Koele in Lanai City. www.golfonlanai.com/koele. ☏ **808/565-4653.** Greens fees $225 nonguests, $210 resort guests. Closed Mon–Tues.

Biking

The **Lodge at Koele** (☏ **808/565-4552**) rents cruiser bikes for $10 an hour to resort guests only.

Horseback Riding

Horses can take you to many places in Lanai's unique landscape that are otherwise unreachable. The **Four Seasons Lanai Resort's Stables at Koele** (☏ **808/565-4424**) offers various daily rides, including slow, gentle group excursions starting at $110 for a 1½-hour **Paniolo Trail Ride,** which takes you into the hills surrounding Koele. You'll meander through guava groves and ironwood trees; catch glimpses of axis deer, quail, wild turkeys, and Santa Gertrudis cattle; and end with panoramic views of Maui and Lanai. Private 1-hour rides can be arranged for $200 per person; 2-hour sunset rides go for $250 per person. Long pants and closed-toe shoes (like running shoes) are required, and safety helmets are provided. Bring a jacket—the weather is chilly and rain is frequent. Children must be at least 9 years old and 4 feet tall, and riders cannot weigh more than 225 pounds.

Horses allow you a chance to visit landscapes that are otherwise unreachable on Lanai.

Tennis

Public courts, lit for night play, are available in Lanai City at no charge; call ☏ **808/565-6979** for reservations. If you're staying at the Lodge at Koele or at Manele Bay, you can take advantage of the lodge's three new Premiere Cushion outdoor hard courts, with complimentary use of Prince racquets, balls, and bottled water. You're also invited to experience the tennis center at the Four Seasons Resort Lanai at Manele Bay, which offers a full pro shop, use of a ball machine, and weekly tennis mixers and tournaments. Courts are $20 per person for resort guests (not open to non-guests). For information, call ☎ **808/565-2072.**

WHERE TO EAT

Lanai is a curious mix of innocence and sophistication, with strong cross-cultural elements that liven up its culinary offerings. You can dine like a sultan on this island, but be prepared for high prices. The tony hotel restaurants require deep pockets, and there are only a handful of other options.

Very Expensive

Main Dining Room ★★★ NEW AMERICAN   The former Formal Dining Room has been revamped under the Four Seasons management and has a new menu. However, the relaxing setting remains, with a roaring fire, bountiful sprays of orchids, sienna-colored walls, and a waitstaff serving in hushed voices. The menu highlights American favorites. The appetizers are so tempting, you could make a meal from the variety of choices: seared diver scallops with sweet spring-pea blini, foie gras and black-truffle parfait, and lava rock–seared Lanai venison. The entrees vary according to the season; when I dined here, the menu included Maui lavender honey–roasted duck breast, mustard-and-herb-roasted rack of lamb, and a buttered poached lobster from the Big Island. The service is impeccable, the atmosphere relaxing. But don't forget your platinum credit card—you'll need it.

At the Four Seasons Resort Lanai, The Lodge at Koele. www.fourseasons.com/koele/dining. ☎ **808/565-4580.** Reservations required. Resort attire recommended; collared shirts and closed-toe footwear requested for men. Main courses $43–$65; 4-course tasting menu $89. AE, DC, MC, V. Fri–Tues 6–9:30pm.

Expensive

Fresco ★ ITALIAN   The former Ocean Grille at the Four Seasons Resort Lanai at Manele Bay has been remodeled and expanded and is now open for lunch and dinner. Located just off the pool, the casual, open-air, Italian-style bistro serves interesting lunches like wraps and sandwiches (such as veggie panini with mushrooms, red peppers, mozzarella cheese, and zucchini), pizza, angus or mahimahi burgers, or fresh-catch fish and chips. At dinner, watch the sun set and the stars come out as you dine on fresh local fish tapenade, pasta dishes, or veal roulade with prosciutto, sage, and polenta.

At the Four Seasons Resort Lanai at Manele Bay. www.fourseasons.com/manelebay/dining. Main ☎ **808/565-2092.** courses $10–$20 lunch, $15–$35 dinner. AE, MC, V. Sun–Mon and Thurs–Fri 11am–4pm and 6–9:30pm, cocktails and antipasti 4–6pm.

Hulopoe Court ★★ HAWAII REGIONAL   This is Manele Bay's informal dining room. It serves one of the best breakfast buffets I've seen in Hawaii, with everything from an omelet station to breakfast meats, daily pancakes, potatoes, rice, and local tropical fruit. The dinner menu leans to upscale steakhouse fare, with choices like grilled mahimahi, mashed potatoes and lime butter; beef tenderloin with Hamakua mushrooms, potato purée, and bordelaise; and barbecued baby back ribs with slaw and cheddar and truffle twice-baked potatoes.

At the Four Seasons Resort Lanai at Manele Bay. www.fourseasons.com/manelebay/dining. © **808/565-2290.** Reservations recommended for dinner. Resort attire recommended. Breakfast main courses $17–$24, buffet $24–$46. AE, DC, MC, V. Daily 7–10am and 6–9:30pm.

Terrace ★★ AMERICAN   Located next to the Main Dining Room in the Lodge at Koele, between the 35-foot-high Great Hall and a wall of glass looking out over prim English gardens, this wonderful spot is the lodge's "casual" dining room. The Terrace is far from your typical hotel restaurant—the menu may be fancy for comfort food, but it does, indeed, comfort. Hearty breakfasts of waffles and cereals, fresh pineapple from the nearby Palawai Basin, Paniola rancheros, and traditional Benedict make a grand start to the day. Dinner choices include skirt steak, meatloaf, roasted chicken, fresh fish of the day, and a vegetarian selection (ricotta and local mushroom risotto with basil and truffle oils).

At the Four Seasons Resort Lanai, The Lodge at Koele. www.fourseasons.com/koele/dining. © **808/565-4580.** Reservations recommended. Resort attire (no T-shirts or flip-flops) recommended. Main courses $16–$24 breakfast, $14–$21 lunch, $27–$50 dinner. AE, DC, MC, V. Daily 7am–2pm and 6–9:30pm.

Moderate

The Challenge at Manele Clubhouse ★ PACIFIC RIM   The view from the alfresco tables here may be the best on the island, encompassing Kahoolawe, Haleakala (on Maui), and, on an especially clear day, the peaks of Mauna Kea and Mauna Loa on the Big Island. You can lunch on salads and sandwiches (Asian tuna salad with grilled ahi, turkey club sandwich, clubhouse burgers with caramelized onions and cheese) or on more substantial entrees, ranging from fish and chips to blackened fish tacos. The clubhouse is casual, the view of the ocean is awe-inspiring, and it's a great gathering place.

At the Challenge at Manele Golf Course. www.fourseasons.com/manelebay/dining. © **808/565-2230.** Reservations recommended. Main courses $15–$25. AE, DC, MC, V. Daily 11am–3pm.

Lanai City Grille ★★ CAJUN/COUNTRY   Celebrated Maui chef Bev Gannon (Haliimaile General Store, Joe's) redesigned the menu in this cute eatery, where the decor consists of pine-paneled walls, chintz curtains, and a fireplace. The menu sticks to whatever is in season and fresh that day, from the fish and seafood to meats and rotisserie chicken.

At the Hotel Lanai, 828 Lanai Ave., Lanai City. www.hotellanai.com. © **808/565-7211.** Reservations recommended. Main courses $28–$40. AE, MC, V. Wed–Sun 5–9pm.

Inexpensive

Blue Ginger Cafe COFFEE SHOP   Famous for its mahimahi sandwiches and inexpensive omelets, Blue Ginger is a very local, very casual, and very reasonably priced alternative to Lanai's fancy hotel restaurants. The four tables on the front porch face the cool Norfolk pines of Dole Park and are always filled with locals who talk story from morning to night. The offerings are solid, no-nonsense, everyday fare: fried saimin (no MSG), very popular burgers on homemade buns, and mahimahi with capers and mushrooms. Blue Ginger also serves a tasty

French toast made with homemade bread and a surprisingly good stir-fried vegetable dish.

409 Seventh St. (at Ilima St.), Lanai City. www.bluegingercafelanai.com. (℗ **808/565-6363.** Main courses under $17 lunch, under $18 dinner. No credit cards. Mon and Thurs–Fri 6am–8pm; Tues–Wed 6am–2pm; Sat–Sun 6:30am–8pm.

Canoes Lanai LOCAL   This ma-and-pa eatery may have changed its name (it used to be Tanigawa's), but it remains the landmark that it's been since the 1920s. In those days, the tiny storefront sold canned goods and cigarettes; the 10 tables, hamburgers, and Filipino food came later. This hole in the wall is a local institution, with a reputation for serving local-style breakfasts. The fare—fried rice, omelets, short stacks, and simple ham and eggs—is more greasy spoon than gourmet, but it's definitely budget-friendly.

419 Seventh St., Lanai City. (℗ **808/565-6537.** Reservations not accepted. Main courses under $14 breakfast, $3–$8 lunch. No credit cards. Sun–Thurs 6:30am–1pm; Fri–Sat 6:30am–8pm.

Coffee Works ★ COFFEEHOUSE   Oahu's popular Ward Warehouse coffeehouse has opened this branch on Lanai, with a menu of espresso drinks, ice cream (including local brands), and a small selection of pastries. It's Lanai City's gathering place, a tiny cafe with tables and benches on a pleasing wooden deck just a stone's throw from Dole Park. Formerly a plantation house, the structure fits in with the surrounding plantation homes in the heart of Lanai City. There are some nice gift items available, including T-shirts, tea infusers, teapots, cookies, and gourmet coffees.

604 Ilima St. (across from the post office), Lanai City. (℗ **808/565-6962.** Most items under $9. AE, DC, DISC, MC, V. Mon–Sat 7am–3pm.

Pele's Other Garden ★★ DELI/BISTRO   Owners Mark and Barbara have turned this small sandwich shop into a popular full-scale deli and bistro. Daily soup and menu specials, excellent pizza, fresh organic produce, and special items, such as top-quality black-bean burritos, make Pele's Other Garden a Lanai City must. Sandwiches are made as wraps or with whole-wheat, rye, sourdough, or French bread, all baked on the island and delivered fresh daily. In the evening, you can dine on china at cloth-covered tables, and the menu expands to include pastas (bow-tie pasta with butterflied garlic shrimp, fettuccine with smoked salmon), pizza, and salads. Beer and wines by the glass (from $6) and a full bar were recently added.

Dole Park, 811 Houston St., Lanai City. www.pelesothergarden.com. (℗ **888/764-3354** or 808/565-9628. Main courses $8–$12 lunch, $17–$20 dinner; pizza from $9. AE, DISC, MC, V. Mon–Fri 11am–3pm and 5–8pm; bar menu 4:30–6:30pm.

SHOPPING

Central Bakery ★ 🎁   This is the mother lode of the island's baked delights—the bakery that is, well, central to Lanai's dining pleasure. If you've noshed on the fantastic sandwiches at the Terrace at the Lodge at Koele or any of the stellar desserts at the lodge's Main Dining Room or at the Four Seasons Resort Lanai at Manele Bay, you've enjoyed goodies from Central Bakery. The bakery supplies all breads, all breakfast pastries, specialty ice creams and sorbets, all banquet desserts, and restaurant desserts on the island. Although it's not your standard retail outlet, you can call in advance, place your order, and pick it up. The staff prefers

Dis 'N Dat is a great place to look for gifts.

as much notice as possible (preferably 48 hr.). Breads (most priced at $6.50) range from walnut onion to roasted potato bacon to olive onion. The bakery also has cookies (chocolate chip, oatmeal, coconut—all for $2), brownies, muffins, croissants (including chocolate croissants), Danishes, and scones, plus an assortment of breakfast pastries (pineapple turnover, hazelnut roll, mascarpone apricot Danish, pistachio chocolate roll, and others). 434 8th St., Lanai. ℂ **808/565-3782.** All orders and pickups go through Richard's Market (see below).

Dis 'N Dat ★★ 🎁 Dis (Barry) and Dat (Susie) visited Lanai from Florida to look at buying a retirement home. They found their home and moved to Lanai to retire. Retirement didn't last. A few years later, outgoing Barry and his wife started searching for unusual, finely crafted teak and exotic wood sculptures and carvings. Along the way, they took a shine to mobiles and wind chimes—the more outrageous, the better. Then they started collecting handmade jewelry, stained glass, and unique garden ornaments and home decor. All this led to this eclectic store, which you have to see to believe. Meeting Barry alone is worth the trip. You'll find T-shirts, pottery, ceramics, batik scarves, hula lamps and whimsical dragonfly lamps, woven baskets, and even waterfalls. There is also a huge collection of Hawaii slipper necklaces, earrings, anklets, and bracelets. You can't miss the vivid green shop with hanging chimes and mobiles leading the way to the front door. 418 Eighth Ave. (at Kilele St.), Lanai City. www.disndatshop.com. ℂ **866/DIS-N-DAT** (347-6328) or 808/565-9170.

International Food & Clothing This store sells the basics: groceries, housewares, T-shirts, hunting and fishing supplies, over-the-counter drugs, wine and liquor, paper goods, and hardware, and even has a takeout lunch counter. I was pleasantly surprised by the extraordinary candy and bubble gum section, the beautiful local bananas in the small produce section, the surprisingly extensive selection of yuppie soft drinks (Sobe, Snapple, and others), and the best knife sharpener I've seen. 833 Ilima Ave., Lanai City. ℂ **808/565-6433.**

The Lanai Art Center offers classes in an array of mediums, plus a gallery with works by Lanai residents for sale.

Lanai Art Center ★ 🎁   This wonderful center was organized in 1989 to provide a place where both residents and visitors can come to create art. The center offers classes and studio time in ceramics, painting and drawing, calligraphy, woodworking, photography, silk and textile painting, watercolor, and glass. There's an impressive schedule of visiting instructors, from writers to folk artists (quilting, lei making, and instrument making) to oil painters. Check out the reasonably priced classes (generally in the $25 range) or browse the gallery for excellent deals on works by Lanai residents. 339 Seventh St., Lanai City. www.lanaiart.org ⓒ **808/565-7503.**

Lanai Marketplace   Everyone on Lanai, it seems, is a backyard farmer. From 7 to 11am or noon on Saturday, they all head to this shady square to sell their dewy-fresh produce, home-baked breads, plate lunches, and handicrafts. This is Lanai's version of the green market: petite in scale (like the island) but charming, and growing. Dole Park, Lanai City.

The Local Gentry ★★ 🎁   Jenna (Gentry) Majkus's wonderful boutique was the first of its kind on the island, featuring clothing and accessories that are not the standard resort-shop fare. (Visiting and local women alike make a beeline for this store.) You'll find fabulous silk aloha shirts by Kahala, inexpensive sarongs, and fabulous socks. There are also great T-shirts, jewelry, bath products, picture frames, jeans, and offbeat sandals. The most recent additions are wonderful children's clothes. 363 Seventh St., Lanai City. ⓒ **808/565-9130.**

Mike Carroll Gallery   If he is on the island, you'll find Mike Carroll at work here on his original oil paintings. After a successful 22-year career as a professional artist in Chicago, Carroll moved to Lanai and has been painting the beauty and the lifestyle of the island ever since. You'll find an extensive selection of his original work, some limited editions, prints, and notecards, plus the work of a dozen or so of Maui's and Lanai's top artists and even some locally made, one-of-a-kind jewelry. 443 Seventh St., Lanai City. www.mikecarrollgallery.com. ℂ **808/565-7122.**

Pine Isle Market   A local landmark for two generations, Pine Isle specializes in locally caught fresh fish, but you can also find fresh herbs and spices, canned goods, electronic games, ice cream, toys, zoris, diapers, paint, cigars, and other basic essentials of work and play. The fishing section is outstanding, with every lure imaginable. 356 Eighth St., Lanai City. ℂ **808/565-6488.**

Richard's Market   The Tamashiros' family business has been on the square since 1946; not much has changed over the years. Richard's is a general store with a grocery section, paper products, ethnic foods, meats (mostly frozen), liquor, toys, film, cosmetics, fishing gear, sunscreens, clothing, kitchen utensils, T-shirts, and other miscellany. Half a wall is lined with an extraordinary selection of fishhooks and anglers' needs. Aloha shirts, aloha-print zoris, fold-up lauhala mats, and gourmet breads from the Central Bakery (see above) are among the countless good things at Richard's. 434 Eighth St., Lanai City. ℂ **808/565-3780.**

LANAI AFTER DARK

The only regular nightlife venues are the two resorts, the Lodge at Koele and Four Seasons Resort Lanai at Manele Bay.

The **Lodge at Koele** has stepped up its live entertainment. In front of the manorial fireplaces in the Great Hall, local artists serenade listeners, who sip port and fine liqueurs while sinking into plush chairs, with contemporary Hawaiian, classical, and other genres of music. The special programs are on weekends, but some form of nightly entertainment takes place throughout the week, from 7 to 9pm. Down at the Manele Bay resort, the **Ahi Ahi Lounge** also has live entertainment nightly from 7 to 9pm.

Occasionally, special events will bring in a few more nightlife options. During the annual **Pineapple Festival,** generally the first weekend in July, some of Hawaii's best musicians arrive to show their support for Lanai (see "Maui, Molokai & Lanai Calendar of Events," p. 46). The **Aloha Festival** (www.aloha festivals.com) takes place at the end of September or during the first week in October, and the **Christmas Festival** is held on the first Saturday in December. For details on these festivals, contact the **Lanai Visitors Bureau,** c/o Maui Visitors Bureau, 1727 Wili Pa Loop, Wailuku, Maui 96793; ℂ **800/947-4774** or 808/565-7600; fax 808/565-9316; www.gohawaii.com/lanai.

WHERE TO STAY

The majority of the accommodations are located "in the village," as residents call Lanai City. Above the village is the luxurious Lodge at Koele (now managed by Four Seasons), while down the hill at Hulopoe Bay are two options: the equally luxurious Four Seasons Resort Lanai at Manele Bay or tent camping under the stars at the park.

In addition to the choices listed below, consider a vacation-home rental like **Hale O Lanai,** in Lanai City (ℂ **808/247-3637;** ww.myhawaiibeachfront. com). It has a fully equipped two-bedroom vacation rental that sleeps up to six; rates range from $125 to $150, plus a $65 cleaning fee.

Don't forget to add 13.42% in taxes to all accommodations bills. Parking is free.

Expensive

Four Seasons Resort Lanai at Manele Bay ★★★ ☺

Located on a sun-washed southern bluff overlooking Hulopoe Beach, this luxury resort enjoys one of Hawaii's best stretches of golden sand. Although not located on the same level as the beach, the U-shaped hotel steps down the hillside to the pool and the beach below. In addition to the ocean view, the garden units (with lush flora, man-made waterfalls, lotus ponds, and streams) are equally serene and promise a relaxing vacation. On the other side, it's bordered by golf greens. The place is a real oasis against the dry, Arizona-like heat of Lanai's south coast.

Designed as a traditional luxury beachfront hotel, it features open, airy rooms, each with a breathtaking view of the big blue Pacific. Sea charts, potted palms, soft camel-hued club chairs, hand-woven kilim rugs, and murals depicting scenes from Hawaiian history fill the lobby. Redone in the clean, crisp style of an elegant Hawaiian resort, the oversize guest rooms have 40-inch flatscreen TVs, huge marble bathrooms, and semiprivate lanai. This resort is much less formal than the Lodge at Koele up the hill and attracts more families. Speaking of families, in addition to the "Kids for All Seasons" child-care programs, the hotel features a teen center with video games, computers, a small pool table, and a 54-inch TV.

The spa offers a variety of massages, facials, wraps, and scrubs (don't miss the signature Ali'i banana-coconut scrub). In addition, the Four Seasons has added a 1,500-square-foot fitness center with the latest cardiovascular and strength-training equipment, free weights, and a wood-floored studio for classes (spinning, yoga, Pilates, and meditation).

1 Manele Bay Rd., P.O. Box 631380, Lanai City, HI 96763. www.fourseasons.com/lanai. © **800/321-4666** or 808/565-2000. Fax 808/565-2483. 236 units. $395–$895 double; from $1,050 suite. Extra person $100. Children 17 and under stay free in parent's room. Packages available. AE, DC, MC, V. Airport shuttle $48 for unlimited use. **Amenities:** 4 restaurants; bar with breathtaking views and live music; babysitting; children's program; concierge; fitness center with classes; golf at the Jack Nicklaus–designed Challenge at Manele; Jacuzzi; large outdoor pool; room service; full spa; tennis courts; complimentary snorkeling equipment. *In room:* A/C, TV/DVD, hair dryer, Wi-Fi ($10–$18 per day), minibar.

Four Seasons Resort Lanai, The Lodge at Koele ★★★ ☺

After some $50 million in renovations, the Four Seasons took over the management of the former Lodge at Koele. This inn, which resembles a grand English country estate, was built in 1991 and needed the makeover. All 102 guest rooms were totally redone, a game room was added, the grounds have been spruced up, and a pagoda imported from China has been constructed on the sprawling English gardens' grounds (not my taste, but I'm sure it will be the backdrop for hundreds of wedding photos).

Inside, heavy timbers, beamed ceilings, and the two huge stone fireplaces of the Great Hall complete the look. Overstuffed furniture sits invitingly around the fireplaces, richly patterned rugs adorn the floor, and museum-quality art hangs on the walls. The guest rooms continue the English theme with four-poster beds, sitting areas (complete with window seats), formal writing desks, and bathrooms with oversize tubs. All rooms have signature Four Seasons beds, 42-inch flatscreen televisions, and high-speed Internet access.

The Four Seasons also retrained the staff to their level of excellent service. Don't expect the sophisticated service you'd get in most Four Seasons around the world—most of the staff have lived on Lanai for generations. Instead, you'll find a charming display of aloha spirit and a strong desire to make sure your vacation is perfect.

Before you reach for the phone, understand that this hotel is not located at the beach (see the Manele Bay resort, above), but rather in the cool mist of the mountains, on 21 acres at 1,700 feet above sea level, 8 miles inland, and a 20- to 30-minute drive to a beach. In the winter, temperatures can drop into the 50s (don't worry, the rooms have heat as well as air-conditioning). Most guests here are looking for relaxation: sitting on the rattan chairs on the porch, reading, watching the turkeys mosey across the manicured lawns, strolling through the Japanese hillside garden, or watching the sun sink into the Pacific.

There are plenty of activities here and at the sister resort down the hill, Manele, so you'll get the best of both hotels. Other pluses include a shuttle to the airport, golf courses, beach, and Four Seasons Resort Lanai at Manele Bay (for a one-time $48 fee), complimentary coffee and tea in the lobby, formal afternoon tea, and twice-daily maid service. Guests can take advantage of the croquet lawns, horseback riding, hiking trails, and garden walks.

1 Keomoku Hwy., P.O. Box 631380, Lanai City, HI 96763. www.fourseasons.com/lanai. ☏ 800/321-4666 or 808/565-4000. Fax 808/565-4561. 102 units. $310–$415 double; from $895 suite. Extra person $100. Children 17 and under stay free in parent's room. Packages available. AE, DC, MC, V. **Amenities:** 2 restaurants; bar with live music; babysitting; bike rentals; children's program; concierge; fitness room; golf at Greg Norman–designed Experience at Koele (p. 357); Jacuzzi; outdoor pool; room service; tennis courts; complimentary snorkeling equipment at Four Seasons Resort Lanai at Manele Bay. *In room:* A/C, TV/DVD, fridge, hair dryer, minibar, Wi-Fi ($10–$18 per day).

Moderate

Hotel Lanai ★ ☺ This hotel lacks the facilities of the two resorts described above, but it's perfect for families and other vacationers who can't afford to spend $310 to $895 (and up) a night. In fact, if you're looking for the old-fashioned aloha that Lanai City is famous for, this is the place to stay. Built in the 1920s for VIP plantation guests, this clapboard plantation-era relic has retained its quaint character and lives on as a country inn.

The entire hotel underwent renovations several years ago—repainting, remodeling, and a general sprucing up. The guest rooms, although extremely small, are clean and outfitted with Hawaiian quilts, wood furniture, and ceiling fans (but no air-conditioning or TVs). The most popular are the lanai units, which feature a shared lanai with the room next door. All rooms have private shower-only bathrooms. The one-bedroom cottage, with a TV and bathtub, is perfect for a small family.

The hotel serves as a down-home crossroads where total strangers meet local folks on the lanai to drink beer and talk story or play the ukulele and sing into the dark, tropical night. Often a curious visitor in search of an authentic experience will join the party and discover Lanai's very Hawaiian heart. Guests have the use of the shuttle to both Four Seasons Resorts, the golf courses (at which they get the same lower rates given to guests at the two resorts), and the beach for a one-time $35 fee.

828 Lanai Ave. (P.O. Box 630520), Lanai City, HI 96763. www.hotellanai.com. © **800/795-7211** or 808/565-7211. Fax 808/565-6450. 11 units. $99–$169 double; $199 cottage double. Extra person $50. Rates include continental breakfast. AE, MC, V. **Amenities:** Excellent restaurant (Lanai City Grille, p. 359); intimate bar; access to 2 resort golf courses on the island; nearby tennis courts; complimentary snorkeling equipment, unlimited shuttle service for entire stay $35. *In room:* Wi-Fi (free).

PLANNING YOUR TRIP TO MAUI

Maui has so many places to explore, things to do, sights to see—it can be bewildering to plan your trip with so much vying for your attention. Where to start? That's where I come in. In the pages that follow, I've compiled everything you need to know to plan your ideal trip to Hawaii.

I strongly advise you to **fly directly into Maui;** doing so can save you a 2-hour layover in Honolulu and another plane ride. If you're heading to Molokai or Lanai, you'll have the easiest connections if you fly into Honolulu.

Next, be sure to read my descriptions of the various areas of Maui (p. 74), to make sure that the destination matches your dreams. Maui accommodations can vary from landscaped luxury resorts in sunny, dry areas to romantic lush tropical rainforests.

And finally, I recommend booking a rental car as soon as you make your plane and hotel reservations. Due to the downturn in the economy, car-rental agencies have cut back on the number of available cars.

GETTING THERE & GETTING AROUND

Getting to Maui

BY PLANE

If you think of the island of Maui as the shape of a head and shoulders of a person, you'll probably arrive at its neck, at **Kahului Airport** (OGG). If you're headed for Molokai or Lanai, you'll have to connect through Honolulu.

For a list of airline websites, see "Airline Websites," at the end of this chapter.

As of press time, the following airlines fly directly from the U.S. mainland to Kahului: **United/Continental Airlines** offers daily nonstop flights from San Francisco and Los Angeles; **Hawaiian Airlines** has flights from San Diego, Portland, and Seattle; **Alaska Airlines** offers flights from Anchorage to Seattle to Kahului; **American Airlines** flies from Los Angeles; and **Delta Air Lines** offers direct flights from Oakland, and flights from San Francisco via Los Angeles.

Other carriers fly to Honolulu, where you'll have to pick up an interisland flight to Maui. (The airlines listed in the preceding paragraph also offer many more flights to Honolulu from additional cities on the mainland.) **Hawaiian Airlines** and **go!Mokulele** offer jet service from Honolulu.

ARRIVING AT THE AIRPORT

If there's a long wait at baggage claim, step over to the state-operated **Visitor Information Center,** where you can ask about island activities and pick up brochures and the latest issue of *This Week Maui,* which features great regional maps of the islands. After collecting your bags from the poky, automated carousels, take a deep breath, proceed to the curbside rental-car pickup area, and wait for the appropriate rental-agency shuttle van to take you a half-mile away to the

PREVIOUS PAGE: **Arriving in Hawaii.**

rental-car checkout desk. (All major rental companies have branches at Kahului; see "Getting Around Maui," below.)

If you're not renting a car, the cheapest way to get to your hotel is via **SpeediShuttle** (✆ 877/242-5777; www.speedishuttle.com), which can take you between Kahului Airport and all the major resorts between 6am and 11pm daily. You'll see taxis outside the airport terminal, but note that they are quite expensive—expect to spend around $92 for a ride from Kahului to Kaanapali and $60 to Wailea.

If possible, avoid landing on Maui between 3 and 6pm, when the working stiffs on Maui are "*pau* work" (finished with work) and a major traffic jam occurs at the first intersection getting out of the airport.

AGRICULTURAL SCREENING AT THE AIRPORTS When you leave, baggage and passengers bound for the mainland must be screened by agricultural officials. Officials will confiscate local produce, like avocados, bananas, and mangoes, in the name of fruit fly control. Pineapples, coconuts, and papayas inspected and certified for export; boxed flowers; leis without seeds; and processed foods (macadamia nuts, coffee, jams, dried fruit, and the like) will pass.

Getting Around Maui

INTERISLAND FLIGHTS

If you must go through Honolulu, you will need to get an interisland flight to Maui. Since the September 11, 2001, terrorist attacks, the major interisland carriers have cut way back on the number of interisland flights. The airlines warn you to show up at least 90 minutes before your flight, and believe me, with all the security inspections, you will need all 90 minutes to catch your flight.

Hawaii has two major interisland carriers: **Hawaiian Airlines** (✆ 800/367-5320; www.hawaiianair.com) and **go!Mokulele** (✆ 888/I-FLY-GO-2 [435-9462]; www.iflygo.com).

Visitors to Molokai and Lanai have three commuter airlines to choose from: **Island Air** (✆ 800/323-3345; www.islandair.com), **go!Mokulele** (✆ 888/I-FLY-GO-2 [435-9462]; www.iflygo.com), and **PW Express** (✆ 888/866-5022

📎 **Cruising Through the Islands**

If you're looking for a taste of several islands, consider a cruise ship. There are a couple that tour the island: **Norwegian Cruise Line** (✆ 800/327-7030; www.ncl.com) and the small **Adventure Smith Explorations** (✆ 800/728-2875; www.AdventureSmithExplorations.com). Norwegian's 2,240-passenger ship *Pride of America* circles the Hawaiian Islands, stopping on the Big Island, Maui, Kauai, and Oahu. Prices range from $1,100 to $2,600. The smaller Adventure Smith

Explorations has a 145-foot boat, *Safari Explorer,* which holds 36 passengers in 18 staterooms for its 8-day and 11-day cruises around the islands. Rates range from $5,000 per person to $8,600 per person. The disadvantage of a cruise is that you won't be able to see any of the islands in depth or at leisure; the advantage is that you can spend your days exploring the island where the ship is docked and your nights aboard ship sailing to the next port of call.

or 808/873-0877; www.pacificwings.com), which all serve Hawaii's small interisland airports on Maui, Molokai, and Lanai. However, I have to warn you that I have not had stellar service on Island Air and recommend that you book another carrier.

Some large airlines offer transatlantic or transpacific passengers special discount tickets under the name **Visit USA,** which allows mostly one-way travel from one U.S. destination to another at very low prices. Unavailable in the U.S., these discount tickets must be purchased abroad in conjunction with your international fare. This system is the easiest, fastest, and cheapest way to see the country.

BY CAR

Hawaii has some of the more expensive car-rental rates in the country. (Even worse is the island of Lanai, where they're very expensive.) To rent a car in Hawaii, you must be at least 25 years of age and have a valid driver's license and credit card. *Note:* If you're visiting from abroad and plan to rent a car in the United States, keep in mind that foreign driver's licenses are usually recognized in the U.S., but you should get an international one if your home license is not in English.

At Maui's airport in Kahului, you'll find most major car-rental agencies, including **Alamo, Avis, Budget, Dollar, Enterprise, Hertz, National,** and **Thrifty.** It's almost always cheaper to rent a car at the airport than in Waikiki or through your hotel (unless there's one already included in your package deal).

Rental cars are usually at a premium on Kauai, Molokai, and Lanai and may be sold out on the neighbor islands on holiday weekends, so be sure to book well ahead.

GASOLINE   Gas prices in Hawaii, always much higher than on the U.S. mainland, vary from island to island. At this writing, average prices for regular gas in Maui are about $4.49 per gallon (except in Hana, where gas was around $5). On Molokai gas was $5.19 and on Lanai gas was $5.49. *Note:* Taxes are already included in the printed price. Check www.gasbuddy.com to find the cheapest gas in your area.

INSURANCE   Hawaii is a no-fault state, which means that if you don't have collision-damage insurance, you are required to pay for all damages before you leave the state, whether or not the accident was your fault. Your personal car insurance may provide rental-car coverage; check before you leave home. Bring your insurance identification card if you decline the optional insurance, which usually costs from $9 to $45 a day. Obtain the name of your company's local claim representative before you go. Some credit card companies also provide collision-damage insurance for their customers; check with yours before you rent.

DRIVING RULES   Hawaii state law mandates that all car passengers must wear a **seat belt,** and all infants must be strapped into a car seat. You'll pay a $50 fine if you don't buckle up. **Pedestrians** always have the right of way, even if they're not in the crosswalk. You can turn **right on red** after a full and complete stop, unless otherwise posted.

ROAD MAPS   The best and most detailed maps for activities are published by **Franko Maps** (www.frankosmaps.com); they feature a host of island maps, plus a terrific "Hawaiian Reef Creatures Guide" for snorkelers curious about those fish they spot underwater. Free road maps are published by *This Week Magazine,* a visitor publication available on Maui.

Another good source is the University of Hawaii Press maps, which include a detailed network of island roads, large-scale insets of towns, historical and contemporary points of interest, parks, beaches, and hiking trails. If you can't find them in a bookstore near you, contact **University of Hawaii Press,** 2840 Kolowalu St., Honolulu, HI 96822 (📞 888/ UHPRESS [847-7377]; www.uhpress.hawaii.edu). For topographic and other maps of the islands, go to the **Hawaii Geographic Society,** 49 S. Hotel St., Honolulu (📞 800/538-3950 or 808/538-3952; hawaiigeographic sociaty@gmail.com).

TIPS ON ACCOMMODATIONS

Maui offers all kinds of accommodations, from simple rooms in restored plantation homes and quaint cottages on the beach to luxurious oceanview condo units and opulent suites in beachfront resorts. Each type has its pluses and minuses, so before you book, make sure you know what you're getting into.

Types of Accommodations

HOTELS

In Maui, a "hotel" can indicate a wide range of options, from few or no on-site amenities to enough extras to qualify the place as a miniresort. Generally, a hotel offers daily maid service and has a restaurant, laundry facilities, a pool, and a sundries/convenience-type shop. Top hotels also have activities desks, concierge and valet services, room service, business centers, airport shuttles, bars and/or lounges, and perhaps a few more shops.

The advantages of staying in a hotel are privacy and convenience; the disadvantage is generally noise (either thin walls between rooms or loud music from a

---

questions TO PONDER

One of the toughest questions in Hawaii is, "What is the carrying capacity of the islands?" How much can be built before Hawaii becomes overbuilt, or unable to support the increased infrastructure and increased population? How many people can Hawaii hold, and how many visitors, before the beaches are too crowded, the lifestyle is gone, and the islands have more concrete than open green spaces?

Along those same lines, the people of Hawaii are constantly debating cultural issues vs. social issues. For example, currently laws regarding ancient burial sites can stop, reroute, or delay construction projects ranging from roads to shopping centers. How much do we protect and preserve vs. how much do we allow new infrastructure or buildings to be built to meet modern wants and needs?

lobby lounge late into the night). Hotels are often a short walk from the beach rather than right on the beachfront (although there are exceptions).

RESORTS

In Hawaii, a resort offers everything a hotel does—and more. You can expect direct beach access, with beach cabanas and lounge chairs; pools and a Jacuzzi; a spa and fitness center; restaurants, bars, and lounges; a 24-hour front desk; concierge, valet, and bellhop services; room service (often 24-hr.); an activities desk; tennis and golf; ocean activities; a business center; kids' programs; and more.

The advantages of a resort are that you have everything you could possibly want in the way of services and things to do; the disadvantage is that the price generally reflects this. And don't be misled by a name—just because a place is called "ABC Resort" doesn't mean it actually *is* a resort. Make sure you're getting what you pay for.

CONDOS

The roominess and convenience of a condo—which is usually a fully equipped, multiple-bedroom apartment—make this a great choice for families. Condominium properties in Maui generally consist of several apartments set in either a single high-rise or a cluster of low-rise units. Condos usually have amenities such as some maid service (ranging from daily to weekly; it may or may not be included in your rate), a pool, and an on-site front desk or a live-in property manager. Condos tend to be clustered in resort areas. There are some very high-end condos, but most are quite affordable, especially if you're traveling in a group.

The advantages of a condo are privacy, space, and conveniences—which usually include a full kitchen, a washer and dryer, a private phone, and more. The downsides are the standard lack of an on-site restaurant and the density of the units (vs. the privacy of a single-unit vacation rental).

BED & BREAKFASTS

Maui has a wide range of places that call themselves B&Bs: everything from a traditional B&B—several bedrooms in a home, with breakfast served in the morning—to what is essentially a vacation rental on an owner's property that comes with fixings for you to make your own breakfast. Make sure that the B&B you're booking matches your own mental picture. ***Note:*** Laundry facilities and private phones are not always available. I've reviewed lots of wonderful B&Bs in chapter 9. If you have to share a bathroom, I've spelled it out in the listings; otherwise, you can assume that you will have your own.

The advantages of a traditional B&B are its individual style and congenial atmosphere, with a host who's often happy to act as your own private concierge. In addition, they're usually an affordable way to go. The disadvantages are lack of privacy, usually a set time for breakfast, few amenities, and generally no maid service. Also, B&B owners typically require a minimum stay of 2 or 3 nights, and it's often a drive to the beach.

VACATION RENTALS

This is another great choice for families and for long-term stays. "Vacation rental" usually means that there will be no one on the property where you're staying. The actual accommodations can range from an apartment to an entire fully equipped house. Generally, vacation rentals allow you to settle in and make yourself at

---

---

home for a while. They have kitchen facilities (at least a kitchenette), on-site laundry facilities, and a phone; some also come with such extras as a TV, VCR or DVD player, and stereo.

The advantages of a vacation rental are complete privacy, your own kitchen (which can save you money on meals), and lots of conveniences. The disadvantages are a lack of an on-site property manager and generally no maid service; often a minimum stay is required (sometimes as much as a week). If you book a vacation rental, be sure that you have a 24-hour contact to call if the toilet won't flush or you can't figure out how to turn on the air-conditioning.

Using a Booking Agency vs. Doing It Yourself

If you don't have the time to call several places yourself to make sure they offer the amenities you'd like, you might consider using a booking agency.

A statewide booking agent for B&Bs is **Bed & Breakfast Hawaii** (© **800/ 733-1632** or 808/822-7771; fax 808/822-2723; www.bandb-hawaii.com), offering a range of accommodations from vacation homes to bed-and-breakfasts, starting at $65 a night. For vacation rentals, contact **Hawaii Beachfront Vacation Homes** (© **808/247-3637;** fax 808/235-2644; www.myhawaiibeachfront. com). **Hawaii Condo Exchange** (© **800/442-0404;** www.hawaiicondo exchange.com) acts as a consolidator for condo and vacation-rental properties.

GETTING MARRIED IN THE ISLANDS

The silky warm weather, the starry nights, the gentle trade winds caressing your skin—Maui is so romantic. That's probably why thousands of people get married on the island. Plus, after the ceremony, you're already on your honeymoon. And the members of your wedding party will most likely be delighted, since you've given them the perfect excuse for their own island vacation.

More than 20,000 marriages are performed annually on the islands; nearly half are for couples from somewhere else. The booming wedding business has spawned more than 70 companies that can help you organize a long-distance event and stage an unforgettable wedding, Hawaiian-style or your style. However, you can also plan your own island wedding, even from afar, and not spend a fortune doing it.

The Paperwork

The state of Hawaii has some very minimal procedures for obtaining a marriage license. The first thing you should do is contact the **Marriage License Office,** State Department of Health Bldg., 54 S. High St., Wailuku, HI 96793 (*C* **808/ 984-8210;** http://hawaii.gov/health/vital-records/vital-records/marriage/index. html), which is open Monday through Friday from 8am to 4pm. The office will no longer mail you the brochure *Getting Married;* you can download it from the website or contact a marriage-licensing agent closest to where you'll be staying in Hawaii (also listed on the website).

Once on Maui, the prospective bride and groom must go together to the marriage-licensing agent to get the license, which costs $60 and is good for 30 days. Both parties must be 15 years of age or older (anyone 15–17 years old must have proof of age, written consent of both parents, and written approval of the judge of the family court) and not more closely related than first cousins. That's it.

After a protracted legal battle and much discussion in the state legislature, civil unions of gay couples is legal as of January 1, 2012. In Hawaii, a civil union gives gay couples the same rights and obligations as heterosexual married couples at the state level.

Planning the Wedding

DOING IT YOURSELF

The marriage-licensing agents, who range from employees of the governor's satellite office in Kona to private individuals, are usually friendly, helpful people who can steer you to a nondenominational minister or marriage performer who's licensed by the state of Hawaii. These marriage performers are great sources of information for budget weddings. They usually know wonderful places to have a ceremony for free or for a nominal fee. For the names and addresses of marriage-licensing agents on Maui and Lanai, call *C* **808/984-8210;** on Molokai, call *C* **808/553-3200.**

If you don't want to use a wedding planner (see "Using a Wedding Planner," below), but you do want to make arrangements before you arrive on Maui, my best advice is to get a copy of the daily newspaper, the ***Maui News,*** P.O. Box 550, Wailuku, HI 96793 (*C* **808/244-3981;** www.mauinews.com). People willing and qualified to conduct weddings advertise in the classifieds. They're great sources of information, as they know the best places to have the ceremony and can recommend caterers, florists, and everything else you'll need.

USING A WEDDING PLANNER

Wedding planners—many of whom are marriage-licensing agents as well—can arrange everything for you, from a small, private outdoor affair to a full-blown formal ceremony in a tropical setting. They charge anywhere from $150 to a small fortune—it all depends on what you want.

Planners on Maui include **Hawaii Weddings** (*C* 800/859-0072; fax 808/ 891-1233; www.hawaiiweddings.com), **White Orchid Weddings** (*C* 800/242-9336; www.WhiteOrchidWeddings.com), **A Dream Wedding: Maui Style** (*C* **800/743-2777** or 808/661-1777; fax 808/876-0804; www.adreamwedding. net), **Romantic Maui Weddings** (*C* **800/808-4144** or 808/249-8484; fax 808/249-8383; www.justmauied.com), and **Dolphin Dream Weddings**

(📞 **800/793-2-WED** [2933] or 808/669-8787; www.dolphindreamweddings. com). For a more complete list, contact the Maui Visitors and Convention Bureau (📞 **800/525-MAUI** [6284]; www.gohawaii.com/maui). And for civil unions, **Gay Hawaiian Weddings** (📞 **800/859-0072;** fax 808/891-1233; www.GayHawaiiWedding.com). Many of the big resorts have their own coordinators on staff as well.

HEALTH & SAFETY

Hiking Safety

Hikers should always let someone know where they're heading, when they're going, and when they plan to return; too many hikers get lost in Hawaii because they don't let others know their basic plans. And make sure you know how strenuous the route and trail you will follow are—don't overestimate your ability.

Before you head out, always check weather conditions with the toll-free **National Weather Service** (📞 **866/944-5025** or check www.prh.noaa.gov) on Maui. Do not hike if rain or a storm is predicted; flash floods are common in Hawaii. Hike with a pal, never alone. Plan to finish your hike at least an hour before sunset; because Hawaii is so close to the equator, it does not have a twilight period, and thus it gets dark quickly after the sun sets. Wear hiking boots, a sun hat, clothes to protect you from the sun and from getting scratches, and high-SPF sunscreen on all exposed areas of skin. Take plenty of water, a basic first-aid kit, a snack, and a bag to pack out what you pack in. Stay on the trail. Watch your step. It's easy to slip off precipitous trails and into steep canyons. Many experienced hikers and boaters today pack a cellphone in case of emergency; just dial 📞 **911.**

Vog

The volcanic haze dubbed *vog* is caused by gases released when molten lava—from the continuous eruption of Kilauea volcano on the Big Island—pours into the ocean. When the winds shift, vog travels over to Maui. Some people claim that long-term exposure to the hazy, smoglike air causes bronchial ailments, but it's highly unlikely to cause you any harm in the course of your visit.

📎 Hey, No Smoking in Hawaii

Well, not *totally* no smoking, but Hawaii has one of the toughest laws against smoking in the U.S. It's against the law to smoke in public buildings, including airports, shopping malls, grocery stores, retail shops, buses, movie theaters, banks, convention facilities, and all government buildings and facilities. There is no smoking in restaurants, bars, and nightclubs. Most bed-and-breakfasts prohibit smoking indoors, and more and more hotels and resorts are becoming smoke free even in public areas. Also, there is no smoking within 20 feet of a doorway, window, or ventilation intake (so no hanging around outside a bar to smoke—you must go 20 ft. away). Even some beaches have no-smoking policies (and at those that do allow smoking, you'd better pick up your butts and not use the sand as your own private ashtray—or else face stiff fines). Breathing fresh, clear air is "in," while smoking in Hawaii is "out."

Don't Get Burned: Smart Tanning Tips

Hawaii's Caucasian population has the highest incidence of malignant melanoma (deadly skin cancer) in the world. And nobody is completely safe from the sun's harmful rays: All skin types and races can burn. To ensure that your vacation won't be ruined by a painful sunburn, be sure to wear a strong sunscreen that protects against both UVA and UVB rays at all times (look for zinc oxide, benzophenone, oxybenzone, sulisobenzone, titanium dioxide, or avobenzone in the list of ingredients). Wear a wide-brimmed hat and sunglasses. Keep infants under 6 months out of the sun completely, and slather older babies and children with strong sunscreen frequently.

If you do get a burn, aloe vera, cool compresses, cold baths, and benzocaine can help with the pain. Stay out of the sun until the burn is completely gone.

Ocean Safety

Because most people coming to Hawaii are unfamiliar with the ocean environment, they're often unaware of the natural hazards it holds. With just a few precautions, your ocean experience can be a safe and happy one. An excellent book is *All Stings Considered: First Aid and Medical Treatment of Hawaii's Marine Injuries,* by Craig Thomas and Susan Scott (University of Hawaii Press, 1997).

Note: Sharks are not a big problem in Hawaii; in fact, they appear so infrequently that locals look forward to seeing them. Since records have been kept, starting in 1779, there have been only about 100 shark attacks in Hawaii, of which 40% were fatal. Most attacks occurred after someone fell into the ocean from the shore or from a boat; in these cases, the sharks probably attacked after the person was dead. Here are the general rules for avoiding sharks: Don't swim at sunrise, at sunset, or where the water is murky due to stream runoff—sharks may mistake you for one of their usual meals. And don't swim where there are bloody fish in the water, as sharks become aggressive around blood.

The waters in Hawaii can range from as calm as glass to downright frightening (during storms); conditions usually fall somewhere in between. In general, expect rougher conditions in winter than in summer. Some 90% of the world's population tends toward seasickness. If you've never been out on a boat, or if you've been seasick in the past, you might want to heed the following suggestions:

- The day before you go out on a boat, avoid alcohol; caffeine; citrus and other acidic juices; and greasy, spicy, or hard-to-digest foods.

- Get a good night's sleep the night before.

- Take or use whatever seasickness prevention works best for you—medication, an acupressure wristband, ginger-root tea or capsules, or any combination. But do it **before you board;** once you set sail, it's generally too late.

- While you're on the boat, stay as low and as near the center of the boat as possible. Avoid the fumes (especially if it's a diesel boat); stay out in the fresh air and watch the horizon. Do not read.

- If you start to feel queasy, drink clear fluids, like water, and eat something bland, such as a soda cracker.

The most common **stings** in Hawaii come from jellyfish, particularly Portuguese man-of-war and box jellyfish. Since the poisons they inject are very different, you need to treat each type of sting differently.

A bluish-purple floating bubble with a long tail, the **Portuguese man-of-war** is responsible for some 6,500 stings a year on Oahu alone. These stings, although painful and a nuisance, are rarely harmful; fewer than 1 in 1,000 requires medical treatment. The best prevention is to watch for these floating bubbles as you snorkel (look for the hanging tentacles below the surface). Get out of the water if anyone near you spots these jellyfish.

> ### Everything You've Always Wanted to Know About Sharks
>
> The Hawaii State Department of Land and Natural Resources offers a website, **www.hawaiisharks.com**, that covers the biology, history, and culture of these carnivores. It also provides safety information and data on shark bites in Hawaii.

Reactions to stings range from mild burning and reddening to severe welts and blisters. *All Stings Considered* recommends the following treatment: First, pick off any visible tentacles with a gloved hand, a stick, or anything handy; then rinse the sting with salt water or fresh water and apply ice to prevent swelling and to help control pain. Avoid folk remedies like vinegar, baking soda, or urinating on the wound, which may actually cause further damage. Most Portuguese man-of-war stings will disappear by themselves within 15 to 20 minutes if you do nothing at all to treat them. Still, be sure to see a doctor if pain persists or a rash or other symptoms develop.

Transparent, square-shaped **box jellyfish** are nearly impossible to see in the water. Fortunately, they seem to follow a monthly cycle: Eight to 10 days after the full moon, they appear in the waters on the leeward side of each island and hang around for about 3 days. Also, they seem to sting more in the morning hours, when they're on or near the surface.

The stings can cause anything from no visible marks to hivelike welts, blisters, and pain lasting from 10 minutes to 8 hours. *All Stings Considered* recommends the following treatment: First, pour regular household vinegar on the sting; this will stop additional burning. Do not rub the area. For pain, apply an ice pack. Seek additional medical treatment if you experience shortness of breath, weakness, palpitations, muscle cramps, or any other severe symptoms. Most box-jellyfish stings disappear by themselves without any treatment.

A new product, just on the market, is **Jellyfish Squish,** made by Coastal Solutions (✆ **912/353-3368;** www.swimoutlet.com/Jellyfish-Squish). It has been getting rave reviews from ocean enthusiasts. It takes away the sting quickly. Best to order it online before you get to Hawaii.

Most sea-related **punctures** come from stepping on or brushing against the needlelike spines of sea urchins (known locally as wana). Be careful when you're in the water; don't put your foot down (even if you have booties or fins on) if you can't clearly see the bottom. Waves can push you into wana in a surge zone in shallow water. The spines can even puncture a wet suit.

A sea urchin puncture can result in burning, aching, swelling, and discoloration (black or purple) around the area where the spines entered your skin. The best thing to do is to pull any protruding spines out. The body will absorb the

📎 Enjoying the Ocean & Avoiding Mishaps

The Pacific Whale Foundation has a free brochure called *Maui Adventure Guide* that introduces visitors to Hawaii's ocean, beaches, tide pools, and reefs. Although written for Maui (with maps showing Maui's beaches), it's a great general resource on how to stay safe around the ocean, with hints on how to assess the weather before you jump into the water and the best ways to view marine wildlife. To get the brochure, call ℭ **808/249-8811**, ext. 1, or visit www. pacificwhale.org.

spines within 24 hours to 3 weeks, or the remainder of the spines will work themselves out. Again, contrary to popular wisdom, do not urinate or pour vinegar on the embedded spines—this will not help.

All **cuts** obtained in the marine environment must be taken seriously because the high level of bacteria present in the water can quickly cause the cut to become infected. The best way to prevent cuts is to wear a wet suit, gloves, and reef shoes. Never touch coral; not only can you get cut, but you also can damage a living organism that took decades to grow.

The symptoms of a coral cut can range from a slight scratch to severe welts and blisters. *All Stings Considered* recommends gently pulling the edges of the skin open and removing any embedded coral or grains of sand with tweezers. Next, scrub the cut well with fresh water. If pressing a clean cloth against the wound doesn't stop the bleeding, or the edges of the injury are jagged or gaping, seek medical treatment.

[Fast FACTS] MAUI

Area Codes Hawaii's area code is 808; it applies to all islands. There is a long-distance charge when calling from one island to another.

Business Hours Most offices are generally open Monday through Friday from 9am to 4pm. Bank hours are Monday through Thursday from 8:30am to 3pm and Friday from 8:30am to 6pm; some banks are open on Saturday as well. Shopping centers are open Monday through Friday from 10am to 9pm, Saturday from 10am to 5:30pm, and Sunday from noon to 5 or 6pm.

Car Rental See "Getting Around Maui," earlier in this chapter.

Cellphones See "Mobile Phones," later in this section.

Crime See "Safety," later in this section.

Customs For details regarding U.S. Customs and Border Protection, consult your nearest U.S. embassy or consulate, or **U.S. Customs** (www.cbp.gov).

You cannot take home fresh fruit, plants, or seeds (including some leis) unless they are sealed. You cannot seal and pack them yourself.

For information on what you're allowed to bring home, contact one of the following agencies:

U.S. Citizens: U.S. Customs and Border Protection, 1300 Pennsylvania Ave. NW, Washington, DC 20229 ((*C* **877/CBP-5511** [227-5511]; www.cbp.gov).

Canadian Citizens: Canada Border Services Agency ((*C* **800/461-9999** in Canada or 204/983-3500; www.cbsa-asfc.gc.ca).

U.K. Citizens: HM Revenue & Customs ((*C* **0845/010-9000** or 020/8929-0152 from outside the U.K.; www.hmce.gov.uk).

Australian Citizens: Australian Customs and Border Protection Service ((*C* **1300/363-263;** www.customs.gov.au).

New Zealand Citizens: New Zealand Customs Service ((*C* **64 9 927 8036** outside of New Zealand, or 0800/428-786; www.customs.govt.nz).

Doctors The West Maui Healthcare Center, Whalers Village, 2435 Kaanapali Pkwy., Ste. H-7 (next to the Westin), Kaanapali ((*C* 808/667-9721), is open 365 days a year; no appointment is necessary. In Kihei, call Urgent Care Maui, 1325 S. Kihei Rd., Ste. 103 (at Lipoa St., across from Star Market), Kihei ((*C* 808/879-7781).

Drinking Laws Beer, wine, and liquor are sold at grocery stores, convenience stores, and liquor stores. There are no state laws limiting when alcohol can be sold, so if the store is open, liquor can be bought. In Maui County (Maui, Molokai, and Lanai) bars and nightclubs must close by 2am.

The legal age for purchase and consumption of alcoholic beverages is 21; proof of age is required and often requested at bars, nightclubs, and restaurants, so it's always a good idea to bring ID when you go out. Do not carry open containers of alcohol in your car or any public area that isn't zoned for alcohol consumption. The police can fine you on the spot. Don't even think about driving while intoxicated.

Driving Rules See "Getting Around Maui," earlier in this chapter.

Electricity Like Canada, the United States uses 110 to 120 volts AC (60 cycles), compared to 220 to 240 volts AC (50 cycles) in most of Europe, Australia, and New Zealand. Downward converters that change 220–240 volts to 110–120 volts are difficult to find in the United States, so bring one with you.

Embassies & Consulates All embassies are located in the nation's capital, Washington, D.C. Some consulates are located in major U.S. cities, and most nations have a mission to the United Nations in New York City. If your country isn't listed below, visit **www.embassy.org/embassies**.

The embassy of **Australia** is at 1601 Massachusetts Ave. NW, Washington, DC 20036 ((*C* **202/797-3000;** www.usa.embassy.gov/au).

The embassy of **Canada** is at 501 Pennsylvania Ave. NW, Washington, DC 20001 ((*C* **202/682-1740;** www.canadianembassy.org). Other Canadian consulates are in Buffalo (New York), NYC, Detroit, Denver, Dallas, Los Angeles, San Francisco and Seattle.

The embassy of **Ireland** is at 2234 Massachusetts Ave. NW, Washington, DC 20008 ((*C* **202/462-3939;** www.embassyofireland.org).

The embassy of **New Zealand** is at 37 Observatory Circle NW, Washington, DC 20008 ((*C* **202/328-4800;** www.nzembassy.com). New Zealand consulates are in Los Angeles, Salt Lake City, San Francisco, and Seattle.

The embassy of the **United Kingdom** is at 3100 Massachusetts Ave. NW, Washington, DC 20008 ((*C* **202/588-6500;** http://ukinusa.fco.gov.uk). Other British consulates are in

Atlanta, Boston, Chicago, Cleveland, Houston, Los Angeles, New York, San Francisco, and Seattle.

Emergencies Dial ☎ **911** for **police, fire,** or **ambulance.** Police district stations are located in Lahaina (☎ **808/661-4441**) and in Hana (☎ **808/248-8311**). For the **Poison Control Center,** call ☎ **800/362-3585.**

Family Travel Maui is paradise for children: beaches to run on, water to splash in, and unusual sights to see. To locate accommodations, restaurants, and attractions that are particularly child-friendly, refer to the "Kids" icon throughout this guide. Be sure to check out the "Especially for Kids" boxes for suggested family activities. And look for *Frommer's Hawaii with Kids* (Wiley Publishing, Inc.).

The larger hotels and resorts offer supervised programs for children and can refer you to qualified babysitters. By state law, hotels can only accept children ages 5 to 12 in supervised activities programs, but they often accommodate younger kids by simply hiring babysitters to watch over them. You can also contact **People Attentive to Children (PATCH),** which can refer you to babysitters who have taken a training course on child-care. On Maui, call ☎ **808/242-9232;** on Molokai and Lanai, call ☎ **800/498-4145;** or visit www.patchhawaii.org.

Baby's Away (☎ **800/942-9030** or 808/344-2219; www.babysaway.com) rents cribs, strollers, highchairs, playpens, and infant seats. The staff will deliver whatever you need to wherever you're staying and pick it up when you're done.

For a list of more family-friendly travel resources, turn to the experts at Frommers.com.

Gasoline Please see "Getting Around Maui," earlier in this chapter.

Hospitals In central Maui, **Maui Memorial Hospital** is at 221 Mahalani, Wailuku (☎ **808/244-9056**). East Maui's **Hana Community Health Center** is on the Hana Highway (☎ **808/248-8924**). In upcountry Maui, **Kula Hospital** is at 204 Kula Hwy., Kula (☎ **808/878-1221**).

Insurance Travel insurance is a good idea if you think for some reason you may be canceling your trip. It's cheaper than the cost of a no-penalty ticket, and it gives you the safety net if something comes up, enabling you to cancel or postpone your trip and still recover the costs.

For information on traveler's insurance, trip-cancellation insurance, and medical insurance while traveling, please visit www.frommers.com/planning.

Internet & Wi-Fi On Maui, branches of the **Hawaii State Public Library System** have computers with Internet access. To find your closest library, check **www.librarieshawaii. org**. There is no charge for use of the computers, but you must have a Hawaii library card, which is free to Hawaii residents and members of the military.

Visitors have a choice of two types of cards: a $25 nonresident card that is good for 5 years (and may be renewed for an additional $25) or a $10 visitor card ($5 for children 18 and under) that is good for 3 months and may be renewed for $10. To download an application for a library card, go to **www.librarieshawaii.org/services/libcard.htm**.

To find Internet cafes in your destination, check **www.cybercaptive.com** or **www. cybercafe.com**.

If you have your own laptop, every **Starbucks** in Maui has Wi-Fi. For a list of locations, go to **www.starbucks.com**. To find other public Wi-Fi hot spots in your destination, go to

www.jiwire.com; its Wi-Fi Finder holds the world's largest directory of public wireless hot spots.

Most major hotels and interisland airports have **Internet kiosks** that provide basic Web access for a per-minute fee that's usually higher than cybercafe prices. Check out copy shops like FedEx Office (formerly Kinkos), which offer computer stations with fully loaded software (as well as Wi-Fi).

Language As in the rest of the United States, English is the language spoken in Hawaii.

Legal Aid Generally, Hawaii has the same laws as the mainland United States. Nudity is illegal in Hawaii. There are *no* legal nude beaches (I don't care what you have read). If you are nude on a beach (or anywhere) in Hawaii, you can be arrested.

Smoking marijuana also is illegal. Yes, there are lots of stories claiming that marijuana is grown in Hawaii, but the drug is illegal; if you attempt to buy it or light up, you can be arrested.

While driving, if you are pulled over for a minor infraction (such as speeding), never attempt to pay the fine directly to a police officer; this could be construed as attempted bribery, a much more serious crime. Pay fines by mail, or directly into the hands of the clerk of the court. If accused of a more serious offense, say and do nothing before consulting a lawyer. In the U.S., the burden is on the state to prove a person's guilt beyond a reasonable doubt, and everyone has the right to remain silent, whether he or she is suspected of a crime or actually arrested. Once arrested, a person can make one telephone call to a party of his or her choice. The international visitor should call his or her embassy or consulate.

LGBT Travelers Hawaii is known for its acceptance of all groups. The number of gay- or lesbian-specific accommodations on the islands is limited, but most properties welcome gays and lesbians like any other travelers.

On Maui check out the website for **Out in Hawaii** (www.outinhawaii.com), which offers "Queer Resources and Information for the State of Hawaii," with vacation ideas, a calendar of events, information on Hawaii, and even a chat room.

For more gay and lesbian travel resources, visit Frommers.com.

Mail As of press time, domestic postage rates are 29¢ for a postcard and 45¢ for a letter. For international mail, a first-class letter of up to 1 ounce costs 98¢ (98¢ to Canada and 80¢ to Mexico); a first-class postcard costs the same as a letter. For more information go to **www.usps.com**.

If you aren't sure what your address will be in the United States, mail can be sent to you, in your name, c/o General Delivery at the main post office of the city or region where you expect to be. (Call ✆ **800/275-8777** for information on the nearest post office.) The addressee must pick up mail in person and must produce proof of identity (a driver's license or a passport, for example). Most post offices will hold mail for up to 1 month and are open Monday to Friday from 8:30am to 4:30pm and Saturday from 9am to noon.

Medical Requirements Unless you're arriving from an area known to be suffering from an epidemic (particularly cholera or yellow fever), inoculations or vaccinations are not required for entry into the United States.

Mobile Phones Just because your cellphone works at home doesn't mean it'll work in Hawaii (thanks to our nation's fragmented cellphone system). Before you get on the plane to Hawaii, check your wireless company's coverage map on its website. There are parts of

Maui (and in some resorts) where coverage is not very good. If you need to stay in touch at a destination where you know your phone won't work, **rent** a phone that does from **InTouch USA** (☏ **800/872-7626;** www.intouchglobal.com).

If you're not from the U.S., you'll be appalled at the poor reach of our **GSM (Global System for Mobile Communications) wireless network,** which is used by much of the rest of the world. Your phone will probably work in most major U.S. cities; it definitely won't work in many rural areas. And you may or may not be able to send SMS (text messaging) home.

Do *not* use your cellphone while you are driving. Strict laws and heavy fines (up to $150) are diligently enforced.

Money & Costs

THE VALUE OF US$ VS. OTHER POPULAR CURRENCIES

US$	C$	£	€	A$	NZ$
1.00	1.02	0.635	0.74	.992	1.30

Frommer's lists exact prices in the local currency. The currency conversions quoted above were correct at press time. However, rates fluctuate, so before departing consult a currency exchange website such as www.oanda.com/convert/classic to check up-to-the-minute rates.

WHAT THINGS COST IN MAUI

	$
Hamburger	6.00 – 12.00
Movie ticket (adult/child)	10.75/7.50
Taxi from Kahului Airport to Kaanapali	85.00
Fare for Atlantis Adventures submarine (adult/child)	109.00/45.00
Entry to Maui Ocean Center (adult/child)	25.00/18.00
Entry to Haleakala National Park	5.00/person or 10.00/car
Entry to Maui Ocean Center (adult/child)	25.00/18.00
Entry to Maui Tropical Plantation (adult/child)	15.00/5.00
Trilogy Sailing Trip to Lanai (adult/child)	159.00/95.00
Old Lahaina Luau (adult/child)	95.00/65.00
20-ounce soft drink at convenience store	3.00
16-ounce apple juice	4.00
Cup of coffee	3.00
Moderately priced three-course dinner without alcohol	50.00
Moderately priced hotel room (double)	150.00–195.00

ATMs (cashpoints) are everywhere in Maui—at banks, supermarkets, Longs Drugs, and in some resorts and shopping centers. The **Cirrus** (**☎** **800/424-7787;** www.mastercard.com) and **PLUS** (**☎** **800/843-7587;** www.visa.com) networks span the country; you can find them even in remote regions. Go to your bank card's website to find ATM locations at your destination. Be sure you know your daily withdrawal limit before you depart.

Note: Many banks impose a fee every time you use a card at another bank's ATM, and that fee is often higher for international transactions (up to $5 or more) than for domestic ones (where they're rarely more than $2.50). In addition, the bank from which you withdraw cash may charge its own fee. Visitors from outside the U.S. should also find out whether their bank assesses a fee on charges incurred abroad.

Credit cards are accepted everywhere except taxicabs and some small restaurants and bed-and-breakfasts.

Multicultural Travelers See "Embassies & Consulates" (p. 379), "Language" (p. 379), "Medical Requirements" (p. 381), "Money & Costs" (above), "Passports" (p. 381), and "Visas" (p. 381).

Newspapers & Magazines The island's daily newspaper is the **Maui News,** P.O. Box 550, Wailuku, HI 96793 (**☎** **808/244-3981;** www.mauinews.com). Publications for visitors include **This Week Maui** (www.thisweek.com), **Maui Visitor Magazine** (www.alohavisitor guides.com), and **101 Things to Do** (www.101thingstodo.com/hawaii/maui/index.php).

Packing Maui is very informal. Shorts, T-shirts, and tennis shoes will get you by at most restaurants and attractions; a casual dress or a polo shirt and khakis are fine even in the most expensive places. Jackets for men are required only in some of the fine dining rooms of a very few ultraexclusive resorts, such as the Lodge at Koele on Lanai—and they'll cordially provide you with a jacket if you don't bring your own. Aloha wear, which does not include T-shirts or sandals, is acceptable everywhere, so you may want to plan on buying an aloha shirt or a muumuu (a Hawaiian-style dress) while you're in the islands.

So bring T-shirts, shorts, long pants, a couple of bathing suits, a long-sleeve coverup (to throw on at the beach when you've had enough sun for the day), tennis shoes, rubber water shoes or flip-flops, and hiking boots and good socks if you plan on hiking.

The tropical sun poses the greatest threat to anyone who ventures into the great outdoors, so be sure to pack a good pair of sunglasses, strong sunscreen, a light hat, and a canteen or water bottle if you'll be hiking—you'll easily dehydrate in the tropical heat, so figure on carrying 2 liters of water per day on any hike. Campers should bring water-purification tablets or devices. Also see "Health & Safety," earlier in this chapter.

One last thing: **It really can get cold in Maui.** If you plan to see the sunrise from the top of Maui's Haleakala Crater, take a warm jacket; an upcountry temperature of 40°F (4°C), even in summer when it's 80°F (27°C) at the beach, is not uncommon. It's always a good idea to bring at least a windbreaker, a sweater, or a light jacket. And be sure to toss some **rain gear** into your suitcase if you'll be in Maui between November and March.

Passports Virtually every air traveler entering the U.S. is required to show a passport. All persons, including U.S. citizens, traveling by air between the United States and Canada, Mexico, Central and South America, the Caribbean, and Bermuda are required to present a valid passport. **Note:** U.S. and Canadian citizens entering the U.S. at land and sea ports of entry from within the Western Hemisphere must now also present a passport or other documents compliant with the Western Hemisphere Travel Initiative (WHTI; see www.getyouhome.gov for details). Children 15 and under may continue entering with only a U.S. birth certificate, or other proof of U.S. citizenship.

Australia Australian Passport Information Service (☎ **131-232,** or visit www.passports. gov.au).

Canada Passport Office, Department of Foreign Affairs and International Trade, Ottawa, ON K1A 0G3 (☎ **800/567-6868;** www.ppt.gc.ca).

Ireland Passport Office, Setanta Centre, Molesworth Street, Dublin 2 (☎ **01/671-1633;** www.foreignaffairs.gov.ie).

New Zealand Passports Office, Department of Internal Affairs, 47 Boulcott St., Wellington, 6011 (☎ **0800/225-050** in New Zealand or 04/474-8100; www.passports.govt.nz).

United Kingdom Visit your nearest passport office, major post office, or travel agency, or contact the **Identity and Passport Service (IPS),** 89 Eccleston Sq., London, SW1V 1PN (☎ **0300/222-0000;** www.ips.gov.uk).

United States To find your regional passport office, check the U.S. State Department website (www.travel.state.gov/passport) or call the **National Passport Information Center** (☎ **877/487-2778**) for automated information.

Petrol Please see "Getting Around Maui," earlier in this chapter.

Police In an emergency, dial ☎ **911** for police. For nonemergencies, call the district station in Lahaina (☎ **808/661-4441**) or Hana (☎ **808/248-8311**).

Safety Although tourist areas are generally safe, visitors should always stay alert, even in laid-back Maui (and especially in resort and beach areas). It's wise to ask the island tourist office if you're in doubt about which neighborhoods are safe. Avoid deserted areas, especially at night. Don't go into any city park at night unless there's an event that attracts a crowd. Generally speaking, you can feel safe in areas where there are many people and open establishments.

Avoid carrying valuables with you on the street, and don't display expensive cameras or electronic equipment. Hold on to your pocketbook, and place your billfold in an inside pocket. In theaters, restaurants, and other public places, keep your possessions in sight.

Remember also that hotels are open to the public and that at a large property, security may not be able to screen everyone entering. Always lock your room door—don't assume that once inside your hotel, you're automatically safe.

Recently, burglaries of tourists' rental cars in hotel parking structures and at beach parking lots have become more common. Park in well-lighted and well-traveled areas, if possible. Never leave any packages or valuables visible in the car. If someone attempts to rob you or steal your car, do not try to resist the thief or carjacker—report the incident to the police department immediately. Ask your rental agency about personal safety, and get written directions or a map with the route to your destination clearly marked.

Senior Travel Always carry identification with proof of your age—it can really pay off. Discounts for seniors are available at almost all of Maui's major attractions and occasionally at hotels and restaurants. The Outrigger hotel chain, for instance, offers travelers ages 50 and older a 20% discount off regular published rates—and an additional 5% off for members of AARP. Always ask when making hotel reservations or buying tickets.

The U.S. National Park Service offers an **America the Beautiful—National Park and Federal Recreational Lands Pass—Senior Pass** (formerly the **Golden Age Passport**), which gives seniors 62 years or older lifetime entrance to all properties administered by the National Park Service (NPS)—national parks, monuments, historic sites, recreation areas, and national wildlife refuges—for a one-time processing fee of $10. The pass must be purchased in person at any NPS facility that charges an entrance fee. Besides free entry, the America the Beautiful Senior Pass offers a 50% discount on some federal-use fees charged for such facilities as camping, swimming, parking, boat launching, and tours. For more information, go to www.nps.gov/fees_passes.htm or call the United States Geological Survey (USGS), which issues the passes, at ☏ **888/275-8747.**

Frommers.com offers more information and resources on travel for seniors.

Single Travelers Traveling in Hawaii is very safe. See "Safety," above.

Smoking Hawaii has some of the toughest antismoking laws in the United States. See the box "Hey, No Smoking in Hawaii" on p. 375.

Taxes The United States has no value-added tax (VAT) or other indirect tax at the national level. Hawaii state general excise tax is 4% on all purchases. Hotel tax is 13.416% added to your hotel bill.

Telephones All calls to destinations on the island are local calls; calls from one island to another via a land line are long-distance, and you must dial 1; then the Hawaii area code, 808; and then the phone number. Many convenience groceries and packaging services sell **prepaid calling cards** in denominations up to $50 (*tip:* Costco's calling card gives you 700 minutes for $20). Many public pay phones at airports now accept American Express, MasterCard, and Visa. **Local calls** made from most pay phones cost 50¢. Most long-distance and international calls can be dialed directly from any phone. **To make calls within the United States and to Canada,** dial 1 followed by the area code and the seven-digit number. **For other international calls,** dial 011 followed by the country code, the city code, and the number you are calling.

Calls to area codes **800, 888, 877,** and **866** are toll free. However, calls to area codes **700** and **900** (chat lines, bulletin boards, "dating" services, and so on) can be expensive—charges of 95¢ to $3 or more per minute. Some numbers have minimum charges that can run $15 or more.

For **reversed-charge or collect calls,** and for person-to-person calls, dial the number 0 and then the area code and number; an operator will come on the line, and you should specify whether you are calling collect, person-to-person, or both. If your operator-assisted call is international, ask for the overseas operator.

For **directory assistance** ("Information"), dial 411 for local numbers and national numbers in the U.S. and Canada. For dedicated long-distance information, dial 1, then the appropriate area code plus 555-1212. There is a fee for the assistance.

Time The continental United States is divided into **four time zones:** Eastern Standard Time (EST), Central Standard Time (CST), Mountain Standard Time (MST), and Pacific Standard Time (PST). Alaska and Hawaii each have their own zone: Alaska Standard Time (AST) and Hawaii Standard Time (HST). For example, when it's 9am in Los Angeles (PST), it's 7am in Maui (HST), 10am in Denver (MST), 11am in Chicago (CST), noon in New York City (EST), 5pm in London (Greenwich Mean Time), and 2am the next day in Sydney.

Daylight saving time is in effect from 1am on the second Sunday in March to 1am on the first Sunday in November in most of the United States. **Hawaii does not observe daylight saving time.** Daylight saving time moves the clock 1 hour ahead of standard time. **Note:** During daylight saving time, Hawaii is 3 hours behind the West Coast and 6 hours behind the East Coast.

Tipping Tips are a very important part of certain workers' income, and gratuities are the standard way of showing appreciation for services provided. (Tipping is certainly not compulsory if the service is poor!) In hotels, tip **bellhops** at least $1 per bag ($3–$5 if you have a lot of luggage), and tip the **chamber staff** $1 to $2 per day (more if you've left a disaster area for him or her to clean up). Tip the **doorman** or **concierge** only if he or she has provided you with some specific service (for example, calling a cab for you or obtaining difficult-to-get theater tickets). Tip the **valet-parking attendant** $1 to $2 every time you get your car.

In restaurants, bars, and nightclubs, tip **service staff** and **bartenders** 15% to 20% of the check, and tip **valet-parking attendants** $1 per vehicle.

As for other service personnel, tip **cab drivers** 15% of the fare; tip **skycaps** at airports at least $1 per bag ($3–$5 if you have a lot of luggage); and tip **hairdressers** and **barbers** 15% to 20%.

Toilets You won't find public toilets or "restrooms" on the streets in most U.S. cities, but they can be found in hotel lobbies, bars, restaurants, museums, department stores, and service stations. Large hotels and fast-food restaurants are often the best bet for clean facilities. Restaurants and bars in resorts or heavily visited areas may reserve their restrooms for patrons.

Travelers with Disabilities Travelers with disabilities are made to feel very welcome in Maui. Hotels are usually equipped with wheelchair-accessible rooms, and tour companies provide many special services. The **Hawaii Center for Independent Living,** 414 Kauwili St., Ste. 102, Honolulu, HI 96817 (✆ **808/522-5400;** fax 808/522-5427), can provide information.

The only travel agency in Hawaii specializing in needs for travelers with disabilities is **Access Aloha Travel** (✆ **800/480-1143;** www.accessalohatravel.com), which can book anything, including rental vans (available on Maui and Oahu only), accommodations, tours, cruises, airfare, and anything else you can think of. For more details on wheelchair transportation and tours around the islands, see "Getting Around" in the individual island chapters.

For more on organizations that offer resources to travelers with disabilities, go to Frommers.com.

VAT See "Taxes," above.

Visas The U.S. State Department has a **Visa Waiver Program (VWP)** allowing citizens of the following countries to enter the United States without a visa for stays of up to 90 days: Andorra, Australia, Austria, Belgium, Brunei, Czech Republic, Denmark, Estonia, Finland, France, Germany, Greece, Hungary, Iceland, Ireland, Italy, Japan, Latvia, Liechtenstein, Lithuania, Luxembourg, Malta, Monaco, the Netherlands, New Zealand, Norway, Portugal, San Marino, Singapore, Slovakia, Slovenia, South Korea, Spain, Sweden, Switzerland, and the United Kingdom. (**Note:** This list was accurate at press time; for the most up-to-date list of countries in the VWP, consult http://travel.state.gov/visa.) Even though a visa isn't necessary, in an effort to help U.S. officials check travelers against terror watch lists before they arrive at U.S. borders, visitors from VWP countries must register online through the Electronic System for Travel Authorization (ESTA) before boarding a plane or a boat to the U.S. Travelers must complete an electronic application providing basic personal and travel eligibility information. The Department of Homeland Security recommends filling out the form at least 3 days before traveling. Authorizations will be valid for up to 2 years or until the traveler's passport expires, whichever comes first. Currently, there is a $14 fee for the online application. Existing ESTA registrations remain valid through their expiration dates. **Note:** Any passport issued on or after October 26, 2006, by a VWP country must be an

e-Passport for VWP travelers to be eligible to enter the U.S. without a visa. Citizens of these nations also need to present a round-trip air or cruise ticket upon arrival. E-Passports contain computer chips capable of storing biometric information, such as the required digital photograph of the holder. If your passport doesn't have this feature, you can still travel without a visa if the valid passport was issued before October 26, 2005, and includes a machine-readable zone; or if the valid passport was issued between October 26, 2005, and October 25, 2006, and includes a digital photograph. For more information, go to **http://travel.state.gov/visa**. Canadian citizens may enter the United States without visas, but will need to show passports and proof of residence.

Citizens of all other countries must have (1) a valid passport that expires at least 6 months later than the scheduled end of their visit to the U.S.; and (2) a tourist visa.

For information about U.S. visas go to **http://travel.state.gov/visa**. Or go to one of the following websites:

Australian citizens can obtain up-to-date visa information from the **U.S. Embassy Canberra,** Moonah Place, Yarralumla, ACT 2600 (© **02/6214-5600**), or by checking the U.S. Diplomatic Mission's website at **http://canberra.usembassy.gov/visas.html**.

British subjects can obtain up-to-date visa information by calling the **U.S. Embassy Visa Information Line** (© **09042-450-100** from within the U.K. at £1.20 per minute; or **866/382-3589** from within the U.S. at a flat rate of $16, payable by credit card only) or by visiting the "Visas to the U.S." section of the American Embassy London's website at **http://london.usembassy.gov/visas.html**.

Irish citizens can obtain up-to-date visa information through the **U.S. Embassy Dublin,** 42 Elgin Rd., Ballsbridge, Dublin 4 (© 1580-47-VISA [8472] from within the Republic of Ireland at €2.40 per minute; **http://dublin.usembassy.gov**).

Citizens of **New Zealand** can obtain up-to-date visa information by contacting the **U.S. Embassy New Zealand,** 29 Fitzherbert Terrace, Thorndon, Wellington (© **644/462-6000; http://newzealand.usembassy.gov**).

Visitor Information The **Maui Visitors and Convention Bureau** is at 1727 Wili Pa Loop, Wailuku, Maui, HI 96793 (© **800/525-MAUI** [6284] or 808/244-3530; fax 808/244-1337; www.gohawaii.com/maui). **Molokai Visitors Association** can be reached at P.O. Box 960, Kaunakakai, HI 96748 (© **800/800-6367** from the U.S. mainland and Canada, 800/553-0404 interisland, or 808/553-3876; www.gohawaii.com/molokai). **Lanai Visitors Bureau** can be reached at 1727 Wili Pa Loop, Wailuku, Maui 96793 (© **800/947-4774** or 808/565-7600; fax 808/565-9316; www.gohawaii.com/lanai). The **Hawaii Visitors and Convention Bureau,** 2270 Kalakaua Ave., Suite 801, Honolulu, HI 96815 (© **800/GO-HAWAII** [464-2924] or 808/923-1811; www.gohawaii.com), provides brochures, maps, and island guides.

Other great websites:

College of Hawaiian Language: **www.olelo.hawaii.edu**

Maui Net: **www.maui.net**

Maui Island Currents (arts and culture): **www.islandcurrents.com**

Water Generally the water in your hotel, or at public drinking fountains, is safe to drink (depending on the island—it may have more chlorine than you like).

Wi-Fi See "Internet & Wi-Fi," earlier in this section.

Women Travelers Travel in Hawaii is very safe. Take the usual precautions you would in your hometown. See "Safety," above.

AIRLINE WEBSITES

Alaska Airlines
www.alaskaair.com

American Airlines
www.aa.com

Continental Airlines
www.continental.com

Delta Air Lines
www.delta.com

go!Mokulele (interisland Hawaii only)
www.iflygo.com

Hawaiian Airlines
www.hawaiianair.com

Island Air
www.islandair.com

United Airlines
www.united.com

US Airways
www.usairways.com

Airline Websites

PLANNING YOUR TRIP TO MAUI

Index

Accommodations

Photo Credits

p. i: ©Ryan Siphers; p. iii-vi: ©Augustin Tabares; p. 1: ©Cara Jalbert; p. 2: ©Ryan Siphers; p. 3: ©GregL / Frommers.com Community; p. 4: ©ian nawalinski / Frommers.com Community; p. 5: ©Ryan Siphers; p. 8: ©Ryan Siphers; p. 10, top: ©Marco Garcia; p. 10, bottom: ©Marco Garcia; p. 11: ©David Fleetham / Alamy; p. 12: ©Douglas Peebles Photography / Alamy; ; p. 13: ©Ryan Siphers; p. 15: ©Courtesy Kapalua Resort; p. 16: ©Courtesy Fairmont Kea Lani; p. 18: ©Courtesy Old Lahaina Luau; p. 19: ©Courtesy Sansei Seafood Restaurant & Sushi Bar; p. 20: ©Ryan Siphers; p. 22: ©Ryan Siphers; p. 24: ©Bruce Omori; p. 25, left: ©SuperStock; p. 25, right: ©Greg Vaughn / Alamy Images; p. 27: ©Carla Jalbert; p. 28: ©Marco Garcia; p. 30: ©Everett Collection Inc / Alamy; ; p. 31: ©Marco Garcia; p. 33: ©Courtesy Mutual Publishing; p. 38: ©Marco Garcia; p. 39: ©Alden Gewirtz; p. 41: ©Ryan Siphers; p. 48: ©Photo Resource Hawaii / Alamy; p. 53, left: ©Bruce Omori; p. 53, right: ©Marco Garcia; p. 55, left: ©Marco Garcia; p. 55, right: ©Carla Jalbert; p. 56, left: ©David Fleetham / Alamy; p. 56, right: ©Douglas Peebles / Alamy; p. 58: ©David Fleetham / Alamy; p. 59: ©dee2travel / Frommers.com Community; p. 73: ©Ryan Siphers; p. 75: ©Carla Jalbert; p. 76: ©Ryan Siphers; p. 78: ©Carla Jalbert; p. 81: ©Kristin Mills; p. 83, top: ©Carla Jalbert; p. 83, bottom: ©Ryan Siphers; p. 84: ©Agustin Tabares; p. 88, top: ©Courtesy Maui Ocean Center; p. 88, bottom: ©Ryan Siphers; p. 89: ©Kristin Mills; p. 90: ©Kristin Mills; p. 92: ©Marco Garcia; p. 94: ©Marco Garcia; p. 95: ©Courtesy HVCB; p. 96: ©Marco Garcia; p. 97: ©Kristin Mills; p. 99: ©Carla Jalbert; p. 100: ©Dana Nadeau / Garden Island Photography; p. 101, top: ©Ryan Siphers; p. 101, bottom: ©Carla Jalbert; p. 103: ©Kristin Mills; p. 104: ©Ryan Siphers; p. 106: ©Ryan Siphers; p. 108, left: ©Agustin Tabares; p. 108, right: ©Ryan Siphers; p. 110: ©Ryan Siphers; p. 111: ©Ryan Siphers; p. 112: ©Ryan Siphers; p. 116: ©Ryan Siphers; p. 117: ©Ryan Siphers; p. 118: ©Carla Jalbert; p. 119: ©Courtesy Maui Ocean Center; p. 120: ©Ryan Siphers; p. 121, left: ©Ryan Siphers; p. 121, right: ©Ryan Siphers; p. 122: ©Ryan Siphers; p. 123: ©Annette Wagner; p. 124: ©Kristin Mills; p. 127: ©Ryan Siphers; p. 128: ©Annette Wagner; p. 129: ©Carla Jalbert; p. 130: ©Ryan Siphers; p. 131: ©Carla Jalbert; p. 132: ©Ryan Siphers; p. 133: ©Carla Jalbert; p. 134: ©Kristin Mills; p. 136: ©Ryan Siphers; p. 138: ©Ryan Siphers; p. 139: ©Agustin Tabares; p. 143, top: ©Courtesy Hotel Hana-Maui; p. 143, bottom: ©Agustin Tabares; p. 145: ©Ryan Siphers; p. 146: ©Ryan Siphers; p. 148, top: ©Ryan Siphers; p. 148, bottom: ©Ryan Siphers; p. 149: ©Ryan Siphers; p. 151: ©Ryan Siphers; p. 154, top: ©Ryan Siphers; p. 154, bottom: ©Ryan Siphers; p. 156: ©Ryan Siphers; p. 157: ©Ryan Siphers; p. 158: ©Kristin Mills; p. 159: ©Carla Jalbert; p. 160, left: ©Ryan Siphers; p. 160, right: ©Ryan Siphers; p. 161: ©Andre Jenny / Alamy; p. 162: ©Ryan Siphers; p. 163: ©Ryan Siphers; p. 164: ©Carla Jalbert; p. 165: ©Ryan Siphers; p. 168: ©Ryan Siphers; p. 170: ©Courtesy Atlantis Adventures; p. 171: ©Kristin Mills; p. 172: ©Judy Skroback / Frommers.com Community; p. 173: ©Ryan Siphers; p. 175: ©Carla Jalbert; p. 176: ©Kristin Mills; p. 177: ©Photo Resource Hawaii / Alamy; p. 178: ©Ryan Siphers; p. 182: ©Agustin Tabares; p. 183: ©Ryan Siphers; p. 187: ©Kristin Mills; p. 188: ©Kristin Mills; p. 190: ©Ryan Siphers; p. 197: ©Courtesy Roselani Ice Cream; p. 203: ©Courtesy Tour da Food Maui; p. 206: ©Courtesy O'o Farm, photo by Anthony Martinez; p. 230: ©Marco Garcia; p. 232: ©Ryan Siphers; p. 233, top: ©Ryan Siphers; p. 233, bottom: ©Carla Jalbert; p. 238: ©Kristin Mills; p. 245: ©Ryan Siphers; p. 246: ©Kristin Mills; p. 247: ©Kristin Mills; p. 248, left: ©Courtesy Old Lahaina Luau; p. 248, right: ©Courtesy of Ulalena at Maui Theatre; p. 255: ©Courtesy Hotel Hana-Maui; p. 257: ©Courtesy Old Wailuku Inn at Ulupono; p. 258: ©Courtesy Four Seasons Hotels and Resorts; p. 259: ©Courtesy Grand Wailea Resort Hotel & Spa; p. 302: ©Pacific Stock / SuperStock; p. 303: ©Marco Garcia; p. 306: ©Marco Garcia; p. 310: ©Marco Garcia; p. 311, top: ©Caroline Commins / Alamy; p. 311, bottom: ©Marco Garcia; p. 312: ©Marco Garcia; p. 313: ©Marco Garcia; p. 314: ©Marco Garcia; p. 315: ©Marco Garcia; p. 317, top: ©Marco Garcia; p. 317, bottom: ©Marco Garcia; p. 318, left: ©Photo Resource Hawaii / Alamy; p. 318, right: ©Marco Garcia; p. 320, top-left: ©Marco Garcia; p. 320, top-right: ©Marco Garcia; p. 320, bottom: ©Marco Garcia; p. 321: ©Marco Garcia; p. 322, top-left: ©Marco Garcia; p. 322, top-right: ©Marco Garcia; p. 322, bottom: